Sculpture in Canada

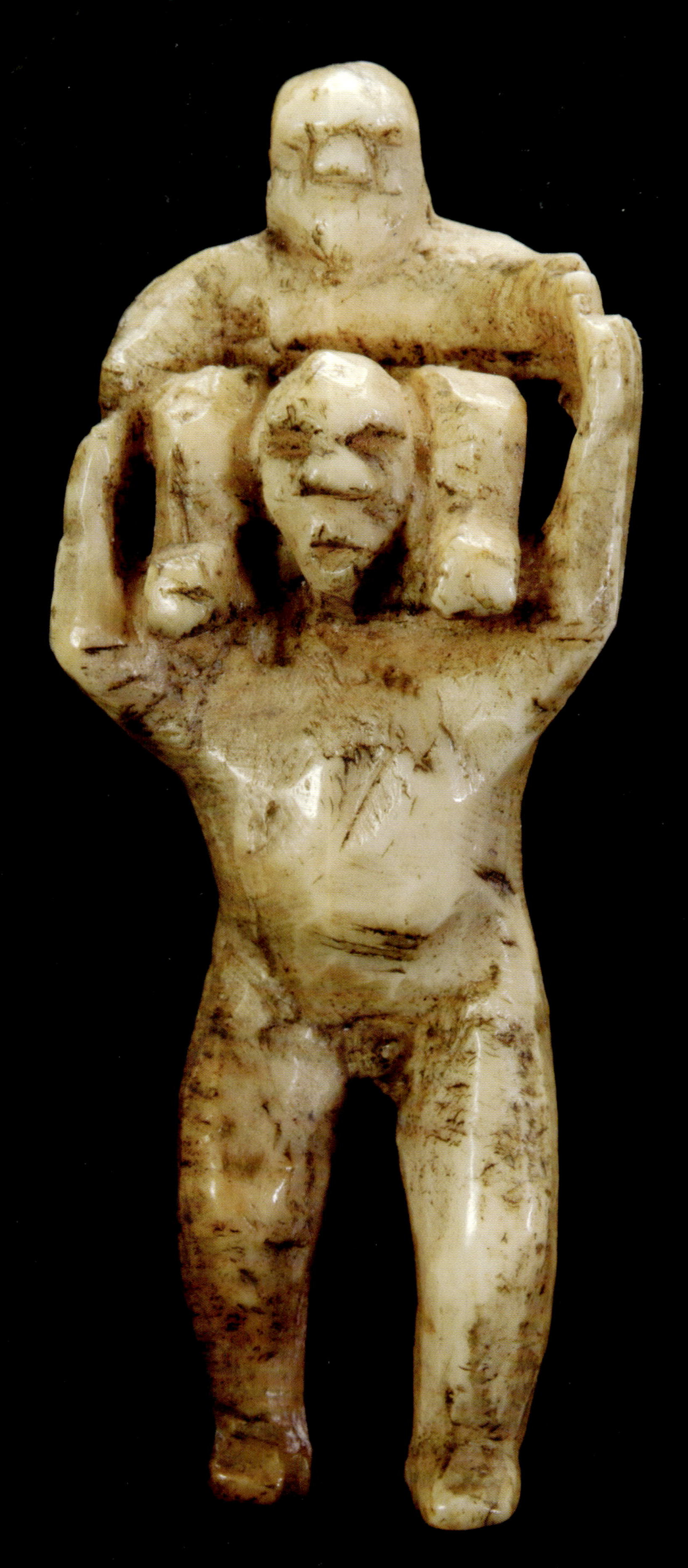

SCULPTURE IN CANADA

A HISTORY

MARIA TIPPETT

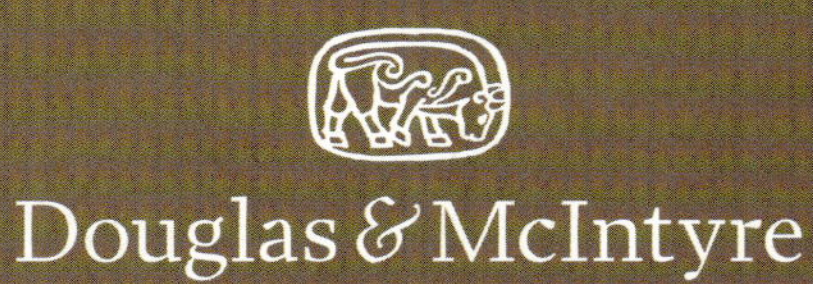

Douglas & McIntyre

Douglas and McIntyre (2013) Ltd.
P.O. Box 219, Madeira Park, BC, VON 2HO
www.douglas-mcintyre.com

Edited by Pam Robertson
Indexed by Kyla Shauer
Text design by Roger Handling
Photo editing with the assistance of Sergei Petrov
Printed and bound in Canada

Photo on p. 2: *Figure of Man and Child*, artist unknown; photo on p. 6: *Construction: Vésuve* by Claude Mongrain. See captions on p. 15 and 214 or List of Works for more details.

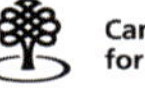 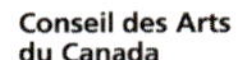 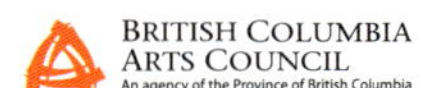 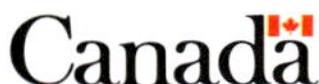

Douglas and McIntyre (2013) Ltd. acknowledges the support of the Canada Council for the Arts, which last year invested $153 million to bring the arts to Canadians throughout the country. We also gratefully acknowledge financial support from the Government of Canada and from the Province of British Columbia through the BC Arts Council and the Book Publishing Tax Credit.

Library and Archives Canada Cataloguing in Publication

Tippett, Maria, 1944-, author
    Sculpture in Canada : a history / Maria Tippett.

Includes bibliographical references and index.
Issued in print and electronic formats.
ISBN 978-1-77162-093-2 (hardcover).—ISBN 978-1-77162-094-9 (HTML)

1. Sculpture, Canadian. 2. Sculpture—Canada. I. Title.

NB240.T57 2017   730.971   C2017-905454-6
                                                     C2017-905455-4

To old friends Diane and Viv Nelles, and
to new friends Sergei Petrov and Mieke Truijen

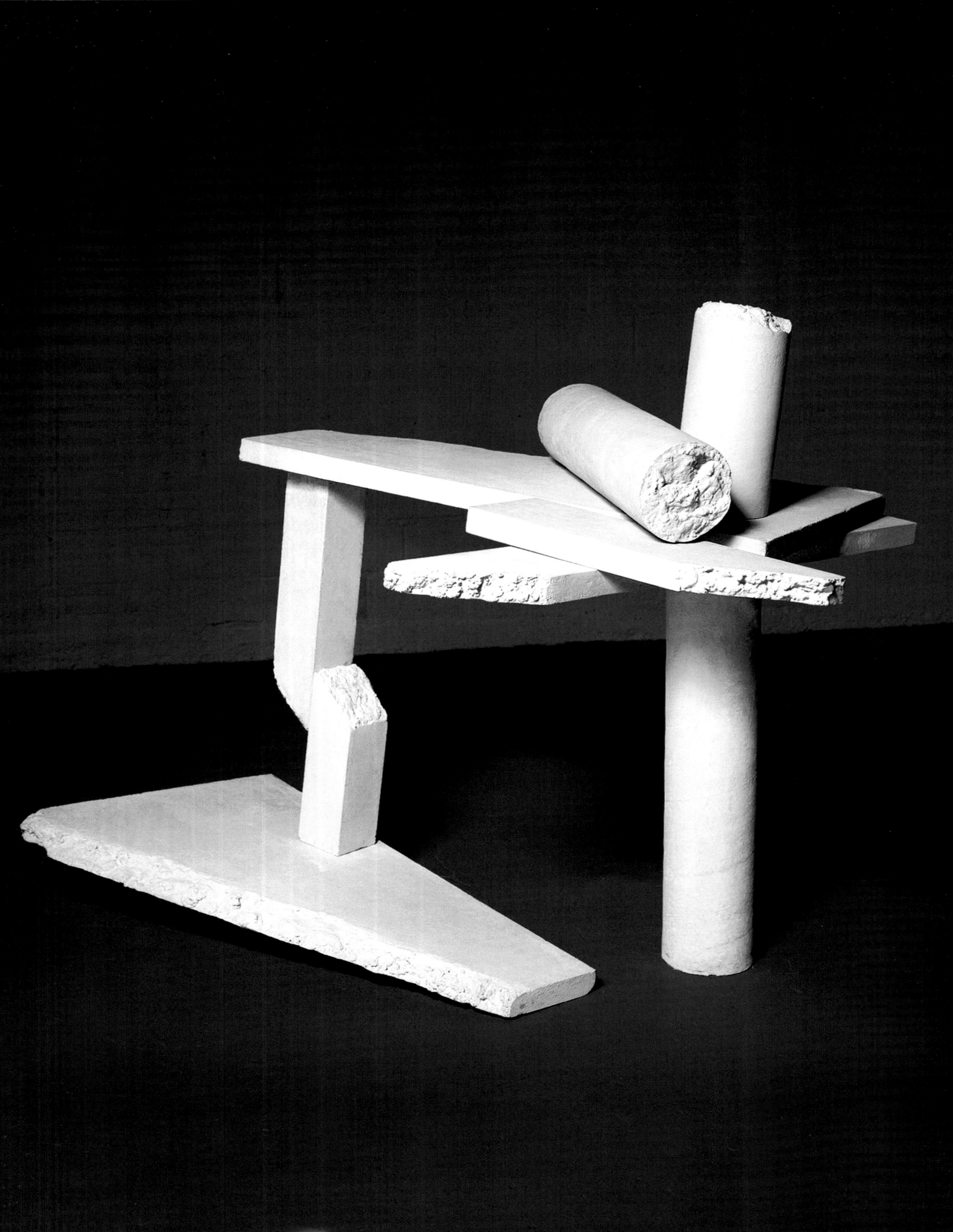

Contents

Introduction

Sculpture has long been the stepchild of painting. Numerically, there are more painters than sculptors, more paintings than sculptures in public galleries and in private collections, more books devoted to painters than to sculptors. Moreover, there is more certainty as to what a painting is. Such generalizations apply to Indigenous and non-Indigenous sculpture alike, and this book attempts to address these lacunae by examining sculpture in Canada over a fifteen-thousand-year period.

The very words *sculpture* and *sculptor* do not roll off the tongue as easily as *painting* and *painter*. Similarly, the processes of creating, storing, exhibiting and marketing these two artistic genres are different. Sculptures are expensive to produce: they take more time, more material and usually more studio space. Because they are generally larger than paintings, they are difficult to transport and, when they arrive at the gallery, require larger exhibition spaces than paintings. Size restricts where sculptures can be exhibited and how they can be stored, and thus who can and will acquire them.

Sculptors in Canada, then, have not had an easy time of it. Up until the last decades of the nineteenth century they were confined to working mainly in wood or stone, or else had to have their works fabricated in foundries—largely in Europe and the United States—to transform their small-scale models, originally made in clay or plaster, into finished bronze pieces. As this book will show, up until the early years of the twentieth century sculptors produced most of their work on commission: for the church or for the government, for their own community or for special interest groups. This meant that they usually worked within prescribed norms established by their patrons. If they wanted more freedom they could produce smaller pieces, but without funding there was little chance that their models would be transformed into full-scale works. Although sculptors seemed freer to dance to their own tune in the twentieth century, the very public nature of their work exposed both Indigenous and non-Indigenous sculptors to criticism from members of the general public, who often had their own opinions about the modernist or postmodernist style in which such pieces might be rendered.

Defining what constitutes a sculpture has problems of its own. As this book shows, a sculpture can be assembled, or carved, or welded, or dug, or chipped or made by a computer. It might take the form of a shard, or a woodcarving or a 3-D computer model. It can be made for utilitarian purposes, or devised to raise social consciousness, or primarily created in the mind of the sculptor with an end product that is secondary. A sculpture can convey a myriad of definitions with thoughts and feelings supplied by the viewer. It need have no meaning other than the very materiality and process involved in its own making. And it might even exist only in photographic reproduction or in the words of its creator. These various kinds of sculpture—with meaning and reception that remains fluid—have their own legitimate claims, established successively by those who make them, by those who view them, by those who exhibit them or acquire them or by those who write about them.

Quite as difficult as defining the ambit of sculpture is deciding who best represents what has been produced in the geographical region we now regard as Canada. The choices I have made here are personal, and I am aware that many other sculptors could have been included. But I had no intention of writing an encyclopedia. I did not want to offer my readers simply a compilation of biographies. Nor did I want to impose my own descriptive analyses or enforce airtight definitions—which may simply indulge the whims of a particular author. *Sculpture in Canada* has a different aim: to explore the historical circumstances under which sculpture has long been produced in Canada, and to assess its reception by galleries, critics and the wider public alike. I want, above all, to introduce Canadians and non-Canadians to the underappreciated wealth of what has been achieved here.

This book is organized chronologically, with its beginnings in the distant pre-historical past and its conclusion in an uncertain present, where the very nature of sculpture is a contested concept. I write as a Canadian woman of European origin. In one sense I am a native, having been born in British Columbia; in another sense I respect the status of the peoples who were long settled on this land before contact was made due to European intrusion. But I do think anyone should have the right to consider such a rich shared history, including the full range of artistic work that has been produced in the land we now call Canada. And although I generally identify the contributions of Diuktai, Inuit and First Nations artists as such, I do not segregate their work into separate chapters. I consider their contributions an integral part of the story I am telling.

It is a long story, beginning further back than I had myself imagined when I first began this project. If I conceive this history rather differently now, it is because I have learned such a lot along on the way. And the mission of this—the first large-scale history of sculpture in Canada—is to lay the foundation for further study and research, and for ongoing discussion and argument, about a field of aesthetic endeavour that has hitherto lacked proper appreciation.

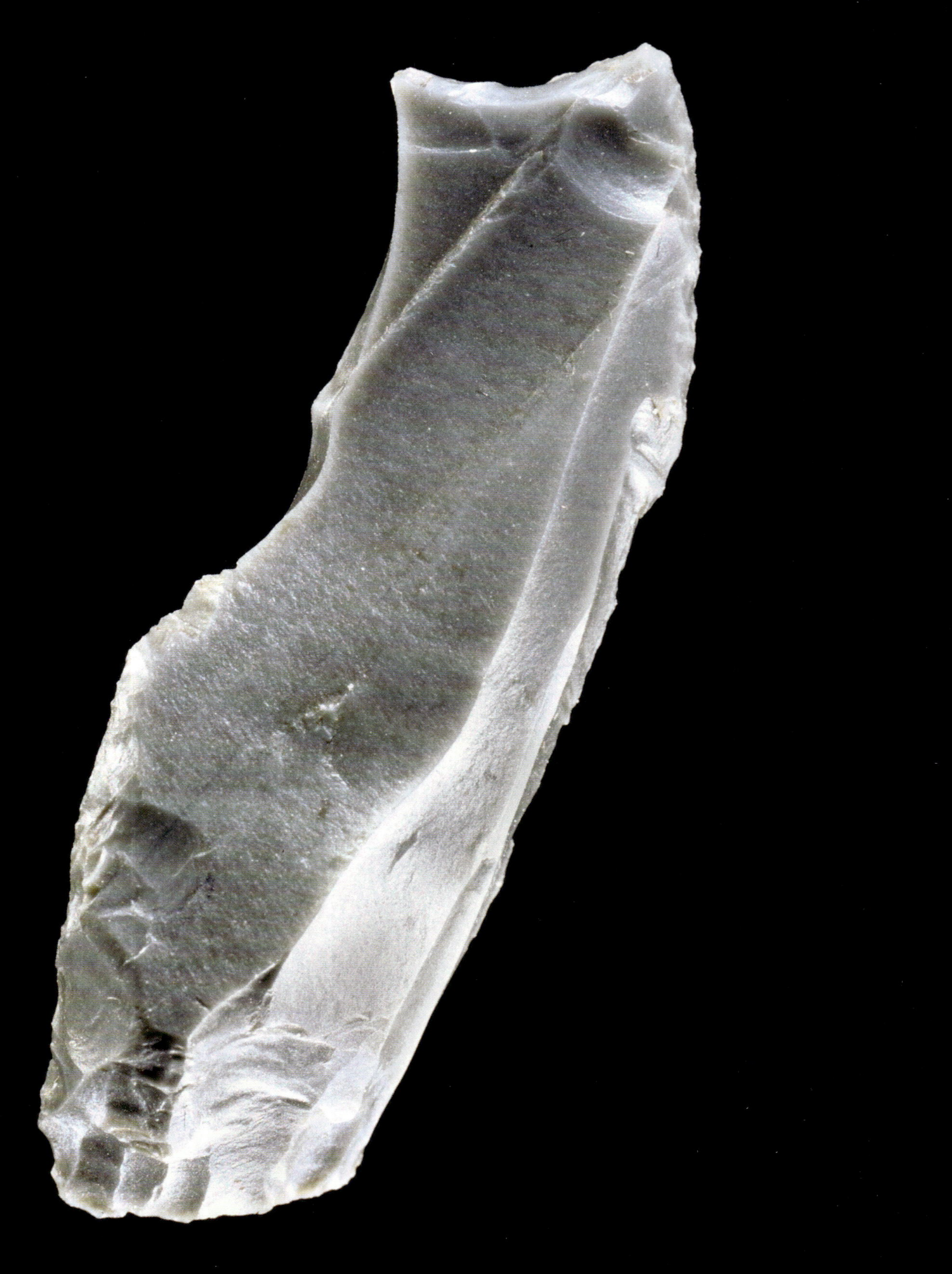

1
Beginnings

Sculpture is the oldest form of the visual arts. It has been practised in the geographical region now called Canada for many millennia. Handcrafted chipped-stone tools and animal-bone shards made during the late Pleistocene epoch, dating back to an estimated 23,000 to 13,000 BCE (previously BC), were recently discovered in the northern Yukon's Bluefish Caves.[1] This implies that the long-extinct Diuktai peoples who had migrated from Siberia to present-day Yukon on ice-free corridors made among the earliest forms of three-dimensional objects on the North American continent.

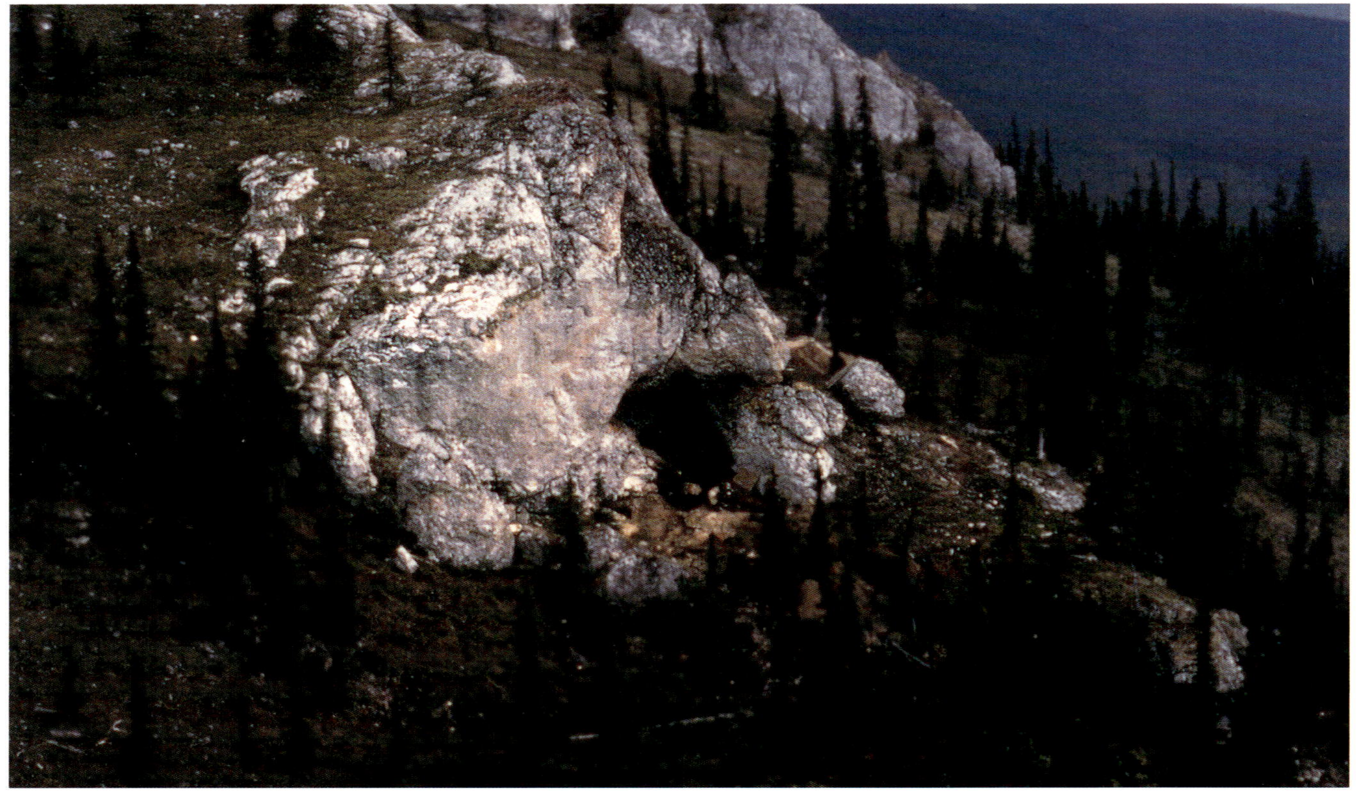

Millennia later, a portrait "maskette" small enough to fit into the palm of a child's hand was produced around 1500 BCE by an artist whose people had inhabited the Arctic Archipelago for 3,500 years. Other highly realistic and abstract representations of humans, animals, birds and human-like spirits, rendered in stone or bone, in antler or ivory, were also made by the late Palaeo-Eskimo, or Dorset people, as they are also known. Later, a century before Europeans began fishing for cod off the Newfoundland coast, the direct descendants of the Thule people, whom we call the Inuit, created similarly diminutive figures from such materials. And on Baffin Island in Nunavut over one hundred life-sized inuksuit still break the horizon on Inuksugasalik Point. Indeed, there used to be over two hundred inuksuit located at this northern acropolis. On the other side of the North American continent, on the coast of what is now British Columbia, the ancestors of the First Nations people who migrated to this region around 9800 BCE also worked in stone. They made bowls in the form of seated human figures. They turned slave-killing clubs into phallic images, and transformed tobacco mortars into vulvar forms. Some of these powerful sculptures that are in today's museums are more than four thousand years old. On the other side of the country, a ten-metre-high ossuary mound was recently discovered in the heart of Toronto. Constructed around 1250 CE (previously AD) by the descendants of the Iroquois Nation, the work might be viewed, in today's parlance, as land art.

These and other objects produced before and soon after the first millennium were created thousands of years before European contact.

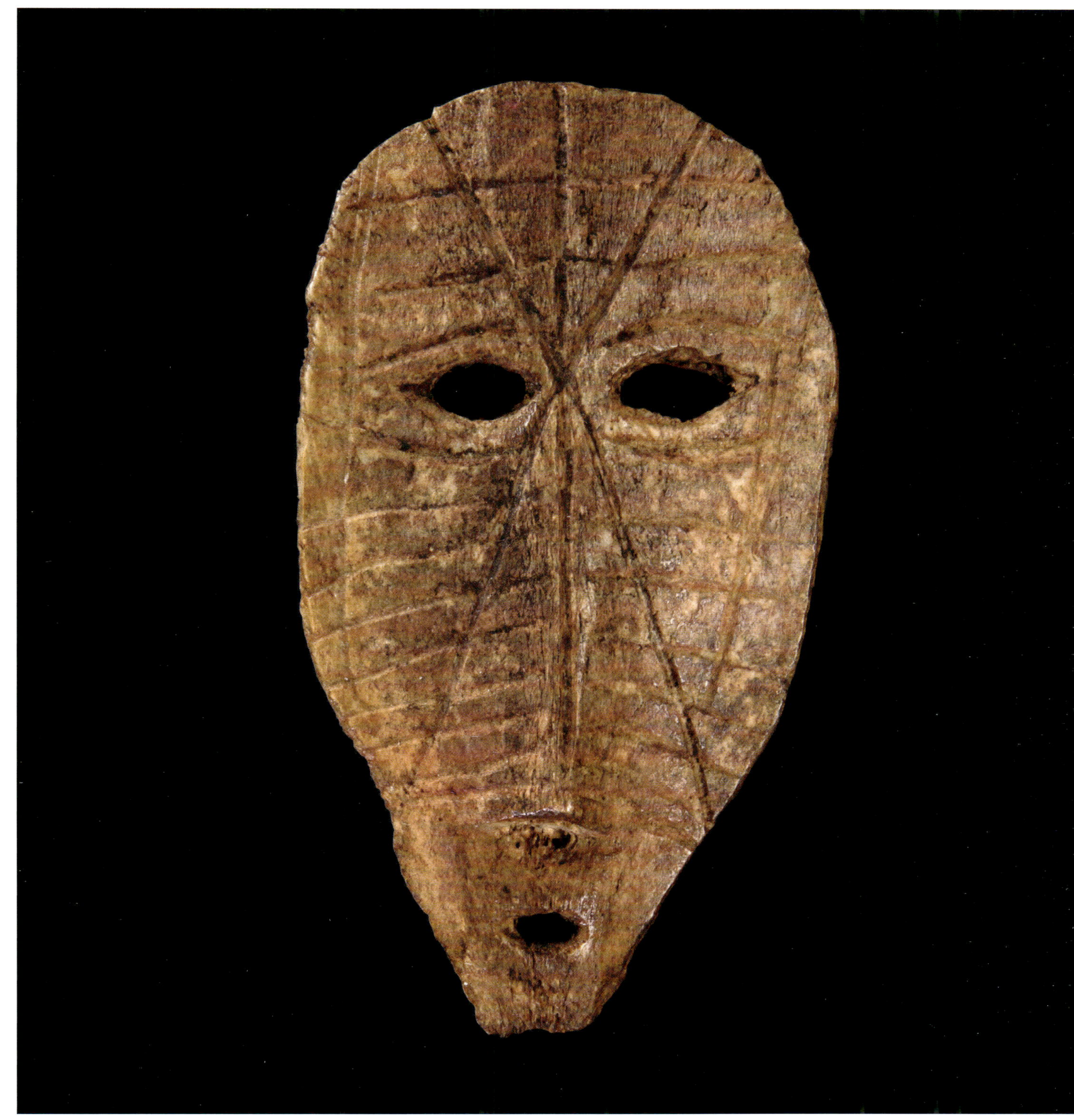

Artist Unknown
Miniature Mask, c. 1500 BCE
A pre-Inuit Palaeo-Eskimo artist created this haunting portrait mask
more than 3,500 years ago. Made from animal bone or antler and incised
with horizontal and diagonal lines possibly representing tattoos, this
carving is small enough to fit in the palm of a child's hand.

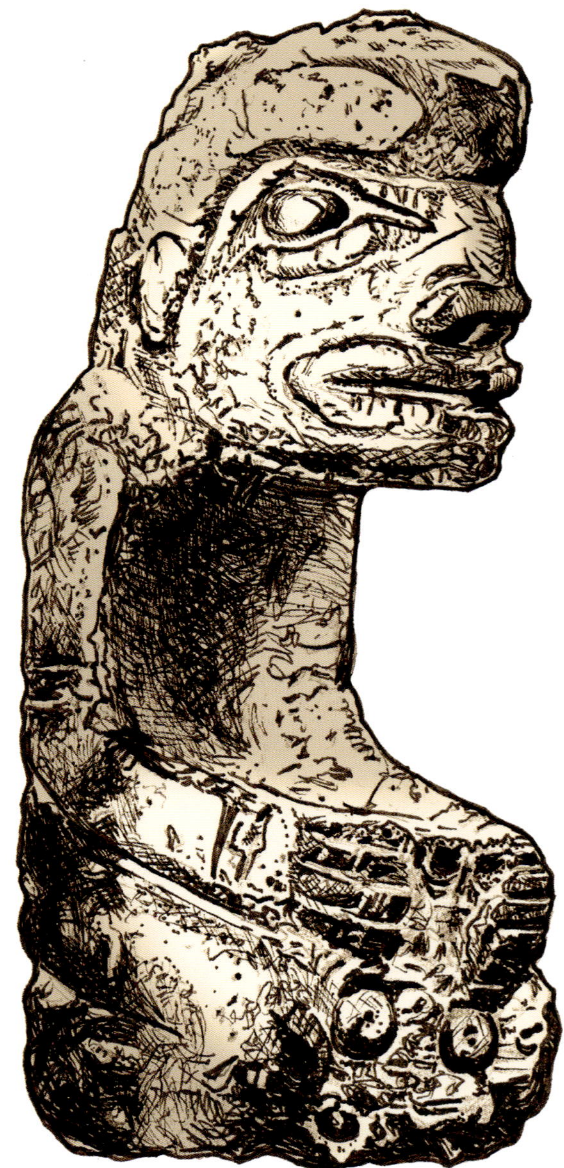

They were variously notched, chipped, ground, shaved, etched, chiselled, carved, dug or constructed. They were produced by two or by many hands. They were made for utilitarian, shamanistic or decorative purposes, or for pleasure. They were venerated or considered ephemeral objects. And the names of the people who produced them are unknown.

Anthropologists and ethnologists call these handcrafted objects "artifacts." They classify them according to type, function, material, location and age. And they can be seen in dimly lit glass cases around the world. But these objects are not simply artifacts. They are singular works of art, which deserve to be treated with the same consideration we would give to a sculpture produced by a non-Indigenous contemporary artist. This is surely how we should consider the hauntingly serene, tattoo-faced portrait maskette fashioned by an early Palaeo-Eskimo artist. Or consider the swimming, crouching, standing or floating bears, with their x-ray skeletal markings, made by the Dorset people. Or the early stone club sculpture

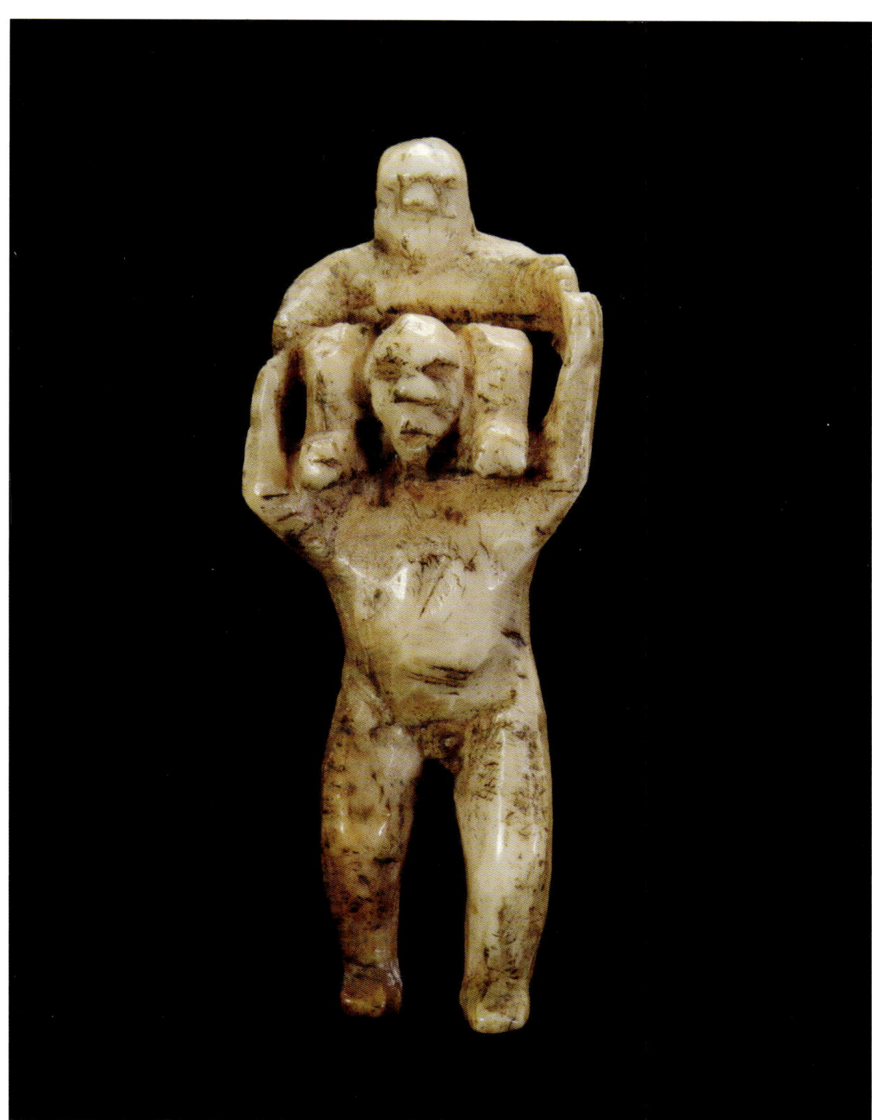

Artist Unknown
Figure of Man and Child, n.d.
An artist belonging to the Dorset people in the eastern Canadian Arctic fashioned this sculpture long before European contact. The sculptor's knowledge of anatomy, technical ability and sense of drama—does this represent a trial of strength or is the man simply carrying his son on his shoulders?—is not diminished by the carving's diminutive size.

Below:
Artist Unknown
Floating or Flying Bear, c. 500 BCE–1200 CE
Carvings of animals like this flying or swimming bear were intended to bring the Inuk hunter luck during the hunt and forgiveness after the creature was slaughtered. This intricately carved sculpture with its deeply incised x-ray style skeletal markings and expressive head was either sewn onto clothing or worn around the hunter's neck.

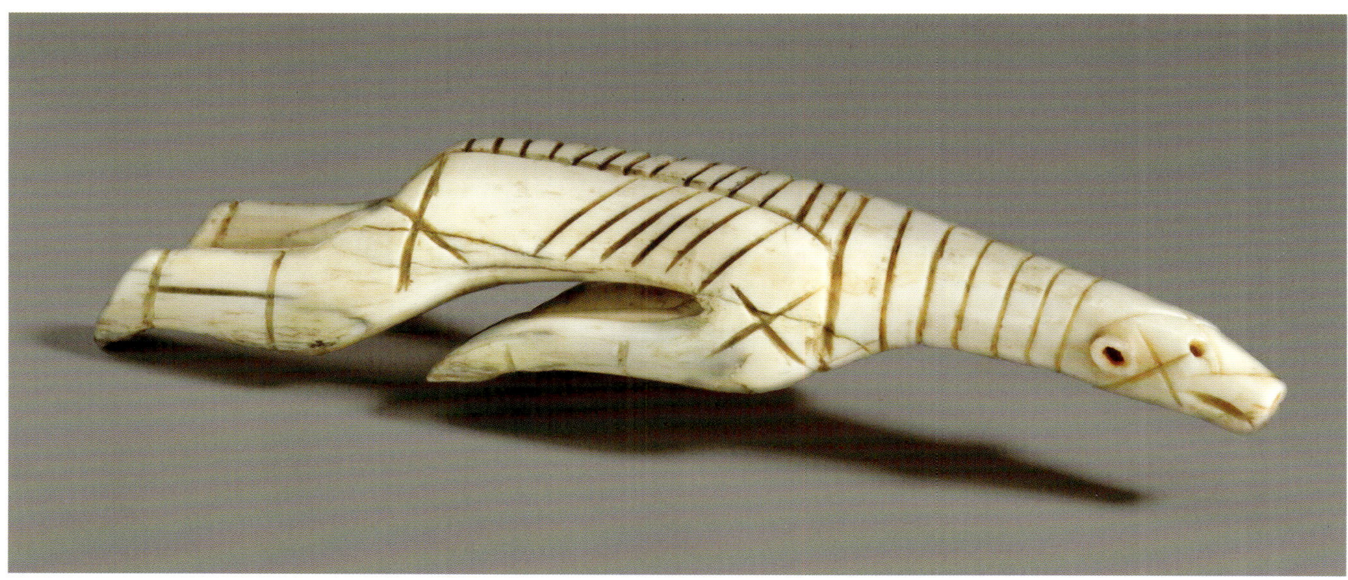

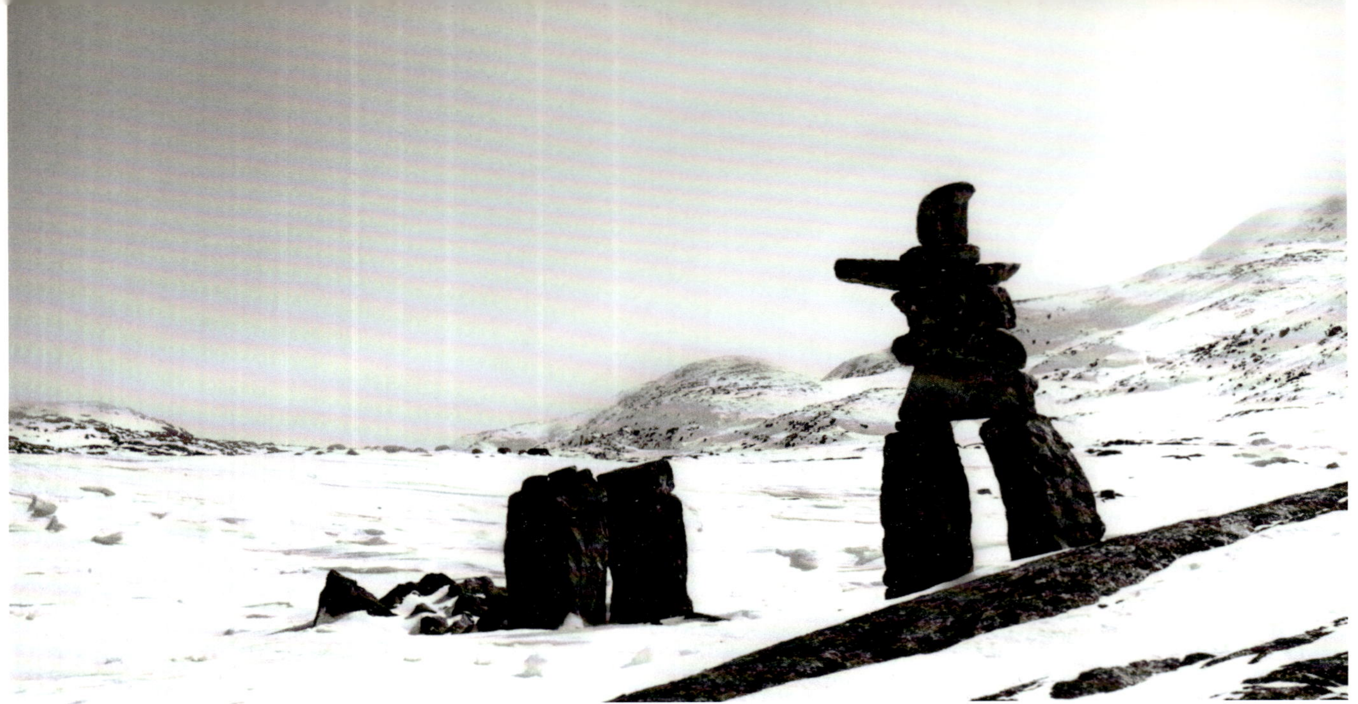

displaying design elements that would provide the structural grid for later generations of Northwest Coast artists. Or the inuksuk composed of rough boulders and stones that are wedged and balanced with precision to make a sculpture in an Inuk's own likeness.

Few of such objects deserve to be dismissed as "artifacts." Instead, they demonstrate that abstract thinking was in place long before the concept was "invented" by early-twentieth-century European artists. They show that the artists who made them had enormous respect for the well-made object. And some of these works reveal that the sculptor's appreciation of the aesthetic quality was so profound that it actually rendered the supposed utilitarian function of the object useless. No matter where or by whom or for what purpose these objects were made, they represent the beginning of the very long history of sculpture in Canada.

And yet most art historians and commentators who write about Canadian culture still seem to cling to the belief of late-nineteenth-century sculptor Hamilton MacCarthy that "the birthplace of the plastic Arts in Canada" began with the settlement of New France.[2] If we follow his line of thinking, this book would surely have to begin in the summer of 1534. That was the year when, during his first voyage to the New World, Jacques Cartier erected a nine-metre-high cross on what is now called Penouille Point in Gaspé Bay. Cartier's makeshift monument proclaimed that this territory now belonged to François I of France. It also symbolized France's conquest of nature and the Roman Catholic Church's attempted domination over First Nations people. Latterly, the cross became a symbol of Jacques Cartier himself.

A hundred years after Cartier arrived in the New World, a cross played an important role in the founding of Ville-Marie, now Montreal. In January 1643, Paul de Chomedey de Maisonneuve hoisted a large wooden cross onto his back. Then, accompanied by a small group of settlers, this thirty-year-old French aristocrat-cum-explorer marched through the thick deciduous forest to the summit of a hill and erected his heavy burden as a monument, to stand in perpetuity. To this day a cross, albeit one made of steel and illuminated by over 150 LED bulbs, stands guard over the city of Montreal on Mount Royal.

By the middle of the seventeenth century other, more sophisticated liturgical carvings conveying the religious values of the Roman Catholic Church appeared. They came in the form of altar screens, tabernacles and calvaries. And they arrived in the hulls of three-masted man-of-war vessels. If the weather was good they could be transported from Le Havre to New France in eight weeks. If the wind and the currents were unfavourable, the whole journey could take up to twenty-four weeks, barring the further possibility of shipwreck.

Little wonder that from the middle of the seventeenth century officials of the Roman Catholic Church seconded French and Belgian sculptors, in addition to master joiners, architects, woodcarvers and carpenters, to travel to New France in order to make religious ornamentation *in situ*. Most of them, like French-born sculptors and master carpenters Samuel Genner and Michel Fauchois, who arrived in New France in 1675, returned to Europe after fulfilling their contracts for the Séminaire de Québec. But a few remained in the French colony, among whom the names Jean Levasseur (1622–1686), Jean Baillairgé (1726–1805) and Philippe Liébert (1733–1804) stand out.

Jean Levasseur and his brother Pierre first set up their workshop in 1651. It functioned for over seventy years. Baillairgé established an even more long-lasting artistic dynasty in Quebec City. Extending over several

Artist Unknown
Stone Club, n.d.
This prehistoric stone club in the shape of a phallus is not a functional weapon; it is an image of a weapon and it represents sexual power. The interplay between literal and metaphorical meaning, life and death, and the relationship of the part to the whole, along with such fundamental First Nations design elements as the formline, illustrate the continuity between prehistoric carvings and Northwest Coast art as we know it today.

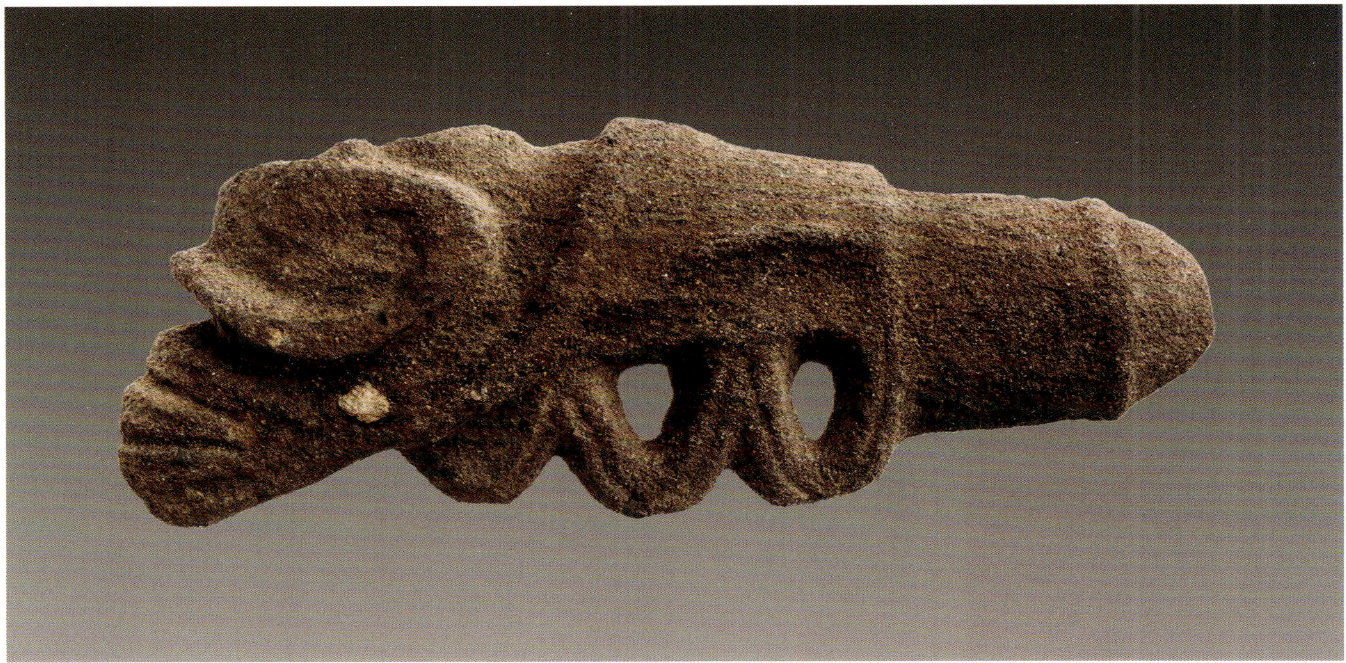

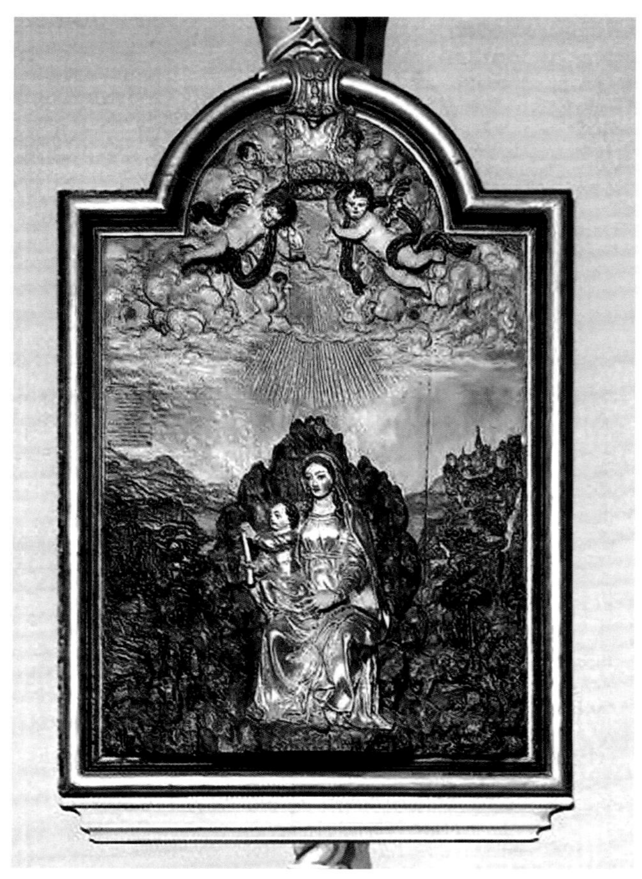

Marie Lemaire des Anges
La Vierge Druidique de Québec, c. 1671–1695
It should not be thought that everyone who carved, painted or gilded liturgical objects was male. Working in the Baroque style, Paris-trained artist Marie Lemaire des Anges inspired her novices and lay pupils at the Ursuline Convent in Quebec. Nor was she a mere copyist. The Virgin Mary in this work wears moccasins and the background landscape is decidedly New World, while the decorative motifs feature local vegetation.

generations, it survived into the twentieth century. These sculpture dynasties, or family firms in today's parlance, ensured that the workshop was trustworthy and reliable. And when one member of the family took religious vows, it gave the family a foot in the door for church patronage.

Liébert did not found a family dynasty, but he did train a host of apprentices. His most accomplished was the Quebec-born artist Louis-Amable Quévillon (1749–1823).

Not every sculptor and craft worker who came to New France during the seventeenth century to produce religious ornamentation for the clergy's newly constructed convents, seminaries and parish churches in and around Quebec City was male. From the moment Marie Lemaire des Anges (c. 1641–1717) arrived in Quebec City in 1671, she carved, gilded *and* painted bas-relief altars and other objects for parish churches run by the Récollet order and later the Jesuits. An adherent of the Baroque style, this Paris-trained artist was unique among her contemporaries, and not just because she was a woman or because she had so many artistic skills to her credit. Lemaire des Anges was ingenious. She incorporated New World motifs such as leaves and flowers alongside First Nations moccasins and the local landscape into reliefs and sculptures like *La Vierge Druidique de Québec* produced for the Jesuit Church around 1685.[3] Working like an early postmodernist sculptor, Lemaire des Anges thus amalgamated the sacred with the profane. She also encouraged her novices and lay pupils at Quebec's Ursuline Convent to participate in the production of liturgical furnishings by teaching them how to carve, paint and gild statues, altarpieces, tabernacles and choir stalls, all of which would aid devotion by deeply moving the viewer.

Sadly, many of the religious carvings—and most of the secular carvings—that were produced during the seventeenth and eighteenth centuries have been lost or are in disrepair. Similarly, we do not know the names of many of the artists who created outstanding works of technical mastery like the earliest surviving free-standing Baroque sculpture *Angel of the Last Judgment* (c. 1670).[4] But we do know something about the functioning of the workshops where these unattributed objects were made.

Some workshops in New France were modelled on the French guild, or *corps de métier*. Others had no official structure. It was here that local journeymen, unskilled workers and apprentices enabled the master sculptor to keep his, and less frequently her, distance from manual labour. A retinue of what might be called horizontal collaborators, including painters, gilders, architects and cabinetmakers, performed their specific tasks in high-ceilinged, high-windowed workshops that afforded ample space and light. Here were artists and their assistants who, following the clergy's instructions, would create a more lavish version of a work that existed in a neighbouring parish church or chapel. Or would produce an outright copy of a famous European work. Or, if the clergy felt that the prefatory drawing adequately

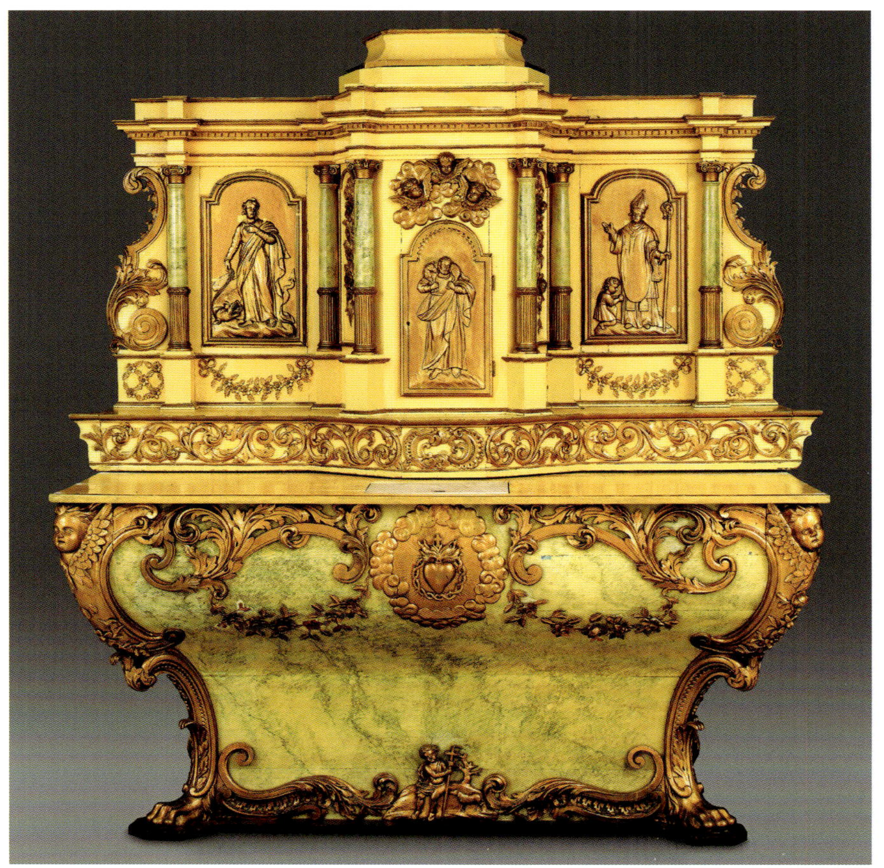

Philippe Liébert
Sacred Heart Altar, 1790
In 1790 the French-born and French-trained sculptor Philippe Liébert and his assistants carved, then painted, then gilded this magnificent altar in gold leaf. Commissioned by the Sisters of Charity, or Grey Nuns, whose order was founded in 1737, the altar's exuberant figurative and decorative motifs are juxtaposed with the restraining columns. This demonstrates how classical order was rendered, during the late eighteenth century, within a Rococo ensemble.

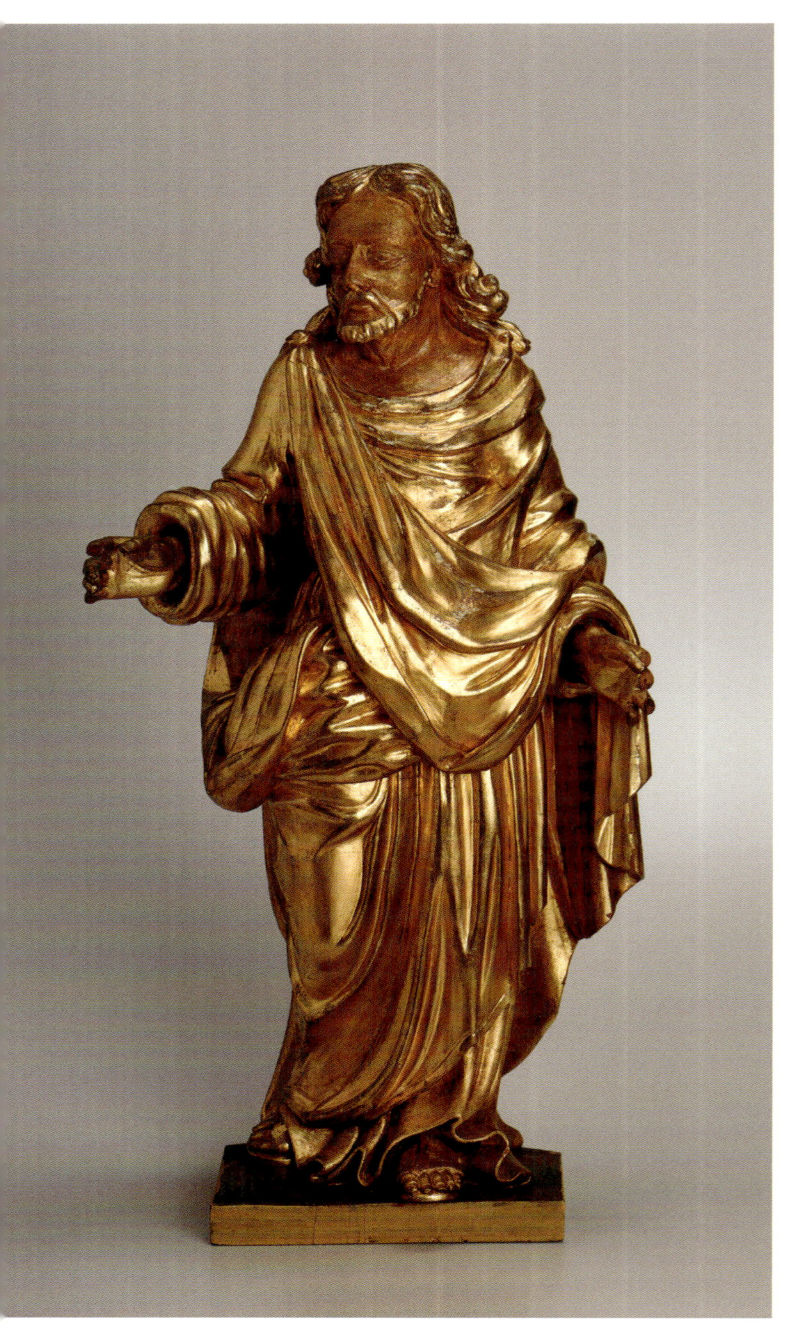

Pierre-Noël Levasseur
Saint Joseph, c. 1750
Quebec-born Pierre-Noël Levasseur was among the first sculptors to
be both born and trained in New France. In keeping with the elements
of Baroque design the artist emphasized the swirling draperies of
Saint Joseph's garments in order to give the saint boundless energy.
Levasseur thereby produced a figure that engaged the congregation in
a visual dialogue every time the mass was given or received.

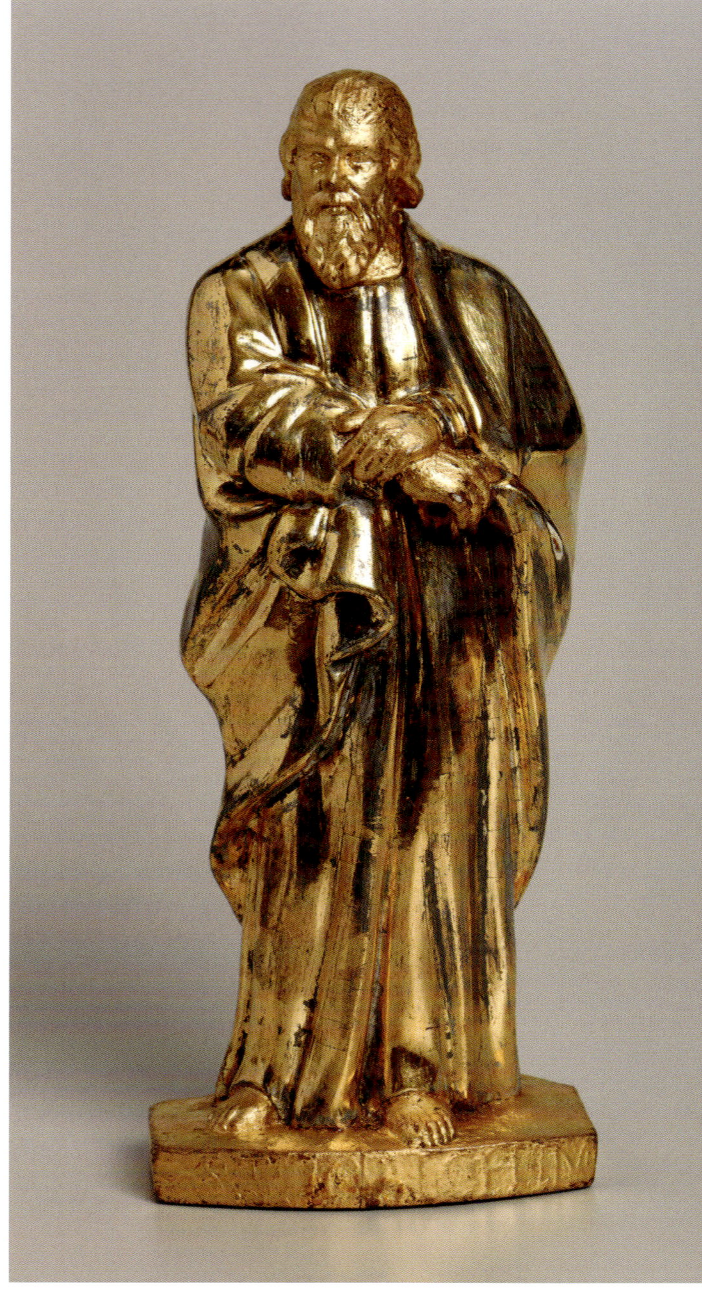

François Baillairgé
Saint Joachim, 1793
François Baillairgé received his initial training in his father's workshop
in Quebec City. But it was during his further study in Paris that he
perfected his skills as both a painter and a sculptor. Using an economy
of detail and restraint typical of Neoclassical style in this sculpture,
Baillairgé challenged the Baroque idiom that had dominated sculpture
in Quebec throughout most of the eighteenth century. He also became
one of Quebec's leading artists.

reflected Roman Catholic doctrines, the sculptor was given free reign. It was also in the workshop that new material like American oak, butternut, basswood and white pine took the place of European wood such as linden, oak and poplar. And it was here that foreign-born artists introduced Quebec-born apprentices to current European styles.

For example, Philippe Liébert passed on the exuberant and flamboyant Rococo style of Louis xv—evident in his *Sacred Heart Altar* (1890), commissioned by the Grey Nuns—to a later generation of artists. Similarly, the Quebec-born Pierre-Noël Levasseur (1690–1770), who studied at the École des Arts et Métiers at Saint-Joachim founded by Bishop François de Laval in 1679, demonstrated in his wood sculpture *Saint Joseph* (1750) that an artist could master the movement and drama of the Baroque style without leaving New France.

It was also from these workshops that some apprentices were singled out for further opportunities. Thus the patronage of the Roman Catholic Church took Jean Baillairgé's talented son, François (1759–1830), to Europe for advanced training. And the results were stunning. Following his return from study in Europe, François Baillairgé had an enormous influence on liturgical sculpture in New France. He challenged the adherents of both the Baroque and Rococo traditions by introducing the Neoclassical style. Baillairgé's sculpture *Saint Joachim* (1793) has great spiritual authority. It is charged with restraint; it was executed with the economy of detail and simplicity that distinguished his work from the flamboyant carvings of his contemporaries. Baillairgé not only introduced Neoclassicism to New France. He removed his sculptures from the confines of the tabernacle and altarpiece, instead integrating them into the architectural fabric of the church. By giving his sculptures their own space, he encouraged anyone who visited the church or chapel to view his carvings as individual works of art. Baillairgé's sculptures were designed to be looked at—more than once.

The sculptures produced by Baillairgé and his contemporaries challenge two conflicting notions. One is that sculpture in New France was produced in a vacuum. The other, to the contrary, is that religious sculpture in New France had all been imported from Europe. Both of these assumptions are wrong. Liturgical sculpture in New France was of a consistently high standard. It was in tandem with—but not imitative of—European trends and styles. And it was anything but colonial.

It could hardly have been otherwise. Sculpture created in New France was produced under very different circumstances than in the mother country. Quebec's population was more urban-based than France's.[5] Unlike post-revolutionary France, Quebec did not experience the dissolution of the Roman Catholic Church, with its subsequent loss of influence and the destruction of its works of art. Paradoxically, therefore, the French Revolution of 1789 worked to the advantage of sculptors in Quebec. This was because the Roman Catholic Church knew that if Quebec was to survive, the Church needed to spread its message *and* create an intellectual elite. The pains the clergy took to reconstruct Quebec City after the damage inflicted during the various battles for the city in the late 1700s and to create new parish churches provided sculptors with plenty of work.

Louis-Amable Quévillon had to hire up to fifteen assistants in order to keep up with the demand for liturgical carvings. François Baillairgé had more commissions than he and his assistants could handle too. But his commissions not only came from the church. During his long career, Baillairgé and his assistants produced dozens of figureheads for the bows of ships built in Kingston and Saint-Jean-sur-Richelieu. And while Baillairgé did not control a large part of the liturgical market like his rival Quévillon, every carving that emerged from his workshop bore the sculptor's distinct style. This enabled Baillairgé to maintain his reputation as the most accomplished artist of his generation.

By the 1840s Quebec's woodcarving tradition was under threat from artists and craftsmen who were producing plaster statues, also known as chalkware. These devotional objects were inexpensive and could be produced more quickly than carvings rendered in wood. Not surprisingly, dozens of foreign-based and foreign-born artists from France and Italy made a good living by marketing plaster-cast replicas of saints and the Madonna. This is not to suggest that sculptors stopped carving in wood. Charles-Olivier Dauphin (1807–1874) and his sons continued to produce liturgical wooden carvings from their atelier in Montreal, as did later generations of woodcarvers in Quebec. But even Dauphin was known to churn out cheap plaster statues for his less prosperous or more impatient clients.

Following the conquest of New France by Great Britain and the signing of the Treaty of Paris in 1763, there was a greater demand for secular sculptures. These were made not only from wood but also from more durable materials ranging from sandstone, marble and concrete to bronze and stone. They came in various forms—columns and obelisks, statues and arches, as well as simple boulders. They were erected in parks, squares and cemeteries—or on the battlefield, or attached to the bows of ships. The people who commissioned these secular works were, as we shall see, often civic councillors, sometimes private businessmen, occasionally military units or government officials and—on one unique occasion—construction workers.

Those chosen to fulfill the commissions—the stonemasons, builders, architects and professional sculptors—came from Europe, the United States and, less frequently, British North America. A sculptor or craftsman could earn a good living by carving figureheads for bows of ships built in Halifax, Lunenburg, Saint John and Quebec City. The most favoured subjects were female torsos and animals, as well as historic and First Nations figures. But there was even more money to be made by producing statues commemorating British royalty, local and foreign statesmen, and military heroes.

One of the earliest secular sculptures erected following the conquest was a head-and-shoulders, larger-than-life marble carving of King George III, who reigned from 1760 to 1820. This competent but undistinguished bust of the British monarch was commissioned following the fire that destroyed a large part of Montreal in May 1765. The artist who designed the work was Joseph

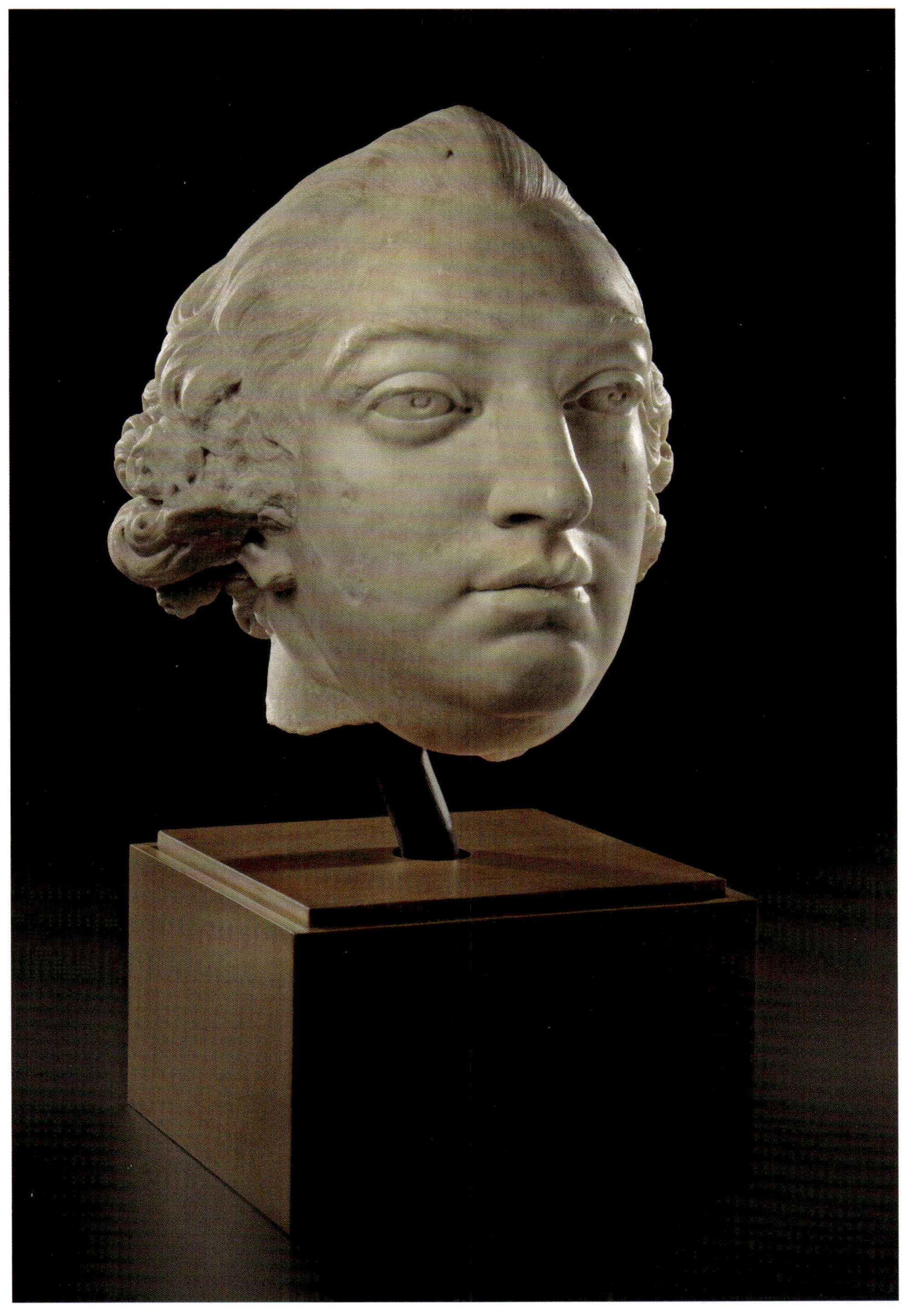

Joseph Wilton
Bust of King George III, c. 1765–1766
A founding member of the Royal Academy of Art, Joseph Wilton was the official artist of King George III, and eighteenth-century commentators often compared him to the Renaissance sculptor Michelangelo. Unlike many artists who produced idealized sculptures of "the mad king," Joseph Wilton portrayed the monarch as flabby-faced and overfed. Erected in Montreal's Place d'Armes in 1773, this bust was a visual reminder to French-speaking residents of Britain's presence in their city.

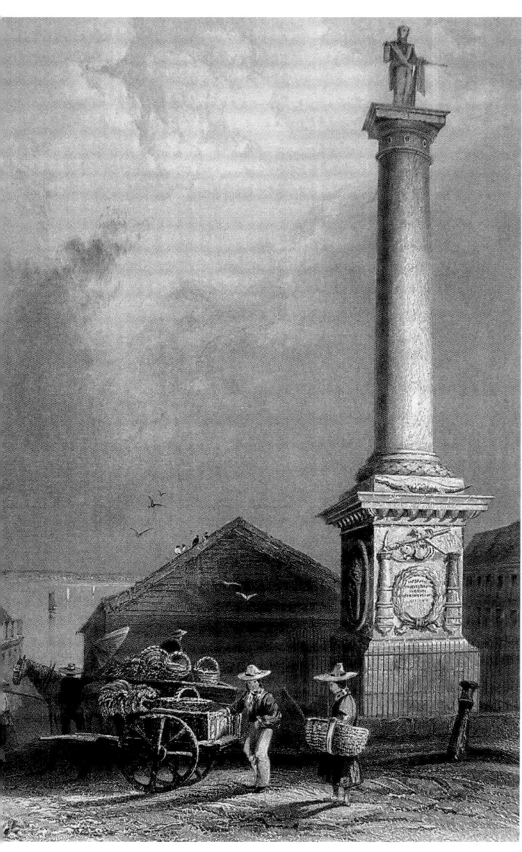

Coade and Sealy of London, design firm; William Gilmore, stonemason
Nelson's Column, 1809
In October 1805 the citizens of Montreal learned that the Royal Navy had defeated the French and Spanish fleets during the Battle of Trafalgar, and that the British commander, Vice Admiral Horatio Nelson, had lost his life. By 1809 English-speaking Montrealers had raised sufficient funds to erect a Neoclassical column, topped with a larger-than-life-sized realistic sculpture of the one-armed admiral, in the city's Place Jacques-Cartier.

Wilton (1722–1803), the official sculptor to the king and a founding member of Britain's Royal Academy of Arts. Wilton's sculpture arrived in Montreal from London in 1766 and seven years later it was duly placed on a pedestal in the core of French-speaking Montreal, the Place d'Armes. Situated across the square from the Notre-Dame Basilica, "the bust," writes scholar Joan Coutu, "was undeniably and unavoidably obtrusive." It was, above all "a constant reminder of the British presence in and control of Montréal."[6]

A monument of a very different kind was erected several years later in the same city. This Neoclassical column did not celebrate a member of the royal family. Rather, it honoured a sailor who had risen through the ranks of the Royal Navy to become an admiral. The column commemorating Vice Admiral Horatio Nelson's victory over the French navy at the Battle of Trafalgar in 1805 was composed of gray compact limestone and a new clay-like material, developed by London-based Eleanor Coade, called Coade stone. Capped by a larger-than-life statue of Nelson, the nineteen-metre-tall column was fabricated in London by the firm Coade and Sealy and shipped to Montreal in seventeen parts. Local stonemason William Gilmore assembled the column at the southern end of Place Jacques-Cartier in Montreal in 1809.[7] Some observers would compare the monument to Nelson with the Vendôme Column erected in Paris's Place Vendôme in 1810. Others looked back in history to the obelisk at Luxor in ancient Egypt. Everyone knew that Nelson's Column stood for military might, male power and political authority. But few observers noted the phallic symbolism of such a column, so well captured in Lawrence Durrell's satirical poem "A Ballad of the Good Lord Nelson" (1943): "Now stiff on a pillar with a phallic air / Nelson stylites in Trafalgar Square / Reminds the British what they once were."[8]

This was not the first column to be erected in British North America. In 1804 a six-metre-high column honouring fur trader and founding partner of the North West Company Simon McTavish was placed on the slope of Mount Royal in Montreal.

Twenty-three years later, stonemason John Phillips produced a monument honouring Generals James Wolfe and Louis-Joseph de Montcalm. The unadorned obelisk was installed in the Jardin des Gouverneurs overlooking the Plains of Abraham, where the generals had died within twenty-four hours of one another during the Battle of Quebec in 1759.

In 1860 the triumphal arch, popularized in ancient Rome, was brought into service during the inauguration of the world's longest bridge: the Great Victoria Bridge spanning the Saint Lawrence River. Two local stained-glass manufacturers, John McArthur and John Spence, were hired to construct and install nine temporary arches between Quebec's dockyard and the entrance to the three-kilometre-long steel bridge. And the person who led the procession through the arches during the bridge's inauguration ceremony was none other than the young son of Queen Victoria, Albert Edward, Prince of Wales.

The same year, in 1860, Scottish-born builder, stonemason and sculptor George Laing (1821–1881) produced a more permanent arch at the entrance to St. Paul's Church Cemetery in the centre of Halifax, Nova

Scotia. The *Crimean War Monument* commemorated two of the men who had died in 1855 at the Battle at the Great Redan during the Crimean War. Derived from classical antiquity, the shouldered flat arch is crowned by the enormous figure of a lion weighing some eleven metric tons. Laing was ahead of his Canadian contemporaries in choosing the lion as a motif for his work. Moreover, it was not until 1867 that British artist Edwin Henry Landseer (1802–1873) popularized this subject in Britain, when he made the clay model from which four lions were cast in bronze then placed at the base of Nelson's Column in London's Trafalgar Square.

There were, of course, commemorative sculptures that did not owe their stylistic origins to ancient Egypt, Rome or Greece. The Irish Commemorative Stone memorial, more commonly known as the Black Rock (1860), was one such work. Composed of a simple boulder, the stone has only one embellishment: an inscription acknowledging the six thousand Irish immigrants who died of typhus at Grosse Ile quarantine station in 1847 and 1848. The origin and financing of the Black Rock also made the work unique. During the construction of the Great Victoria Bridge, a group of workers discovered the mass grave containing the Irish immigrants' bodies. It was they who paid for the modest memorial out of their own pockets.

Generally, however, it was the public who financed memorial and commemorative sculptures. A memorial committee, composed of the community's most prominent citizens, would persuade the local government to donate a site. They would choose an artist to produce a sculpture, and then organize a public subscription campaign to raise the money to pay for the work. However, public subscription campaigns often did not yield the desired result. When this happened, the work was delayed and payment was withheld from the commissioned sculptor until the

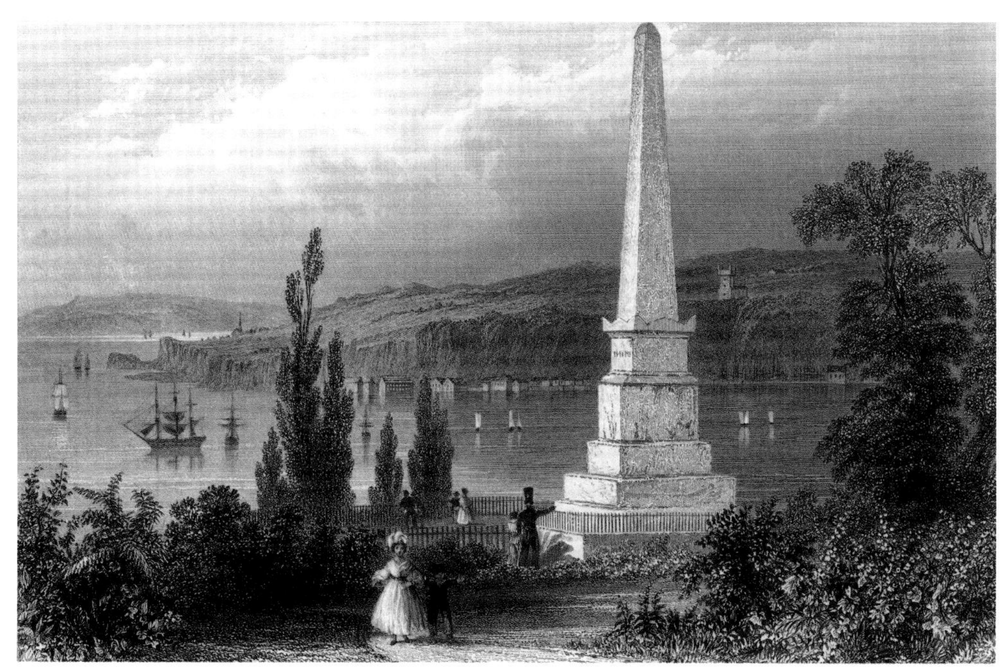

John Phillips, stonemason
Monument to Wolfe and Montcalm, 1827
This stark twenty-metre-high obelisk, located in Quebec City, commemorates the deaths of Generals Wolfe and Montcalm, who died within twenty-four hours of one another on the Plains of Abraham during the Battle of Quebec in 1759. A Latin inscription, etched on a brass plate on the monument's foundation stone, translates as, "Military virtue gave them a common death. History a common fame. Posterity a common monument."

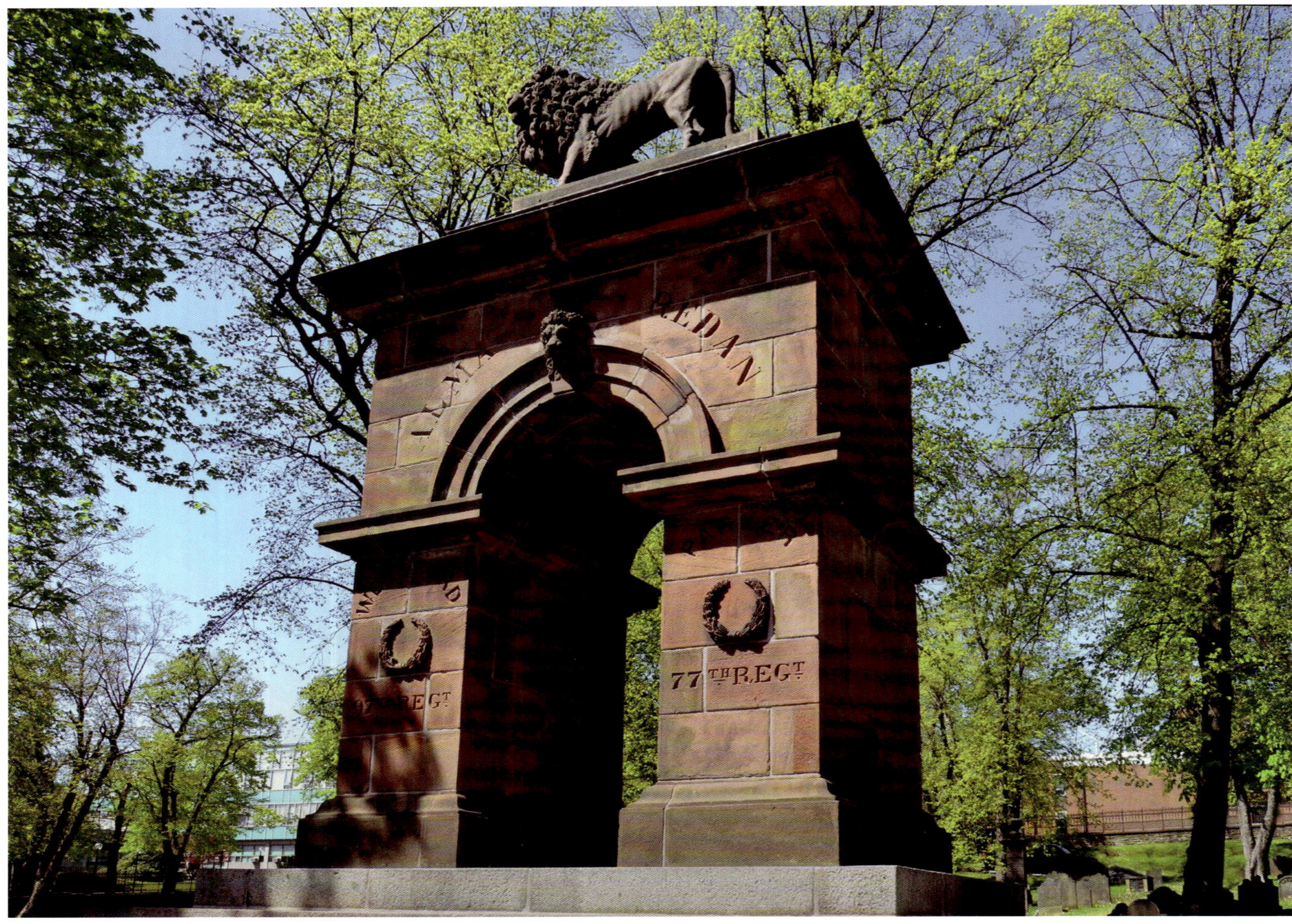

George Laing
Crimean War Monument, 1860

George Laing's *Crimean War Monument*, featuring a shouldered flat arch dominated by a magnificent lion weighing eleven metric tons, stands at the entrance to the Old Burying Ground (St. Paul's Church Cemetery) in Halifax, Nova Scotia. Although the monument was commissioned to honour Major Augustus Welsford and Captain William Parker, who died at the Battle of the Great Redan (1855), the arch has come to represent all members of the Halifax and Dartmouth Volunteer Companies who lost their lives during the Siege of Sevastopol (1854–1855).

funds were in place. This was the case with both Nelson's Column and the *Crimean War Monument*.

Other groups had more luck in raising funds. England-based merchant-philanthropist Jonas Hanway had no difficulty accumulating enough money through public subscription to pay for the bust of King George III, erected in 1773. In the 1830s it was British soldiers, posted in Quebec City, who paid for the helmet and sword that topped the second memorial column honouring General James Wolfe. Two decades later, with Napoléon III now in power as the French emperor, Prince Jérôme-Napoléon showed himself eager to mark the centenary of the French victory over the British at the Battle of Sainte-Foy during the Seven Years War, in which 1,124 British soldiers had died against only 833 French casualties. The prince gave Quebec's Saint-Jean-Baptiste Society a statue of Bellona, the Roman goddess of war. In 1860 the imposing sculpture—designed by a member of the famous Baillairgé family, Charles Baillairgé (1826–1906)—was placed on top of an almost fourteen-metre-high fluted Doric column that had been paid for by public subscription. Three years later, in 1863, the *Monument aux Braves* was unveiled near Quebec City.

Once the memorial or commemorative sculpture was erected and paid for, an elaborate unveiling ceremony, replete with backslapping speeches, uniformed bands and festive crowds, took place. But there was no guarantee that a monument, so enthusiastically celebrated during its dedication ceremony, would remain an object of veneration. The memorial column in Montreal dedicated to fur trader Simon McTavish was allowed to deteriorate, and was eventually torn down. The nine arches celebrating the opening of the Great Victoria Bridge were demolished as soon as Britain's future king left Montreal. Almost one hundred years after its fabrication, Nelson's Column in Montreal needed a facelift. Funds were raised, the column was repaired and a rededication ceremony was held in 1900. In 1997 it was the statue of Nelson himself at the top of the column that needed attention. It had deteriorated to such an extent that it was irreparable. A copy now stands in its place, but the original statue can still be viewed at the Centre d'Histoire de Montréal.

The memorials, obelisks, statues, busts and columns erected in squares, parks and battlegrounds in British North America were about more than stone, rock and bronze. They were about more than those who had paid for them, or the stonemasons, craftsmen, architects or sculptors who had created them. They were about power. The bronze bust of King George III proclaimed to all—particularly French-speaking residents of Montreal—that they had a British king to whom their loyalty was demanded. The rededication of Nelson's Column in 1900 reminded Montreal's divided community of the admiral's service to the British Empire. The French and English inscriptions written on the nine arches celebrating the opening of the Great Victoria Bridge professed both groups' allegiance to Great Britain—but proved temporary.

We need to ask, then: Whose past, whose myths and whose memory was being invoked by these works? The modest boulder at the entrance to the same bridge was a reminder that thousands of hopeful immigrants had lost their lives during their voyage to the New World. The monument celebrating the last French victory under the Chevalier de Lévis at the Battle of Sainte-Foy showed that French soldiers were capable of winning a victory against the odds. And the lion mounted on the *Crimean War Monument* left no doubt that the sculpture stood for the valour and strength of the British Empire.

Moreover, the meanings associated with many of these secular and religious monuments had a limited sell-by date, with contests over their symbolism. In response to the Quebec Act of 1774, which guaranteed the Québécois their language, religion and civil law, a faction of British merchants who opposed the act vandalized the marble bust of King George III. An award was offered for the names of the culprits who had painted the bust black, draped it in a rosary of rotten potatoes and attached a banner that read *Voilà le Pape du Canada et le sot Anglais.* No one came forward to claim the reward. During the American invasion of Montreal a year later, the bust disappeared altogether. It surfaced fifty years later, however, when construction workers found it at the bottom of a well. No effort was made to restore and reinstall the much-altered sculpture—it was without neck and shoulders—of the supposedly mad British king.

A truncated column honouring General James Wolfe erected in Quebec

City in 1832 suffered a different fate. On their pilgrimage to the Plains of Abraham, where the general had died, admirers would chip a piece off the column as a memento. By 1849 the column was in such bad disrepair from the actions of enthusiastic souvenir hunters that it had to be dismantled. It was replaced with an eleven-metre-high Doric column protected by a sharply pointed iron fence. As for Nelson's Column in Montreal, Quebec sovereignists threatened to blow it up in 1890. Seven years later someone proposed moving the monument to an Anglophone district of the dominantly French-speaking city. But the suggestion came to naught and Nelson's Column remains in its original location to this day.

As noted earlier, the French and British settlers were not the only—or indeed the earliest—inhabitants of this land. Nor were they the only people for whom such aesthetic objects were invested with significance and ambiguity. What about the meaning and making of Indigenous sculpture following European contact, occupation and settlement of North America? What did visitors to the New World see when they confronted Northwest Coast art? And to what extent did First Nations artists themselves alter their art form following contact?

European and Russian explorers, who made landfall on the northwest coast in the late eighteenth century, saw intricately carved columns—which we now call totem poles—standing in front of, or as a structural part of, enormous cedar-plank-and-beam "big houses" that served the communities. In villages on the archipelago of Haida Gwaii (called the Queen Charlotte Islands throughout most of the nineteenth and twentieth centuries), animals, humans and mythological figures were carved along the conical shape of a cedar log. In the Tlingit, Nisga'a and Tsimshian villages that hugged the north coast and inland rivers, maritime explorers and traders encountered totem poles featuring human and animal figures that were stacked as though separated by a horizontal line. Further south they found a more dramatic art form. The Kwakwaka'wakw carved and painted frontal house poles featuring thunderbirds whose enormous beaks opened and closed to admit the inhabitants to the entry of the community house. The Coast Salish and Nuu-chah-nulth peoples' artists likewise often departed from the conical shape of the log. Their welcome figures and memorial poles were usually carved in the round.

For some European visitors totem poles and other carvings associated with Northwest Coast peoples were objects for scientific inquiry. While Captain James Cook's ships, the HMS *Discovery* and HMS *Resolution,* were anchored at Friendly Cove (Yuquot) in the spring of 1778, for example, the expedition's artist, John Webber (1751–1793), sketched anthropomorphic beings that were carved into two interior house posts of a Nuu-chah-nulth cedar-plank big house. He also made drawings of two masks, a seal decoy and a rattle. These drawings were later "refined" by an engraver back in London, then tipped into Captain Cook's posthumously published *A Voyage to the Pacific Ocean* (1784). Captain Cook acquired several Nuu-chah-nulth

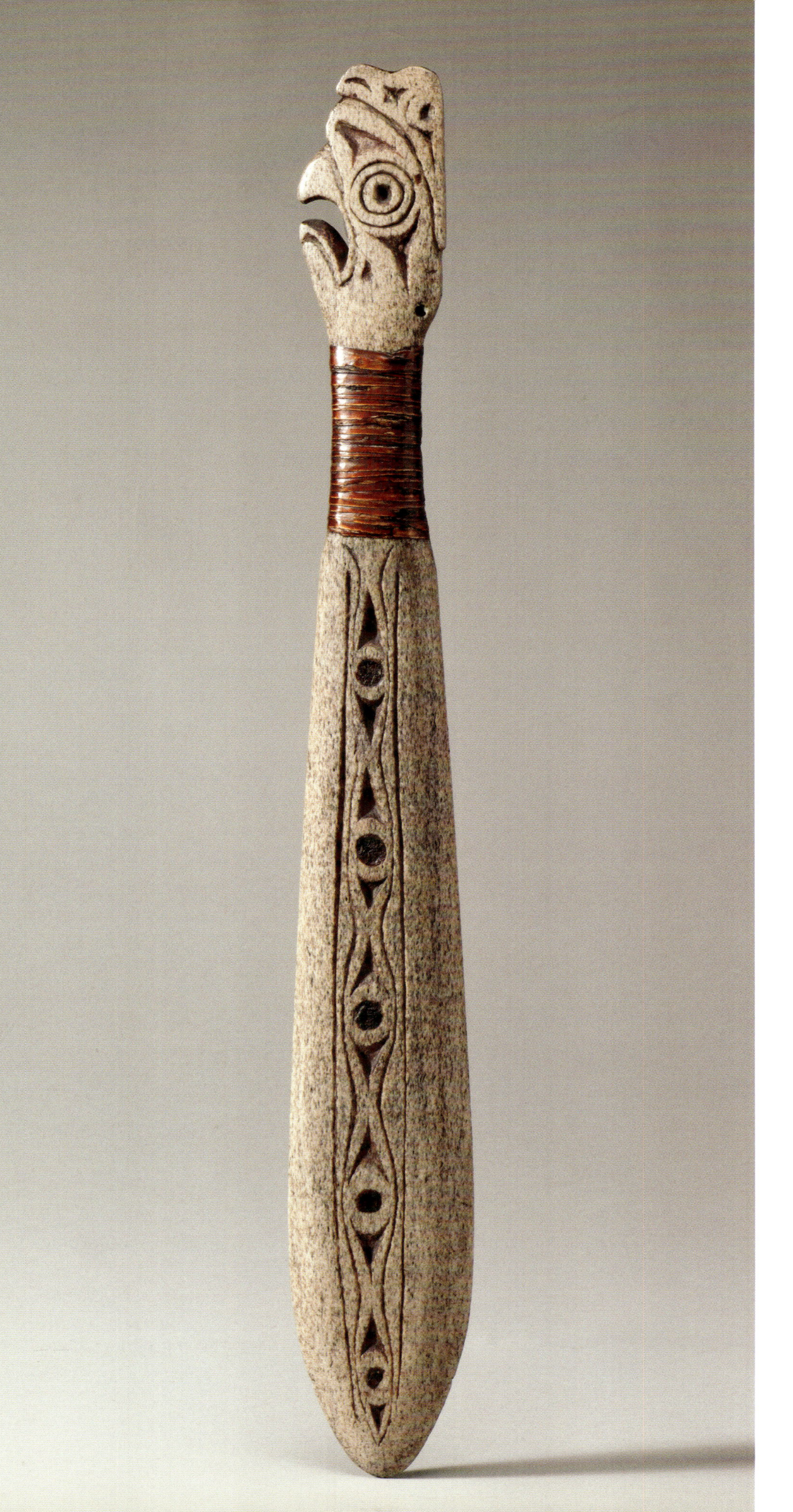

Artist Unknown
Whalebone Club, c. 1778
Captain James Cook collected this club,
made from the dense lower jawbone
of a whale, during his visit to Friendly
Cove (Yuquot) in northern Vancouver
Island's Nootka Sound (Mowichat)
in 1778. At the hilt of the club is an
open-beaked thunderbird thought by
the Nuu-chah-nulth people to have the
power to hunt whales. Flowing down
the club's blade are incised lines and
decorative motifs that might represent
the feathers of the mythical bird.

carvings when he made landfall at Friendly Cove during his third voyage to the New World. The most remarkable is a finely sculptured *Whalebone Club* (c. 1778) whose handle is in the shape of a bird's head and the shaft of which is incised with geometric designs—representing feathers, perhaps—typical of Nuu-chah-nulth carving. Fifty years later a maritime trader, in search of sea otter pelts along the Inside Passage between Vancouver Island and the mainland, collected a sensitively carved representation, Haisla *Face Mask* (c. 1830), produced by a Tsimshian artist.[9]

Most visitors to the northwest coast during the first half of the nineteenth century, however, had little or no interest in looking at or acquiring Indigenous art. They viewed it as monstrous and crudely made, the product of an uncivilized and heathen people. This line of thinking reinforced the Euro-American settlers' sense of superiority over Indigenous people, justified their possession of their lands and legitimized the efforts of both the Catholic and Protestant Churches to convert their peoples to their God.

For First Nations peoples, their totem poles were not, as many visitors to the New World assumed, objects of worship. The stylized crest figures depicted on these monumental sculptures had other functions: they signified a family's lineage; they validated a family or clan's rights and privileges; they confirmed family status; they commemorated events. And all of this gave a visual confirmation of the spiritual and social order of the community. Nor were Indigenous peoples "heathens." They possessed their own creation myths, their own gods and their own spirits. Moreover, the ceremonial and utilitarian objects they made were anything but crudely rendered. The intricate carving, the sense of rhythm and the dramatic presentation were as technically proficient as anything created by the artists' contemporaries in eighteenth-century Europe.

Above all, First Nations people were good at trading. They were well

Artist Unknown
Carved Panel Pipe, early 1800s
In the early decades of the nineteenth century, Haida artists began carving napkin rings, platters and decorative pipes from the fine-grained sedimentary black shale known as argillite. Made largely for the "tourist trade," these items often combined European motifs with Indigenous designs. The artist who carved this sculpture made First Nations design secondary to the European seamen and their boat.

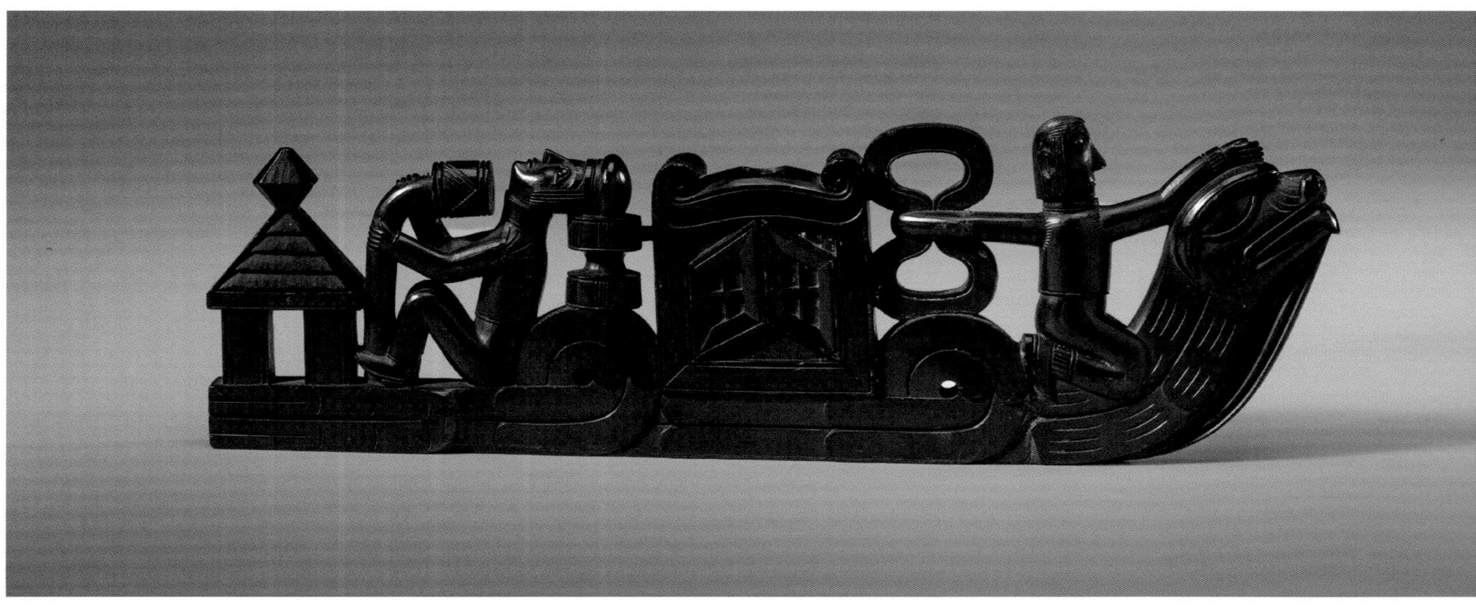

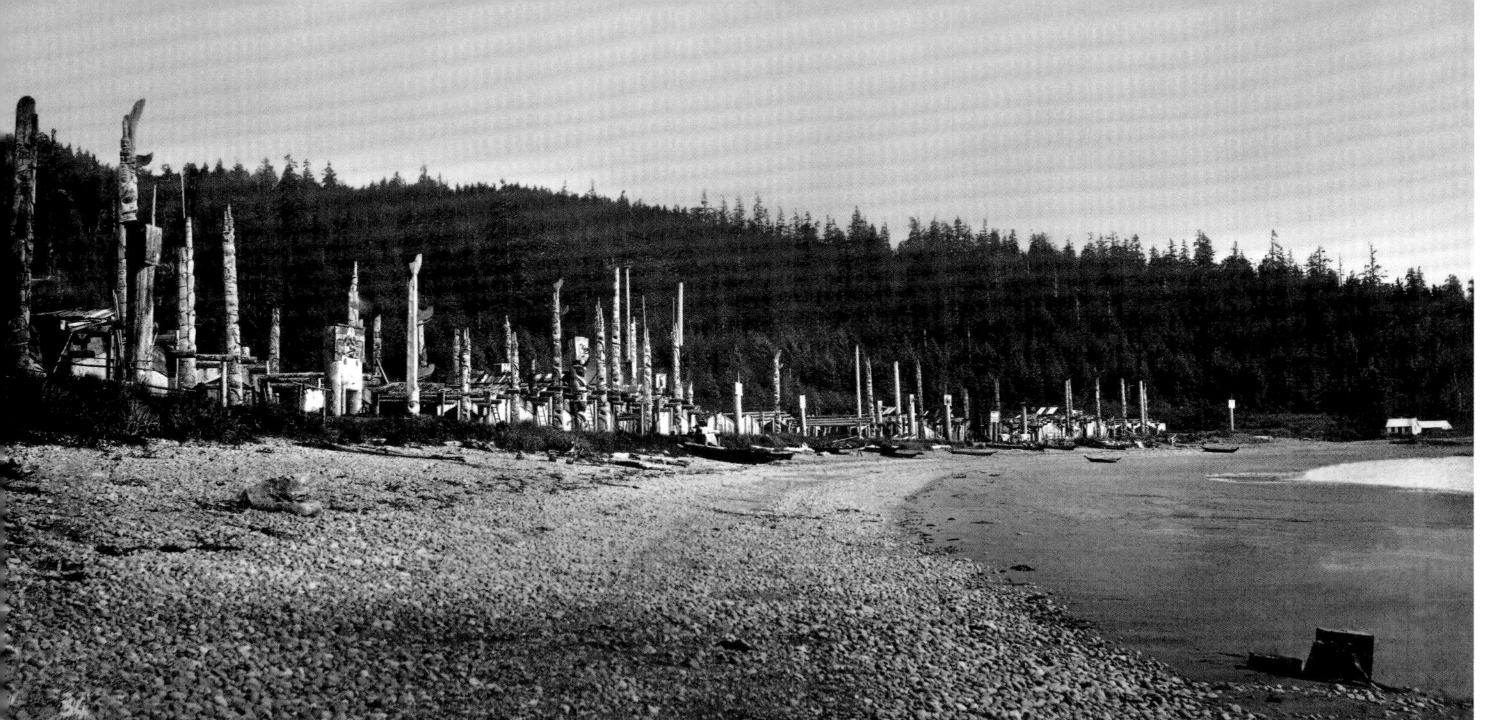

used to bartering otter pelts—they knew how to trade "soft gold" for the European goods they needed for their own purposes. In doing so, they simultaneously upgraded their technology and expanded their market. Access to iron and steel tools enabled Indigenous artists to replace their traditional carving implements of stone, shell and beaver teeth. Access to Euro-American maritime explorers and traders gave them new customers for their artwork. And the demand for what were pejoratively called "curios" grew exponentially as the first generation of settlers and even missionaries began collecting Indigenous works of art.

First Nations artists were masters at adapting their own aesthetic interests to the requirements of their non-Indigenous patrons. They produced dozens of miniature carvings of totem poles, canoes and big houses. They even expanded their repertoire to include napkin rings and brooches. And, departing from tradition once again, they combined Indigenous motifs with non-Indigenous ones. For example, it was not unusual for an artist to integrate an American eagle or a European sailor into a sculpture.

Although largely produced for trade, these carvings were rarely cheaply crafted. Most were stunning pieces of sculpture that rose out of a mature art form and drew on artistic skill and an imaginative sense of how to adapt Indigenous designs and subject matter for their non-Indigenous clientele.

During the early decades of the nineteenth century artists in Haida Gwaii met the demand for such curios in a novel way. They transformed the black carbonaceous shale known as argillite into miniature totem poles, canoes and panel pipes that would not smoke—primarily for the non-Indigenous market. A piece called *Carved Panel Pipe*, created by a Haida artist during the first period of argillite carving, 1800 to 1835, offers a good example of how fine, lattice-like carving combining disparate human and mythical figures gives this material an apparent lightness that defied the sculpture's actual weight.

**The Haida village of Skidegate, Haida Gwaii
July 26, 1878**
When George Mercer Dawson of the Geological Survey of Canada took this photograph in 1878, he counted more than fifty totem poles in Skidegate Inlet. This display belied the fact that the population of the former fur-trading centre had fallen drastically due to introduced diseases and ceremonial objects were being removed to museums around the world. Moreover, proselytizing Methodist ministers, and later government officials, made the ceremonial traditions that gave a visual and oral confirmation of the social and spiritual order to the community illegal. By 1932 only three poles remained standing in Skidegate; two decades later there was only one.

Photo by George Mercer Dawson, Collection of the Canadian Museum of History, 2007.171.184.

The European presence had an enormous impact on Indigenous art and culture. Trade in otter pelts gave First Nations people more wealth and more power. Initially, there were more potlatches and winter feasts, with a consequent demand for more ceremonial objects and totem poles. And as indicated earlier, with the introduction of iron and steel tools, artists produced carvings more quickly and on a larger scale. Totem poles were now more often rendered as free-standing sculptures rather than a structural part of a big house. A photograph of the Haida village of Skidegate taken in the summer of 1878 demonstrates the extent to which the area between the high-tide mark and the big houses was festooned with a forest of totem poles.

But there was a price to be paid for this newfound wealth, power and artistic achievement. By the early decades of the nineteen century, the sea otter trade had become so successful that the animal was near extinction. By the middle of the same century, Indigenous people were feeling the mixed effects of the government's assimilation policies and of the Church's attempts to convert them to Christianity. And then, more alarmingly, there was the effect of diseases—tuberculosis, whooping cough and measles—to which First Nations people had no immunity.

When Spanish maritime explorers made landfall on Haida Gwaii in 1774, there were probably over 10,000 Haida living on the islands. By 1835 the population had fallen to 6,693, and by 1870 to a pitiful 1,244. New contacts had spread new diseases. The population of First Nations people in Haida Gwaii and in villages along the northwest coast continued to decline with the impact of smallpox in 1862. Villages were abandoned overnight. Power vacuums were created within decimated Indigenous communities and families. By the end of the century the population of Haida Gwaii had fallen to 800.

The introduction of disease decimated First Nations populations. Maybe there were fewer potlatches and winter ceremonies, and consequently less demand for totem poles and other ceremonial objects within a smaller community. Yet, "almost ironically," as anthropologist Aldona Jonaitis puts it, "during this period of increasing oppression by whites and population decimation, Northwest Coast artwork flourished as never before, as taller totem poles, more impressive houses, and more dazzling costumes had to be made in order to satisfy the needs of the remaining Indians who wished to use their art to convince the world of their prestige and importance."[10] Thus, quality was not sacrificed.

What happened on the west coast had, in important ways, been prefigured further east, where Europeans had first settled—or intruded. The Iroquois, or Haudenosaunee, people, who inhabited 3,800 square kilometres near the Saint Lawrence and the eastern Great Lakes certainly knew the extent to which disease had impacted upon the cultural life of their community.[11] Contact with Europeans in the middle of the seventeenth century had not only led to the occupation of Indigenous traditional lands; the introduction of viruses to which the Iroquois were not immune led to a series of disfiguring diseases like smallpox ravaging their communities.

When traditional curing rites failed to eradicate these foreign-induced epidemics, the Iroquois re-evaluated the spirit forces that governed their medicine societies. The result was the production of False Face masks, sacred objects that became both agents and healers of disease. The masks were mental constructs representing the dreams and mythology of the producer and wearer who hoped to be healed. The masks' broken and bent noses, deeply furrowed brows and deep-set eyes, along with their protruding or lolling tongues, twisted mouths and distended lips, prompted one anthropologist to describe them as "memorials to generations of nightmares."[12] False Face masks were carved from the living tree, and most artists preferred to work in basswood. After the mask was sketched out, the artist removed it from the tree, refined the carving, applied either black or red paint and then added horsehair. Like the ceremonial carvings made by West Coast First Nations artists, False Face masks were brought to life when members of the False Face Society wore them during the spring and autumn healing, or right of purification, ceremonies.[13]

Across the continent the demand for First Nations art did not simply continue within the Indigenous community. Nor was interest confined to a few early traders and settlers. By the middle of the nineteenth century, sculptures made by Indigenous artists were traded throughout British North America, directly and indirectly. They were also displayed at agricultural fairs across the country. For example, it was not uncommon to see birchbark boxes or model canoes among the objects made by the Mi'kmaq at Halifax's annual Industrial Exhibition. Nor was it unusual to find Northwest Coast First Nations carvings further afield; they became a feature of the Canadian display booths at international fairs like London's Great Exhibition in 1851. As will be shown, during the last two decades of the nineteenth century anthropologists and curators would scramble to acquire both "old" and "new" First Nations carvings for their museums around the world.

There is a common dimension to the experience of those producing and consuming the sculptures of both the Euro-American and Indigenous peoples alike. When we look at what happened in New France, and later in all the provinces and territories of what is now Canada, we see that the meanings and lessons proclaimed by the religious, secular and Indigenous monuments and sculptures were not always shared. There were competing memories. There were convenient and sometimes inconvenient "truths" relating to past events and personages. These were competitive and idealized visions of the past, working at different levels. We should be in no doubt, as one historian has put it, that "commemoration is closely related to power: it reveals an ongoing contest for hegemony."[144] This was as true when Cartier planted the cross at Gaspé Bay in the summer of 1534 as it was when a group of citizens in Montreal erected Nelson's Column in 1809, when the first Iroquois artist carved a False Face mask and when Haida sculptors raised their totem poles on Haida Gwaii.

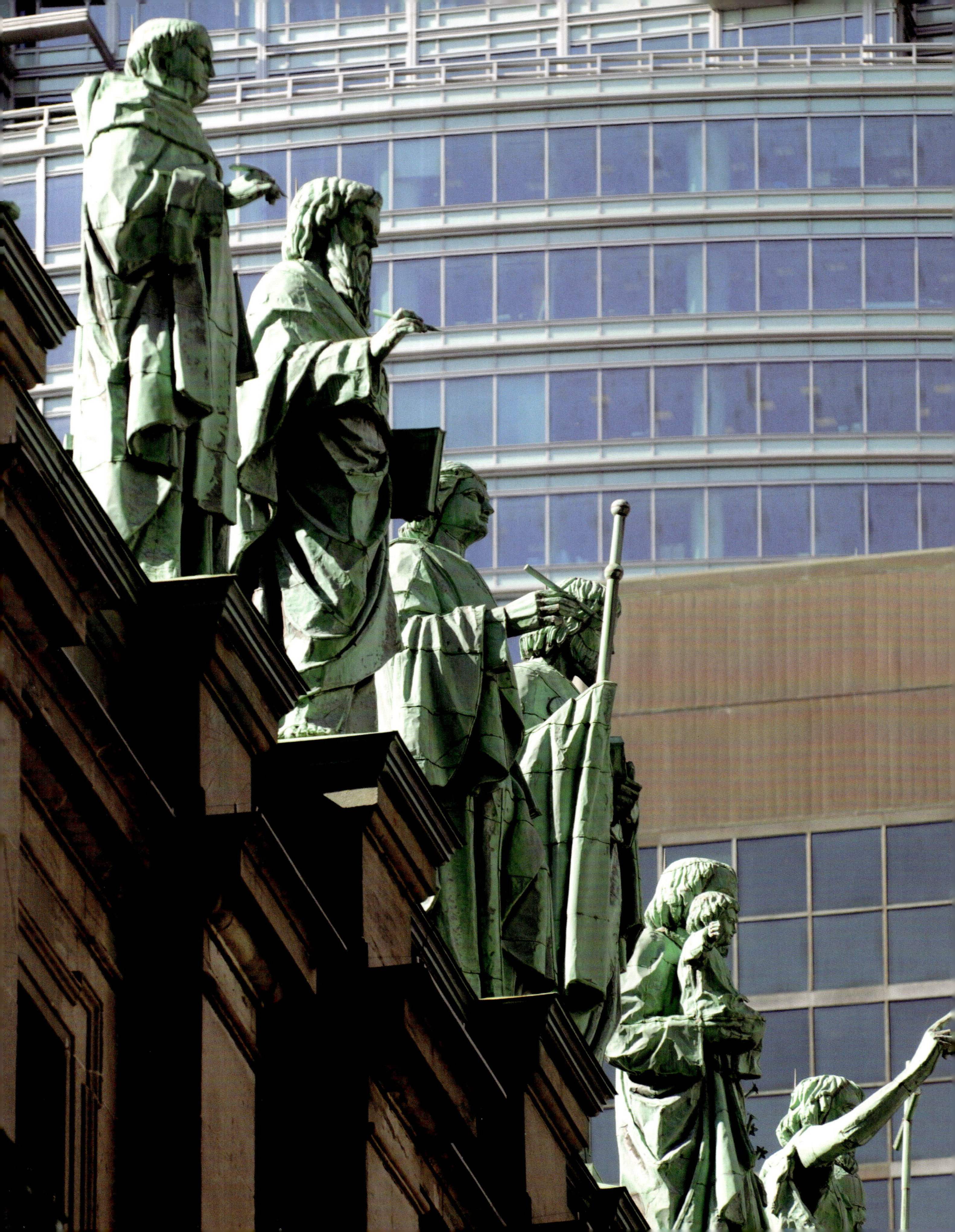

2

Sculpture for a New Country

In May 1881, an enormous sculpture depicting the mother of Christ was put on display in Quebec City and then in Montreal. To see it, adults were charged ten cents and children five. This was probably the first time people had ever paid to view a sculpture, yet the price of admission was worth every penny.

Standing seven and a half metres high and weighing over three thousand kilograms, the *Statue de Notre-Dame-du-Saguenay* (1881), or *Our Lady of Saguenay*, as the sculpture also became known, was the attraction. It was carved from three enormous blocks of pine. These had been clad in lead and then given several coats of white paint to make the finished work resemble marble. No one who viewed the colossal sculpture disputed the claim that it was the largest work of its kind in North America—at least until 1886, when the thirty-three-metre-high Statue of Liberty by Auguste Bartholdi (1834–1904) was installed in New York Harbor.

Opposite:
Olindo Gratton
Detail of *Thirteen Saints*, 1892–1900
(see page 39)

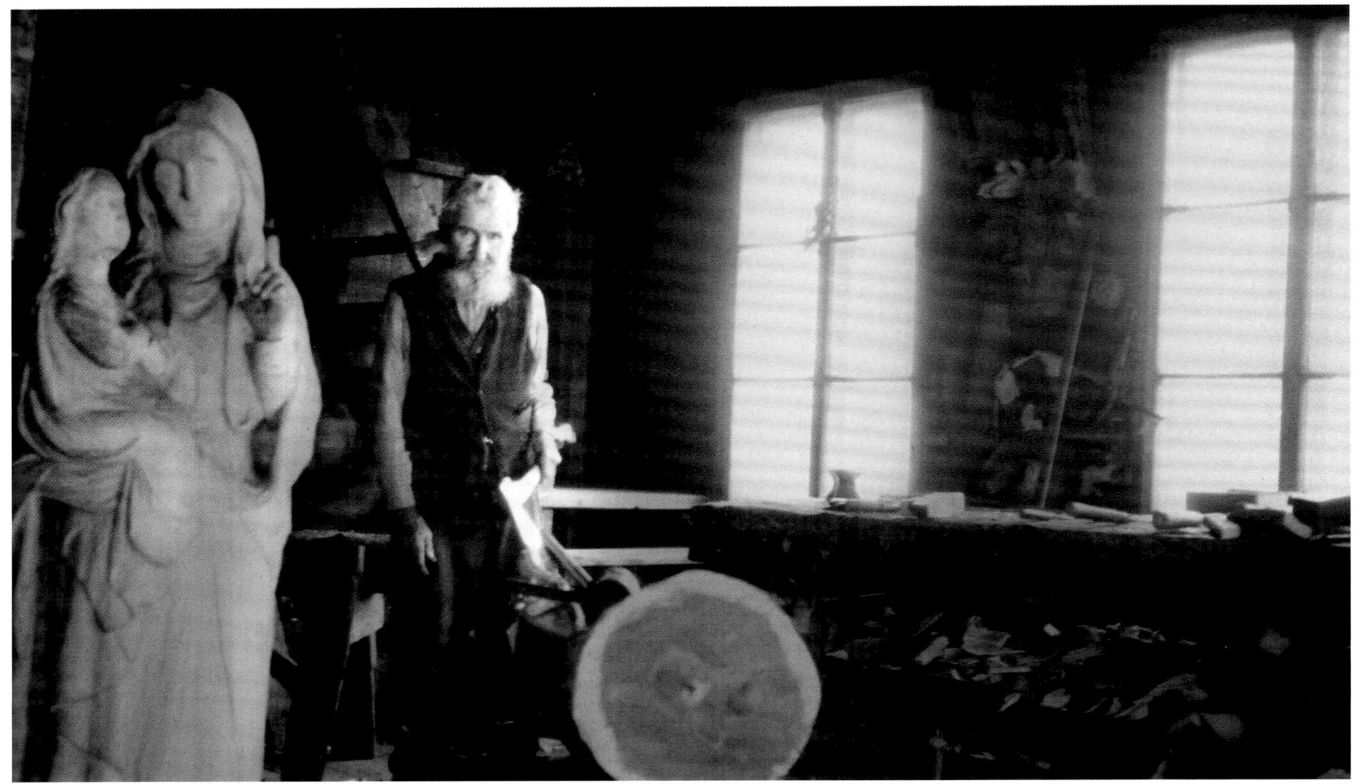

Louis Jobin in his studio next to a statue of the Virgin Mary and Infant Jesus, 1926.

Photo by Frank Oliver Call, Collection of the Canadian Museum of History, 80-1132.

Few paused to wonder why the Madonna eventually came to rest in a remote area on the south shore of the Saguenay River in rural Quebec, or why the donor who led the public subscription to pay for this work chose to celebrate her when the cult of the Virgin Mary was already past its peak at the time.

People were, of course, already well accustomed to seeing roadside shrines and *ex votos* throughout the province. The Church had always ensured that the Madonna's visual representation in wood and in plaster carried both a patriotic and a religious meaning for Roman Catholic parishioners in Quebec. It seemed natural, then, that it was to the Madonna that Charles-Napoléon Robitaille had prayed when his horse-drawn sleigh fell through the ice as he crossed the Saguenay River, and natural that the Madonna clearly had answered the drowning man's prayers by saving him from certain death—an event that he wished to commemorate.

When the sculptor Louis Jobin (1845–1928) accepted Robitaille's consequent commission to produce a statue of the Madonna, he was thirty years old. He was living in Quebec City where, many years earlier, he had apprenticed with woodcarver and architect François-Xavier Berlinguet (1830–1916) before working as an assistant to New York City sculptor William Boulton. Returning to Quebec City in 1875, Jobin and his assistants had set up shop carving religious statuary, ships' figureheads, storefront signs and statues in wood—and even producing ice sculptures for Quebec's winter carnivals.

The work that Jobin undertook for Robitaille was very different from

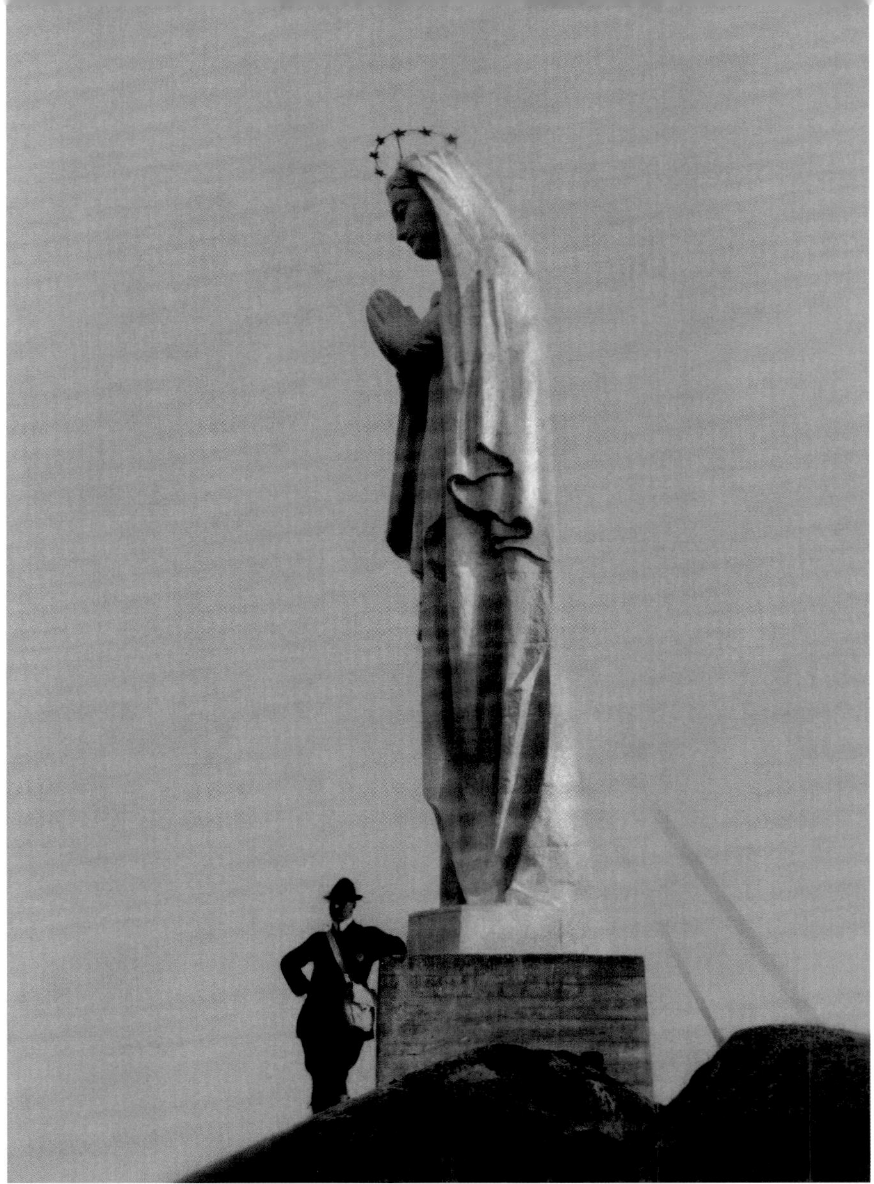

Louis Jobin
Statue de Notre-Dame-du-Saguenay, c. 1881
Sculptures of the Virgin Mary were everywhere in late-nineteenth-century Quebec. But until the Statue of Liberty was erected in 1886, the *Statue de Notre-Dame-du-Saguenay* was the largest sculpture in North America. This work is not only remarkable because of its colossal size, nor because the sculptor developed a way to protect it from Quebec's harsh winters by cladding the wood in lead. The *Statue de Notre-Dame-du-Saguenay* is particularly notable because shortly after its installation high above the banks of the Saguenay River it became a place of pilgrimage.

his previous commissions. It allowed him to work on a grand scale. And it enabled him to experiment with a new material: lead. Using the metal to cover his work would earn Jobin a reputation for having found a solution for protecting wooden sculptures from Quebec's harsh winters. The siting of the *Statue de Notre-Dame-du-Saguenay* at Cap Trinité was equally significant. The sculpture was in the direct line of vision of everyone who sailed down the Saguenay River. And in spite of its remote location, Jobin's Madonna became a place of pilgrimage for Québécois, just as the Virgin Mary at Lourdes was for the French. This assured Jobin that his sculpture— and his name—would be maintained in perpetuity.[1]

In 1901 Jobin moved his studio to Sainte-Anne-de-Beaupré, where he continued to fulfill commissions for clients in and around Quebec City as well as across the rest of Canada and, indeed, throughout North America. An astute businessman, Jobin had plenty of work. His prices were competitive: in order to promote sales he sold his work at 40 per cent less than his European rivals and he covered shipping costs to anywhere in North America. Even so, although Jobin continued producing secular and religious carvings until the age of eighty, he died a pauper in 1928 at the age of eighty-three.[2]

There were other artists in late-nineteenth- and early-twentieth-century Quebec who also earned a living as full-time sculptors. Jean-Baptiste Côté (1832–1907) proclaimed "My time is over" in response to competition from low-cost religious plaster statuary imported from Italy, but he nonetheless found plenty of work outside of the Church.[3] This came from town councillors, ship owners, shopkeepers and ships' captains, as well as from private individuals and organizations. In 1880 the national convention of French Canadians invited Côté to produce a statue in wood of Saint Jean Baptiste, the patron saint of French Canadians. And during the winter months Côté, just like Jobin, was not too proud to carve ice sculptures for the carnivals.

Côté also demonstrated in works like *Le Chanteur* (c. 1865) that sculpture could have a lighter side. Working in wood, he carved life-sized, stick-like caricatures of public figures and, lower down the social scale, depicted habitants, lumberjacks and snowshoers—all of which showed how sculptors could apply their wit and artistic skills to satirical works of art.

Among other sculptors, Côté's slightly younger contemporary Olindo Gratton (1855–1941) was different because he produced virtually all of his work for the Church. After leaving the family farm in Sainte-Thérèse-de-Blainville in 1871, the young Gratton had moved to Montreal, where he enrolled at the École Normale Jacques-Cartier. During his early years in Montreal, Gratton found a patron in the European-trained painter Napoléon Bourassa (1827–1916) who, in line with church teaching, believed that both religion and loyalty to one's native land could be realized through the production of liturgical works of art. In 1872, Gratton joined the atelier of the well-established Montreal sculptor Charles-Olivier Dauphin (1807–1874), famous for his intricate liturgical carvings. Gratton continued to work alongside Dauphin's three sons after their father's death, and oversaw the production of fine wooden sculptures, relief panels and ornamental decorations for a number of religious institutions. Acknowledging his need for further technical training, Gratton then enrolled in free evening courses offered at the Council of Arts and Manufactures in Montreal, where the city's nascent painters and sculptors studied alongside working-class tradesmen.

Gratton got his first real break in 1881 when he entered the Montreal studio of the well-known sculptor Louis-Philippe Hébert (1850–1917). It was as a member of Hébert's atelier that Gratton found his career blossoming. Working from European sales catalogues and from little-known images proposed to him by the clergy, Gratton produced dozens of ornamental and religious carvings for the interiors of Neo-Gothic churches. He prepared the moulds used for the bronze casting of religious figures. And he continued to study at the Council of Arts and Manufactures in Montreal. When Hébert left for Paris in 1887, Gratton moved to Boston but was soon back in Montreal where he and another sculptor, Philippe Laperle (1860–1934), opened their own workshop. That partnership came to an end in 1891, and Gratton was awarded his most prestigious commission the following year. It was to produce thirteen statues representing the

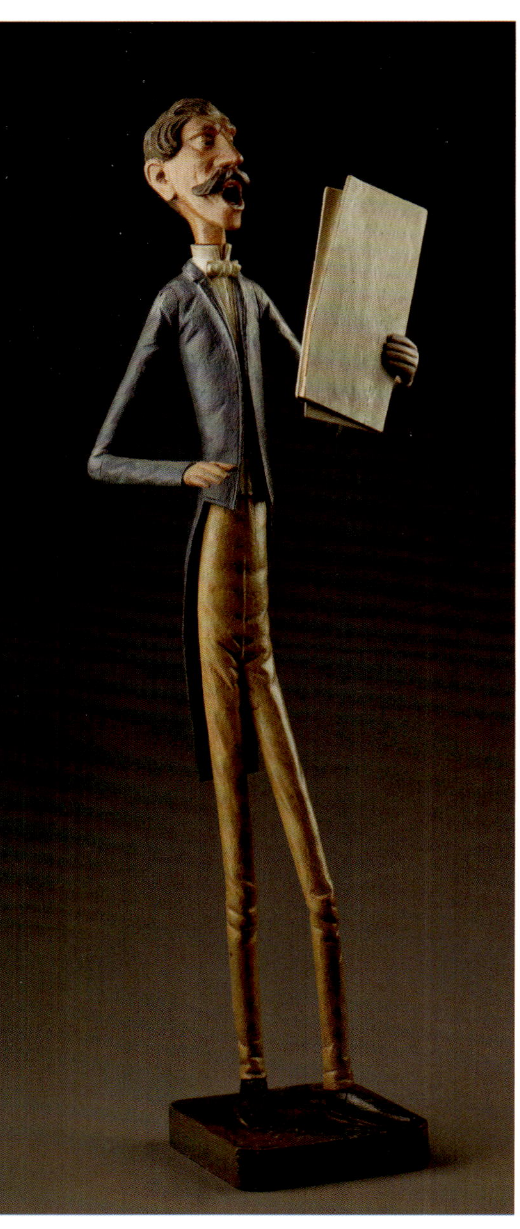

Jean-Baptiste Côté
Le Chanteur, c. 1865
Although he trained as an architect, Jean-Baptiste Côté made his living as an illustrator and sculptor. In protest against Quebec's impending confederation with Canada, he produced over six hundred engravings and three hundred woodcuts for magazines like *La Scie Illustrée*. Côté also carved everything from devotional representations of the Virgin Mary to cigar-store images of Indigenous people, political leaders and other citizens like this drawing-room vocalist. Côté's sculptures introduced wit and humour into Quebec sculpture.

patron saints of Montreal's thirteen parishes for Quebec's largest Roman Catholic church: the Marie-Reine-du-Monde Cathedral.

Gratton's larger-than-life carvings, duly mounted above the building's facade, gave the cathedral a great sense of presence and gravitas. Carved in wood, then covered with sheets of copper, the saints not only appeared to be as solid as marble, but to be stepping forward into space. Their size, their animation and their dominant position on the building all demonstrated that religious carvings were free-standing works of art in their own right, rather than architectural embellishments.

Though the completion of these imposing figures in 1900 established Gratton's reputation as one of the finest woodcarvers of religious sculpture in the province of Quebec, there is little that intrinsically distinguishes them from the religious statuary of his contemporaries. Indeed, during his lifetime, some critics claimed that his sculptures were unimaginative, amateurish, boring and even derivative. Yet, as art historian Bernard Mulaire writes, we can now see that rather than simply "imitating" the Renaissance masters, Gratton was actually "participating in the stylistic

Olindo Gratton
Thirteen Saints, 1892–1900
Olindo Gratton, who produced over three hundred sculptures between 1877 and 1939, was among the last artists in Quebec to derive his entire income from the patronage of the Church. During his lifetime many felt he was incapable of working outside of the codified and referential constraints demanded by the commissioning clergy. However, Gratton's figurative sculptures of the patron saints of thirteen Montreal parishes exceeded everyone's expectations by doing justice to the facade of Quebec's most revered cathedral.

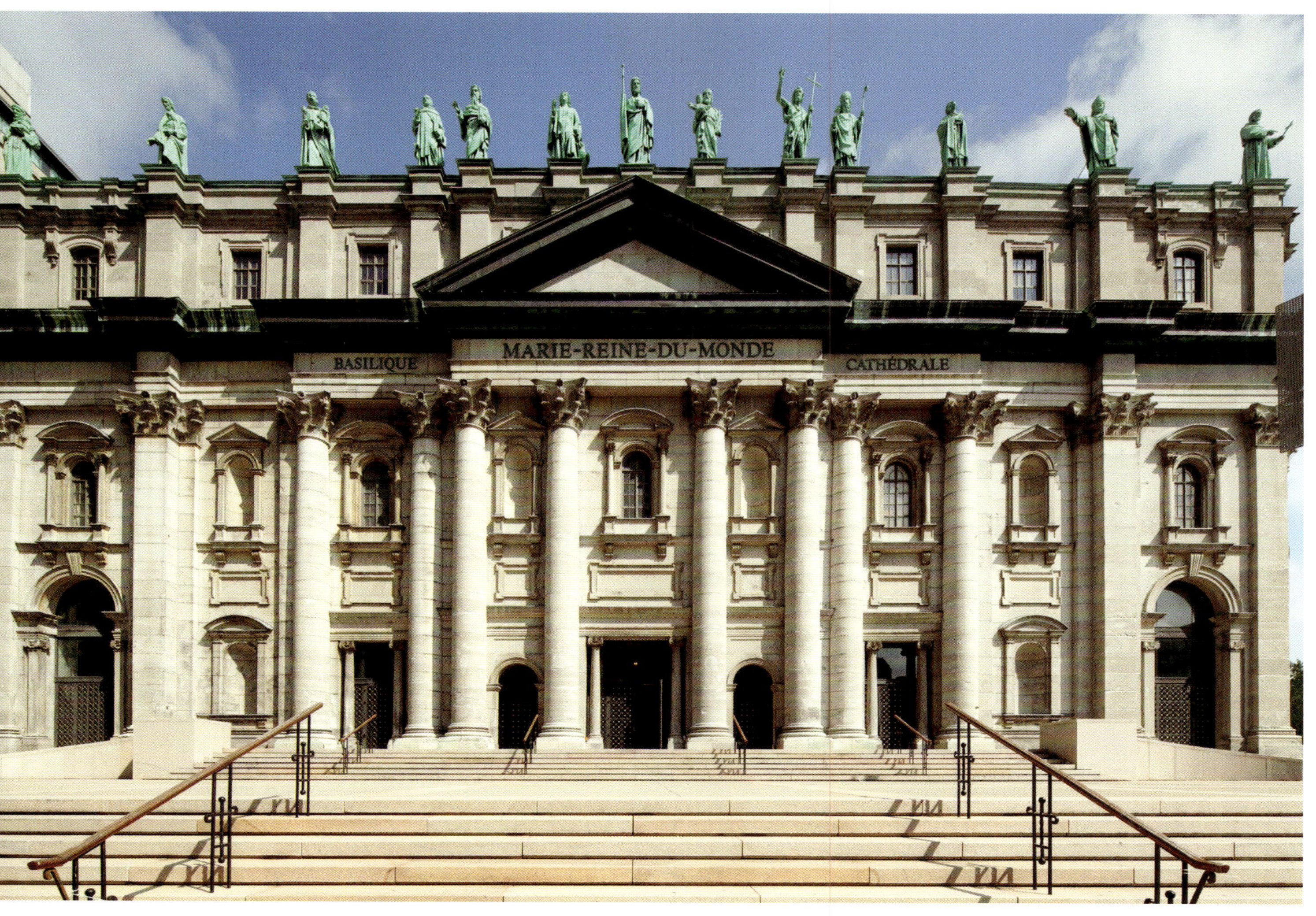

Revival movement of the time."[4] By partaking in what has been called religious triumphalism, the artist was ensuring that his work was in fashion and, above all, always in demand.

Gratton would have liked to work in bronze. That medium was more durable than wood or wood clad in copper or lead. Unlike wood, bronze grew more interesting as it acquired the patina of age. Gratton also wanted to make statues of significant historical and contemporary figures. Sculptors who produced secular works could work on a larger scale, and they had more freedom; religious sculptures were codified and referential. And, by the end of the nineteenth century, sculptors in the secular market had more status and frequently secured more lucrative commissions.

But despite the growing demand for self-definition in both French- and English-speaking Canada following Confederation, Gratton himself failed to break into the commemorative market. Unlike his first teacher, Bourassa, or his employer, Hébert, he lacked the sophistication to make the right connections in the secular art world. He had not studied in Europe. Moreover, after completing the sculptures for the cathedral in Montreal, he took himself out of the province's centre of art by moving back to the village of his birth, Sainte-Thérèse-de-Blainville.

True, he maintained his links with Montreal through his membership in the Club Saint-Denis, formed in 1911 to give largely French-Canadian artists an alternative to the anglophone Art Association of Montreal. And in 1918, he had a solo exhibition at Montreal's Bibliothèque Saint-Sulpice. Seven years later, in 1925, he did receive a much longed-for memorial commission: to produce a bronze sculpture of the founder of the Séminaire de Sainte-Thérèse, Charles-Joseph Ducharme.[5] By this time, however, Gratton was seventy years old and, although he would enjoy another sixteen years of productive life, it was now too late for him to make his career in the secular market.

Following the Confederation of Canada in 1867, an ambitious ethic of citizenship fostered a sense that the arts had an important role to play in shaping the identity of the new country. Writing in 1893, W.A. Sherwood opined that "a country's national standing was measured by its cultural achievement."[6] More than a decade earlier the Earl of Dufferin (governor general of Canada from 1872 to 1878) had already suggested that "the cultivation of art" was "a most essential element in our national life."[7] And during his own tenure as governor general (1878–1883), the Marquis of Lorne and his sculptor-wife Princess Louise had helped establish an academy of art "for the purpose of cultivating and improving the arts of painting, sculpture, architecture, and industrial design."[8] The founding of the Royal Canadian Academy of Arts, along with their proposal for a National Gallery of Canada, came to fruition in 1880. Sculptors now had a place to study at the Royal Canadian Academy's school, and a prestigious gallery where they could aspire to exhibit their finest work.

Federal politicians were equally aware of the beneficial role that culture could play in nation building and, during the economic boom lasting from the 1890s to the 1910s, they had the funds to pay for it. From the time of his election to parliament in 1874, and influentially during his fifteen-year tenure as prime minister (1896–1911), Sir Wilfrid Laurier supported funding for the National Gallery and the Royal Canadian Academy of Arts. He saw to it that Canadian painting and sculpture were represented at international expositions and fairs. And, promising "to do all in his power to help," he encouraged artists to visit him in Ottawa.[9]

The premiers of Canada's provinces, who oversaw the construction of legislative buildings across the country, also encouraged the arts by making commemorative sculptures an integral part of their building programs. The architects of Quebec's new Legislative Assembly Building offered a counterpart to the overwhelming influence of the British Empire by celebrating the province's secular saints, like Jacques Cartier, who were thought to possess Christian *and* French virtues in equal measure. Conversely, on the other side of the country, government officials in the newly created province of British Columbia hired an immigrant Italian sculptor-tinsmith, Franz Cizek, to decorate its legislature with stone carvings of British writers, British statesmen and, on top of the dome, a bronze figure of British seaman Captain George Vancouver.

Although private patronage was less forthcoming, the Art Association of Montreal, founded in 1860, got a building of its own in 1879 thanks to a bequest from art collector and wealthy merchant Benaiah Gibb. In Toronto, the Ontario Society of Artists founded a public art gallery in 1900 and three years later the Art Museum of Toronto got a permanent home when Goldwin Smith bequeathed his Toronto mansion.

John Edgcumbe Staley claimed in 1914 that secular sculptures, were "a potent force in the molding of national characteristics." Many Canadians, especially in English-speaking Canada, agreed with him. Yet, as Staley further observed, Canada was at a "rather crude and material stage" of its development, largely because "the energies of the people are concentrated on laying the foundations of future greatness, and there has not been sufficient time to develop the artistic and idealistic qualities of a people who are still lying to a great extent dormant."[10] Since homegrown sculptors were generally perceived to be less qualified and less able, they frequently lost out to foreign-born artists on many of the post-Confederation commissions.

For example, it was Belgian-born French artist Paul Chevré (1867–1914) who was chosen by the Saint-Jean-Baptiste Society of Quebec to produce a sculpture of Samuel de Champlain. This bronze statue, 4.23 metres high, was erected beside Quebec City's magnificent Château Frontenac in 1898. Much to the chagrin of the local press, Chevré was also commissioned to produce a sculpture honouring Honoré Mercier (who had become the first nationalist prime minister of Quebec in 1886). Chevré's bronze sculpture of Mercier was installed on the grounds of Quebec's Legislative Assembly in 1909.

Unlike the European-born Chevré, some of the sculptors who produced commemorative memorials for Canada never even crossed the Atlantic. Scottish sculptor David Watson Stevenson (1842–1904) had created a full-figure bronze statue of Scotland's most celebrated poet, Robert Burns, for the

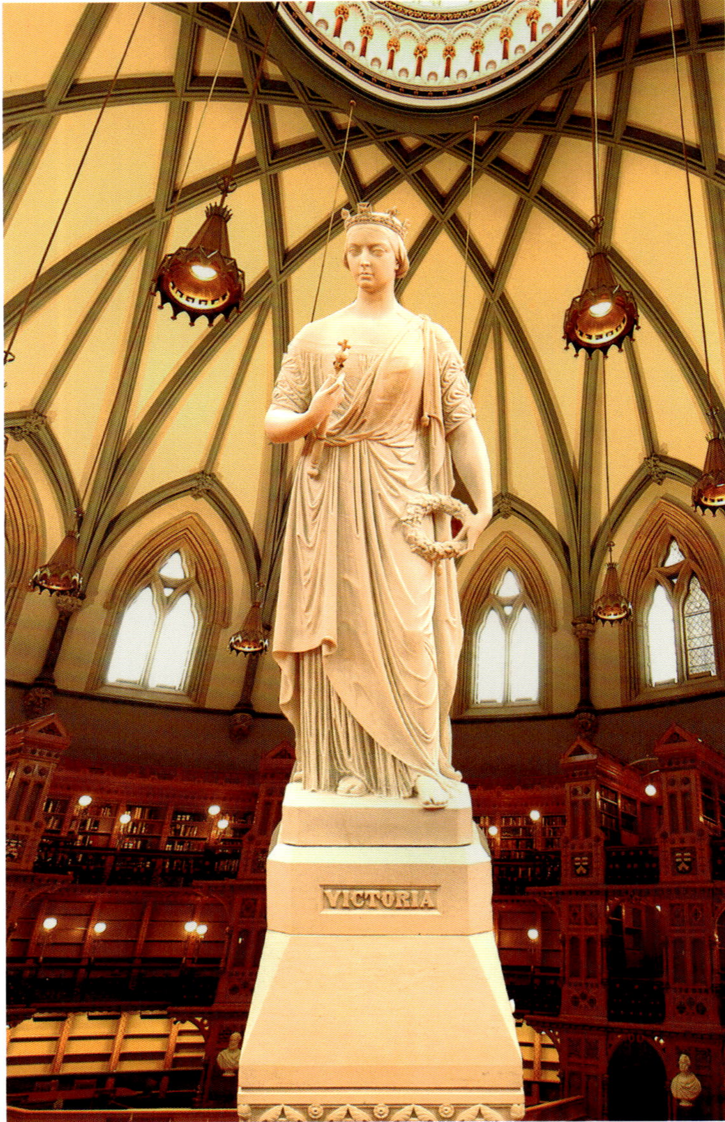

Marshall Wood
Queen Victoria, 1871
Queen Victoria disliked sitting for her portrait. And after the death of her husband in 1861, when the stout and somewhat dowdy monarch only wore coal-black gowns, she became a less appealing subject for artists. When Marshall Wood began this sculpture of the queen she was almost fifty years old. Yet Wood chose to depict a much younger queen. He dressed her in classical garments and gave her a blank and impersonal expression. This full-length, 2.33-metre-high, 1,550-kilogram work was so popular that the sculptor made several copies for governments in India and Australia.

Scottish town of Leith in 1898, and several copies of this work duly found their way from his studio in Scotland to cities throughout the British Empire, including one situated in Toronto's Allan Gardens in 1902. It was the same for another British-based artist, the Italian-born sculptor Mario Raggi (1821–1097). A copy of his bronze sculpture of Queen Victoria, originally created for Hong Kong, eventually found its way, in 1901, to Toronto's Queen's Park.[11]

Even the future prime minister of Canada, W.L. Mackenzie King, was among those who preferred foreign to local sculptors. Distraught by the death of Henry Albert Harper, who had died attempting to rescue a drowning girl during a skating party in Ottawa, King wished to memorialize the young man's sacrifice. And he was instrumental in choosing an American sculptor, E.W. Keyser (1875–1959), to produce the bronze sculpture *Sir Galahad* (1905), which was installed on Parliament Hill in Ottawa.[12]

British sculptor Marshall Wood (1834–1882) did take up residence

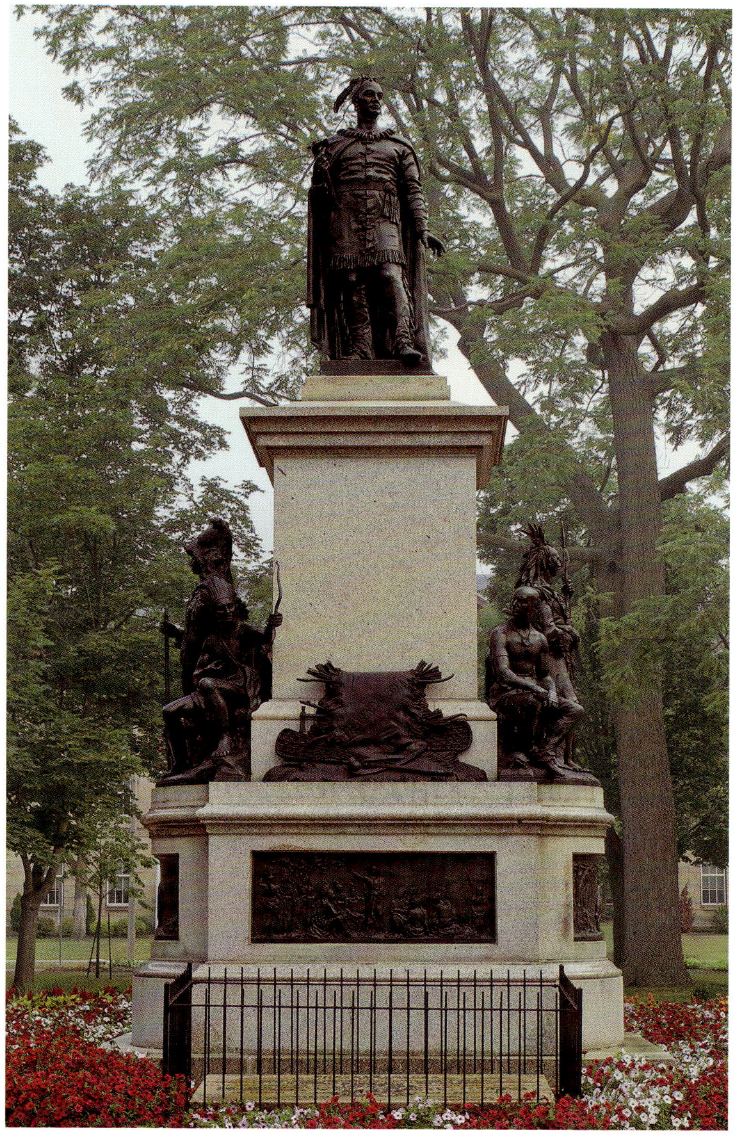

in Canada from 1871 to 1873. An exhibitor at London's Royal Academy since the mid-1850s, Wood had a high reputation in London ("admirable" wrote the *Times*) for producing likenesses of royal personages and literary figures.[13] Not least, Wood also knew how to please and whom to please. In 1873 he presented the first Canadian prime minister with a flattering marble sculpture in which Sir John A. Macdonald wore antique robes and displayed the order of Knight Commander of the Bath.[14] But it was Wood's statues of Queen Victoria that were most popular, defying the notion that fame was uniquely masculine. Wood arrived in Canada with three statues of the queen—one marble and two in bronze—and sold them all. In the larger-than-life marble sculpture (2.33 metres high) of the youthful queen, Wood presented the British monarch as a Roman goddess. It was purchased by the Canadian government for two thousand guineas (worth at least $300,000 today) and was installed in the Library of Parliament in

Ottawa. No one in Canada seemed to worry that Wood went on to produce replicas of the work for the federal governments of Australia and India.

The sculptor's son, Percy Wood (1860–1904), got into the commemoration game too. In the mid-1880s he was commissioned to create a bronze sculpture of Six Nations chief Captain Joseph Brant for the town of Brantford, Ontario. The resulting *Joseph Brant Memorial* (1886) depicted Brant as "a wise leader whose Christian faith, allegiance to Britain, and admiration for the monarchy made him a figure worthy of imitation."[15] A year before the bronze sculpture was inaugurated, Louis Riel had led the Northwest Rebellion. The image of Brant, whose "loyal" troops had helped the British during the American Revolutionary War, thus offered a reassuring contrast, implicitly suggesting that the exploitation and forced relocation of Indigenous peoples did not prevent their assimilation into the national identity of anglophone and francophone Canada.

Percy Wood had done his homework. During the course of making preparatory sketches of what he felt were "ideal types" of First Nations people in and around Brantford, Ontario, he was made "a full feathered chief of the Turtle tribe."[16] Nor did Wood's association with the Six Nations people end when he left the country. A year after the unveiling of his highly idealized portrait of Brant surrounded by bare-breasted warrior chiefs with their war-making accoutrements, Wood attended a dinner for the Golden Jubilee celebration of Queen Victoria in 1887 at the Savoy Hotel in London. Dressed "in full war paint" for the occasion, the "astonishing savage" (so the newspapers reported) whooped and hollered and ate his dinner off the floor.[17] The sculptor had clearly "gone Native." While Wood was among the first sculptors to place an Indigenous person at the top of the plinth instead of below it, his work inevitably reinforced contemporary stereotypes and negative ways of thinking about First Nations people.

The fact is that some influential foreign sculptors did receive their commissions through personal contacts without ever setting foot in Canada. Such was the case with self-taught British sculptor George Edward Wade (1853–1933). According to one of his contemporaries, art historian M.H. Spielmann, "it cannot be said that there is any striking or marked individuality in the work of Mr. Wade, or that the modelling calls for special comment."[18] Nonetheless, with the patronage of the Canadian High Commissioner in London, Sir Charles Tupper, as well as the Marquis of Lorne, Wade duly won the commission to produce a life-sized sculpture of Canada's first prime minister, Sir John A. Macdonald, with the first bronze cast installed in the crypt of St. Paul's Cathedral in 1892. Working from photographs, Wade was able to complete his commission while avoiding the inconvenience of crossing the Atlantic. He also took advantage of the multiple castings afforded by working in bronze to have several copies of his work reproduced. They found their way to Hamilton, Montreal, Kingston and London, Ontario. These were usually erected on a simple granite plinth, but in the case of Montreal, Macdonald was placed under an architecturally designed baldachin, or canopy, supported by Corinthian columns and surmounted with British lions, seven children—symbolizing the country's youth—and an allegorical female figure of Canada.

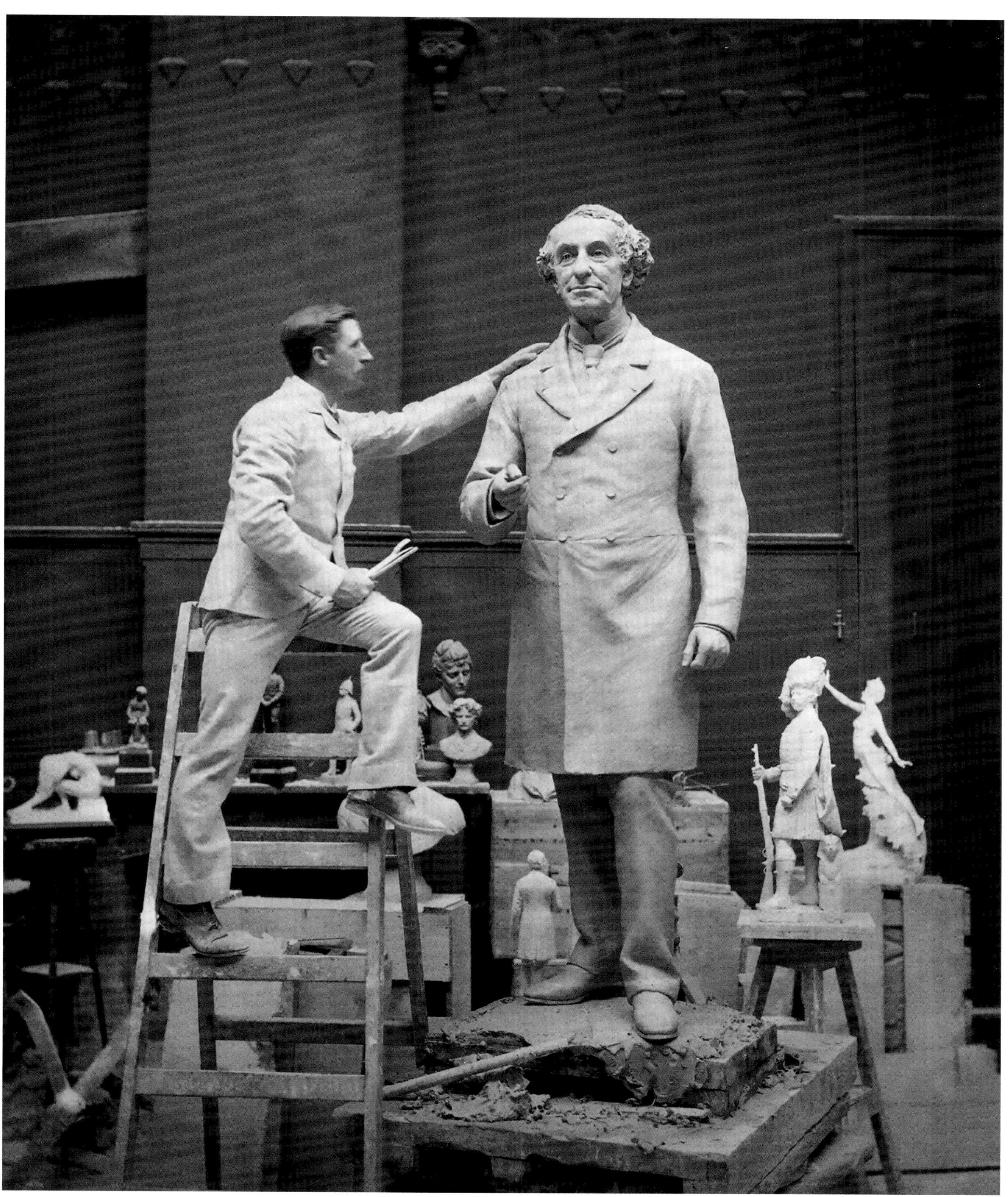

It was through similarly privileged contacts that another favoured British sculptor received prominence. In 1893 Princess Louise, the wife of a former governor general, the Marquis of Lorne, made a life-sized copy of a bronze sculpture of her mother, Queen Victoria. The work was accepted by and installed in front of Montreal's Royal Victoria College, McGill University, in 1899.

The first Canadian-born sculptor to offer a serious challenge to his foreign-born counterparts was Louis-Philippe Hébert (1850–1917). Like Olindo Gratton, Hébert was born and raised in humble surroundings in the Bois-Francs region of rural Quebec. But the similarity between the two men ended there. At the age of nineteen Hébert travelled to Rome with the Canadian contingent of the international volunteer army, known as the Papal Zouaves, who were committed to helping Pope Pius ix resist the unification of Italy. Although the surrender of the Papal States in September 1870 curtailed Hébert's military service, visiting Rome's churches and museums, as he later wrote, "rekindled my longing for beauty [and] whetted my desire to become a sculptor."[19]

Upon returning to Canada in 1872, Hébert studied woodcarving with Adolphe Rho (1839–1905) in Bécancour, on the south shore of the Saint Lawrence River in central Quebec. In 1873 Hébert submitted a small wooden bust of the prolific French poet and chansonnier Pierre-Jean de Béranger to the Provincial Agricultural Fair in Montreal. The painter and writer Napoléon Bourassa saw the carving on display and was so impressed that he invited the young man to become his apprentice.

Hébert studied drawing and modelling with Bourassa at his atelier on Rue Sainte-Julie in Montreal for six years. He taught at Montreal's Council of Arts and Manufactures. Under Bourassa's direction he completed liturgical sculptures and statuary ensembles for churches like Ottawa's magnificent Notre Dame Cathedral. Then, in collaboration with Canon Georges Bouillon (1841–1932), who was both priest and architect, and assisted by Olindo Gratton and Philippe Laperle, Hébert set up his own workshop, where he continued to win commissions, primarily for the Roman Catholic Church. Eventually, however, Hébert turned from wood to clay, making him one of the first sculptors in Quebec to cast his work in bronze. Having earned his reputation by fulfilling commissions for the clergy, Hébert turned to the secular market.

Hébert entered the secular commemorative memorial market at the right time. In 1857 Queen Victoria had designated a small lumber town lying at the confluence of the Ottawa, Gatineau and Rideau Rivers as the country's future capital. Bytown, as the city was known until 1855, had been the site of westward expansion and a centre for First Nations people. Its future identity—as one lowly member of parliament and future prime minister of Canada, Sir Wilfrid Laurier, ambitiously hoped in 1893— would be as the Washington of the north. It was becoming common at the time to use sculpture as a vehicle for moral improvement and civic pride, and as a way of celebrating the country's statesmen. Responding to the late-nineteenth-century "City Beautiful" movement, the federal, provincial and local governments alike were committed to adorning their squares, parks and boulevards with sculptures.

In 1881 Hébert entered an international competition. The federal government of Canada wanted a life-sized bronze sculpture of Sir George-Étienne Cartier, the well-known francophone supporter of Confederation who became a member of both the Parliament of Canada and the Legislative Assembly of Quebec. The work was to be the first memorial sculpture erected in the country's capital city. In a competition open to sculptors both local and international, each entrant was invited to submit a drawing and a "maquette"—a scaled down version of the work—for the consideration of the selection committee. The sculptor chosen to render the work was Louis-Philippe Hébert.

After completing the sculpture of Cartier in 1885, Hébert went on

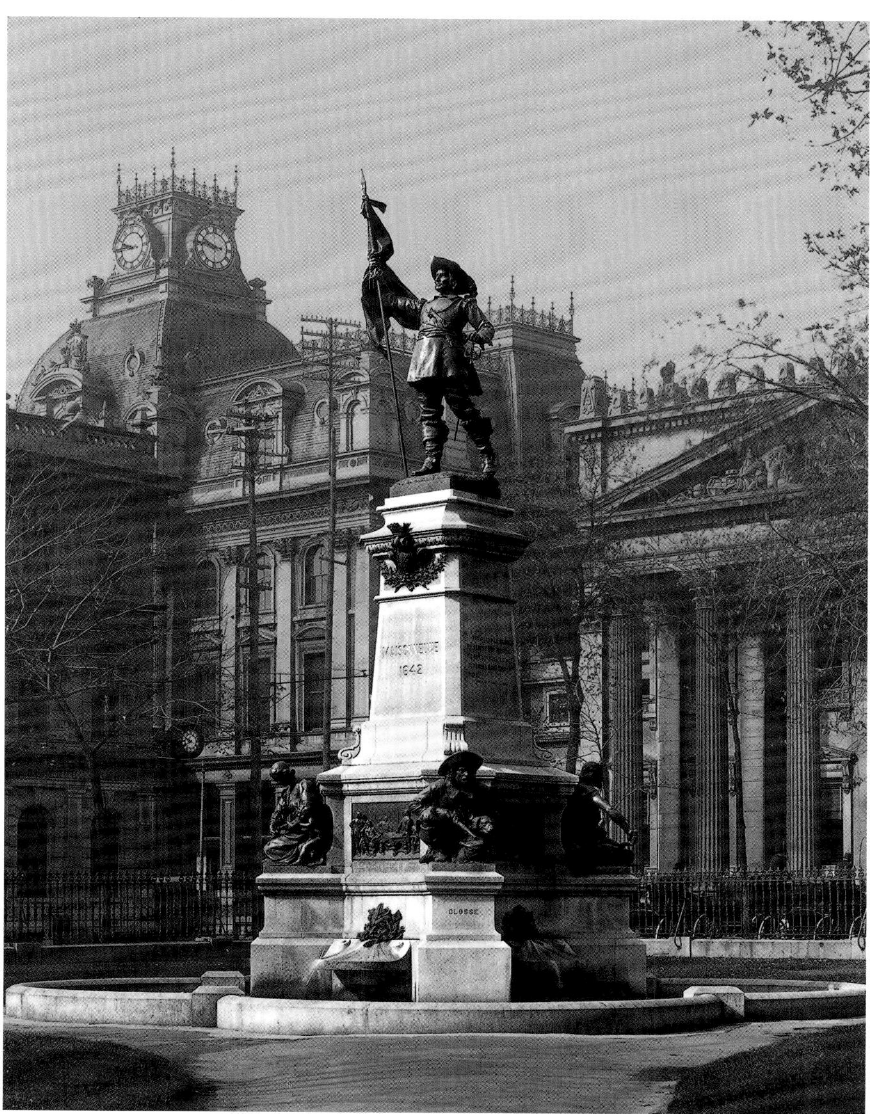

Louis-Philippe Hébert
Maisonneuve Monument, 1895
Perched on top of a decorative plinth that stands in the Place d'Armes in Old Montreal is an image of the city's founder, Paul de Chomedey de Maisonneuve. Holding the French flag in one hand and his sword in the other, the French aristocrat-cum-soldier and first governor of Montreal has the air of a swaggering cavalier. Hébert placed four figures at the corners of the monument: French-born Charles Le Moyne, the merchant Lambert Closse, the founder of the first hospital in New France, Jeanne Mance, and an unidentified First Nations Iroquois warrior.

to win other commissions depicting both contemporary and historical figures. Working in the late-nineteenth-century academic style he produced full-scale bronze sculptures of Sir John A. Macdonald (1895) and Queen Victoria (1897), and both were erected on Parliament Hill in Ottawa. Working under the direction of architect Eugène-Étienne Taché, Hébert produced ten sculptures—some secular, some religious—for the new Legislative Assembly Building in Quebec City. He also oversaw the production of bronze busts of Montreal's leading citizens for installation in the Notre-Dame-des-Neiges Cemetery. In 1895 Hébert completed perhaps his most accomplished commemorative work: a dramatic rendering of Montreal's founder, Paul de Chomedey de Maisonneuve, that could be seen from every viewpoint in Place d'Armes.

Moreover, Hébert won commissions outside of Ottawa and the province of Quebec. He produced a bronze statue of Nova Scotia's most loved politician, Joseph Howe, for Halifax in 1904 and, ten years later, an equestrian sculpture for Calgary, the *South African War Memorial*, commemorating the fallen in the Boer War. Working on a smaller scale he made a number of busts, medallions, medals and tabletop or drawing-room bronzes that were not only affordable for bourgeois consumption but gave Hébert's imagination free reign.

Hébert had a knack for making connections that enabled him to win commissions from his upper-middle-class clients. He also knew how to exploit his connection with the newly established cultural institutions. He became an associate member of the Royal Canadian Academy of Arts and a regular exhibitor at the National Gallery of Canada, which not only showed but also purchased his work. He also exhibited his work with Montreal's Canadian Art Club and Toronto's Ontario Society of Artists. In addition, responding to Laurier's invitation for artists to contact him, Hébert exercised his indomitable charm once more.

Hébert also demonstrated that Canada's sculptors were producing work not only worthy for display in the Canadian pavilions at industrial and agricultural exhibitions, but also at world fairs, including Philadelphia's in 1876, Antwerp's in 1885, Paris's in 1900 and Glasgow's in 1901.[20] Likewise, bronzes by Hébert of Queen Victoria and explorer Sir Alexander Mackenzie were shown at the Canadian pavilion of the Exposition Universelle in Paris in 1900 before they were installed on Parliament Hill in Ottawa.

Such commissions did not come easily. Even after his initial selection, Hébert had to submit drawings and maquettes to the sponsors, who often demanded alterations and sometimes the approval of foreign artists. And his reputation as Canada's premier sculptor did not prevent selection committees from giving commissions to foreign-born sculptors instead. It was, Hébert wrote later, partly in order to compete with foreign-trained sculptors for commissions and thereby "acquire the knowledge and taste necessary for the production of outstanding works" that he moved his atelier to Paris in 1887.[21] Although Quebec had a foundry run by Louis-Joseph Hévard that produced works in bronze by 1878, Hébert also wanted to have access to the best foundries in the world—one of which was Thiébaut Frères in Paris.

This was to be the first of Hébert's several visits to the French capital, in a series of extended residencies. During his time in France, Hébert improved his modelling skills. By studying the work of other sculptors he was introduced to the mélange of European styles from Classical and Neoclassical to Symbolism. While visiting the foundries, he became familiar with the intricacies of casting sculptures in bronze.[22] A sociable man, Hébert made connections with local artists and intellectuals who no doubt facilitated the inclusion of his work at the Paris Salon, the Société des Artistes Français and at the Exposition Universelle in 1900. As his reputation grew among his fellow European artists, art gallery curators and members of exhibition societies, official honours duly followed. In 1901 Hébert was made a Chevalier of the Légion d'Honneur in France, and in 1903 a Companion of the Order of St. Michael and St. George by Britain; eleven years later, Italy awarded him a knighthood in the Order of St. Gregory.

Hébert's accomplishments outside of Canada were thus as important as those at home. First and foremost, by shifting the practice of woodcarving to modelling in clay he was an example to every sculptor in Quebec. By distinguishing himself in Europe, he raised the profile of Canada's sculptors. Not least of all, Hébert showed that sculpture could pay. Upon his death in 1917 the artist's estate was valued at $100,000 (worth several million dollars today).

Louis-Philippe Hébert was indeed regarded by the critics as "the first Canadian sculptor of commemorative statues."[23] But he was far from the only one in this field. At his Marble and Granite Works studio in downtown Montreal, sculptor Robert Reid produced commemorative works, sometimes commissioned from far afield. One, titled *Little Black Devils Volunteer Monument* (1886), honoured the volunteers of the Ninetieth Winnipeg Battalion who died in 1885 during the Northwest Rebellion; the sandstone and marble sculpture of Britannia that dominates the *Canadian Volunteers Monument* (1870) was dedicated to the University of Toronto student volunteers who defended Upper Canada during the Fenian Raid in 1866.

Another English-Canadian sculptor from Quebec, George William Hill (1862–1934), had, like Hébert, assimilated to the academic traditions exemplified by the Classical and Neoclassical styles. This privileged him in a competition with his fellow Montreal sculptor Alfred Laliberté (1878–1953) to complete a sculpture destined for Montreal's Mount Royal Park to celebrate the one hundredth anniversary of the birth of Sir George-Étienne Cartier in 1914. It was a commission that Hill indeed won—rightly or wrongly, with some claiming that Laliberté's rejected maquette for the monument was "the most beautiful work of art ever made in Canada."[24] In 1913 Hill also got a good share of work on Parliament Hill in Ottawa creating sculptures of George Brown and Thomas D'Arcy McGee, two journalists and politicians who had been founding fathers of Confederation.

More difficult to place, Hamilton MacCarthy (1846–1939) claimed both

British and Canadian ancestry, having arrived in Toronto from England at the age of thirty-nine. Born in London, MacCarthy received his initial instruction from his sculptor parents before studying in Antwerp, Belgium. Upon completing his education, he quickly made a name for himself by exhibiting with fine art societies in Bristol, Yorkshire and Glasgow. When he moved to Toronto from England in 1885, MacCarthy lost little time in exhibiting with the Royal Canadian Academy of Arts and the Toronto-based Ontario Society of Artists, becoming a member of both. These institutions provided the British-born sculptor with the necessary connections to win memorial commissions not only in Ottawa and Toronto, but also in such cities as Halifax, Annapolis Royal, Quebec City, St. John, Brockville and Charlottetown.

Of the works that MacCarthy produced after his arrival in Canada, virtually all of them celebrated statesmen, military figures, explorers and educators: among them General Sir Isaac Brock, Egerton Ryerson, Samuel de Champlain and Sir John A. Macdonald. MacCarthy's work, like that of Hébert, Reid and Hill, brought together a mélange of those late-nineteenth-century academic styles suited to the celebration of heroism, manliness and success. His commemorative sculptures thus captured and defined a historical moment; yet it is difficult today to see quite what distinguished them from the run-of-the-mill academic sculptures of his contemporaries.

MacCarthy was not only a successful sculptor: he was also an accomplished writer. In 1899 he wrote the first extensive essay on Canadian sculpture for J. Castell Hopkins's multi-volume *Canada: An Encyclopaedia of the Country* (1898). MacCarthy's essay "The Development of Sculpture in Canada" paid tribute to Quebec's formative liturgical sculptors. He singled out his contemporary, Louis-Philippe Hébert, and, referring to his most accomplished sculpture, the *Maisonneuve Monument* (1895), noted how its "composition of base, pedestal and fountain shows unity of design combined with the strength of form and grace of outline."[25] He was not shy in talking about his own work, noting that his bust of Queen Victoria had been produced for the monarch's Diamond Jubilee in 1897. And he even gave a backhanded compliment to "old Jobin," whom he cheekily acknowledged as having "decorated nearly all the doors of the cigar shops throughout and beyond the Province with statues in wood of Turks, Indians, Squaws, Sailors, Negroes, and *Habitants*."[26]

MacCarthy reserved his severest criticism, however, for the English sculptor George Edward Wade—especially for the Montreal version of his sculpture depicting Sir John A. Macdonald (where MacCarthy had a vested interest as a rival, of course). In this work, Wade's red granite pillars and bronze Corinthian capitals—with British lions, male youths representing the seven provinces and a female figure representing Canada—formed, in MacCarthy's view, "not a happy *tout-en-semble*."[27] And while the "likeness" in this sculpture of Macdonald was acknowledged as "good and the figure and robes carefully modeled," MacCarthy felt that it was, "not altogether characteristic of the late Premier."[28]

"A nation's history is written in its monuments," MacCarthy proclaimed in 1904. Memorial sculptures thus encouraged "a national and patriotic pride in the noble deeds of the country's history makers" when "deeds of heroism

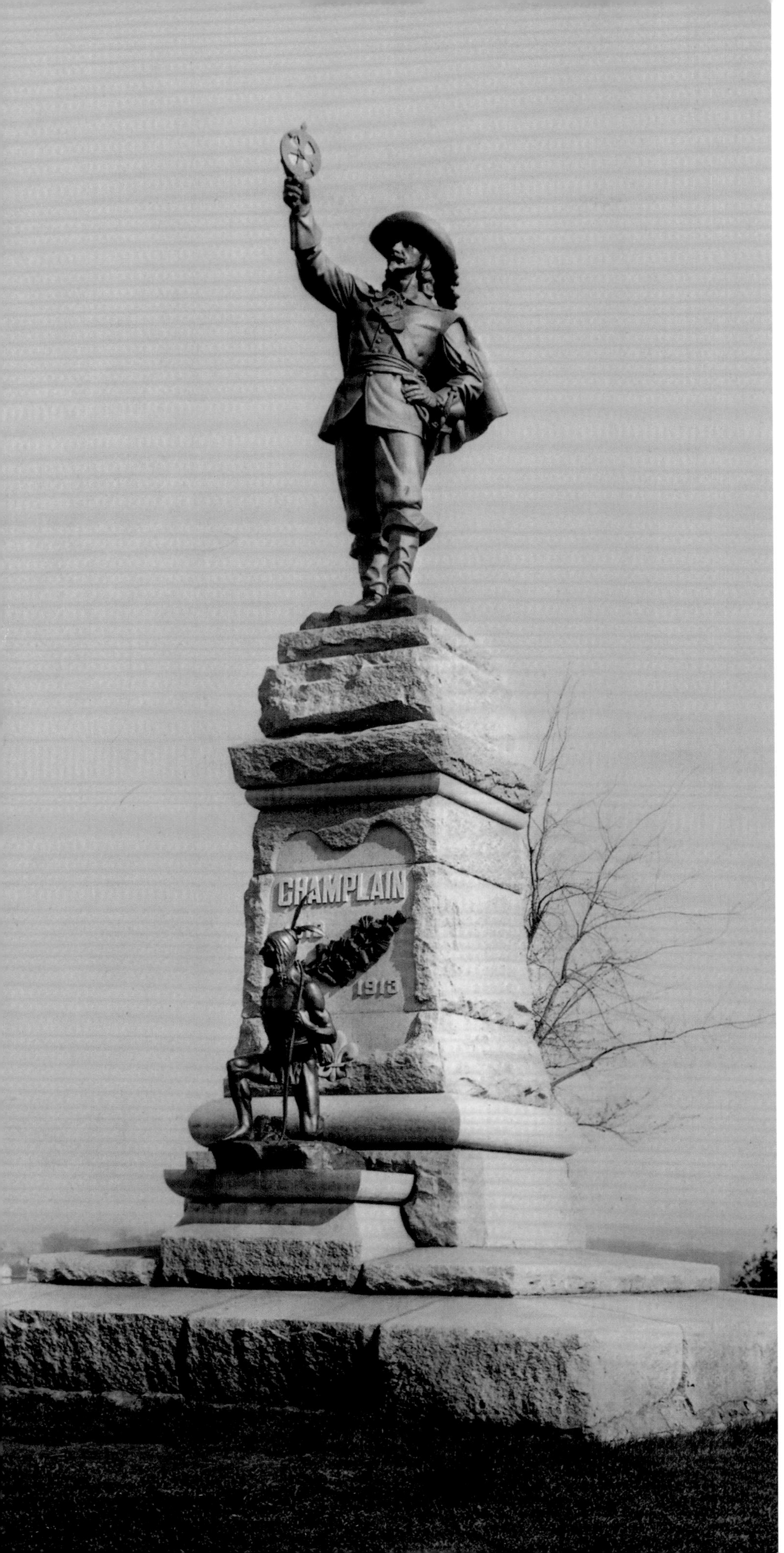

Hamilton MacCarthy
Samuel de Champlain, 1915

In 1915 Hamilton MacCarthy won the commission to produce a sculpture commemorating the three hundredth anniversary of the founding of New France by French navigator, soldier and cartographer Samuel de Champlain. Although he was among the leading sculptors of the day, MacCarthy was not the most accurate one: the explorer holds an astrolabe upside down when it should have been suspended from a rope. Three years after completing the work MacCarthy reinforced the notion that Champlain was a man of science by adding a bronze sculpture of the bare-breasted Anishinabe scout who had helped Champlain navigate the waters of the Ottawa River. By adding the scout to the base of the monument MacCarthy not only suggested the gulf that lay between the "educated gentleman" and the "noble savage," he reinforced the national narrative that erased the exploitation and forced relocation of First Nations people.

and beautiful incidents" were "commemorated in enduring bronze."[29] It was therefore important that his fellow sculptors seek the best possible likeness of the figure they were modelling. Upon the death of the country's first prime minister, MacCarthy had himself taken a death mask of Macdonald to ensure the accuracy of his own work. "Carefully modeled" figures and robes were considered equally important. So was the sculptor's attempt to make a bronze sculpture as smooth as possible, giving no indication of the sculptor's manual gestures or other marks left from the modelling of the clay. Getting the insignias correct enhanced the stature and importance of the subject. And MacCarthy further declaimed, "The highest plane in Statuary is reached in the *Ideal single figure*, commonly armed and emblematic, expressing some emotion, passion, or attribute of man's inner being."[30] Below that was "the *Ideal group* of two or more figures."[31]

MacCarthy believed that this could be realized by showing the figures in contrapposto pose—this entailed setting the right leg back in order to make the figure seem to be advancing when viewed from the side. And, in order to capture a defining moment, a political figure might be shown in full-swing debating style, often with an outstretched hand grasping a document. Similarly, dignity and repose were also important. So were the overall design of and the harmony between the plinth—which was usually in the hands of marble carvers and architects—and the bronze sculpture above it, which was the work of the artist.

Memorial sculpture had another purpose, according to this notably vocal advocate of the genre: the "embellishment of our cities, our parks and gardens and places of interest, with ideal Statuary, Fountains and other sculptured adornments," all of which, MacCarthy continued, "would raise them in dignity, attractiveness and beauty." Hence "sculpture through its beauty and *al fresco* endurance is especially fitted to present and express the incidents and achievements of history; heroes, heroines and patriots who have built up their country and the Empire upon which the sun never sets."[32]

But who were the heroines? Women had never been admirals, generals, politicians, commercial leaders or part of the "heritage elites" that were thought to be worth commemorating. Confined largely to the home, Canadian women occupied a separate sphere from their male partners. Indeed, women rarely appeared above the plinth—unless they were Queen Victoria or an allegorical figure representing Canada, peace, Bellona, a winged goddess or Britannia. Nor, until the beginning of the twentieth century, were women likely to be represented in contemporary dress: instead they were swathed, fully or partially, in robes that owed their inspiration to ancient Greece or classical Rome. And if, in works like Louis-Philippe Hébert's small-scale, exquisitely modelled and, above all, sensuous female nude *La Fée Nicotine* (1902), they had no clothes at all: they were representations of allegorical figures.[33]

Indeed it was not until the first decade of the twentieth century that, working on a small scale, Hébert represented his female subjects in contemporary clothing. He also, at that point, elevated three women to the status of secular saints: Laura Secord, who in 1813 warned British soldiers of an attack from the Americans; Madeleine de Verchères, who at the age of fourteen thwarted a raid by the Iroquois on Fort Verchères; and the Acadian heroine Evangeline.[34]

And when it came to *making* sculptures, only high-born artists like Princess Louise and female members of the clergy had been tolerated. Even then, rumours went around that it was Princess Louise's teacher, the British sculptor Sir Joseph Edgar Boehm (1834–1890), not herself, who had created her sculptures. Until the very end of the nineteenth century, memorials and memorial making were largely a subject and an activity for men. This remained the case until a young woman from Ontario by the name of Katherine Wallis came onto the scene.

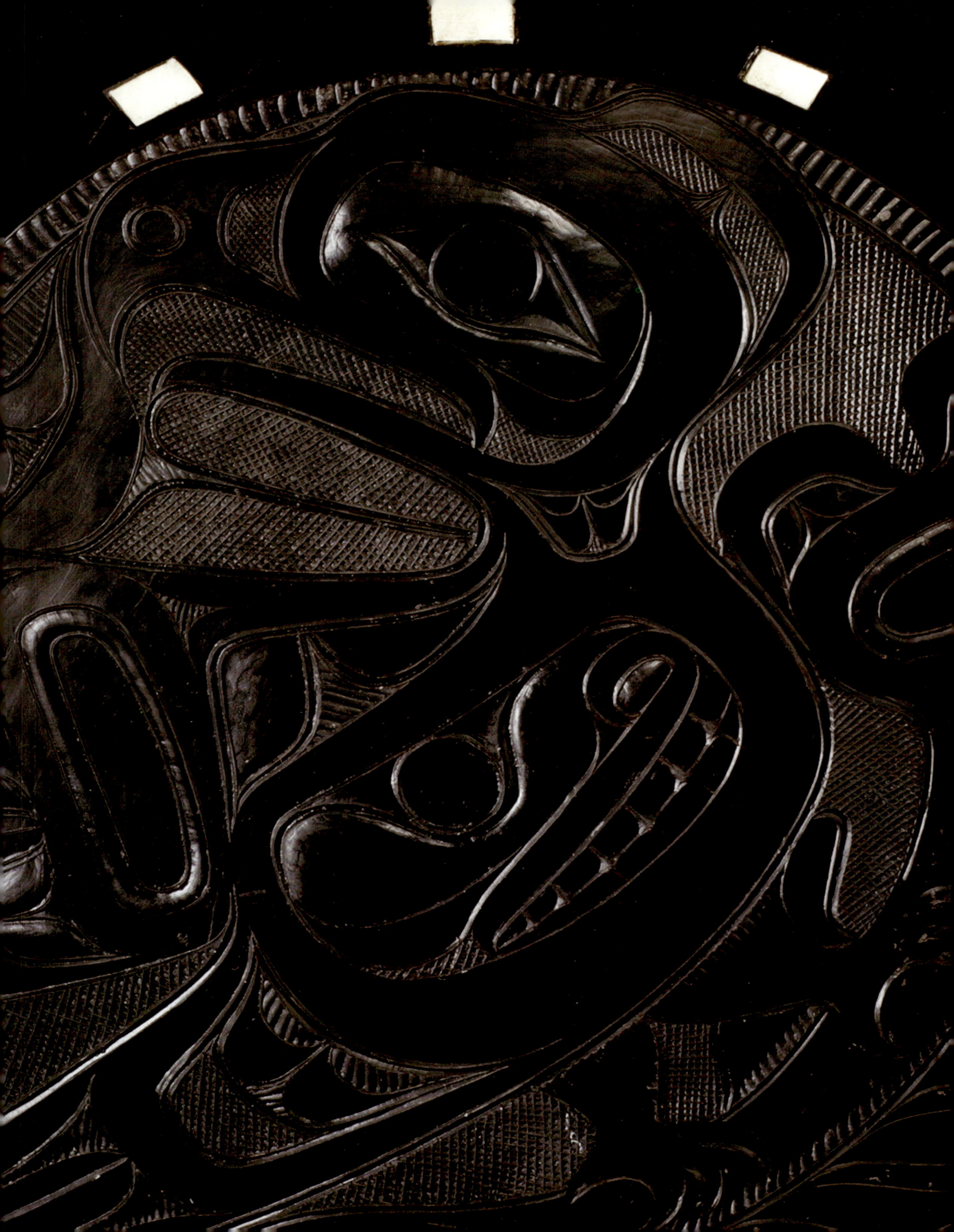

3

At Home and Abroad

As we have seen in the previous chapter, there was no greater authority on Canadian sculpture than writer and sculptor Hamilton MacCarthy. At the beginning of the twentieth century, his own work and that of other sculptors like Louis-Philippe Hébert showed the extent to which commemorative sculpture could be used to create a national narrative by celebrating political leaders—and to bury national narratives by ignoring First Nations people and women. Yet, even in the apparent prime of MacCarthy and Hébert's influence, the commemorative genre was beginning to lose its pre-eminent status, just as these artists' work, though technically proficient, was frequently arid and mediocre. Moreover, it became increasingly clear that religion, nationalism and commemoration were not the only themes suitable for sculptural work.

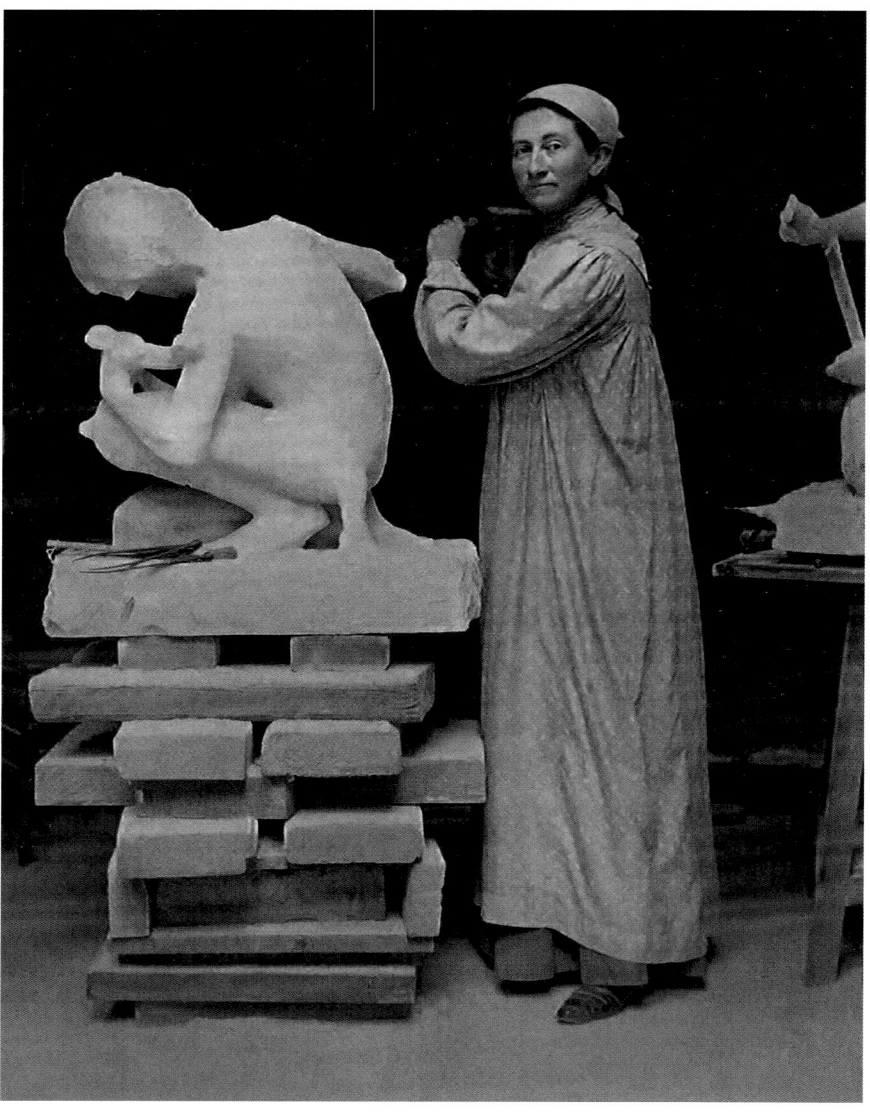

Katherine Wallis and *Mercury* in the artist's Paris studio, pre-1914.

Collection of the Trent University Archives, Katherine E. Wallis fonds, 69-002 Box 1.

Increasingly sculptors could not only create a work without having to reconcile their own style with a client's expectations, but also had more say in setting the price. A sculptor's patron did not have to be the clergy or the state; it might well be a private citizen, an art gallery or an art association. Nor did the sculpture itself have to be life-sized or colossal, realistic or idealistic; it did not have to be perched on a plinth or surrounded by allegorical figures. A sculpture could be small enough to fit on the mantelpiece or placed in a garden.

No one exemplified this important turn in the history of Canadian sculpture more than Katherine E. Wallis (1861–1957). Here was a woman who made an indelible mark in a man's world. Born in Merino, outside of Peterborough in rural Ontario, Wallis spent the formative years of her life on the family farm. It was there that she found role models in her mother's friends, among whom were the writers Catharine Parr Traill and her sister Susanna Moodie and the painter Anne Langton. These strong, creative women encouraged Katherine Wallis and her sister Adah to pursue their artistic studies in Britain, where their own talents had been shaped before they had exchanged their lives there for log cabins in the Ontario bush. Following Anne Langton's advice—"If you wish to attain your dream, you cannot stay here"—Katherine and her sister left for Europe in 1878.[1]

True, Ontario already had an art school where Katherine and Adah could have acquired basic training. Founded in 1876, Toronto's Ontario College of Art, known today as the Ontario College of Art and Design University, had been part of the Toronto Normal School since 1856; but the art classes were segregated and drawing from the undraped model was unheard of. Since 1872 the province also had an active group of professional artists. But although the Ontario Society of Artists admitted women, its female members were prohibited from attending the society's meetings and from serving on the society's council.

It was during her husband's tenure as governor general that Princess Louise sought "to stimulate her Canadian sisters to cultivate at once mental gifts and physical vigour."[2] Although it was under their residence in Canada that both the National Gallery of Canada and the Royal Canadian Academy of Arts came into being, the latter august body would only elect one woman, the painter Charlotte Schreiber (1834–1922), who could neither vote nor attend the academy's meetings. It was another nine years before Mary E. Dignam (1857–1938) was moved "to do something to open the doors for women" because they "had no recognition or place." In 1889 this art activist, painter and teacher formed the province-wide, Toronto-based Women's Art Club for "professional" and "serious" women artists.[3]

Meanwhile, the young Katherine Wallis initially pursued her ambitions in Scotland. When she began her studies at the Edinburgh School of Art in 1878 her "joy knew no bounds." At the end of two years she had sold a few paintings and, according to her diary, was "now qualified as a professional artist!"[4] Convinced that "one must travel to attain in Art," Wallis "begged to get more knowledge in the beloved Edinburgh."[5] But her mother was now dying and her father was unwell. Someone had to oversee the running of the farm. The call of duty brought Wallis and her sister back to Merino, Ontario.

It was not until thirteen years after her first visit to Great Britain that, now thirty-two, Wallis had the freedom, with financial support from her brother, to resume her studies. In 1893, accompanied by her sister and their governess, Miss Buchanan, and following in the footsteps of Anne Langton, the party travelled overseas and then spent two years visiting Europe's major cathedrals, museums and art galleries. Towards the end of the tour, "sculpture made its first real impression" on Wallis. The experience of viewing an early Augustan sculpture depicting Psyche and Eros at the Castle of Baia in Naples was, she recalled, like "facing something more living and with a higher beauty than anything I had ever seen before."[6] Wallis was now convinced that sculpture was "the Art of Arts!" Although she had enrolled in the painting department at the Royal College of Art, when she returned to London in 1895 she moved to the college's sculpture department.[7]

It did not take Wallis long to discover that sculpture was a messier genre than painting: at once more physically demanding and less independent.

Even before the sculptor began modelling a figure, a wooden or iron armature had to be constructed to support the clay. Once the clay model had been finished and this material had sufficiently dried and shrunk, it was handed over to craftsmen at the foundry who transformed it into a more durable object. Following the lost wax process, sculptors in India had been casting bronzes since 5000 BCE. The process entailed several stages. The clay model was covered with plaster; then the clay was removed from the plaster mould, which was used to make a casting in a bronze alloy consisting of 85 per cent copper and 5 per cent each of lead, tin and zinc. Only after the bronze cast had been made, burnished and sometimes chased, was it returned to the sculptor, who was left to choose a suitable patina for the surface of the piece.

While creating a sculpture in stone did not involve so many hands, it was equally messy and its outcome just as unpredictable. There was dust. There was the possibility of chipping, fracturing or splintering the stone when the chisel or a mallet struck it. Further damage could occur when a sculpture, weighing perhaps five hundred kilograms, was transported from an artist's atelier to the home of the commissioning patron, an exhibition hall or a private art gallery.

Katherine Wallis was taught at the Royal College of Art by the French-born sculptor Édouard Lantéri (1848–1917). A former pupil of the famous Neoclassical painter Jacques-Louis David (1748–1825), Lantéri was a regular exhibitor at the Royal Academy of Art. Long after Wallis had been his pupil, Lantéri published his *Modelling: A Guide for Teachers and Students* (1902), which gives some idea of how Wallis would have acquired her basic training. Lantéri insisted that his students learn how to produce an accurate drawing of the model or bust before they began to model or carve the work in clay or stone. He also insisted that his students acquire a thorough knowledge of anatomy. It was only then, according to Lantéri, that a sculptor had "the necessary power to express truthfully the personal sentiment with which Nature has endowed him."[8]

Wallis knew how to draw. After all, she had spent two years at the Edinburgh School of Art, during which she had made a modest living from selling her copies of famous paintings. She had a sound knowledge of the skeletal structure of animals because her father had been an ardent taxidermist. But it was only under Lantéri's guidance that Wallis became thoroughly acquainted with every facet of the human body—the skeleton, the muscles and the ligaments—by copying plaster-cast replicas of works by Michelangelo and Donatello and by working from life. Doing this taught Wallis about mass and about the significance of the negative space between masses. And it helped her to transfer the correct proportions of a living model to her clay model or block of stone or marble.

By the end of her first year, Lantéri's training had reinforced Wallis's love of classical sculpture. More significantly, he introduced her to what became known as "the New Sculpture," whose followers produced small-scale bronzes of domestic subjects, including women, children and animals, in a variety of late-nineteenth-century styles.

Wallis's ability to give distinction and suppleness to the human figure won her the Royal College of Art's bronze medal. One work in line with the naturalism characteristic of the New Sculpture, *A Young Canadian Fiddler* (c. 1898), was accepted at the Royal Academy for exhibition. Wallis also won the Modellers' Free Scholarship, which enabled her to pursue her studies for another two years. In 1899, at the end of three years at the Royal College of Art, Wallis relocated to Paris. Intending to visit the city for six months, she remained there—with short visits to England, Canada and Germany—until the outbreak of the Second World War in 1939.

Within a year of arriving in Paris, Wallis had met several like-minded female sculptors who, like her, had chosen to pursue what was generally considered to be a man's profession. It was not an easy life for these largely single women. Making a sculpture was a more expensive activity than making a painting. Materials were costly. Studio spaces had to be large in order to accommodate the work. And while there were many foundries in Paris by the 1890s, casting a clay or plaster model into bronze was not cheap.

Many female sculptors paid for their atelier and materials by modelling for male sculptors, or by working as their studio assistants—the most famous being Auguste Rodin's lover, source of inspiration and assistant, Camille Claudel (1864–1943), who was an accomplished sculptor in her own right. Few female sculptors like Katherine Wallis had the luck to find private patrons willing to buy their work outright, or an art gallery willing to give them a solo exhibition. Most female sculptors made their reputations by getting a sculpture accepted for display at one of the annual Paris Salon exhibitions, in the hope that an art critic would write a favourable review of the work and thereby bring it to the notice of the larger public.

There were, however, some advantages to being a sculptor—even if you were a woman. A sculptor could hire a professional carver to enlarge a stone or bronze maquette to any size with the aid of a "pointing machine." Moreover, as the technique of bronze casting improved, and advances in mining and smelting reduced the price of material, multiple copies of the original work could be cast in bronze. This meant that, by the middle of the nineteenth century, owning a small-scale sculpture, or statuette, was no longer reserved for the social and financial European elite, for whom owning a gilt bronze had previously been a highly esteemed status symbol. The middle classes could afford to own bronze sculptures too.

Though women had been admitted to the state-run École des Beaux-Arts two years before Wallis arrived in Paris in 1899, most chose to study at the more intimate Académie Julian or Académie Colarossi, where they could work from the nude model in unsegregated classes. It was at the Académie Colarossi that Wallis's interest in domestic subjects that had been popularized by an earlier generation of female painters—most notably Mary Cassatt (1844–1926) and Berthe Morisot (1841–1895)—was reinforced. The Colarossi was also where Wallis became familiar with the work of sculptors Jules Dalou (1838–1902) and Jean-Antoine Injalbert (1845-1933). These painters and sculptors were famous for capturing the private, intimate moments of women and children. But even more important for Wallis was a chance encounter, while sketching animals in the Jardin des Plantes in central Paris, with the leading Swiss-born *animalier* sculptor,

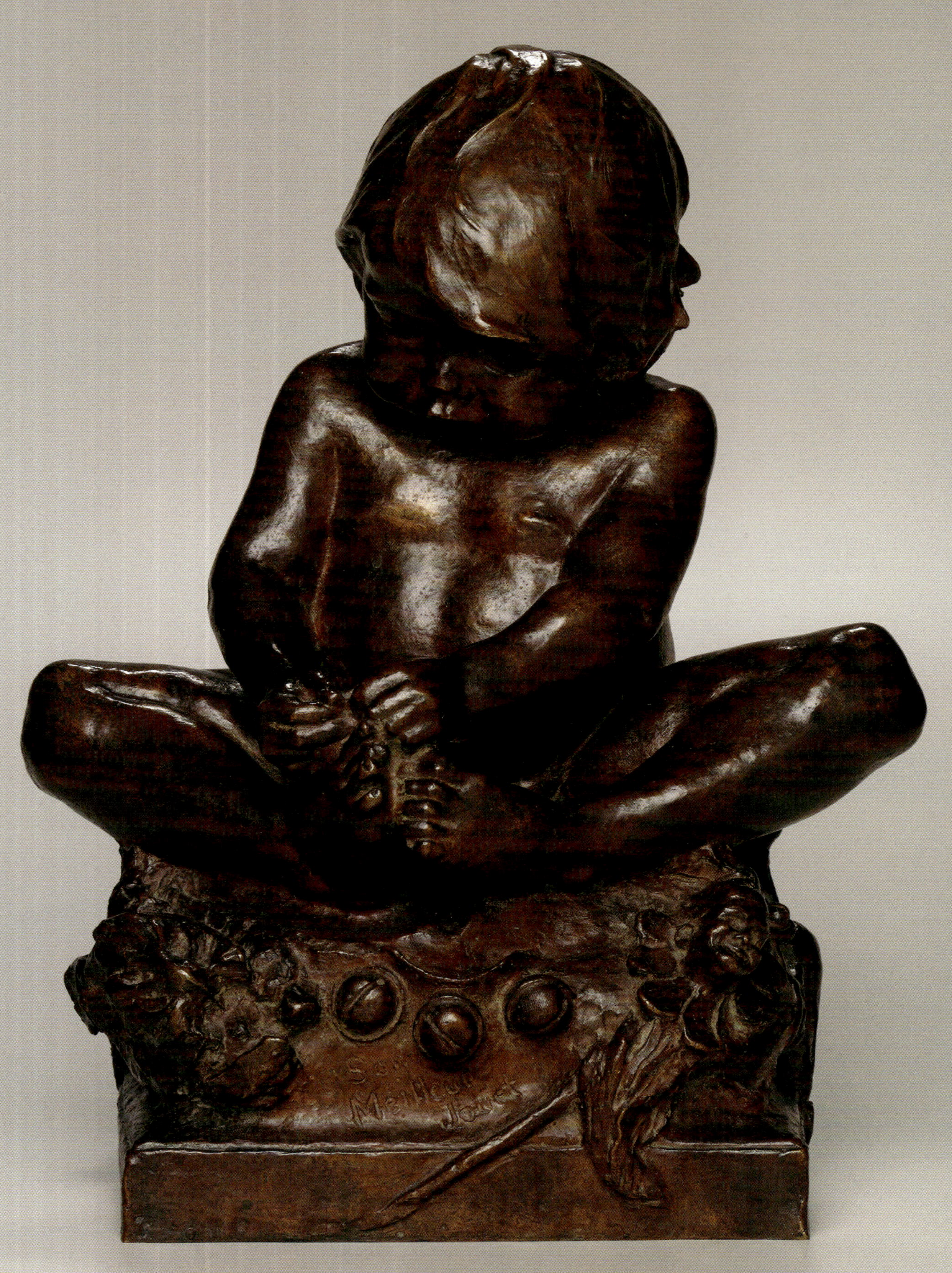

Oscar Waldmann (1856–1937). Their resulting association gave her the confidence to add another theme to her small-scale bronze statuettes and larger marble sculptures: animals.

During her third year in Paris, Wallis also met the leading sculptor of the day—perhaps of the twentieth century. Auguste Rodin (1840–1917) was at the height of his career when a fellow female sculptor introduced Wallis to him in 1902. Largely self-taught, Rodin had transformed sculptural practices by showing that sculpture did not have set rules of the kind laid out by Hamilton MacCarthy and practised by the majority of commemorative sculptors in Canada. A figurative sculpture by Rodin was stripped down to the bare essentials. The surface of his finished bronzes possessed a rough, unfinished or *non finito* quality that revealed marks from the sculptor's hand and fingers. In making the finished bronze no different from the clay model, Rodin revealed the process involved in making a sculpture.

In setting aside a realistic rendering of his subject, Rodin transformed an abstract idea, concept or emotion into concrete form. And, just as his sculptures often had no story and no finished look, they often had no plinth. What Rodin's sculptures did possess, however, was energy, movement and a life force that fused form with feeling and the concrete with the imaginary. It could be said that Rodin was the first artist to make a sculpture for sculpture's sake.

With a view to helping Katherine Wallis understand and develop her own technique, Rodin encouraged her to make drawings of the sculptures at the Louvre. He gave Wallis a critique of her work in which he praised her "solid construction." And Rodin also asked to see more of her work. But Wallis demurred. As she later explained, "I could not avail myself of his kind permission to bring everything I did for him to see, as modeling is not easily transportable and I was getting all I could absorb from the Maitre [Oscar Waldmann] and had also helpful criticisms from Injalbert [her teacher at the Académie Colarossi] from time to time."[9] Although Wallis reflected in later life that it had been "a great privilege to watch him work," she felt that Rodin's "criticisms were not helpful." She attempted to justify this by saying that his eyes were very short-sighted and therefore he looked at his work closely, while she was long-sighted "and had difficulty always in suppressing details."[10]

The fact was that Wallis was clearly not prepared, as Rodin was, to tap into her emotions—or to abandon the naturalistic rendering and finished "look" of her subject. Like her mentors Waldmann, Dalou and Injalbert, who adhered to the practices of the New Sculpture, Wallis's works were less emotional, less personal and less imaginative than Rodin's. Wallis's subjects, as seen in *His Best Toy* (pre-1910), *Lioness, Mercury* and *Mon Petit Chou*, were domestic and allegorical.[11] These works, executed during the first decade of the century, possessed a formal naturalism and a detailed rendering of the work's surface that was admired by public galleries and private patrons alike but was far different from the sculpture of Rodin.

Wallis won prizes and awards. She saw her work exhibited at the Paris Salon and at international expositions like Paris's Exposition Universelle in 1900. Galleries and museums acquired her work; Wallis's *Lioness* was purchased by the Art Gallery of Toronto while *Mon Petit Chou* was bought by the Walker Art Gallery in Liverpool. International expositions displayed her sculpture; private and public individuals and institutions in Dresden, London, Leeds and Glasgow gave her commissions. And she got plenty of praise. Wallis's large marble carving *Mercury* was considered by one critic to have been executed "in the tradition of Michelangelo."[12]

In 1904 Katherine Wallis travelled to Canada where she hoped, at last, to establish her reputation in her native country. True, she exhibited her work at the Royal Canadian Academy of Arts during her visit. But when she attempted to submit her work to St. Louis's International Exposition, she found that Canada's contribution did not include painting or sculpture; Wallis returned to Europe without exhibiting in the United States. When the fifty-three-year-old sculptor was about to make another trip to Canada, with the intention of making a second attempt to establish her name, it was 1914 and the First World War broke out in August of that year. Wallis closed her studio on the Rue de Fleurus in Paris and worked as a nurse in a Canadian hospital. When the war ended she re-opened her studio and remained in Paris until the outbreak of the Second World War in 1939. Now in her late seventies, she moved to Santa Cruz, California, where she lived until her death in 1957.

Writing in her memoir toward the end of her long life, Katherine Wallis was proud that she had never wavered from what she called her "ideal." For Wallis, as for many of her contemporaries in Europe, sculpture was not "found in the great 'ordered' work," evident in major memorial commissions, but in her own ideal. And Wallis expressed that ideal "naturally or decoratively" and with a sincerity that she hoped would "give a message to the world which will enrich it."[13]

Wallis's work remained naturalistic and allegorical—and perhaps sometimes cloyingly sentimental. Her largely domestic subject matter belonged to the late-nineteenth- and early-twentieth-century followers who adhered to the New Sculpture. Not surprisingly, she deplored the modernist sculptors whose work she would have seen in the second decade of the twentieth century at the Paris Salon.

While few Canadian sculptors of Wallis's generation possessed her technical ability or received her level of international recognition, she never succeeded in establishing a name for herself in Canada. In her generation, the fact that she was a woman limited her opportunities as a sculptor and excluded her from full membership in art societies like the Royal Canadian Academy and the Ontario Society of Artists. Yet she had spent three decades of her early life in Canada, leaving precisely to pursue her art, and later enjoyed the recognition that was denied to her in her own country.

Canadians living in Montreal were introduced to the sculpture of Auguste Rodin in 1907 when the Montreal Museum of Fine Arts acquired one of the twenty-eight full-scale castings of his famous work *The Thinker* (1902).

But two sculptors from Montreal—Louis-Philippe Hébert and Alfred Laliberté—were already familiar with the sculptor's work. They had viewed it several years earlier at the Paris Salon, where Katherine Wallis had also exhibited her sculpture.

Rodin's example had more influence on Hébert than on Wallis. After Hébert's exposure to the French artist, he gave his own sculptures a less intense, looser rendering that brought the viewer closer to the original clay model. He began working outside of the severe, didactic subjects demanded by adhering to the commemorative genre. And as can be seen in the Symbolist-inspired sculpture *Inspiration* (1904), Hébert made himself and his female muse—and the very process of making a sculpture—the subject of his work.

Laliberté went even further than Hébert in demonstrating his debt to Rodin. In *Sketch for "Corn-husking"* (c. 1906–1907) Laliberté left his fingerprints and marks from the tooth-edged modelling stick on the

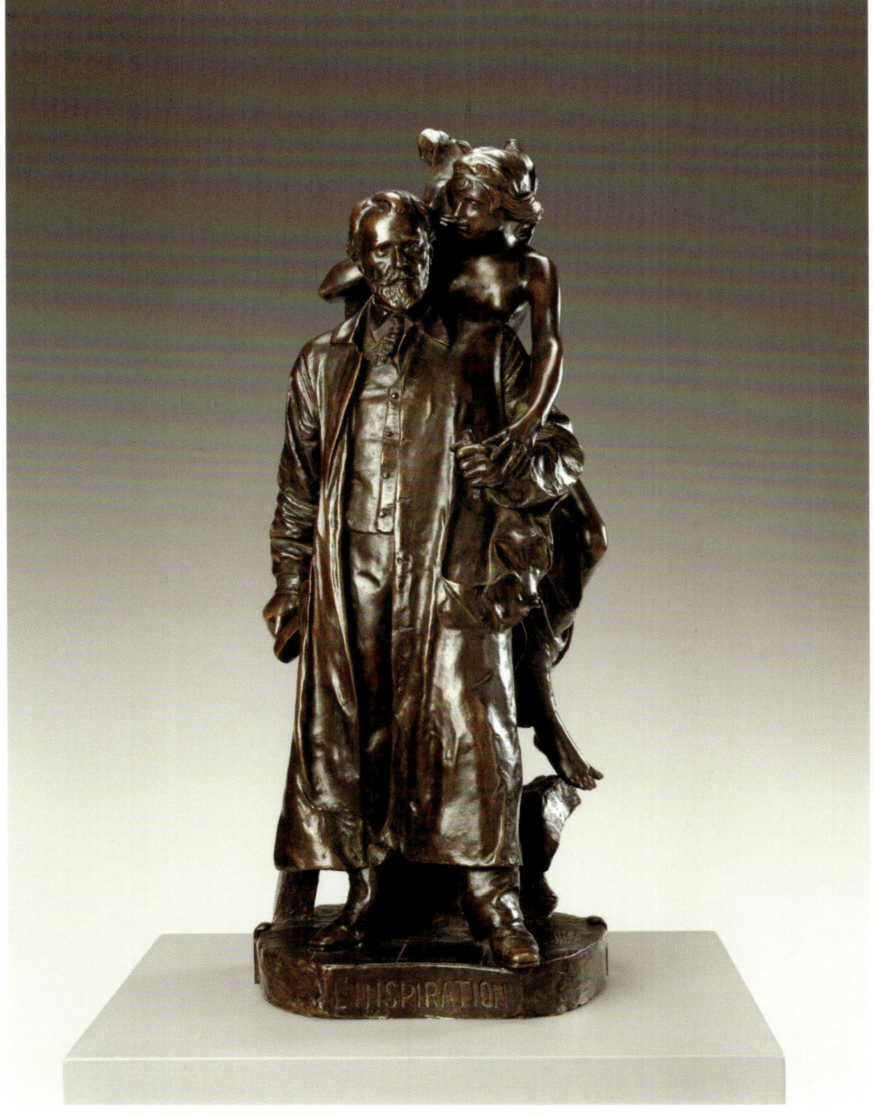

Louis-Philippe Hébert
Inspiration, 1904
This loosely rendered self-portrait is a refreshing contrast to Hébert's realistic figurative sculptures of politicians and military personages. Drawing on the late-nineteenth-century Symbolist tradition, Hébert explored the creative process. Thus a winged muse whispers words of advice and encouragement into the Montreal sculptor's ear as she guides his chisel.

Alfred Laliberté
Sketch for "Corn-husking," c. 1906–1907
After Alfred Laliberté won first prize at the provincial exhibition in Quebec City for a life-sized bust of Sir Wilfrid Laurier, Montreal's Council of Arts and Manufactures funded his studies at the École des Beaux-Arts in Paris. It was there that the young sculptor was introduced to the work of Auguste Rodin. Laliberté had the courage to follow his mentor by leaving his fingerprints on the surface of a finished work in order to introduce his viewer to the process of creating a sculpture.

surface of the finished bronze. Even more remarkable, he abandoned any attempt to give a realistic representation of the two figures, making this work among the first Impressionistic sculptures to be produced by a Canadian artist.

Even so, Laliberté could also give a more realistic, more controlled and less Impressionistic rendering of a subject. In this sense, he was closer to the painter Gustave Courbet (1819–1877) who, beginning in the late 1840s, had depicted rural subjects in an unromantic and unidealized manner. Laliberté was equally sympathetic to Jules Dalou (1838–1902) and Constantin Meunier (1831–1905), who were concerned that manual skills were being lost as a result of mechanization and the depopulation of the countryside, and that they needed preserving in their sculptural works. And this is not surprising: Laliberté had been raised on a farm in rural Quebec where he had "tilled the soil, with axe, spade, pick in hand."[14]

Unlike Hébert, Laliberté had bypassed a workshop apprenticeship and taken his initial training as a sculptor at the Council of Arts and Manufactures school in Montreal. Then, with the support of his local member of parliament Sir Wilfrid Laurier and the Council of Arts and Manufactures, as well as funds raised by public subscription, Laliberté travelled to France. He spent five years, from 1902 to 1907, studying with Katherine Wallis's former teacher, Jean-Antoine Injalbert, and also with

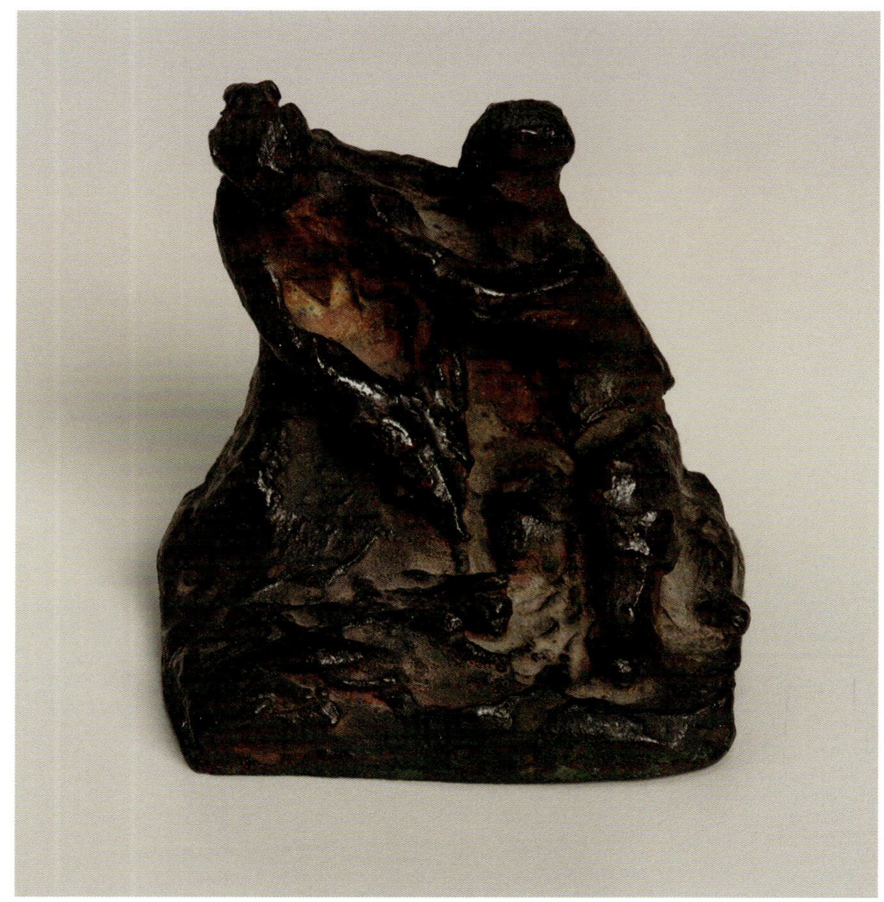

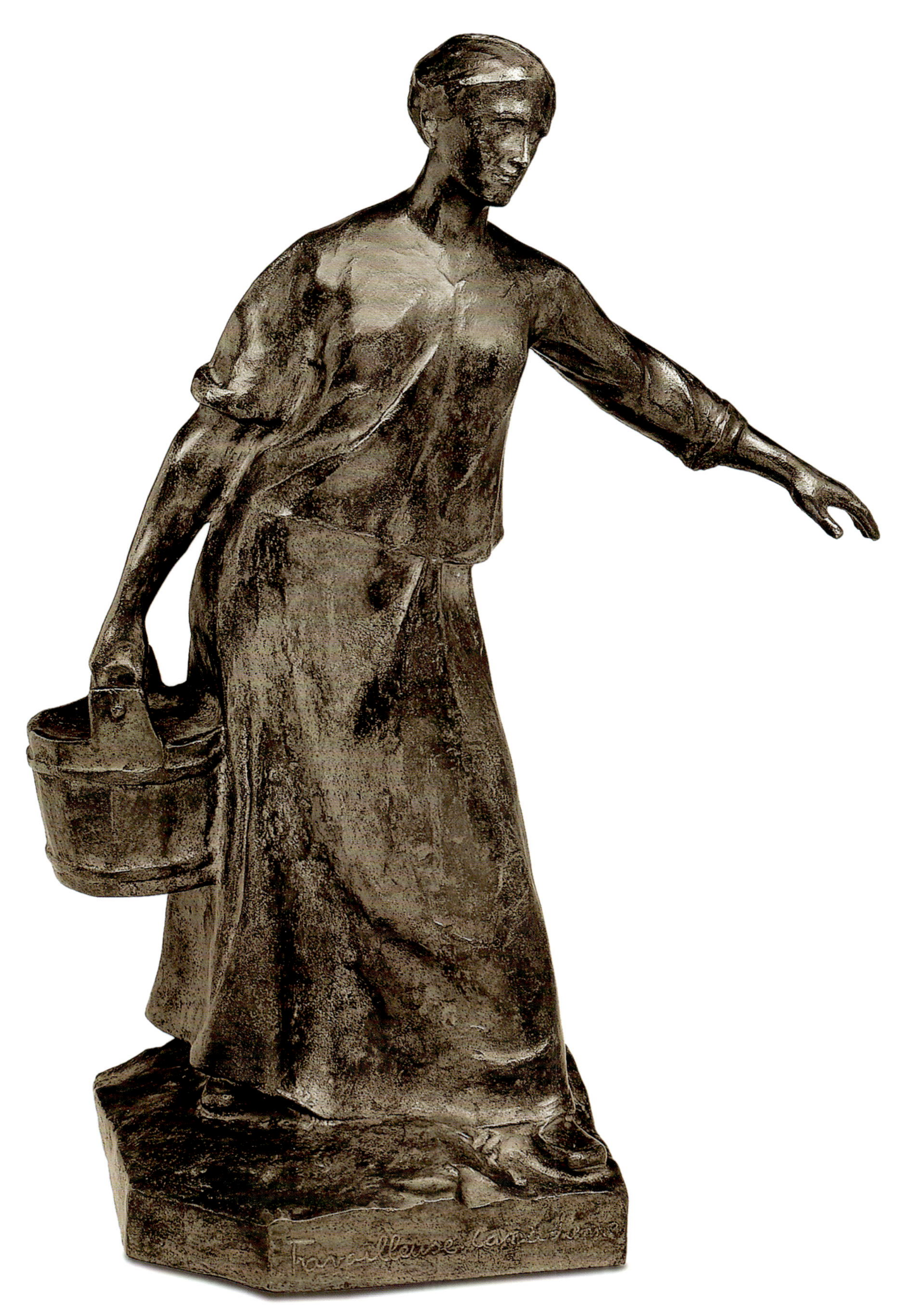

Gabriel-Jules Thomas (1824–1905), whose sculpture was firmly rooted in the academic tradition. Laliberté also enrolled at Paris's École des Beaux-Arts where students were encouraged to produce monumental sculpture replete with allegorical and classical imagery.

When he returned to Montreal in 1907, the cachet of having studied in Paris landed Laliberté a teaching position at his old school. It was now that he established his name by producing memorial sculptures for the Notre-Dame-des-Neiges Cemetery in Montreal and two works, memorializing the seventeenth-century French Jesuit missionaries Fathers Jacques Marquette and Jean de Brébeuf, for the facade of the Legislative Assembly Building in Quebec City. In 1910 Laliberté returned to the French capital to oversee the casting of these two sculptures in bronze at the Andro Foundry. But the sculptor's association with France ended a year later.

Canada, and specifically Quebec, would remain Laliberté's real home. He exhibited his work at the annual exhibitions of the Art Association of Montreal and the Royal Canadian Academy of Arts and in the showroom of Montreal's Johnson and Copping Gallery. He cast his sculptures at Montreal's Robert Mitchell Foundry, and taught at the Council of Arts and Manufactures school. He made a name for himself by producing realistic small sculptures that gave a romanticized view of rural life in Quebec as it had been in the 1880s. And he expanded his repertoire of subject matter.

Less than ten years after returning to Quebec from France, Laliberté accepted a commission that came to symbolize his oeuvre as a whole. *La Fermière* (1914) was made for the centrepiece of a fountain in Montreal. The work had its genesis in the small studio piece *Travailleuse Canadienne* (c. 1903–1906). Laliberté made several castings from this piece, one of which fell into the hands of his patron, Sir Wilfrid Laurier.

What made *Travailleuse Canadienne* and its up-scaled version, *La Fermière*, so popular was that Laliberté chose to depict a female farm worker in contemporary dress. The critics applauded Laliberté's choice of subject. They liked his spare style. And they appreciated the artist's visual representation of the habitant, who occupied an important place at the heart of French-Canadian rural life. Indeed, as one commentator noted, *La Fermière* was "a manifestation of his patriotism and nationalism."[15] Yet another critic went further, claiming that the sculpture was "a living symbol of French Canada, of the spirit that reigned over our settling in this country, a spirit that has been preserved until this day and can still be found in the farthest corners of the countryside, where mores have retained all their pristine purity, their distinct character, clearly carved from the severe, sober and virtuous way of life of our forefathers."[16]

La Fermière was thus infused with a particular sense of identity, linked to a culture that was specific to largely one part of Canada. But this demotic turn towards a new kind of realism and a new kind of subject was now paralleled elsewhere by other work, albeit in different idioms, but likewise showing that Canadian sculptors had more options than simply to depict a famous person or to serve the Roman Catholic Church.

This was also true during the Boer War (1899–1902), also known as the South African War, when the rendering of a heroic general gave way to the representation of the lowly soldier. A host of sculptors, including Louis-Philippe Hébert, Hamilton MacCarthy and George William Hill, produced memorial sculptures of non-commissioned Anglo-Canadian soldiers for many cities across the country. Adapting the iconography made familiar in late-nineteenth-century battle paintings and in on-the-spot newspaper sketches, sculptors depicted soldiers waving their hats or rifles or standards high above their heads. Or mounted on a trusty steed. Or in the midst of attempting to control a high-spirited horse. However the largely anonymous non-commissioned soldiers were depicted, accuracy was foremost in the minds of the citizens' committees and local councils who commissioned the works. Concerned that Louis-Philippe Hébert provide an accurate rendering of the horses that had outnumbered the five-hundred-strong contingent of western Canadian soldiers known as the "Rough Riders," one enterprising citizen in Calgary, Pat Burns, shipped a western Canadian horse to the artist's studio in Montreal.

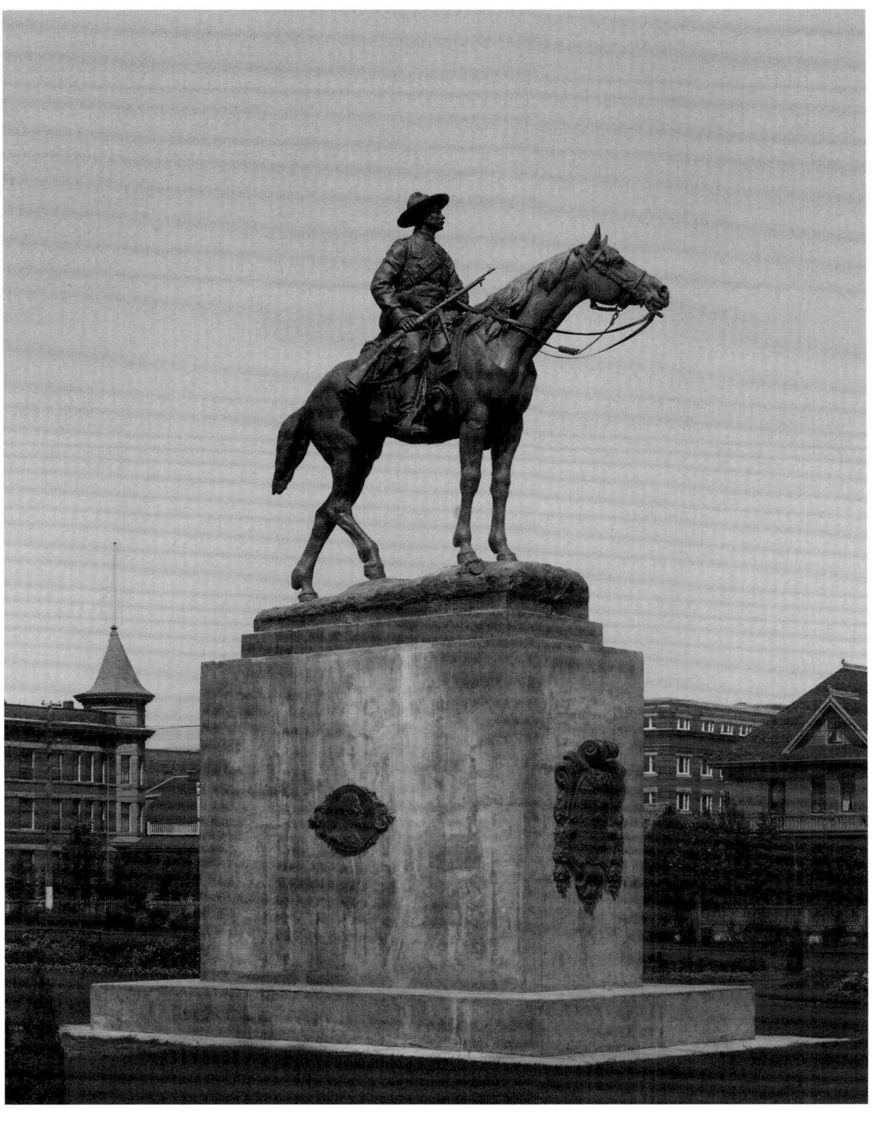

Louis-Philippe Hébert
South African War Memorial, 1914
During the Boer War western Canada sent a contingent of five hundred volunteers, known as the Rough Riders, and an even larger number of horses to South Africa. When the war ended in 1902 and Canadian sculptors began memorializing the men who had fought for "King, Country and the British Empire," these hardy, strong and agile horses accompanied their riders on the tops and bases of plinths across the country. Eager to ensure that Hébert made an accurate depiction of the western Canadian horse, a businessman in Calgary shipped one to the artist's studio in Montreal.

Ontario sculptor Robert Tait McKenzie (1867–1938) also created figurative sculptures of unidentified people. But his figures were not romantic idealizations of the unnamed soldier or the habitant. Following Aristotle's notion of the ideal form, McKenzie rendered smooth-skinned athletes, of which *The Relay* (1910) is the best example. Other sculptors preferred to depict specific Canadian themes—particularly those associated with the past. During his training at Paris's École des Beaux-Arts and Academies Colarossi and Julian, Marc-Aurèle de Foy Suzor-Coté (1869–1937) came under the influence of the French Impressionists and the earlier generation of Neoclassical sculptors like François Rude (1784–1855), who regarded scenes from everyday life as a worthy subject for small-scale sculpture. In *The Old Canadian Pioneer* (1912) Suzor-Coté set

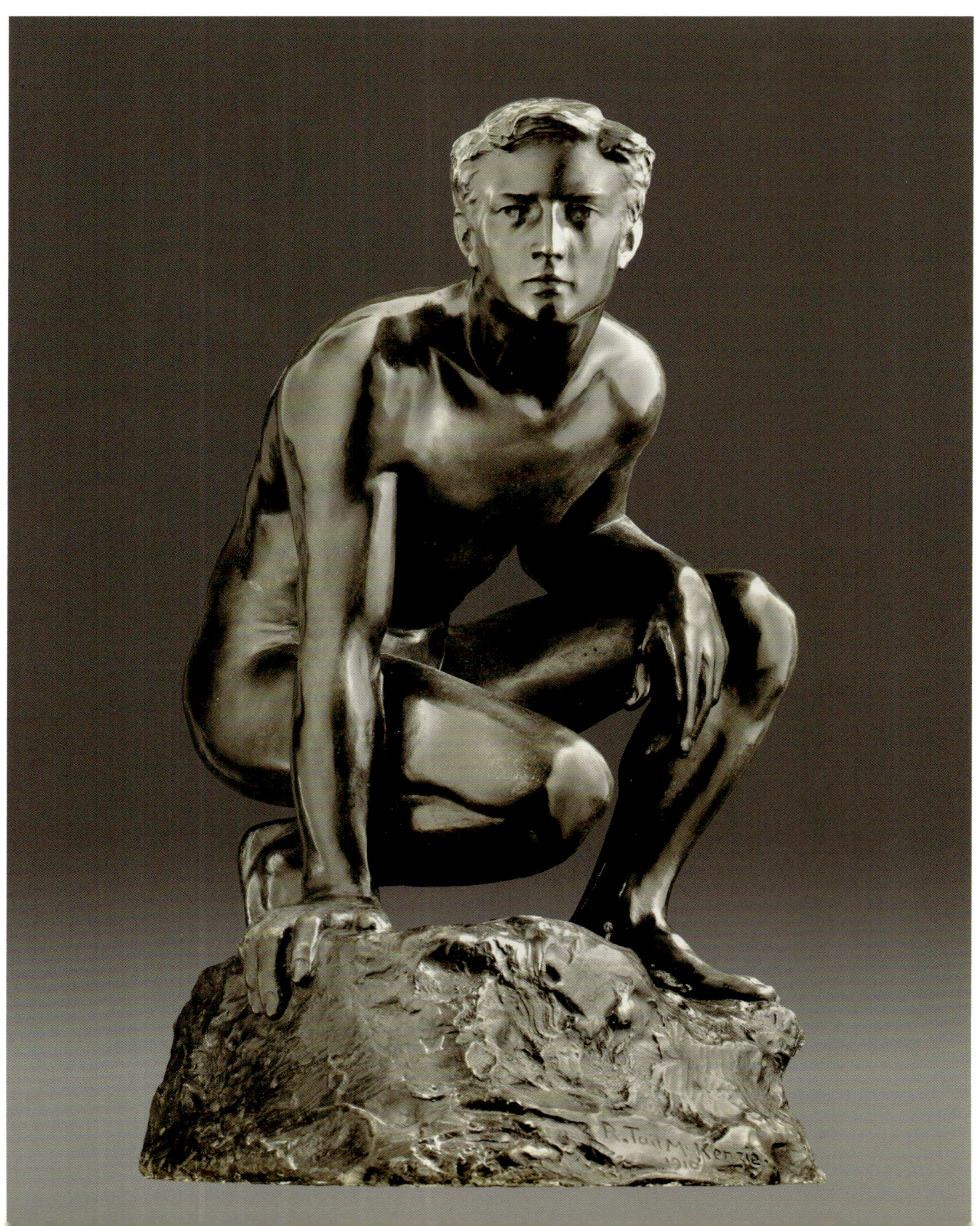

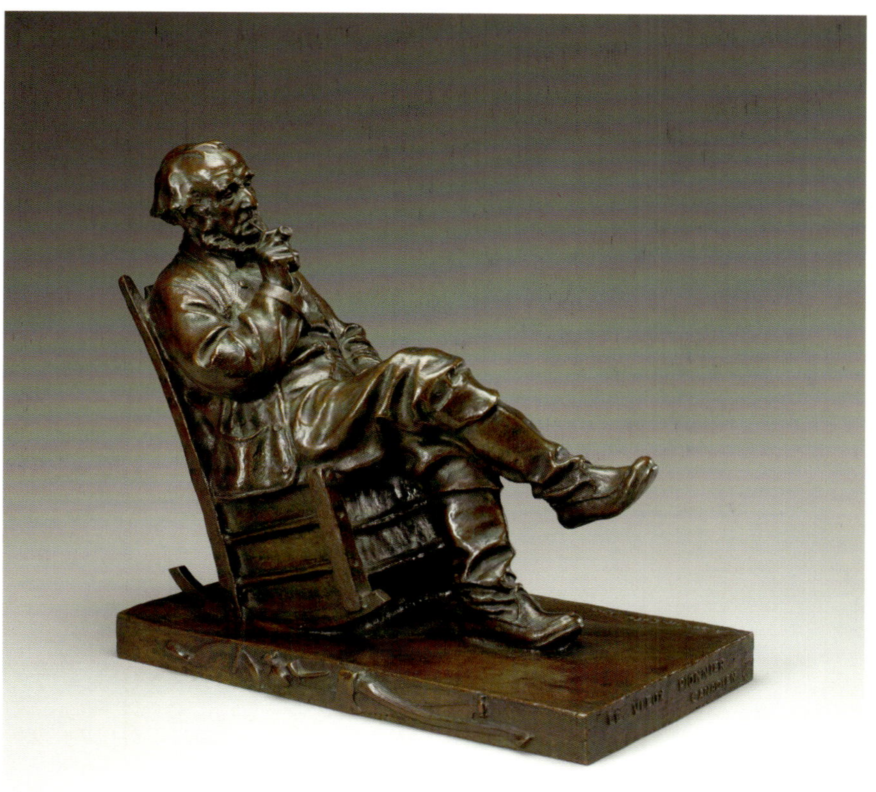

Marc-Aurèle de Foy Suzor-Coté
The Old Canadian Pioneer, 1912
Like many sculptors of his generation who studied in Paris, Suzor-Coté came under the influence of the French Impressionists and of Neoclassical sculptors who belonged to an earlier generation of artists. Convinced that scenes from Canada's rural past offered his urban-based public in Montreal lessons in self-reliance and endurance, Suzor-Coté created small-scale sculptures like *The Old Canadian Pioneer*.

aside any emotional relationship with his subject and any concession to beauty. He also gave a realistic treatment of a way of life that might have disappeared but continued to offer lessons in the virtues of hardiness and self-reliance to the increasingly urban-bound citizens of Montreal.

Another theme that was peculiarly North American was First Nations culture. During the closing decades of the nineteenth century, European sculptors were fascinated by themes they saw as exotic. And when Buffalo Bill Cody romanticized the "Native Indian" in his Wild West show, First Nations people suddenly offered a poignant subject for Canadian sculptors. Most, however—other than Joseph Brant—were depicted at the base of the plinth, not atop it. But in 1896 Hamilton MacCarthy produced a head-and-shoulders sculpture of the American-born Shawnee chief Tech-kum-thai, famous for helping General Sir Isaac Brock prevent an American invasion of Canada. The sculptor could have based his *Portrait Bust of Tech-kum-thai (Tecumseh)* (1896) on an anonymous sketch that had been made from life in 1808 and was later reproduced in Benson Lossing's *Pictorial Field-book of the War of 1812* (1868). But MacCarthy chose to give a blank-faced, idealized portrait of the Shawnee chief.

The story of a later work by MacCarthy is perhaps more significant to us today in illustrating the changing visibility of Indigenous peoples in Canada. In 1915 MacCarthy was responsible for a memorial situated on Nepean Point overlooking Parliament Hill in Ottawa. Unveiled by no less

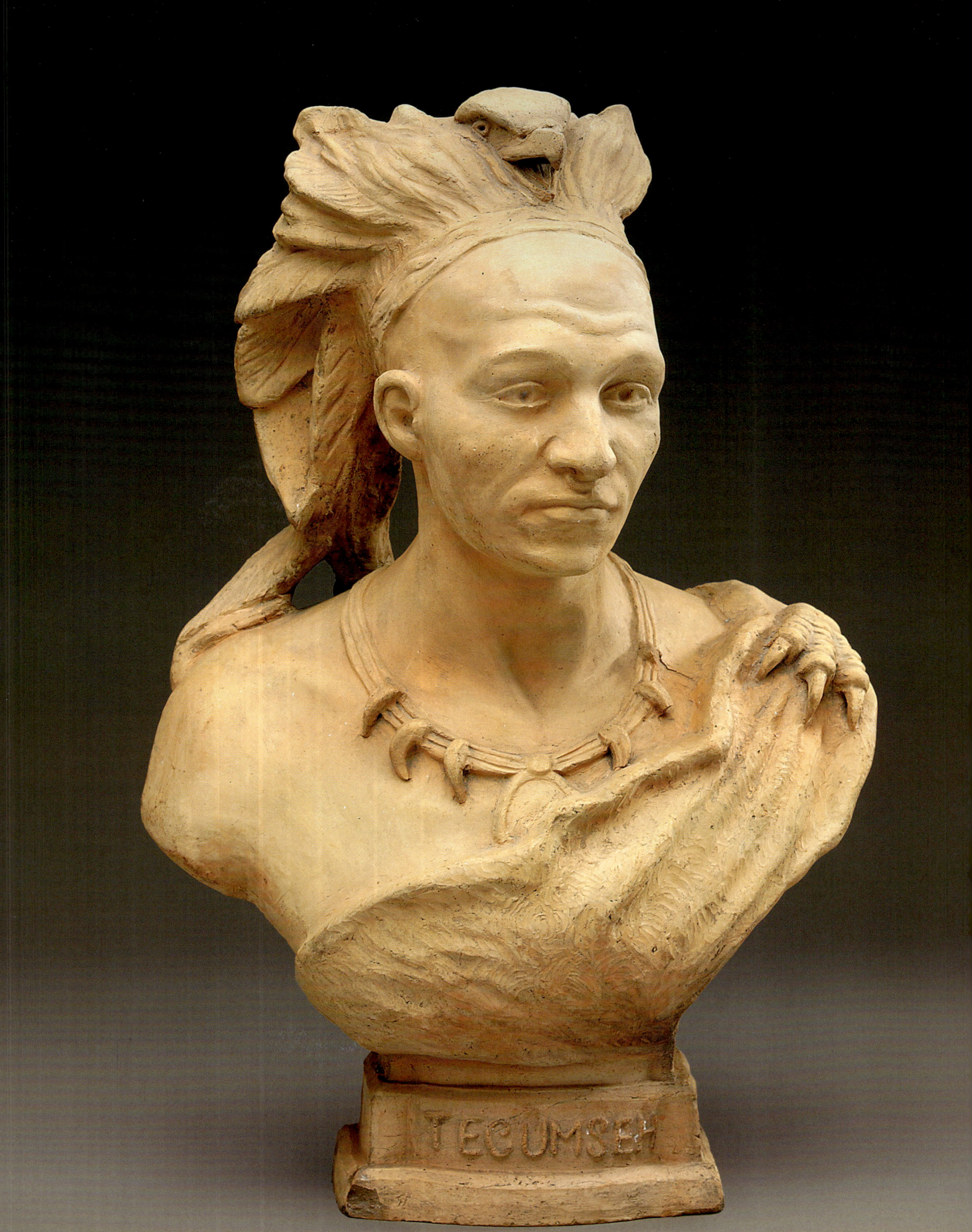
TECUMSEH

a figure than the governor general of Canada, the Duke of Connaught, MacCarthy's sculpture celebrated the landing in Ottawa of Samuel de Champlain in 1613: a great French hero, of course, fittingly commemorated amid the current perils of a war in which France, Britain and Canada were all now allies. But three years later, as though to remedy a wartime oversight, MacCarthy added an Anishinabe scout in a lowly position at the base of the monument.

Louis-Philippe Hébert had not hesitated to exploit similar images. He had rendered the anonymous "Indian" in small-scale terracotta sculptures like *The Last Indian* (1901) and also in more imposing works, like the four sculptures of an Abenaki family, *La Halte dans la Forêt*, he created for Quebec's Legislative Assembly in 1889 while living in Paris. Alfred Laliberté had also celebrated First Nations peoples' hunting skills in *Young Indians Hunting* (c. 1905), while in *Le Scalp* (c. 1906) he explored the theme of anxiety and pessimism that was popularized by French Symbolist sculptors and painters.

Indigenous people were therefore used and abused by Euro-Canadian sculptors in various ways. As we have seen they were sometimes portrayed as brave warrior-assistants to the colonial project; sometimes as a people who had once belonged to a noble but doomed race. In Quebec, more ambiguously, they could serve as an allegory of French Canada itself, since French Canadians—like Indigenous people—could claim to have been colonized and dispossessed of their land, and thus now occupied a subservient position.[17] However Indigenous peoples were depicted, though, they were seldom attired in non-Indigenous clothing, ensuring that they were viewed in the past, rendering them less visible in the present.

In 1896, when the nineteenth century was pressing against the new century, a group of women belonging to Montreal's Women's Art Association (formerly called the Women's Art Club) echoed Alfred Laliberté's concern that mass-produced goods were replacing traditional crafts. In 1902 the association's Home Arts and Handicrafts Committee held an exhibition of Indigenous and non-Indigenous crafts at the Art Association of Montreal. Three years later they severed their ties with the association and, calling themselves the Canadian Handicrafts Guild (CHG), set their agenda. The CHG hoped to stimulate production and thereby prevent the loss and degradation of traditional crafts; they aimed to give artists and artisans alike a market for their work; and they wanted to make the public view craftsmen and craftswomen as artists.

The founders of the CHG made efforts to achieve this by collecting and even commissioning work, which they then showed and sold at their annual exhibitions in Montreal. They established branches of their organization across the country, and by the end of the 1930s had branch offices in every province from British Columbia to Prince Edward Island. It is true that the CHG did not organize an exhibition of Inuit sculpture at the McCord Museum in Montreal until 1930, or hold its first sale of Inuit art at their

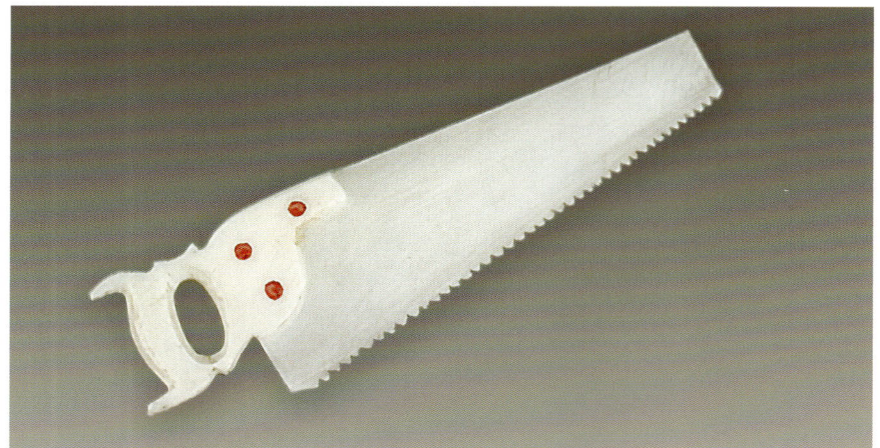

Artist Unknown
Model Saw, pre-1912
This ivory sculpture of a Euro-Canadian tool is a far cry from the diminutive carvings of people and animals that the Inuit had immemorially fixed to their parkas or added to their graves. Made for "strangers," objects like this saw provided Inuit artists with a much-needed income. In this way they were "compensated" for the disruption of their traditional way of life by the very people to whom the carvings were sold.

Montreal premises until 1949; but they had, from their founding, been attracted to preserving and supporting Inuit sculpture and Inuit artists.

The members of the CHG were drawn to this genre of Indigenous sculpture for several reasons. They believed that Inuit sculpture was made by "primitive" artists and thereby shared an unbroken link with Stone Age art. Inuit sculpture was untainted by decadent Western ideas and values;

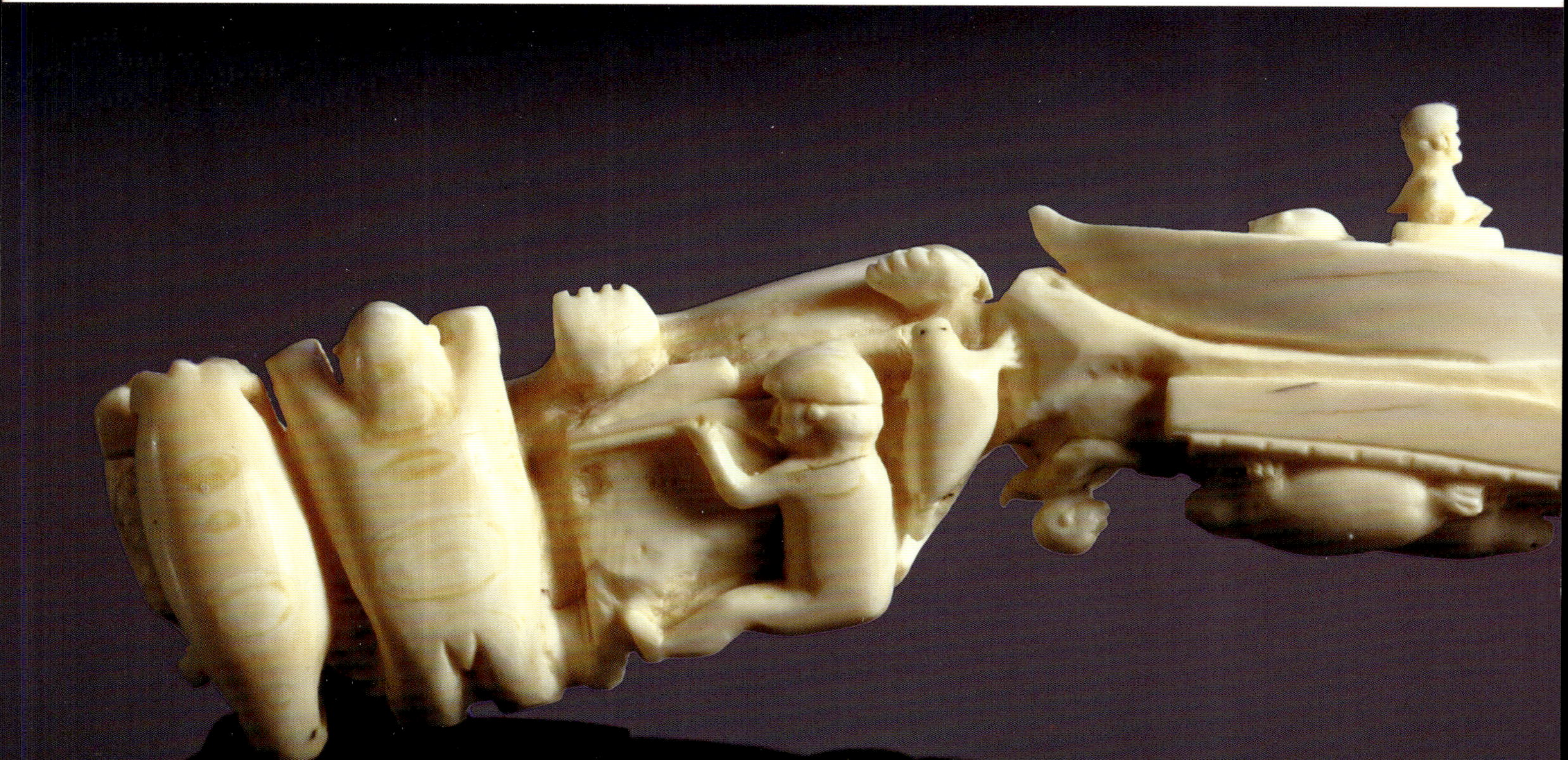

it was not subject to Western standards of art criticism, where change and progression were the goals. Moreover, in a country where national symbols were in the process of being created, the CHG also believed that Inuit carvings could reinforce the notion that even urbanized Canadians were a northern people, and thereby different from their American neighbours to the south.

The CHG were not the first to collect Inuit sculpture or to hold these misguided views. Inuit artists had been trading their small-scale carvings, as well as their navigational and whaling skills, with European and North American whalers since the late eighteenth century, in exchange for tobacco, metal objects, tea and cloth. In the next century, when there was even more demand for their work, Inuit artists began making miniature replicas of their seal oil lamps and knives, of their harpoons and their snow houses, specifically for trade. And during the first half of the twentieth century, when land-based traders, missionaries and schoolteachers successively came to the Arctic and disrupted the Inuit's traditional way of life, the sale of carvings provided a much-needed source of income. Inuit artists began making larger sculptures and expanding their repertoire. They made replicas of their newly acquired trade goods, such as saws and oil lamps. And as one Inuit artist living in the District of Ungava (a region that would now cover parts of Quebec, Labrador and Nunavut) demonstrated, they

Artist Unknown
Scene of Traditional Life, c. 1904–1905
This delicately rendered carving is not, as its title suggests, a scene of traditional life. True, the Indigenous artist who produced it lived in the District of Ungava in northern Quebec. True, the carving was made from the tusk of a walrus. And, true again, an Inuk hunter paddles his kayak towards an ice floe populated with seals. But any association with traditional hunting practices ends at the opposite end of the carving, where another hunter shoots a bear with a rifle. This is a wonderful example of how, by the end of the nineteenth century, Inuit artists were incorporating old and new traditions into one work.

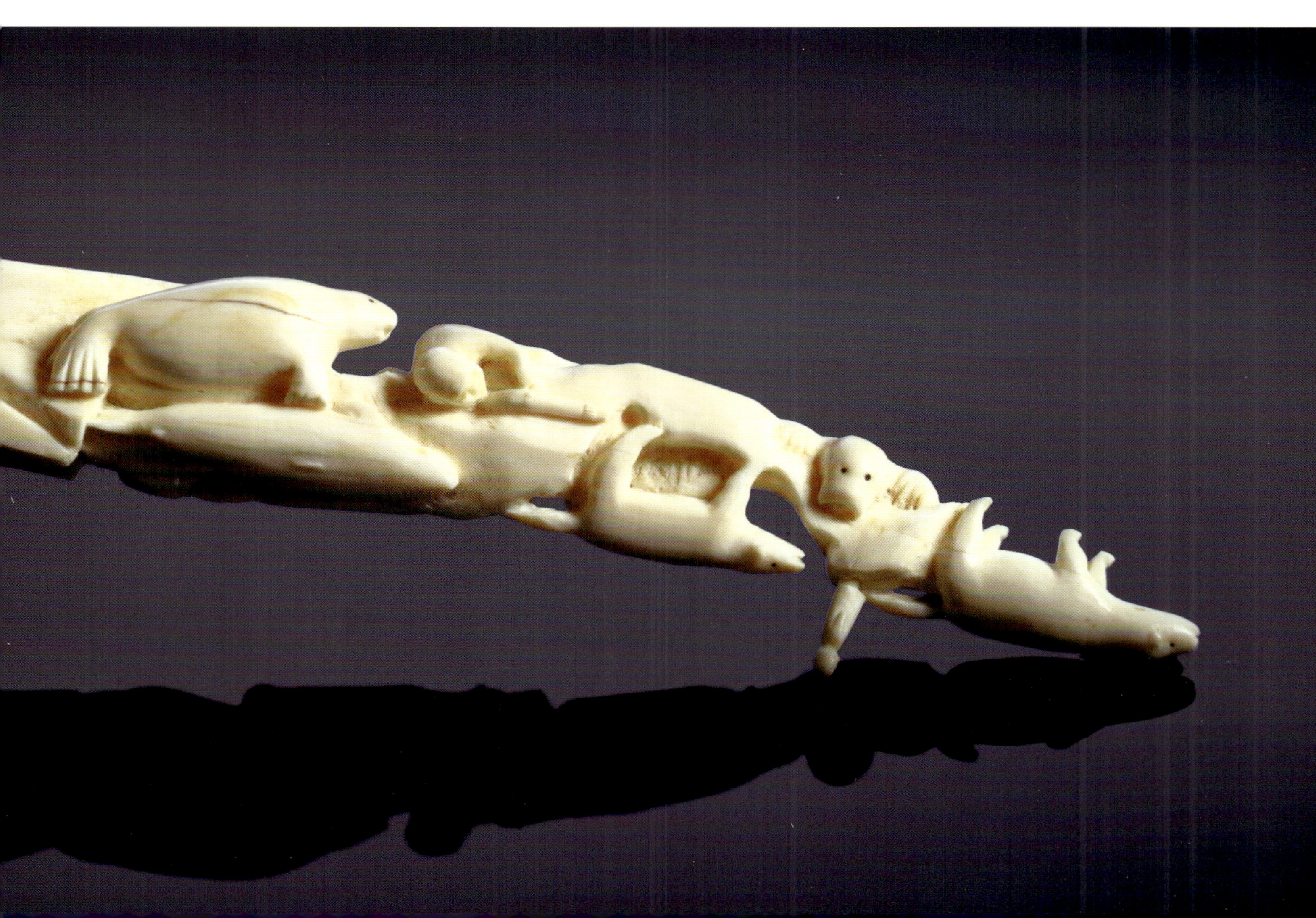

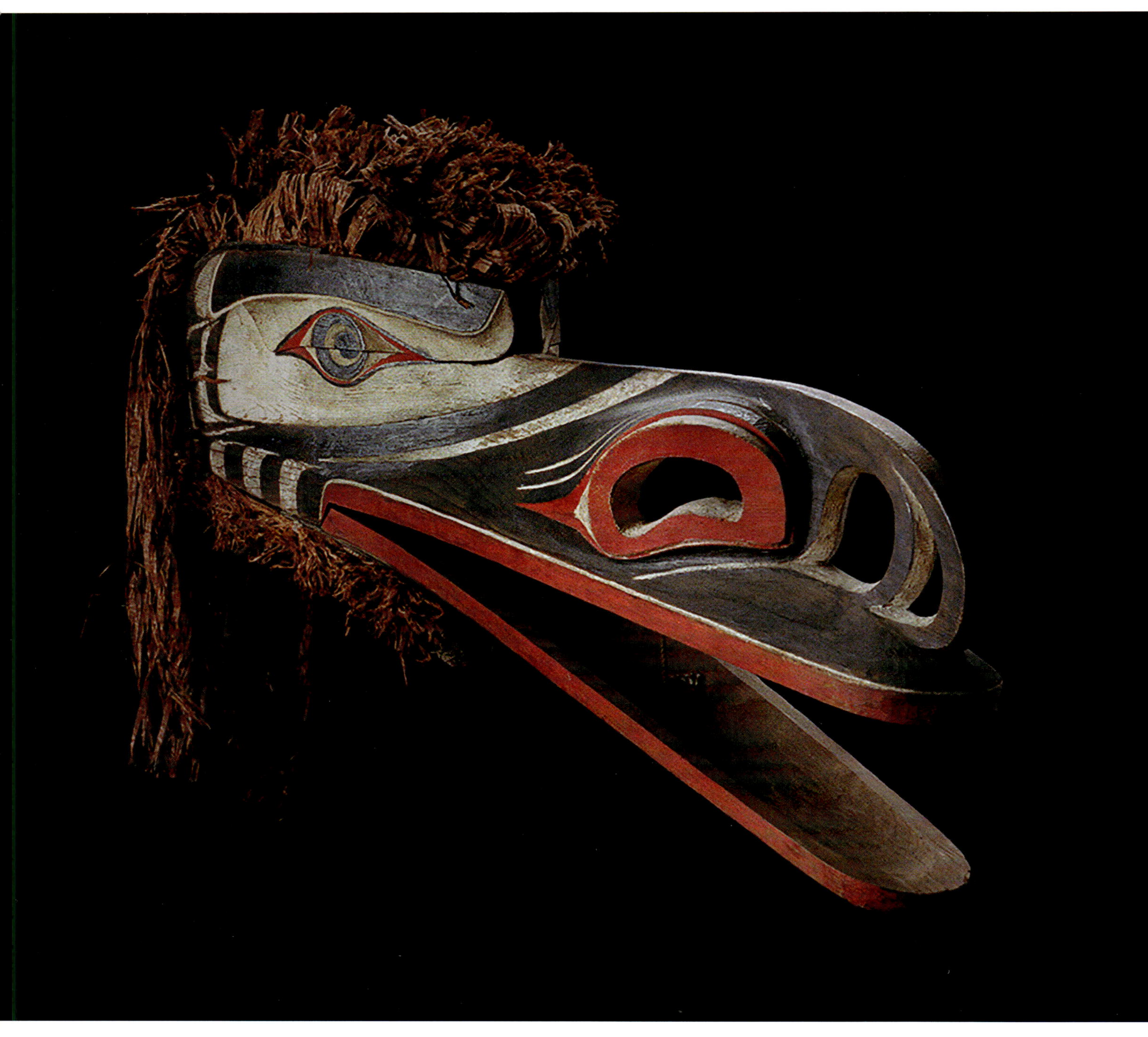

Willie Seaweed
Cannibal Bird (Raising Top or Crooked Beak) Mask, c. 1910
This Hamatsa mask, performed during the Kwakwaka'wakw people's
initiation ceremony, or *tseyka*, was associated with the man-eating raven
spirit Baxwbakwalanuksiwe'. Willie Seaweed showed the extent to which
an art object could provide his people with a concrete visualization of and
contact with this mythical creature in the spirit world. Seaweed went on
to make fourteen more Hamatsa, or crooked-beak, masks.

sometimes combined new and old tools in one carving. In the intricately carved *Scene of Traditional Life* (c. 1904–1905), for example, one hunter pursues the seals that rest on an ice floe in his traditional kayak, while another hunter shoots a bear with his newly acquired rifle.

The Canadian Handicrafts Guild's interest in and promotion of Inuit sculpture was largely due to the Arctic's remoteness in relation to southern Canada. The Inuit were rarely seen and rarely shunned. This was hardly the case, however, when it came to First Nations people. Often living in or within easy reach of white communities and towns, they were far from invisible. First Nations carvings lacked the kind of romantic narrative that attracted the CHG and their white clientele to Inuit art. Moreover, while the CHG recognized that First Nations art had flourished during an earlier era, most of its members wrongly believed that the culture was dead or dying.

It is certainly true that the Indian Act of 1884 banned the gift-giving ceremony known as the potlatch in an attempt to eradicate any vestige of First Nations culture. Around the same time, the government also attempted to assimilate First Nations peoples into white society by forcing children to attend residential schools, where cultural expression was prohibited. In this wider ambition, the government was unsuccessful in its measures. Despite everything, First Nations artists continued to produce carvings in wood and in silver for family members. They made ceremonial carvings for their chiefly patrons. Some made objects specifically for the tourist trade, or sold their work to government agents, or to private collectors, thus keeping on the right side of the law and keeping their carving skills alive. A few Indigenous artists were commissioned to produce work for anthropologists and museum collectors who were in the process of building the world-class collections that survive today.

Traditional objects also continued to be made for secretly held illegal potlatches, feasts and other winter ceremonies. In 1906 a Haida artist, Robert Davidson Senior, carved a canoe. The art of carving and painting canoes—as well as totem poles—was also kept alive further down the coast by Nuxalk sculptors in Bella Coola (Komkotes Village), by Nuu-chah-nulth carvers living at the mouth of the Nitinat River at Clo-oose, by Kwakwaka'wakw carvers at Alert Bay, Blunden Harbour and Fort Rupert, and, closer to what is now Vancouver, by Musqueam carvers. Thus, many sculptors persisted in using their art for traditional and work-related cultural practices—or for the more lucrative tourist trade.[18] But two names can truly be termed totemic: Willie Seaweed and Mungo Martin.

The Kwakwaka'wakw artist Chief Willie "Smoky Top" Seaweed (Kwaghitola and Heyhlamas) (c. 1873–1967) was among a generation of artists who produced outstanding sculptures. Born in a cedar-plank big house in the village of Ba'a's at Blunden Harbour, in Queen Charlotte Strait, Willie Seaweed apprenticed to his half-brother Johnny Davis Seaweed. Willie Seaweed carved totem poles and painted community house fronts. And he produced numerous drums, rattles, masks and whistles that were "performed" at illegal social gatherings, secretly held potlatches and at traditional winter ceremonies. Seaweed thus continued to put his carvings in the social and cultural context of his community. Around 1910, for

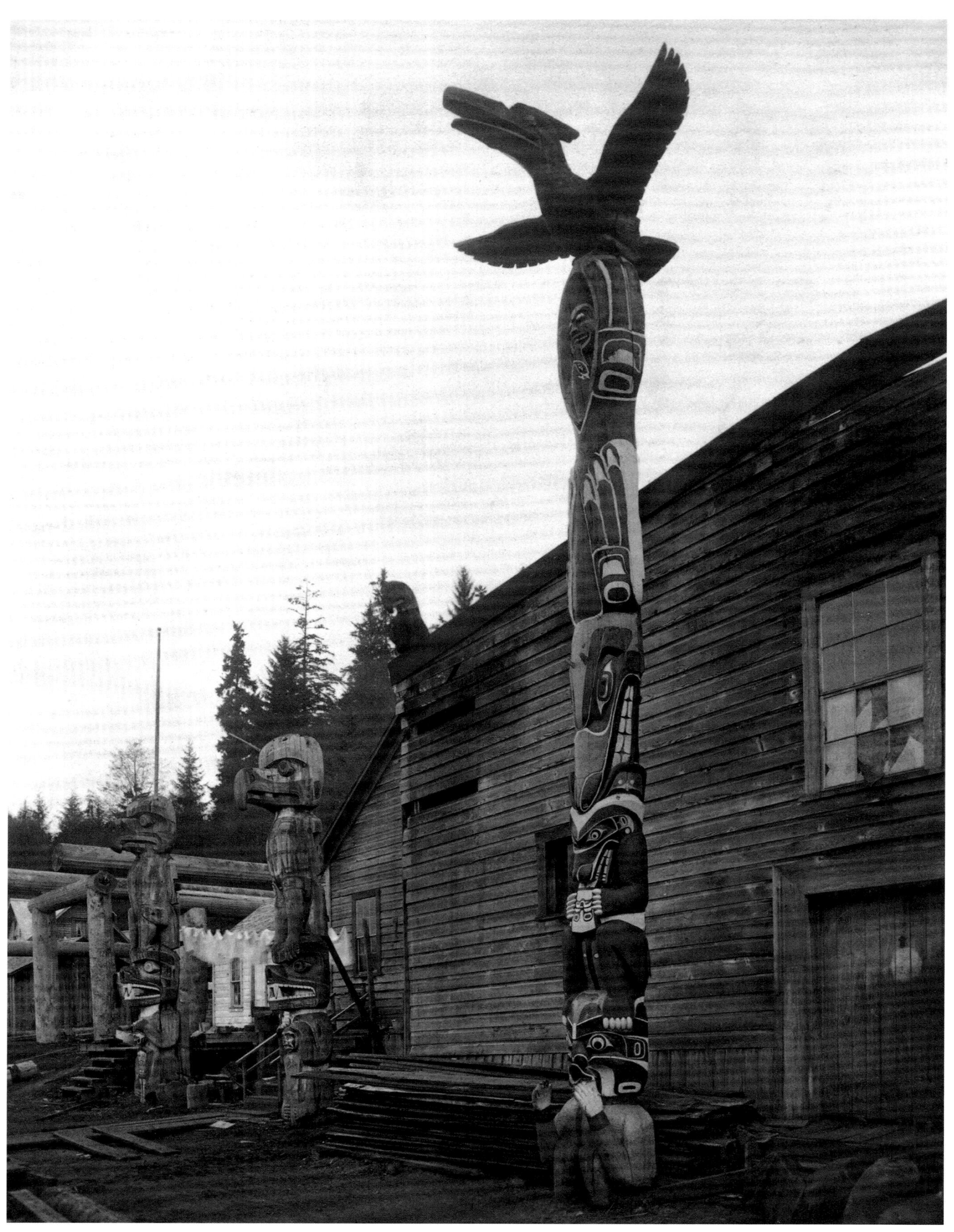

example, he carved, painted, then danced the mask *Cannibal Bird*, also known as *Raising Top* or *Crooked Beak Mask*, during a ceremony to celebrate the birth of his infant son. Seaweed gave the work a dramatic flair by exaggerating the wide, flat mouth and mobile beak. *Cannibal Bird* was the first, but not the last, of Seaweed's crooked-beak masks associated with the man-eating raven spirit Baxwbakwalanuksiwe' and performed during the initial ceremony known as *tseyka*.

A similar story unfolded in Fort Rupert (Ts'axis), where singer, songwriter and, above all, master artist Mungo Martin, Chief Nakapenkem, (1879–1962) made his mark. Like Seaweed, Martin did not attend a residential school, declared compulsory by the federal government in 1884. Rather, he was apprenticed as an artist to his paternal uncle, then to his stepfather Charlie James (1875–1938), who was known for his flamboyant style and high-keyed palette. Like James and Seaweed, Martin pushed the limits of Kwakwaka'wakw design and defied the anti-potlatch law when

Opposite:
Mungo Martin
Raven of the Sea, c. 1900
Totem poles were owned and inherited by a particular group or clan. They denoted wealth and power. Mungo Martin carved and painted the human, mythical and animal figures on this totem pole by using D-edges, curved knives, elbow adzes, chisels and wedges, and by making his own pigments from copper, shells, berries, charcoal and moss. The combination of subtle colours and deep carving on this pole offered a contrast to the unadorned big house in front of which the pole stands.

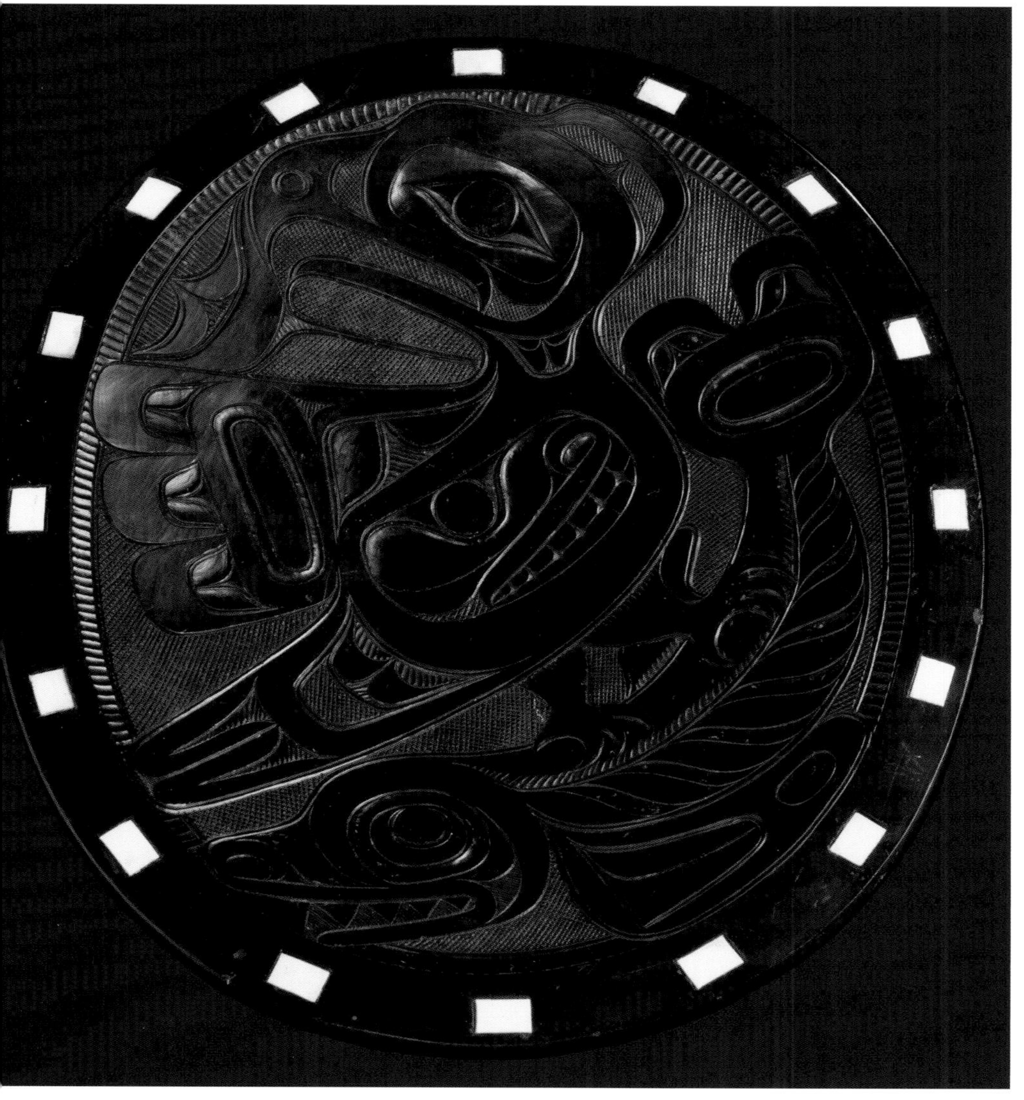

Charles Edenshaw
Argillite Plate, pre-1899
This elegant argillite platter, in which a raven sits on the back of a whale, was probably made for the tourist trade. Nevertheless, Edenshaw did not miss an opportunity to explore new ways of dealing with space, tension and release. In fact the design elements enclosed in this circular composition are so finely balanced that they give the work an inherent energy resembling that of a tightly coiled spring.

he produced the totem pole *Raven of the Sea* (c. 1902) in Alert Bay. The human, animal and mythical figures, with their protruding lips, forward-thrusting beaks, wings and arms, cover three-quarters of the pole's surface. By doing so Martin obliterated the original shape of the western cedar log. He also gave this large-scale sculpture a dramatic touch by crowning the top of the pole with a magnificent spread-winged raven, apparently about to take to the air from its perch.

While the masks and totem poles made by Seaweed and Martin might have departed from tradition, they were to be performed by their own people. Yet some such works were sold to outsiders. In 1914 Dr. C.F. Newcombe, a Victoria-based amateur ethnologist who was collecting carvings by First Nations artists for the British Columbia Provincial Museum of Natural History and Anthropology (now known as the Royal BC Museum), purchased Seaweed's *Cannibal Bird*. Seaweed regarded such a mask as primarily a vehicle for conveying ceremonial privileges. He also took the view that, as an outsider, Newcombe did not possess the ceremonial privileges to perform the Hamatsa, or so-called "cannibal ritual," associated with winter ceremonies, which would have given the mask meaning. Following the ceremony during which this mask was "danced," Seaweed felt free to sell it to the museum collector, and made another Hamatsa mask to replace it. Likewise, Seaweed knew that the model spread-winged totem poles that he made for the tourist trade had no meaning for their purchasers either. He made them in order to keep alive the making of Indigenous art on a legal basis. This made it easy for Seaweed to distinguish between tourist and museum art, on the one hand, and, on the other, work that was inseparable from his people's customs and rituals, including dance, theatrical enactment and ceremony.

Working further north in Haida Gwaii, Charles "Chinni" Edenshaw (1839–1920), also known as Tahayghen or 7idansuu, acquired a comparable reputation. He transformed silver coins into exquisite bracelets; he turned wood into masks, model canoes and bentwood boxes; and he fashioned argillite into miniature totem poles, platters and compotes. Taught by his uncle, Chief Albert Edward Edenshaw (also known as Gwaaygu or 7idansuu), who had enlisted his nephew to help him carve totem poles, the young Edenshaw began carving when he was a youth.

Like Martin and Seaweed, Edenshaw was familiar with the myths and customs of his people, as well as with the design elements that formed the basis of West Coast First Nations art: the formline, the ovoid and, among others, the U-shape. He handled space and balance, tension and release in a way that pushed these design elements into a new realm. Every motif Edenshaw painted, every figure he carved or engraved, was charged with movement, and with a latent energy that resembled a tightly coiled spring.

And Charles Edenshaw was an innovator. He expanded the formal design elements inherent in Indigenous art by rounding his formlines. He stacked or interwove or overlapped one U-shape onto another in order to give the sense that there was no end and no beginning to the sculpture.[19] He introduced narrative into First Nations art. He combined images from

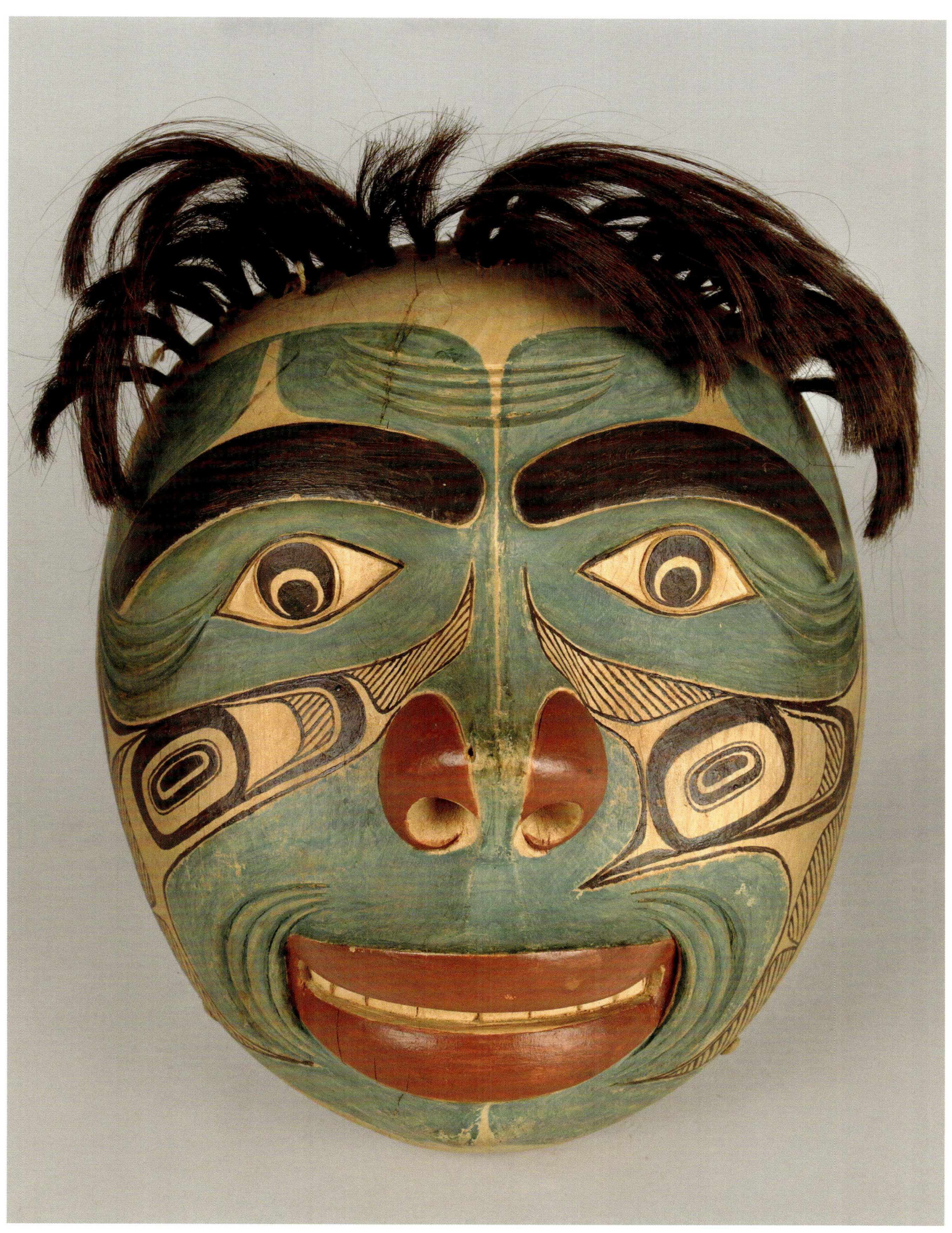

the pages of *The Illustrated London News* that were pinned to the walls of his workshop/studio with Haida heraldic emblems and crest figures. And he broke with tradition again by giving his *Humanoid Mask* (1902) the suggestion of a smile and a look of surprise. As his great-grandson, Haida artist Robert Davidson (b. 1946) put it, Edenshaw's masks were so realistic that "the sculpture looked like it was winking at me."[20]

Edenshaw was, above all, an avid promoter of his own work. His clients came from his own community as well as from outside of Haida Gwaii. He travelled to the trading post at Port Essington on the mouth of the Skeena River, where the trader and merchant Robert Cunningham sold his work. He fulfilled commissions for anthropologists, ethnologists and museum collectors as well as for private collectors and dealers. He won the respect of German anthropologist Franz Boas who, in his writings, was among the first Euro-American scholars to propose elevating Indigenous art from an exotic craft to an art form.[21]

Edenshaw's non-Indigenous collectors could not get enough of his model totem poles, his argillite chests and platters, his gold and silver bracelets, and his delicately carved masks. And, not surprisingly, many agreed with Dr. C.F. Newcombe, who wrote in 1902 that Edenshaw was "the best carver in wood and stone now living."[22]

These are indeed great names. Yet there were, of course, other First Nations sculptors living on the northwest coast; others who made a living from their art; others who promoted their work inside and outside of the First Nations community; others who incorporated new subject matter and design elements; and others who did so without losing the integrity of the traditional art form. But few of them had the privilege of having their work so well documented by non-Indigenous people. And above all, few of them produced work that complemented Western standards of aesthetics.

The mythical, animal and human figures wrapped around Edenshaw's model totem poles and the realistic expression rendered in works like *Humanoid Mask* were haunting rather than threatening. There were no broken noses or twisted faces characteristic of the masks Iroquois artists like Gus Yellow produced for the False Face Society. There were no protruding beaks or outstretched arms and wings characteristic among the work of other First Nations artists living in coastal British Columbia. And there were certainly no frightening figures like the man-eating Baxwbakwalanuksiwe' rendered by Kwakwaka'wakw artists. Judged through the perceptual lens of the anthropologist and storekeeper, the agent and the tourist, it was Edenshaw's ability to reconcile traditional styles and values with non-Indigenous themes and sensibilities that made him "the first modern Haida artist."[23]

When Edenshaw died at the age of eighty-one in 1920, much had changed for him, as well as for other First Nations artists. The settler population had exploded while the First Nations population had declined by 90 per cent—largely due to disease—and would not begin to increase for more than another decade. Children had to attend residential schools in southern British Columbia, the extraction of coal and oil in Skidegate Inlet was evident, and a Hudson's Bay Company post had been established in Old Massett. And then there were the missionaries, who had been the drive behind the anti-potlatch laws. In spite of these devastating changes, however, many First Nations artists up and down the west coast never lost their cultural traditions. Ultimately, the Canadian government's arrogant view that this heritage could be eradicated proved a failure. It was Edenshaw's descendant Jaalen Edenshaw (b. 1980) who explained why every First Nations artist had a sense of taking over from "what your uncle [Charles Edenshaw] built." As the Haida artist put it: "Whether you lift it higher or drop it lower, is up to me, but you are starting at that point."[24]

First Nations and Inuit peoples inevitably formed relationships with the non-Indigenous settler population. They dealt with social and cultural disruption and with disease, not only by exchanging their trading and hunting skills and their knowledge of the land, but also through their art. They showed an ability to accommodate a difficult situation by drawing on their heritage. In this sense, they saved themselves from simply being victims. By persisting in producing their art, whether for the tourist trade or for their own symbolic purposes, they became more than survivors. They lost a great deal, but they did not lose everything, least of all what really mattered to them and to their sense of identity: their art.

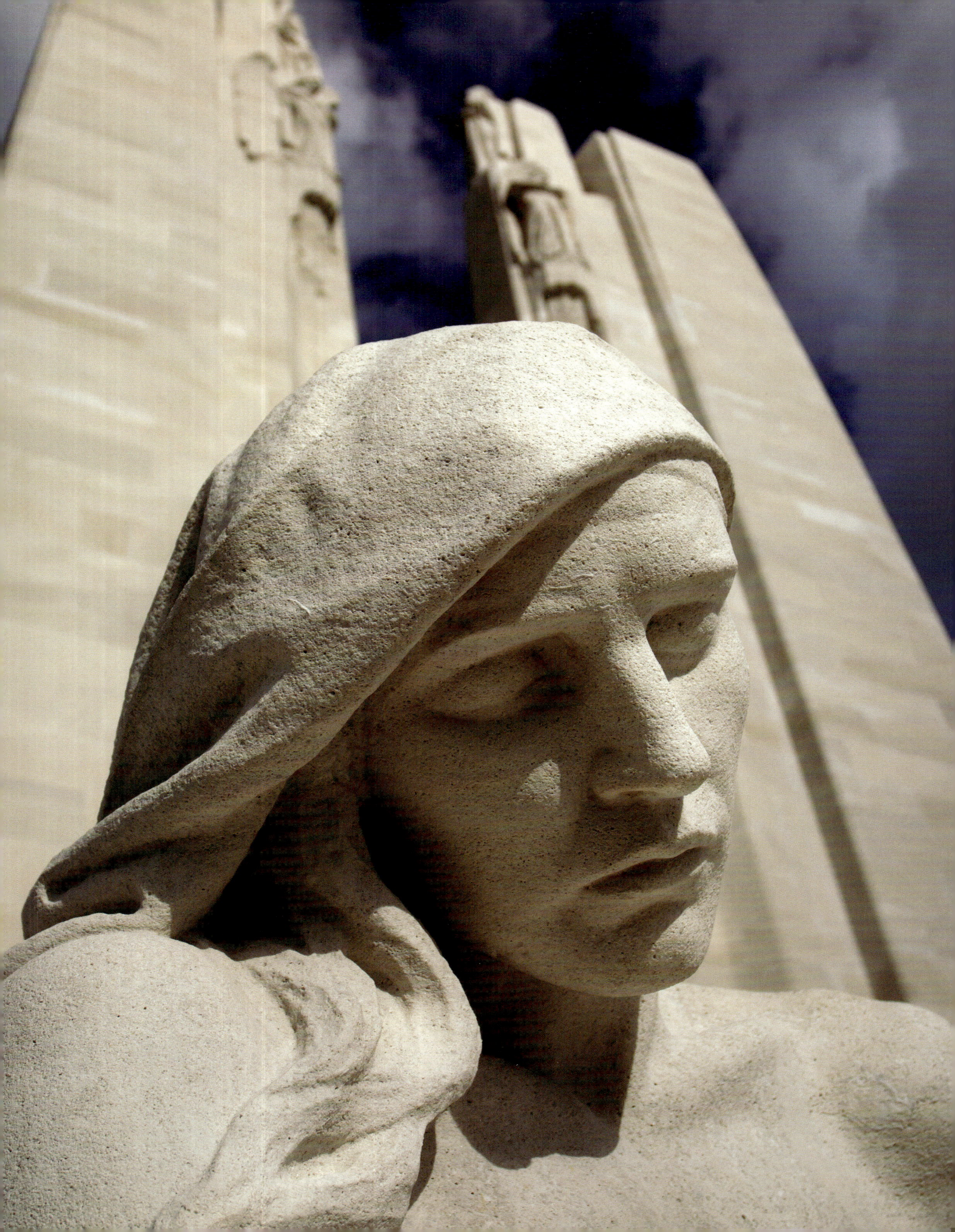

4

Sculpture at the Service of War

In 1910 the art critic Augustus Bridle stated despondently that being a sculptor was "the most precarious career" in the country.[1] Within just over a decade, however, Bridle's observation was certainly refuted—happily, in that most of Canada's sculptors had more work than they could handle, but with tragic implications as to why this was so. Arguably, it was during the Great War that Canada came of age; certainly, it was in that bitter and prolonged conflict that many Canadians—both men and women—met their deaths, mainly in Europe. They were to be mourned by even larger numbers at home. Human tragedy and national identity were interwoven themes, each of them now perceived more acutely than before.

Opposite:
Walter Seymour Allward
Detail of the *Canadian National Vimy Memorial*, 1936
(see pages 104–5)

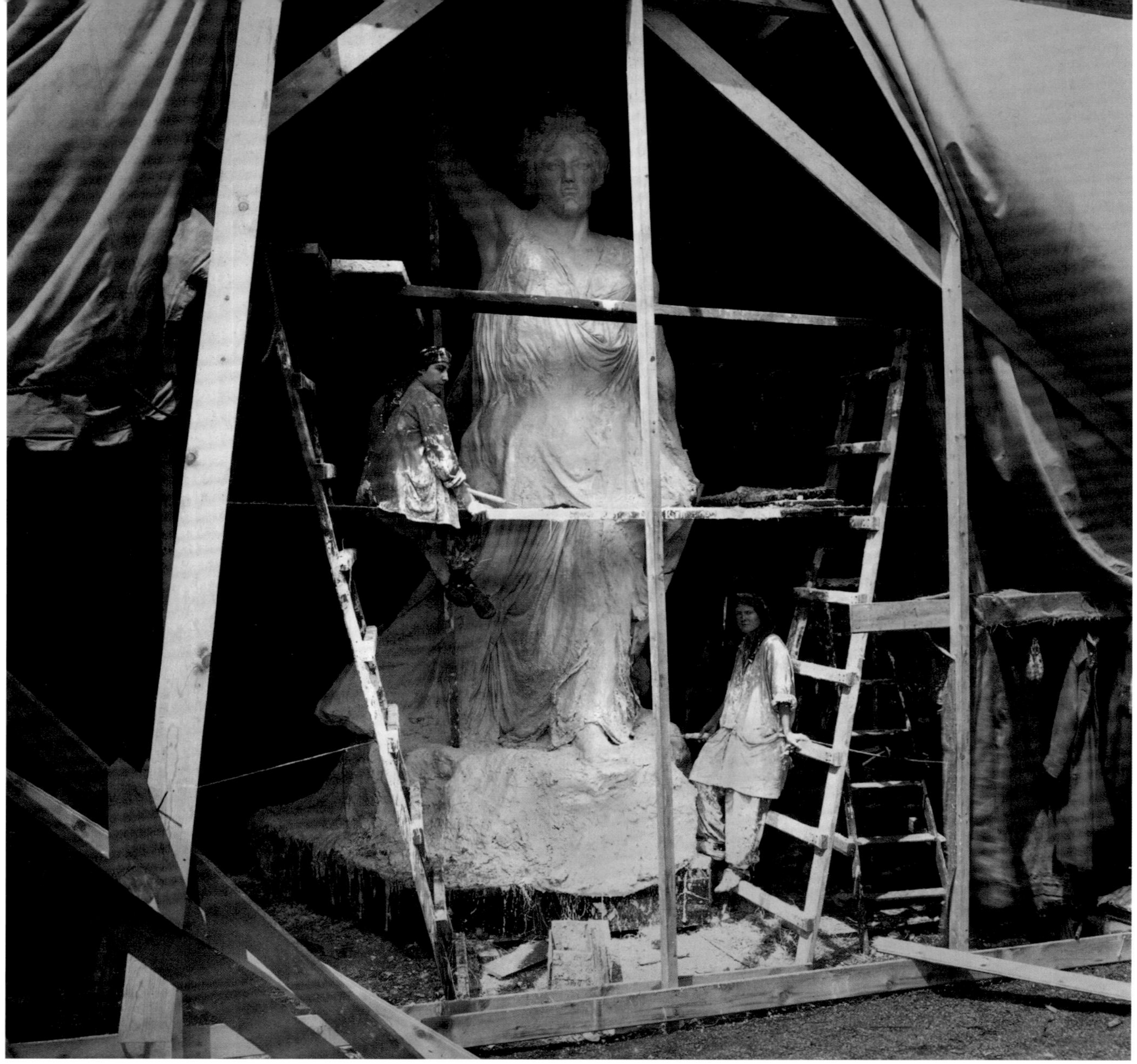

Frances Loring (on the scaffold) and her assistant Margaret Scobie creating *Miss Canada*, c. 1917.

Photo: Collection of the Archives of Ontario, Sears Canada Inc. Fonds, F229-308-0-1089.

Canadians had to come to terms with estimates of the war dead that swelled to over 60,000. In addition, of the 424,000 men who had gone overseas with the Canadian Expeditionary Force, over 172,000 of those who did make it back to their homeland were maimed or gassed or psychologically damaged. A two-minute silence was introduced in 1924 on the eleventh hour of the eleventh month, a sombre moment when sons and daughters, wives and husbands, needed a place to publicly mourn their dead. And the patch of earth on which a cenotaph, column, obelisk, plaque or cross was erected was sacred. This consecrated ground, chosen in every village, town and city across Canada, provided a site for remembering, for grieving and ultimately for mourning the country's loss. Thus began what Susan Elizabeth Hart has aptly described as a "monument-building frenzy."[2]

At the outbreak of war in August 1914, the prospects for painters, sculptors and art institutions across Canada had looked bleak. For example, the National Gallery of Canada found that three-quarters of its operating budget was slashed. And things got worse in 1916 when a fire destroyed the Centre Block of the Houses of Parliament and the National Gallery was consequently forced to give up most of its space in the Victoria Memorial Museum to the government. Art societies like the Royal Canadian Academy of Art, Montreal's Pen and Pencil Club and the Ontario Society of Artists had difficulties too. They lost a large percentage of their funding from federal and provincial governments.

The president of the Royal Academy, William Brymner, was saddened by the impact of war in producing a declining art market and people who seemed to be "thriving on munitions."[3] The public did not share Brymner's view. Many wondered whether it was unpatriotic to spend money on art rather than on Victory Bonds. Sir Edmund Walker, who had been collecting Japanese prints before the war, was exceptional in now making a point of spending his money on Canadian art. As the war progressed, however, private art galleries discovered that patriotism and profit could march hand in hand. Rather than close their doors they could cater to the public's appetite for seeing and investing in anything relating to the war— including wartime posters, photographs and cartoon sketches.

Not only art collectors and art galleries initially feared accusations of indulging in luxuries. Newspapers featured articles querying the role of artists during the hostilities. Most artists did not question whether they had a right to practise their art when war broke out in August 1914, nor did they agree with the charge that Canadian artists were "given over to idleness and depression."[4] In due course, some sculptors made an effort to show that they did have a role to play in the war. An early example, produced in 1915 by Emanuel Hahn (1881–1957), was the Impressionistic painted plaster "sketch" *War the Despoiler.*[5]

Here is an artist who, as will become clear, can be seen in different dimensions, through different lenses. The young Emanuel Hahn had immigrated to Canada as a boy from Germany with his middle-class family in 1888. He enrolled in part-time classes in design and modelling at the Toronto Technical School, while supporting himself and his family by designing bronze reliefs for Toronto's McIntosh Marble and Granite Company and the Canada Foundry Company. In 1906, wanting more training as a sculptor, Hahn naturally returned to Germany, where he took courses in modelling and woodcarving at Stuttgart's renowned Kunstgewerbeschule.

At the time, such links proved professionally helpful. After three years of study and extensive travel in Europe, Hahn began building his career as a professional sculptor in Toronto. He became a part-time teacher at the Toronto Technical School and in 1912 became head of the sculpture department at the Ontario College of Art. During these years Hahn exhibited his Symbolist-inspired studio pieces with the Ontario Society of Artists and the Royal Canadian Academy. He also designed funerary statuary and commemorative monuments. At the outbreak of the Great War, Hahn's connections with Ontario's leading artists and societies and his reputation as the chief designer for the Thompson Monument Company duly brought him

more commemorative commissions. But although his work for the company
appeared across the country, a warning is signalled, as will become clear, by
the comment that his employers "rarely promoted him by name after the war
lest his German roots lose them business."[6]

After the war broke out in 1914, Emanuel Hahn exchanged his
Symbolist style for Impressionism in an attempt to express his revulsion to
warfare. *War the Despoiler* was thus a personally apt title for the work. And
it expressed a wider mood, shared by two other artists. Alfred Laliberté's
Allegory of War (1917) and the more dramatic sword-brandishing figure
1914 (c. 1918) by Henri Hébert (1884–1950) are small-scale pieces
rendered, like Hahn's, in the style of Rodin, and focusing on the feel and
the plasticity of clay in its prefabricated state.[7] However, as we shall see,
these Impressionistic tendencies, with their emphasis on process and
material, would soon be replaced by academic realism. And the hardware
of warfare—the trench and the tank—and the human dimension—the
non-commissioned soldier and the munitions worker—would become
preferred subjects for the painter and sculptor alike.

It was towards the end of the war that another sculptor, Frances Loring
(1887–1968), responded to the war in her small-scale work *Grief* (1918).[8]

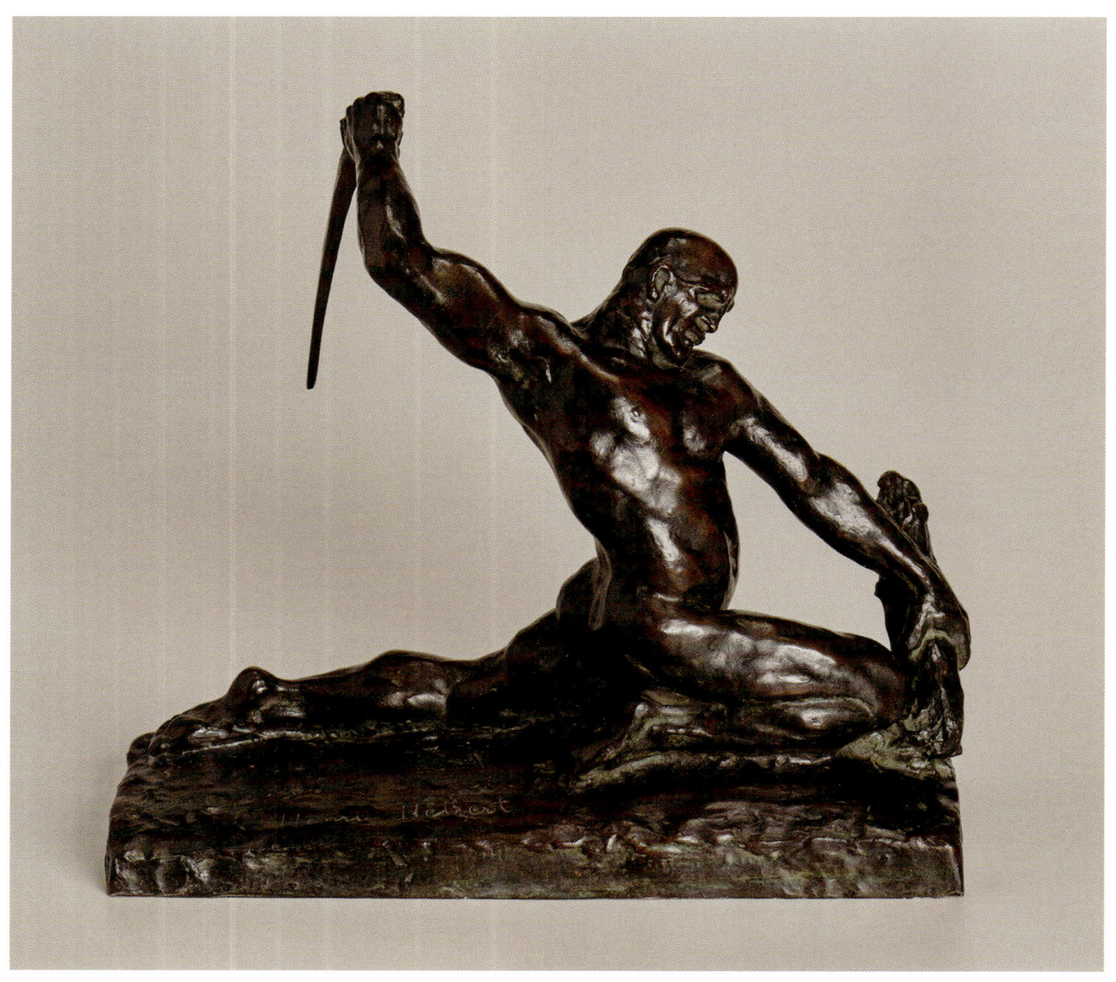

Loring, like Hahn, had a cosmopolitan background. She had studied sculpture in Geneva, Paris and Munich before entering the Art Institute of Chicago in 1905, where she met her future lifelong partner, Florence Wyle (1881–1968). Both of them had been born in the United States. In Chicago, Loring and Wyle studied under Lorado Taft (1860–1936) who variously practised the Beaux-Arts, Impressionist and Symbolist styles popularized by largely French and Belgian sculptors in the late nineteenth and early twentieth centuries. But Taft, who considered sculpture to be a "masculine art," was hardly encouraging to female sculptors.[9]

Loring and Wyle therefore moved to New York City, where they encountered the work of the Ashcan School of artists, known for portraying scenes of daily life in an academic style. However, Loring preferred "to be a big figure in a small pool," so she and her partner moved their sculpture studio to Canada.[10] Loring and Wyle thus arrived in Toronto in 1911 and 1912, respectively, to discover that neither their gender, nor their subject matter, nor their birthplace was a barrier to acceptance as Canadian sculptors.

Within a few years, "the Girls," as they were known, became frequent contributors to the Toronto Industrial Exhibition. They were elected as associate members of the Royal Canadian Academy of Art and became members of the Ontario Society of Artists and the Women's Art Association of Canada. Their figurative sculptures, rendered largely in the pre-war Beaux-Arts academic style, came to the attention of Eric Brown, director of the National Gallery, and to wealthy art collectors like Sir Edmund Walker. And sculptors and painters in Ontario and Quebec warmly received "the Girls" and their work, too. As art critic Estelle M. Kerr wrote a couple of years after their arrival in Canada, everyone was gratified that "two such talented young American sculptors should come to live amongst us."[11] Moreover, their subsequent status as Canadian sculptors was not to be compromised by the nationalist emotions of wartime, in the way experienced by Emanuel Hahn.

Few could have imagined at the outset the extent to which the Great War would alter the cultural landscape of Canada. Sculptors saw few immediate opportunities to put their skills to any military use. Ontario-born sculptor Robert Tait McKenzie, who was living in the United States when the war broke out, joined Britain's Royal Army Medical Corps in 1915. It was only when he returned to Canada from Britain in 1917 that he found he could adapt his modelling skills to help surgeons reconstruct the disfigured faces of soldiers. But as the numbers of casualties rose during the course of the war, it became clear that sculptors also needed to focus on commemorating officers and non-commissioned soldiers alike. The cenotaph, the plaque and the figurative sculpture rendered in bronze, marble or stone met this need; it gave Canadians a sacred site on Canadian soil for remembering, for grieving—and, more controversially, for warning the next generation against the dangers of engaging in future wars.

Long before the hostilities ended in November 1918, private citizens

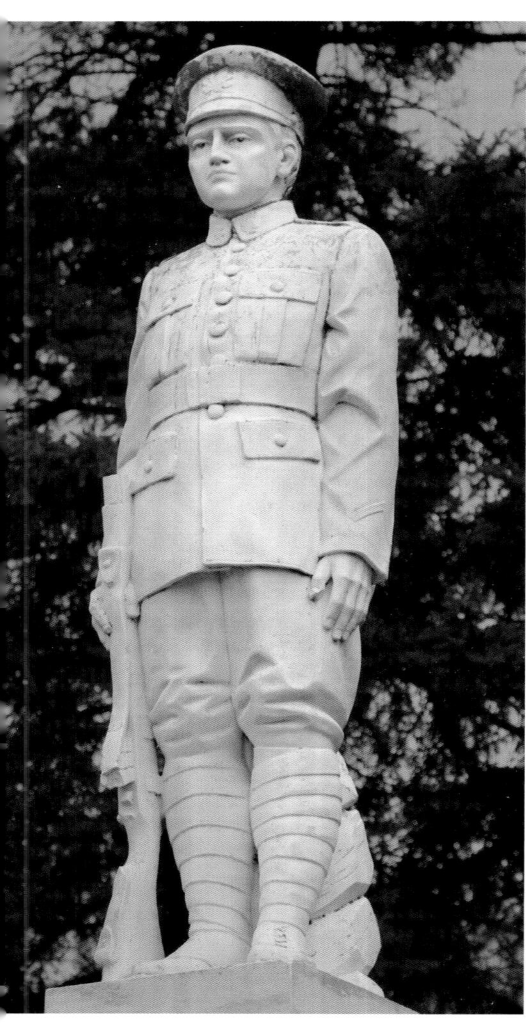

Artist Unknown
Canadian Soldier, n.d.

It was less expensive to order a ready-made figurative sculpture of a Canadian soldier from Italy than to commission a Canadian sculptor to produce an original work. It may well be that over half of the four hundred or so figurative works commemorating Canada's participation in the Great War were in fact mass-produced in Carrera, Italy. But there was a risk in ordering a marble or bronze Italian-made figure from a pattern book. The uniforms were often wrong—soldiers were shown with soft rather than hard hats, for example—and the pose was often stiff and the gaze was distant.

and public organizations formed memorial committees across the country. After raising funds by public subscription, they hired a sculptor, or sometimes a stone carver and possibly an architect or a memorial maker, to design a figurative sculpture and a plinth. Initially war memorials came in various sizes and genres. In the small prairie community of Treesbank, Manitoba, a modest wooden shrine festooned with a Union Jack and an inscription bearing the names of the men "who have fought, and are fighting and will fight for King and Country, for freedom and for civilization," was constructed in 1917.[12]

At T. Eaton Company's flagship store in downtown Toronto, a 4.9-metre-high plaster allegorical statue entitled *Miss Canada* (1917) was installed. Draped in Grecian robes and surrounded by nine coats of arms representing Canada's provinces, the sculpture became "a symbol of the brave and dauntless spirit of Canada's young men and women." Warming to this theme, the same commentator claimed that *Miss Canada* also "symbolized splendidly the Spartan-like Canadian woman with her whole-hearted spirit of service and sacrifice."[13] Fittingly, perhaps, this was the work of Frances Loring. The popularity of *Miss Canada* inspired another critic to claim: "We need not go out of Canada for any work we want done. Canadians can do anything."[14]

Though a few Canadian sculptors—now including Frances Loring—did receive a number of war-related commissions, many communities and organizations that could afford it preferred to hire a foreign-born sculptor. After holding an international competition, the Bank of Montreal chose the well-known American sculptor James Earle Fraser (1876–1953) to commemorate the company's 230 employees who had died in the war. Two of Fraser's models, one in bronze and the other in marble, were transformed into sculptures for the bank's head branches in Montreal and Winnipeg respectively. Less prosperous than the bank, the small community of Saint-Boniface, Quebec, did not have the funds to commission their own sculptor. What they could afford was one of the nine hundred copies made of the sculpture *Le Poilu Victorieux*, depicting a French soldier, designed by French artist Eugène Bénet (1863–1942). Replicas of the sculptor's original work were marketed by the Durenne Foundry in Paris. The copy that ended up in rural Quebec was one of the few sculptures in Canada to feature and thereby celebrate a French, not a Canadian, soldier.[15]

There was obviously a risk in commissioning a foreign sculptor to depict Canadian soldiers. James Earle Fraser's bronze figure at the Bank of Montreal's branch in Winnipeg purports to feature a Canadian soldier—but one dressed in an American uniform. Italian monument makers produced over half of Canada's figurative war memorial sculptures for towns and cities across the country. But there was a downside to these made-to-order memorials as well. The Carrara-based sculptors often depicted Canadians wearing soft rather than hard hats. They dressed them in uniforms that have a disturbing similarity to those worn by soldiers from New Zealand and Australia.[16] And they rendered them in stiff stand-to-attention poses. Many Italian sculptors clearly felt that they had fulfilled their Canadian commission if they had placed a maple leaf on a soldier's hat or collar.

In 1916, through the launch of a significant wartime initiative, an even larger number of foreign artists found themselves employed to depict Canada's war effort; and these foreign-born painters and sculptors, moreover, were to create their work on the Western Front and in England. For in 1916 the London-based Canadian War Memorials Fund (CWMF) was established as a charity, paid for out of the pockets of two London-based newspaper barons: the New Brunswick–born Max Aitken, who became Lord Beaverbrook in 1917, and his friend Lord Rothermere.[17] Convinced that painters and sculptors were capable of reconstructing unrecorded events relating to the war and of recording events as they happened, Beaverbrook and Rothermere began commissioning artists to make "suitable Memorials in the form of Tablets, Oil-Paintings etc., to the Canadian Heroes and Heroines in the war."[18] By the end of the war, the CWMF had variously employed over fifty painters and sculptors who were not only British but also Belgian, Australian, Danish and Croatian. A collection of nearly one thousand paintings and sculptures was the result and the legacy.

When news reached Canada that no Canadian painter or sculptor had been invited to join the CWMF, the country's artistic community was understandably outraged. Officials at the National Gallery of Canada wondered why Beaverbrook's organization had fifteen thousand pounds to spend on art when their own budget had been severely reduced. Canadian artists demanded to know why others were being paid to paint and model their country's soldiers. Members of the Ontario Society of Artists and Montreal's Pen and Pencil Club protested that their members had been overlooked. One journalist penned an article with the headline: "Canadian Artists Not Included."[19]

Beaverbrook, caught on the hop, was quick to respond to these complaints. In 1917 he invited a handful of Canadian artists, among whom were future Group of Seven members F.H. Varley (1881–1969) and A.Y. Jackson (1882–1974), to join the Canadian Expeditionary Force in France and Belgium as official war artists. He also suggested that Canadian officials should hire painters to record activities relating to the aircraft, munitions and shipbuilding industries, whose thriving business helped to bring the Canadian economy out of its pre-war slump.

Although Beaverbrook had included two British sculptors and one Croatian, no official on either side of the Atlantic proposed inviting a Canadian sculptor to join the CWMF program until a few months before the end of the war.[20] In September 1918, while walking around Toronto's Canadian National Exhibition, the director of the National Gallery of Canada, Eric Brown, saw female munitions workers dressed in their overalls. Persuaded that they might be "very fine subjects for a series of small bronzes," he invited Frances Loring to join what had now become the home front branch of the Canadian War Memorials Fund project.[21]

Both Frances Loring and Florence Wyle were immediately sent to sketch in munitions plants and aircraft factories, on farms and in training camps in Ontario and Quebec. When they returned to their studio in Toronto they transformed their sketches into over a dozen plaster models that were,

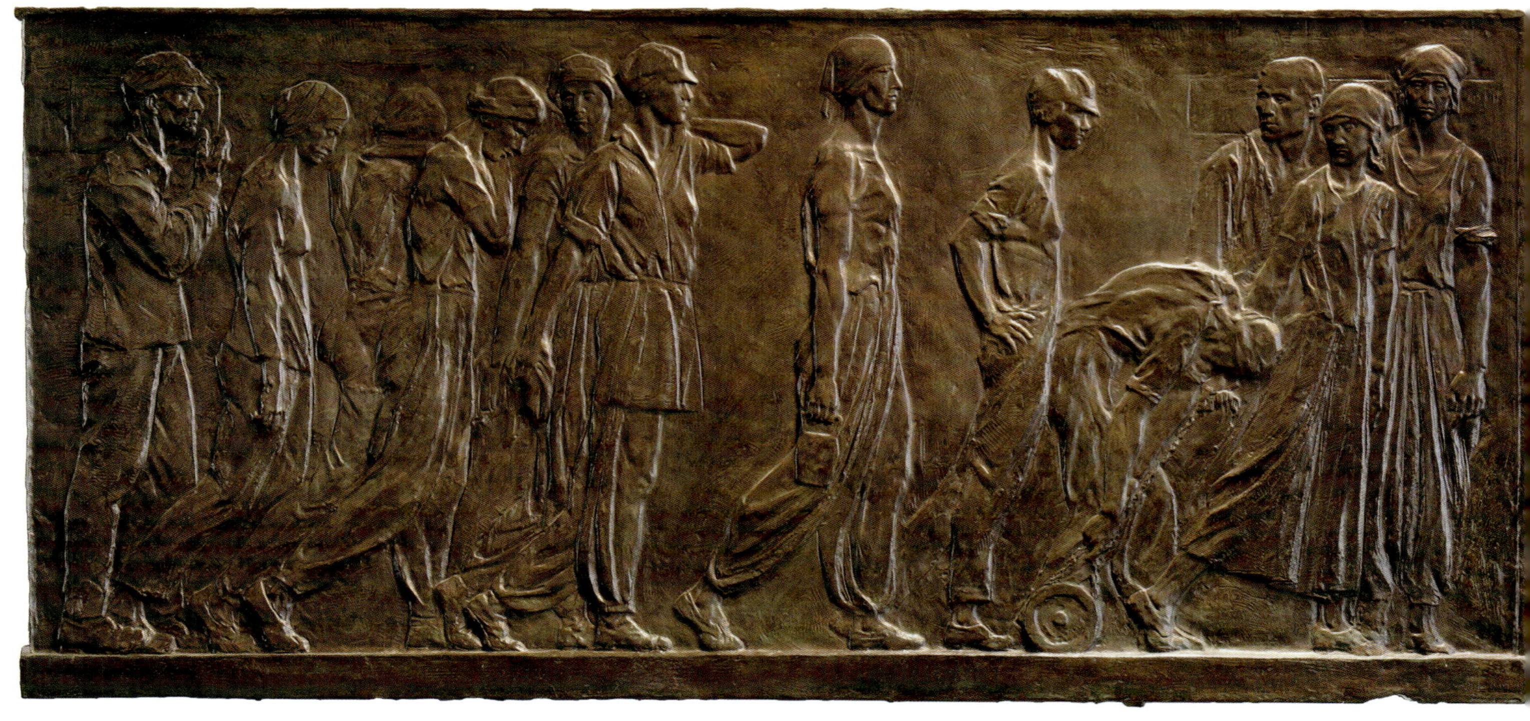

Frances Loring
Noon Hour in a Munitions Plant, 1918–1919
During the Great War women worked as nurses in Canadian field hospitals; they raised funds for Victory Bonds; and they worked on farms, in munitions factories and in shipbuilding plants across the country. Frances Loring's elegant bronze relief of female munitions workers during their lunch break offered an uplifting image that reinforced the dignity of labour. The women's stoical commitment to their job is more akin to the unflinching martial figures that skirt a Greek vase than to the typical image of factory workers.

in turn, transformed into bronze by the Gorham Manufacturing Company in New York and William A. Rogers Limited—later F.G. Tickell and Sons— in Toronto.

Like the Canadian painters who recorded events on the home front, Loring and Wyle showed that many options were open in recording twentieth-century warfare. A war memorial did not have to portray the horrible wastage of life in the trenches or, sidestepping the horrors associated with the Western Front, depict highly stylized allegorical figures like Loring's own earlier sculpture, *Miss Canada*. And though it was once fancifully claimed that Loring "didn't like to do pieces unless she had to climb a ladder to get at them," she and Wyle actually discovered that a sculpture could be small and still convey its message.[22]

Influenced by the down-to-earth subject matter of New York's Ashcan School, Wyle and Loring's sculptures demonstrated that women did not have to be depicted as passive victims, or sexual objects, or grieving widows dressed in Grecian or Roman robes. The dress and the posture of the women Wyle and Loring rendered in their sculptures were very different. Their female workers had strong, sinewy arms that were capable of turning steel rods, finishing shells and stoking furnaces in the munitions factories. In Loring's *Noon Hour in a Munitions Plant* (1918–1919) and Wyle's *The Furnace Girl* (1918–1919) the message was clear: these women were as heroic, in their way, as the soldiers who went "over the top" into battle. It has rightly been claimed that Loring and Wyle's portrayal of women made no small contribution in taking "Canadian sculpture out of its fledgling phase of historical hagiography into the next important stage of monumentalization."[23]

Such memorials not only assuaged the loss felt by the public and celebrated the contribution that women were making to the war effort, they boosted a special line of business. Already thriving from the increased demand for private grave memorials, the Toronto-based firms that benefitted from the surge in memorial building included the McIntosh Granite Company and the foundry department of the William A. Rogers Limited Company. The Robert Mitchell Company of Montreal and Toronto had even more trade. It was the same for memorial companies in other parts of Canada. For example, in the province of Manitoba, the Memorial and Tile Company, the Sunderland Company, the Hooper Marble Works and the Guinn and Simpson Company found new customers. Thus, employees of monument

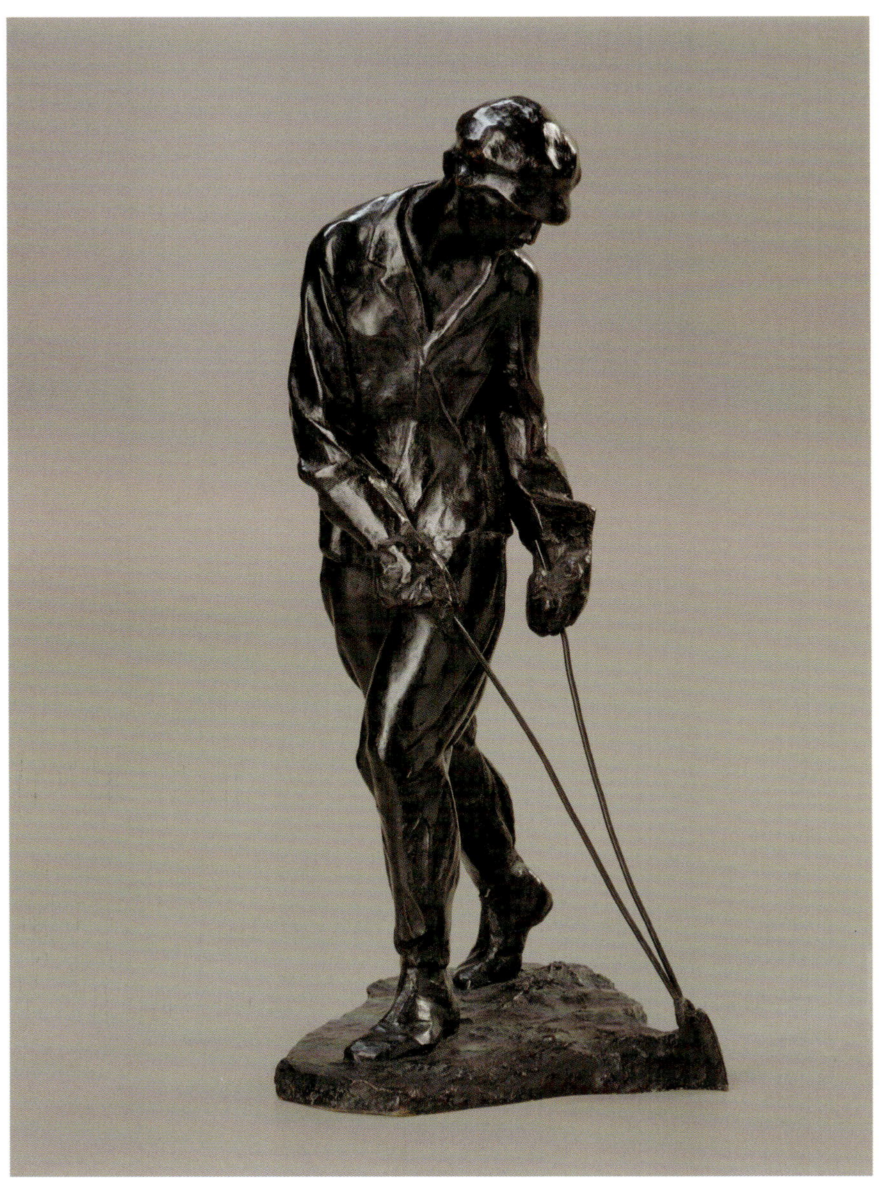

Florence Wyle
The Furnace Girl, 1918–1919
With a wartime shortage of labour, many Canadian women took over the jobs of the men who joined the Canadian Expeditionary Force. Working as a welder or a rod turner in a munitions factory or steel plant required strength, stamina and endurance. And Florence Wyle's depiction of a "furnace girl" leaves no doubt that women were up to the task. This work, along with Frances Loring's sculptures of female factory and plant workers, offers a contrast to the conventional images of women as grieving victims with little agency of their own.

companies who had previously designed everything from gravestones to fire hydrants now found themselves making war memorials. Most of the designers who worked for these monument companies were confined to producing the pedestal and the inscription. But a few designers modelled the figure on top of the plinth in clay, to be cast into bronze or transformed into marble, limestone or granite, often in Europe or the United States.

Some communities found a novel way to commemorate their war dead. At the end of the hostilities the Canadian government had acquired over three thousand German machine guns. Some of the guns found their way to the tops of plinths under which the names of the community's war dead were duly inscribed in stone or written on bronze plaques.[24] The federal government wanted a more imposing monument to honour the Canadians who had lost their lives during the hostilities. A competition was held to design and produce a national war memorial for the country's capital. The winner was British-born sculptor Vernon March (1891–1930). Although he had the distinction of being the youngest exhibitor at Britain's Royal Academy of Arts, March had no formal education. What he did have, however, were the right connections among Canadian government officials based in London and Ottawa. One of March's most enthusiastic supporters was none other than the country's prime minister, W.L. Mackenzie King. In 1928 Pathé News filmed the prime minister admiring *The Response*'s progress during his visit to the sculptor's studio in Farnborough, Kent.[25]

Communities and organizations that wanted Canadian sculptors to create their war monuments hired sculptors like Alfred Laliberté, who produced *Monument aux Braves de Lachine* (1925), located at Parc Stoney Point in Lachine, now a borough of Montreal. Or they hired Frances Loring to supervise Italian carvers at the famous marble quarry in Carrara, Italy, to transform her full-sized plaster cast of *These Laid the World Away* (1928) into marble. Most Canadian sculptors, though, did not have the backing of powerful organizations like the Law Society of Upper Canada, which is what allowed Loring to accompany her plaster model to Italy. Thus communities had to settle for a ready-made sculpture imported from Italy. This meant that all they had to do was provide the plinth and the plaque on which the names of the war dead were inscribed.

By the 1920s, however, Canadian sculptors and monument designers— like their Italian counterparts—were also creating plaster or clay models that could be turned into multiple bronze copies, or into the less expensive and less durable marble or sandstone. In Toronto, for example, the Italian-born stone carver Louis Luigi Temporale (1909–1994), who had emigrated to Canada in 1927, transformed the drawings, models and maquettes of work produced by Francis Loring, Florence Wyle and Emanuel Hahn, among others, at the family business known as Canadian Art Memorials Limited, which was run out of a former ice house in Port Credit, Ontario. Earlier, Montreal-based Coeur de Lion MacCarthy (1881–1979), son of the more famous Hamilton MacCarthy, had produced a sculpture variously known as *The Angel of Victory* or *Winged Victory* (1922) for the Canadian Pacific Railway (CPR), to commemorate the company's loss of over one thousand employees in the war. The work depicted a soldier ascending to

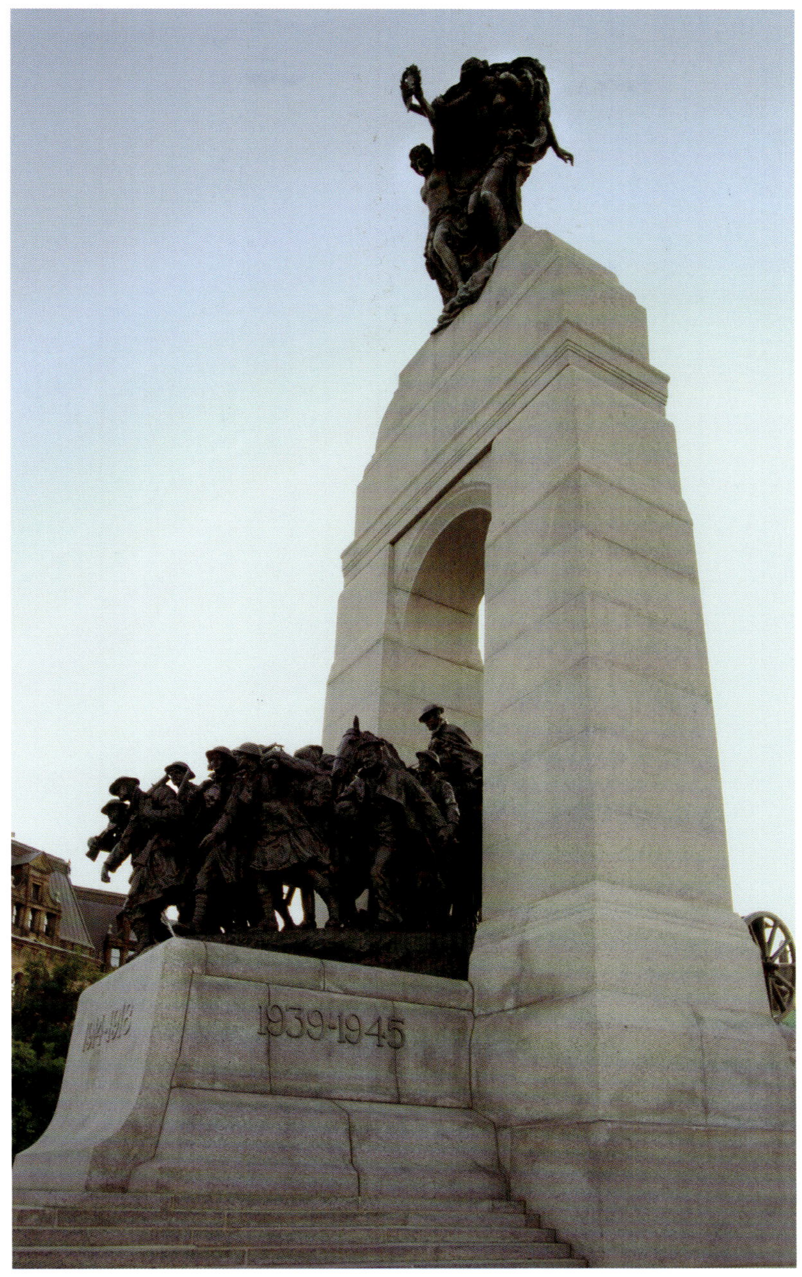

Vernon March
The Response, **1939**
Canada's *National War Memorial, The Response,*
was placed within view of the Parliament
Buildings in Ottawa. Honouring everyone who
had participated in the conflict, the site became a
place of reverent pilgrimage and a venue for public
ceremonies commemorating the First and—in due
course—Second World Wars. One of Canada's most
conventionally rendered sculptures, this work was
completed by March's seven siblings following the
sculptor's death in 1930 and was unveiled in Canada
nine years later.

heaven in the arms of a Christian angel—or, as historian K.S. Inglis has
mused, was the figure a messenger from the classical gods?[26] Three copies
of *The Angel of Victory* were installed near the entrances to or in the foyers
of CPR's stations in Montreal, Winnipeg and Vancouver. For Christians, the
sculpture was visual proof that every soldier who died was redeemed and,
like Jesus Christ himself, had ascended into heaven.

Already known for his monuments dedicated to the fallen in the Boer
War, Quebec sculptor George William Hill made a good living following
the war designing multi-figurative plaster models that were replicated in
bronze and installed in communities from Sherbrooke and Westmount,

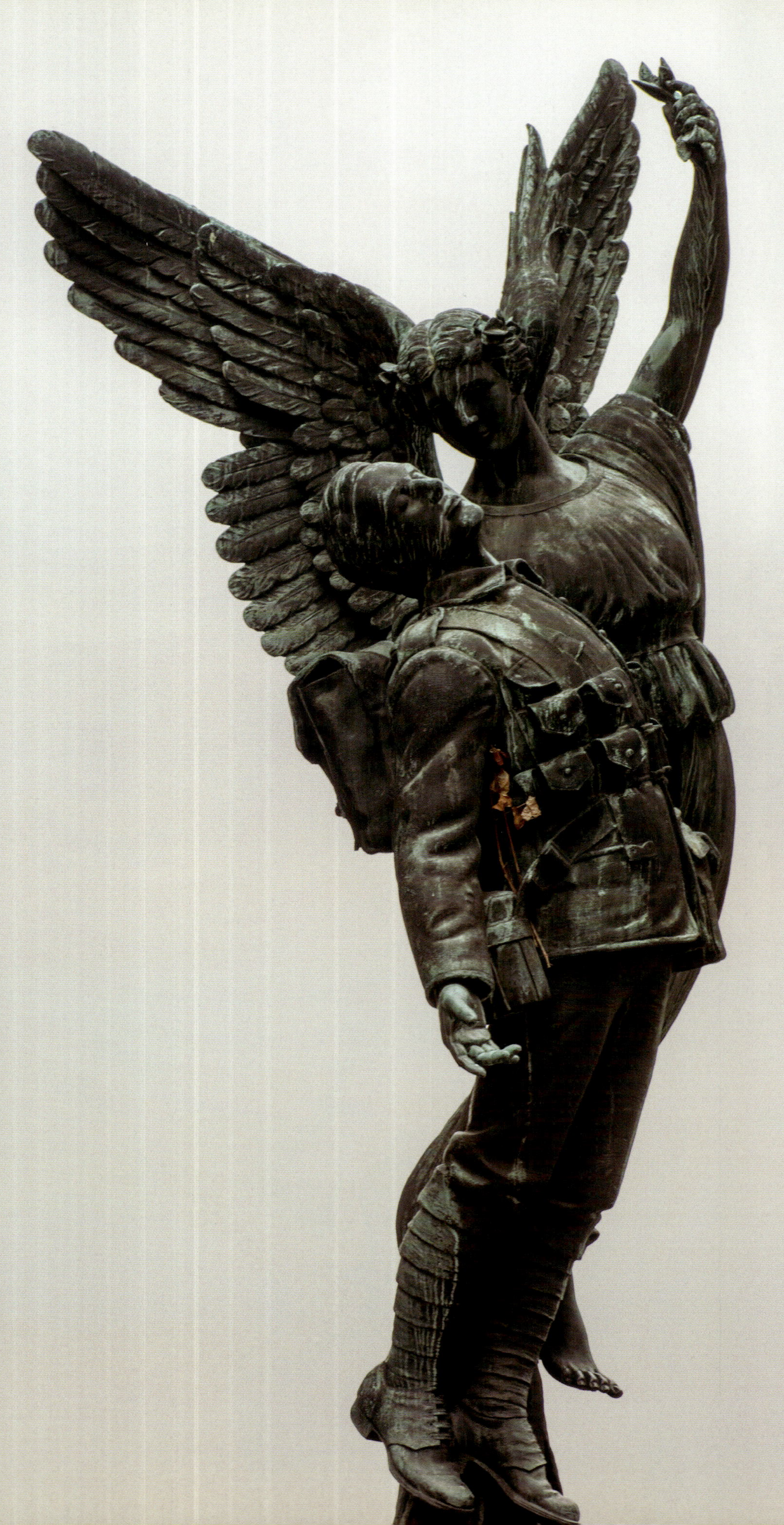

Quebec, to Pictou, Nova Scotia, to Charlottetown, Prince Edward Island. Born and trained in London, Toronto-based sculptor Alfred Howell (1889–1978) fashioned war memorials in the French Neoclassical style that were also commissioned by and installed in communities across the country.

While Loring and Wyle's sculptures of female workers were making a valuable contribution to the war effort, most sculptors, including Hill and MacCarthy, continued to display women as allegorical figures, perhaps in the form of Britannia, or that of Canada. A woman might also appear as a large-winged angel of victory, or directing a marching soldier into battle. Indeed, a grieving woman represents sacrifice in Henri Hébert's Art Nouveau–inspired *Monument aux Braves d'Outremont* (1925). In Vernon March's more realistic rendering, *The Response*, we see two female nurses, possibly added as afterthoughts, at the rear of the procession of soldiers who, having responded to the call of duty, march toward victory. And as for the two figures—"man the Defender and woman the Giver"—featured on the *Welland-Crowland War Memorial* (1934–1939) by Elizabeth Wyn Wood (1903–1966), the female figure, as has been cogently suggested in the inscription on the plinth, represents "sacrifice and service," and is little more than an "object, foil to the figure of man who is the true subject of the nation."[27]

Only occasionally, as we have already seen, did sculptors depart from depicting women as allegorical figures. One such work, honouring a British

Opposite:
Coeur de Lion MacCarthy
The Angel of Victory, 1922
This monument was commissioned in commemoration of more than a thousand employees of the Canadian Pacific Railway killed in the Great War, but its scope is plainly more ambitious. Sculptures of the winged goddess of victory originated in classical Greece, though it was not until the American Civil War that the goddess embraced fallen soldiers to show that their sacrifice had not been in vain. Building on this visual trope, MacCarthy's angel suggests both the triumph of Christianity and the barbarity of the "irreligious" Germans.

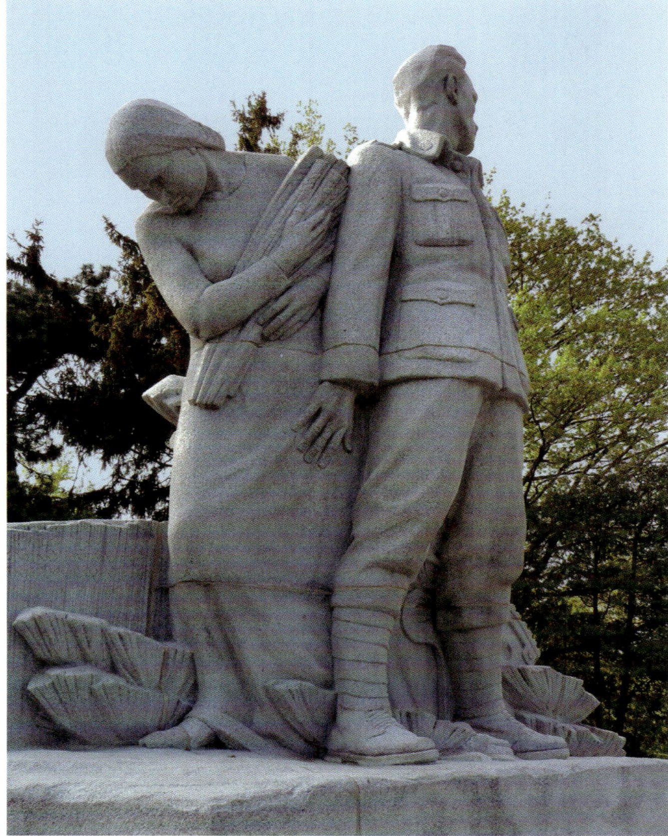

Elizabeth Wyn Wood
Welland-Crowland War Memorial, 1934–1939
During the two decades following the Great War, Elizabeth Wyn Wood emerged, in the view of one critic, as "the most advanced and adventurous sculptor working in Canada today." Yet when it came to designing the *Welland-Crowland War Memorial* in the early 1930s, Wyn Wood reverted to traditional stereotypes of gender roles. According to the inscription on the monument, the female figure represents sacrifice while the male soldier represents service. Any indication that women had contributed to the war effort is erased by the conventional image of the woman taking refuge behind her husband.

nurse who had been shot by a German firing squad for assisting Allied soldiers, was Florence Wyle's *Edith Cavell Memorial* (1921), a bronze tablet. Commissioned by Toronto General Hospital, Wyle's realistic depiction not only memorialized Cavell: it paid tribute to the three thousand nursing sisters who served in the Royal Canadian Army Medical Corps—forty-five of whom had died.

Most sculptors produced work that dealt more directly with the war. George William Hill's war memorial at Charlottetown's Legislative Assembly on Prince Edward Island depicts three rifle-brandishing soldiers running through a war-torn landscape; in Emanuel Hahn's monument at Saint-Lambert, Quebec, the soldier goes over the top; in Coeur de Lion MacCarthy's *Monument des Braves* at Trois-Rivières the soldier is about to plunge his bayonet into the enemy; and in the *Brockville War Memorial* by Nicolas Pirotton (1882–1943) the soldier is in the midst of throwing a grenade.

Dead soldiers were less popular unless, like MacCarthy's *The Angel of Victory*, they were ascending into heaven in the arms of a winged guardian angel. Or unless they represented an alleged event. *Canada's Golgotha* (1918) by Francis Derwent Wood (1871–1926) depicted the alleged crucifixion of a Canadian soldier during the Second Battle of Ypres in April 1915. The highly realistic sculpture was touted as "Canada's sternest memorial to her sons' sufferings."[28] And when plans were being made to exhibit *Canada's Golgotha* at the Canadian War Memorials Exhibition at Burlington House, home to Britain's Royal Academy of Arts, in January 1919, newspapers predicted that it would be "the ghastliest thing in the

Henri Hébert

Monument aux Braves d'Outremont, 1925

The bronze figure poised against the unadorned wall in *Monument aux Braves d'Outremont* might be seen as an ordinary woman or Canada herself. There is no question, however, that the figure embodies a grief that needs no words to be conveyed. Hébert heightened the emotional intensity inherent in this work in two ways, first by giving his figure the sort of expressive pose that was being popularized in the silent movies of the day. And, second, by relying on the delicate sinuosity of Art Nouveau style.

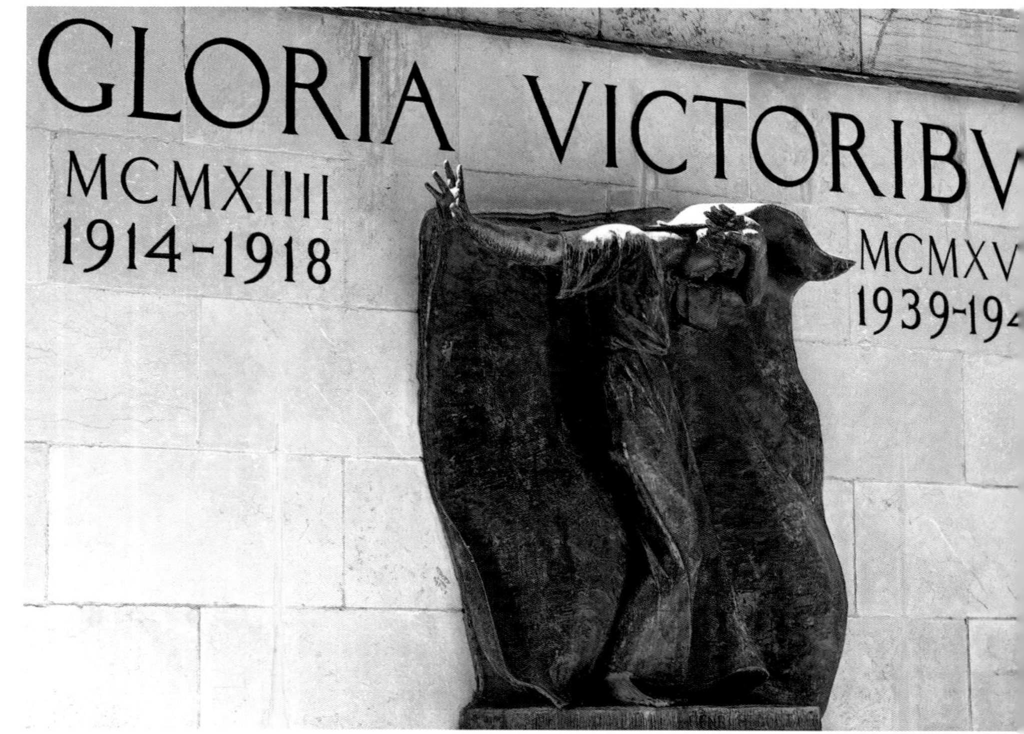

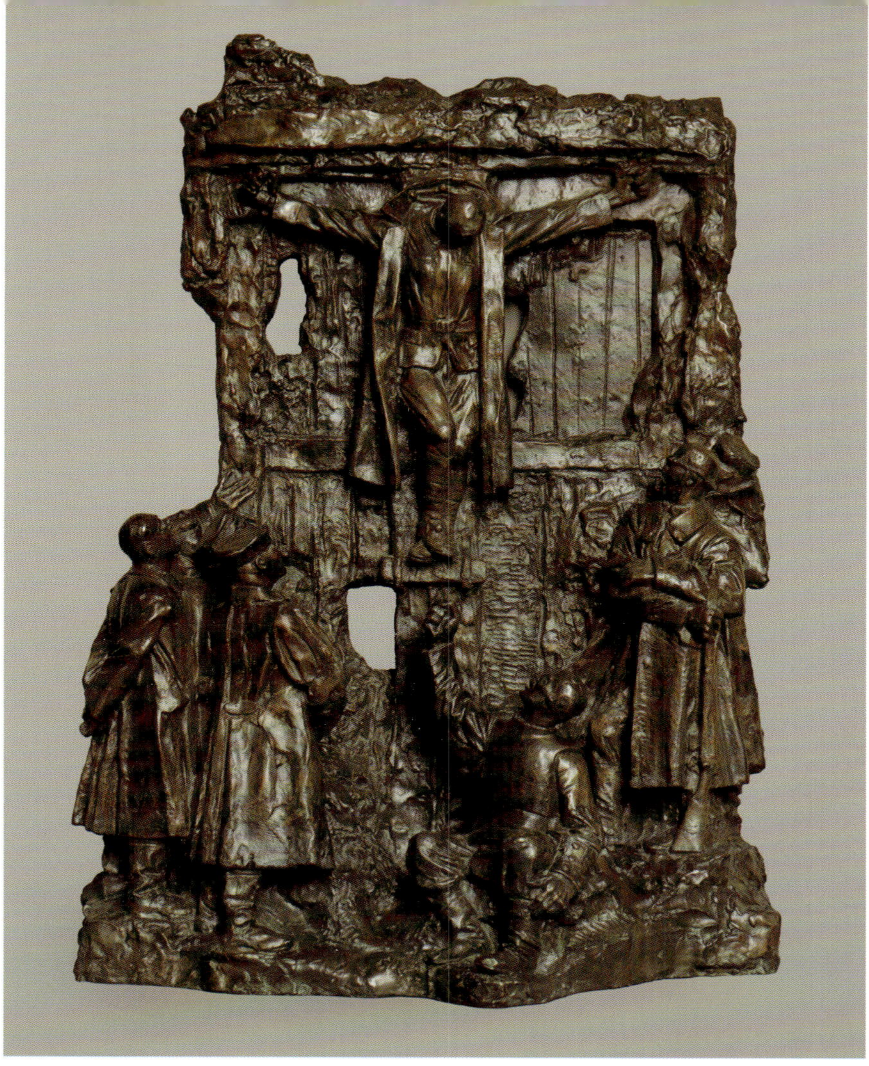

Francis Derwent Wood
Canada's Golgotha, 1918
Canada's Golgotha, freighted with its reference to the crucifixion of a Canadian soldier during the Second Battle of Ypres in April 1915, became the most controversial sculpture produced during the Great War. And it was not the literal and academic rendering of the subject that came into question. It was the work's stark message: the jeering soldiers (obviously German) are presented as sacrilegious criminals on a footing with the executioners of Christ himself. True or false? Canadian officials were unable to prove that the incident had actually taken place and the sculpture was withdrawn from public exhibition. It has only recently become available again.

rooms… [whose paintings and sculptures depicted] courage, agony and death."[29] This was not far from the truth. When the CWMF displayed the sculpture in New York City later that year, *Canada's Golgotha* was confined to a special room. And when the same exhibition was about to make its rounds to major cities across Canada, officials withdrew Derwent Wood's sculpture from exhibition.[30]

The gory depiction of a crucified Canadian soldier surrounded by fist-clenching, sacrilegious, jeering German soldiers provoked a morbid fascination among everyone who saw it. But while *Canada's Golgotha* might have helped justify the Canadian public's loss, Derwent Wood's sculpture proved an embarrassment for the Canadian government when they could not verify that the incident had actually taken place.[31] But there was something else that made the work exceed its sell-by date: the sculpture was a tool of war, and the war was now over.

The public wanted less realistic depictions of warfare following the Armistice in November 1918. They wanted sculptures that embodied an idea that could reflect any meaning the viewer wished to give it—sacrifice, waste, sorrow, pride and even redemption—rather than a realistic portrayal of an event. One example is Emanuel Hahn's life-sized bronze *Tommy in his Greatcoat* (1922), erected in Lindsay, Ontario. By the time it was exhibited at

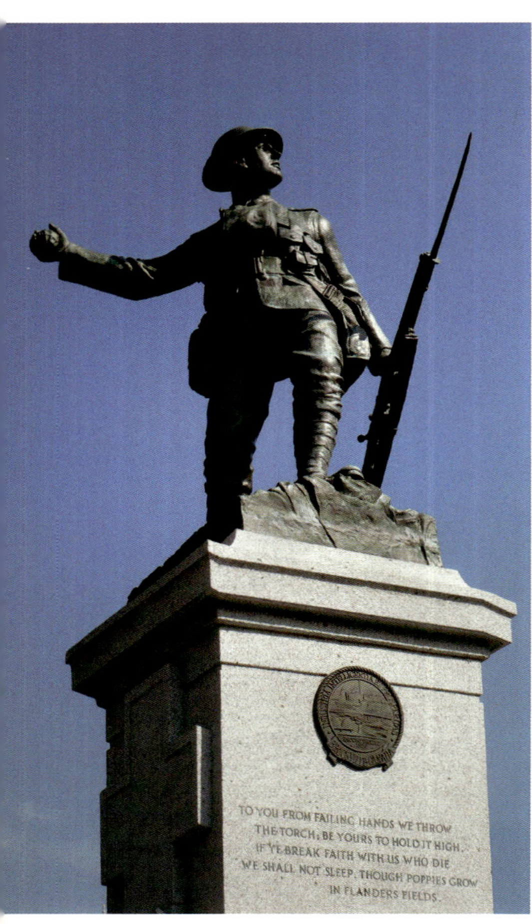

Nicolas Pirotton
Brockville War Memorial, 1924
Matter-of-fact representations of soldiers going
"over the top" and brandishing their guns had their
origins in the drawings and paintings popularized
during the nineteenth century by on-the-spot
sketch artists and painters. Transferred into plaster,
marble and bronze by sculptors during and after
the Great War, such images were rendered in a
no-nonsense academic style. In Nicolas Pirotton's
Brockville War Memorial the soldier is throwing a
grenade. Such action sculptures were so popular
that monument companies in both Canada and Italy
produced multiple copies that could be ordered from
their sale catalogues.

the Canadian National Exhibition in 1923, bronze replicas of the work had
already been installed in Lindsay and in Hanover, Ontario, and Moncton,
New Brunswick. *Grieving Soldier* (1922) was also designed by Hahn,
and ten copies were made of the sculpture. Available in either granite or
bronze from Thomson Monument Company, the figurative sculpture was
inscribed with the title of John McCrae's famous poem "In Flanders Fields"
(1915). Hahn's *Grieving Soldier* was installed in communities from Fernie,
British Columbia, to Westville, Nova Scotia. Coeur de Lion MacCarthy
and the self-taught stone carver Nicolas Pirotton also produced multiple
copies of figurative sculptures depicting soldiers in repose that found their
way to rural communities across the country. So popular were these less
belligerent single-figure images that William A. Rogers Limited developed
their own prefabricated larger-than-life Italian-made bronze statue.
Described simply as "Pensive Soldier" in the company's catalogue, it was
the work most frequently ordered by communities throughout Canada.

Commemoration of the war, in short, had largely determined the artistic
agenda in postwar Canada. It was the opinion of artist A.Y. Jackson,
a member of the Group of Seven, which was formed in 1920, that "the
discipline the artists subjected themselves to in painting things of little
aesthetic interest has done them a lot of good."[32] But it riled Frances
Loring, who complained to the director of the National Gallery of Canada,
Eric Brown, that she and Florence Wyle had "wasted a lot of time on fool
monuments."[33]

Loring and Wyle had special reason for complaint, for they had run up
a considerable debt in order to meet foundry expenses, and were worried
on business lines. In fact, once the government reimbursed the Girls, they
were able to buy an old wood-framed church in Toronto's Moore Park
and convert it into a home/studio. And it remained true that fulfilling war
memorial commissions had prompted both Loring and Wyle to depict
Canadian women in a new way. It had also brought them to the attention
of their peers and the Canadian public. After viewing their wartime
sculptures displayed at Toronto's CWMF exhibition in 1920, A.Y. Jackson
was so impressed that he wanted "to knock down all the statues in Toronto
and let [Wyle and Loring] replace them with anything [they wish]."[34] Many
others, including Eric Brown, felt much the same.

The fact was that some artistic reputations were made out of the tragedy
of war, and not only in Ontario but on the other side of the country, too.
After Earl "Bunny" Clarke (1879–1954) completed a bronze war memorial
commemorating the teachers and students of Victoria High School who had
died in the war, British Columbia's lieutenant-governor gave the promising
sculptor and art teacher a scholarship for a year's study in Europe. In 1927
Clarke returned to Victoria High School, where he remained an inspiring
teacher until his retirement in 1945.

In Toronto Ivor Lewis (1882–1958), a former Ontario College of
Art student, was pulled from the ranks of the art department at Eaton's

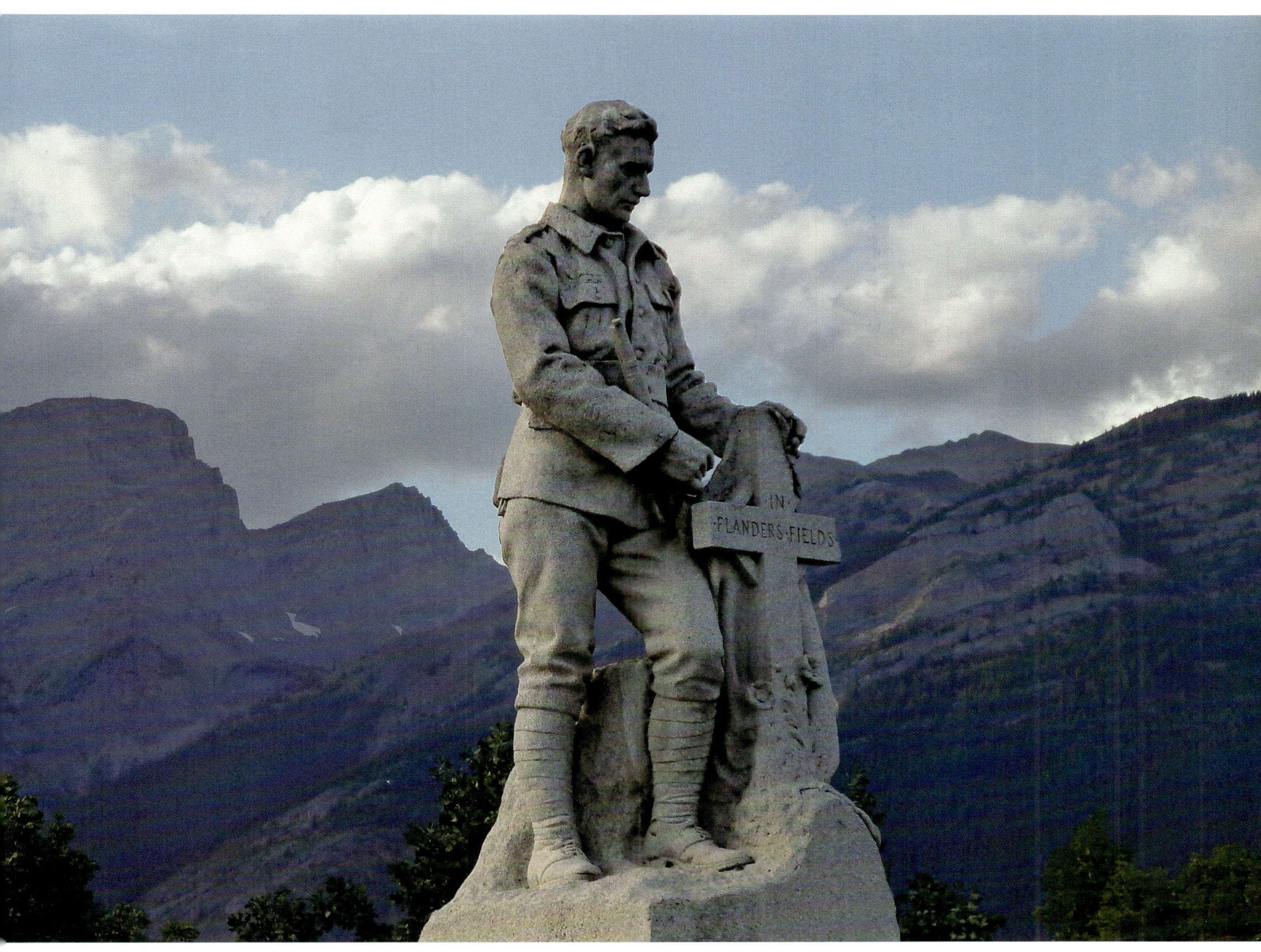

department store in order to design a life-sized bronze statue of the founder of the store, Timothy Eaton. Lewis's seated figure, executed in the pre-war Beaux-Arts style, was installed at stores in Toronto and Winnipeg. The sculpture not only commemorated the store's fiftieth anniversary, it celebrated the company's generosity to members of their staff who enlisted in the Great War. During the war Eaton's employees had received full or half pay, depending on their marital status, and were ensured a job when they came home. Lewis rose through the ranks of the company and in 1942 became the director of Eaton's.

It would be misleading to tell a simple feel-good story here, however. Some Canadian sculptors were indeed earning a good living by fulfilling war-related commissions in the form of commemorative statues, reliefs, medals and coins. At the same time, as Frances Loring's comment to

Emanuel Hahn
Grieving Soldier, 1922
By the 1920s many Canadians wanted a more positive, more reflective and less belligerent image of their soldiers. Taking John McCrae's famous poem "In Flanders Fields" as a starting point, German-born Emanuel Hahn produced one of the most moving—and ambiguous—sculptures of the period. Is this pensive soldier mourning the death of his comrades? Is he distraught by the wastage of war? Or is he fearful that it might happen again? Hahn's image allowed everyone to invest it with their own meaning.

Eric Brown suggests, making sculptures to order could be an inhibiting constraint on artistic expression and opportunity.

Sculptors had, of course, been subjected to the scrutiny of the person or group who had commissioned the work long before the Great War. The making of a public monument had always been a co-operative business, entailing the sculptor-designer-modeller, the stone carver and even an architect. Sometimes the ethnicity of the sculptor had been a relevant consideration, whether in the choice of British artists by groups affirming their loyalty to the Empire or in the patronage of francophone artists celebrating their Québécois identity. But the commissions for war memorials accentuated a new kind of sensitivity—or prejudice—about the participation of sculptors of German or Austrian origin.

Emanuel Hahn, again, provides a prominent example. As we have seen, he had already won high esteem as a Canadian sculptor in the pre-war years, with his visits to Germany enhancing his professional credentials. During the war, likewise, his work expressed a sense of the pity of war, such as many other Canadians felt. In 1925, then, it was of little surprise that this distinguished sculptor applied for and won a commission against more than forty competitors to design Winnipeg's cenotaph. But a year later, the city changed its mind when it discovered that the winner had been born in Germany.

Hahn had long been a naturalized Canadian; his eminence in his field was well attested; the fact that his memorials already stood in town squares across the country was not in dispute. Such points made no difference to the Winnipeg Board of Trade, to the Imperial Order Daughters of the Empire or to the War Widows' Association, all of which were prominent in making the case for the sculptor's dismissal. In the end Hahn was allowed to keep his fee, but the commission was withdrawn.

The Winnipeg War Memorial Committee held another competition. This time the winner was the sculptor Elizabeth Wyn Wood. The committee duly praised her work for its originality and heroic proportions that were "bound to arrest the passer-by." Alas, their failure in due diligence was exposed when they subsequently discovered that the brilliant sculptor whom they were now lauding was married to Hahn.[35] Again, embarrassment and prejudice were unhappily intermingled in the withdrawal of the commission for a second time. The Winnipeg War Memorial Committee justified their actions by suggesting that the memorial must represent the views of both the public and the veterans.[36]

But their exclusion of sculptors—or those married to sculptors—of German or Austrian ethnicity begged a bigger question: For whom were these memorials being created? What kind of soldier was being represented? Evidently there was no image of an Austrian-born or German-born Canadian soldier. Nor was there commemoration of the 225 Canadians of Japanese ethnicity who had volunteered, fifty-four of whom had died on the Western Front with the Tenth Canadian Infantry Battalion in 1916. Indeed, in 1919 the Japanese community raised funds for their own war memorial. And in 1920 the city of Vancouver gave the Japanese committee a site in Stanley Park for the *Japanese Canadian War Memorial*

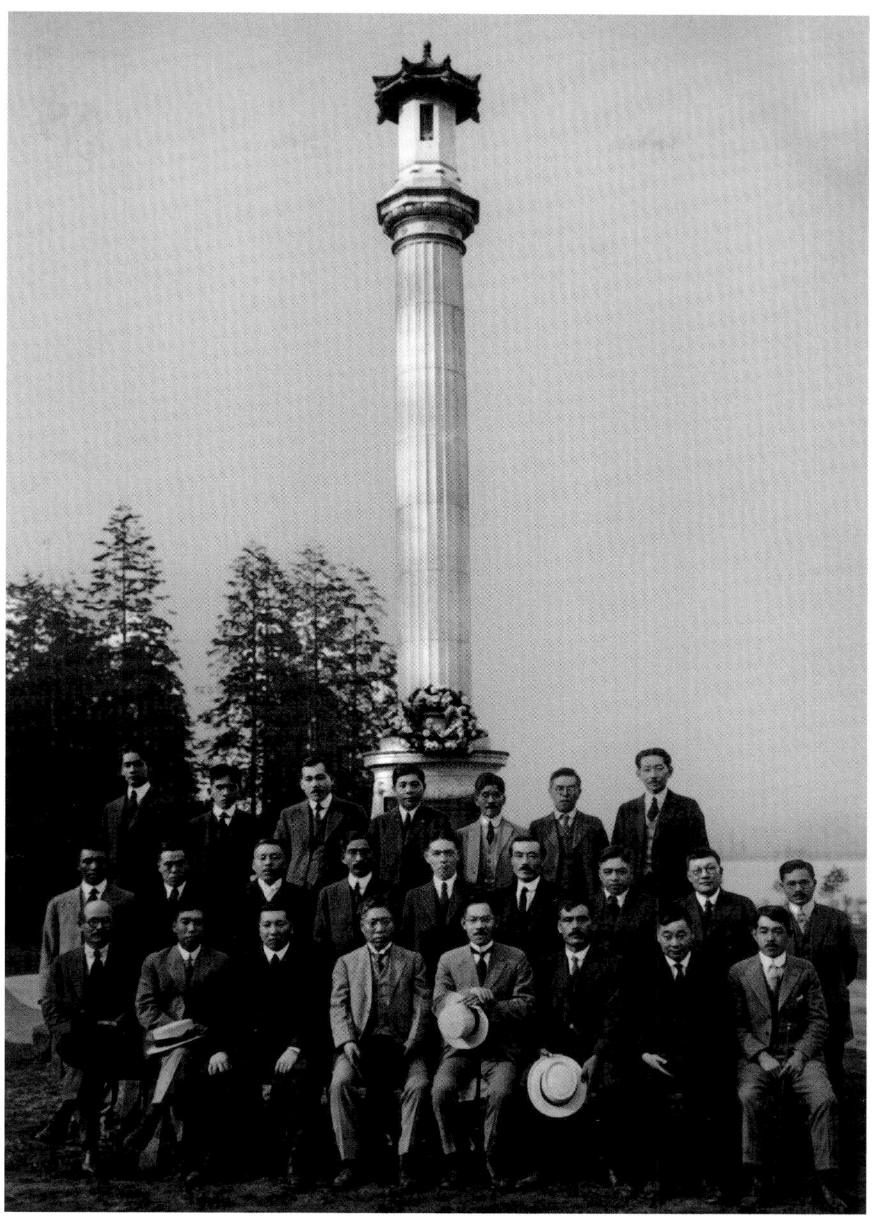

(1920), which brilliantly merged Western design with ancient Kasuga lanterns typical of shrines in Kyoto.

The issue was not so much immigrant status as ethnicity. After all, those of European stock were hardly the earliest surviving inhabitants of Canada. Before contact with Europeans, First Nations people raised no pillars or inscriptions to commemorate intertribal warfare. Yet, during the Great War, while over four thousand Indigenous people had been integrated into various battalions of the Canadian Expeditionary Force, they continued to be represented as half-clad scouts or noble savages below the plinths, of which the British sculptor Vernon March's *Samuel de Champlain Monument* (1925), erected in Orillia, Ontario, is just one example.[37] Nor were the two hundred Chinese Canadians who laid the tracks that took supplies to the front lines commemorated; nor the one thousand African Canadians who formed Atlantic Canada's No. 2 Construction Battalion.

The commemoration of Quebec's soldiers who partook in the Great War for the usual complex of emotional and financial reasons was nevertheless perplexing since many of the men had volunteered for service. Yet it was also true that, following the Military Service Act (1917), there had been riots in Quebec against the imposition of conscription the following year. Even so, more than one hundred war-related monuments throughout the province of Quebec honoured the 35,000 French Canadians who served overseas. The most popular among them comprise a simple cross. Erected in cities and towns and along country roads, the cross remained a symbol of the religious spirit that had founded Quebec. But during the war, and particularly following the Conscription Crisis, the cross became a place where Québécois prayed to save their sons from being *recruited* into the army.

The kind of soldier depicted on Canada's war memorials rarely resembled anyone who belonged to the country's minority groups. He was a sensitive, virile and resourceful white male, shaped by Canada's wilderness landscape and harsh climate. The only place where war memorials represented every soldier who had contributed to the war effort was at the base. It was there that the names of the war dead were listed, usually in alphabetical order and without distinction of ethnicity, rank or status. In this at least they were equal in the sight of God.

Just as the soldier at the top of the plinth fitted the identikit image of the average Anglo-Canadian, so the style in which memorial sculptures were created was equally determined. To follow what the art critic for *Canadian Magazine* called the "ultra-modern art that had its birth in Germany" might have been seen as unpatriotic.[38] But the fact was that working in an idiom that reflected European modernism was never a question for Canadian sculptors.

While some Canadian painters adapted modernist styles to their depiction of warfare, as we have seen, Canada's sculptors clung to the more traditional Beaux-Arts, Symbolist and Art Nouveau styles that had dominated sculpture before the First World War. Thus, most Canadian sculptors were more concerned with content than with style. Loring and Wyle's sculptures of munitions and farm workers displayed at the Canadian War Memorials Exhibition in Toronto in October 1919 embodied, as Eric Brown put it, Canada's "determination to win the war."[39] Derwent Wood's reconstruction of the alleged crucifixion of a Canadian soldier left "future generations a damning indictment of the nation whose soldiers crucified a Canadian soldier and mocked his long-drawn-out agonies."[40] Reflective solitary figures, as depicted by Hahn, among others, and even soldiers ascending into heaven, were not seeking to glorify war in the idiom made familiar during the nineteenth and early twentieth centuries in more formal battle paintings.

One way or another, by the end of the 1920s the idea that wartime sculpture had to be heroic had been subverted. Sculptors were no longer tied to depicting actual events. In accordance with popular expectations, the war-memorial sculpture became a blank slate on which any emotion—sorrow, loss, hope for Canada's future or quiet heroism—could be projected. And when Canada's largest war memorial, at Vimy Ridge in northeastern France, was commissioned, this was the implicit prospectus for the work.

Walter Seymour Allward (1876–1955) was the artist eventually chosen. A Toronto-born sculptor, he had sound credentials for the job. The 1913 and 1925 surveys of Canadian art both agreed that Allward was the country's most distinguished sculptor. Indeed, James Mavor wrote in 1913 that Allward had "no competitor."[41] Moreover, known for respecting the "best traditions of sculpture," Allward was adjudged unlikely to slip "into the realm of those whose tendencies in sculpture are similar to the cubists' tendencies in painting."[42]

Apart from a few modelling courses at the Toronto Technical School, Allward was largely self-taught. Remarkably, he had spent four years as an apprentice in an architectural firm before joining the Don Valley Brick Works, where he designed ornamental figures and decorative architectural designs. He got his first break at the age of nineteen when he won a competition to design a monument to be installed in Toronto's Queen's Park, to commemorate the men who had died during the Northwest Rebellion in 1885. Many other commissions followed the completion of the *Northwest Rebellion Monument* (1895). Among them were two memorializing the Boer War—the *Boer War Memorial Fountain* (1906) in Windsor, Ontario, and the *South African War Memorial* (1910) in Toronto—and the *Bell Telephone Memorial* (1917) in Brantford, Ontario.

But when the Canadian Battlefields Memorial Commission chose Allward for the *Canadian National Vimy Memorial*, this was a far larger project than he had previously undertaken. The site on Hill 145, some 250 acres at Vimy Ridge on the edge of the Douai Plain in northern France, was already a significant place in Canada's history. It was here that the Canadian Expeditionary Force had fought as a unit for the first time, here that they captured the ridge in April 1917, and here that over 10,500 men were killed or wounded during the assault. It would take Allward more than ten years to memorialize this event in stone.

It was a colossal undertaking. It took two years to haul 10,000 metric tons of concrete to provide a base for the work. It took a year for Allward to find the right material for the body of the work—he chose Seget limestone from an ancient quarry near Split in present-day Croatia. And it took several more years to transport this material to France, where it was bonded to a frame of cast concrete.

In 1922 Allward moved his studio from Toronto to London, where he designed a large part of the memorial. The monument's basic feature is two thirty-metre-high pylons, each bearing a large cross, a maple leaf and a fleur-de-lys, in tribute to Canada and to France; and it is topped by winged angels. Drawing on stylistic elements evident in his earlier work, like the *Bell Telephone Memorial*, Allward made twenty-two life-sized plaster moulds, based on his own original plaster models. These figures were transported to France, and with the help of a pointing machine and

Following pages:
Walter Seymour Allward
Canadian National Vimy Memorial
(front view), 1936
Almost as soon as the war ended in 1918, travel agencies met the needs of the families and friends who wanted to see where their loved ones had died by offering tours to the war-devastated front. Today many Canadians make the same pilgrimage. And the place they visit most frequently is the imposing national memorial that overlooks the Douai Plain in France. This is where more than 10,500 Canadians met their deaths during the Battle of Vimy Ridge in 1917. The *Canadian National Vimy Memorial* remains one of the most prominent war memorials in Europe.

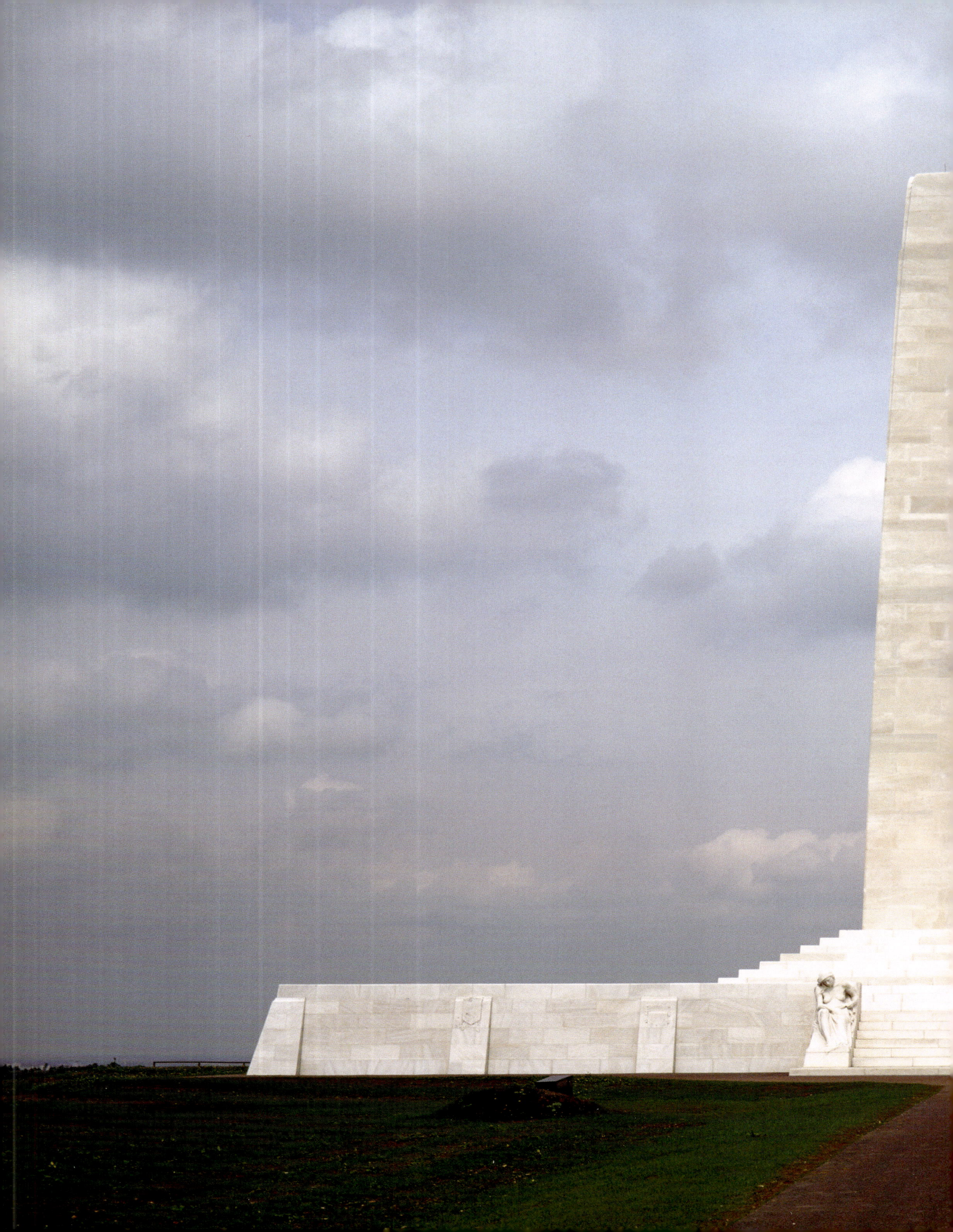

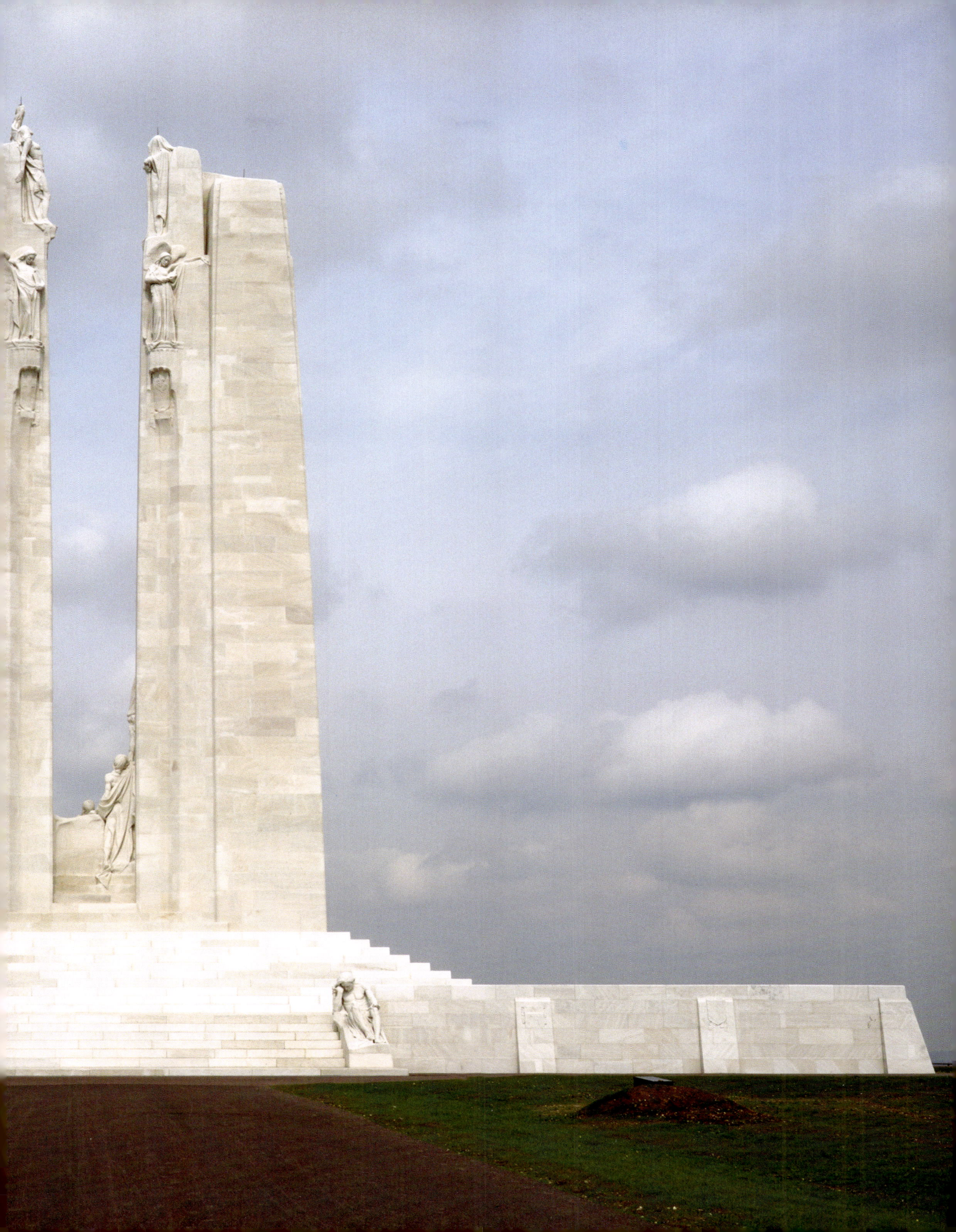

the skill of Italian stone carvers, they were doubled in size. Indeed, the central figure, *Canada "Bereft,"* which serves as a focal point for the whole work, was carved from a thirty-metric-ton block of stone.

While the designers of the ANZAC *Memorial* (1932) in Sydney, Australia, ignored references to classical sculpture and focused on the soldier, Allward took his inspiration from Michelangelo's Medici tomb in Florence and from sculptors who continued to follow the Neoclassical style.[43] Sacrifice, grief and mourning were represented by figures depicting a spread-eagled soldier and a cloaked figure of a young woman—Canada mourning the loss

Walter Seymour Allward
Canada "Bereft": **maquette for the** *Canadian National Vimy Memorial*, **c. 1921**
Until the outbreak of the Great War women were generally unpopular subjects for Canadian sculptors. In designing the Canadian war memorial at Vimy, however, Walter Allward did not hesitate to feature women. Rendered in the Neoclassical and Art Nouveau styles, his females were not personalized but symbolic images expressing sorrow, grief and mourning. Allward's combination of grief with nationhood in his plaster maquette *Canada "Bereft"* won general acceptance of the figure as a fitting centrepiece for the memorial.

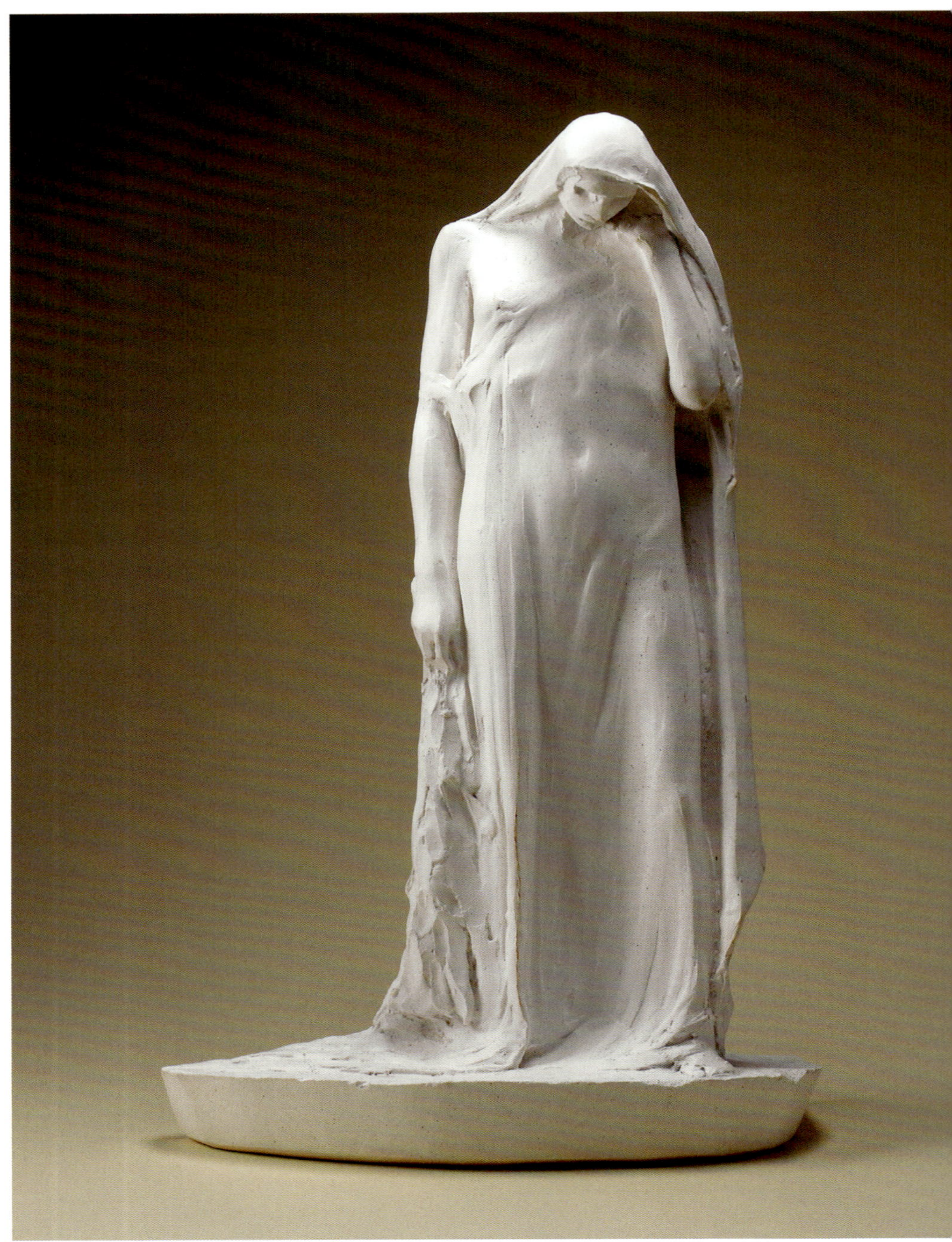

of her people. Bereaved parents were accompanied by muscular allegorical figures representing universal virtues: peace, truth, justice, hope, charity, honour and faith.

The *Canadian National Vimy Memorial* is a tour de force. The head of the Canadian Expeditionary Force, Sir Arthur Currie, may have been a great general but he hardly represented general opinion in describing Allward's memorial at Vimy Ridge as "another enormous thing with steps and railings" and deeming it a waste of money.[44] The hundred thousand people who gathered at the Vimy memorial's inauguration in July 1936 thought differently, most of them finding it a fitting commemoration of the place where the Canadian Expeditionary Force had experienced such loss of life in capturing Vimy Ridge. King Edward VIII, French president Albert Lebrun and Canadian prime minister W.L. Mackenzie King were present at the unveiling ceremony.

The Vimy Ridge memorial was from the first a place of pilgrimage for those Canadians who could afford to travel to Europe—in particular those who were unable to locate the grave of their loved one. And during the Second World War, rumours that the Germans had destroyed Canada's most revered memorial were dispelled when Adolf Hitler himself, ironically admiring its peaceful nature and its references to classical sculpture, visited it. So great was the Führer's admiration for Allward's monument that Waffen-ss troops were detailed to protect the memorial from destruction by either the Allied or German forces during the remainder of the war. No other work by a Canadian sculptor had received this kind of attention—by friend or foe—and it remains a site of memory today.

Though it hardly seemed so at the outbreak of hostilities in August 1914, the war proved a good thing for Canadian sculpture. With war-related memorials in virtually every city and town, sculptors had a new prominence. War-related commissions allowed many to support themselves both during and after the war. The artistic establishment, hitherto all too quick to hire foreign-born sculptors, discovered that the male and female sculptors in their midst were just as capable of producing good work that could appeal to the average Canadian. And perhaps it did not matter that an Italian monument maker working at the quarry in distant Carrara might have created a city or town's memorial sculpture, or that work by a Canadian sculptor, too, was suitable for reproduction across the country, or that unlike Canada's commissioned painters, the country's sculptors adhered to pre-war styles. What mattered most was that sculpture now had a visual presence, not just in Ottawa or Montreal, but also in large and small communities across the country, reaching out to the average Canadian. In sculpture too, the Great War had a major role in nation building.

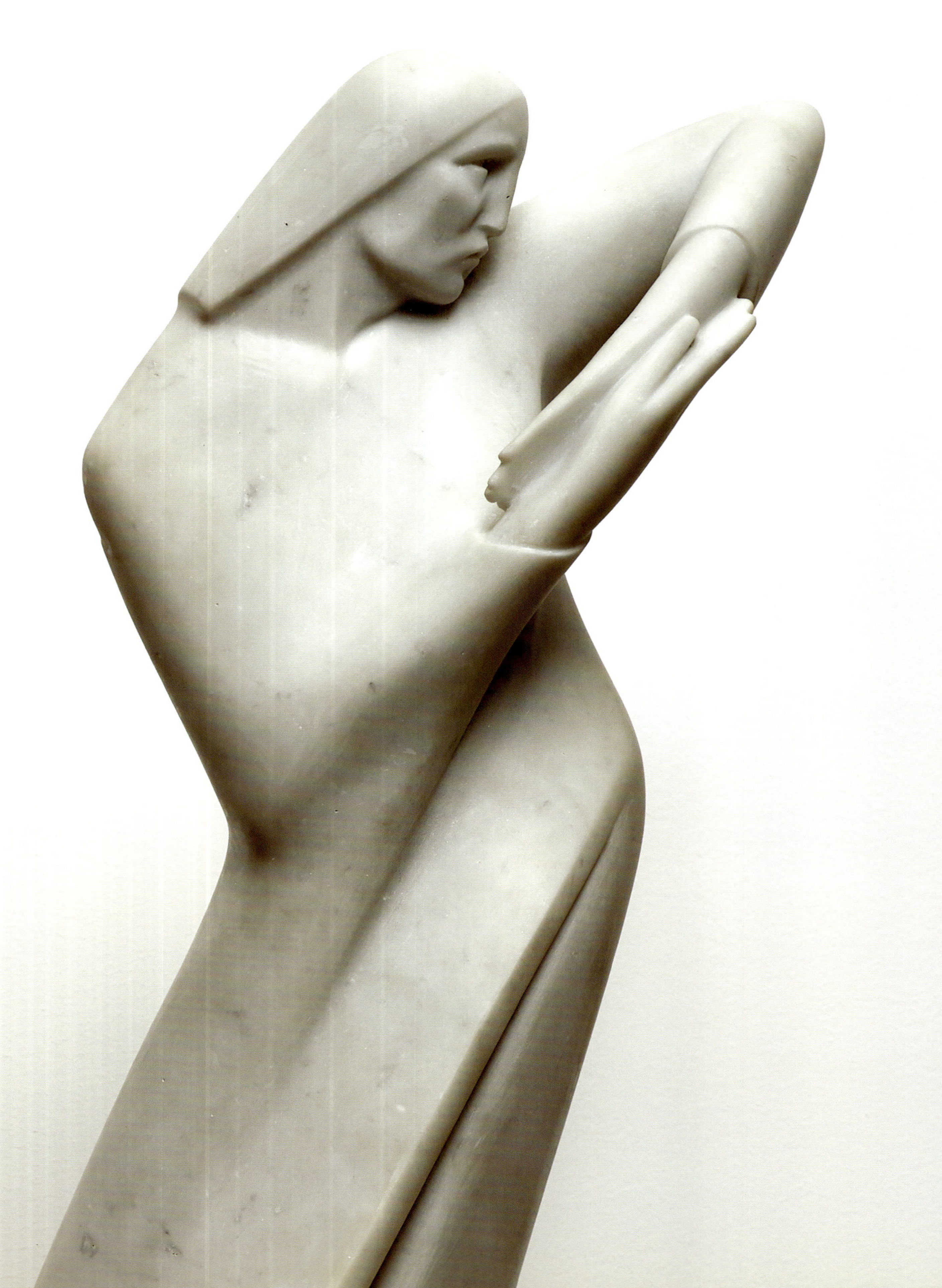

5
Reorientation

In 1938 Walter Seymour Allward closed his London studio and returned to Canada. His great achievement in designing and overseeing the construction of Canada's war memorial at Vimy Ridge had taken its toll, sapping the sixty-two-year-old sculptor's energy and dampening his spirits. "I have been eating and sleeping stone for so long," he complained, that "it has become an obsession with me, a nightmare."[1]

Much had happened during Allward's fifteen-year absence from Canada. The public had a new relationship with sculpture—after all, there were more "typical" soldiers at the tops of plinths than statesmen or other prominent figures.

Opposite:
Elizabeth Wyn Wood
Detail of *Gesture*, 1927
(see page 116)

Equally, the art gallery establishment had a new relationship with the Canadian artists in their midst, and the Canadian artist with society. Canadian painters and sculptors had turned from mourning Canada's war dead to celebrating the country's future. Under the influence of isolationist and pacifist sentiments, most sculptors and painters seemed to have forgotten about the war. Instead, they found new themes that set them apart not only from the Americans to the south but also from the old-world European culture across the Atlantic. Symbols of the solitary or fighting soldier, of the grieving widow or of the allegorical figure of Miss Canada now found themselves displaced by images of the wilderness landscape of northern Ontario, the Canadian Arctic and the Inuit, the habitant, the prairie immigrant, the miner and the hockey player.

Simeone Quppapik (1909–1995) carving in Cape Dorset (Kinngait), April 30, 1962.

Photo by Charles Gimpel.

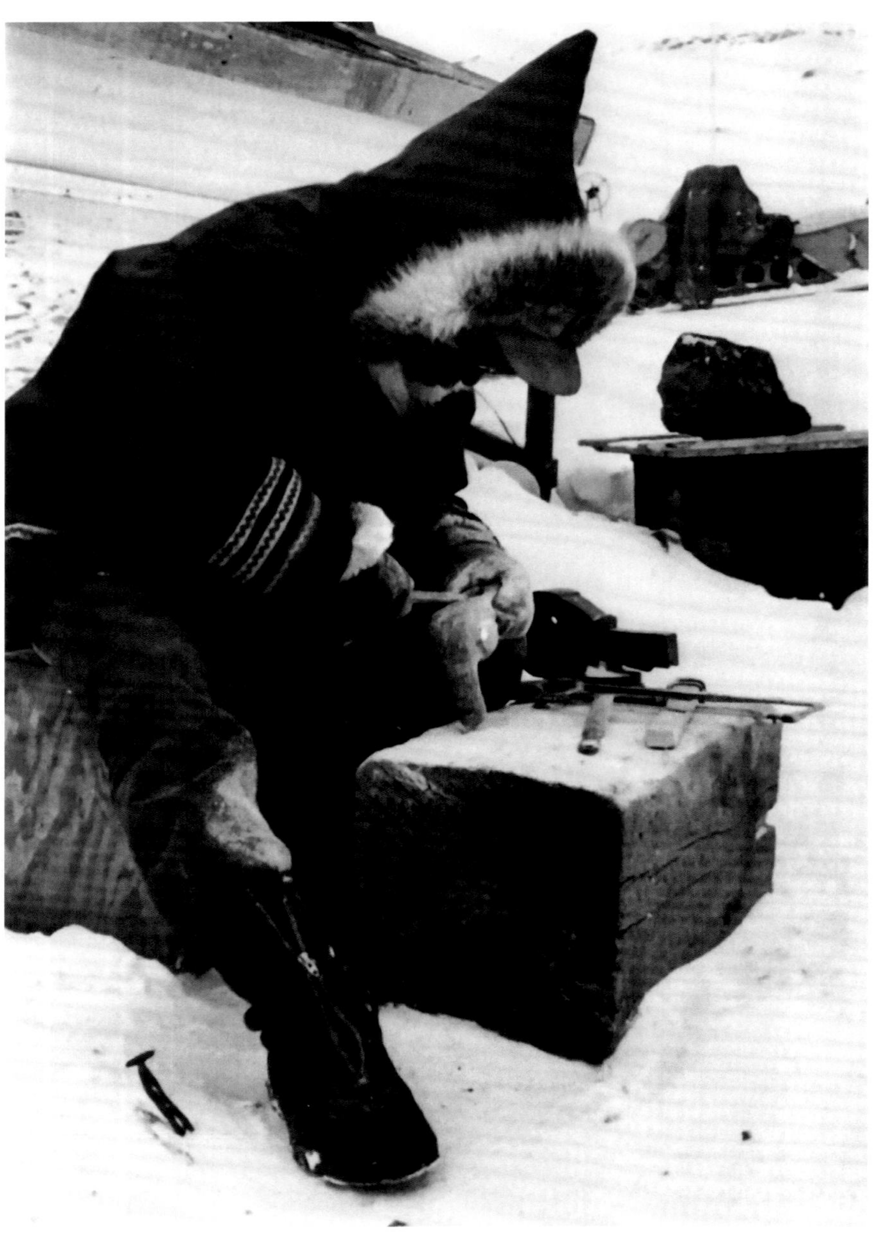

The economic prosperity of the 1920s made Canadian sculpture more visible at home and abroad. Private collectors purchased more commemorative busts, plaques, statues and outdoor sculptures than ever before. A new generation of architects commissioned sculptors to make large-scale panels and reliefs, free-standing statues and decorative ornamentation for prominent buildings. Sculptors like Charles Marega (1871–1939) of the Vancouver School of Decorative and Applied Arts (Now Emily Carr University of Art and Design) found themselves engaged in a variety of commissions. The Italian-born Marega was versatile; he was responsible for the lions on Vancouver's imposing Lions Gate Bridge, and he carved and cast sculptures of King Edward VII and Joe Fortes—a popular Vancouver swimming instructor originally from Trinidad—respectively. Marega also produced caryatids for the cornices of Vancouver's Sun Tower, a whole series of portrait sculptures for the new library addition to the Parliament Buildings in Victoria and a bust of Benito Mussolini that remains in the bowels of the Vancouver Art Gallery.

The availability of funds during the first decade of the interwar years not only gave sculptors employment on-site in construction: it augmented the budgets of the art institutions that prominently displayed their work. In 1915 the Art Gallery of Toronto had mounted the first Canadian exhibition devoted entirely to sculpture.[2] Eleven years later, in 1926, the gallery built a sculpture court in the heart of the museum. Not to be outdone, the National Gallery of Canada included Canadian sculpture in its nationwide travelling exhibitions and at the British Empire Exhibitions at Wembley (a new stadium in north London) in 1924 and 1925. During the next decade, Canadian sculpture was also featured at the 1939 World's Fair in New York City. The National Gallery in Ottawa likewise expanded its mandate to acquire not only the greatest foreign art that was available to them but to purchase work by Canada's leading sculptors.

An art critic for Britain's *Manchester Guardian* made the observation in 1937 that Canada was "too big [a country] to carry on without an outside stimulus."[3] It was certainly true that many provincial and federal art galleries had made it a priority to bring foreign exhibitions to Canada. And it is also true that Canada's sculptors benefitted from being exposed to the work of internationally recognized sculptors from abroad. In 1925 and 1927, for example, the Art Gallery of Toronto sponsored two seminal exhibitions of modern art. Two years later the exhibition *Contemporary Russian Art* and the *International Exhibition of Modern Art* featured the work of Ivan Meštrović (1883–1962), Jacob Epstein (1880-1959) and Aristide Maillol (1861–1944), among other leading European sculptors. And in 1927 the National Gallery of Canada hosted the exhibition *Selected Group of Modern European Sculpture.*

Art schools and colleges also now gave Canadian sculptors a place in their expanding institutions. Walter Seymour Allward's former assistant, Emanuel Hahn, headed the sculpture department at the Ontario College of Art and his wife, Elizabeth Wyn Wood, taught modelling at the Central Technical High School, escaping in cosmopolitan Toronto the anti-German prejudice that had dogged them on the Prairies. Also in Toronto,

Alfred Howell became the first head of sculpture at the Central Technical High School. Allward's rival in Quebec, Henri Hébert, had lived in the shadow of his famous father, Louis-Philippe Hébert, until the latter's death in 1917. Henri Hébert, who had attended Paris's École du Soir de la Ville de Paris and École Nationale des Arts Décoratifs, now found his own métier as a sculptor in Montreal, teaching at both McGill University's School of Architecture and at the Monument-National. In Toronto, Frances Loring and Florence Wyle offered informal art lessons in their church-cum-studio/home and helped launch the careers of Dora de Pédery-Hunt (1913–2008), Rebecca Sisler (b. 1932) and Frances Gage (b. 1924). In Vancouver, Beatrice (or "Bee," as she preferred to be called) Lennie (1904–1987) established her own school of sculpture. And in Winnipeg, Alberta-born Evelyn Fay "Byllee" Lang (1908–1966) named the de Marin School of Sculpture—which ran from 1936 to 1940—after her husband who was killed in the Spanish Civil War.

The philanthropists Rosa and Spencer Clark inaugurated the Guild of All Arts on their large estate on the Scarborough Bluffs outside of Toronto. There they gave one hundred local painters, sculptors and craft workers equipment, materials and studio space in an attempt to "revive an interest in arts and crafts" and to encourage artists "to earn their living as artists by creating public acceptance of their work."[4] Institutions outside of Canada like the Carnegie Corporation and the Rockefeller Foundation provided assistance to arts organizations by funding cultural groups and institutions across the country.[5]

Art critics and journalists now not only promoted sculpture in the local newspaper, but also wrote about it in newly founded art journals. Believing that Quebec needed to be taken out of its regionalist thinking, a group of Montreal artists, musicians, architects and writers launched the bilingual publication *Le Nigog* in 1918. Even though this particular periodical collapsed after less than a year, in that time *Le Nigog* served as "a kind of antidote to what its founders and contributors perceived as the stultifying conventions of the past and the hopelessness of the present" by introducing European modernist ideas to Quebec.[6] There were few equivalent arts journals in the rest of Canada until 1940. Assisted by sculptor Violet Gillett (1898–1996) and funded by the Carnegie Corporation, Acadia University professor Walter Abell founded *Maritime Art*. Three years after it was launched, the journal was renamed *Canadian Art* and relocated from Wolfville, Nova Scotia, to Ottawa, where it came under the aegis of the National Gallery of Canada.

It was hardly a peculiarity of sculpture alone that, like so much of Canadian cultural activity, it was to be found disproportionately concentrated in the cities of Toronto and Montreal. This tendency was reinforced in 1928 when the Sculptors Society of Canada (ssc) was formed, with many familiar names providing its motivating force: in particular Frances Loring and, of course, Florence Wyle, along with Elizabeth Wyn Wood and Emanuel Hahn, all of them based in Toronto. They joined forces with the Quebec luminaries Henri Hébert, Alfred Laliberté and Marc-Aurèle de Foy Suzor-Coté. Other less prominent members of the ssc were Alfred Howell and Lionel Fosbery (1879–1956).[7]

Like its American counterpart, the National Sculpture Society (1896), the ssc's mandate was to bring sculptors together for "the encouragement, improvement, and cultivation of the art of sculpture."[8] This entailed seeing to it that more sculpture was included in exhibitions at home and abroad—and not exhibited with its back to the wall, precluding an all-round view. The ssc was equally concerned with monitoring the quality of public monuments and ensuring that public commissions were awarded to Canadian sculptors. The ssc also saw to it that the Royal Canadian Academy made Canadian sculptors full-fledged members rather than associates.[9] It prompted the National Gallery of Canada to add more Canadian sculpture to its permanent collection—in the 1920s works by foreign sculptors still far outnumbered those by Canadians. The ssc also encouraged the press to aspire to a level of discourse and critical analysis in their discussion of sculpture that had thus far been reserved for painting. All told, the ssc aimed to give sculpture a higher profile with higher public esteem, and thereby convince both the public and the patrons who commissioned works that the country's sculptors could do rather more than produce gravestones, public war memorials, garden ornaments and architectural decorations.

The Sculptors Society of Canada's inaugural exhibition opened in October 1928 at the Art Gallery of Toronto; it then moved to the National Gallery in Ottawa and then to the Montreal Museum of Fine Arts. At all three venues, the exhibitions were well attended by the public and art critics alike. Commenting on the 170 works on display, a writer for the *Toronto Daily Star* captured a sense of rather naive enthusiasm: "Few of us knew that Canada had enough moveable sculpture to fill one room, let alone three." Augustus Bridle was equally gratified that the artists had maintained "the fine balance between progressiveness and traditional reserve, without flamboyant radicalism."[10] By the time that the ssc's fourth annual exhibition was held in 1935, Arthur Lismer (well known as a former member of the Group of Seven, which had disbanded in 1932) assured his readers in the literary magazine *Curtain Call* that the day had passed when Canadian sculpture could be put into the corners at exhibitions dominated by paintings. Sculpture was now, he wrote, "a force to be reckoned with."[11] Bertram Brooker, painter and editor of the *Yearbook of the Arts in Canada 1928–1929*, had another reason to be proud. Suzor-Coté, Hahn, Hébert and other members of the ssc now found their work exhibited alongside that of leading European sculptors like Auguste Rodin, Ivan Meštrović and Jacob Epstein in Canada's leading art galleries.[12]

All of this was new. Yet we need to appreciate that most of the leading members of the ssc were by no means apostles of modernism. The ssc was, above all, popular because most of its members adhered to traditional styles made familiar in the hundreds of war memorials that could be seen across the country. Modernism had not simply been kept at bay during the war. Wyle and Loring were never prepared to abandon the idea that

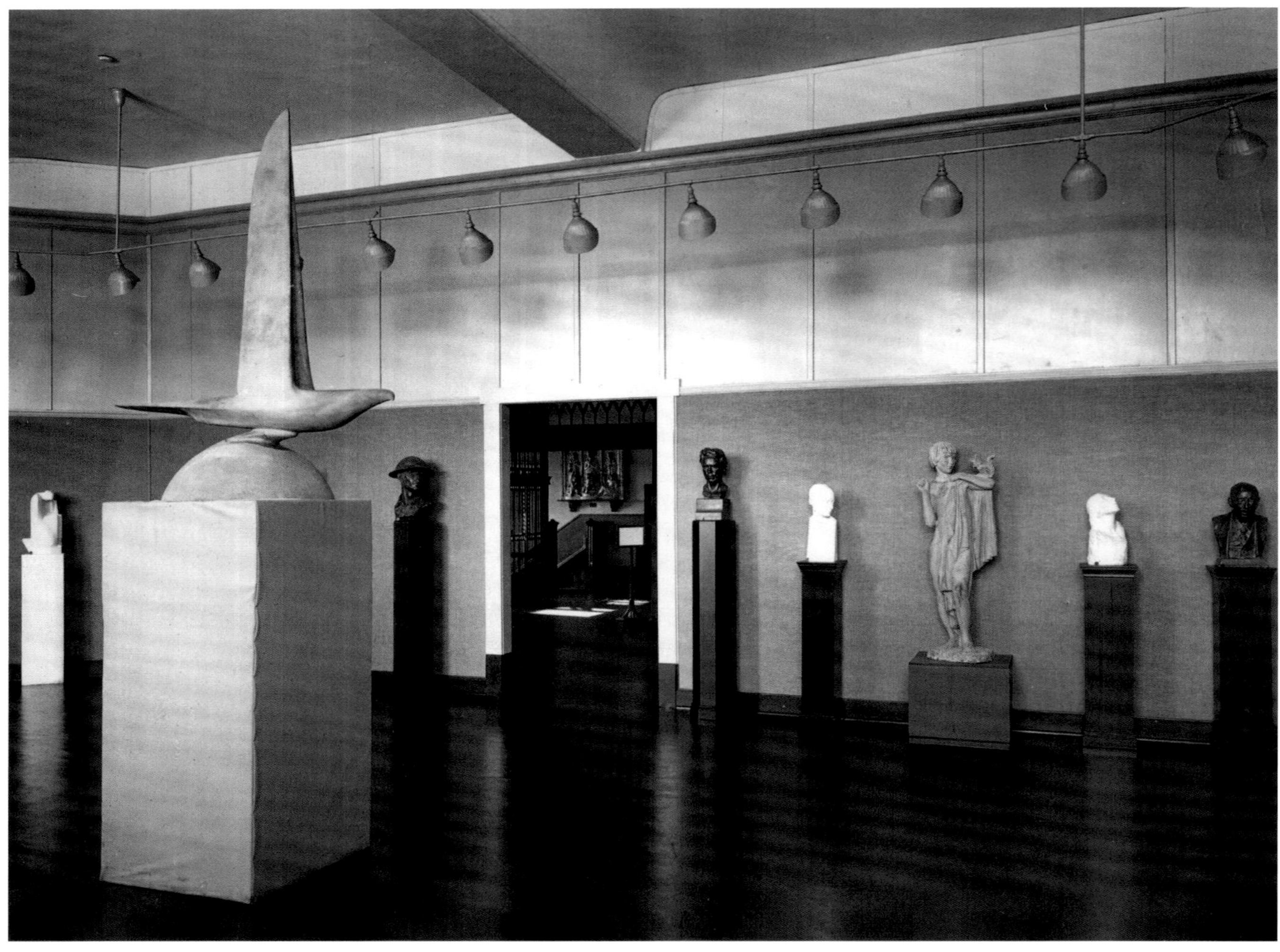

The Sculptors Society of Canada's first exhibition, 1928

Canada was late in forming an organization devoted entirely to the promotion of sculpture, lagging some thirty years behind Australia's Yarra Sculptors' Society (1898). This photograph of the Sculptors Society of Canada's first exhibition in 1928 shows Emanuel Hahn's sensitive evocation of a bird in *Flight* (c. 1926–1928). It was the most modernist work in the exhibition—most of the contributors clung to the academic style of the late nineteenth century.

Photo courtesy of the National Gallery of Canada Library and Archives, Ex 0099 b, 2/7.

a sculpture should be uplifting and beautiful. They shared Katherine Wallis's abhorrence of what she called the "willful use of ugliness and deformity" evident in the experiments of her modernist contemporaries in Paris.[13] Henri Hébert, whose own work remained largely allegorical and decorative, was more tolerant of the importance of significant form and the move to abstraction advocated by British art critic Roger Fry in 1909.[14] He felt that "Canadian artists, like those of every other nation, should have the right to represent abstractions, to translate ideas."[15] This too was part of the ssc's agenda, as its inaugural exhibition demonstrated with the prominence given to the work of one of its most active members. Even so, while many of Emanuel Hahn's sculptures from the late 1920s clearly had their origin in the organic abstract tradition established by an earlier generation of modernist sculptors like Constantin Brâncuşi (1876–1957) and Jean Arp (1886–1966), most of the ssc's members clung to pre-war modes and practices. This helped to thwart the incorporation of modernist tendencies into the mainstream of Canadian sculpture at the time.

Indeed, the ssc was popular because like many sculptors across the country its members were offering new subjects that reinforced the nationalist sentiment evident in Canada during the interwar years. Emanuel Hahn commemorated the exploration of the Canadian Arctic in his bust of Vilhjalmur Stefansson in 1929.[16] Beatrice Lennie celebrated Canada's bourgeoning airline industry, seen in the founding of Air Canada in 1937, in her sculpture *Night Flight* (1938).[17] In Winnipeg, "bedrock realist" sculptor Byllee Lang paid homage to manual labour in her bronze relief *Coal Miners* (c. 1944), commissioned by the Canadian Bureau of Miners in Ottawa.[18] Moving away from an abstract rendering of the figure, evident in *Gesture* (1927), Elizabeth Wyn Wood portrayed the broad-shouldered, bare-footed, courageous and above all recognizable women who had helped settle the Canadian Prairies. Her larger-than-life plaster cast *Linda* (c. 1932), along with *Woman Holding Skein* (1934–1935), captured the plight, especially during an era of droughts and economic depression, of the eastern European immigrants who had worked so hard to make a new life in Canada.[19]

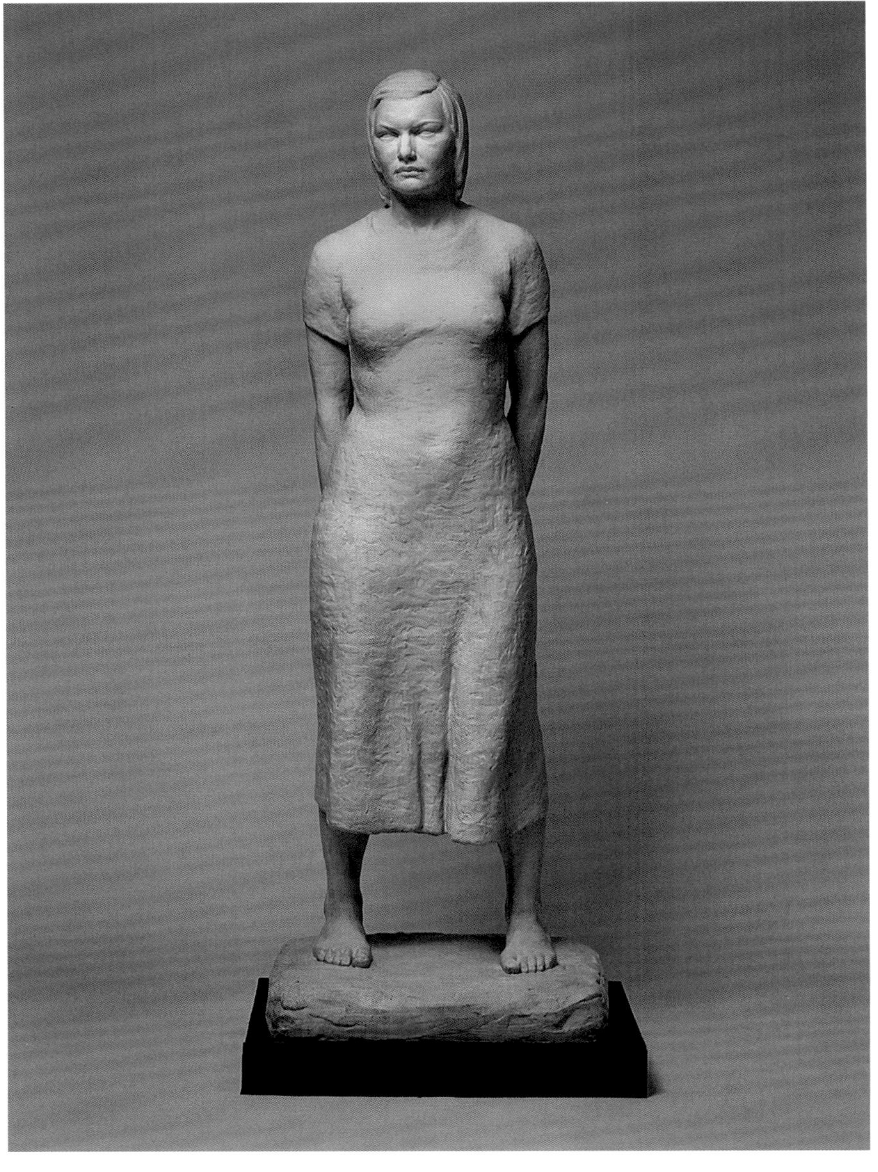

Elizabeth Wyn Wood
Linda, c. 1932
The interwar Depression saw farm incomes cut drastically, by as much as half in real terms, in Manitoba, Alberta and Saskatchewan. Responding to such economic realities, Wyn Wood set aside the high optimism inherent in her earlier Art Deco–style sculptures and turned to Social Realism. Speaking to the human figure and to the human condition, this style was well suited to her depiction of this steadfast farm girl, struggling to make ends meet during hard times on the Prairies.

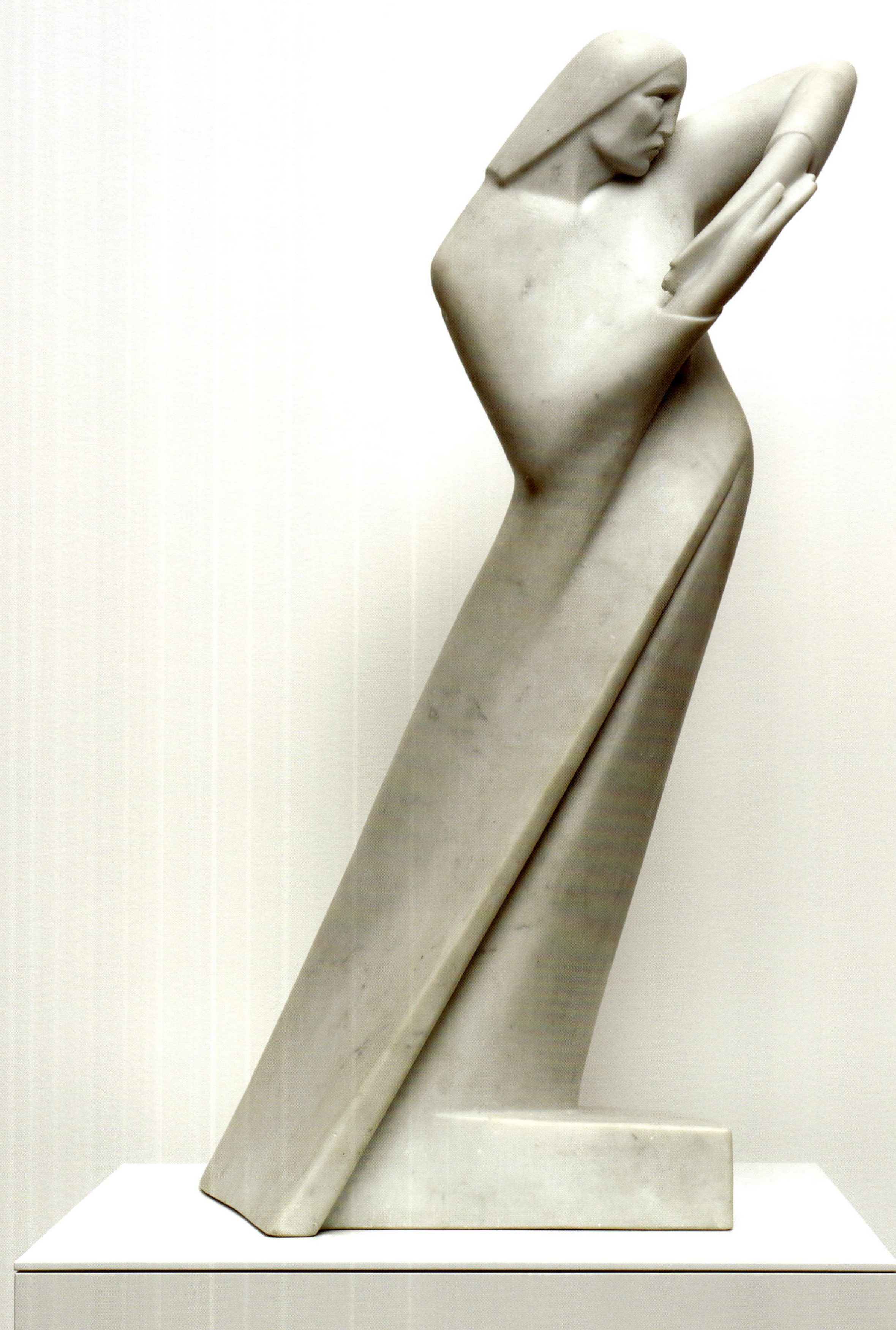

Non-Indigenous sculptors did not leave First Nations and Inuit people out of the new memorialization game, either. Marc-Aurèle de Foy Suzor-Coté created an arresting sculpture titled *Caughnawaga Women* (1924). Another Québécois, Sylvia Daoust (1902–2004), produced an equally realistic bust, *Young Huron*, in 1936.[20] Robert Flaherty's photographs and his widely viewed film *Nanook of the North* (1921) were the source of inspiration for Frances Loring's *Inuit Mother and Child* (1938).[21] And after making two successive visits to First Nations villages in British Columbia in the late 1920s, Loring's partner, Florence Wyle, turned her pencil sketches of totem poles along the Skeena River into plaster models of miniature totem poles.[22]

In 1935 Frances Loring paid tribute to Canada's favourite sport: ice hockey. The Socialist Realist style, evident in her heroic 2.3-metre-high *Goal Keeper* (c. 1935), did not look out of place when it was exhibited in Moscow in an exhibition sponsored in 1944, at the peak of wartime admiration for the Red Army, by the National Council for Canadian-Soviet Friendship.[23] But no other theme, not even ice hockey, expressed the nationalist sentiment in Canada more than the land. And, in the late 1920s, it was the landscape of northern Ontario that Elizabeth Wyn Wood took as her subject.

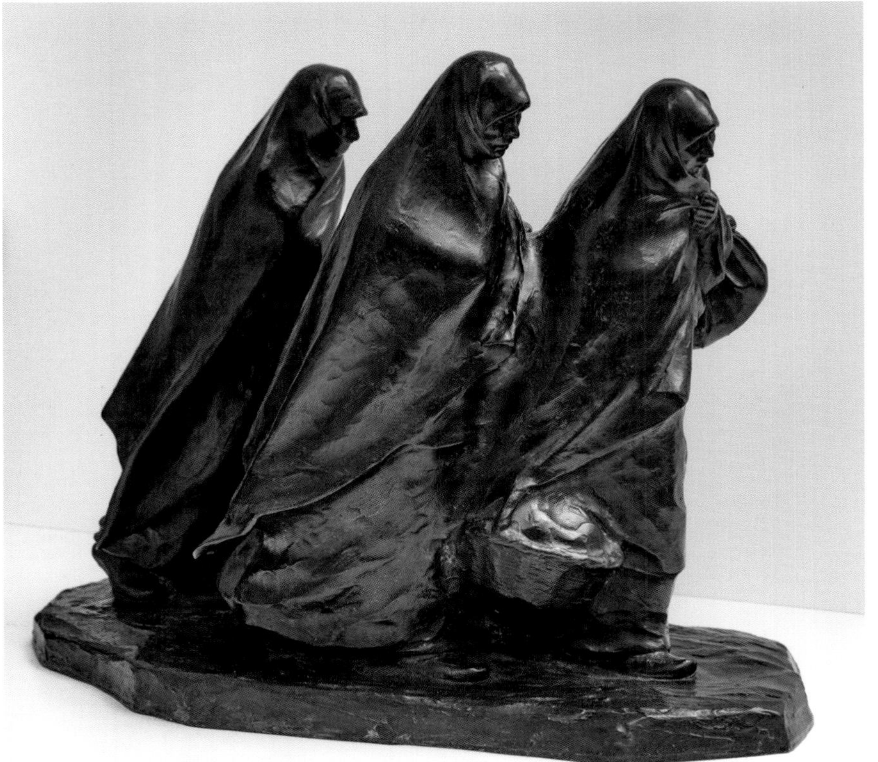

Marc-Aurèle de Foy Suzor-Coté
Caughnawaga Women, 1924
Painter and sculptor Marc-Aurèle de Foy Suzor-Coté, from Arthabaska, Quebec, was among the many Canadian artists who studied in Paris in the late nineteenth and early twentieth centuries. At Paris's École des Beaux-Arts, he encountered the work of Swedish sculptor Carl Milles (1875–1955), whose sculptures of Indigenous people clearly influenced the Canadian sculptor's depiction of three Caughnawaga (Kahnawake) women from the easternmost part of the Iroquois Confederacy's territory. Exhibition in Paris brought rewards to Suzor-Coté, who won the grand prize at the Paris Salon in 1894.

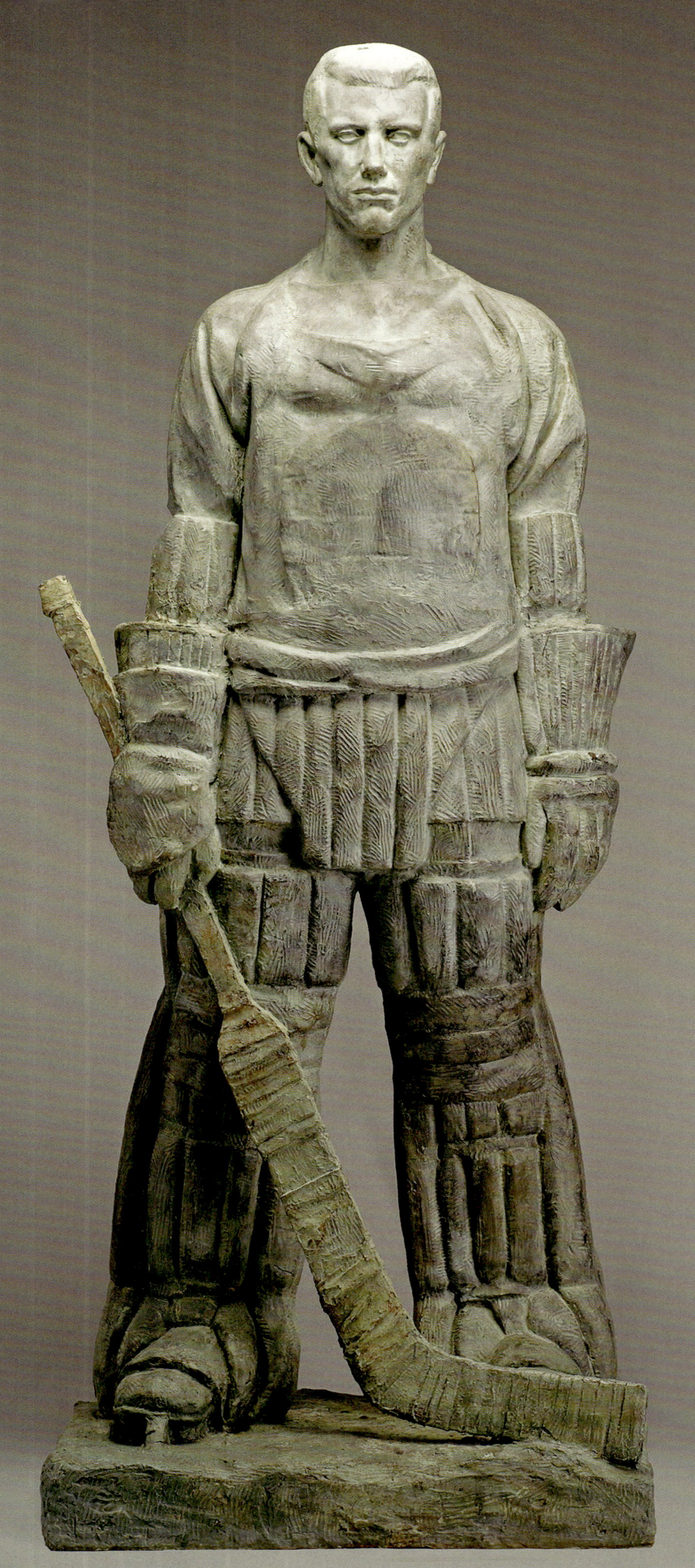

Born in Ontario in 1903, Elizabeth Wyn Wood had attended the Ontario College of Art before moving to New York City. There she studied modelling under Edward McCartan (1879–1947), the director of the sculpture department of the Beaux-Arts Institute of Design, and practised carving under the French-born figurative sculptor Robert Laurent (1890–1970). Before returning to Toronto, Wyn Wood was also exposed to the pioneer of modernist sculpture, the Romanian-born Constantin Brâncuşi, and to the highly expressive work of the nationalist Croatian artist Ivan Meštrović, whose figurative sculptures lay between the romanticism of Rodin and the more radical exponents of Social Realism. It was indeed Meštrović's work that resulted in Wyn Wood's highly stylized yet expressively abstract sculpture *Gesture* (1927).

Wyn Wood was equally responsive to the spirit of the machine age, as expressed over a decade earlier in the sculpture of Russian Constructivists like Naum Gabo (1890–1977) and in the writings of Walter Benjamin.[24] Like Gabo and Benjamin, Wyn Wood believed that new technologies and new materials could be adapted to contemporary sculpture. "Today we mine large quantities of tin in Canada," she commented, arguing that it was "a beautiful material of our plastic expression."[25] Tin was "a noble material" in Wyn Wood's eyes, and much under-valued. "No one would believe it was more expensive than bronze—they thought of tin cans, which are in fact iron."[26]

Following her sketching trips to Georgian Bay and the Muskokas, Wyn Wood reduced her sketches of glaciated rocks, twisted pines, solitary islands and turbulent weather to what art critic Jehanne Biétry Salinger described as "self-contained, serene, solemn [and even] austere" landscape sculptures.[27] The subjects that Wyn Wood chose to render in *Northern Island* (1927) and *Reef and Rainbow* (1927), and later in *Passing Rain* (1928–1929) and *Dead Tree* (1929), had already been popularized in the paintings of the Group of Seven.[28] But, according to one critic, Wyn Wood displayed a technique that was more brilliant than even the landscape paintings of the Group of Seven themselves.[29]

By the time the ssc formed in 1928, Wyn Wood was already casting her clay or plaster models in pewter, copper, brass, tin and aluminum rather than in bronze. And, just like Brâncuşi, who a generation earlier had heralded the end of monolithic sculpture by reducing the human figure into cubes and ovoids, Wyn Wood was now presenting the land as a series of geometrically simplified shapes and masses. Indeed, Bertram Brooker called her "a sister of Brancusi [*sic*]" in *The Yearbook of the Arts in Canada 1928–1929*.[30]

Yet Wyn Wood's achievements were all her own, as her contemporaries could now see. In embracing new materials and introducing themes that spoke to the country's nationalist sentiment, she achieved due recognition. No wonder that one observer saw Wyn Wood's combination of native subject matter and austere modernism—"the two well-nigh irreconcilable halves of Canadian inspiration today"—perfectly united in *Passing Rain*.[31] No wonder that Wyn Wood's plaster model for this work, carved in Orsera marble by sculptors at the Natale Pieri Workshop in Florence, shared first

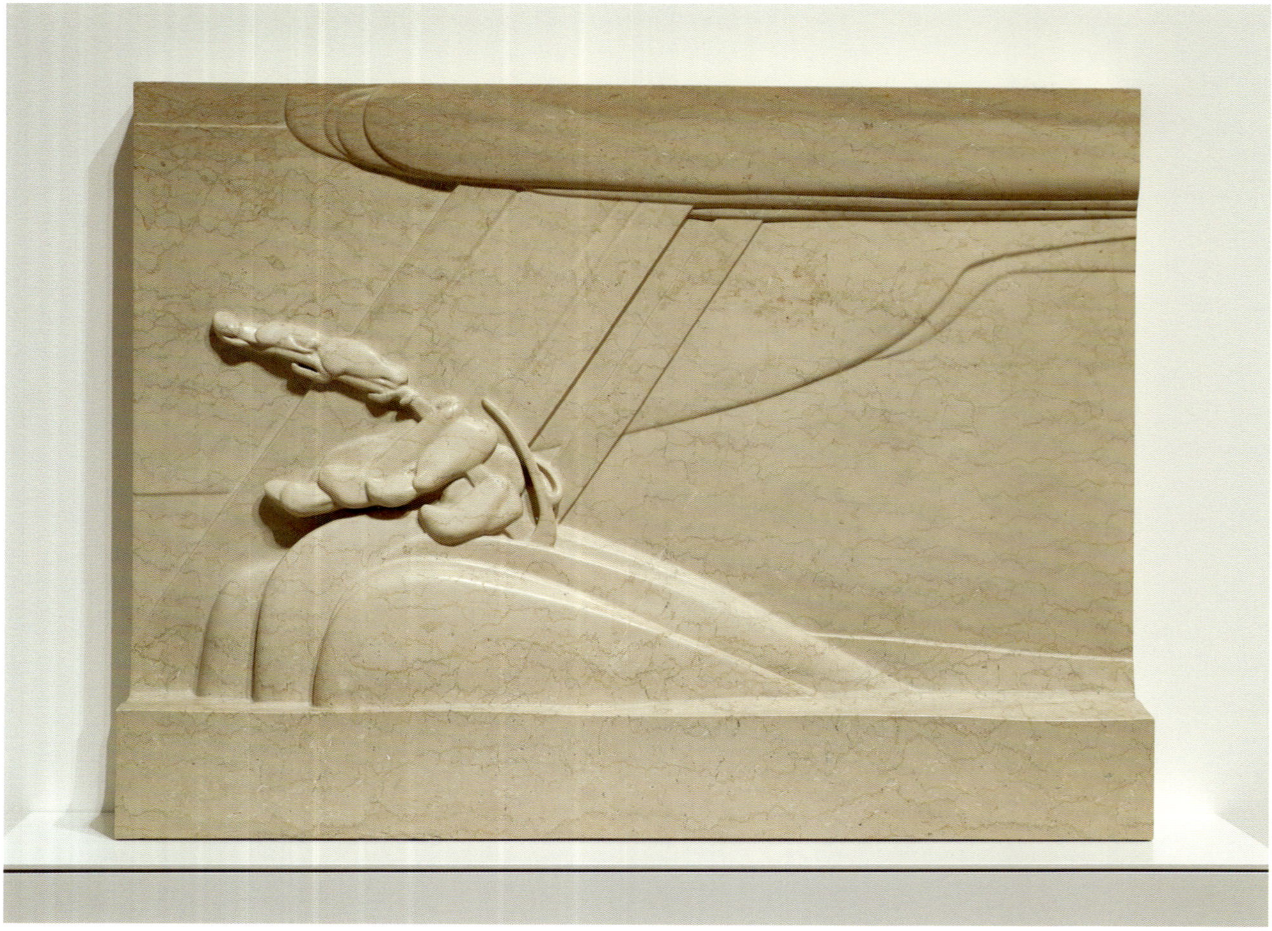

Elizabeth Wyn Wood
Passing Rain, 1928–1929
Elizabeth Wyn Wood tackled a subject that was at the heart of the Canadian psyche: the landscape. It had already been explored in a modern idiom on canvas by the Ontario-based Group of Seven, but Wyn Wood brought volume and mass to the subject. Using new materials and mechanical precision characteristic of the machine age, Wyn Wood rendered her vision of the northern Ontario landscape in *Passing Rain*. By so doing she demonstrated that wind-bent trees, solitary islands and quickly changing weather were subjects as well suited to sculpture as to painting.

prize with a sculpture by Montreal's Sylvia Daoust at the inaugural Lord Willingdon Competition in 1929. And no wonder that one of the country's leading art critics, Blodwen Davies, called Wyn Wood "perhaps the most advanced and adventurous sculptor working in Canada today."[32]

In Quebec, the story was rather different. There, sculptors like Alfred Laliberté and Sylvia Daoust were attempting "to legitimize French-Canadian society through reference to a mythical French peasant base," and to rekindle liturgical sculpture.[33] At first glance, Alfred Laliberté's *L'Ère de la Méchanique* (1934), might suggest that he had created a transitional work positioned somewhere between Rodin and Wyn Wood. But this is surely a misleading impression. For Laliberté was not embracing the machine age in *L'Ère de la Méchanique,* but rather denouncing the invasion of the machine into sculpture.

Technological, scientific and industrial changes that were taking place in Quebec affected rural areas quite as much as the province's cities. The impact was manifested in a sense of alienation, displacement and anomie—feelings with which traditional forms of religion were unable to cope. And the cultural community in Quebec, as seen in the years before the Great War, often responded by looking to the past. Nova Scotia folklorist Helen Creighton collected habitant songs, a process begun in the 1860s by pioneering folklorist and historian Ernest Gagnon. Years later, from the mid-1920s, National Museum of Canada ethnologist Marius Barbeau organized folk festivals that were sponsored by the Canadian Pacific Railway. Not surprisingly, when the nationwide festivals were held in Quebec they featured eighteenth- and nineteenth-century religious carvings alongside contemporary religious and secular folk art sculpture,

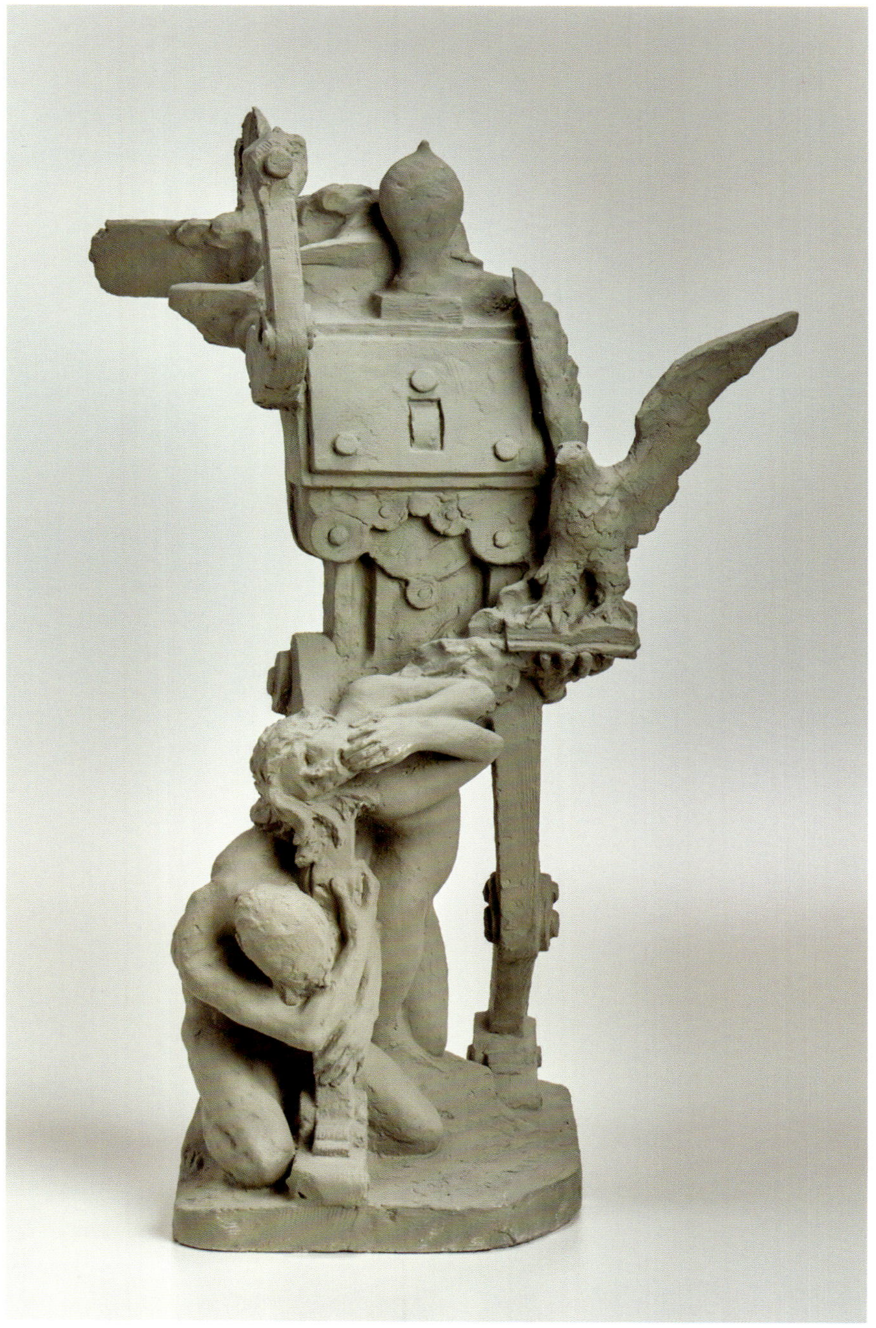

Alfred Laliberté
L'Ère de la Méchanique, c. 1934
For Montreal-based artist Alfred Laliberté, industrialization was both an agent of the Anglo-Canadian ruling class and an invasion from the United States—all of it contributing to the destruction of the traditional rural life of Quebec. The Depression accentuated this negative view: in May 1933, 1.5 million Canadians were dependent upon government funds for their survival. Like the machine in Charlie Chaplin's 1936 film *Modern Times*, Laliberté's machine-like creature has gone out of control as it pounds the man and the woman. What was worse, it seems to ask: employment or unemployment?

produced by Georges E. Tremblay (1878–1939), Joseph Georges Trudelle (1877–1950), Médard Bourgault (1897–1967), Louis Parent (1908–1982) and Lauréat Vallière (1888–1973).

Art galleries also mounted exhibitions that spoke to the tradition of religious and secular carving in Quebec. The Art Gallery of Toronto's *Painting, Sculpture and Wood Carving of French Canada* accompanied the paintings of the Group of Seven in 1926. In 1935 the Art Association of Montreal paid tribute with the exhibition *Traditional Arts of French Canada: Unbroken Tradition*. And in 1946 the Detroit Institute of Arts showed religious carvings of the seventeenth and eighteenth centuries alongside hand-woven rugs and folk art in *The Arts of French Canada, 1613–1870*.

During the interwar period, Laliberté built on his earlier interest in rural Quebec. A commission from the Provincial Secretary of Quebec saw him produce a series of sculptures on the legends, trades and customs of the habitant. Within five years he had cast over two hundred clay models into bronze. Departing from his pre-war focus on rendering not more than two figures, many of these new works, like *L'Apprentissage d'Art* (1928–1932), had even more. Multi-figurative sculptures like this reinforced the view, promoted by art historians and in Laliberté's own writings, that an unbroken thread existed between Quebec artists of the past and the present.[34]

This was an influential claim, increasingly accepted during the interwar

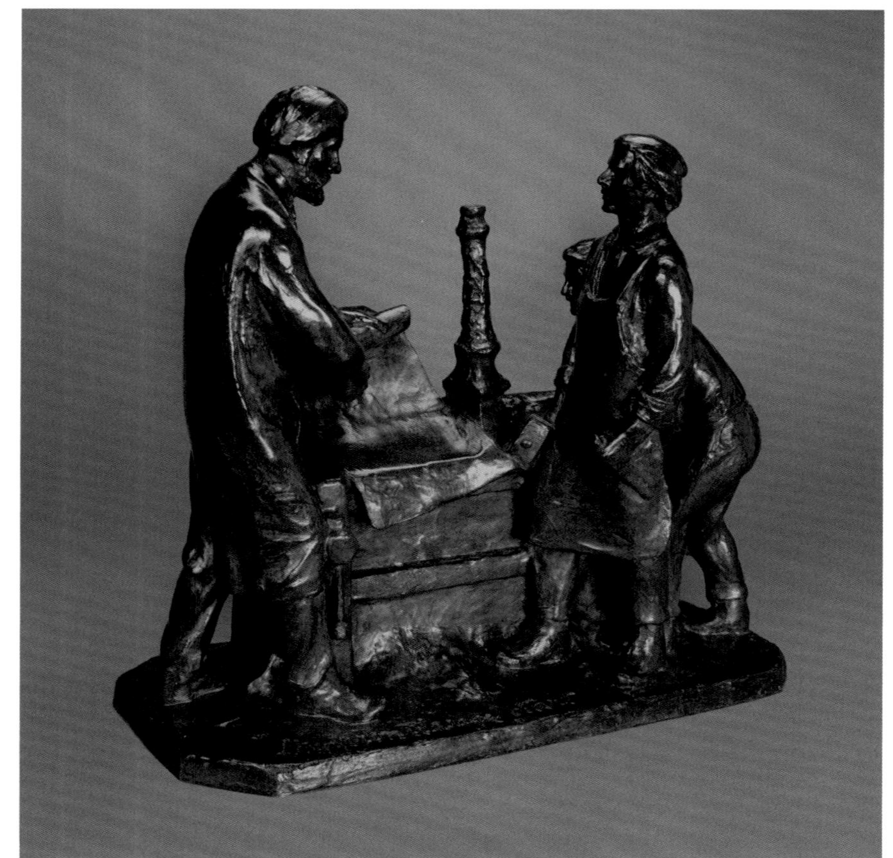

Alfred Laliberté

L'Apprentissage d'Art, **1928–1932**

In 1928 Alfred Laliberté received a commission from the Provincial Secretary of Quebec to produce sculptures depicting rural life in Quebec. Within a couple of years he had made over two hundred small-scale, realistic works in bronze, of which *L'Apprentissage d'Art* is one. Though it depicts only two students, at the height of sculptor Louis Quévillon's career—the late 1700s to early 1800s—his workshop had given board and lodging as well as instruction to up to fifteen apprentices, who had helped him fulfill commissions for no fewer than forty parishes in Quebec. Laliberté thus sought to invoke the inspiration of an unbroken link between sculptors in eighteenth- and nineteenth-century New France and his own contemporaries in interwar Quebec—not just in technique but in their role in sustaining an organically united way of life.

years. Indeed, one critic reaffirmed Laliberté's belief that his work "would serve as an invaluable document for future generations."[35] Another saw Laliberté's habitant series as providing a "living instruction" and a valuable document "for future generations."[36]

Thus, ideas associated with Quebec's nationalism and patriotism held, as historian Nicole Cloutier has pointed out, "the center-stage in politics and literature, and Laliberté's sculptures, providing concrete illustrations of them, were timely."[37] The Art Association of Montreal and the Musée du Québec were among the institutions to put Laliberté's new work on show. But here the reception was mixed. One critic wanted a more realistic representation of the habitant. In Léo-Pol Morin's view, Laliberté's sculptures were "more literary and symbolic than sculptural."[38] While another commentator wondered how a sculptor of Laliberté's standing could "squander his talent on anecdotal works, treating subjects that belong to painters and writers."[39] In the end Laliberté's group tableaux were anecdotal. They were an exercise in nostalgia.

The government of Quebec only acquired 100 of the 214 works that Laliberté produced for the commission. Laliberté attempted to sell the rest through the Watson Art Galleries. But, as the account books of the Montreal gallery show, this was not the kind of work that private collectors wanted. Insisting in his memoir that posterity was "the greatest glory, and the only one that I aspire to," Laliberté was, not surprisingly, dismayed.[40]

If Laliberté had his own agenda, so did another sculptor from Quebec, Sylvia Daoust. She responded less to the newly politicized interest in the habitant than to the revival of religious carving, thus reinforcing Newton MacTavish's belief that "the Latin races," as the art critic termed French Canadians, shared a "fondness for carvings and images in their church."[41] Daoust's rendering of religious subjects did not begin, however, until after her meeting in 1937 with Benedictine monk and architect Paul Bellot (1876–1944).

In making her career as a sculptor, Daoust had attended the Montreal School of Fine Arts, the Montreal Council of Arts and Manufactures (1915–1916) and the École des Beaux-Arts (1923–1930). Receiving a government scholarship in 1929, she then studied in France with the French liturgical sculptor Henri Charlier (1883–1975). In Paris, and later in New York City, Daoust also encountered the sculpture of Auguste Rodin, Charles Despiau (1874–1946), Antoine Bourdelle (1861–1929) and Ivan Meštrović. On her return to Canada in 1930, Daoust taught at the École des Beaux-Arts de Québec from 1930 to 1943 (and at the Montreal School of Fine Arts from 1943 to 1968). And, as noted earlier, she initially rendered secular themes in works like *Young Huron* (1936).

In 1937, however, all of this suddenly changed. Prompted by Bellot's revulsion at the cheap religious plaster of Paris statues that had flooded the market since the middle of the nineteenth century, Daoust set aside secular themes and supported Bellot's mission by reviving religious subject matter. Working from her Dorval studio on the outskirts of Montreal, she now abandoned the flamboyant Beaux-Arts style and clay modelling characteristic of her earlier sculptures and began carving directly in stone

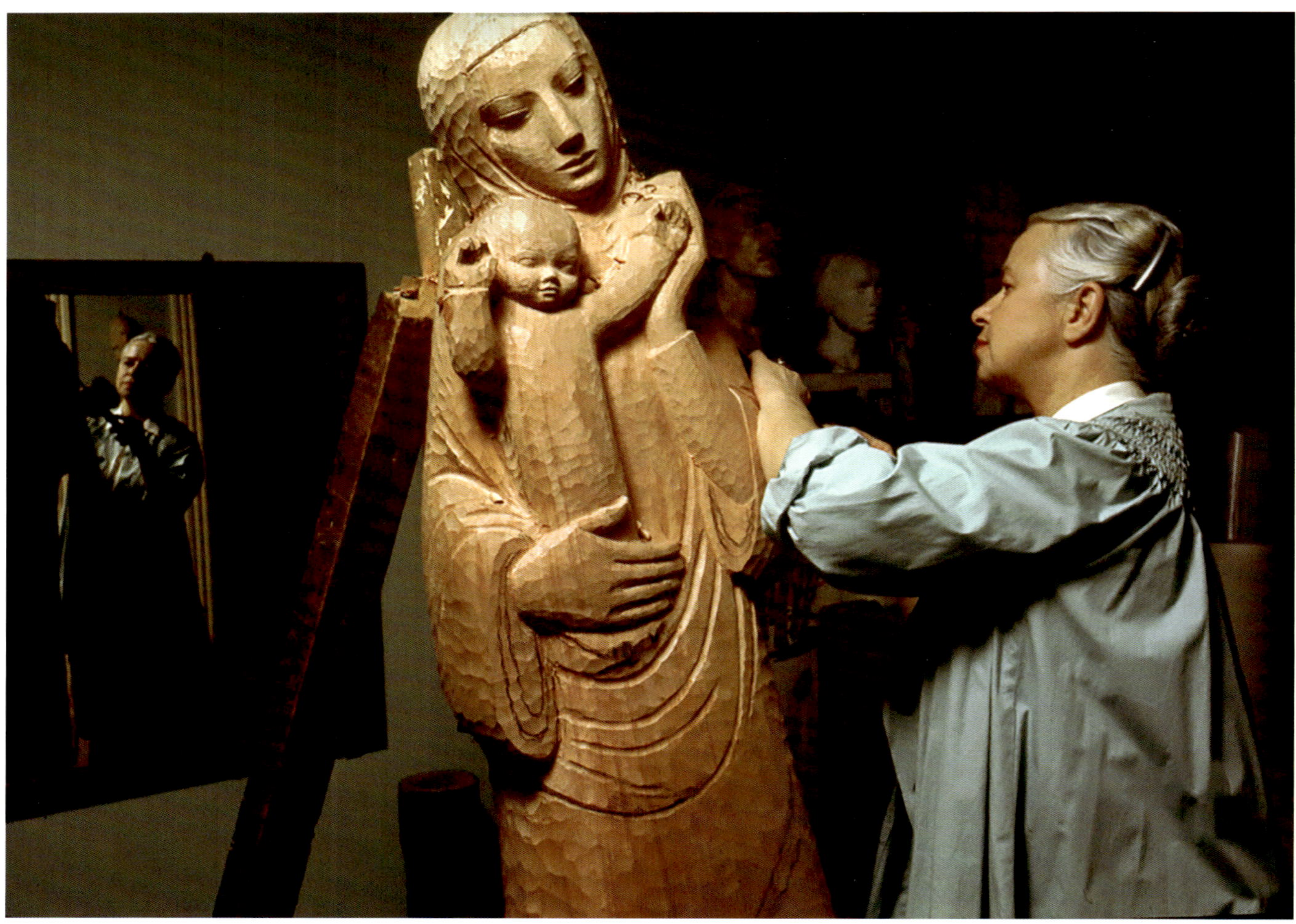

and wood. Over the course of the next few decades she produced dozens of Madonnas and other religious figures for cathedrals and churches throughout Quebec.

To many, it seemed that Daoust had revived religious carving in Quebec through her own spontaneous expression of religious feeling. But she did not do this simply by drawing on the stylistic vocabulary of Quebec's seventeenth- and eighteenth-century sculptors. Rather, Daoust combined the formal characteristics of line and volume inherent in the modernist idiom with the austerity of the unadorned sculpture of the Middle Ages. "Rarely," as Walter Abell observed, "did the more baroque Madonnas of earlier French Canada equal this modern one either in depth of feeling or in unity of design."[42] Described in Bertram Brooker's *Yearbook of the Arts in Canada* (1929) merely as "romantic in conception and delicate in modeling," Daoust's sculptures showed—despite Brooker's dismissively sexist comment—that carving directly in wood or in stone was as well suited to religious themes in the twentieth century as it had been during the seventeenth and eighteenth centuries in New France.[43]

Daoust was not the only sculptor in the country to set modelling in clay or plaster aside in favour of direct carving. In the 1920s the art critic for the *Montreal Herald* had noted that Paris-based Katherine Wallis was "the apostle of an entirely new cult in the realm of mallet and chisel."[44] And, during the late 1930s, a new generation of sculptors, among them Alberta-born E.B. Cox (1914–2003) and the Québécois Julien Hébert (1917–1994) and Charles Daudelin (1920–2001), likewise preferred to carve rather than model their sculptures. In doing so, they rejected the example of the clay modellers, many of whom had a penchant for detail and, in casting their clay model into bronze, were usually one step away from the original work. Similarly, they avoided Rodin's emotional engagement with his subject. These young sculptors, whose careers would blossom after the Second World War, were more in tune with British sculptor Henry Moore (1898–1986), who declared in 1930 that "Sculpture in stone should look honestly like stone… to make it look like flesh and blood, hair and dimples is coming down to the level of the stage conjuror."[45]

Beatrice Lennie was in the first graduating class at the Vancouver School of Decorative and Applied Arts. After she left the city's first art school in 1929, Lennie moved to California, where she studied life modelling and carving under left-leaning sculptor Ralph Stackpole (1885–1973) at the California School of Fine Arts in San Francisco. Armed with the example of Stackpole's monumental Socialist Realist style, Lennie returned to Vancouver in 1934 and soon became the province's leading sculptor. She supported herself by teaching at the short-lived BC College of Art as well as at her own sculpture school and by giving classes at the Vancouver Art Gallery. Lennie also fulfilled numerous public commissions: for the Hotel Vancouver, the newly constructed Pattullo Bridge spanning the Fraser River, and for the Federal Building in downtown Vancouver. And, when she had time, Lennie created non-commissioned sculptures.

As was evident in Katherine Wallis's earlier experience in Paris, making a career as a sculptor in a man's world required physical strength and stamina—attributes art critics rarely assigned to women. Such a career was out of tandem with the widely held view that, due to their "biological, social and environmental" situation, female painters and sculptors could not "emerge—as men occasionally do—triumphant."[46] Like Wallis, however, Beatrice Lennie was more concerned with form and mass, with light and shadow, than with the views of her sexist critics. And, like Wallis again, she did have supporters. To the art critic of the *Canadian Review of Music and Art*, the "simple massiveness" of Lennie's sculpture *Repose* (c. 1934) evoked "the bulk and volume of Crown Mountain which dominates the Burrard Inlet and Harbour [in Vancouver]." J. Delisle Parker approvingly suggested that this work's primitive force reminded him of the sculptures of Henri Gaudier-Brzeska (1891–1915), who had perished in the Great War. The art critic also commented: "For a woman of no special physical strength but armed with courage and vision—behind her goggles to ward off the dangerous chips—admiration and praise are due in no small measure." It is true that, after Beatrice Lennie, the notion that modellers were the conceivers of a sculpture, whereas carvers were mere artisans, came to seem obsolete. Indeed, as Parker further declared, Michelangelo would have approved of Lennie's work.[47]

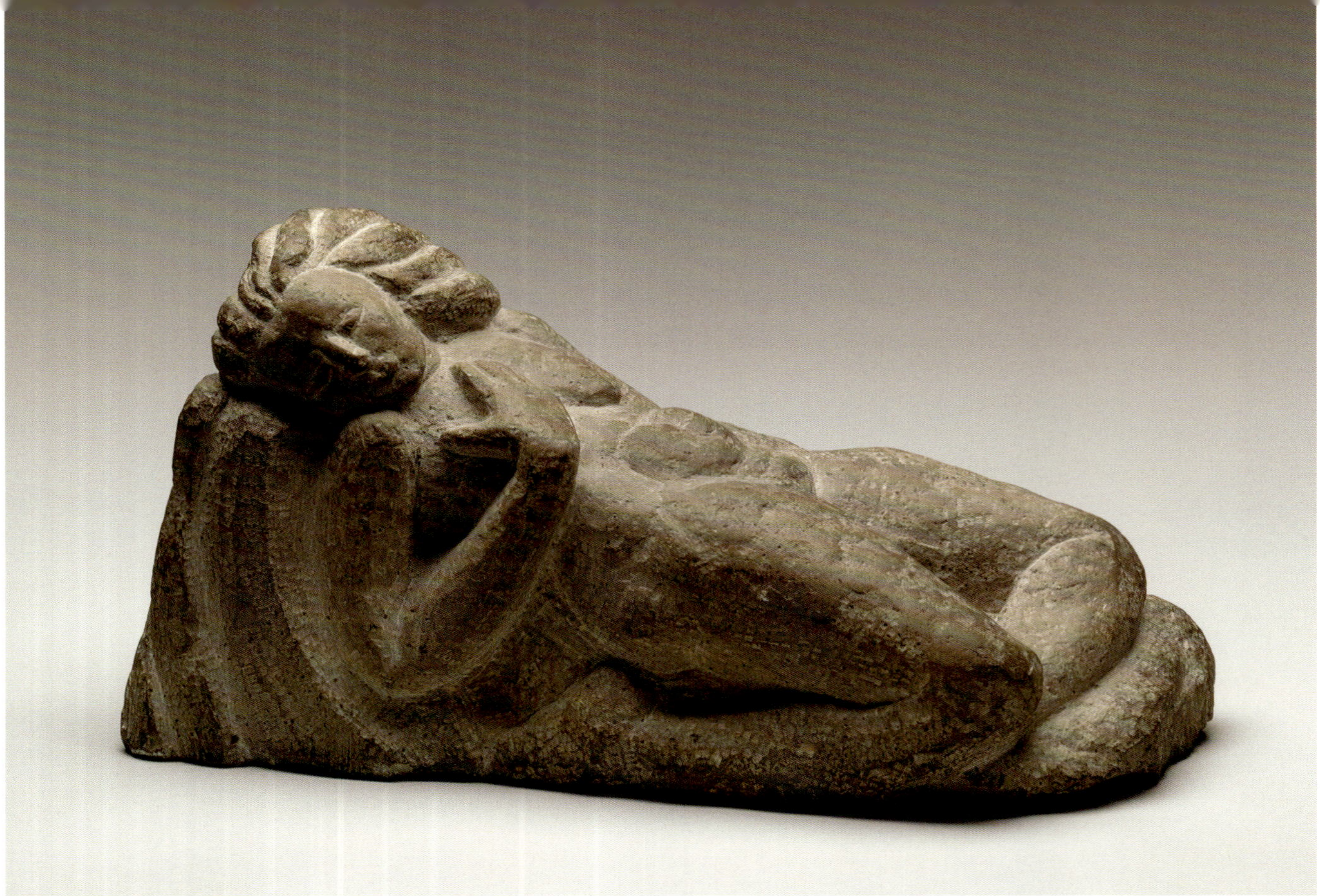

Beatrice Lennie
Repose, c. 1934

When Beatrice Lennie arrived at the California School of Design in 1929 she had been modelling her sculptures in clay and faithfully rendering her subjects. By the time she returned to Vancouver five years later, she was carving directly in stone—just like the First Nations artists who worked in that material thousands of years before European contact. And also like her Indigenous counterparts, Lennie was more concerned with representing an idea than a realistic representation of her subject.

These were high claims, but Parker went further—much further. He made clear in his admiring article that Lennie was not the only sculptor in the province to have carved directly in stone. He compared her sculpture *Repose* with the "rugged vitality of design and purpose of artistic expression" that was characteristic of the three-thousand-year-old sculpture *Sechelt Image* (c. 1600 BCE), housed in the Vancouver Museum. In this way Parker had discerned a continuity—rather in the manner of contemporary art critics in Quebec—by affirming "an unbroken tradition" between non-Indigenous contemporary modernist sculpture and Northwest Coast Indigenous stone sculpture. "In the whole history of Art," Parker insisted, there is "a straight line of tradition in creative sculpture."[48]

True, First Nations and Inuit artists had been carving in stone and wood—and many other materials—for millennia. During the 1920s the Canadian Pacific Railway encouraged First Nations artists to demonstrate their carving skills at their folk festivals, and since 1889 the Banff Indian Days in the Rockies had featured the arts and culture of the Stoney-Assiniboine people. First Nations families had also participated in itinerant Wild West and medicine shows in Atlantic Canada, using the public performance space as a venue to sell their art.[49] Working from their outposts in the eastern Arctic, officials of the Hudson's Bay Company (HBC) had encouraged the Inuit to produce carvings for sale in their department stores in the south. Knowing that their clientele possessed romantic notions about the "primitive," "untutored" Inuit who lived on the land, HBC factors wanted Inuit artists to produce carvings that featured traditional themes. As we have already seen, however, many Inuit artists preferred to make sculptures that spoke to the rapid acculturation of their people, like *Man in Rocking Chair Playing Concertina* (c. 1929–1931), carved by an unidentified artist near Pond Inlet on Baffin Island.

But, as pointed out in an earlier chapter, it was only since the early decades of the twentieth century that the Canadian Handicrafts Guild (CHG) had been marketing Indigenous art, and only since the Great War that civic, provincial and the federal governments, along with art galleries and museums, devoted limited attention to Indigenous culture. Some non-Indigenous people saw the marketing of First Nations and Inuit art as a means for alleviating poverty. Others saw it complementing the burgeoning tourist industry. While still others sought to exert some measure of influence over Indigenous culture in order to bring it within the ambit of the broader Canadian nationalist project.

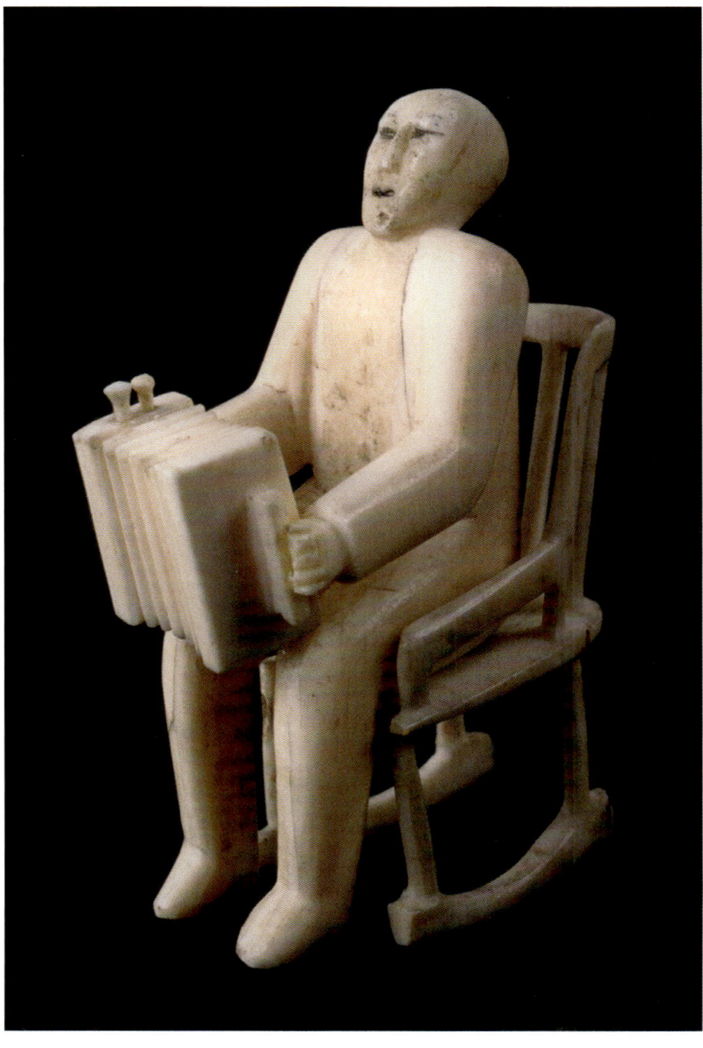

Artist Unknown
Man in Rocking Chair Playing Concertina,
c. 1929–1931
The recruitment of a white clientele for Inuit art in southern Canada reinforced a conventional preference for carvings of animals and Inuit men and women. This was a function of the market rather than of the innate intentions of the artists who obligingly produced "art for strangers." But this artist from Pond Inlet on Baffin Island in Nunavut clearly preferred to depict the present, not the past. Moreover, the technical ability with which the artist portrays a man playing an accordion is a tour de force.

This created a role for government intervention. Fearing "that an increase in demands for curios and souvenirs, coupled with a changing material culture, would soon lead to the disappearance of native articles," the Department of Indian Affairs, now called Indigenous and Northern Affairs Canada, recognized a potential in the production of what they called "Eskimo handicrafts."[50] During the 1920s the department thus encouraged Indigenous students in residential and industrial schools across the country to produce traditional carvings. Hoping that the sale of their work would provide a much-needed income once young Indigenous men and women left school, the government also began marketing it at industrial and agricultural fairs in Brandon, Regina, Edmonton and Calgary.

But First Nations sculpture was tolerated within the dominant society if it was either "old" or transformed by non-Indigenous artists for business or exhibition purposes. In 1917, at the Victoria Memorial Museum, Canada's national museum, archaeologist Harlan I. Smith wrote a paper titled "The Use of Prehistoric Canadian Art for Commercial Design." "These motifs," Smith suggested, "may be used as they are or may be conventionalized or dissected or multiplied or developed in several of these ways."[51] Ten years later, the Victoria Memorial Museum joined the National Gallery in mounting the *Exhibition of Canadian West Coast Art—Native and Modern*. This seminal exhibition set the landscape paintings of Emily Carr and the Group of Seven and the bronze totem pole sculptures of Florence Wyle alongside the "primitive" carvings of largely anonymous with the exception of Haida artist Charles Edenshaw—First Nations artists. As Eric Brown made clear in the catalogue accompanying the exhibition, his intention was "to mingle for the first time the art work of the Canadian West Coast tribes with that of our more sophisticated artists in an endeavor to analyze their relationships to one another, if such exist, and particularly to enable this primitive and interesting art to take a definite place as one of the most valuable of Canada's artistic productions."[52]

Brown seemed to forget, or was unaware, that this was not the first time that Indigenous carvings had been exhibited with non-Indigenous paintings and sculpture. In 1905, under the patronage of Governor General Earl Grey, portraits of Chiefs Poundmaker, Big Bear and Crowfoot by Edmund Morris (1871–1913) had been exhibited with "artifacts" produced by un-named First Nations artists. And a few months before the *Exhibition of Canadian West Coast Art—Native and Modern* opened in Ottawa in 1927, Paris's Musée du Jeu de Paume opened *La Première Exposition d'Art Canadien à Paris*, displaying the sculpture of Northwest Coast artists together with paintings by the Group of Seven, among others. Assuming that the Group of Seven would steal the show, Canadian officials were taken aback when French art critics, who had a penchant for Surrealist art, made it clear that they preferred the "exceptional sculptures" of Canada's Indigenous people.[53]

The idea that totem poles could promote tourism prompted the government-owned Canadian National Railway (CNR), in conjunction with the Department of Indian Affairs and the Victoria Memorial Museum, to launch a "salvage" operation of totem poles in Gitxsan villages along the Upper

Skeena River in 1924. Some totem poles were moved closer to the tracks and then covered with garish-coloured house paint in order to enhance their visibility to passing railway tourists. Other totem poles from the same area were sawn up, covered in a coat of "preservative" black paint and shipped to Toronto, where two of them were reassembled, "restored" and installed in the stairwell of Toronto's Royal Ontario Museum, where they can be viewed to this day.[54]

The mantra that Indigenous culture was dead or dying was itself a long time dying. In the 1920s most officials still subscribed to the notion that Indigenous art existed only in the past and not in the present. They justified the restoration and removal of totem poles, and the appropriation of Indigenous culture for their museums and businesses alike, by claiming that Indigenous people did not "value their own artistic monuments."[55] Only at the end of the interwar period was this notion challenged in a few quarters by the counter-claim that Indigenous people were not only *still* producing sculpture but that what they produced was *art*.

In 1941 the Vancouver Art Gallery became one of the first institutions to display contemporary works by Indigenous artists alongside the historic sculptures of their ancestors. A year later, the provincial museum followed suit by launching an annual *Exhibition of Modern Indian Arts and Crafts*. Both exhibitions thus put contemporary work, albeit of largely anonymous First Nations artists, into a public art gallery.

And before this, in 1939, the federal government, committed to adorning the entrance of the Canadian pavilion at the New York World's Fair with totem poles, turned to Kwakwaka'wakw artist Mungo Martin for help when they encountered difficulty in finding suitable "old" totem poles for display. Martin produced rough sketch designs of two poles. The Indian agent for Alert Bay, M.S. Todd, approved them and Martin was commissioned to carve two 5.2-metre-high totem poles, for which he would be paid the well-deserved sum of $500.[56] When the country's prime minister, W.L. Mackenzie King, saw Martin's carvings at the entrance of the Canadian pavilion, he was apparently "shocked"—perhaps as though seeing a ghost.[57]

When Mungo Martin received his commission in 1939, carving totem poles was technically illegal, and the ban on holding a potlatch was not rescinded until 1951. Yet it was only common sense that, as one First Nations person who attended an illegal potlatch hosted by chiefs from Hazelton and Gitsegukla, BC, in November 1939 observed, "there was no more harm in Indians passing out gifts in such occasions than there was in whites making gifts during the Christmas season."[58] Moreover, when Willie Seaweed raised a memorial pole that acknowledged the death of King George V in 1936, the government turned a blind eye. Dedicating a totem pole to a British sovereign enabled Seaweed and his fellow artists at Kingcome Inlet to "demonstrate their loyalty to the Crown and reposition themselves as valuable citizens of the nation"—all of which, as art historian Leslie Dawn has suggested, "reversed the situation in which Native culture was appropriated by the nation; instead, imperial figures were appropriated into Native culture." The underlying irony here was defiance: "if it was

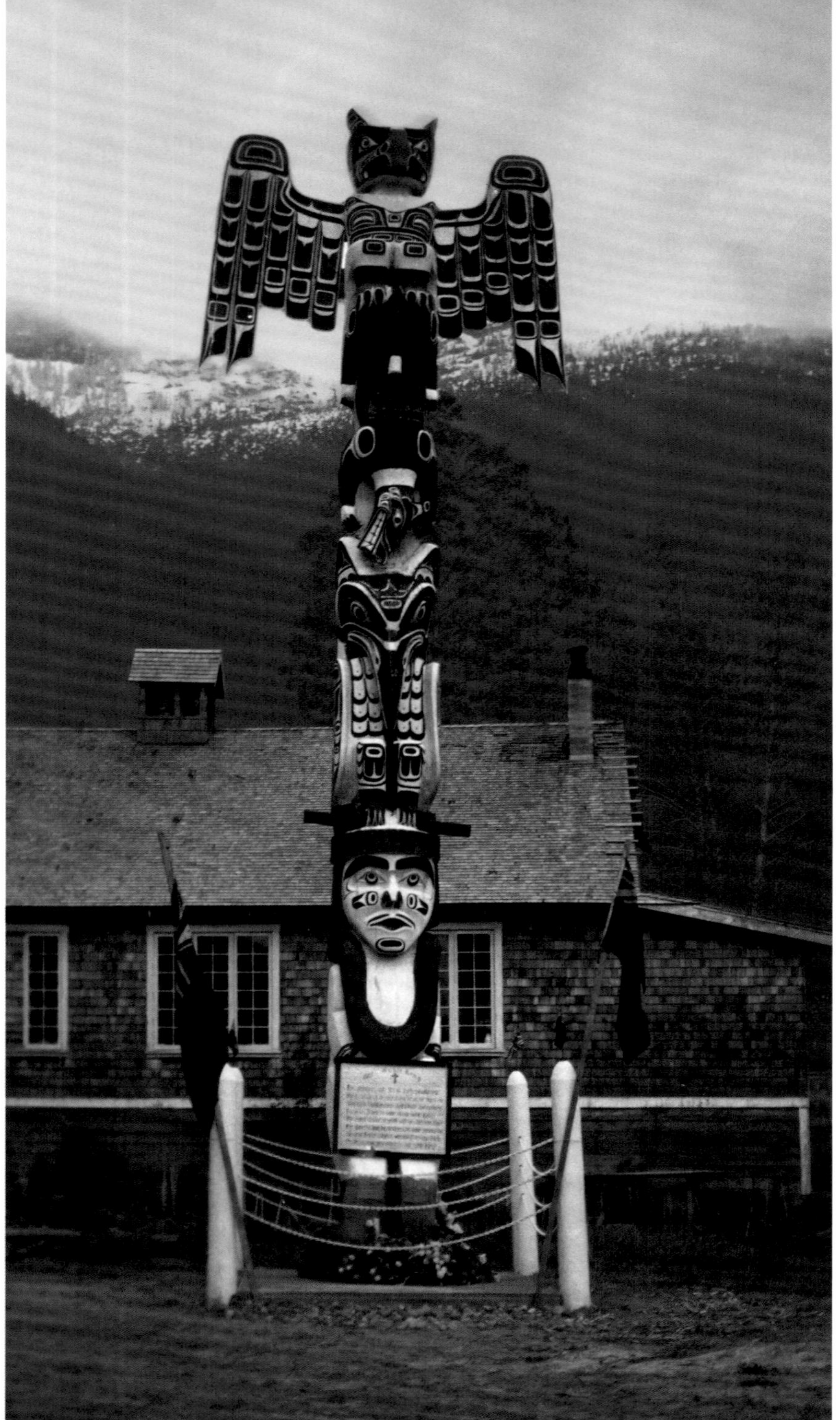

Willie Seaweed
Memorial Pole to Commemorate the Death of King George V, **1936**
During the 1930s, Willie Seaweed broke every convention. He used high-gloss red, orange, black, blue and green enamel paints; he employed a compass and a straight-edge to make his carvings more precise. Culturally too, he challenged convention. With the assistance of Kwakwaka'wakw artists Tom Patch Wamiss and Herbert Johnson, he incorporated the imperial figure of King George V into First Nations culture on this totem pole, which was raised in the monarch's memory in 1936.

permissible to hold ceremonies celebrating the ascension of the king, then why," Dawn continued, "would the nation view similar ceremonies for the ascension of a chief as illegal?"[59]

Mungo Martin was aware of this irony. And it was reinforced four years before the anti-potlatch law was rescinded, when his niece, the sculptor Ellen Neel (1916–1966), also known as Kakaso'las, invited him to help her restore and carve new poles for the University of British Columbia's Totem Park.

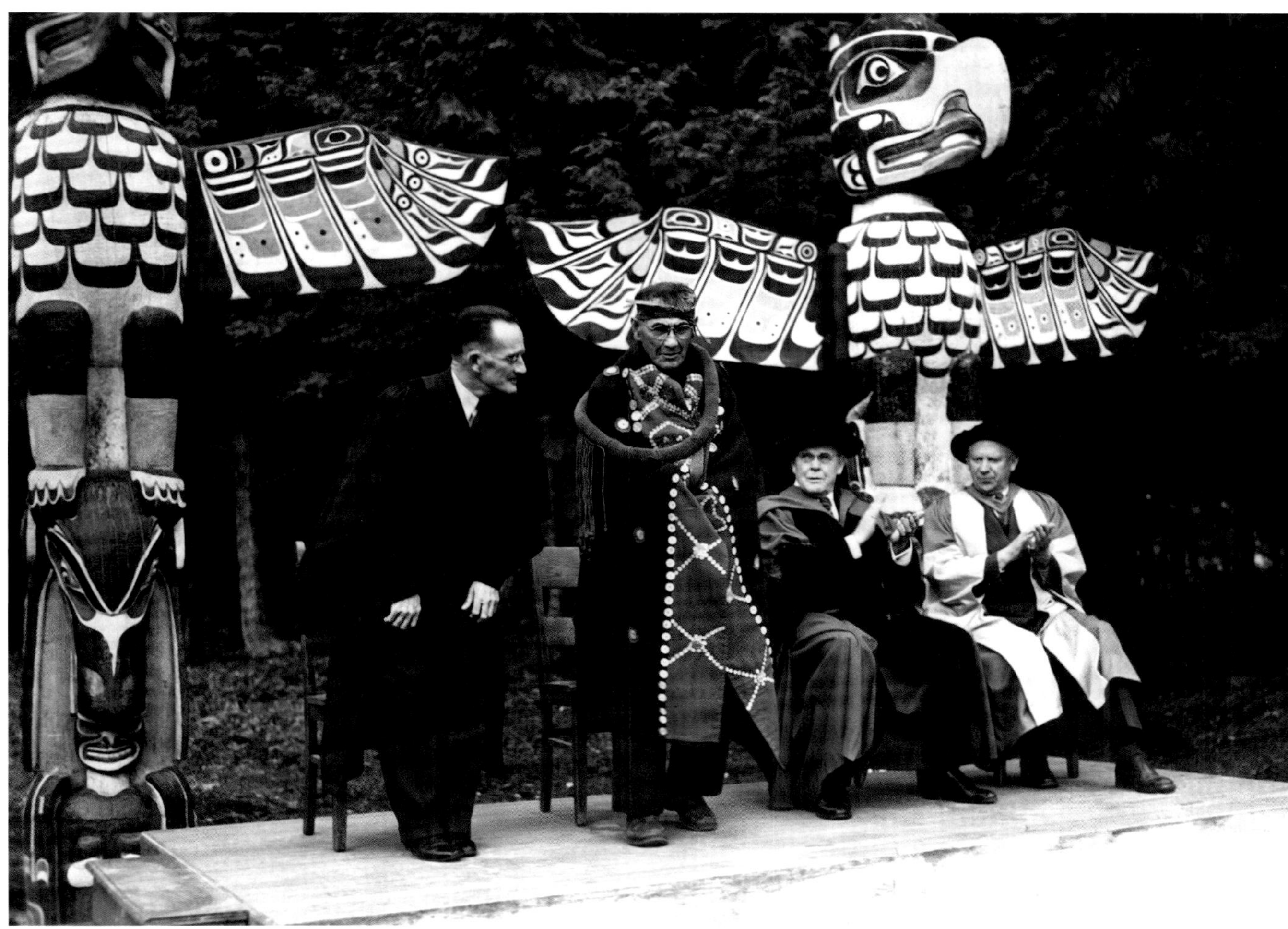

By 1947 Neel had made a name for herself. Speaking at the Vancouver Conference on Native Indian Affairs in 1948, she told an assembled crowd of educators, curio dealers and government officials that "Our art must continue to live for not only is it part and parcel of us, but it can be a powerful factor in combining the best part of the Indian culture into the fabric of a truly Canadian art form." Neel thus confronted curio dealers, whom she felt had cheapened First Nations carving for their own profit. Instead of accepting the notion of a dying tradition, confined by its own historic methods and resources, Ellen Neel pleaded that modern Indigenous artists "be allowed to use new and modern techniques, new and modern tools, new and modern materials."[60] Three years later, in 1951, the Massey Commission's *Royal Commission on National Development in the Arts, Letters, and Sciences*, known as the *Massey Report*, recognized Indigenous sculpture as art. In 1954 the Vancouver Art Gallery allowed two First Nations women, Hatti Fergusson and Ella Gladstone, to mount an exhibition, *The Arts and Handicrafts Show*, featuring contemporary Indigenous artists from all areas of the province. In the spring of 1955 the editors of *Canadian Art* chose a drawing by Mungo Martin for its cover. And ten years later, in 1965, the House of Commons would pass

Hunter Lewis introducing Mungo Martin at the opening of Totem Park
May 16, 1951
This photograph of Mungo Martin being honoured by dignitaries at the University of British Columbia was taken in the year that the federal government finally amended the Indian Act to legalize the making of First Nations art and the holding of traditional ceremonies. But Mungo Martin had already been breaking the law. Since the late 1940s, along with his niece, Ellen Neel, he had been repairing totem poles for the University of British Columbia's Totem Park, and in some cases—like the carvings we see here—making new copies from the originals. Martin's work in Vancouver, and later in Victoria, would spawn a host of Indigenous artists who worked under his tutelage.

Photo: UBC Historical Photograph Collection, UBC 1.1/9773.

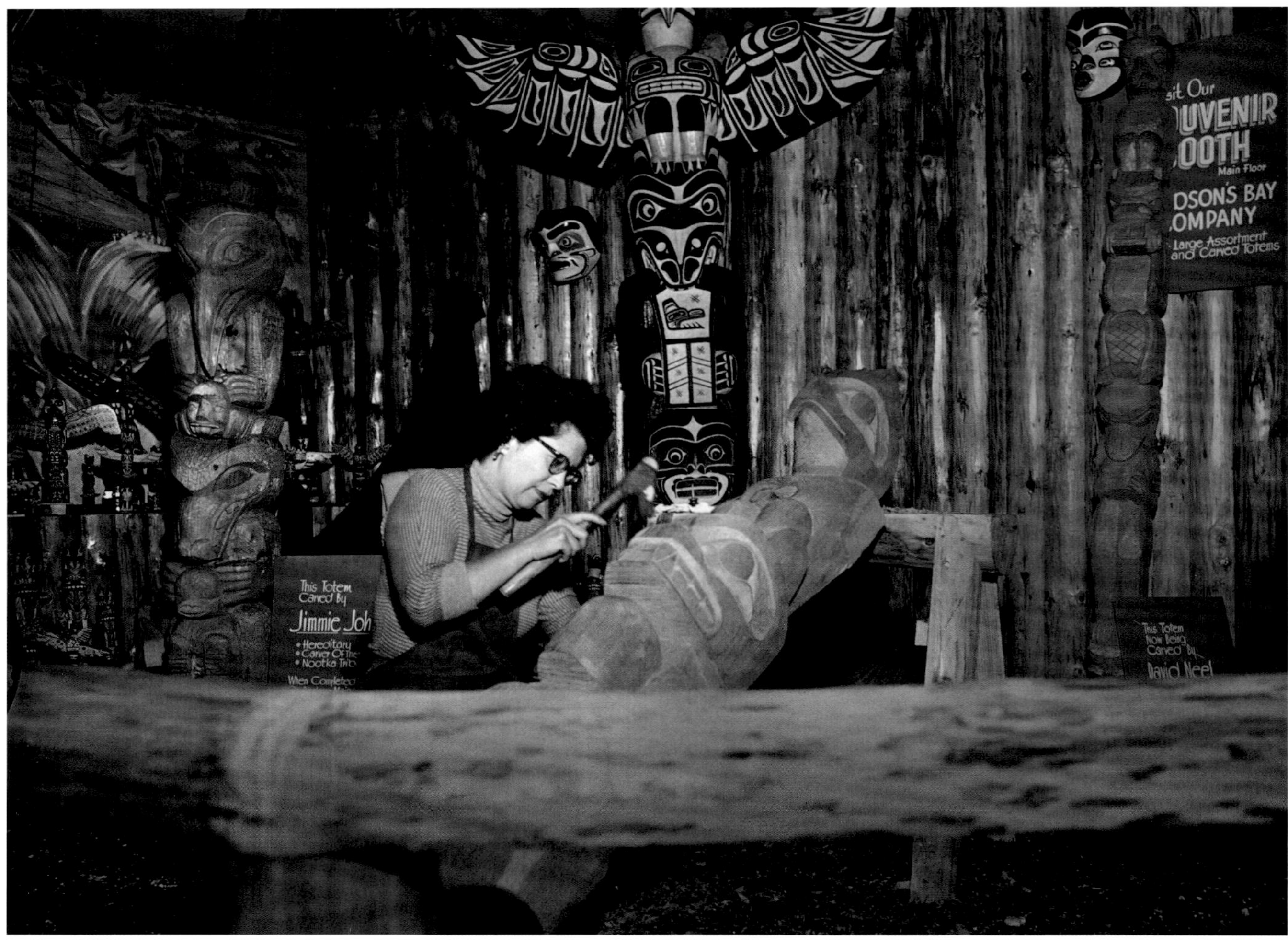

Kwakiutl carver Ellen Neel carving totem pole 1953

Ellen Neel might have been criticized for pandering to the tourist trade when she set up her Totem Art Studios in Vancouver's Stanley Park in the 1940s. But what alternative was open to her? Neel knew that, at a time when producing work for ceremonial purposes was illegal, making "curios" for the tourist trade was the only way of keeping the tradition of carving alive. Unlike most British Columbians, she did not subscribe to the notion that First Nations art was dead or dying. Rather she saw it as a vital force for First Nations people themselves and for Canadian culture in general.

Photo: City of Vancouver Archives, CVA 180-2362.

Bill C-4, "An Act to Preserve and Promote Native Indian and Eskimo Arts and Crafts."[61]

Ellen Neel had come to Vancouver from Alert Bay with her non-Indigenous husband and six children in 1943. Described in the *Province* newspaper as a "girl" carver, Neel proved herself rather more than that; almost single-handedly she played a crucial role in winning respect among the non-Indigenous community for contemporary Northwest Coast sculptors.[62] Following the Vancouver Conference on Native Indian Affairs in 1948, the Vancouver Parks Board allowed Neel to establish Totem Art Studios in Stanley Park. It was from there that she sold her work to tourists and fulfilled larger commissions, including a 4.9-metre-high totem pole, *Victory Through Honour* (1948).[63] Neel herself soon rode the bus from the Totem Art Studios in Stanley Park to the University of British Columbia's Totem Park. The university had invited her to restore several historic Kwakwaka'wakw totem poles, including one carved by her grandfather and teacher Charlie James. Working on such a large scale was strenuous. Many of the poles were beyond repair, and the job interfered with Neel's souvenir business. And that was when she called on her uncle, Mungo Martin, for help.

Like Neel, Martin found that most of the poles at the University of British Columbia were irreparable. He offered to carve new ones and the university hired him at carpenter's wages of $2.79 an hour. After he had carved two totem poles for the university, the director of the provincial museum in Victoria, Wilson Duff, invited him to copy and restore a few of the salvaged poles that stood in Thunderbird Park, which had been established next to the museum in 1941. Relocating to Victoria in 1952, Martin set about restoring old poles and carving new ones; he also built a large cedar plank big house—Wawadit'la. And it was at Wawadit'la in December 1953 that Martin hosted the first legal potlatch, after such events had been decriminalized two years earlier. Representatives of twenty-eight First Nations groups, along with government officials and the wider public, watched the dances, listened to the singing and saw the masks and rattles being performed. The production and the performance of First Nations art were now out in the open.

On the other side of the country the Canadian Handicrafts Guild (CHG) had held the first exhibition of "Eskimo" arts and crafts in 1930. They made little effort, however, to identify the artist, to date the work or to distinguish between the unpolished, austere, low-relief basalt carvings produced by artists living in Clyde River (Kanngiqtugaapik) and Eskimo Point (Arviat) and the realistic, animated, gravity-defying and highly polished stone sculptures produced by artists in Cape Dorset (Kinngait). Thus, while it is true that a number of private and public organizations were giving Inuit and First Nations artists larger markets and thereby increasing their incomes, they were also encouraging the production of assembly-line sculptures, turned out to order by anonymous artists. This not only reinforced a sense of the undistinguished homogeneity of both First Nations and Inuit sculpture, but also relegated the carvings to the handicraft shop, and less frequently honoured them with display in a gallery.

While contemporary First Nations and Inuit sculptors were finding new markets and beginning to have their work taken seriously as art outside of their communities, non-Indigenous sculptors were floundering at the outbreak of the Second World War in September 1939. Beatrice Lennie found it difficult to sustain an active career as a sculptor with the demands of teaching. Byllee Lang, who had set up her own school of sculpture in Winnipeg in 1937, was wooed in 1940 to teach at the Winnipeg School of Art, only to find herself without a job at the end of 1943; she was unable to fill her classes since many young men had signed up for war service. The rationing of lead, wire, clay and plaster was another problem that confronted non-Indigenous sculptors. Materials were not only scarce; foundries were fully committed to producing munitions. Sculptors scrounged wire from newspaper bundles, gathered twigs and rooted about garbage dumps for "priority" materials in order to continue producing their work.[64]

Writing of the Sculptors Society of Canada's exhibition in 1944—their seventh exhibition since 1928—the art critic Page Toles was not only disappointed by the work on show. She felt that it "showed little of the wartime influence so noticeable in current exhibitions of painting and graphic art."[65] This observation was neither fair nor true. Elizabeth Wyn Wood produced a bust, *Munitions Worker* (1944), whose stylized industrial clamp and sickle spoke to the Socialist Realist sculpture of Canada's war ally, the Soviet Union.[66] Florence Wyle celebrated women's contribution to war—as she had done during the First World War—by also producing a bust of a munitions worker. In *Mourning Figure, Female Nude* (c. 1940), Walter Allward resurrected a motif in his Symbolist and Art Nouveau style familiar from his Vimy Ridge memorial.[67] British-born painter and sculptor Violet Gillett, who taught at Saint John Vocational School, addressed the economic hardship suffered in New Brunswick during the Depression and Second World War in her sculpture *Freedom from Want* (1944). And Frances Loring did something entirely different. She created a

Violet Gillett
Freedom from Want, 1944
The slogan "freedom from want" was well known in the forties as one of the "Four Freedoms" enunciated by President Roosevelt as an Allied war aim. In 1944 the Canadian federal government passed the Family Allowance Act and its significance was not lost on Violet Gillett. New Brunswick, where she had taught at the Saint John Vocational School since 1928, remained one of the poorest provinces in the country. This work, rendered in the New Sculpture style of an earlier generation of sculptors that included Katherine Wallis, remains one of Gillett's most significant sculptures.

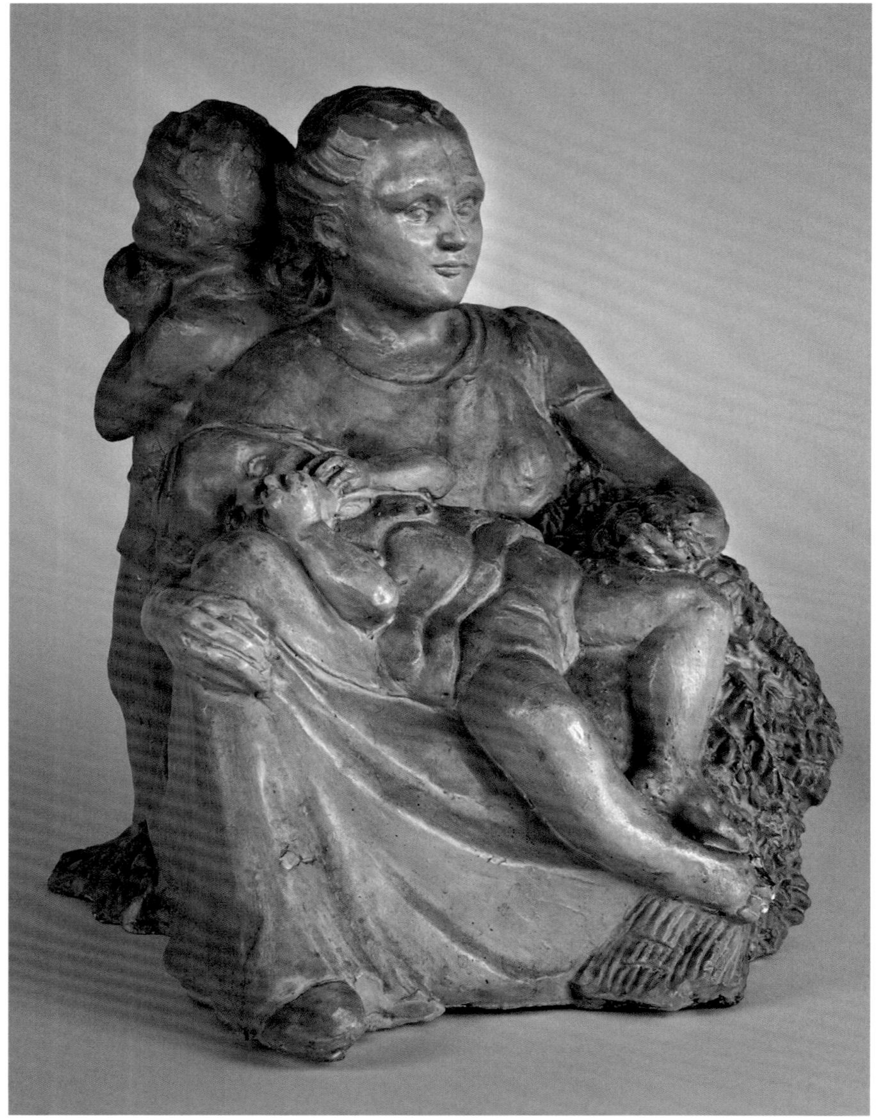

kit called *How to Get Started: Woodcarving for Pleasure* to keep soldiers in the Canadian Army and sailors in the merchant marine occupied during their spare time.

Confident that painters and sculptors had demonstrated that they had a role to play in society during the interwar years, Violet Gillett hoped that the war would create "an unprecedented demand for the work of the artist."[68] But sculptors had little chance to become a part of an official war art program, and even less chance to win the support of the prime minister. Conditioned by high Victorian romantic idealism, W.L. Mackenzie King was focused on collecting architectural ruins for his estate during the war—most recently from the Palace of Westminster, bombed in 1941. Indeed, while Mackenzie King was organizing the transfer of the rubble from Westminster in the hull of a Canadian destroyer to his estate in Gatineau, north of Ottawa, Canadian artists and sculptors were assembled in Kingston at the first national conference of Canadian art. One of the many resolutions the delegates at the Kingston Conference of Canadian Artists put forward urged the federal government to "set up machinery for the creation of works of art recording the various phases of the Dominion's war effort."[69]

Halfway through the war, in February 1943, the federal government did second a few artists to record the activities of Canada's soldiers, sailors and airmen; but they were all painters—including the female artist Molly Lamb Bobak (1922–2014). As Elizabeth Wyn Wood later lamented in the *Journal of the Royal Architectural Institute of Canada,* "no one thought it worthwhile to commission any Canadian sculptors as war artists."[70]

Violet Gillett also hoped that the war would "produce new forms" for the sculptor.[71] This did not happen. By 1937 Wyn Wood's modernist experiments were over; she had produced her finest work by the early 1930s and was now working in the Socialist Realist style.[72] Other sculptors, also cut off from the American and European centres, clung to pre-war styles ranging from the Beaux-Arts, Impressionist, Symbolist and Art Deco traditions. Nor were public commissions for new memorials forthcoming. The names of the new war dead were simply added to the plinths, including that of the *National War Memorial* in Ottawa, that had been built to commemorate the war dead in the First World War. In 1945 Walter Abell justified the lacuna of Second World War memorials by writing in the prestigious London-based *Studio* magazine that we were now living "in an un-monumental age."[73]

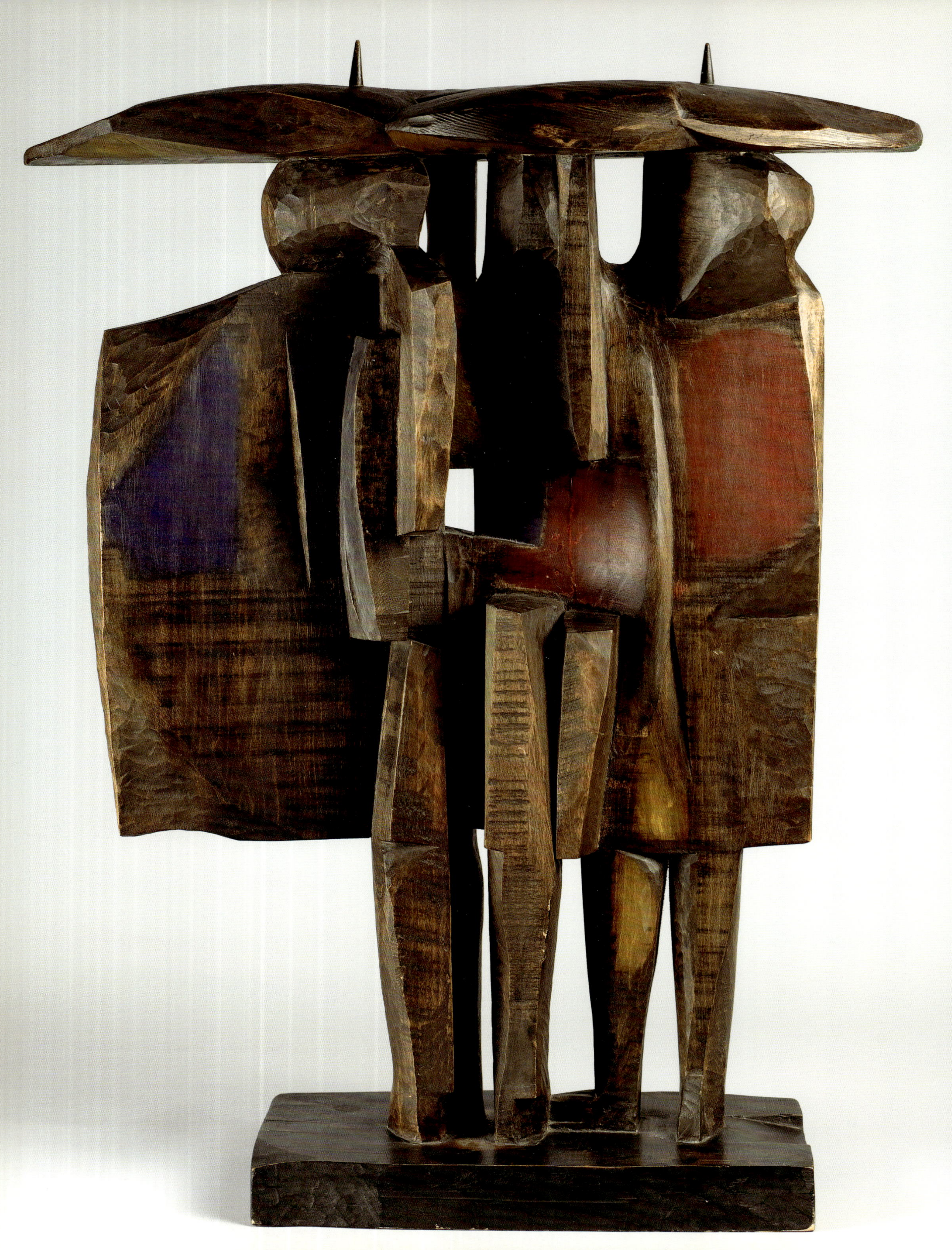

6

Off the Plinth

During the two decades following the Second World War, sculpture seemed to be everywhere. Thanks to the patronage of federal and provincial governments and of private patrons and industry, sculpture was to be found in public squares, in private and public galleries, in airports, on university campuses, at international expositions and, providing the work was small enough, on the coffee tables and mantelpieces of private collectors.

There were many reasons for this change. Many sculptors had relocated their studios and workshops—from the studio to the factory, or from the countryside to the city, or from their homeland to the United States or Europe. In the cities of Montreal, Vancouver and Toronto sculptors increasingly worked with architects to create a new "cityscape."

Opposite:
Anne Kahane
Rain, 1958

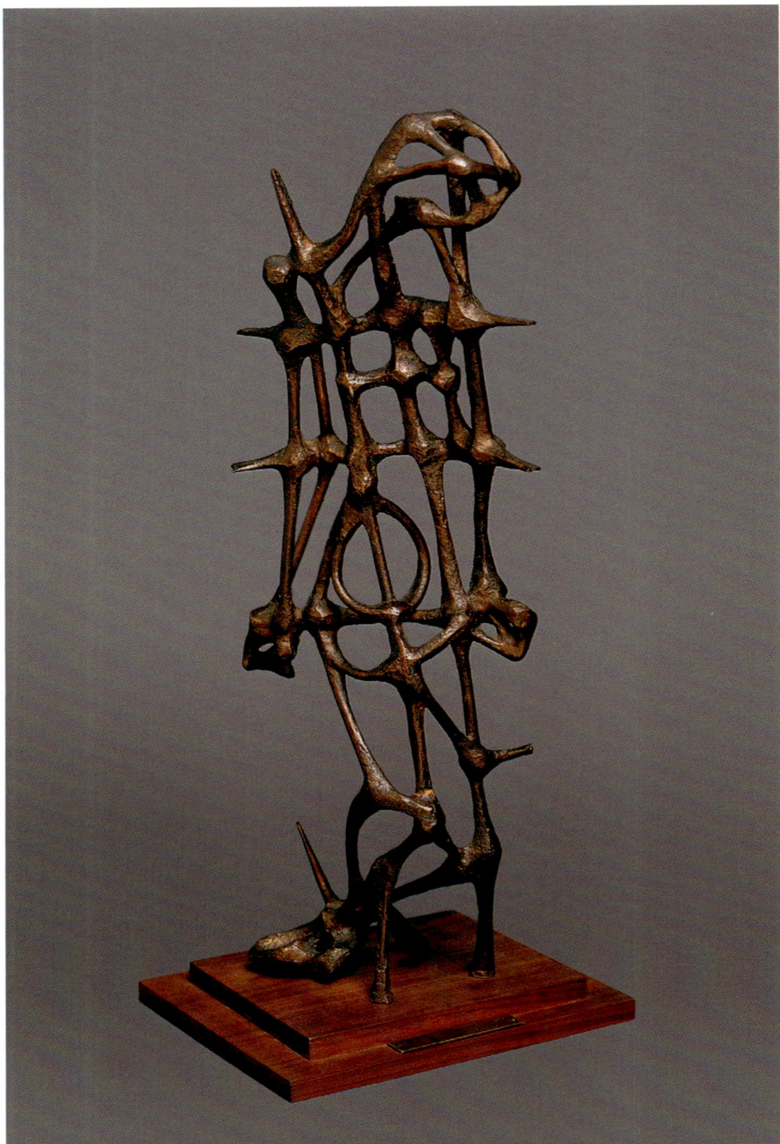

Anne Kahane
Maquette for the Unknown Political Prisoner, 1953
The 1953 international competition for a sculpture dedicated to "The Unknown Political Prisoner" was intended to pay tribute to all the men and women who, during imprisonment, had lost their lives in the cause of human freedom. Anne Kahane's submission did not win the competition but the Institute of Contemporary Arts in London did single out her work for honourable mention. Line can express many things—energy, emotion, movement or rigid control. Departing from the solidity of her previous figurative work, Kahane created a skeletal structure by using copper tubing to enclose space, thereby establishing the suffocating boundaries of the prisoner's cell.

Sculptors also discovered new ways of exhibiting and marketing their work, inside and outside the gallery, inside and outside the country. Some formed exhibition groups; others worked in splendid isolation.

Nor were Inuit and First Nations artists ignored. As we shall see in the following chapters, it was following the Second World War that they entered the art scene as sculptors in their own right, rather than as an appendage to nationalist-inspired programs. Some played a part in curating their own exhibitions. And, like their non-Indigenous contemporaries, they lobbied every level of government, demanding their right to partake in making the new postwar society.

Much of the work that emerged among Canadian sculptors following the Second World War was charged with vitality and power. It might be composed of traditional materials like bronze, wood and stone or it might be constructed, assembled or fabricated from industrial materials or found objects. It was frequently devoid of any reference to nature. And it was often controversial.

After the First World War, many established Canadian sculptors had received the largest share of their income by designing memorials to honour the country's war dead, in a one-off explosion of commissions that had run its course by the time the *Canadian National Vimy Memorial* was unveiled in 1936. "Young sculptors today," Frances Loring warned a gathering at the University Women's Club in Toronto in 1939, were now "finding difficulty in beginning a career" and were thus facing poor prospects. "Most drop out before they reach the professional stage because the years of training are longer and the time needed for production longer than in any other art."[1] True, the generation younger than Loring's seemed to have fewer opportunities, precisely because they had not established their names during the "war memorial frenzy."

After the Second World War, as mentioned previously, new war memorials provided little employment. Even so, many sculptors found adequate compensation through the spin-off from the postwar building boom. The availability of funds, the desire to create more attractive cities, and the attention given to urban planning allowed sculptors to turn their hand to public art. Writing in the *Journal of the Royal Architectural Institute of Canada* in 1948, Elizabeth Wyn Wood suggested that "the most vigorous Canadian sculpture" was to be found in one of two places: either in permanent installation on buildings or else in parks.[2] As Vancouver sculptor Lionel Thomas (1915–2005) put it in 1955: "Now that the modern style in architecture prevails to the point of becoming a commonplace, architects and their clients are finding that painting and sculpture can relieve the aesthetic puritanism of purely functional design."[3] Hence the bas-reliefs that could soften and break up the space of the austere facades and foyers of office buildings designed in the International Style. Hence the sculptures that could give a focal point to newly created civic spaces, to parks, fountains and squares. Hence, too, the sculptures that gave the public reflective moments amid the steel, concrete and glass of the country's new airports, shopping malls and universities.

Even before the Second World War, the government of Quebec had directed a percentage of public funds towards providing art for government buildings, and this policy continued. Thus, in Montreal the building of the Place des Arts in 1963 gave commissions to, among others, Louis Archambault (1915–2003), who had already proven himself to be among Quebec's leading Abstract sculptors, for example in exhibiting *The Iron Bird* (1951) at the open-air *International Exhibition of Sculpture* during London's Festival of Britain in 1951. Canada's federal government had proved less supportive. When the Massey Commission—mandated in 1951 to investigate the state of the arts and sciences in Canada—received a submission from the Sculptors Society of Canada, the body expressed regret that the recent capital plan had made no place for sculpture in the government's building program.[4] Step by step, however, this neglect was remedied. From 1964, all federal buildings under the Department of Public Works applied a policy to implement a provision for sculpture.[5]

Private businesses had long been ahead of the government in embellishing their buildings with sculpture. The architectural firm Marani and Morris, feeling that bas-relief carvings could give the facade of the projected building for the Bank of Montreal in Toronto an illusion of depth as well as a focal point, secured this important new commission in 1946. It sought help from British-born Jacobine Jones (1897–1976), dubbed by one commentator as a stone carver "without equal in Canada," who was joined by five other well-established sculptors—Elizabeth Wyn Wood, Florence Wyle, Walter Allward, Frances Loring and Emanuel Hahn—together with the lesser-known sculptor Donald Stewart (1912–1977), from Toronto.[6] Working largely in the Art Deco style, popularized at Paris's Exposition des Arts Décoratifs in 1925, these sculptors produced ten bas-reliefs for the facade and interior of the bank, representing the different provinces of Canada. Among their chosen subjects were animals, including a skunk, and the climate, storm and calm. Rendered with spare lines and mechanical precision, the Cubist-inspired reliefs offered a challenge to the prevailing academic style.

The Bank of Montreal Building opened in 1949 to a mixed response. One critic liked the fact that this prominent and imposing new building had been designed by Canadian architects and embellished by Canadian artists. But others suggested, with some reason, that the Canadian motifs such as Elizabeth Wyn Wood's panel representing Saskatchewan and Frances Loring's representing the province of Quebec reflected a sentiment and a style more in tune with the 1920s and 1930s than with the late 1940s. Still other commentators, including one astute observer in the *Journal of the Royal Architectural Institute of Canada*, judged the reliefs as small and unimpressive and not well integrated with the overall design of the building.[7]

There still remained, however, an honoured place for the liturgical arts. Following the Second World War, ecclesiastical patrons once again became important for sculptors. With the hope that religion was to play a significant role in postwar Canada, many churches were built or renovated and sculptors were called upon to decorate them. As art historian Robert Pincus-Witten observed, "notions of patriotic sentiment, guilt and social responsibility" now stimulated this largely unforeseen development.[8]

In the postwar years, then, Sylvia Daoust continued to carve religious themes in wood and stone. Similarly, steeped in the ideas of the religious revival movement which had gripped many sculptors during the interwar years, Louis Parent fulfilled a major commission that saw him produce seventeen stone and marble carvings representing the Stations of the Cross, known as *The Way of the Cross*, in the grounds of Saint Joseph's Oratory on Mount Royal in Montreal. Begun in 1943, the project took the Montreal sculptor over a decade to complete.

Spanish-born sculptor Jordi Bonet (1932–1979) wanted to create "an authentic public art like that of the cathedrals in the Middle Ages" when

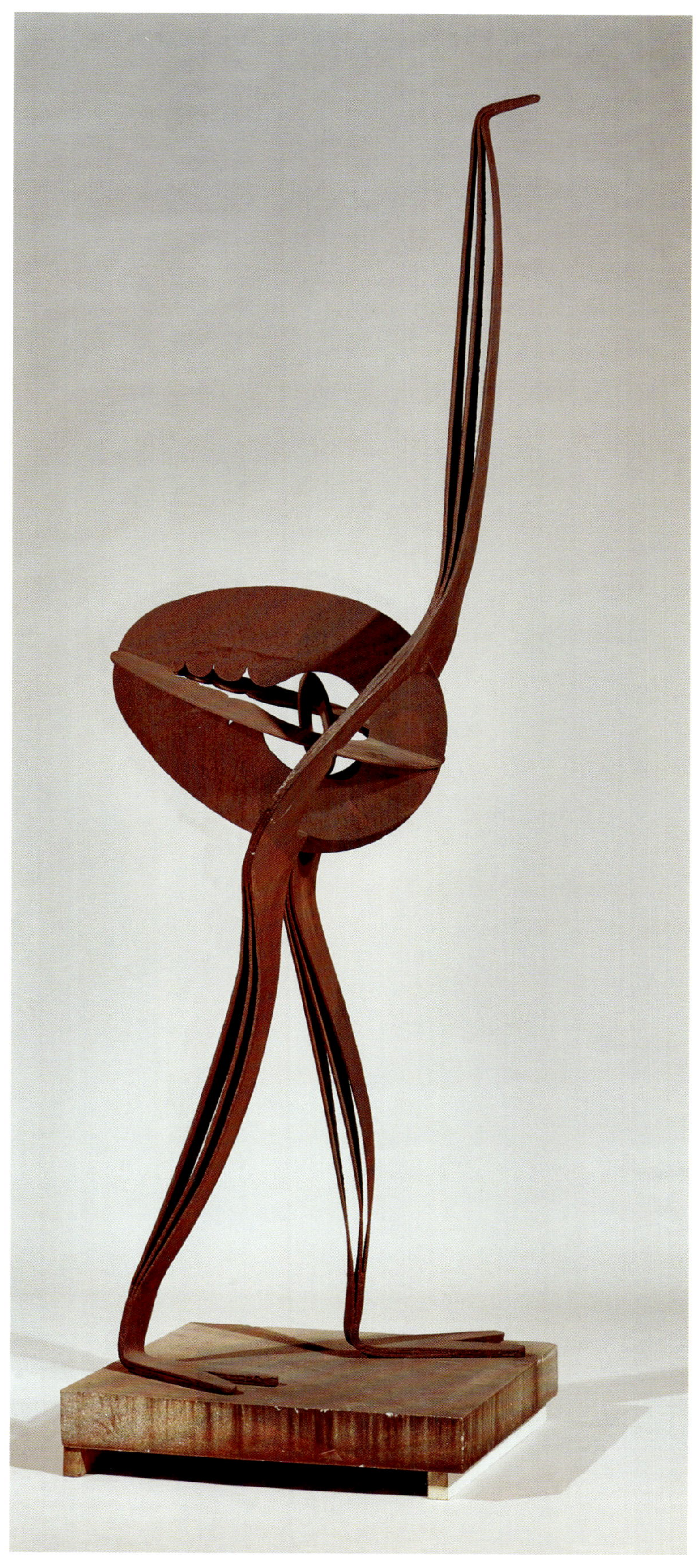

Louis Archambault
The Iron Bird, 1951

The Iron Bird was included in the Festival of Britain, staged in postwar London to celebrate the British contribution to science, technology, architecture and the arts. Though exhibited alongside sculptures by Britain's Barbara Hepworth and Henry Moore, Archambault's graceful, steel-plated ostrich-like bird had more in common with the work of Surrealist Swiss sculptor Alberto Giacometti. Following the festival, *The Iron Bird* would become a feature in Canada's pavilion at the Brussels World's Fair in 1958; two years later it was repatriated to the National Gallery of Canada.

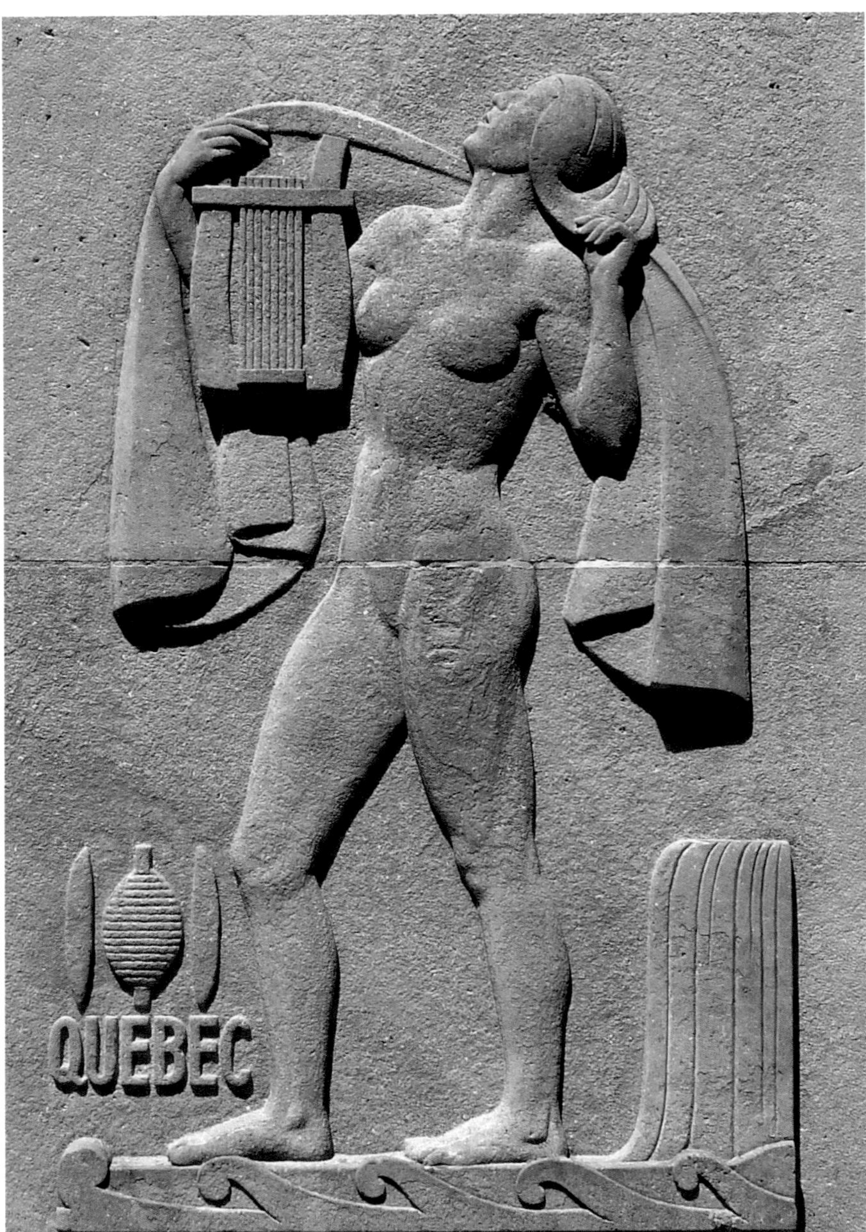

Frances Loring
Quebec, c. 1949
At Guildwood Park's open-air museum in Scarborough, Ontario, there are a number of sculptural fragments, rendered in granite, limestone or marble, that once adorned public buildings. This low-relief limestone panel, produced by Frances Loring, adorned the facade of Toronto's Bank of Montreal Building until the bank's demolition in 1968, when the sculpture was moved to Guildwood Park. Following the spare Art Deco style, with its aesthetic roots in the art of ancient Egypt, *Quebec* aligns stylistically with modernist European art of the interwar period.

he arrived in Canada in 1954.[9] Within a few years Bonet, assisted by more than a dozen employees in his studio/factory in Mont-Saint-Hilaire, was producing bas-relief wall murals for churches and secular buildings—all reflecting the audacious Spanish architecture of Antoni Gaudí (1852–1926). Constructed from tile and aluminum, Bonet's wall reliefs were not simply architectural add-ons. Through his collaboration with architects and designers, so it has been argued, he sought to elevate a building "beyond the function of true architecture."[10] And with an eye to the individuality and exuberance of Gaudí, Bonet did "everything" that his more traditional liturgical artist colleagues "disdained."[11]

Liturgical sculpture was not just confined to Quebec. Toronto's Emanuel

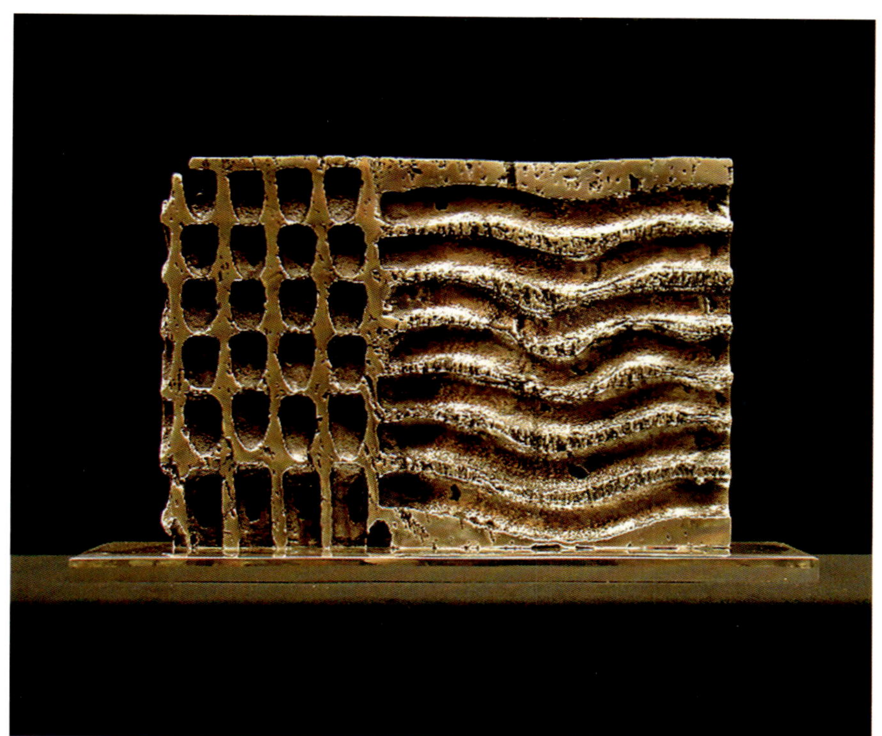

Jordi Bonet
Mouvement de Vague, c. 1964
This Spanish-born artist was known for the imposing ceramic and aluminum abstract murals that he and his assistants produced in limited editions for churches throughout the province of Quebec. But he also produced more intimate sculptures for the secular market, like this highly detailed, jewel-like work, which captures the movement of a wave through the repetition of undulating lines. Drawing on natural forms and on the organic style evident in the buildings of Spanish architect Antoni Gaudí, *Mouvement de Vague* is among the most exquisitely crafted works of the postwar period.

Hahn carved a life-sized crucifix for the Chapel of the Mission House for the Society of Saint John the Evangelist at Bracebridge in Muskoka, Ontario. The first major commission received by Katie Ohe (b. 1937), following her study in New York City, was to carve a wooden pulpit, communion table and baptismal font for the chapel at Calgary's Grace Presbyterian Church. Working in concrete, Ohe further completed a mural for Saint Michael's Roman Catholic Church in the same city, depicting the banishment of Lucifer from heaven. Saskatchewan-based sculptor John Nugent (1921–2014) was likewise committed to producing spiritually uplifting art. Settling in the rural community of Lumsden, Saskatchewan, in 1948, this liberal Roman Catholic from Montreal established a studio and foundry. Working in the modernist idiom, Nugent cast numerous bronze crucifixes and tabernacles. Victor Tolgesy (1928–1980), who arrived in Ottawa from Hungary in 1951 and founded the Guild Studio of Contemporary Liturgical Art, had sufficient commissions to enable him to work full-time as a sculptor.[12]

If many liturgical sculptors clung to traditional styles and dealt with realistic subject matter in order to win commissions from their religious patrons, similar pressures were felt from architects, as recognized in the *Massey Report* in 1951. Many sculptors accordingly feared that their "creative work" would suffer if it were too closely bound with the demands made upon them. Lionel Thomas influentially insisted in 1955 that one of the two cardinal principles that should govern the relations between the artist and the architect was that "there must be no artistic compromise—an attempt to impose academic 'realism' must be resisted."[13]

It seems to be true that sculptors working with architects in the construction of the new airports, universities and shopping malls found themselves increasingly liberated from external dictates.[14] They seized new chances to realize their own vision within the architectural context, enlivening the impact of austere structures. As Toronto's Gerald Gladstone (1929–2005) now confidently argued, metal's physical character not only allowed it "to relate to monumentality naturally," but also had "great outdoor coloring potential" of a kind often "lacking in our dull grey and pale yellow facades."[15]

In 1963 Ontario premier John Robarts announced that art works would be included in and around the Macdonald Building, the largest single edifice in Toronto.[16] When the commissions were duly handed out a few years later, Walter Yarwood (1917–1996) produced a free-standing bronze "screen" that convincingly expressed the sculptor's own emotional experience. "As I walk slowly past this wall of bronze," critic Iris Nowell noted of *Pines* (1968), "I imagine I see what Walter saw as he canoed in a gorge, silently floating through his beloved pines, feeling at home with himself and his world."[17] On the Prairies, too, sculptors took the chances that they were now offered. George Swinton (1917–2002), a teacher at the Winnipeg School of Art, designed a free-standing work for the country's first covered shopping mall, Polo Park Shopping Centre. Also in Winnipeg,

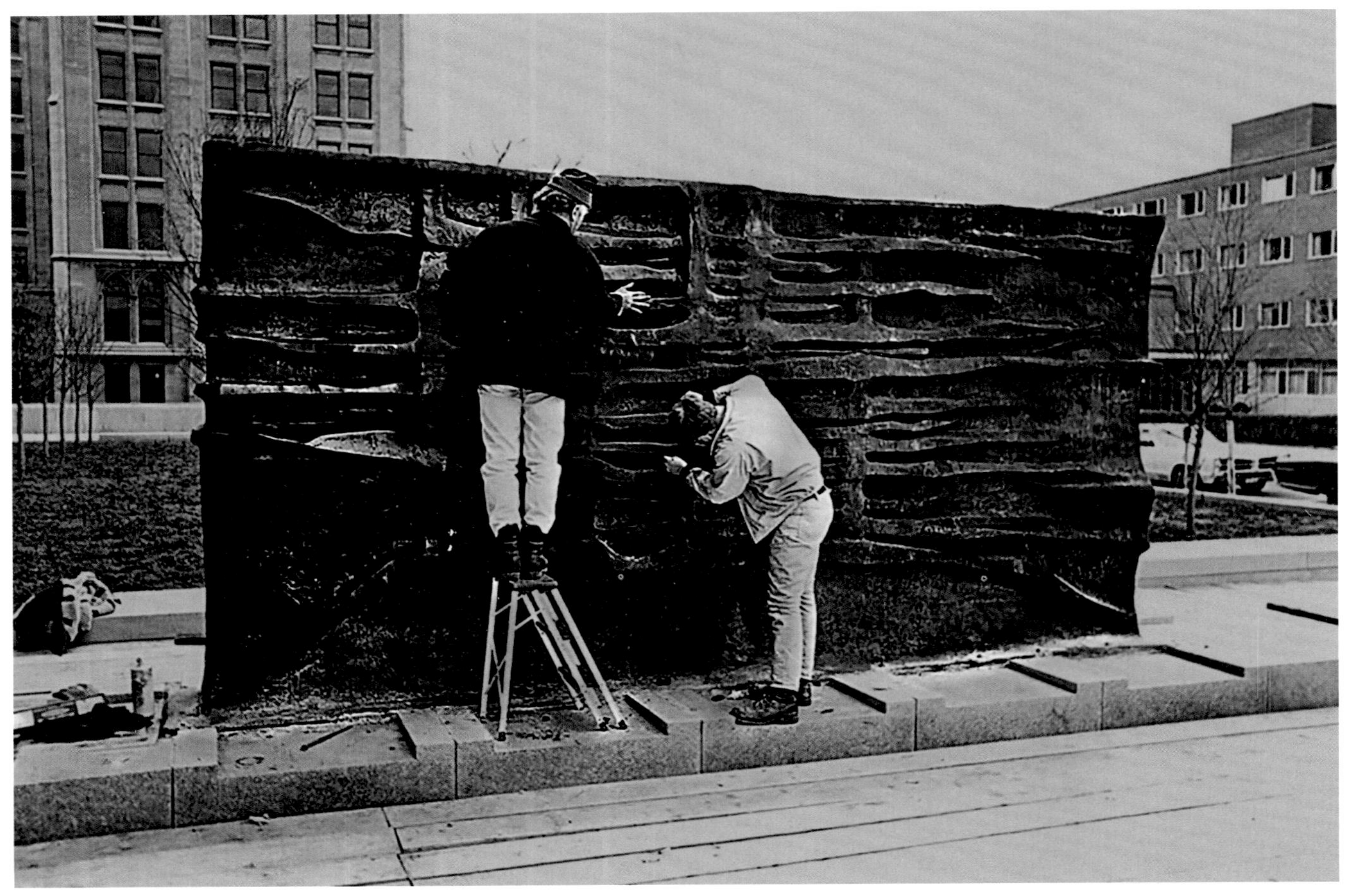

Richard Williams (1921–2013) created a wall relief in stainless steel for the Investors Syndicate Building. Not to be outdone, architects in Saskatoon gave art teacher Eli Bornstein (b. 1922) free rein to produce a fountain/sculpture in 1956 for the Saskatchewan Teachers' Federation Building; and three years later, another teacher, Robert Murray, born in Vancouver in 1936, who was to soar to international prominence, was given free scope in his commission for Saskatoon's city hall.

Sculptors became beneficiaries of still other projects during the postwar building boom. In Vancouver, for example, the University of British Columbia commissioned a number of free-standing and relief works for the forecourts and walls of their new buildings. Some consisted of welded Cor-Ten steel or sheet copper. Others were cast in bronze or concrete. Among the new generation of sculptors for these works were Jack Harman (1927–2001), Gerhard Class (1924–1997), Robert Clothier (1921–1999), George Norris (1928–2013) and Lionel Thomas.

In 1958, the federal government's Department of Transportation made an important decision to devote 1 per cent of all airport construction to sculpture in bas-relief for the facades and foyers of its airports. At a time when airports were being constructed in virtually every major city in the country, this gave major commissions to Robert Murray and Louis Archambault in Vancouver, Toronto and Ottawa, in each case for larger-than-life-sized sculptures.

It may be true that the majority of the country's architects and town planners encouraged sculptors to produce works that inspired introspection and contemplation; yet, it should not be assumed that the general public and the press were always happy with modernist work. In 1949, for example, Robert Roussil (1925–2013) made the mistake of leaving his sculpture *La Famille* (1949) outside of the Montreal Museum of Fine Arts' school overnight. The work, depicting a nude man and woman and a small child, did not conform to traditional views or uphold conservative values, and was thus distasteful to the public. Under the cover of darkness, the police carted off the "obscene" work in a paddy wagon.

In the 1960s John Nugent also ran into difficulty over his proposal of a work to commemorate Metis leader Louis Riel, who had led the Northwest Rebellion in 1885. The maquette of a welded steel tower that Nugent submitted was reminiscent of a model, *Monument to the Third International*, that the Russian Constructivist sculptor Vladimir Tatlin (1885–1953) had produced in the Soviet Union in 1920. But Nugent's proposal, like Tatlin's before it, never advanced past the model stage. Instead, Saskatchewan's premier, Ross Thatcher, wanted a realistic representation of Riel. Nugent was sent back to his studio. This time he emerged with a maquette of an expressionistic figure of a naked Louis Riel, which Thatcher liked no better. Fearing that the commission was slipping from his hands, Nugent agreed to drape Riel's naked figure in a cape and in 1968 this less imaginative *Louis Riel Memorial* was installed on the grounds of the Saskatchewan legislature in Regina.

At the beginning of the same decade, and in the same province, Robert Murray found himself defending his welded steel fountain sculpture

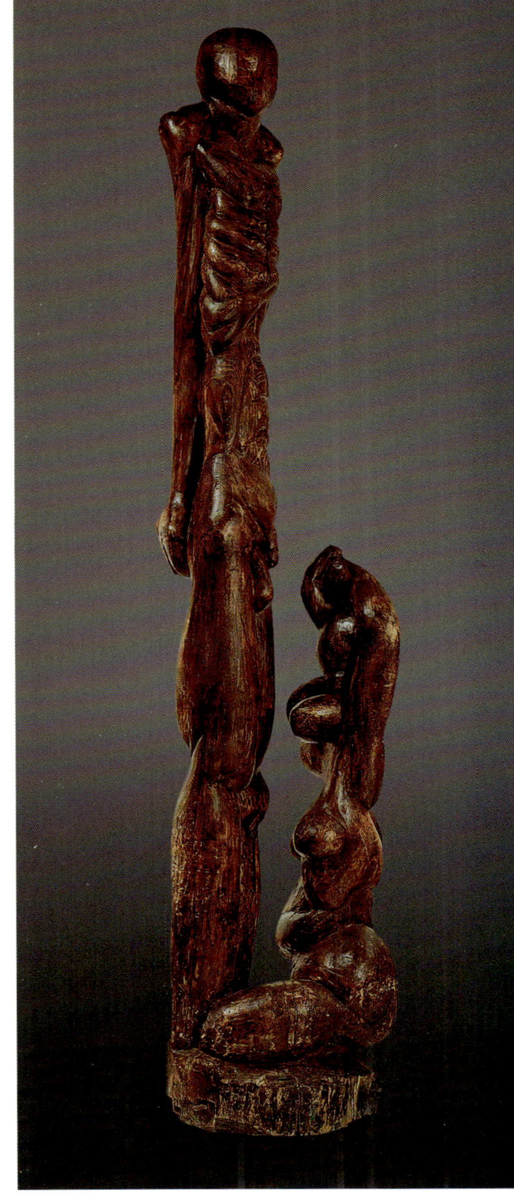

Robert Roussil
La Famille, 1949
Left mistakenly outside the Montreal Museum of Fine Arts in 1949, this "obscene" work was famously "arrested" by the police and sent to jail. Yet it would be wrong to think of *La Famille* only as an object of controversy. Its sensual, even erotic, depiction of a naked man, woman and child challenged the notion that figurative sculpture had to be true to life. Robert Roussil escaped Quebec's conservative art scene in the late 1950s, as Montreal painter Jean-Paul Riopelle (1923–2002) had earlier, and enjoyed a successful career in France until his death in 2013.

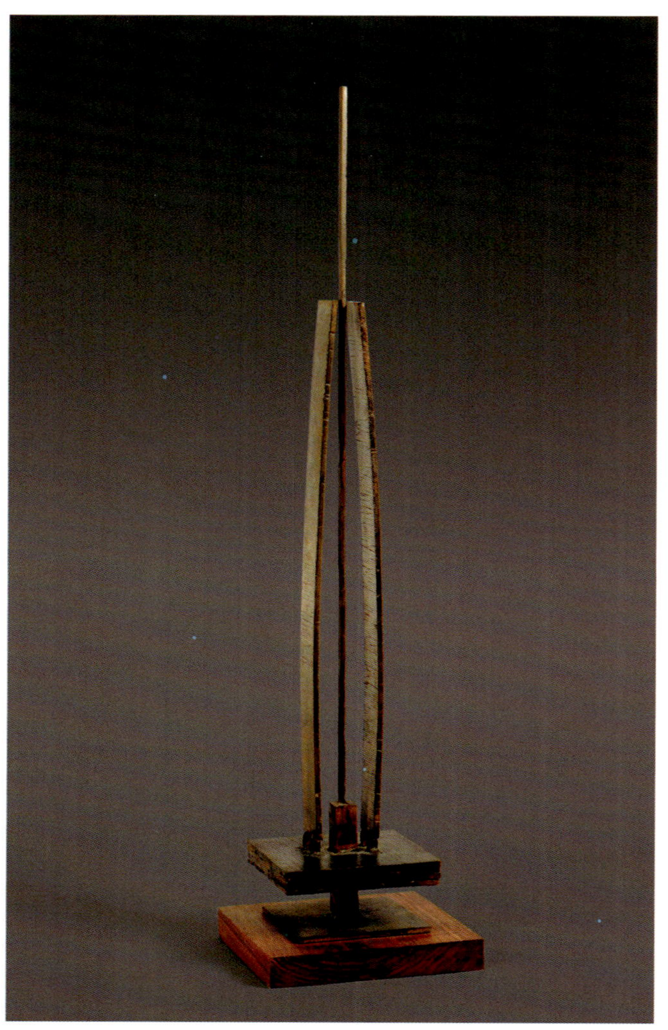

John Nugent
Design for *Louis Riel Memorial*, 1968
This maquette honouring Louis Riel, whose defiance of the Canadian
government led to his execution in 1885, is plainly no literal representation
of its subject. Had Nugent's maquette been transformed into a finished work,
it would have been the only modernist sculpture in the country to embrace
the ideas of the Russian sculptor Vladimir Tatlin, whose Constructivist project
sought to bring art and technology into accord. But Saskatchewan's premier,
Ross Thatcher, who wanted a realistic representation of Riel, brusquely
foreclosed this possibility.

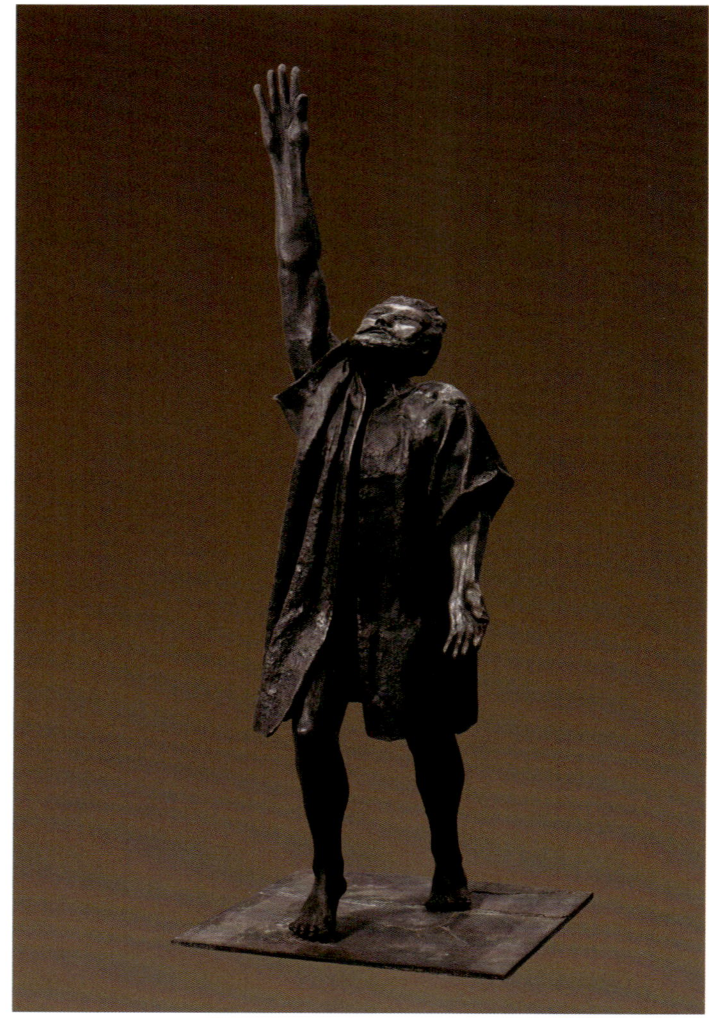

John Nugent
Louis Riel Memorial, 1968
If Nugent's controversial first proposal for a memorial to Louis Riel marked a move
away from figuration to abstraction, his second proposal—giving flesh and bones to
his portrayal of Riel—reversed that process. However, Nugent's revised sculpture of
Riel drew as much controversy as its predecessor and his marvellously expressionistic
nude figure had to be draped in a cape. Moreover, the Metis community was
understandably upset because they had no input into the revised design, while
others questioned why the "mad religious fanatic" was being commemorated at all.
Nugent's *Louis Riel Memorial* stood in Regina's Wascana Park for twenty-three years
before being incarcerated in the storerooms of the MacKenzie Art Gallery.

Rainmaker (1960). The public had anticipated a realistic sculpture featuring the province's economic activity. But Murray had made the material itself, and its sweeping arcs and curves, the subject of his sculpture. The public and critics had also expected Murray to do the work himself, rather than supervise a skilled welder doing it for him. Murray responded to his critics by claiming that he had "attempted to create a work which will have a purposeful relationship in its physical situation and at the same time remain expressive of a subject idea."[18] He further noted that during the process of creating *Rainmaker*, a valuable exchange had taken place "between the fabricator, the men working on the piece and myself."[19] The public, however, were still puzzled as to why Murray had exchanged the romantic isolation of the artist's garret for the factory floor.

When Armand Vaillancourt (b. 1929) was commissioned to produce a war memorial for Chicoutimi, Quebec, he announced, "I wasn't going to do one of those things with one soldier knifing another."[20] But the result, the

Robert Murray
Working Model for *Fountain Sculpture* (*Rainmaker*), 1959
Vancouver-born sculptor Robert Murray had just returned to Canada after studying at Mexico's Allende Institute in San Miguel de Allende when Saskatoon's city councillors commissioned him to produce a sculpture for the centrepiece of a fountain. The simplicity, elegance and gravitas of the resulting work was lost on the public. Persuaded that *Rainmaker* did not represent anything—or that the welders at Saskatoon's John East Iron Works, rather than the artist, had created the work—the public duly vented their outrage at the time. Today we can see that what made *Rainmaker* unique in the Canada of 1959 was the fact that it exemplified sculpture-as-process rather than sculpture-as-representation.

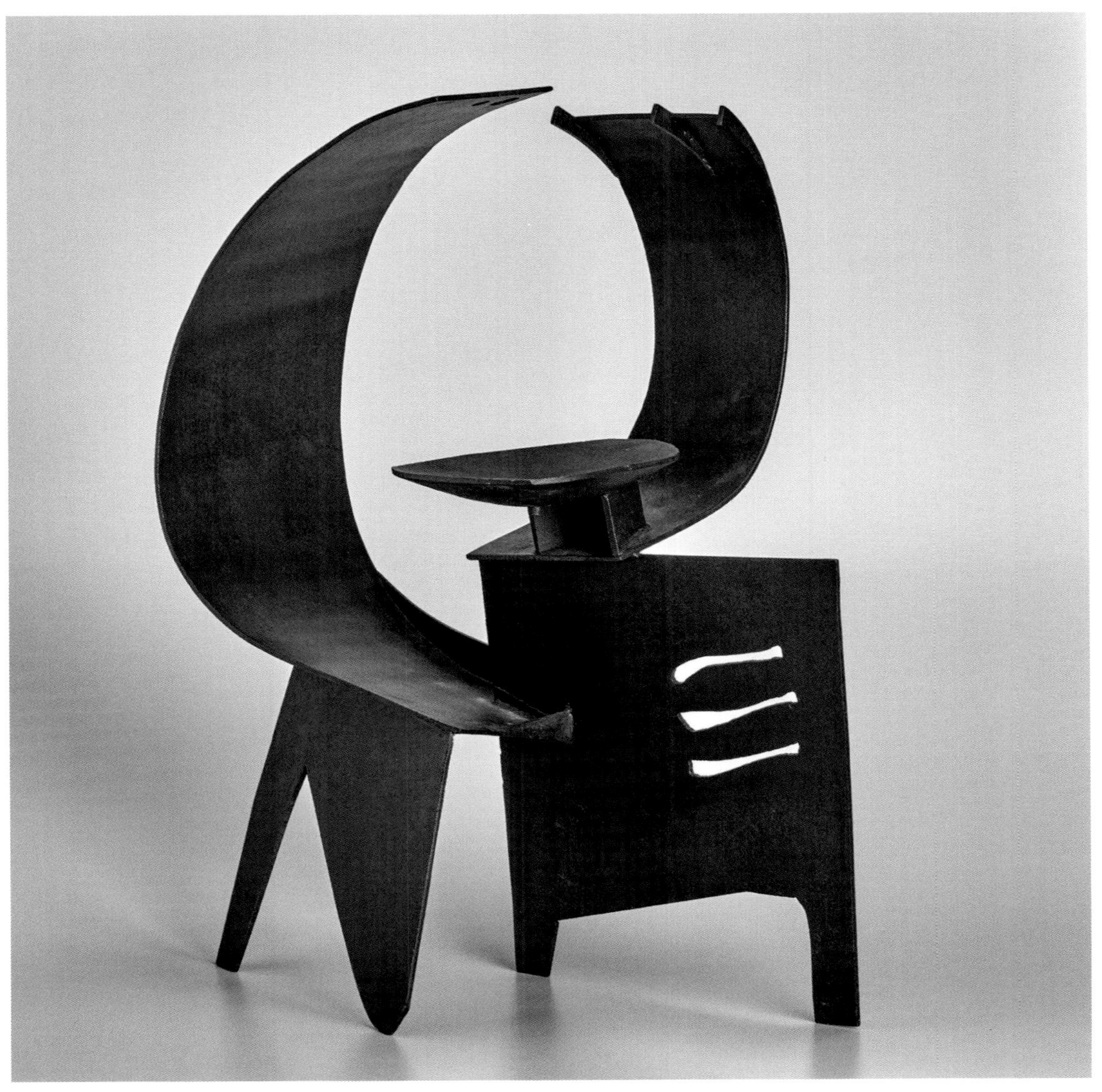

five-metre-high *Cénotaphe de Chicoutimi* (1959), was, to one commentator, nothing more than "a bristling jungle of scrap metal that lunges skywards like an anti-aircraft gun."[21] A few years later another public commission came Vaillancourt's way. *L'Humain* (1963), representing the sculptor's response to the Cuban Missile Crisis, was so unpopular that the citizens of Asbestos, Quebec, where the sculpture was installed, founded an anti–modernist art group—Mouvement pour l'Opposition au Monument.

Nor was a work of sculpture immune from criticism when it was exhibited within the walls of a public or private gallery. In 1955 the Winnipeg Art Gallery's seminal exhibition, featuring contemporary Canadian painting and sculpture, included work by Anne Kahane (b. 1924), Eli Bornstein and Louis Archambault. It provoked, at best, a mixed reception. "If you squint your eyes," one grudging commentator observed, the "abstractions look quite naturalistic."[22]

Nobody in Canada who showed any interest in sculpture could have been unaware of the changes that were now taking place within the country and abroad. Reproductions of Abstract sculptures were not only illustrated and discussed in the pages of *Canadian Architect* and *Canadian Art*. New art journals—*Arts et Pensées* (1951), *Vie des Arts* (1956)—along with long-established foreign publications like *The Studio* (London) and *The American Magazine of Art* introduced the public and Canadian sculptors to new ideas, and sometimes even featured their work. Exhibitions of foreign art helped to keep Canadian sculptors abreast with the latest trends, notably *Contemporary Art in France, Britain and the USA* (1950) at the Montreal Museum of Fine Arts and *Recent British Sculpture* (1962) at the Art Gallery of Toronto (renamed the Art Gallery of Ontario in 1966). Furthermore, when travel restrictions eased in the postwar period, the availability of grants and bursaries gave many sculptors an opportunity to see the work for themselves by travelling to Europe and the United States.

Montreal had always been more cosmopolitan than cities in the rest of Canada. For sculptors living there, access to foreign collections and study abroad had long been normal. Art schools, along with the provincial government, offered travelling scholarships and prizes like the Grand Prix de la Province de Québec. From 1946 to 1948 Charles Daudelin lived in Paris on a bursary from the French government. There he produced the limestone sculpture *Crouching Woman* (1947), very clearly influenced by the rhythmic movement and organic curvilinear forms of the French sculptor Henri Laurens (1885–1954), with whom he studied; indeed Laurens had himself explored the same theme in his earlier *Crouching Woman* (1926).[23] Though Claude Tousignant (b. 1932) spent a year in Paris in 1952, it was in New York, a decade later, that the colour-field paintings of Barnett Newman (1905–1970) prompted him to produce large monochrome sculptures, thus enabling him "to say as much as possible with as few elements as possible."[24]

After returning to Montreal following war service, Robert Roussil took advantage of the offer of a Veterans Affairs grant to study at home, in the Art Association of Montreal's school, where he worked with Louis Archambault. But in 1956 Roussil left the country for France. From his base in Provence he became a frequent exhibitor at the Creuse Gallery in Paris, and in 1958 he exhibited his sculpture in the French pavilion at the Brussels World's Fair. The career of Montreal's Suzanne Guité (1927–1981) was even more multifaceted and peripatetic. Following the war, she worked in Paris under Brâncuși, who left his mark on her simplified, even severe, figurative stone sculptures like *Le Chercheur d'Espace* (1948). In 1951 Guité relocated to Florence, studying at the Academy of Fine Arts; then in 1953 she attended the National Polytechnical Institute in Mexico. After that, Guité re-crossed the Atlantic in order to visit archaeological sites on the Greek islands of Crete and Rhodes.

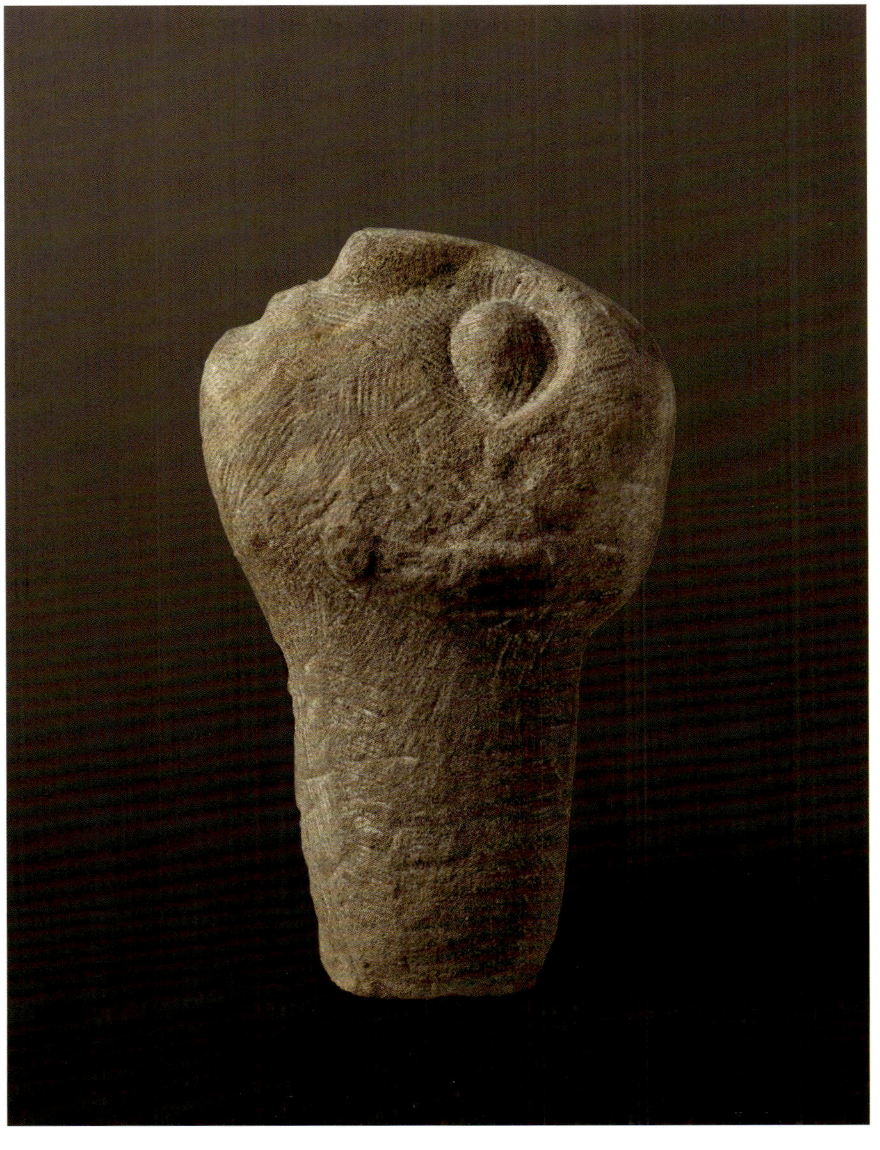

Suzanne Guité
Le Chercheur d'Espace, 1948
Suzanne Guité might have seemed over-educated, having studied with so many leading sculptors, including László Moholy-Nagy, Alexander Archipenko and Constantin Brâncuși. She had also visited archaeological sites and art galleries in North and South America as well as in Europe, and she had exhibited her own sculptures widely, including at the Venice Biennale in 1958. *Le Chercheur d'Espace*—or Space Seeker—uses direct carving in stone to create a compact, simplified head that speaks to the sculpture of ancient civilizations, to the Surrealist movement and to the quest for universal themes. Yet Guité didn't live long enough to bring these influences to fruition—in her mid-fifties, she was murdered by her second husband.

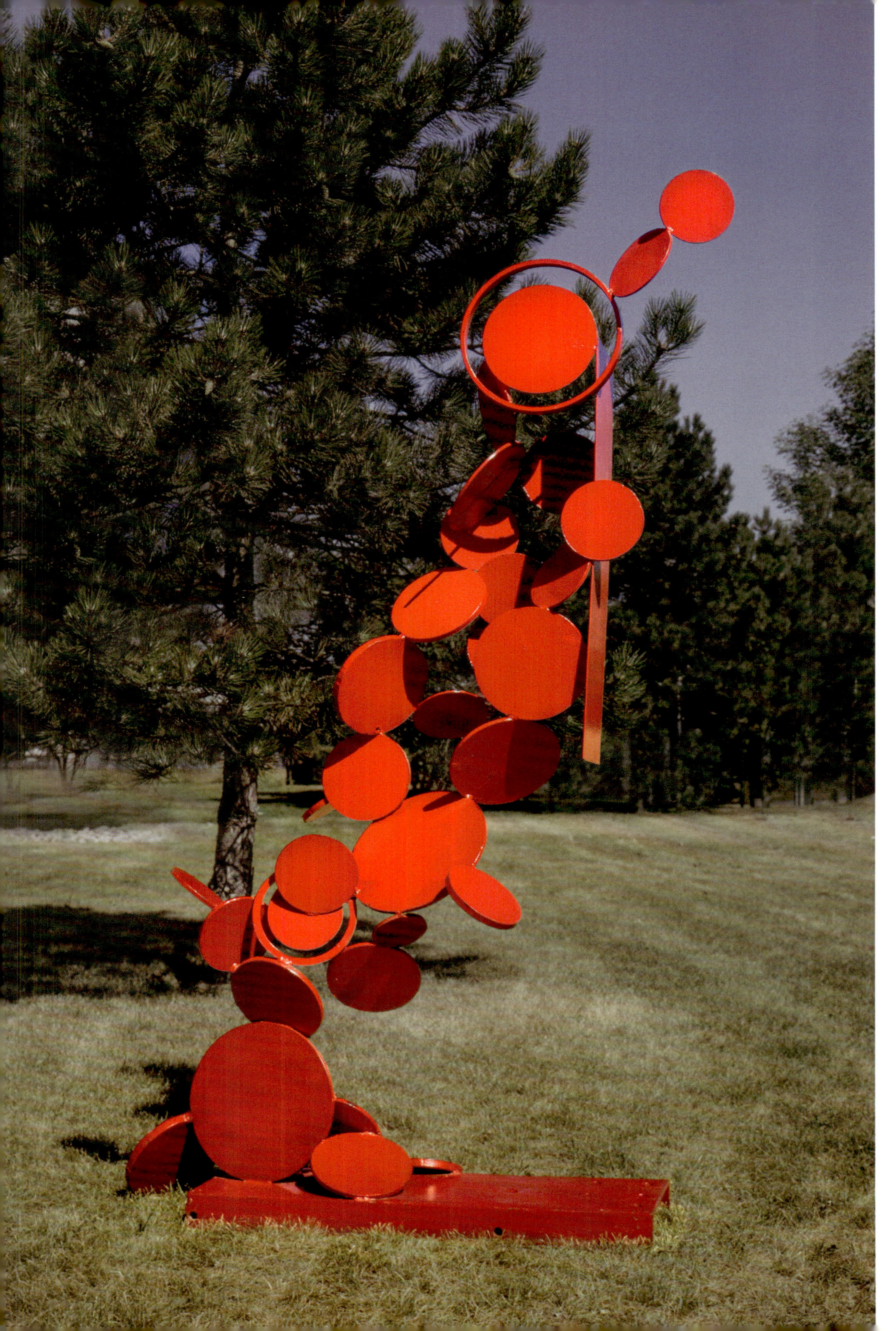

Armand Vaillancourt had been exposed to arc-welding and folded-metal techniques during a trip through the United States in the early 1950s. This knowledge had enabled him to produce the *Cénotaphe de Chicoutimi* as well as to pass on his technical skills to other sculptors like Françoise Sullivan (b. 1925). This Montreal-based artist had studied dance in New York under Franziska Boas and Martha Graham. After meeting Vaillancourt, Sullivan combined his welded-metal techniques with her knowledge of dance to charge her gravity-defying sculptures, like *Chute en Rouge* (1966), with a sense of movement and energy unmatched by her colleagues in Quebec. The Polish-born sculptor Esther Wertheimer (b. 1926), following her study at the Montreal School of Fine Arts, attended the International Academy of Austria and won a one-year scholarship at the Academy of Fine Arts in Florence, where she remained for several years, before immersing herself in classical Italian art and contemporary Italian sculpture. Anne Kahane, another Quebec-based sculptor, studied architecture, industrial design and woodcarving at New York's Cooper Union Art School from 1945 to 1947.

The Department of Veterans Affairs had offered artists returning from war service a choice between money ($5,000), a job in the public sector or a three-year grant to study. Yet relatively few took advantage of the latter offer; and outside Quebec relatively few Canadian sculptors went to Europe. Peter Sager (1920–1985), a former pupil of Vancouver's Beatrice Lennie, was unusual in receiving a scholarship from the French government that enabled him to continue his studies in France. He spent four years in Paris, where he was taught by Swiss sculptor Alberto Giacometti (1901–1966).

It was in the late 1950s that sculptor Robert Hedrick (b. 1930), from London, Ontario, went to study at the Allende Institute in San Miguel de Allende. So did Robert Murray, who began as a painter and printmaker but turned to sculpture while in Mexico. Within a decade Murray's sculpture was characterized by an apparent weightlessness and buoyancy and by an understated volume, all enhanced by the fact that his work was installed on the ground not on a base or plinth. Another rising sculptor was Jack Hardman (1923–1996). (He is, of course, easily confused with the previously mentioned Jack Harman, who was to build the first large foundry in British Columbia for casting large sculpture in 1963.) It was Hardman who scraped together funds from his high-school teaching position and travelled in the early 1950s to England. He enrolled at the Slade School of Fine Art in London, where he came under the spell of Henry Moore and Barbara Hepworth (1903–1975).

Most Canadian sculptors had to wait until 1957 before they qualified for public funding to travel and study abroad. The idea that the state should support the arts had been fermenting since the end of the nineteenth century but it was the Kingston conference in 1941 that influentially challenged the romantic notion that the artist was a remote figure pursuing her or his vision of what truth was without any connection to the larger world.[25] The argument was that, if democracy was to survive, it needed the artist, as the custodian of the values that civilization was struggling to preserve, to help build a better society. The artist, on the other hand, also needed the support of the state. These ideas formed the core of the recommendations that both

Opposite:
Françoise Sullivan
Chute en Rouge, 1966
Françoise Sullivan spent the formative years of her career as a painter and as a dancer. When she turned to sculpture, she brought this multidisciplinary approach to her work, combining modern dance with her interest in Fauvism, Cubism and Abstract Expressionism. The title of this work, *Chute en Rouge*, or Fall in Red, may suggest that the brightly coloured discs cascade to the ground—or do they, depending on your viewpoint, soar into the air? This magnificent sculpture, which playfully articulates the interplay of space through a series of welded discs, is about movement, process and colour.

artists and sculptors put forward to the national inquiry into the arts and sciences mentioned earlier. But the plan set out in the *Massey Report* in 1951 was only fully realized when the succession duties from the estates of two entrepreneurs from the Maritimes, Sir James Dunn and Isaak Walton Killam, fell into the government's coffers. From the year of its formation in 1957, the Canada Council could now offer unprecedented opportunities for foreign travel—not least to sculptors.

By the late 1950s many felt that New York rather than Paris was the centre of modern art, but Europe continued to attract many recipients of Canada Council grants. Toronto's John Ivor Smith (1927–2003) was awarded a Canada Council Junior Fellowship that enabled him to travel to Italy in 1957 and 1958, ostensibly to acquire both new and ancient casting techniques. There he worked in cast stone and bronze, and experimented with fibreglass-reinforced epoxy, of which *Florentine* (n.d.) is the best example.[26] He was also influenced by figurative Italian sculptors including Marino Marini (1901–1980) and Giacomo Manzù (1908–1991).

In 1959 another Canada Council recipient, Gerald Gladstone, was able to give up his job as the art director of Toronto's MacLaren Advertising Company and study at the Royal College of Art. During his time in London he met Henry Moore. More significantly, Gladstone began using new materials, as he later recalled: "I watched some guys near King's Cross welding fire-escapes and I wondered what they'd do with the scrap. I asked them to give it to me—and they did."[27] Gladstone's use of metal rods, as we shall see in the next chapter, were by no means "sculptural gimmickry." As art critic Charles Spencer continued in a respectful review of Gladstone's show at London's Molton Galleries in 1962: "This combination immediately creates its own relationships and reminds one, for instance, of the anatomical drawings of Leonardo or Stubbs with their tensions and sinuous forms; also space travel, even science fiction."[28]

In 1960 Montreal's Ulysse Comtois (1931–1999) forsook painting for sculpture after seeing the welded steel sculptures of Julio González (1876–1942) at the Spaniard's solo exhibition in New York. But it was only in 1963 and 1964, while on a Canada Council grant in Europe and Israel, that he began assembling laminated wood or aluminum plates in interlocking spirals, thereby producing elegant works like *Column* (1967–1968).

Other itinerant sculptors never left North America. In 1961 John Nugent perfected his bronze-casting skills in a New York foundry. Living in New York City, he worked in clay, plaster, aluminum and stone; he saw impressive exhibitions and works by Giacometti and Brâncuşi. It was also in New York City that another Canada Council recipient, Calgary sculptor Katie Ohe, was introduced to "welding, metal spinning, chrome plating, high speed cutting equipment and materials such as Cor-Ten steel, anodized aluminum, plastics and resins," and to the work of Julio González, David Smith (1906–1965) and Isamu Noguchi (1904–1988).[29] Using these materials and importing new ideas allowed Ohe to break away from a strict rendering of the anatomical structure of the figure. As she put it: "I felt liberated, free to express myself with the dynamics and aesthetics of pure form."[30]

Opposite:
Ulysse Comtois
Column, 1967–1968
Painter and sculptor Ulysse Comtois was one of the artists who benefitted from the establishment of the Canada Council in 1957. He had previously been on the fringe of the Montreal-based Automatistes, who introduced their own style of Abstract Expressionism to the Canadian art scene. In the early 1960s, inspired by the sculptures of Julio Gonzáles, whose work he had first viewed in New York City, Comtois received a travel grant that took him to Europe and Israel. Afterwards, he became distinctive in painting or varnishing the twisting and interlocking rings of his sculptures, made initially from laminated wood, and eventually from metal.

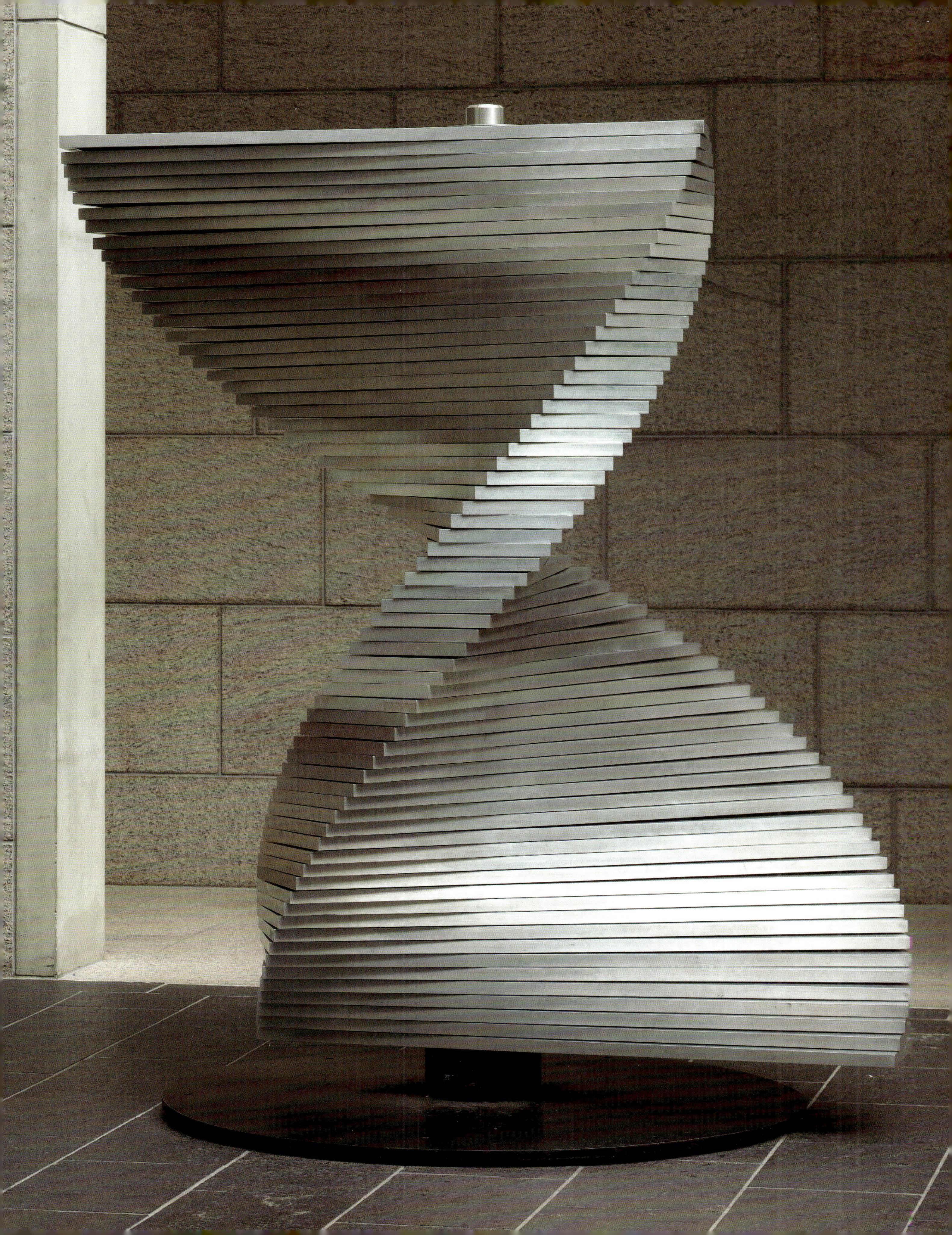

It may be too simple to speak of such contacts as bringing cultural imports into Canada; but there is no ignoring the influence that the work of non-Canadian sculptors exerted during this formative period. In 1961 John Nugent paid a notable visit to the American sculptor David Smith at Bolton Landing, New York, and his viewing of the American sculptor's metal constructions made a major impact on his own work, prompting him to "cast bronze or welded precut steel in planar geometric combinations."[31] Likewise, following study at the Vancouver School of Art, Ronald Bladen (1918–1988) moved to San Francisco and then in 1956 to New York, where he made his first free-standing Minimalist sculptures out of painted plywood. He too visited David Smith's studio and sculpture park.

In 1945, at the tail end of the Second World War, Walter Abell had claimed, as pointed out earlier, that that year marked the beginning of the "un-monumental age of sculpture."[32] His suggestion seemed plausible enough at the time. For many sculptors, including Anne Kahane, John Ivor Smith, Jack Hardman and Sybil Kennedy (1899–1986), the figure remained at the centre of their work. And it was not the realistic representation of the human form that mattered to these artists. Rather, for Kennedy and her colleagues the figure was a vehicle for expressing "the emotional significance of an idea through a rhythmic composition of line, form and space."[33]

But were these figurative sculptors simply lagging behind? "Compared to the more emotional and immediate arts," Elizabeth Wyn Wood wryly observed in 1948, sculpture was "long and slow."[34] Or was there something else at work, as the Vancouver expatriate painter Joe Plaskett (1918–2014) implied when he told an audience at the Vancouver Art Gallery in 1956: "We who were young abstractionists and who went to Europe were all shaken up when we saw the Sistine Chapel or Saint Mark's in Venice… We no longer accept anything because it is abstract, because it looks different and daring, because it looks original. We demand content and we demand style."[35] At the time there was no agreed view of the direction in which Canadian painting and sculpture was now moving, still less on the quality of the work being produced. One critic, Andrew Bell, declared the Sculptors Society of Canada's 1949 exhibition to be "dull and depressing."[36] Yet major developments, as we have seen, were in gestation.

The extent to which the modernist idiom was increasingly accepted and championed elsewhere became evident in the attention attracted by the international competition held by the Institute of Contemporary Arts in London in 1953 for a sculpture honouring "The Unknown Political Prisoner." Three of the forty-one finalists were Ontario's Robert Norgate (1920–1956), Quebec's Julien Hébert and Anne Kahane; and it was Kahane who received a commendation from the London-based jury for her maquette.

A visual metaphor of a cage or cell enclosing a writhing body, Kahane's *Maquette for the Unknown Political Prisoner* (1953) was composed of copper tubing and plastic wood bound together by wire. The work would have satisfied Julien Hébert's view that a sculpture was capable of expressing a particular theme by balancing form and content.[37] Stylistically, Kahane's spiky rendering simultaneously harked back to wire compositions created by Pablo Picasso (1881–1973) in the late 1920s and reached forward to David Smith's landscape drawings-in-space of the early 1950s. At the same time Kahane's work fulfilled the maxim of another sculptor living in Montreal, Sybil Kennedy, that a statue "should always be made Pyramidal, Serpentine."[38] Even so, here was an expressive work that, having moved away from figuration toward abstraction, was on the cusp of being non-objective. Kahane's work duly received recognition not only in London but also when the maquette was later displayed back in Canada.

Seeking a better life following the Second World War, many of Europe's finest painters and sculptors fled to North America where they had a chance to re-establish their reputations in more prosperous circumstances. Canada got its fair share of sculptors among the new immigrants, who often brought with them an understanding of modernist painting and sculpture. Dora de Pédery-Hunt (1913–2008), who had been trained at the Hungarian Academy of Fine Arts in Budapest, sought refuge in Canada in 1948 and became a prominent medal maker—she designed the Canadian Centennial Medal in 1967. Others passed on their skills to the country's new generation of sculptors through teaching. In 1959 Yugoslavian-born sculptor Zeljko Kujundzic (1920–2003) founded and became the director of the Kootenay School of the Arts in Nelson, British Columbia. Likewise, Jan Zach (1914–1986) arrived in Victoria from Czechoslovakia in 1951 and "provided something approaching a miraculous transformation of the artistic scene."[39] Before he left the city permanently, to teach at the University of Oregon in 1958, Zach demonstrated to young sculptors like Elza Mayhew (1916–2004) how, by turning the growth and movement of abandoned beach logs into roughly hewn sculpture, European Constructivism could be expressed through regional particularities. Determined to avoid cloning his students, he told them: "Don't try to catch the train; try to establish your own railroad."[40] Irish-born sculptor George Wallace (1920–2009) arrived in Canada in 1957 and three years later became a professor of fine arts at McMaster University in Hamilton. He was a disciple of British sculptor Reg Butler (1913–1981), who had been the overall winner of the "Unknown Political Prisoner" competition, and the influence is obvious. Determined to represent the human condition, Wallace produced a formidable group of welded-steel sculptures featuring criminals and religious figures, among whom were Christ, Peter, Lazarus and *The Benevolent Angel* (1963).

Dancing to an entirely different aesthetic, American-born Eli Bornstein brought what he called "structurist" sculpture to Saskatoon in 1950. Bornstein was an inspirational teacher at the University of Saskatchewan until his retirement in 1990. The magazine *The Structurist,* which he founded in 1960, gave him a further outlet for his "extensive writings on art, technology, architecture and ecological issues."[41] The magazine, which exists to this day, also provided a fitting compendium to the sculptor's

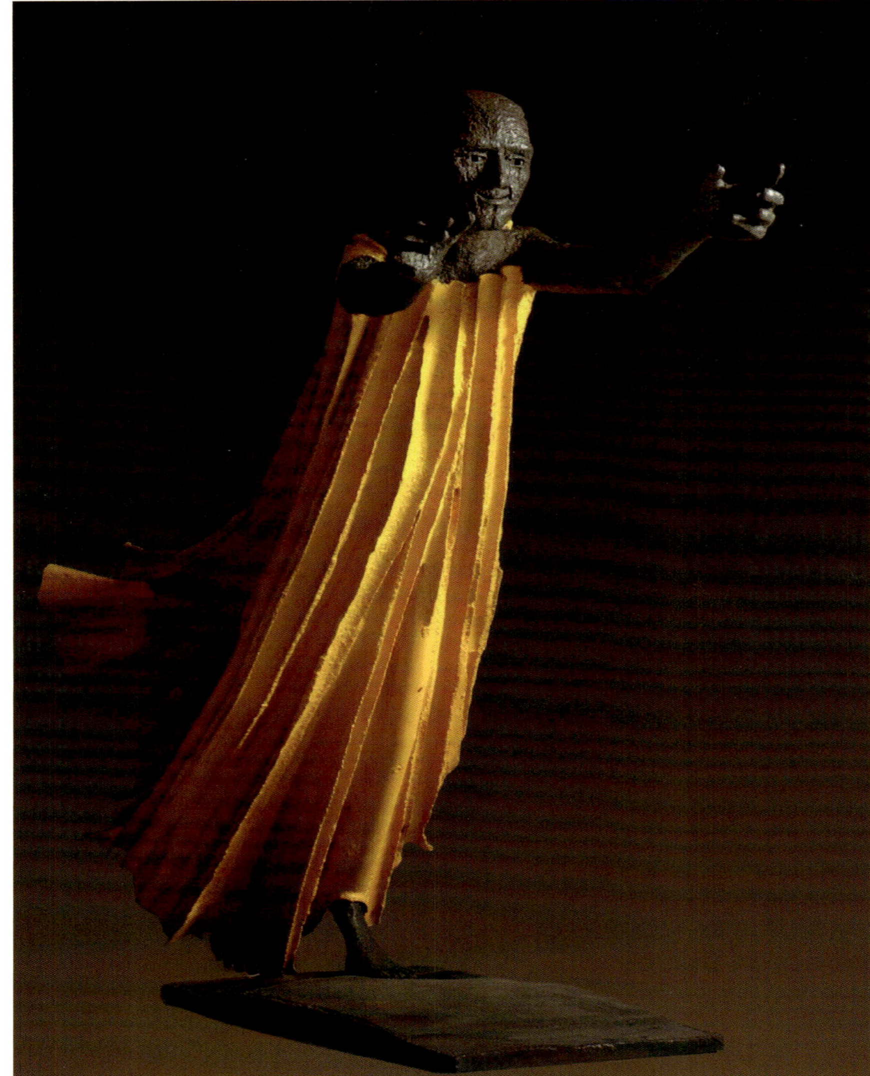

George Wallace
The Benevolent Angel, 1963
During his early years, Irish-born artist George Wallace had envisioned becoming a priest. Instead he became a sculptor and, after taking up a post at McMaster University in Hamilton, an art teacher. During his long teaching career—from 1960 to 1985—this romantic humanist never lost his interest in the spiritual side of the human condition, nor in making gravity-defying sculptures. He produced dozens of highly expressionistic sculptures of angels and saints. He explored the darker side of life by making thieves and hanged men subjects for his work. And, looking back to archaic Greek statuary, Wallace introduced colour into his sculptures.

explorations in light and colour, as resolved in his birchwood blocks and aluminum multi-plane configurations. Works like *Structurist Relief No. 18-II* (1958–1960) were a hybrid of painting and sculpture: "I couldn't think of one as more important than the other and I couldn't let one go in favour of the other," Bornstein explained. "Once I started looking at things, I seemed to be attracted to colour and light as well as to form and structure."[42]

There were, of course, postwar sculptors, painters and theorists who came to Canada and did not stay. Fernand Léger (1881–1955) and Ossip Zadkine (1890–1967), respectively French and Russian sculptors who were associated with the early days of Cubism, came to Quebec for brief periods of time, as did André Breton (1896–1966), a leading figure of Surrealism, and Father Marie-Alain Couturier (1897–1954), a French advocate of both modern art and the renewal of religious art.

Russian sculptor Alexander Archipenko (1887–1964), who had immigrated to the United States in 1923, acquired an enormous reputation

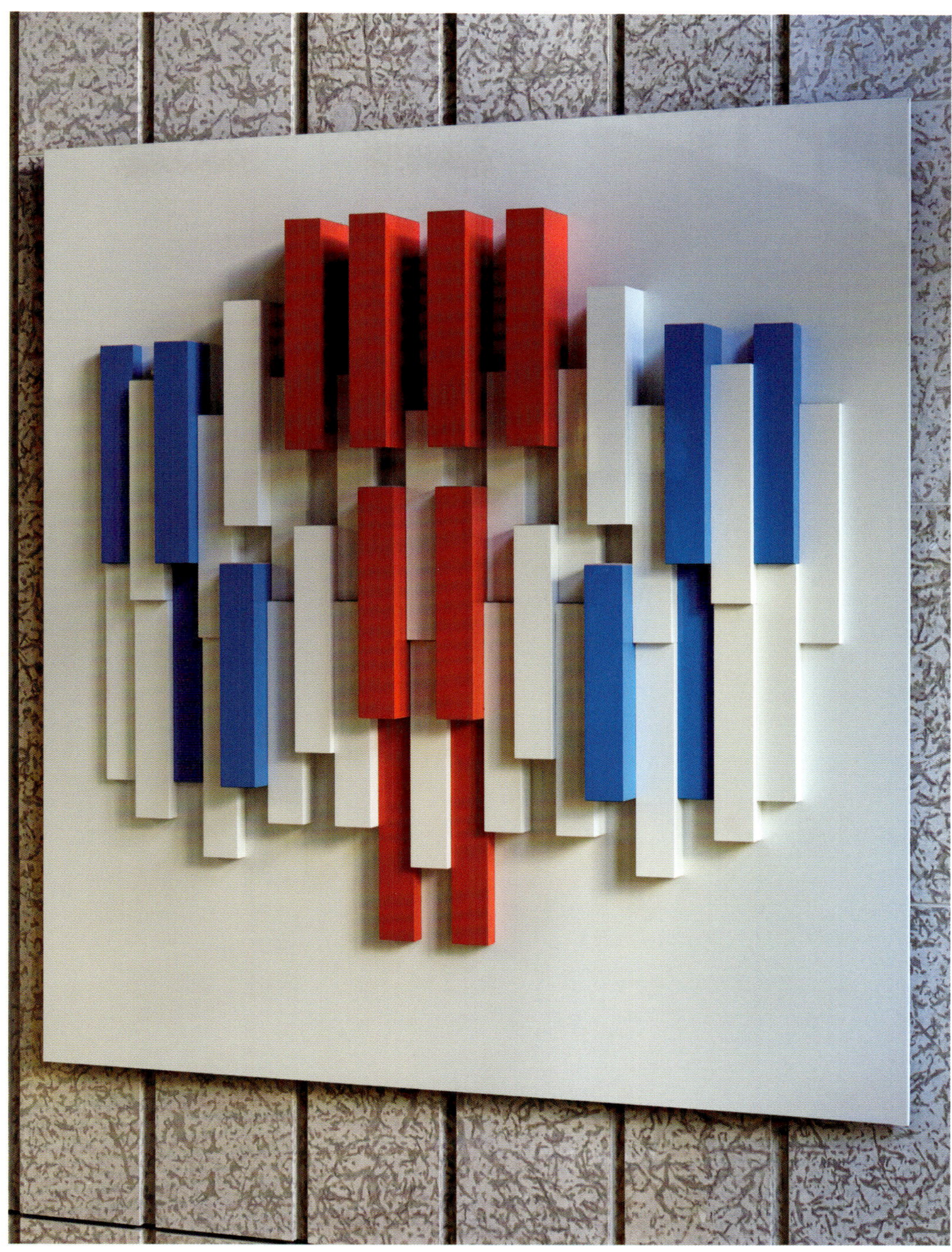

Eli Bornstein

Structurist Relief No. 18-II, 1958–1960

This American-born sculptor, who from 1950 made his living as a teacher and sculptor in Winnipeg, decided early in his career that the only way left open for both the sculptor and the painter was to create strictly geometric abstract constructions. Eli Bornstein built on the ideas of not only the American abstract sculptors but also of Russian sculptors, including Antoine Pevsner (1886–1962) and Kazimir Malevich (1879–1935). And he used a multi-plane, grid-like structure to make the colours and geometric forms of his bas-relief and free-standing sculptures expand into space.

among several Canadian sculptors. Working frequently in terracotta, Archipenko departed from Neoclassical tradition by opening up the sculptural mass and by enclosing space. The visual interplay between space and volume, between concave and convex forms, is evident in the work of Suzanne Guité, Irène Legendre (b. 1904) and Sybil Kennedy, all of whom studied with Archipenko in either Chicago or New York City. The same could be said of Jack Hardman, who met Archipenko at the University of British Columbia, where the Russian artist spent the summer in 1957. Other sculptors in Canada also broke out of the monolithic representation of the figure thanks to Archipenko.

In the postwar world, a perceived reversal of roles and relative importance between North America and Europe had an obvious impact in Canada. Europe was devastated and impoverished. Its art scene was in tatters. Conversely, Canada had experienced prosperity from shipbuilding and airplane and munitions production—all a product of the Second World War. Material circumstances obviously played a part in reinforcing a sense of the coming pre-eminence of North American over European art.

Sculpture was given high prominence in the articulation of this ambitious claim. In 1949, Clement Greenberg, the most influential art critic in the United States, announced that sculpture was "to be entirely abstract" and its lightness was to "negate the mass and solidity of traditional monolithic sculpture." Significantly, Greenberg predicted that sculpture was poised to overtake painting as the supreme art.[43] And his followers were now determined to set the agenda and, in Greenberg's view, surpass their contemporaries in Europe.[44]

New York may have seemed an appropriate place for such ambitions to be declared. Emma Lake, Saskatchewan, was perhaps a less likely spot for them to be realized. Yet, as Greenberg affirmed in a well-publicized visit there in 1962, it was where hopes of a renaissance of Canadian sculpture became focused. Founded in 1955, the Emma Lake Artists' Workshops at Murray Point in northern Saskatchewan were, according to Regina College teacher and artist Kenneth Lochhead (1926–2006), "a partial answer to the problem of isolation."[45] The Co-operative Commonwealth Federation (now the NDP) was elected as the first socialist government in North America in 1944 and was among the first provincial governments in Canada to fund the arts, by creating the Saskatchewan Arts Board, modelled on Great Britain's Arts Council, in 1948. Emma Lake was funded accordingly.

The (largely female) "students" who attended the workshops were professional painters, teachers and sculptors from western Canada. The (largely male) instructors who taught them were prominent western Canadian artists like Vancouver painter Jack Shadbolt (1909–1998). It was in 1957 that the teaching took a new direction. Prompted by some frustration—"If we can't get out, then let's bring someone from the outside to us"—invitations to give workshops at Emma Lake went out to Will Barnet (1911–2012), John Ferren (1905–1970), Barnett Newman (1905–

1970) Anthony Caro (1926–2013) and Donald Judd (1928–1994), all of whom adhered to the modernist critical aesthetic of Clement Greenberg.[46] During the 1960s and 1970s, these painters and sculptors from Great Britain and the United States made Emma Lake seem, in one critic's view, "more an outpost of New York rather than a part of the Canadian art scene."[47]

Barnett Newman's visit to Emma Lake in 1959 had profound consequences for two Vancouver-born Canadian sculptors. Newman's famous quip was that "sculpture is what you bump into when you back up to see a painting," yet if this suggested that he was unsympathetic to the art form, nothing could have been further from the truth.[48] Newman had a devotion to the flat surfaces and pure colour characteristic of Minimalist sculpture, self-evidently free of any association with outmoded images. We are, so the Quebec painter Paul-Émile Borduas (1905–1960) put it, always making ourselves out of our own feelings. Newman preached a similar gospel to his students. "He suggested that we didn't need him, we needed a psychiatrist," Robert Murray recalled. "That had to do with the sense of paranoia and lack of confidence that he saw in many of us, which came from the isolation of living in the middle of Canada, where interest in our work from the Eastern establishment was almost non-existent."[49]

Newman did not show his own work to his students at Emma Lake, nor did he advance any theory or art dogma. What he actually did was give the workshop participants confidence that if they took a professional approach to their work they could produce paintings and sculptures that were on a level with their contemporaries in New York. "From that point on," Murray recalled, "it was inevitable I would come to New York."[50] In 1960 Murray gave up his position at Saskatoon Technical Collegiate and accepted an assistantship from Newman. Reacting to the excesses of Abstract Expressionist painting, Murray went on to produce elegant, brightly painted, welded-metal constructions. Though he made his career and his reputation in the United States, Murray made a practice of returning to Canada during the summer months. Above all, during the 1960s he continued to partake in exhibitions in which he had no equal among his Canadian peers.

Here was the context, then, for Greenberg's own visit to the Emma Lake Workshops in 1962. Like Newman, three years earlier, Greenberg spoke rather than painted. As one account puts it, "he encouraged the artists to find and transmit the essence of what made them truly individual in their work, persuading them to avoid imitation while still celebrating the ideas of the modernist aesthetic that he had done so much to popularize."[51] This too echoed Newman. Greenberg's utterances were reported in awed tones to his receptive audience. It was clear that the prophet had spoken, with a success "based on respect for his eye and his ideas, and on his talent for creating win/win situations."[52]

Greenberg behaved almost like an American football coach, set on raising the morale of his team. After a tour of western Canada in the year following his visit to Emma Lake, he went on, in a highly publicized article published in *Canadian Art* in the spring of 1963, to lavish his praise on what these artists were doing. "The vitality of art in Regina does constitute an unusual phenomenon," he pronounced, while Calgary's Katie Ohe, not to be overlooked, was hailed as "a good abstract sculptor, doing tight and beautifully sensed little monoliths in terra cotta."[53] Eli Bornstein earned Greenberg's praise for his welded aluminum sculpture made for the Teachers' Federation Building; its "open and 'drawn' geometrical construction" and its "over-all conception" were "magnificent."[54]

The extent of Greenberg's influence, however, should not be exaggerated, nor all his comments accepted at face value. Above all, the New York spectacles through which he viewed Canadian art do not give an objective impression of what Canadian artists were really doing. One thing this distinguished visitor did not note was the extent to which Bornstein's work was not only inspired by the writings of John White on pictorial space but also by the Constructivist reliefs of the American artist Charles Biederman (1906–2004) whose interest in colour, light, intersecting abstract planes and new materials beginning in the late 1930s formed the basis of Bornstein's work.[55] John Nugent, who attended the Emma Lake Artists' Workshops in the 1950s and early 1960s, brought the Formalist Abstraction of the New York School together with his own brand of Constructivist sculpture. Barnett Newman's suggestion that Nugent move to the United States was ignored. He preferred to remain on his farm, in Saskatchewan, where he fulfilled commissions across the country producing collages and by combining prefabricated elements.

Nugent was by no means alone in not succumbing to Greenberg's magic. Many other artists flooded *Canadian Art* with demands as to why the magazine had asked an outsider to comment on their work. In Toronto John Ivor Smith was already wary of what he called "the cult of New York." In his view this was "the most dangerous and debasing feature of the contemporary art scene."[56] In western Canada, Vancouver artists were equally guarded about stepping onto Greenberg's bandwagon. During his visit to Vancouver in the early 1960s, the art critic was "boring, boring, boring"—at least that was the opinion of Myra Hardman, the wife of sculptor Jack Hardman. "All he did," she maintained, "was prose on about Modern Art and the avant-garde and blah, blah, blah, while everybody sat at his feet." The fact that they sat there, of course, was itself significant. "None of us had the wit to say that it was just one of many styles," and, in order to explain why no one took him on, she simply offered the comment: "We were all Canadians. We were too polite." More surprisingly, Greenberg's wife, Jenny Van Horne, likewise declared that her husband was "so boring." She found the lack of response remarkable. "Why," Van Horne asked the assembled group of painters and sculptors, "is everybody listening to him?"[57]

In Vancouver, Greenberg had clearly found himself among artists who were not devotees of the New York School. Jack Hardman, working as Alexander Archipenko's assistant at the University of British Columbia, was now adapting the Russian sculptor's unique form of figurative Cubism and terracotta material to his own sculptures. Having just returned from England, the Alberta-born but Vancouver-based sculptor David Marshall (1928–2006) remained a follower of Henry Moore. Elza Mayhew, who explored the themes of sacrifice, authority and ritual, was equally

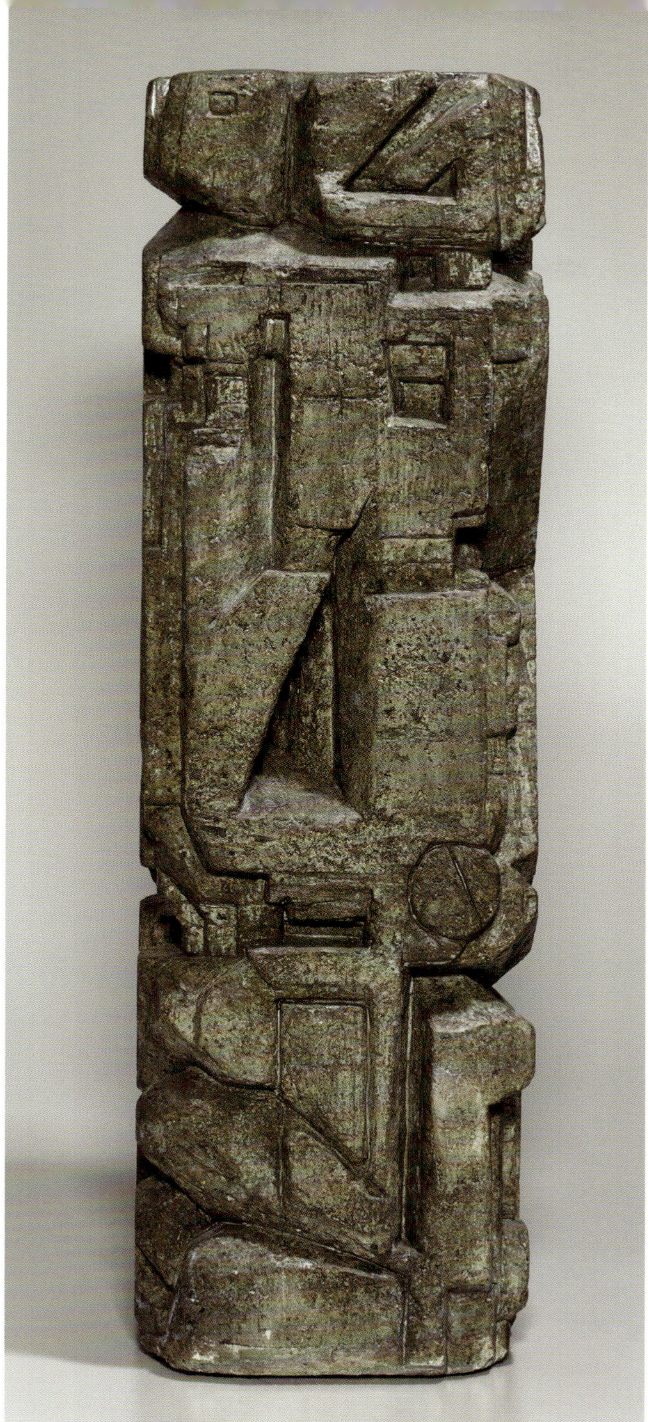

ambivalent towards Greenberg and American Abstract Expressionism. This Victoria sculptor's monolithic columns melded the unique landscape and Indigenous art of her native province with the sculpture of ancient Mayan, Etruscan, Assyrian and Minoan civilizations. "In the sense that the work is mainly monolithic and totemic, I am a traditionalist, dominantly concerned with the old inevitable sequence of past, present and future," she explained. On the other hand, her efforts in "opening up space within the volume in various ways" in her bronze and stone sculptures were, she claimed, "a denial of the monolithic character, as are the protrusions which extend out from the block."[58]

Thus, for Hardman, Mayhew and Marshall alike, there was little craving for Greenberg's patronage, approval or support. Indeed, Vancouver's first art gallery devoted entirely to contemporary art and sculpture, the New Design Gallery, had given them a venue for their work since 1955. And when Marshall joined with sculptors from Washington State to found the Northwest Institute for Sculpture in 1956, British Columbia's sculptors enjoyed their first outdoor exhibition at the University of British Columbia. Together with Quebec's open-air exhibition at Île Sainte-Hélène in the same year, it was among the first outdoor exhibitions of sculpture in the country.

It is not surprising that the director of the National Gallery of Canada, Alan Jarvis, noted that "a mini-Renaissance" had taken place in Vancouver during the 1950s, though the city's coolness to the rest of Canada might be viewed as a reaction against central-Canadian nationalist thinking, as promoted by the Canada Council.

A group of sculptors in the conservative farm belt of Ontario also proved that they did not need Clement Greenberg's support and were perfectly capable of mounting their own exhibitions, marketing their own work, producing their own magazines and working in a range of styles and mediums. Sculptors from London, Ontario, including Ed Zelenak (b. 1940), Tony Urquhart (b. 1934), Walter Redinger (1940-2014) and Jeffrey Rubinoff (1945–2017), shared an abhorrence of the market-driven system, dominated by the art centres of Toronto and Montreal. At the same time, they were conscious of what was going on outside of the country. Because they strove to be part of the international art world, they saw themselves as internationalists, not nationalists; and as cosmopolitans, not regionalists. They displayed their work in a number of artist-run galleries and co-operatives, which gave them control over the content, display, sale and distribution of their work. In 1966 the National Gallery of Canada paid tribute to some of them in an exhibition titled *The Heart of London*. It is no surprise, then, that by 1969 London should be dubbed "the most important art center in Canada and a model for artists working elsewhere, 'the site of Canada's first regional liberation front.'"[59]

Sculptors in Quebec, for their part, were undaunted by Greenberg's claim that the new and vigorous art typified by the New York School was simply "Made in the USA." In 1947, Paul-Émile Borduas and his Surrealist-inspired colleagues, who had formed Les Automatistes in 1943, held their first exhibition of non-objective, gestural (or action) paintings, presented as metaphors of the inner thoughts and feelings of the artist rather than as their "rational" objective representation of the world around them. Some would go on to produce sculpture, namely Borduas himself, Jean-Paul Riopelle (1923–2002), Françoise Sullivan and Marcel Barbeau (1925–2016). But the members of Les Automatistes were largely painters and, not least, political activists who, in their manifesto *Refus Global* (1948), challenged the backward-looking Church and the province's authoritarian premier Maurice Duplessis, leader of the Union Nationale government.

Although Les Atomatistes had an enormous presence in Quebec, other groups, including Prisme d'Yeux (1948) and Les Plasticiens (1955), reacted against what they felt was the group's overly intellectual stance and its use of art as a vehicle for emotional states. In 1956 Armand Vaillancourt and Robert Roussil were instrumental in founding the Association des Arts Plastiques à Montréal. Here was a forum where poetry, jazz, performance and teaching could take place in the mid-1950s. Their May 1953 exhibition, featuring 350 works created by a wide range of painters and sculptors, was held in the Place des Arts. Openly critical of the Duplessis government, and accordingly considered a vehicle for subversive purposes, the exhibition was closed by the police under the infamous "Padlock Law." No wonder Roussil and Vaillancourt were thought to be the first "to bring modern sculpture into the public sphere and, in so doing, to present a different aspect of monuments than those we were used to seeing."[60]

While established institutions largely ignored their sculptures, the public could not have missed Vaillancourt's experimental performance-sculpture and environmental work *L'Arbre de la Rue Durocher* (1953–1954). The Montreal-based artist worked outdoors on this sculpture for over two years, and did so in the manner of the German artist Joseph Beuys (1921–1986), variously described as sculptor, installation artist and interventionist. Vaillancourt figuratively brought a dying tree back to life by cutting, carving, burning and sculpting it, using burners, hand tools and an axe.[61] Over the next decade, as we have seen, Vaillancourt became a public activist, linking public sculpture to political, social, environmental and cultural concerns. Animated by the idea that sculpture was a spectacle, he created large abstract metal sculptures like *Je Me Souviens* (1967).[62] Vaillancourt transported the 310-metric-ton sculpture to Toronto for exhibition at the International Sculpture Symposium in High Park but the political nature of the work's title prompted the exhibition committee to reject it. Vaillancourt had to hire eight tow trucks to transport the work back to Quebec.

Anne Kahane, too, might be thought of as a social commentator; but apart from her *Maquette for the Unknown Political Prisoner,* her sculptures were quiet, satirical works. Her assemblages in wood and aluminum subtly questioned and observed, rather than overtly challenged, social conventions. Kahane portrayed the human condition in suspended motion, with implied or interrupted action: a group of people watching a ball game, or sheltering under an umbrella. Yvette Bisson (b. 1926) and Yves Trudeau (b. 1930) were also actively at work, and well known through the society they founded in 1961, the Association des Sculpteurs de Québec.

Montreal showed itself less impressed by New York than was the case in Toronto. There the members of Painters Eleven (1953) prominently embraced Abstract Expressionism and the New York School and in 1957 invited Clement Greenberg to view their work in Toronto. Two painters in the group turned to sculpture: not only Walter Yarwood (1917–1996) who, according to fellow artist Tom Hodgson's assessment in 1963, made the other painters "look like Boy Scouts," but also Kazuo Nakamura (1926–2002), who manifested an interest in science, time and space.[63] By 1965,

Armand Vaillancourt
L'Arbre de la Rue Durocher, 1953–1954
Armand Vaillancourt's sculptures rarely failed to
engage the public in Quebec, and elsewhere in
Canada, by challenging established aesthetic norms
and by questioning conservative social values and
political beliefs. During the early 1950s, Montrealers
watched as Vaillancourt integrated nature into
modern sculpture by working both with and against
it. He cut, burned, scratched and dismembered a
tree, and eventually gave it a new life in the form
of an organic sculpture. Among the first installation
or performance sculptures in Canada, the colossal
L'Arbre de la Rue Durocher took Vaillancourt two
years to produce.

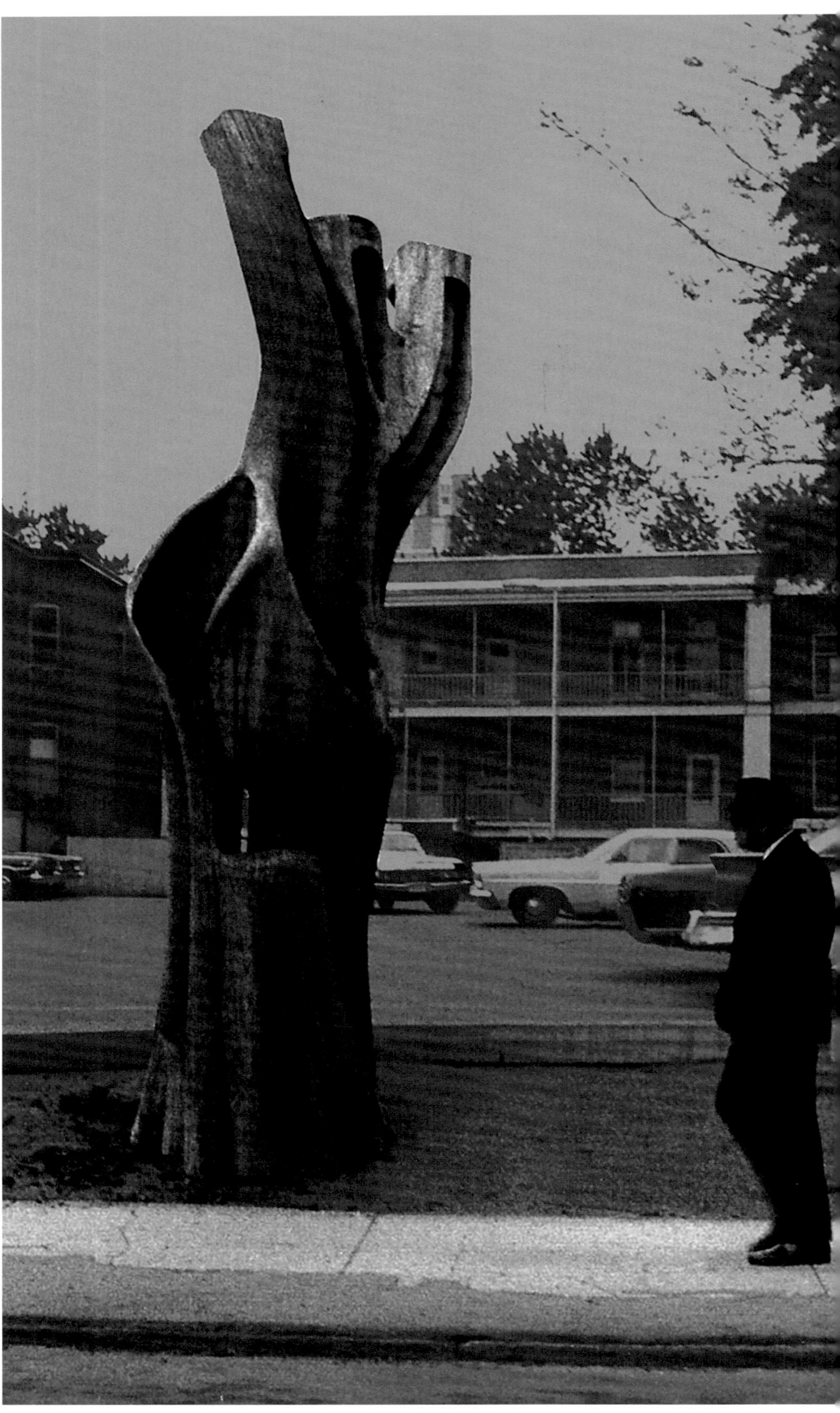

after five years of working as a sculptor, Yarwood was using his totem theme to produce cast-aluminum lattice columns with surfaces that had been sheered and picked away with the help of acid.[64]

Like Yarwood, sculptors Henry Saxe (b. 1937), David Partridge (1919–2006), Ulysse Comtois, Yosef Drenters (1930–1983), Robert Murray, Michael Snow (b. 1929), Tony Urquhart and Gerald Gladstone had all begun as painters. Yarwood admitted that he "wasn't really a success as a painter." Looking back on his paintings, he felt "they were paintings with sculptural ideas."[65] Although Gladstone turned to sculpture in 1960, the same year as Yarwood, he did not stop painting. Sorel Etrog (1933–2014) arrived in Canada in 1959 from Romania, via Israel and then Brooklyn; and his dynamic figurative bronzes and Symbolist abstractions were inspired by the rich simplicity of Oceanic and African carvings and pre-Columbian clay figures. His own subject-based, knotted and painted constructions seemed to Etrog himself "neither painting nor relatively shallow sculptural relief," and he instead claimed them as "both."[66]

Claude Tousignant, who had also begun as a painter, found the question equally difficult—or perhaps equally easy—to answer. "For the artist, the distinction between painting and sculpture is not very important because the painter is the sculptor and vice versa."[67] The same could be said of Robert Hedrick (b. 1930), from Windsor, Ontario, whose sculptural reliefs carried on a dialogue with his non-objective gestural paintings. As a filmmaker, musician and a painter, Michael Snow displayed various influences in his work, enabling him to blur the margin between painting, film and sculpture, as seen in his *Walking Woman* series, begun in 1961 while he was living in New York.

Whether or not the average Canadian subscribed to modernist or traditional forms of sculpture, by the early 1960s sculpture could not be ignored because it was in the public square, in private galleries, in the church and, depending on its size, in the home. And these works, as the sculptor John Ivor Smith noted in 1962, not only showed a plethora of styles and a plethora of materials, they prompted a feeling that sculpture was "approaching a flowering, in Canada no less than elsewhere, and the rapid increase in popularity we see today may promise an adequate audience."[68] Writing in *Maclean's* in 1963, the journalist Robert Fulford was forthright: "Whether they like it or not, Canadians will see a great deal more sculpture in the next few years than they've seen in the last few."[69] The art critic Hugo McPherson made a stronger case for sculpture a year later. It was no longer the "Cinderella of the arts," taking second place to two-dimensional painting.[70] Instead, in Canada "sculptors were no longer the orphans of the art scene: indeed, as the season ended it was clear that—for the first time since the age of Quebec's wood carvers—Canada's sculptors were shining more brightly than her painters."[71]

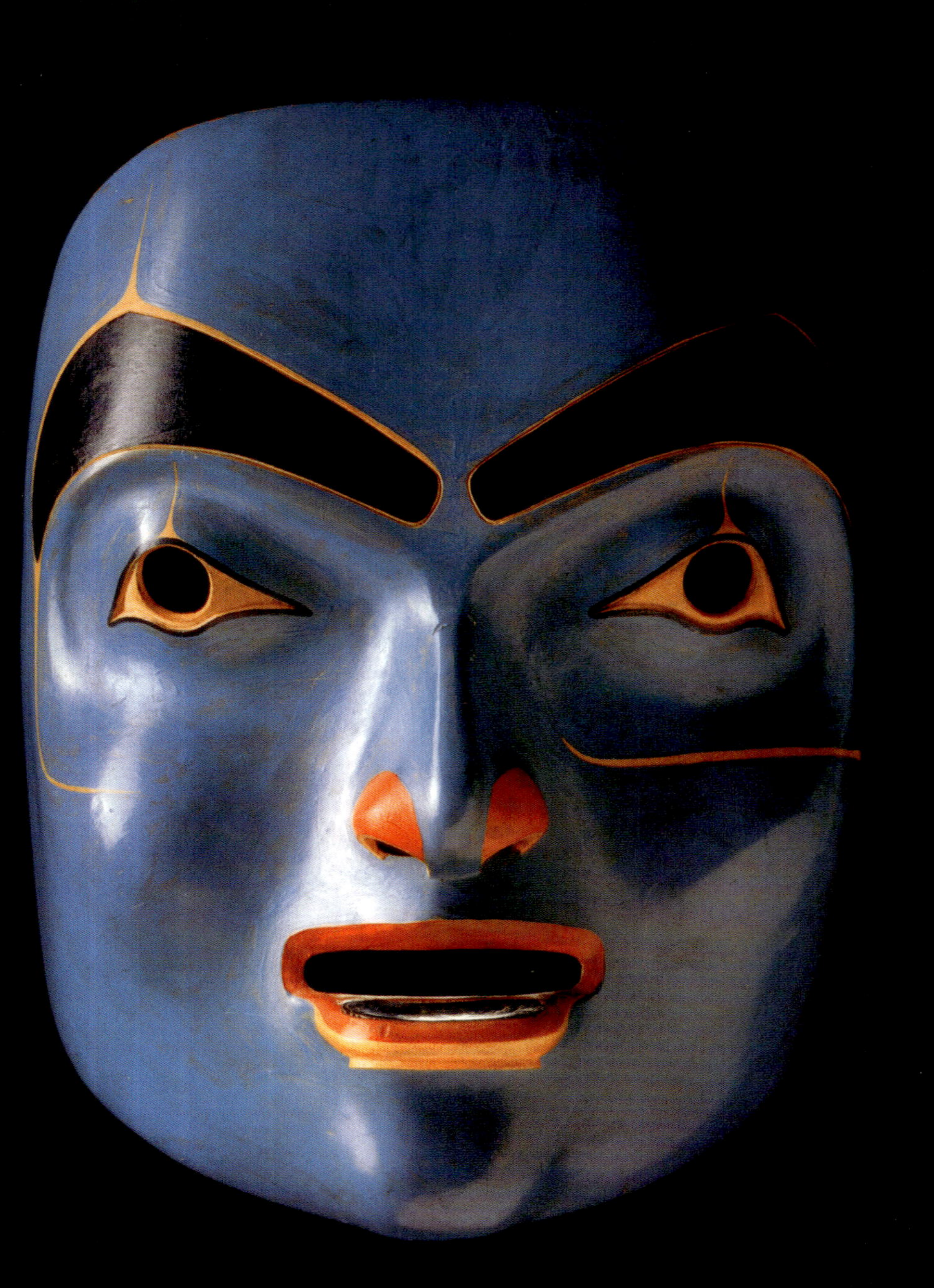

7
Centennial Sculpture

It was an uphill struggle to gain official recognition for modernist sculpture in Canada. The National Gallery of Canada had been slow to embrace Clement Greenberg's call in the late 1940s for a "New Sculpture" movement. Under the direction of Harry McCurry, who had taken over from Eric Brown in 1939, the National Gallery was still characterized in 1955 as "a crusty, dark and forbidding institution" and downright "tomb-like" in the Canadian edition of *Time* magazine.[1]

The fact that it was housed in the Victoria Memorial Museum seemed to say it all. It was not just the material structure of the public building—at this time one still had to pass through the stuffed animals to get to the galleries above—it was the institution's policies. There were simply too few purchases of contemporary sculpture from public funds. As Elizabeth Wyn Wood put it in 1948: "As far as the public Art Galleries are concerned they have all but, as the psychologists might say, 'unconsciously rejected' the art of sculpture."[2]

Things began to improve when Alan Jarvis (1915–1972), a sculptor himself, took over the National Gallery in 1955.[3] His declared ambition was to build "a museum without walls" and the new director did this in several ways. He sent dozens of travelling exhibitions, including sculpture, across the country. He had a hand in choosing Jean-Paul Riopelle and Paul-Émile Borduas, both Surrealist-inspired members of Les Automatistes, for inclusion in the third São Paulo Exhibition in Brazil in 1955. Likewise, Montreal sculptor Louis Archambault was chosen to represent Canada at the Venice Biennale in 1956. Jarvis also saw to it that Archambault and Vancouver sculptor Bill Koochin (b. 1927) were commissioned to produce work for the Canadian pavilion at the Brussels World's Fair in 1958 (though it did not help that the work displayed in front of the Canadian pavilion was dominated by a high blank cinema wall belonging to the Russian pavilion). And in 1966, a pioneer of Abstract sculpture from Montreal, Yvette Bisson, exhibited some of her stone sculptures at the Rodin Museum in Paris.

Alan Jarvis not only saw to it that Canadian sculpture was shown abroad. He made a point of visiting artists' studios and of giving lectures on painting and sculpture across the country. He appointed publicists to promote the National Gallery, including one based in the Maritimes and one in western Canada. And, a decade before his friend, British art historian Kenneth Clark, hosted the famous television series *Civilisation*, in 1958 Jarvis invited Canadians to watch a thirteen-part series, *The Things We See*, on CBC Television. During the eighth episode Jarvis showed that he was not afraid to get his hands dirty when he applied heavy daubs of clay to Jacob Epstein's well-known bust of George Bernard Shaw in an attempt to "deflate the stuffy pretensions of art and gallery-going."[4]

It was a significant step in 1959 when Jarvis moved the entire collection of the National Gallery itself from the upper floor of the Victoria Memorial Museum to the seven-storey Lorne Building near the Parliament Buildings. Personally he preferred traditionalist sculptors like Frances Loring and Florence Wyle. He remained averse to the New York School of Abstract Expressionist artists. And he was committed to spending the largest share of the gallery's annual budget on European "masters."

Admittedly, Jarvis added some early European modernist sculptors, including Jean Arp, Jacques Lipchitz (1891–1973), Alberto Giacometti, Jacob Epstein and Henry Moore, to the gallery's collection. And he did acquire work by Canadian sculptors: not only his favourite, Louis Archambault, but also Anne Kahane, Dora de Pédery-Hunt and Victor Tolgesy. But the irony, as one historian puts it, was that "under the most conspicuously cosmopolitan director in its history, the National Gallery became the equivalent of a national customs post for art, excluding those forms that might pose the greatest challenge to the alleged uniqueness of the home-grown product"—a policy through which Jarvis implemented an "aesthetic *cordon sanitaire* even as he promoted Canadian 'abstraction.'"[5]

Such was Jarvis's legacy on leaving the National Gallery in 1959. His successor, Charles Comfort (1900–1994), had been a war artist as a painter during the Second World War, but was also a sculptor. This helped ensure that three-dimensional art was not ignored. Indeed in 1962 and 1964, under Comfort's direction, the National Gallery sponsored two outdoor exhibitions of modernist sculpture that included artists from across the country. There were contributions from Nova Scotia painter and sculptor Thomas De Vany Forrestal (b. 1936), Toronto's Gerald Gladstone and Les Levine (b. 1935), Alberta's Katie Ohe and Vancouver's Jack Hardman, along with Jordan Hammond Smith (b. 1936) and Yves Trudeau from Montreal. Was this enough to signal a change of heart?

The National Gallery's uncomfortable relationship with contemporary art came to a head in 1965. During the course of mounting an exhibition by New York artist Andy Warhol (1928–1987), Toronto gallery owner Jerrold Morris ran into Canadian import laws. Photographs of the pop artist's boxes of Brillo soap pads and tin cans of Campbell's soup were put before Charles Comfort as director of the National Gallery. He duly declared that they were not sculpture and were therefore subject to 20 per cent duty on commercial value attributed to merchandise. According to Comfort, sculpture "must be in metal or stone, or other materials in black and white, as opposed to the painted wooden boxes of Warhol."[6] It was not until the arrival of Jean Sutherland Boggs in 1966 that the gallery's disdain for contemporary American art was fully overcome.

Up until then, it was not in Ottawa that the pace was set, nor even in Montreal, which had led the art scene during the 1940s and 1950s. From the late 1950s, Toronto was perceived as the centre of modernist art in Canada, for a variety of reasons, some of them not intrinsically aesthetic. Montreal may have had claims to challenge the priority of New York in pioneering Abstraction in modern art, but Toronto was now where sculptors from all over the country wanted to go to and to be seen. The city's size, cosmopolitan flavour and urban vitality allowed nationalist and regional backgrounds to be forgotten.

Most cities in Canada had, at most, one commercial gallery devoted to modern art. Vancouver had its New Design Gallery; Ottawa had both the Robertson Gallery and the Blue Barn. Montreal certainly did better than this: in 1955 an exclusively non-objective gallery opened, the Galerie l'Actuelle. The city also had Galerie Antoine, the Dominion Gallery, Galerie Denyse Delrue and Galerie Agnès Lefort, not to mention the short-lived Place des Arts, which was more than a gallery: it was a resource centre and political forum—and a thorn in the side of the city of Montreal, which closed it down. Crowning this was the founding in 1964 of the first public gallery in the country devoted solely to modern art: the Musée d'Art Contemporain de Montréal. Some sites shared space with another activity. Madame Lespérance's flower shop was a venue for artists like Charles Daudelin; the Librairie Tranquille was a bookstore with space for monthly exhibitions; some restaurants, like L'Échourie and the Hélène de Champlain Restaurant, on Île Sainte-Hélene, also provided a venue for Montreal's sculptors.

Yet it was Toronto that set the pace in the 1960s. It had the largest number of commercial galleries willing to display the work of contemporary sculptors to a wider, more affluent and more receptive public. The city had the Greenwich Gallery, later known as Isaacs Gallery, along with the Roberts Gallery, the Park Gallery, the Carmen Lamanna Gallery, the Morris Gallery, the Gallery Pascal and the Helen Mazelow Gallery (originally a framing shop)—all of which had been established by the 1960s. The most important venue for sculptors, however, was the Here and Now Gallery, founded in 1959 and renamed the Dorothy Cameron Gallery in 1962. It was not long before its owner, Dorothy Cameron (1924–2000), was acclaimed as "the midwife of modern Canadian sculpture."[7]

This high claim was well deserved. With her overriding commitment to putting modernist sculpture before the public, Cameron found difficulty in turning a profit, but she certainly succeeded in giving new prominence to the works displayed: as one commenter put it, "A Cameron exhibition was always a unique, audaciously curated, beautifully staged, carefully produced art event."[8] A producer of mixed-media sculpture herself, Cameron cast her net widely. Her visits to artists all over Canada were reflected in the solo exhibitions during the six years that she was a gallery curator: in the early 1960s showing the work of Ulysse Comtois, Yosef Drenters, Gerald Gladstone, Robert Hedrick, Victor Tolgesy, Claude Tousignant and Elza Mayhew.

It was Cameron's two-part sculpture exhibition *Canadian Sculpture Today*, held during the spring of 1964, that marked the apogee of her influence. Featuring no fewer than fourteen sculptors, here was "a commercial venture on a scale hitherto undreamed of in Canada."[9] The quality of the work on display heralded a new era, moving beyond nationalist attempts to portray the land or monumental carvings of the country's leaders or organic carvings in the style of Henry Moore.[10] The work on view challenged the time-worn conventions of beauty, realism and perfection. And not one member of the Sculptors Society of Canada, viewed since 1950 as "relatively cautious and conservative," was invited to contribute to the exhibition.[11]

Instead, the artists whose work was chosen represented the younger generation of sculptors. There were John Ivor Smith's Surrealistic cast-stone heads; there were bronze figures by the Romanian-born Sorel Etrog; there were the sensuous ceramic sculptures of the American-born Arthur Handy (1933–2004). Also prominent were Elza Mayhew's bronze structures evoking Aztec monuments, along with the broken-line motifs of Anne Kahane's whimsical assemblages in wood and metal. Walter Yarwood's cast-iron sculptures, Armand Vaillancourt's bronzes and Robert Murray's austere, unreconstructed modernist works were there too. Attempting to generalize the importance of the exhibition, critic Hugo McPherson observed that these sculptors had defied "firmly but not rebelliously the philistine demand for decorative and representational objects; each is intent on exploring a personal vision." He also noted that "though their vision is contemporary and their techniques inventive, most prefer to work in a durable and even rich medium."[12]

In 1967 Canada's one hundredth birthday became more than an official commemoration of a constitutional anniversary. It opportunely unleashed a celebration of national identity with a powerful social and cultural impact. This fostered much more widespread recognition of how much had been achieved, not just in the course of the past century, but specifically in the previous two decades. The Indigenous and non-Indigenous sculpture on show at Expo '67 was seen through that lens, and not always in an inward-looking way. Instead, it was gratifying that more Canadian sculptors than ever before were incorporating the latest trends from abroad into their work, or reworking old themes, or developing new forms of expression.

A writer for the *Chicago Tribune* was one of fifty million people who rode the monorail to Expo '67's site at the Mackay Pier, La Ronde, Île Sainte-Hélène and Notre Dame Island. "There is," Vincent Price observed, "hardly a corner, plaza, platform, or what have you, that doesn't brag a piece of sculpture moving, still, or literally, belching fire or water at you." This actor-cum-art-collector saw sculptures on rooftops, in squares, inside or in front of pavilions, in reflecting ponds and even under water. But, as Price commented, "the real clincher was that the majority of works were not the product of established or old or modern masters but of young artists from all over the world, especially Canada, and that a lot of it was first rate."[13] Indeed, there was so much sculpture on display by Canadian and foreign sculptors alike that the art critic for *Time* magazine was prompted to observe that "In its entirety, Expo '67 could be viewed as one long contemporary art gallery."[14]

Sculptures representing sixty-two nations were displayed. They included work from well-known international sculptors, ranging from Britain's Henry Moore and the United States' Alexander Calder to the master of Italian Renaissance sculpture, Michelangelo. But, as William Withrow made clear in the catalogue, *Sculpture Canadienne / Canadian Sculpture, Expo 67*, there were a sufficient number of home-grown works to give "Canadians, and the whole world, a fine opportunity to assess the state of Canadian Sculpture today."[15]

Thus, there were murals by André Biéler (1896–1989) and Ulysse Comtois as well as by Armand Vaillancourt, whose three-storey-high concrete work adorned the entrance of the Expo '67 Administrative Building on the Mackay Pier. There was also a reworked version of Vaillancourt's *L'Arbre de la Rue Durocher* (1953–1954); Louis Archambault's figurative and much larger sculpture *Une Grande Couple* (1967); and Sorel Etrog's *Flight* (1967)—a larger version of his contribution to the Venice Biennale in 1966. Jordi Bonet displayed five sculptures cast in aluminum in the Place des Nations, having "exhausted all technical and creative possibilities of ceramics," as one critic commented.[16] In *Meditation Piece* (1967), Elza

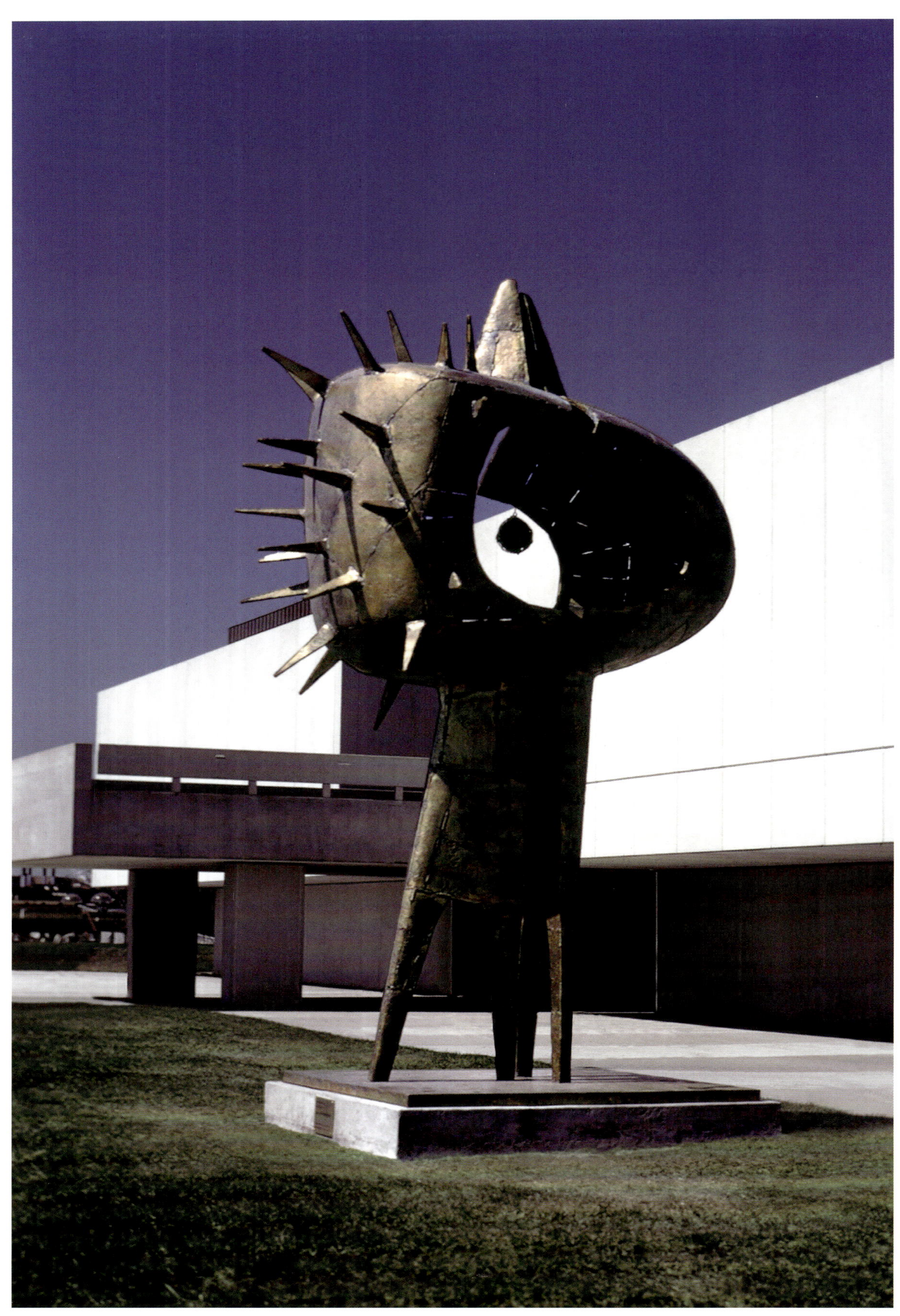

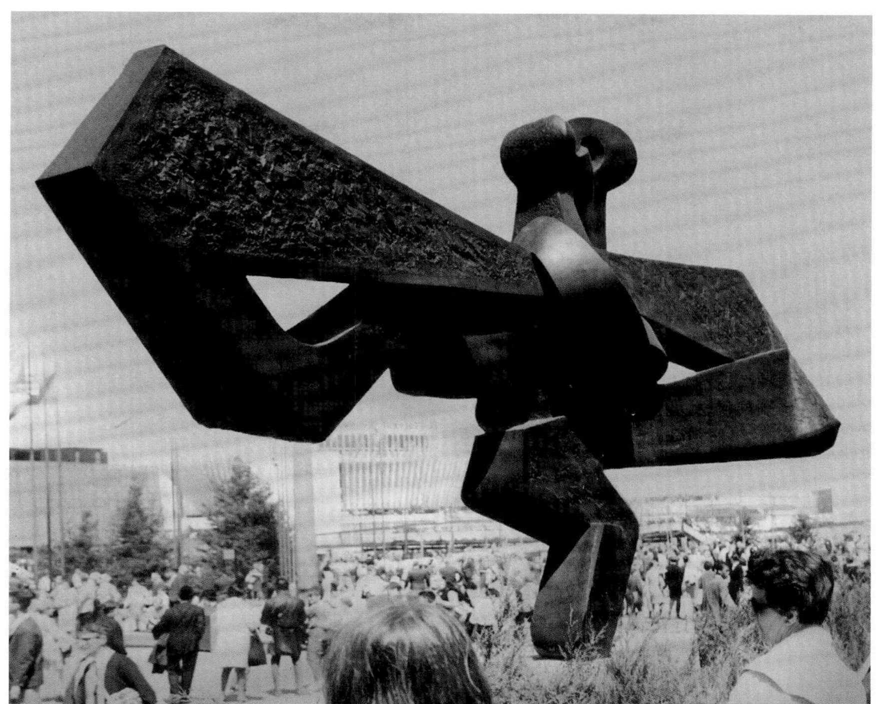

Mayhew was less adventurous.[17] Though now working on a larger scale, she maintained the totemic theme, favoured modelling her work in clay and casting it in bronze rather than carving directly on the stone. Two other sculptors from Montreal, Germain Bergeron (b. 1933) and Anne Kahane, implemented new methods: the first by welding industrial scrap iron and the second by laminating mahogany planks, which exemplified Clement Greenberg's observation that such works were "not so much sculpted as constructed, built, assembled, [and] arranged."[18] Contributions from other female sculptors, including Françoise Sullivan and Suzanne Guité, likewise helped to reinforce the notion that sculpture was no longer exclusively a male art. Conversely, Michael Snow, who never claimed to be a sculptor in the first place, produced eleven stainless steel cut-out figures of women. First conceived in New York in 1961, his *Walking Woman* was the centrepiece of the Ontario pavilion.

If the works of the fifty-one Canadian artists at Expo '67 shared anything, it was diversity. They did not adhere to a single style that might have been identified as typically Canadian. Like so many artists who had emerged after the Second World War, Françoise Sullivan wished to rid sculpture "of all non-sculptural forms, and the superfluous imagery so often confused with 'style.'"[19] "Canadian sculpture as an individual statement" did not exist for Gerald Gladstone, while Armand Vaillancourt felt that his work could only be called Canadian insofar as it was executed in Canada.[20] As Toronto sculptor Maryon Kantaroff (b. 1933) reflected a few years later: "To be, or to try to be, self-consciously 'Canadian' is to lose the personal integrity without which art cannot come into being."[21] The "modernism" to which most of the sculptures on display at Expo '67 adhered had, in

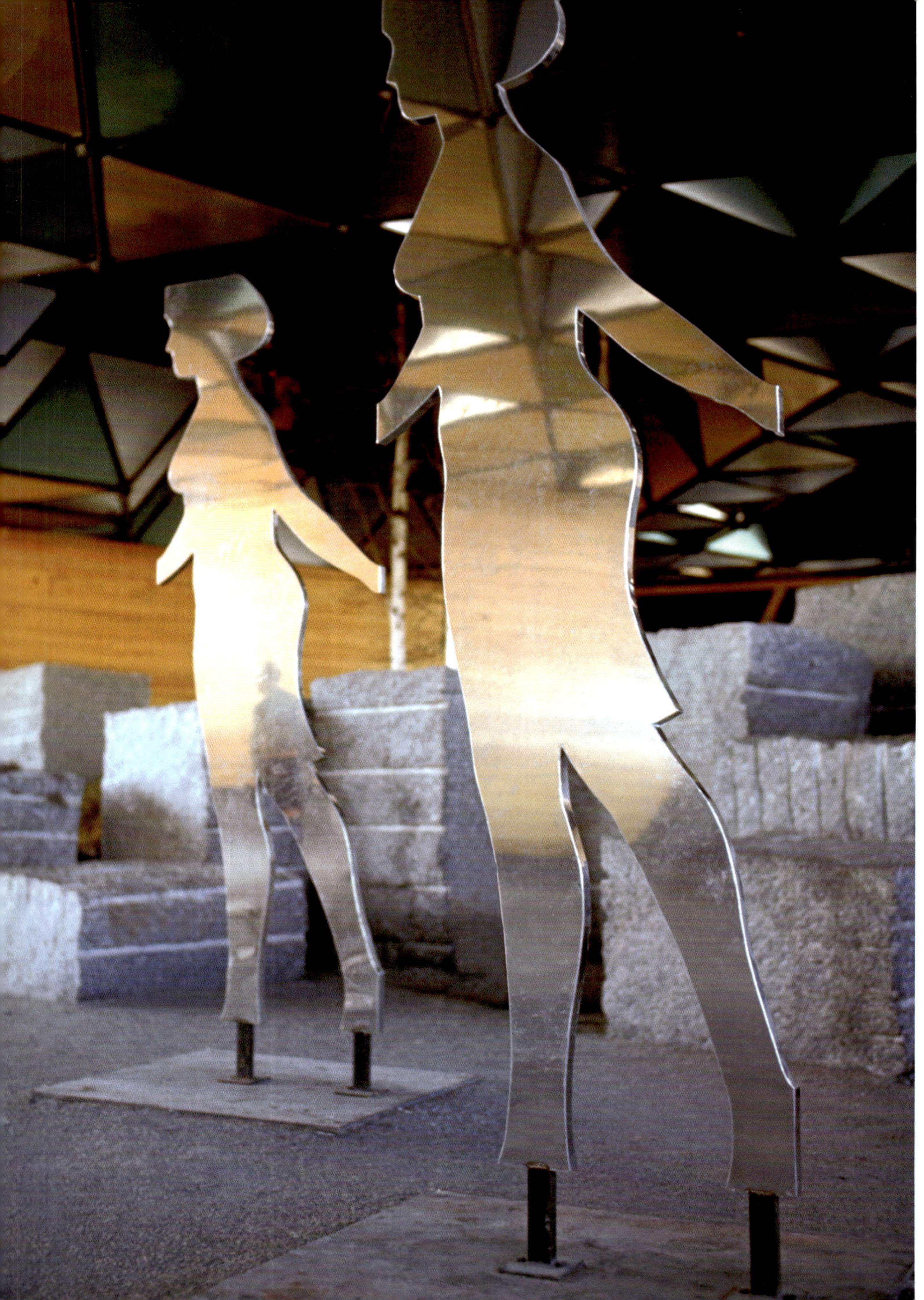

the minds of many viewers, no style, no ethnicity, no identifiable country of origin and no political message promoting national or local causes like Quebec's Quiet Revolution, which was very much on the minds of most Canadians following President Charles de Gaulle's famous "Vive le Québec libre" speech at Expo '67 in July 1967. Just like the fair, to which admission could only be gained by showing an ersatz "passport," the non-traditional work on display provided a common ground, one that was "necessary for building the future world."[22] Or so it seemed to the many visitors who put current fears of atomic warfare aside as they walked around the sixty-seven pavilions covering the islands.

The Canadian sculpture on show did not always relate to the exposition's declared theme: "Man and His World." This had been inspired by Antoine de Saint-Exupéry's memoir *Terre des Hommes* (1939) and transformed into the exposition's logo by the sculptor-cum-designer Julien Hébert. Indeed,

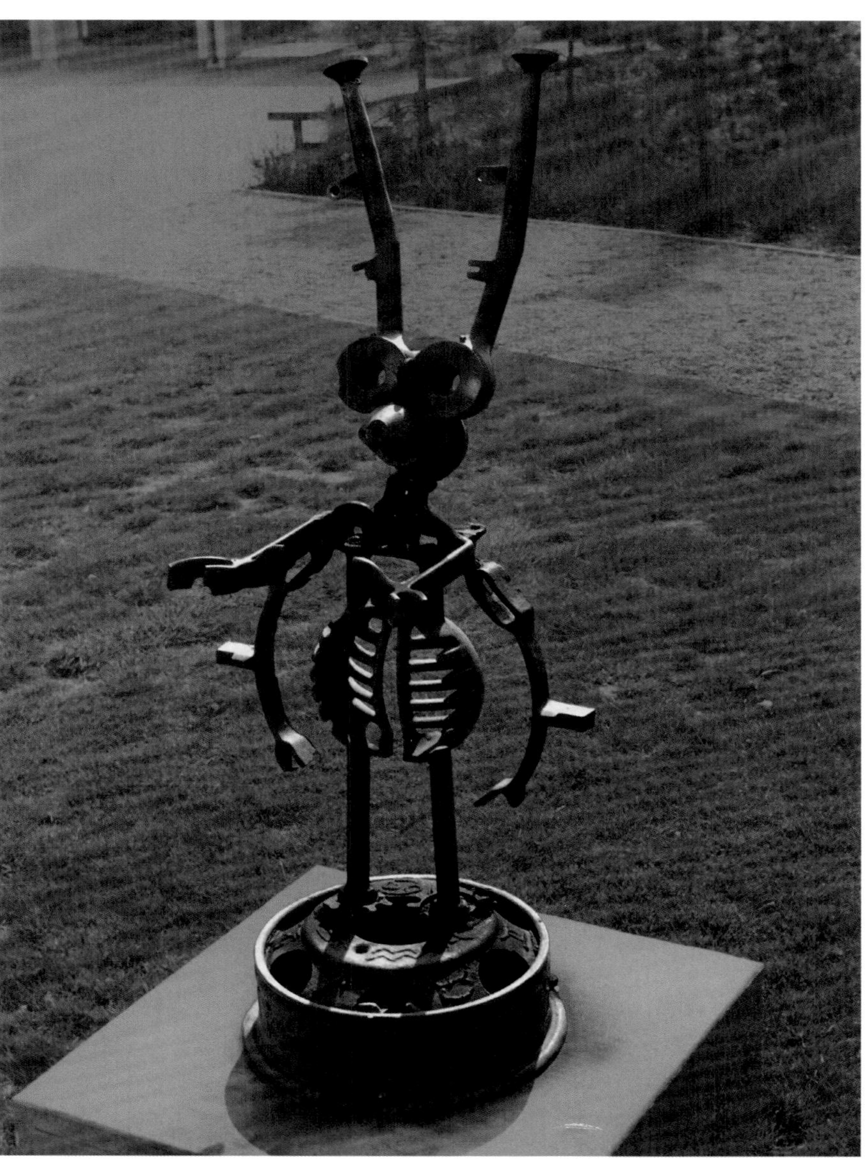

Yves Trudeau created this work at a time when the electrification of lanterns in Canada's lighthouses was almost complete, making the lighthouse keeper almost obsolete. But Trudeau was not looking to the past when he fabricated this nine-metre-tall robot-like lighthouse, sited alongside the Man the Explorer pavilion. *Phare du Cosmos* or *Cosmic Lighthouse*'s coloured and textured surfaces, along with its kinetic nature, proclaimed that this sculpture represented the future.

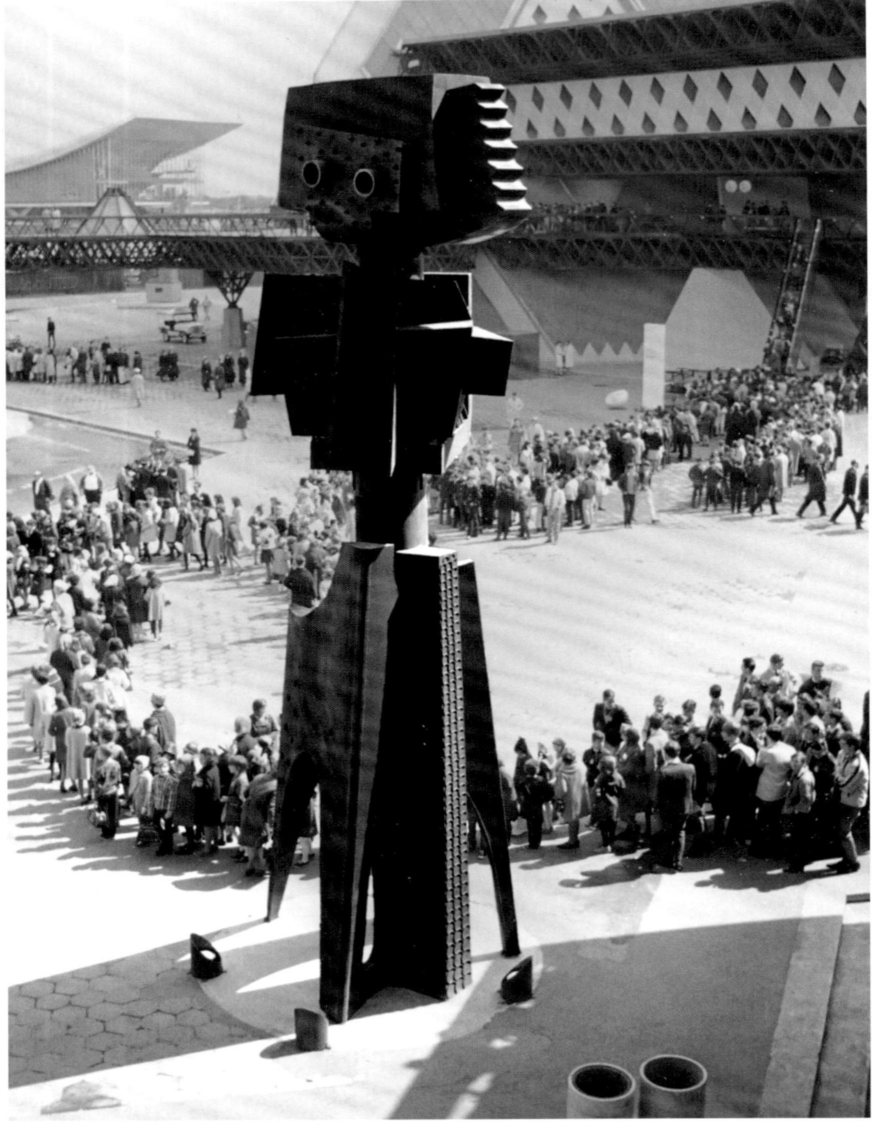

Bergeron's *Robot, Man* and *The Venetian* (all 1967) and Kahane's wood sculpture *Man On His Head* (1967) showed that man was not so much *of* this world but *at odds* with it.[23] Nor was the sculpture on display confined to one particular medium. Works were fashioned from wood and bronze as well as from steel and concrete. Nor was there a prescribed way of making a work: a sculpture could be cut, assembled, welded, riveted, carved or forged, or modelled in clay or plaster. Equally, three-dimensional objects could be pierced, broken or punctured, just as space could move through as well as around a work. Nor was every sculpture a "stabile" or a motionless piece. Yves Trudeau's steel *Le Phare du Cosmos,* installed outside the Man the Explorer pavilion, moved its robot-like head and, it was commented, emitted a "strange electronic power."[24] Alternatively, Gerald Gladstone's sculpture *UKI* (1967), inspired by tales of Huron and Iroquois "monsters," was only visible every half hour when it emerged from the man-made lake.

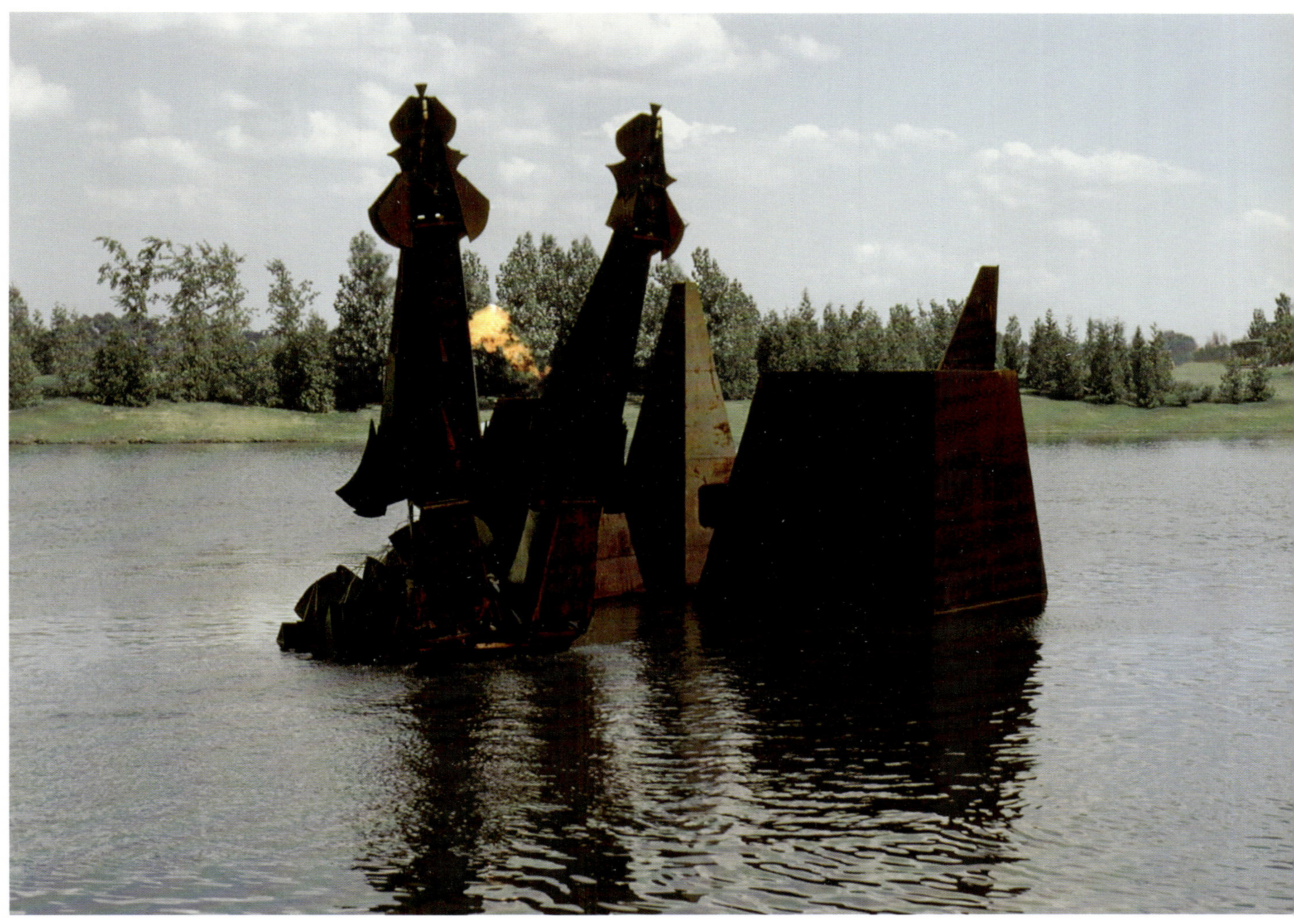

Reactions to the Canadian sculptures on show were mixed. William Withrow affirmed that Expo '67 was "fairly representative" of the full range of Canadian sculpture—a view endorsed by Vancouver's New Design Gallery owner and critic Alvin Balkind. However, the editor of *Canadian Art* magazine, Barry Lord, and Toronto art critic Robert Fulford both felt differently.[25] The fifty-one sculptures on display, according to Lord, "did not represent the current status of sculpture."[26]

True, there were notable exclusions. Neither Calgary's Katie Ohe nor Montreal's Hugh LeRoy (b.1939) nor Vancouver's multimedia sculptor Iain Baxter (b. 1936) had been invited to submit work. Two other British Columbians, Jack Hardman and Jack Harman, were also left out, as was Les Levine, a native of Montreal but a resident of New York City since 1964.[27] The Newfoundland-born sculptor Fred Willar (b. 1939) did contribute one work but he was the only representative from the four Atlantic provinces.[28] Barry Lord also complained that, while Gerald Gladstone and Armand Vaillancourt had three works included and John Ivor Smith and Yves Trudeau were invited to contribute two, "our greatest talent in this field," Robert Murray, had only received one commission.[29]

Gerald Gladstone
UKI, 1967
Gerald Gladstone's commission at Expo '67 offered him an opportunity to do something entirely new and on a grand scale. *UKI* was composed of hundreds of cones and spheres made out of a steel alloy known as Stelcoloy that rusted relatively slowly, thus protecting the steel from deterioration. And it depicted one of the four giants, the Great Serpent—or Monster Serpent—that had terrorized the Wendat people of the Huron Nation. *UKI* was kinetic: the entire work was only visible when it emerged from a man-made lake at half-hour intervals. And it was dramatic: when the sculpture surfaced, two mechanical serpents spewed fire. Gladstone's sculpture thus brought welded sculpture, modern technology and new materials together with the oral history of one First Nations group.

But there was another reason why, in the eyes of Lord and Fulford, the Canadian sculpture on display in Montreal was "a major disappointment."[30] The fact was that Expo '67 had competition. Running concurrently with Montreal's extravaganza was an exhibition called simply *Sculpture '67*. It was held, of course, in Toronto; and almost inevitably curated by Dorothy Cameron, the best-known Toronto gallery dealer, and also supported by the National Gallery of Canada. The works were installed in and around the periphery of the new city hall in Nathan Phillips Square in downtown Toronto. "Where EXPO looked to its own needs and its own ideas," Robert Fulford observed, "Miss Cameron looked to arts."[31]

Cameron's aim, as she wrote in the catalogue accompanying the outdoor exhibition, was to give "Canadian sculptors a chance and a challenge to demonstrate what they could do on a major scale, freed of the restrictive red-tape of specific commissions."[32] And this is what she did. Of the fifty-four sculptors drawn from New Brunswick to British Columbia, most were involved, in varying degrees, in the exploration of new forms, new spatial concepts and new materials. Now established as a teacher at the University of Oregon, Jan Zach produced flexible kinetic sculptures out of rolled and folded stainless steel. Toronto-based sculptor Kazuo Nakamura created simple geometric forms out of concrete. Montreal's Guido Molinari (1933–2004) and Françoise Sullivan, and Vancouver-born Tom Burrows (b. 1940) and Robert Murray, along with Newfoundland's Wallace French (b.1940), all enlivened their sculptures by applying colour to them. Ted Bieler (b. 1938) and Archie Miller (b. 1930) produced work in a relatively new material: reinforced plastic, commonly known as fibreglass.

Such diverse artists, as Fred Willar put it, were producing sculptures "quite beyond the traditional definitions." And one might have added that unlike their counterparts at Expo '67, whose adherence to the exposition's theme often resulted in weak figurative abstract works that represented a superficial kind of modernism, these sculptors were free to produce what they wanted. If they were united by anything it was, as Willar claimed, by a "tough integrity that transcended fashion and obliterated such terms as 'old hat' and 'with it.'"[33] One participant, Françoise Sullivan, enthused: "you find neither dogmatism nor uniformity: you participate in effervescence."[34]

Yet not all went well for the organizers or the sculptors of this exhibition. There was a constant tug-of-war between the National Gallery of Canada's new director, Jean Sutherland Boggs, and Dorothy Cameron, who was denied additional funding to match the twenty-four-hour surveillance afforded to the sculptures at Expo '67. As a result, many of the works displayed without protection in downtown Toronto were damaged. Some were walked on; others were skated on; still others were defaced. As a result, the National Gallery lost face, the artists saw some of their works vandalized and Dorothy Cameron's exhibition was forced to close on July 17—seven weeks ahead of schedule. As one commentator reflected in *artscanada* seven years later "*Sculpture '67* fell victim to the convenient but facile notion that public sculpture is the frail and difficult child that is a nuisance to look after."[35]

All in all, the art critics had plenty to argue about: over who was and who was not chosen to exhibit their work at Expo '67; over how many commissions each artist received; over whether or not the submissions fairly represented current work in the host country and the theme of the fair. Yet the one form of sculpture that was largely exempt from such criticisms was the Indigenous work on display. It escaped the public's antipathy to the frequently mystifying works fashioned in the modernist idiom, and its popularity became driven above all by a belief that Indigenous sculpture was a truly Canadian art form.

This was, of course, something new. Contemporary Indigenous art had not generally been popular among the Canadian public in the early twentieth century. Indeed, many people in that era did not think that it was art at all. In 1945 the founding editor of *Maritime Art*, Walter Abell, had been a lonely voice in predicting "that Canadians can look ahead to sculpture from West Coast Indians as well as carvings, dance masks, and ivory miniatures from the Eskimos in the Arctic."[36] Although the acceptance of contemporary Indigenous art was incremental, within twenty years Abell was to be proved right.

As we saw earlier, it was notably through the work of Charlie James, then of his granddaughter Ellen Neel and her uncle Mungo Martin, that the tradition of First Nations art among the Kwakwaka'wakw people had been not only kept alive but revived and recognized. This was the context that permitted the emergence of Bill Reid (1920–1998), formerly a CBC radio announcer with a large public following, as a jeweller and Indigenous artist. It was Reid, with his upbringing as a highly educated man who had barely acknowledged his own family's First Nations roots, who proved uniquely equipped to enlist sympathetic attention for Indigenous art, precisely because he stood in such an ambiguous position himself.

Beginning in the mid-1950s, Reid made exquisite jewellery with both Indigenous and non-Indigenous motifs; he gave radio talks; and he made films focusing on contemporary and historic First Nations art. Reid was also befriended by curators, like Wilson Duff at BC's provincial museum, and by Audrey and Harry Hawthorn at the fledgling anthropology museum at the University of British Columbia. In 1954 Bill Reid became part of an expedition sponsored by the Totem Pole Preservation Committee that resulted in the removal of totem poles from Haida Gwaii and their transport to the provincial museum and the University of British Columbia.

In 1956, he took a further step in reclaiming his heritage. When he heard that Mungo Martin had been commissioned by the provincial museum to carve a Haida pole for Thunderbird Park, Reid humbly became the distinguished carver's apprentice. Over the course of two weeks, Martin taught Reid how to use a D-edge, an elbow adze and a curved knife, in addition to chisels and wedges. Three years later, in 1959, Reid resigned from his job at the CBC and, with the help of Douglas Cranmer (1927–2006), also known as Pal'nakwala Wakas or Kesu', and funding from the Canada Council, embarked on creating totem poles for a Haida village on the grounds of the University of British Columbia. During the next three years Reid and Cranmer mixed and matched crests and used power saws to rough out the designs—all of which marked a departure from traditional First Nations practices and traditions.

By the late 1950s Reid was moving seamlessly between the Indigenous and non-Indigenous world. He worked alike with museum people and government officials, and with First Nations artists like the Haida-born Robert Davidson, who became his apprentice in 1966 and would go on to become one of the province's leading First Nations artists. Reid also joined forces with Seattle anthropologist, artist and museum curator Bill Holm, and wrote the seminal book *Northwest Coast Indian Art: An Analysis of Form* (1965). And throughout the 1950s and 1960s he helped curate and publicize exhibitions, including *People of the Potlatch* (1956) and *100 Years of BC Art* (1958).

Here was the essential background for the seminal exhibition that took place at the Vancouver Art Gallery during Canada's centennial year, *Arts of the Raven: Masterworks by the Northwest Coast Indian* (1967). Today we might criticize *Arts of the Raven* for including non-Indigenous artists who, like Ottawa sculptor E.B. Cox, combined Iroquois and Haida styles in his masks, animals and human torsos. And we would wonder why First Nations artists had not been given a prominent role in choosing and installing the work, or in writing about it in the exhibition catalogue. But, at this particular time, the exhibition was a milestone. The inclusion of contemporary carvings—ranging from gold and silver bracelets and pendants, to argillite platters, totem poles and panel pipes, to a wolf mask and a crouching bear carved from cedar—left few in doubt that the work on display was art. As a writer for Seattle's *Post-Intelligencer Weekender Magazine* proclaimed, "the unique form in Northwest coastal art is very much part of the present, to be repeated and appreciated by all—Indian and non-Indian alike."[37]

Yet the First Nations sculpture at Expo '67 was presented in a very different way. Bill Reid's exquisite 22-carat gold *Eagle and Bear Box* (1967) was displayed alongside work by Mohawk ceramicist Elda Smith (1919–2013) of the Turtle clan of the Six Nations community; but they were put among the "crafts" in the Canadian pavilion, rather than with the work of the Euro-Canadian artists and sculptors who participated.[38] And other contemporary First Nations work was dominated by historic pieces created by largely anonymous artists in the pavilion designated for the "Indians of Canada." Outside it was erected the twenty-metre-high totem pole carved by Kwakwaka'wakw artists Henry Hunt (1923–1985) and his son Tony (b. 1942). This pavilion's location on the edge of the exhibition grounds, as commentators have recently pointed out, "symbolized the place for First Nations in 1960s Canada: of but not in the country."[39]

Tactically if not strategically, many of the decisions on how to display Indigenous art at Expo '67 were in the hands of curators recruited from the First Nations themselves: Tom Hill, an Ohsweken from the Six Nations community in Brantford, and Alex Janvier, of Dene Suline and

Saulteaux descent, from Alberta. Clearly it was not the aesthetic status of the sculpture on display that concerned them. Instead, both men were understandably focused on raising the public's awareness of the continuing plight of First Nations people. Upon entering the Indians of Canada pavilion, the visitor was confronted with large accusing banners: "You have stolen our native land, our culture, our soul…" Another read: "An Indian child begins school by learning a foreign tongue." An archival and photographic display that exposed the effects of ongoing colonization, economic destitution and systematic racism was underscored by the findings in the federal government's *Hawthorn Report* (1966–1967).[40] It was the Cree folksinger Buffy Sainte-Marie who pithily summed up the propaganda function for the Indians of Canada pavilion: "like a classroom, but that's what's needed."[41]

The design of the pavilion, comprising an enormous teepee and a big house, reaffirmed the neo-colonial perspective, as did the choice of Indigenous art for display. Featuring historic carvings made the work acceptable because it had little to do with the First Nations people that Euro-

Bill Reid and Douglas Cranmer
Poles and Houses at the Haida Village,
1959–1962

In 1959, Bill Reid already had a successful career behind him—but as a radio announcer, not a sculptor. Then, with only a ten-day carving lesson from Chief Mungo Martin, Reid and his assistant, Douglas Cranmer, began creating a Haida village at the University of British Columbia, commissioned through a grant from the Canada Council. Working for carpenters' wages, Reid and Cranmer used power saws to rough out their designs and they combined figures not because they told a story but simply because they looked good. Thus their totem and mortuary poles, which blurred the distinction between invention and tradition, were hardly faithful to the history and experiences of the Haida people.

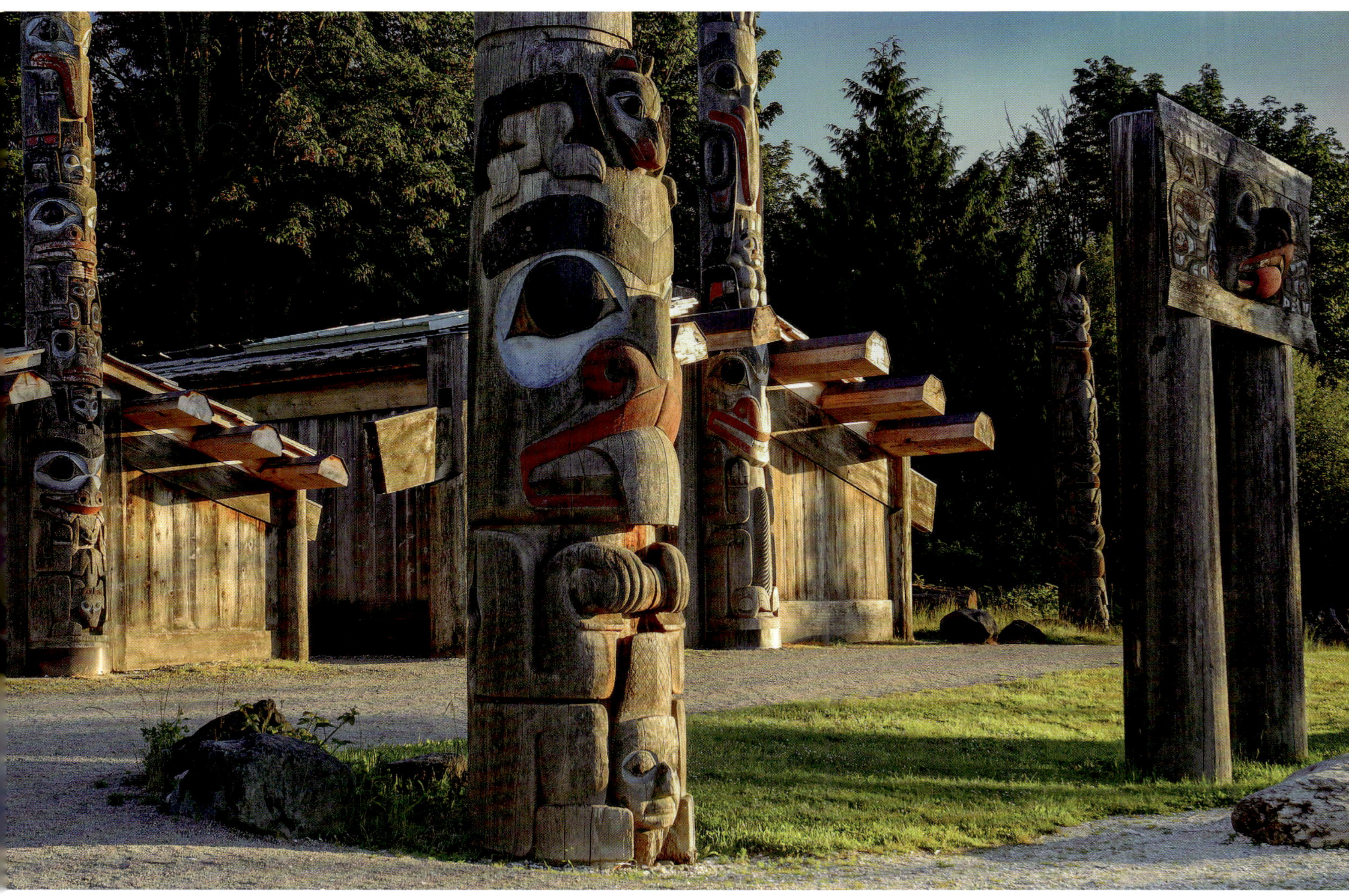

Canadians encountered in everyday life. All too easily, this reinforced the notion that First Nations art was dead, not living. Moreover, the work on show pre-empted the sort of aesthetic judgment and criticism to which the non-Indigenous sculpture was subjected.

Here, then, was the problem in presenting contemporary Indigenous art in a political rather than an artistic context. Ingo Hessel later noted the same dilemma when discussing Inuit art: to do so "in terms of Western concepts of style and art history is to be accused of ethnocentrism and cultural assimilation; yet to treat Inuit art separately from Canadian art is to be accused of ghettoizing it and pandering to political correctness."[42] Exhibiting contemporary First Nations sculpture alongside contemporary Canadian crafts in 1967 thus perpetuated the belief that it was handicraft, not fine art. And shielding it from critical judgment still inhibited First Nations sculpture from being accepted on its own aesthetic merit.

A similar dilemma shrouded the reception in southern Canada of Inuit art. Created by so-called "primitive" artists, it was regarded as immune from art criticism, where change and "progression" were the goalposts. Yet this did not prevent it from being a highly visible feature at Expo '67, where an inuksuk stood at the entrance to the Canadian pavilion. The architectural structure of the pavilion itself was an inverted nine-storey-high pyramid in the form of a katimavik ("meeting place" in Inuktitut). Inside the Canadian pavilion a 280-square-metre mural, carved in plaster by Cape Dorset (Kinngait) artists Elijah Pootoogook (Pudlat) (b. 1943) and Kumakuluk Saggiak (b. 1944) and depicting pre-contact life in the north, covered the walls of the Tundra Restaurant. And there were carvings by Pootoogook, Elizabeth Okalik (b. 1924) from Whale River and Thomassiapik Sivuarapik (1941–2009) from Puvirnituq in northern Quebec, as well as work from numerous other Inuit artists, many of their identities unknown.

In 1967 Inuit art was already a commercial success story. By 1952 over twenty thousand carvings had been brought out of the Arctic; exhibitions of Inuit sculpture had been held not only at Toronto's Royal Ontario Museum, with its historical and cultural criteria, but also at the National Gallery of Canada, signalling aesthetic acceptance. By the end of that decade, Cape Dorset had become known as the "Florence of the North." Inuit artists were beginning to be recognized as individuals by institutions in the south. For example, the Sculptors Society of Canada elected the Puvirnituq sculptor Charlie Sivuarapik (1911–1968) as a member, recognizing him as "one of the greatest sculptors of our day."[43] This election was made in 1958, the same year in which the art critic William Dale observed that what had formerly been "a pastime for hunters of walrus, polar bear and seal has now become an industry."[44]

By the late 1950s a carving by an Inuit artist was so sought after that the market was flooded with mass-produced imitations made from plastic, ceramic and even stone, and often sold at minimal prices. The Canadian government responded by attaching what was called an "igloo tag" to every carving. Then, at the beginning of the next decade, the government was instrumental in helping artists establish their own co-operatives for marketing their work in the south.[45]

This postwar success of Inuit art—public, critical and financial alike—clearly needs explanation; and the story is one that is impregnated with many ambiguities that defy simple stereotypes. At the time, a common view was based on a misguided belief that Inuit artists were untainted by decadent Western ideas and values. As the London art dealer and photographer Charles Gimpel wrote in 1953, in the catalogue accompanying his gallery's coronation exhibition, *Eskimo Carvings*, "nowhere in the world do we find people so undisturbed by the surge of civilization."[46] This idea was reinforced by the depiction of traditional themes, such as hunting and fishing, in the sculpture on display at the Gimpel Fils Gallery; and likewise by the many figurative carvings of Inuit men and women.

A similar stereotype of a pristine and uncorrupted habitat was equally evident in the Tundra Restaurant mural in the Canadian pavilion at Expo '67. Like the glossy photographs of the ever-smiling Inuit in the magazine *The Beaver*, this mural presented Inuit peoples as living on the land in a semi-primitive—though happy—state. Watching Pootoogook and Saggiak create that work, critic Barry Lord reinforced the image of the Inuit's "otherness" when he commented that the artists were "not at home in the exhibitionist atmosphere of the fair."[47]

Inuit carvings were popular partly because they offered many southern Canadians a cultural link to the country's resource-rich hinterland, romanticized as an expansive yet little-explored northern frontier. Inuit art offered such Canadians an exotic yet accessible alternative to the difficult-to-understand modernist paintings and sculptures championed by professional curators and art historians. At the same time this supposed link with the "primitive" Inuit, however factitious, gave prosperous, white, urbanized Canadians a new sense of their own identity. This was significant in a country where national symbols had always been in short supply. So, just like the country's new flag and its new national anthem, Inuit art was a talisman, reminding Canadians that they were at heart a northern people and essentially different from their American neighbours to the south. This was surely why an Inuit carving of a stalking bear, a supine seal or an Inuk hunting had long been the most socially acceptable gift the Canadian government could present to a visiting head of state.[48] Moreover, the support of Inuit sculpture offered by the Department of Northern Affairs and National Resources allowed the federal government to claim that it possessed a liberal-minded policy towards the country's Indigenous peoples.

But there was another reason why the Canadian government became increasingly interested in supporting Inuit art: it was a response to the economic plight of the Inuit people themselves. The Inuit had long been subjected to the fluctuating cycles of the international economy, to changing company policies and to trends in fashion. They had coped with these fluctuations and incursions while remaining on the land. In the middle of the twentieth century, however, things changed.

The federal government's effort to incorporate the Inuit into the social, economic and political sphere of southern Canada now forced Inuit children to live in residential schools far from their homes. There they were prohibited from speaking Inuktitut and from practising their customs and beliefs; there too they became more susceptible to disease—particularly tuberculosis. The lifestyles of the children's parents, which previously blended subsistence with trade, also changed. The collapse of the white fox industry in the early part of the twentieth century was now coupled with the decline of the caribou population. This prompted the abandonment of camp life and a move to centralized settlements. In search of alternative forms of employment, some Inuit men took on construction jobs at newly established weather and radar stations. Others helped build airstrips. And a smaller number worked in the copper and zinc mines on Hudson Bay. Even so, while some began to prosper, many families went hungry; some even starved to death.

Seeking to remedy the economic crisis in the north, the government hired Toronto-based artist James Houston (1921–2005), whose career and impact deserves to be better understood. Born in Grand'Mère, Quebec, Houston had studied at the Ontario College of Art, then at the Académie de la Grande Chaumière in Paris. In 1948, while on a sketching trip to Arctic Quebec, he was introduced to Inuit sculpture. The following year Houston extended his travels to the eastern and central Canadian Arctic, where he purchased Indigenous "crafts" for the Canadian Handicrafts Guild's annual sale in Montreal. Four years later Houston was working for the arts and crafts section of the Canadian government's Department of Northern Affairs and National Resources. By 1956 Houston had convinced government officials that he would be in a better position "to encourage a new and exciting field of Canadian art" if he were permanently based in the Arctic.[49]

It was then, in Cape Dorset (Kinngait) on the south coast of Baffin Island, that Houston mounted his quest to make Inuit art more palatable to audiences in southern Canada and to create a viable market. Over the course of the next few years, he did much to change both the iconography and the style of historic Inuit art by making it comply with Western standards of art. Houston had already created a manual in 1951, *Sanajaqsaq: Eskimo Handicrafts.* Some of Houston's simple line drawings were inspired by the work of British sculptor Henry Moore, who himself had been influenced by Inuit sculpture at a formative stage of his career.[50] The drawings in Houston's handbook explicitly showed the Inuit what sort of carvings would be "useful and acceptable to the white man." Carvings with a pedestal, Houston indicated, made them suitable for display on a mantelpiece or in an art gallery's glass showcase. A favoured viewpoint, he explained, was preferable over works that were carved in the round. Carvings with a smooth finish were more likely to appeal to the southern Canadian buyer, so Inuit carvers were given sandpaper for this purpose. Houston offered advice on the most highly sought-after motifs: in order of

Opposite:
Lucy Tasseor Tutsweetok
Mother and Children, c. 1960
Lucy Tasseor Tutsweetok initially carved Arctic animals in stone as well as in caribou antler. But it was after her move from Kangiqlliniq (Rankin Inlet) to Arviat (Eskimo Point) that she began working in a stone called steatite. Prompted by the memory of her grandfather's figurative sand drawings, Tasseor Tutsweetok now took mothers and children as her major theme, and always let the original flat, dull, grey stone determine the shape of her work. Thus heads, arms and sometimes legs emerge from the edges of the carving, while drawings are incised on the flat surfaces. Non-Indigenous critics called her work, in Western art parlance, Minimalist.

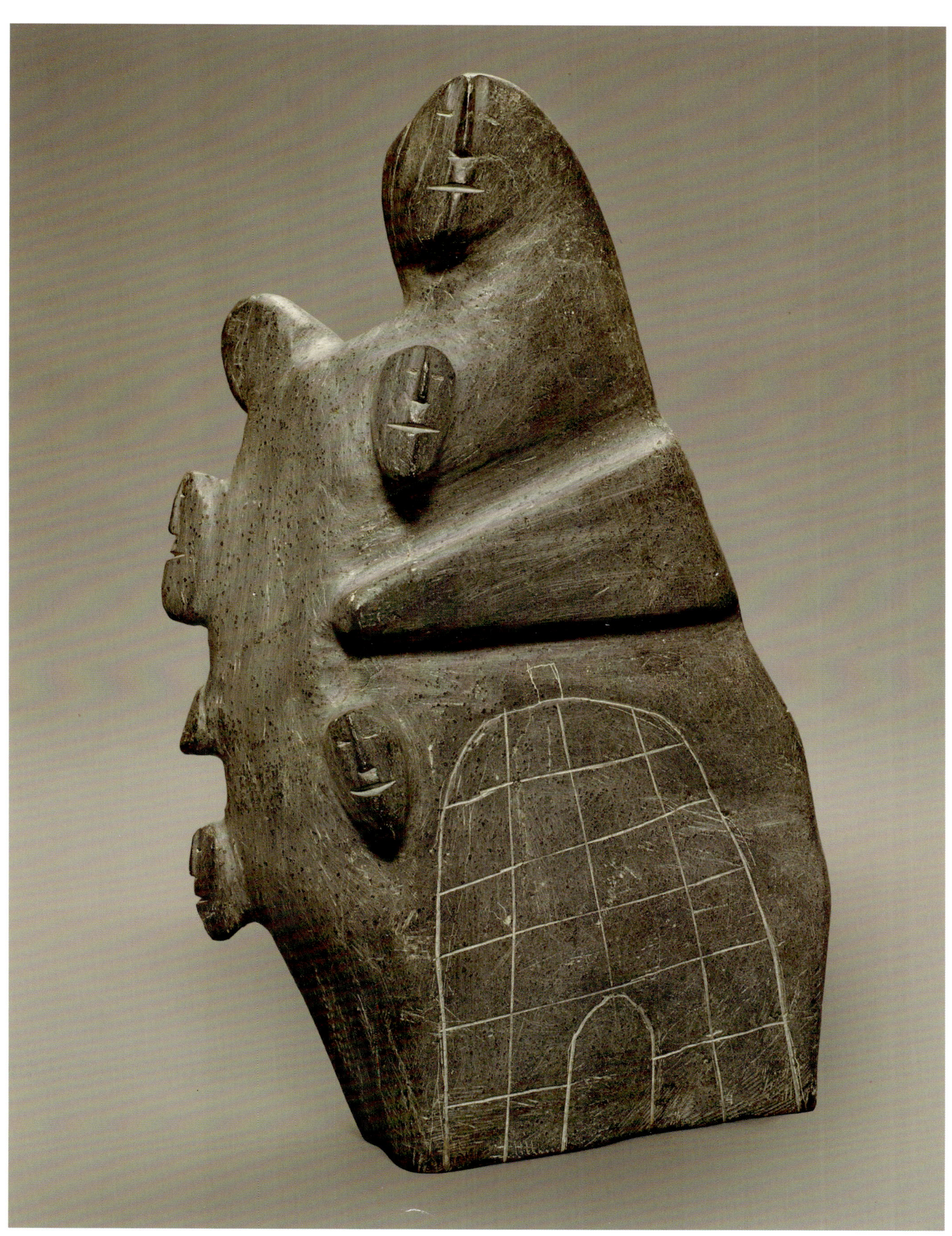

preference, he listed people, walrus, bears, seals, caribou, birds and fish.[51]

"The work is abstract, legitimately abstract—not like children's art or even, for that matter, much more modern abstract art," Richard T. Lambert wrote admiringly in *Canadian Forum* in 1955. And what really "floored" him was "that these people are producing work similar to that which is best and most acceptable in our contemporary sculpture." He was taxed to explain this extraordinary convergence, for example in the work of Osuitok (or Oshaweetuk) Ipeelee (1923–2005). "Modern sculpture is in great part, derived from or influenced by primitive art," Lambert suggested. "It may seem obvious to point out similarities with modern sculptors… just put some of this sculpture down beside Moore, Epstein. Then compare *Mother Child* (1956) by Osuitok Ipeelee with Moore's work and his fascination for negative shapes. How have they and we arrived at the same thing at the same time?"[52]

The question of affinity here masks a question of influence. Certainly, some of the Inuit carvings could be called modernist in Western art parlance. This was certainly true of the figurative sculptures of mothers and children produced by sculptor Lucy Tasseor Tutsweetok (1934–2012), based at Arviat (formerly known as Eskimo Point) on Hudson Bay. Moore's figurative sculptures, as mentioned, had informed Houston's drawings in *Sanajaqsaq: Eskimo Handicrafts*. And Houston's on-the-spot sketches, made during his travels, proved equally influential. "Saumik [Houston] drew a picture of an iglu to show me what he wanted me to make," Cape Dorset sculptor Sheokjuk Oqutaq (1920–1982) candidly explained. "He gave me a file. That was when I started carving."[53]

Some carvers, like Manasie Akpaliapik (b. 1955), felt qualms over the impact of this kind of tutelage upon Inuit artists—"If they do something different, it might not sell"—and remained fiercely independent.[54] Cape Dorset artist Paulosie Sivuak (1930–1986) remembered seeing Houston's instruction manual but "didn't follow his advice because I didn't like those drawings at all."[55] More ambivalently, Peter Pitseolak (1902–1973) noted a growing confidence among Inuit artists, which was itself perhaps an indirect tribute to Houston's impact. "You could very easily notice that people started being their own bosses," Pitseolak commented. "They didn't listen any more to what was the right or wrong thing to do. They following [*sic*] their own ideas."[56]

Whatever the direct influence of Houston's pedagogy, Inuit artists quickly caught on to the tricks of the white trade. They produced larger carvings because they sold better than smaller ones. They made multiple copies of work that had sold well. And when heavy duties were imposed on the export of stone carvings, Inuit artists began to carve non-taxable whalebone. Inuit artists also discovered that the work of some artists fetched higher prices than that of others—thus prompting the celebrated printmaker Kenojuak Ashevak (1927–2013) to sign drawings that had in fact been done by her more obscure husband, Johnniebo.[57] In such ways, the final product was enterprisingly adapted to the market. "The Qablunaq (white man) likes shiny finish, while the Inuit like to see a rough finish," sculptor Simon Tookoome (1934–2010) observed. "If I took such a carving to you, you would pay less because it wasn't highly polished and you would tell me if I do more work and make it look [the way you like], you'll pay me more."[58]

Told that their southern clients had a preference for animals and for carvings of an Inuit man or woman, as well as for narrative scenes, many Inuit sculptors stopped making the ashtrays and chessboards that had been their stock and trade. Osuitok Ipeelee produced hawks sometimes standing on one leg and Pauta Saila (1916–2009) carved a series of dancing bears in various sizes and shapes. Though both sculptors injected energy and movement into their finely balanced figurative carvings, their "smiling" whimsical bears and dynamic hawks were in danger of becoming caricatures of the creatures they were depicting.

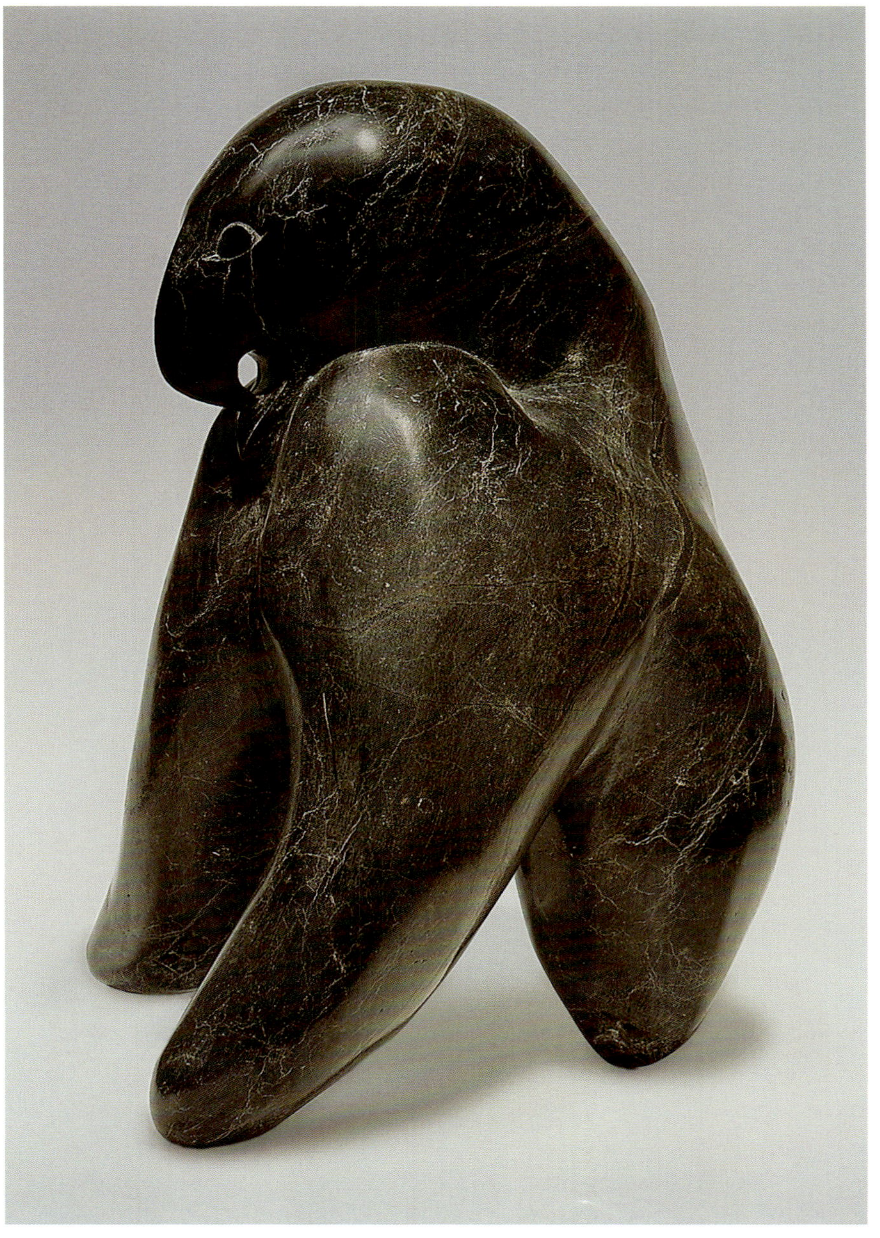

Osuitok Ipeelee
Hawk, 1968
Osuitok Ipeelee was a Cape Dorset artist who had been taught by his father, Ohotok, to carve in soapstone and to make prints, while living "on the land"—in skin tents (*tipuq*) in the summer and in snow houses (*iglu*) in the winter—during his formative years. His work was already well known when James Houston arrived on Baffin Island in 1951. But it was Houston who encouraged Ipeelee and made the artist's work known through sales and international exhibitions in southern Canada and elsewhere. Ipeelee became a teacher and mentor to many artists in Nunavut, but few of his contemporaries ever produced carvings of birds and animals that were so finely detailed, so charged with energy and movement, and so delicately balanced.

Looking back, with a purposeful sense of retrospect, these subjects came easily to many artists. "When I carve, I try to convey what it was like for Inuit in the early 1940s," stone sculptor Uriash Puqiqnak (b. 1946) reported in 1991.[59] Manasie Akpaliapik's goal was "to record the legends. These are important to us because we use them as guide posts to the old days."[60] For example, a story featuring forty people who had been caught on an ice floe during the course of travelling to new hunting grounds on an island in Hudson Bay became a much repeated subject for one artist. Using sealskins, rope and wood from their sleds, the survivors had

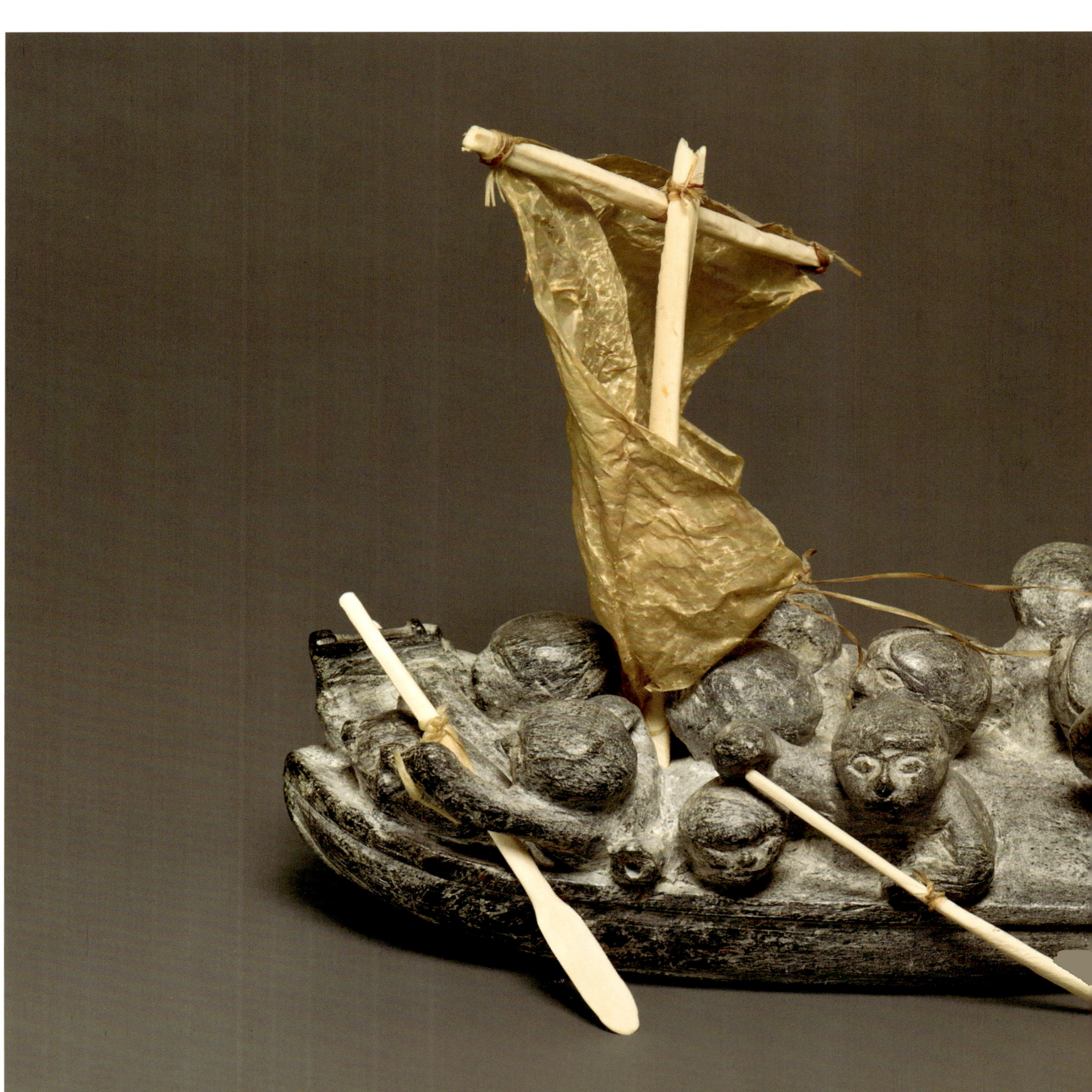

constructed an umiak, or skin boat, which enabled them to eventually reach land. This tragic incident resulted in *Migration* (c. 1965), the work of a Puvirnituq artist from northern Quebec, Joe Talirunili (c. 1906–1976). Inuit sculptors thus captured past events, illustrating an earlier way of life; and, drawing on their rich oral tradition, they also depicted mythical figures, of which *Stone Sea Goddess "Taleolaya"* by Mannumi Shaqu (1917–2000) is just one example.[61]

It should not be thought that Inuit carvers were naive. George Akikuluk (1940–2015) had been relocated to Baffin Island's most northern settlement,

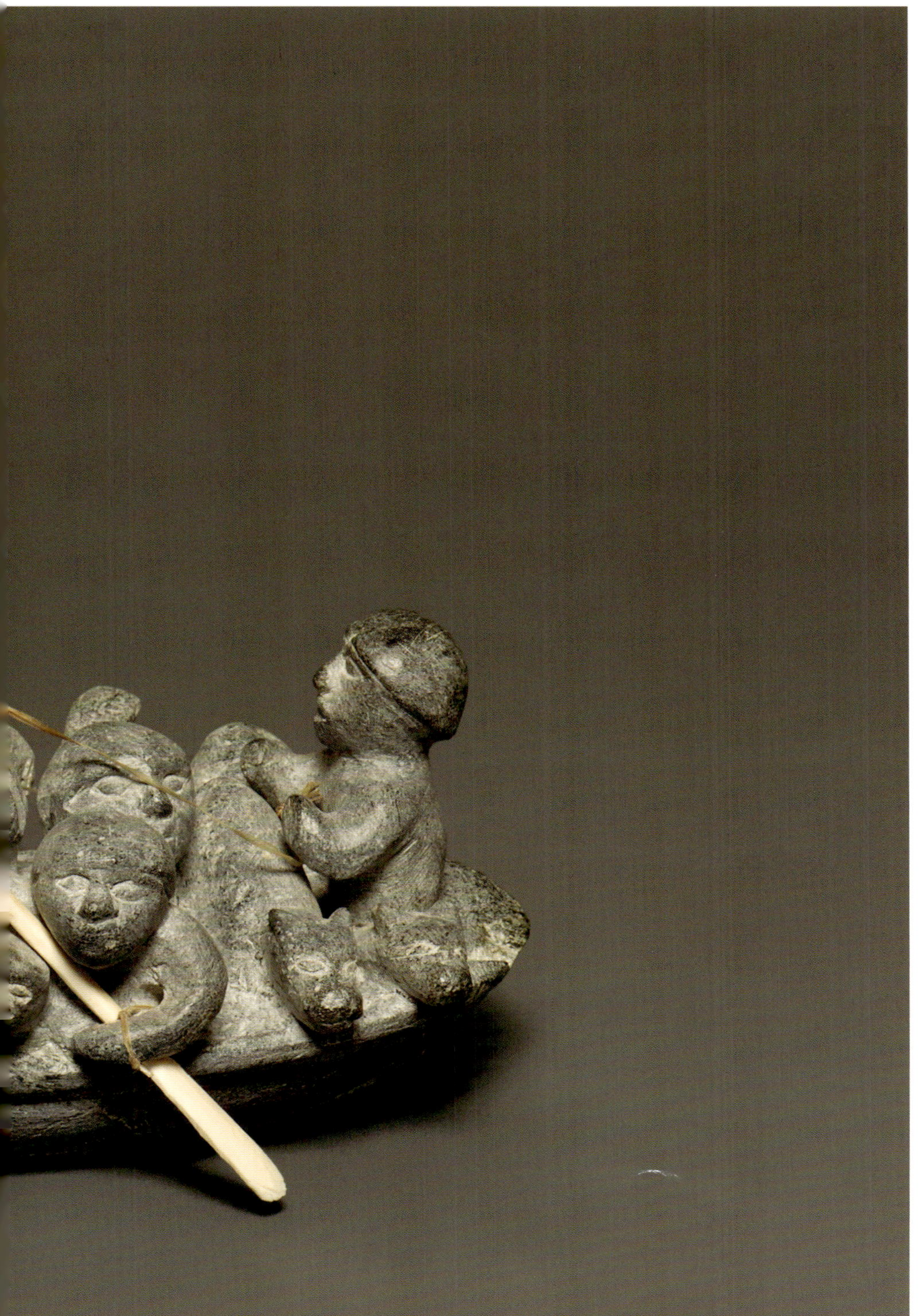

Joe Talirunili
Migration, c. 1965
Many Inuit artists tell a story in their carvings. Joe Talirunili found one that was worth repeating—many times. It concerns the shipwreck of some forty people and their escape onto an ice floe, where, working against the melting ice, they constructed a skin boat (umiak) from sealskins, rope and wood from their sleds. The survivors floated for several days before reaching the safety of land. Rather like the seal hunters in *Lost Party Waiting* (1972) by Newfoundland printmaker David Blackwood, Talirunili's *Migration* captures the anxiety of a people who are both dependent upon an environment that they know, but pitted against the odds in the harshness of the northern climate.

Pauta Saila
Bear, 1962

Like many artists in the Canadian Arctic, Pauta Saila learned to carve by watching his father. But unlike most of his Inuit contemporaries, Saila liked to carve what he felt, not what he saw. He also knew that he could best keep his family from starving by producing work that would sell in the south and accordingly he hit upon a subject that would earn him a good living: the bear. He produced dozens of carvings of bears: lying down, resting on their sides, or standing on one leg, or on two. Saila's stylized "dancing bears," with their weightlessness and their whimsical expressions, belie the fierce image of the polar bear.

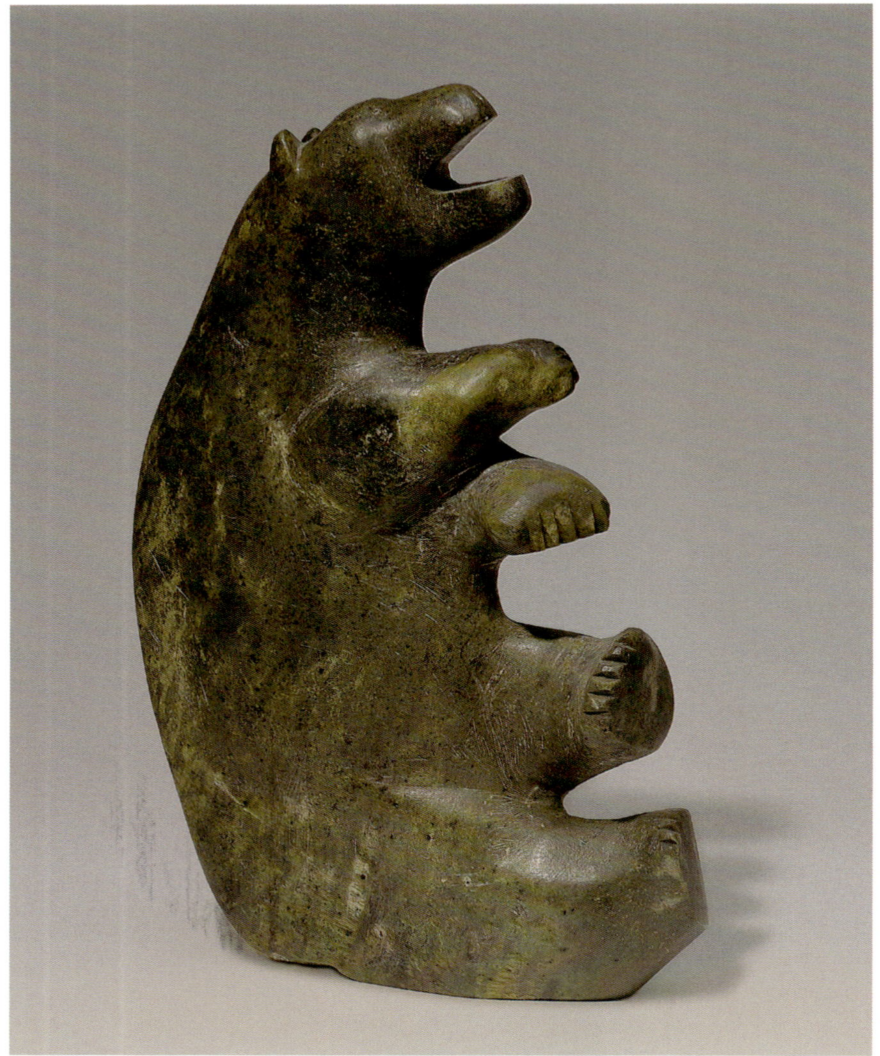

Arctic Bay (Ikpiarjuk), during the government's ill-fated "resettlement" scheme in the mid-1950s. He was not alone in wondering whether Inuit art was being used "to make a lot of profit for a lot of people" in the south.[62] The irony of being asked to recapture the past was not lost on one artist from Baker Lake (Qamani'tuaq) who observed in 1976 that: "Years ago all the qallunat (white men and women) who came here told us to get rid of angakut (shamans) and all the beliefs in turngat (evil spirits), and we did. Now the qallunat asks us all the time, 'Where are the angakut and turngat among your people and your art?'"[63]

Aesthetics apart, Houston's impact on the economy of virtually every settlement in the eastern Canadian Arctic and in northern Quebec is undeniable. By 1967, 70 per cent of the adult residents of Cape Dorset, for example, were carving or making prints, thus providing the community with half of its annual income. A sculptor could earn from fifty cents to two and a half dollars for a carving. As Kenojuak Ashevak observed: "In times of need, and when hunting was poor, we carved."[64]

All of this was only possible, of course, because James Houston and his assistant Terry Ryan—along with a few others—cultivated an interest in Inuit art in southern Canada. In 1952 Houston helped the National Gallery of Canada mount the seminal exhibition *Eskimo Art*. Houston wrote numerous articles for popular magazines and exhibition catalogues in which he extolled the uniqueness of the "primitive," "emotionally stimulating," "intellectually rewarding" and "intuitive" art form. Speaking on lecture tours across Canada and in the United States in 1954, Houston told his audiences that contemporary Inuit art had an unbroken link with prehistoric art. With an eye to promoting quick sales, he reminded his audiences that Inuit art was vulnerable to extinction.[65] Yet he also claimed that Inuit art was "created for the artist's satisfaction, not just for commercial ends."[66]

Not everyone was persuaded. Winnipeg-based sculptor and art historian George Swinton, who spoke of this process turning the Inuit into "a bunch of cultural phonies," was a notable skeptic. "The good Eskimo carvers don't care any more," Swinton claimed in 1958. The demand for assembly-line carvings was stunting creativity and "doing irreparable harm to the Eskimo's dignity." Swinton fired a direct salvo at Houston when he said that "Northern Affairs officers are not only making the Eskimo dependent on the white man by carving, but are telling him what to make."[67] Nevertheless Inuit art remained popular and sales continued to increase. Commercial galleries dealing only with Inuit art opened across the country.

Praise him or blame him, it was James Houston who remained the impresario of Inuit art. He was the living link between the Indigenous culture of the Canadian north and the modernist perspectives of international sculpture. Southern Canadians who shied away from non-Indigenous contemporary works that they found difficult to comprehend found Inuit sculpture more congenial. Yet the irony, of course, was that without their exposure to modernist works of art in the first place the public in southern Canada would never have been able to appreciate the inherent abstract nature of First Nations and Inuit art.

The Surrealists had glimpsed this when Northwest Coast Indigenous art was shown in Paris just before the Second World War. In the postwar period, Charles Gimpel, who promoted modernist British sculptors in his London gallery, mounted the first of a series of exhibitions of Inuit art in 1953. In this sense, it might be said that First Nations and Inuit art was accepted by the European and Canadian public through the back door. And while the public might not always have understood the modernist work on show, the Indigenous work at Expo '67 confirmed modernism's supremacy over traditional sculpture, heralding its acceptance through the front door.

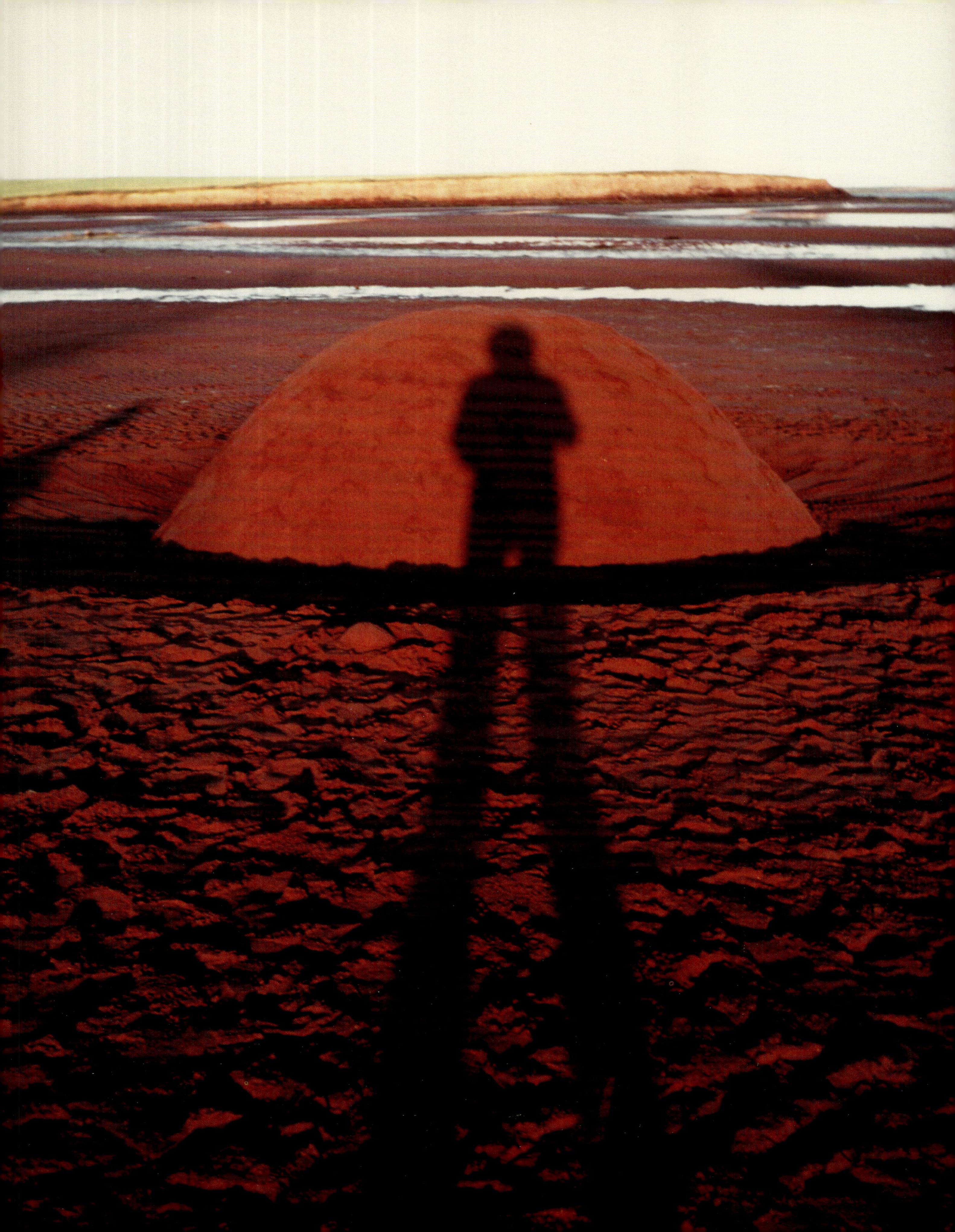

8

Sculpture Shock

If we ask what characterized sculpture during the era following the late 1960s, it was surely not just the variety of materials employed, nor the ways in which a sculpture was made, nor where it was installed or made: it was diversity itself. Not only was the concept of space challenged in new ways; so was the permanence of what was created. And the role of the viewer was no longer that of a passive observer gazing at a sculpture that had an elevated position upon its plinth.

Opposite:
Bill Vazan
Detail of *Sand Form Made at Low Tide Sand Flats at Paul's Bluff Inlet,*
***Victoria Prince Edward Island*, 1969**
(see page 210)

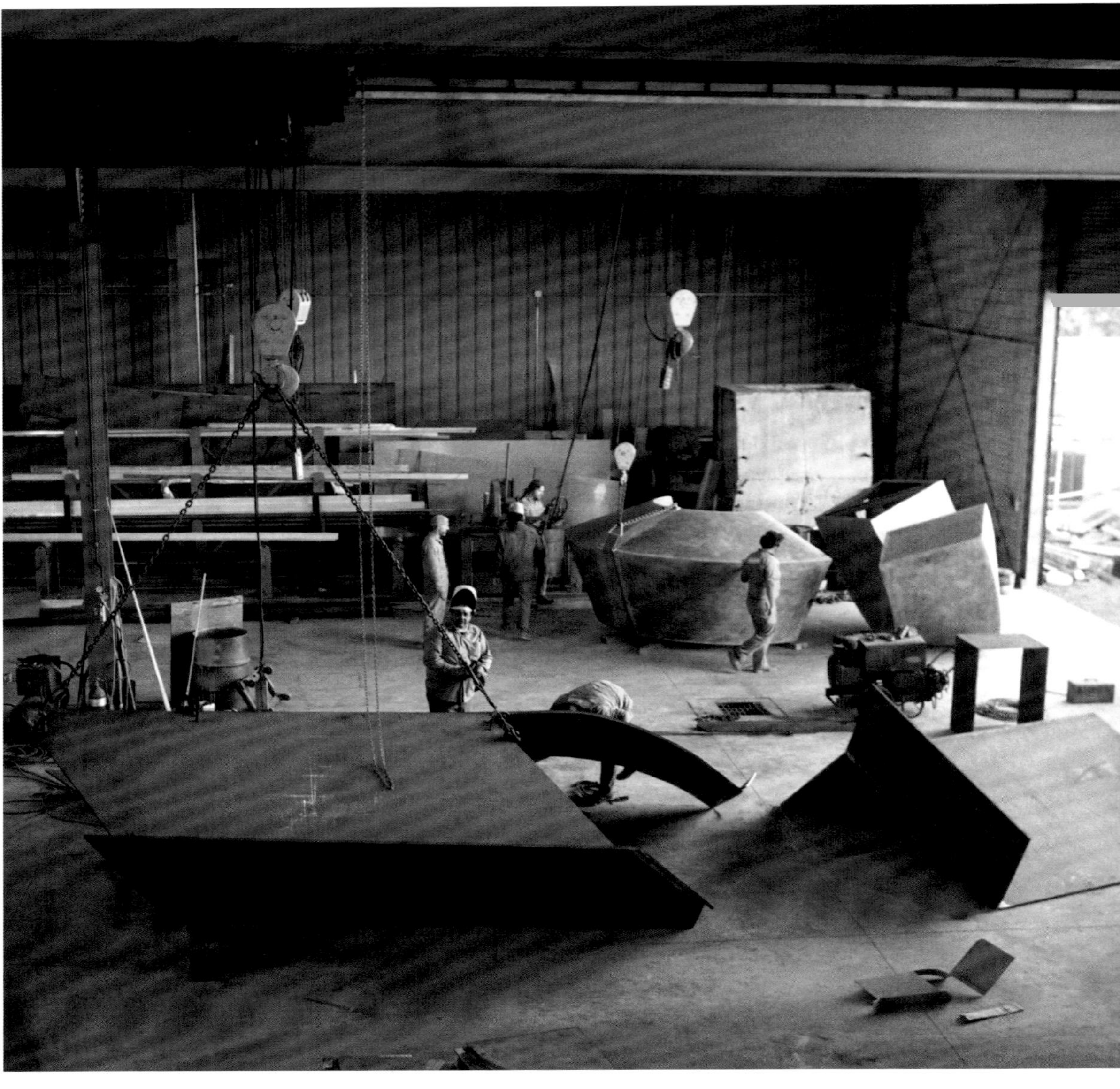

What we see from the late 1960s is a disordering of the conventional world, which necessarily makes it difficult to give an ordered account of a process that is still in flux today. More than ever before there was a relentless striving for the new, which now drove many sculptors to break with modernist aesthetics. As Judith Collins suggested in her seminal book *Sculpture Today* (2007), the three-dimensional art form was no longer figurative and vertical, neither modelled nor carved, but now horizontal, or stacked, or scattered.[1] There is undoubted insight in this generalization, but a look at what was produced in Canada from the late 1960s to the early years of this century tells a more complex story, with jarring inconsistencies and loose ends that cannot easily be tied together.

It is true that new forms of sculpture were created largely as an alternative to the modernist tradition. Its heroic image of the artist and its masterpiece-making were things that had shaped avant-garde practices since the early years of the twentieth century, giving its own cachet to sheer novelty among those who bought the work. As *Globe and Mail* art critic John Bentley Mays observed ironically in 1989 of the apparent demands of the art market: "If you were an artist, you couldn't make art thornily complicated or politically radical or otherwise un-buyable enough."[2]

From the middle of the 1960s on, as it seemed to many, there was no prescribed way of making a sculpture and no hierarchy of styles or mediums. A sculpture could now be monolithic or ephemeral, vertical or horizontal. It could now be painted or left to the vagaries of the weather. It could now be combined with other artistic practices, from architecture and photography to music and video. It could now consist of several objects, sometimes related to one another and sometimes not. A sculpture could express the social, political and economic concerns of the postwar generation or be concerned with nothing other than the material from which it was made. As for the finished product, it might indeed still be capable of being stored in a gallery's vault; but, if it had been created on a computer, it could be deleted with the touch of a button; if created on the land or shore, it could disappear with the next rainfall or high tide.

New ways of thinking about the creator—or creators—of a work of sculpture and about the viewer have given rise to various forms of contemporary work including Installation, Minimalism and Conceptualism. These all fall under the rubric of postmodernist art and have presented a challenge to the critics and to art historians alike. As Denise Leclerc put it, what failed to emerge along with new trends was "an entirely appropriate language for speaking about abstract art to the public at large."[3] The absence of traditional procedures of evaluation was a worry, and curator Karen Wilkin pointed to the perils of an "uncritical acceptance of dubious efforts."[4] It was true that conceptual art "lent itself to art-making that was philosophically provocative," as Joan Murray acknowledged, but the questions did not always generate convincing answers. "In the end, the work seems far less significant in itself than as part of an era in which an art world liberating itself from Abstract Expressionism was searching for a new direction."[5]

Critics and commentators were often bemused. They looked increasingly to the sculptors' own words, along with their videos and photographs, for an understanding of their work. It has thus often been left to the artists to explain what they do and how they think. And this has generated confusion in the face of diversity. "Sculpture," claimed Montreal artist David Altmejd (b. 1974), "is a self-contained object around which you can walk." Conversely, in his view: "Installation is made of different elements that don't necessarily touch each other."[6] For others, as we will see, sculpture, installations and interventions on the land meant something else, and had other purposes.

When sculptors began to mix two-dimensional and three-dimensional art, it challenged the canon. The result was often, as Todor Todorov (b. 1951) has engagingly put it, a kind of genetically modified art (GMA), in which more than one form of art fought "for supremacy in the same work."[7] In this metaphor, GMA might be easier to produce, it could be cultivated with much less effort, it yielded more dividends—but it was often tasteless. Further questions can also be posed. How was the consumer to be protected? Was the product adequately labelled? How was it to be marketed?

It is tempting to blame Columbia University art historian Rosalind Krauss for generating confusion here, with her suggestion in 1979 that sculpture could be anything.[8] This was possible because, unlike a painting, a sculpture, in her view, was "located at the juncture between stillness and motion, time arrested and time passing."[9] Admittedly, another American academic, Udo Kultermann, had noted almost a decade earlier that "everything has become material for the sculptor today."[10] But it was Krauss, with her much repeated phrase "sculpture in the expanded field," who was credited with giving sculptors licence to produce work that had no fixed boundaries, no fixed rules and no fixed spatial context. Indeed, the new pluralism and the total tolerance in art, as philosopher Arthur Danto observed in the late 1990s, now ruled out nothing.[11]

When David Burnett and Marilyn Schiff wrote their seminal book on contemporary art in Canada in 1983, they collected all difficult-to-categorize works into a chapter and called it "Alternative Modes."[12] Likewise, Joan Murray's survey of Canadian art published in the final year of the twentieth century put Installation sculpture into a chapter titled "Alternate Practice."[13] And it was not until 2014 that the Canadian journal *Espace*, with its influential circulation in the sculptural world, created a new logo for its cover, one that represented "the diversity of art practices related to sculpture, installation or any other art form associated with spatiality."[14]

To tell this story simply within an art-historical context would give a very narrow view. Literary theorists and critics certainly had a hand in prompting new ways of seeing, of making, of situating and of thinking about sculpture. During the 1960s French writers Roland Barthes and Michel Foucault questioned the status of the author as creator and redefined the role of the reader, listener and viewer in the essays "The Death of the Author" (1967) and "What is an Author?" (1969). A decade earlier, University of Toronto–based philosopher and communication theorist Marshall McLuhan had examined the impact that advertising and the communications media were having on society and culture. He questioned the distinction between "high" art and popular culture and, long before the Internet, predicted the impact that electronic media would have on visual and oral culture.[15] By the middle of the 1960s McLuhan's aphorism "the medium is the message" and his metaphor of "the global village" had made him a household name far beyond Canada, imperishably testified by Woody Allen giving McLuhan a walk-on part in the popular film *Annie Hall* (1977). Thus, McLuhan had himself become a walking, talking global villager, listened to around the world.

Educational institutions played an important role in transmitting such ideas. The University of British Columbia sponsored the Festival of the Contemporary Arts in 1964, during which Marshall McLuhan spoke on the fine arts and popular culture, thus inspiring followers among a new generation of artists. Art schools across the country revised their curriculums. Entrance requirements in some schools were dropped. Drawing, modelling and anatomy were frequently eliminated. And sculpture and painting were amalgamated in studio-based courses. The notion was that artists were communicators and suppliers of ideas, not of objects; that the contemporary communication media had a role to play in shaping a work of art; and, above all, that the purpose of a work was not to set up traditional norms and ideas but to knock them down. Students were thus encouraged to address issues in a wider world, beyond the conventional narrative of art history.

The Nova Scotia College of Art and Design (NSCAD) was at the forefront of art schools across Canada in promoting these ideas. American-born sculptor and curator Gerald Ferguson (1937–2009), who was brought to NSCAD as the first director of its Anna Leonowens Gallery in 1968, made the college the centre of Conceptual sculpture in Canada by showing that a work was created in the mind of the artist and that the actual object was an afterthought. Ferguson's 1979 installation *1,000,000 Pennies* dematerialized the art object; it ignored the financial value of the objects comprising it, it put no premium on their scarcity and, above all, it correspondingly devalued the skill required to produce a sculpture.

Ferguson and his colleagues Garry Neill Kennedy (b. 1935) and Les Levine created Conceptual works that were anti-art, anti-form, anti-style and—above all—anti-modernist (in the prevailing sense of "modernism" in the art world). They addressed contemporary political, social and economic concerns. And, reinforcing the point that they were part of an anti-modernist movement, these teachers introduced their students to international theorists, critics and artists, among whom were Canadians Ingrid Baxter (b. 1938) and Iain Baxter (b. 1936), British sculptor John Chamberlain (1927–2011), Americans Robert Smithson (1938–1973) and Robert Morris (b. 1931), and German Joseph Beuys. Teachers at NSCAD also established student exchange programs and the college's association with American contemporary sculpture was sealed in 1973 when they leased a loft in Lower Manhattan in New York City. No wonder students wrote on the walls of the college's Mezzanine Gallery, "I will not make any more boring art."[16]

How this worked out in practice was less easy to specify. One former NSCAD student, Alberta-born Robin Peck (b. 1950), spent many years remaking the standard black box, thus challenging his modernist predecessors by side-stepping skill and authorship and the emergence of new artistic forms and styles. Another former NSCAD student, Teresa Marshall (b. 1962), built on Gerald Ferguson's idea that students should engage with political and social concerns in their work. Of Scottish-Canadian and Mi'kmaq descent, Marshall created multimedia installations that confronted "the way our lives have been altered from the original connectedness with the land."[17] One work, *Elitekey* (1990), includes a canoe, a woman wearing Mi'kmaq dress—in fact the artist's grandmother—and a half-masted Canadian flag, all rendered in concrete. It thus consists of items that have been appropriated

Following pages:
Gerald Ferguson
1,000,000 Pennies, 1979
Conceptually, *1,000,000 Pennies* is different from the monolithic works that were scattered around the Expo '67 site. It is also anti-style, anti-form, anti-artificial and—above all—anti-modernist. True, Gerald Ferguson and his colleagues at the Nova Scotia College of Art and Design sought to work outside traditional sculpture norms and practices; they did so by drawing attention to the commodification of the art object and also by challenging the cultural authority of the art gallery. Yet this work is itself owned by an established art gallery, displayed in it, and written about by people in the art-world establishment.

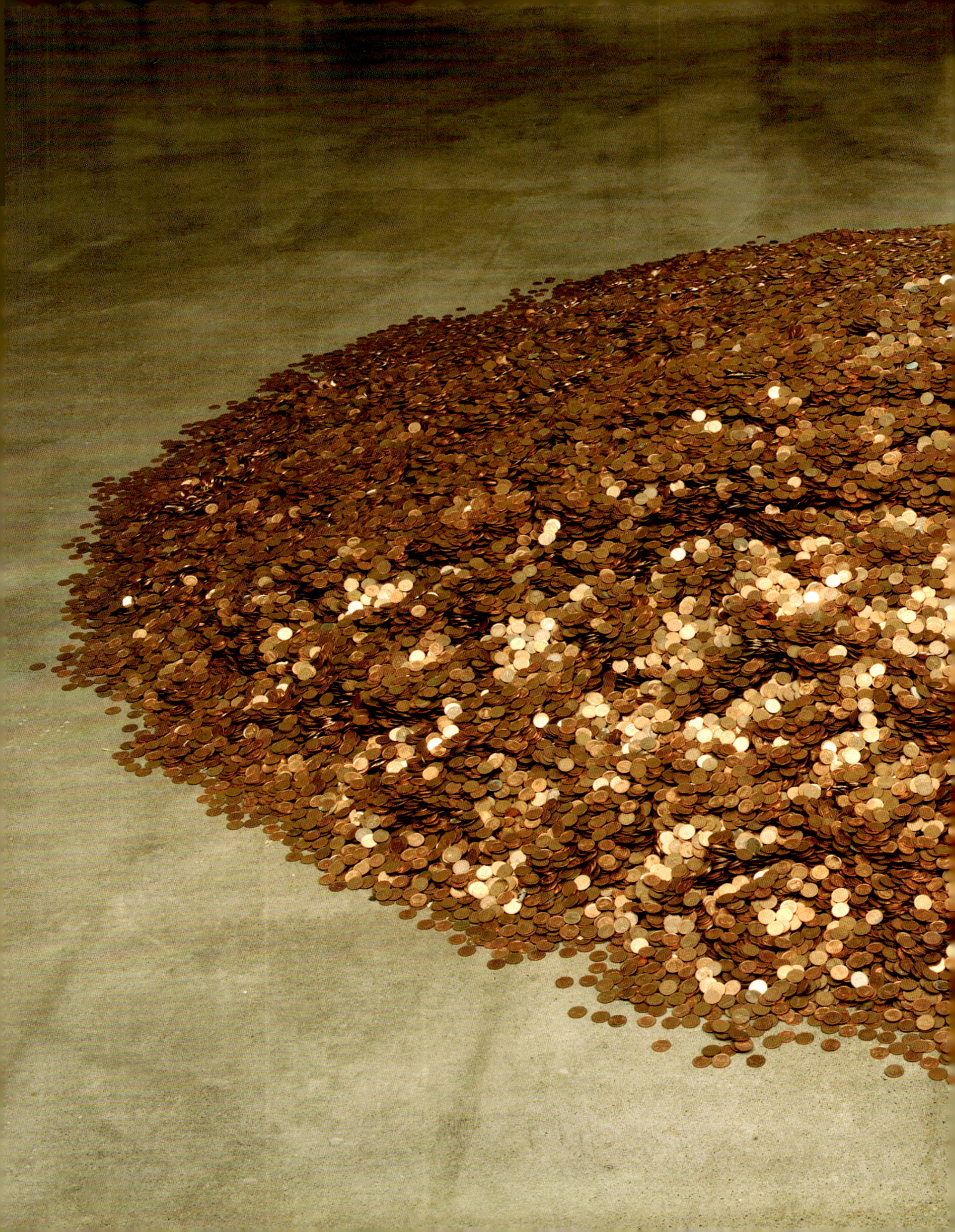

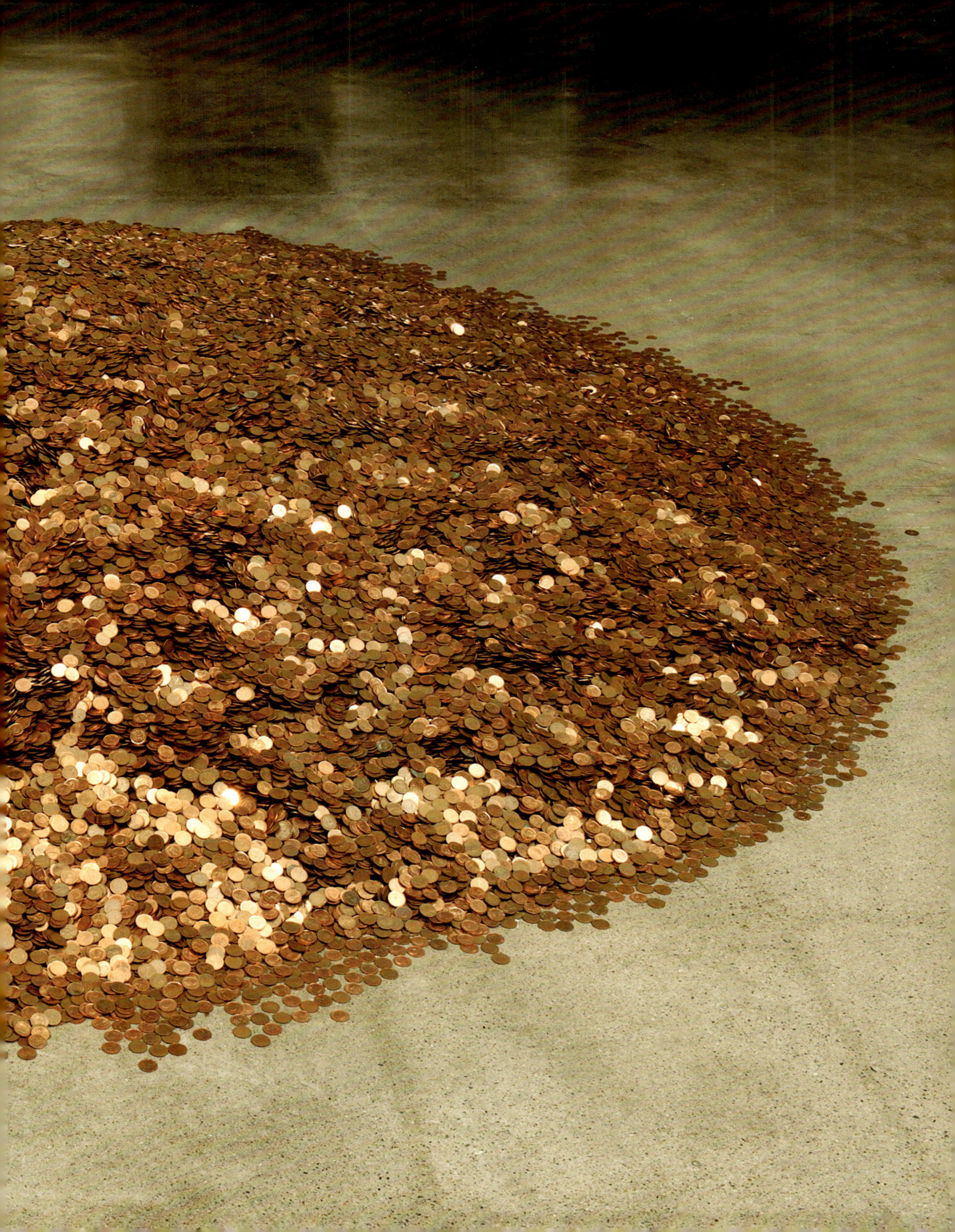

by the dominant non-Indigenous culture, or are associated with a Canadian ideal to which Indigenous people have long been forced to conform.[18]

Inuit sculptor Manasie Akpaliapik did not look to the past, but to the present challenges confronting the Inuit living in Nunavut. "A lot of the time my art helps me cope with things," the sculptor recalled. "Sometimes there are things that I can't talk about, but it will come out in my art."[19] Combining whalebone, Brazilian soapstone, antler, ivory, muskox horn and shell, in *Untitled* (1991) Akpaliapik explores the problem of alcoholism that has inflicted the community of Arctic Bay.

Although the National Gallery of Canada largely ignored contemporary Indigenous art until the end of the twentieth century, the gallery's director, Jean Sutherland Boggs, did appoint a curator of (non-Indigenous)

Manasie Akpaliapik
Untitled, 1991

Not every sculpture that came out of the Canadian Arctic was made out of material from the north, especially when shortages of indigenous "soapstone" prompted the importation of stone from Brazil. Likewise, by the last decades of the twentieth century some Inuit artists were making sculptures that dealt with contemporary, and often controversial, situations. Yet they were taking a financial risk by producing sculpture that did not— as collectors in the south desired—depict how the Inuit had lived in the past. Artists like Manasie Akpaliapik instead showed how, during the last half of the twentieth century, the Inuit were affected by relocation programs, by the residential school system and, as we see here, by the introduction of alcohol from southern Canada.

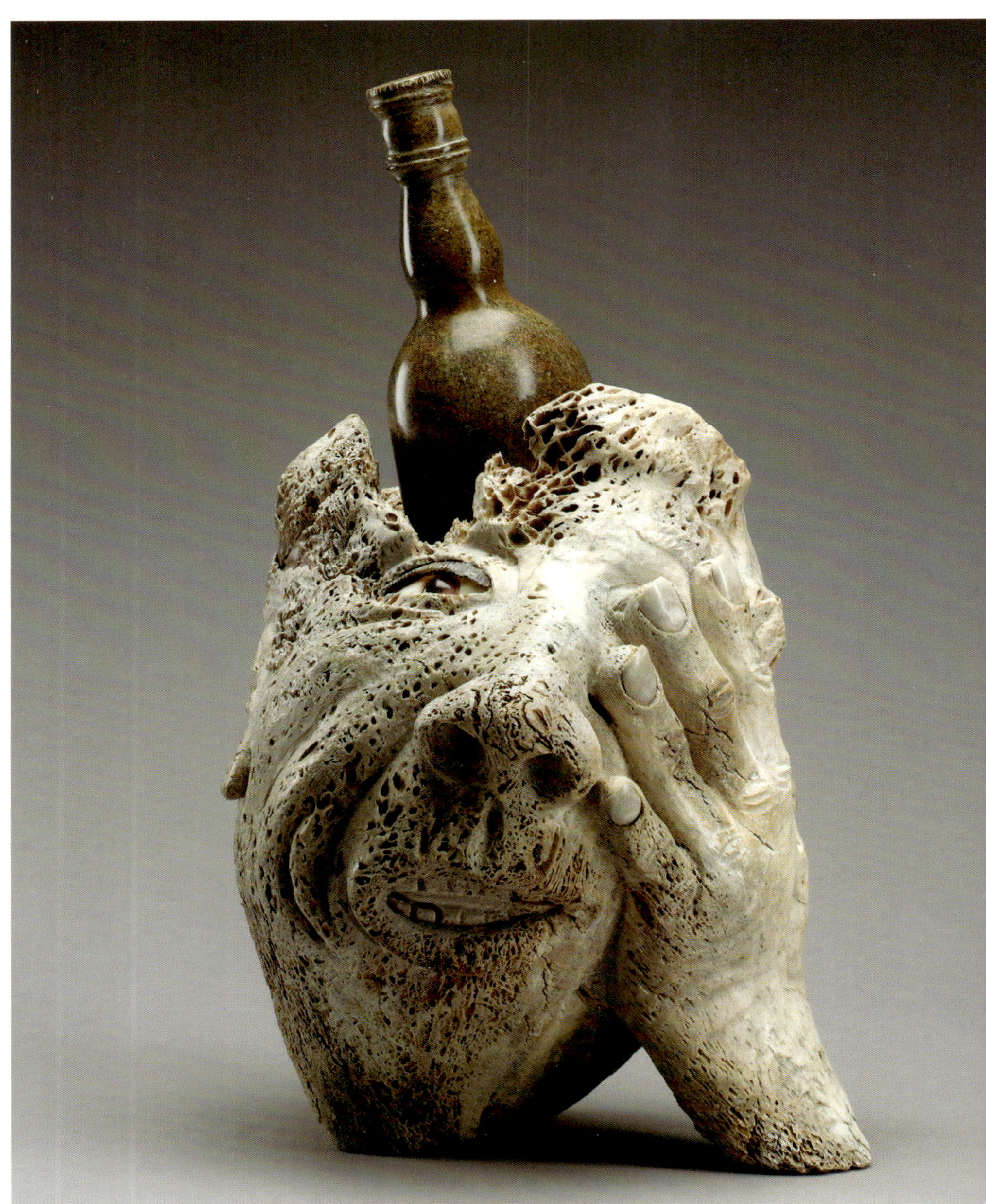

contemporary Canadian art in 1968. Within a year of joining the National Gallery, Pierre Théberge invited the interdisciplinary and collaborative leaders of N.E. Thing Co., a Vancouver-based art collective, to set up an installation in the foyer of the gallery's Lorne Building. Replete with office furniture, typewriters and secretaries, the gallery was mistaken for an office building by the many potential visitors who, instead of viewing the installation, innocently walked by. This was, of course, the point that Ingrid and Iain Baxter were making. Placed within the foyer of the country's leading public art gallery, the installation questioned the sanctity of a work of art, its material value and the aura surrounding the artist who had created it. This also underscored the corporate context in which art is displayed, marketed and consumed.[20]

N.E. Thing Co. was by no means unique. Other multimedia art collectives, including Toronto's General Idea (1969) and A SPACE (1971) and Vancouver's Intermedia (1967) and Western Front Society (1973), now sought to demystify the artistic process by replacing the seriousness of "high art" with play, pastiche and parody. They were all successful in challenging the art establishment and in getting their work displayed in public galleries. By the early 1980s, as *Montreal Gazette* art critic Lawrence Sabbath noted, museums had gone from being "repositories and preserves of the past" to institutions where "novelty" had become a virtue—indeed a selling point in a new market.[21]

Likewise, Montreal-based sculptor Irene Whittome (b. 1942) questioned the sanctity of the museum by taking on the role of artist, curator, ethnographer and ethnologist. *The White Museum v* (1975) consists of a series of "totemic" objects that Whittome wrapped, categorized, then enclosed in glass-fronted museum display cases.[22] A few years later Victoria-based sculptor Mowry Baden (b. 1936) constructed a 14.5 by 8.5–metre room within a room on the fourth floor of the National Gallery of Canada. Titled *Ottawa Room* (1979–1980), Baden's non-functional room was judged successful since it conveyed "a critical and definite sense of 'lived space' to a building which has none of its own."[23] The sculptures comprising Brian Jungen's *Prototypes for New Understanding* (1998–2005) were not only stunningly clever: their acceptance by museums across the country and around the world showed how some public art institutions were willing to support sculpture that questions their very own practices. Jungen (b. 1970) is a sculptor of Swiss and Dane-zaa descent, who left Fort St. John in northern British Columbia in order to attend the Emily Carr College of Art and Design in Vancouver. He successively challenged the way in which First Nations art had been interpreted, consumed, assimilated, exploited and displayed in Canada's museums and galleries. Working rather in the manner of Marcel Duchamp, he dematerialized the art object by reconfiguring Nike Air Jordan running shoes into First Nations masks in such works as *Prototype for New Understanding #2* (1998).

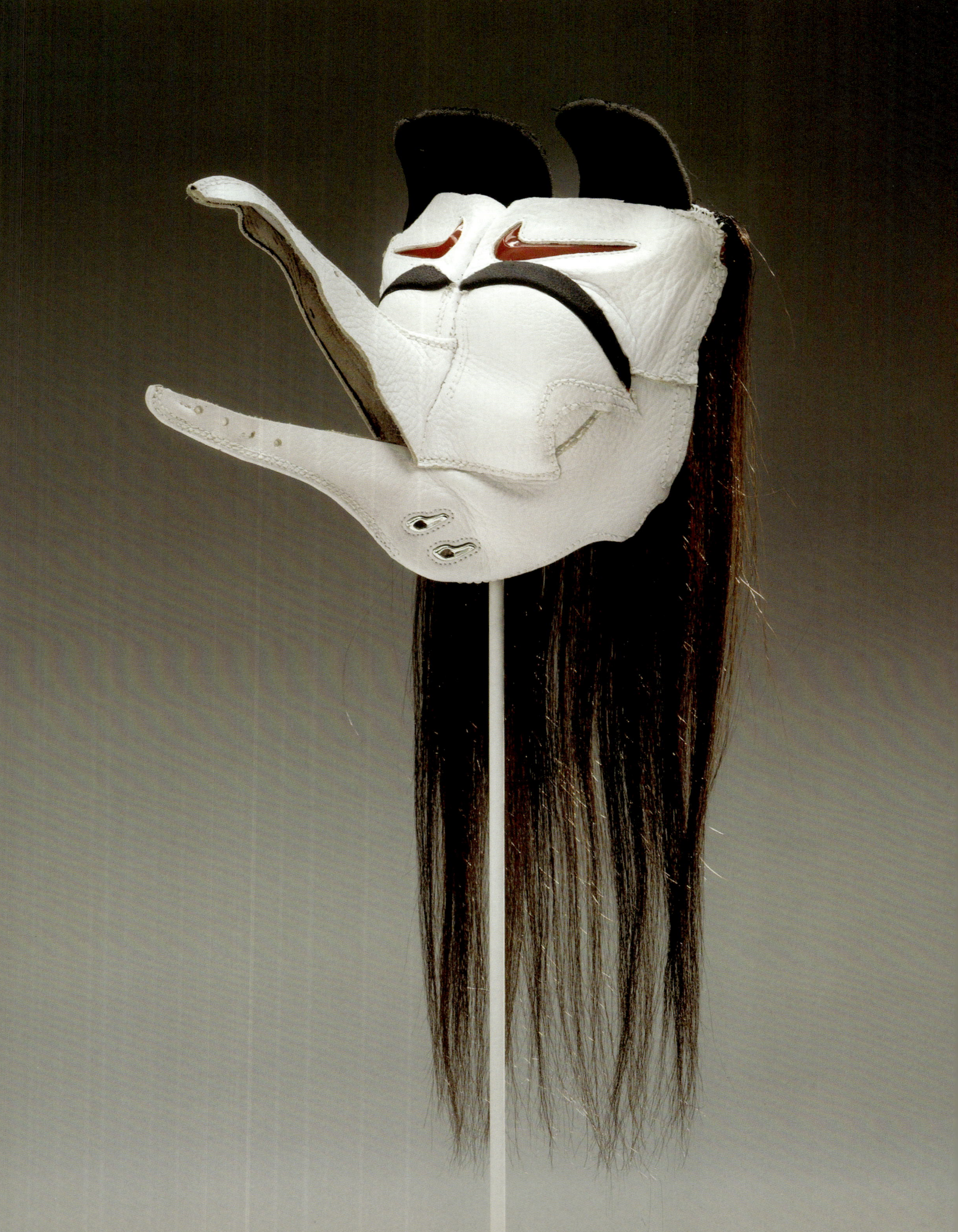

Museums, galleries and collectors all encouraged the novelty that had become a virtue for many sculptors right across the country. They did this, as one newspaper article put it, "by exhibition and purchase of works by living artists thus conferring instant Orwellian fame, while they're still young and before the next new wave rolls over them."[24] In this perspective the new iconoclasm in sculpture had proved a conspicuous success, in grabbing attention, in getting talked and written about, and in stretching the tolerance of public as well as private galleries for work that challenged the historic canon.

But if the medium was the message, it was often a message that struggled for public appreciation. German sculptor Joseph Beuys was not alone in his belief that artists could bring about social change, by heightening awareness of the Cold War confrontation, the Vietnam War, the AIDS epidemic and the nuclear arms race, along with the rights of Indigenous people and women. The Toronto-based multimedia co-operative General Idea addressed the HIV/AIDS crisis with an installation at Toronto's Power Plant Gallery titled *One Day of AZT/One Year of AZT* (1991). Consisting of hundreds of capsules arranged in daily, monthly and yearly dosages, the work took on more meaning when two members of General Idea's collective, Felix Partz— born as Ronald Gabe in Winnipeg in 1945—and Italian-born Jorge Zontal (b. 1944), died of AIDS three years after the work was completed.

Jana Sterbak (b. 1955) addressed several themes, ranging from the exploitation of women and eating disorders to fashion and the consumer society, in her controversial work *Vanitas: Flesh Dress for an Albino Anorectic* (1987). Composed of more than twenty kilograms of raw steak

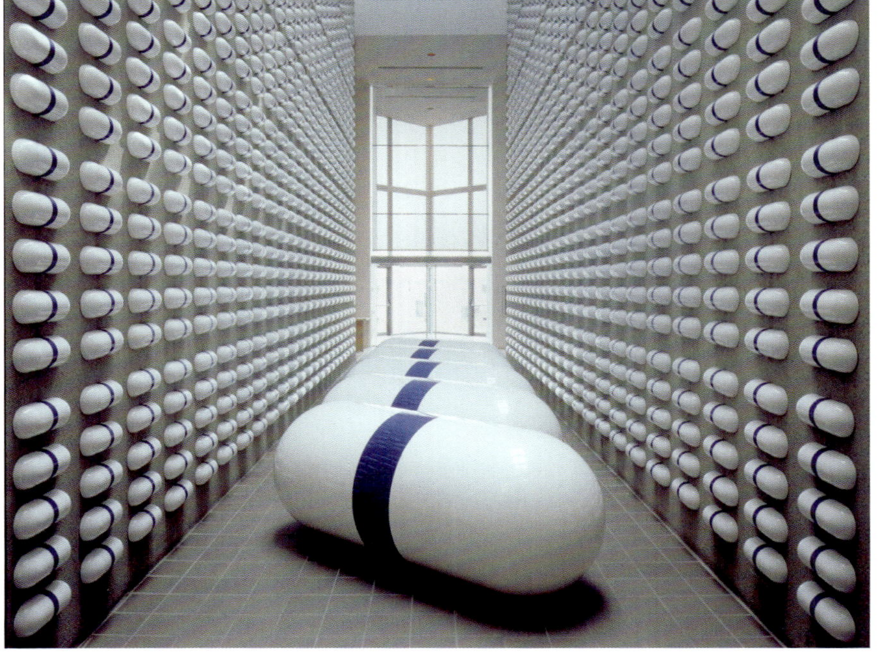

General Idea
One Day of AZT/One Year of AZT, 1991
When the artists associated with General Idea made this work in 1991, AZT was the only drug available—for those who could afford it—for treating HIV-positive patients. Exhibited at the height of the AIDS epidemic, *One Day of AZT/One Year of AZT* sets out one year's supply of the drug in daily, monthly and annual quantities. The members of General Idea—A.A. Bronson, Felix Partz and Jorge Zontal—had reason to hope that the installation would help to change people's negative ideas about the disease. Sadly, Partz and Zontal died of AIDS-related symptoms three years after the work was first shown.

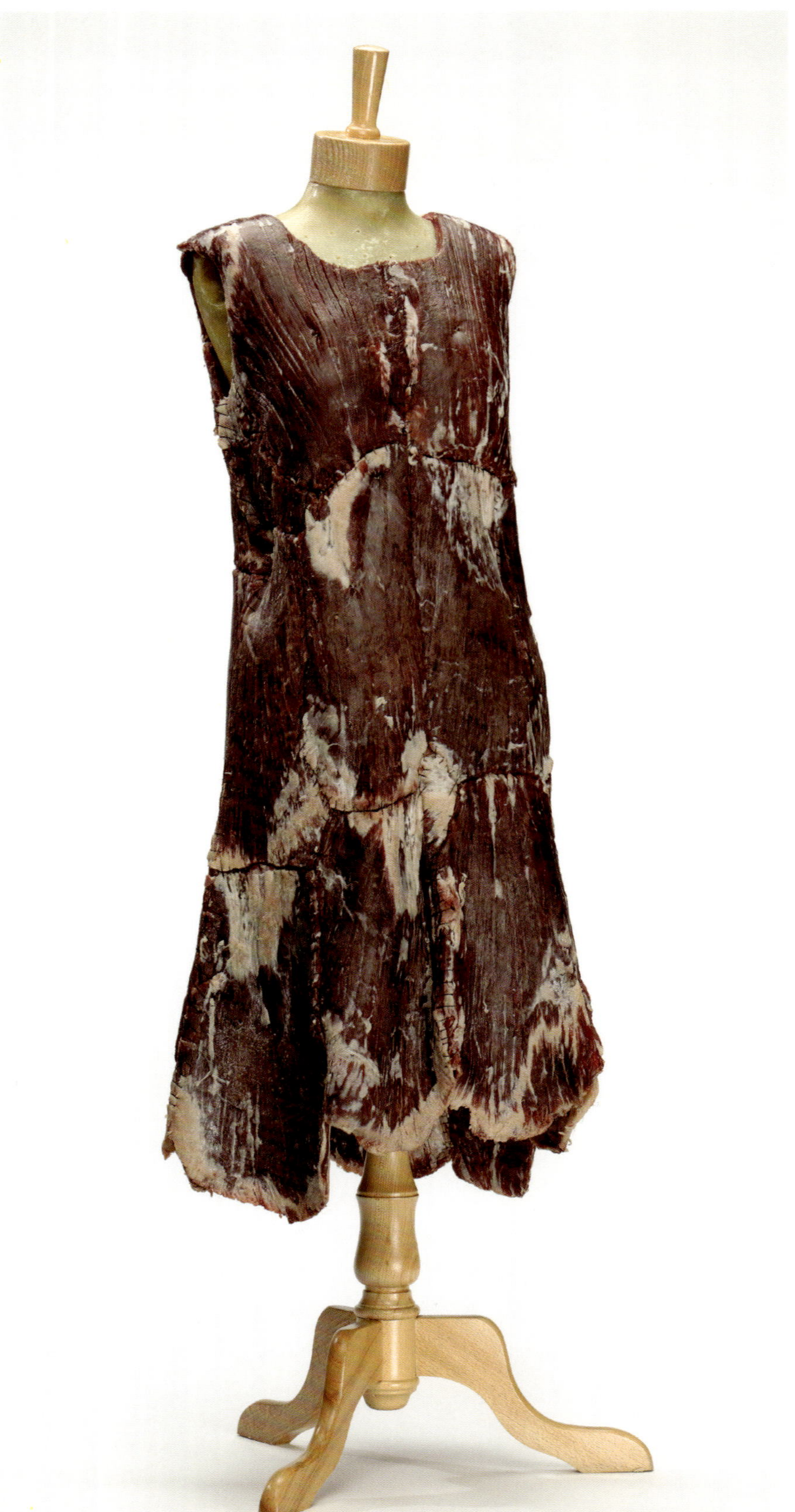

Jana Sterbak

Vanitas: Flesh Dress for an Albino Anorectic, 1987

This work, which addresses the fashion industry's
exploitation of women, might be called a renewable
sculpture. Indeed, every time that Jan Sterbak's
Vanitas: Flesh Dress for an Albino Anorectic is put on
show, some twenty kilograms of raw flank steak
must be acquired, then sewn together and hung
on a tailor's dummy in order to complete the work.
During the course of exhibiting this extraordinary
piece, the meat dries and flakes—and smells—
thereby reinforcing the themes of death, decay and
the transience of life, much as these tropes were
immortalized in a different idiom by Flemish still-
life painters in the seventeenth century.

that was sewn together and then draped on a mannequin, the work made her one of the most contentious sculptors in the country. It was first shown at the Galerie René Blouin in Montreal; then in 1991 it was included in the National Gallery of Canada's exhibition *Jana Sterbak: States of Being*. The work caused uproar among members of parliament and the public alike. Some felt that the sculptor had wasted food. Others complained that fresh meat was an inappropriate material for a work of art. While still others simply feared that the work was a health hazard, since the once-fresh meat decomposed during the course of the exhibition. In fact, *Vanitas* had a historical precedent in seventeenth-century Flemish still-life compositions, where the inclusion of rotting meat represented the transient and impermanent nature of life. Aware of this, both the Walker Art Center in Minneapolis and the Centre Pompidou in Paris acquired versions of Sterbak's work.

Shary Boyle (b. 1972), based in Toronto, also focused on the body. Her lace-draped porcelain figures broke down the barrier between the decorative arts and sculpture. Her battered, bound and headless women not only gave her a vehicle for confronting female abuse, it gave her an opportunity "to celebrate what is disordered, out of control, even flawed."[25]

Working on a grander scale, Tom Dean (b. 1947) summoned "the god Frankenstein" to help him assemble "his newborn monster from fragments of the freshly dead." Dean's unsettling installation *The Whole Catastrophe* (1999) features bronze castings of charred babies, swollen penises, hands and legs, and female pelvises, among other severed body parts.[26] Judged by one critic as "sculptures rather than bodies, objects that tweak the relations between consciousness and corporeality, representation and actuality," Dean's installations are more than this.[27] They depict chaotic scenes, from global catastrophes to sexual violence.

Architect and sculptor Melvin Charney (1935–2012) had a very different agenda for his work. He questioned the standardization and commodification of urban space and the extent to which modernist architecture had alienated the public. From the middle of the 1970s, Charney constructed site-specific replicas of historic facades on vacant city lots from which the original buildings had been removed. Charney's first life-sized installation, *Les Maisons de la Rue Sherbrooke* (1976), "reconstructed" two nineteenth-century grey stone heritage townhouses that had been demolished during the frenzy of urban renewal. The recuperation and reconstruction of one section on Rue Sherbrooke was too much for Montreal's mayor Jean Drapeau, especially during the Olympics in Montreal. The night after the work was built, city officials tore down the scaffold-backed plywood facades. Undeterred, Charney persisted in such work and his "ruins and phantoms" of historical buildings appeared on vacant lots in Ontario, Quebec, Nova Scotia and across North America.[28]

Such episodes generated controversy; they became news stories; they drew attention to what this generation of artists was doing within a genre that still claimed to be sculpture. An awkward question remained: had the public really been persuaded? Or had sculptors widened the gap between themselves and the public by responding to the private and public galleries' installation and purchasing practices? It seemed clear that embracing the latest styles of work did not succeed in boosting attendance figures at the country's public art institutions; nor did the explicit politicization of the work. As National Gallery of Canada director Hsio-Yen Shih told a gathering at the Windsor Art Gallery in the autumn of 1978, "the wall between the artists and the public has never been greater."[29]

Melvin Charney was not the only sculptor to react against the confines of the "white-cube" gallery, with its controlled climate, artificial lighting and neutral walls. In his installation *Le Grand Rassemblement* (1986–1996), Montreal's Marcel Gagnon (b. 1945) produced 120 life-sized concrete figures that could only be viewed when the Saint Lawrence River was at low tide. A decade earlier, and on the other side of the country, one had to venture to the Maplewood Mudflats on the outskirts of Vancouver to view sculptures by Tom Burrows (b. 1940). Composed of recycled industrial materials, they not only challenged conventional ways of representing the landscape, but also, like Gagnon's sculptures, were intentionally created as works that would not last.[30]

Jeffrey Rubinoff, a sculptor from London, Ontario, chose his own distinctive way of avoiding the confines of the white-cube gallery. In 1971 he purchased two hundred acres of land on a difficult-to-reach island in British Columbia. Over several decades, and with the assistance of John Kirk, Rubinoff transformed an old farm and the wilderness landscape surrounding it on Hornby Island "into a vision of a large conceptual piece," by creating berms and mounds, by digging small ponds and trenches, and by clearing trees and underbrush.[31] Then, using a former barn as his studio, Rubinoff fabricated all of his ambitious pieces without assistance. Initially, in *Series 1*, he created a group of stainless-steel cubes and oblongs that self-consciously drew upon the work of the American sculptor David Smith, especially upon his abstract *Cubi* series (1963–1965). Then, with the work of British sculptor Anthony Caro and American Richard Serra (b. 1938) in mind, Rubinoff embarked on two further series of gravity-defying quasi-mechanical works that variously combined shafts and pistons, T-sections, triangular brackets and heavy welded steel plates, as well as joints, spheres and tubular forms. By the third and fourth series, Rubinoff had found his own voice within modernist sculpture. Using Cor-Ten steel or stainless steel he explored negative and positive space, balance and counterpoint. Once *in situ*, the works not only spoke to one another, unfolding the sculptures' journey from one series to the next, they also interacted with the surrounding landscape, with the changing light, with the vagaries of the weather, and—not least—with the growth of moss and lichen on their burnished surfaces.

Rubinoff's work is *in* but not *of* the environment in which it stands. This was a key difference, then, between him and those who were known variously as land, earth, environmental or destination artists. True, they had also installed their work in remote locations in order to escape the art

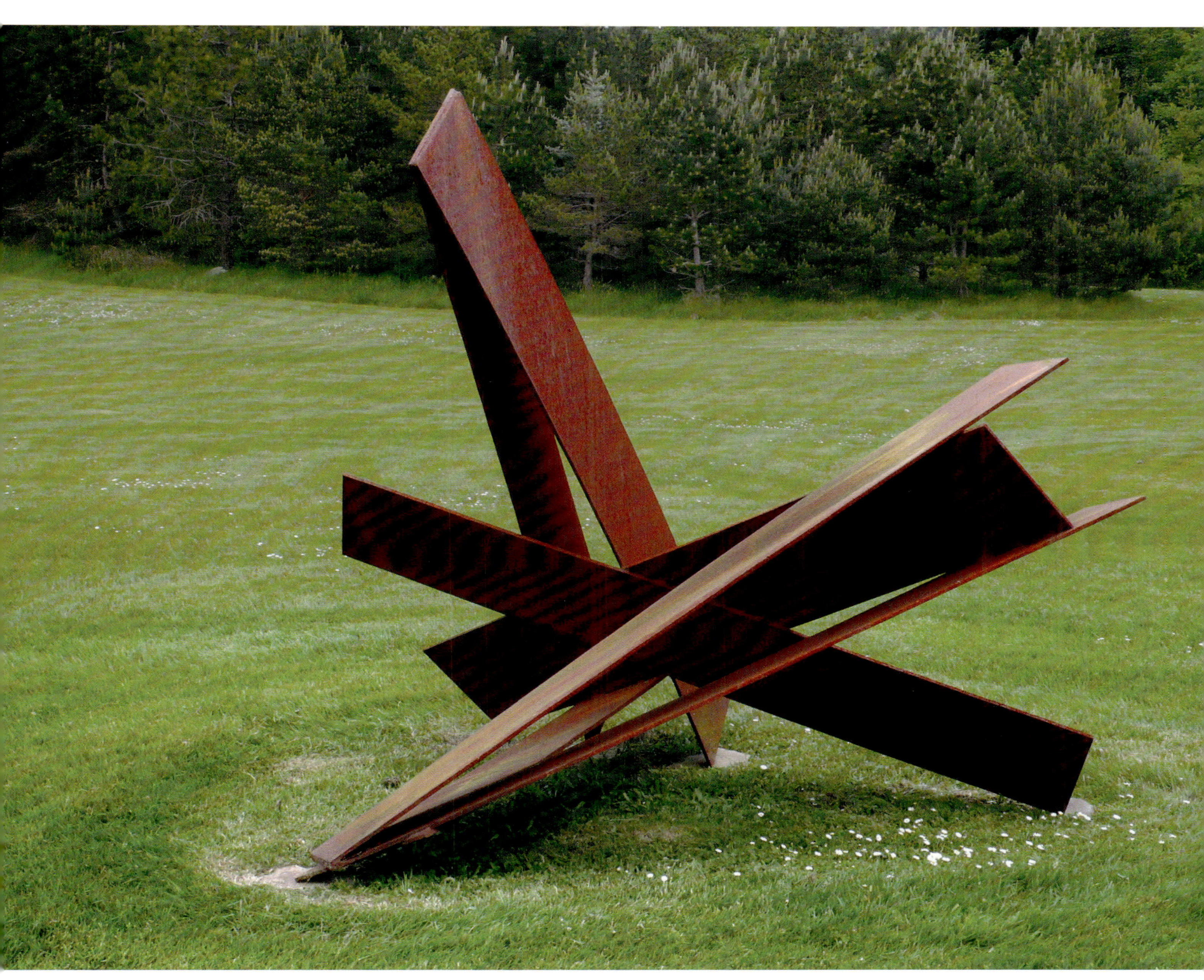

Jeffrey Rubinoff
Series 3-5, 1983

American sculptor David Smith and British sculptor Anthony Caro popularized the use of Cor-Ten steel; but it was Canada's Jeffrey Rubinoff who took that material in so many more directions. Working like a sorcerer's apprentice in a large barn, surrounded by chains and sanders, by grinding wheels, by oxyacetylene torches and casting equipment, Rubinoff fabricated each piece without the help of assistants. The sculptures from *Series 3* (see previous page) and *Series 4* seen here rekindle the spirit of early modernism by exploring balance and weightlessness, negative and positive space. Equally they speak to Rubinoff's belief that sculpture is music in plastic space by "describing" the counterpoint at work in the late string quartets of Ludwig van Beethoven.

market and the confining space of private and public art galleries. But for them, the land was indeed their studio; it provided them with material as well as being the showroom for their ephemeral installations.

Foreign artists made some of the first landscape interventions in Canada. In 1970, American sculptor Robert Smithson created a non-site work, *Glue Pour*, whereby several metric tons of glue were poured down a hill on the outskirts of Vancouver. (The Vancouver Art Gallery sanctioned the work at the time.) The following decade, using only his bare hands and "found" tools, British land artist Andy Goldsworthy (b. 1956) built a series of snow arches north of the Arctic Circle near Grise Fiord (Aujuittuq).

Like their American and British counterparts, Canada's land sculptors were not interested in simply depicting the landscape as such, but in transforming it. The mounds, mazes, circles, squares and furrows, among other ways in which they transformed the landscape, were not intended to be permanent works of art. Indeed, most of their work exists only in photographs or on videotape; or, even more transiently, in the memory of those who witnessed or participated in the making of the work. One of the earliest installation land artists in Canada was Bill Vazan (b. 1933). In 1969 this Montreal-based artist created *Sand Form Made at Low Tide Sand Flats at Paul's Bluff Inlet, Victoria Prince Edward Island*. Because the mound of sand disappeared completely after seven high tides, it now only exists in the large-format photographs taken by the sculptor.

Land artists have not simply forsaken the notion of permanence. They have also forsaken the studio, the foundry, the marketplace, the art gallery and the urban space. They have used materials outside the artistic realm, avoiding traditional methods of making sculpture—and of marketing it too. And they have also sought unique ways of addressing social and environmental concerns. Described in 2001 by one critic as "a tree-hugging ecologist who plunders nature in order to ennoble it," Reinhard Reitzenstein (b. 1949) removed the soil from the roots of eight coniferous trees, then after peeling off the bark he turned them upside-down and placed them around the circumference of a circle eighteen metres in diameter.[32] In *No Title* (1987) this Toronto artist and teacher hoped to draw attention to First Nations land claims by placing the work on contested ground on Topsail Island near Sault Ste. Marie. The protest had little political effect, however, and Reitzenstein's intervention was subsequently bulldozed.

In Saskatchewan Edward Poitras (b. 1953) also made the displacement and survival of First Nations people the subject of his work. In 1988 he exchanged a rectangular strip of sod from the lawn of the Mendel Art Gallery in Saskatoon with a similar strip from the Gordon First Nation community near Fort Qu'Appelle, Saskatchewan. He made his point when the strip of grass from the Mendel Art Gallery flourished on the reserve while the sod of grass transplanted from the reserve to the gallery lawn withered and died. *Offensive/Defensive* (1988) was, as the title suggests, not only a metaphor contrasting the difference between urban and rural life. It was about the survival of the Metis people, who had memorably resisted at the Battle of Batoche under their leader, Louis Riel.

In Quebec the group known as Boreal Multimedia took the idea of

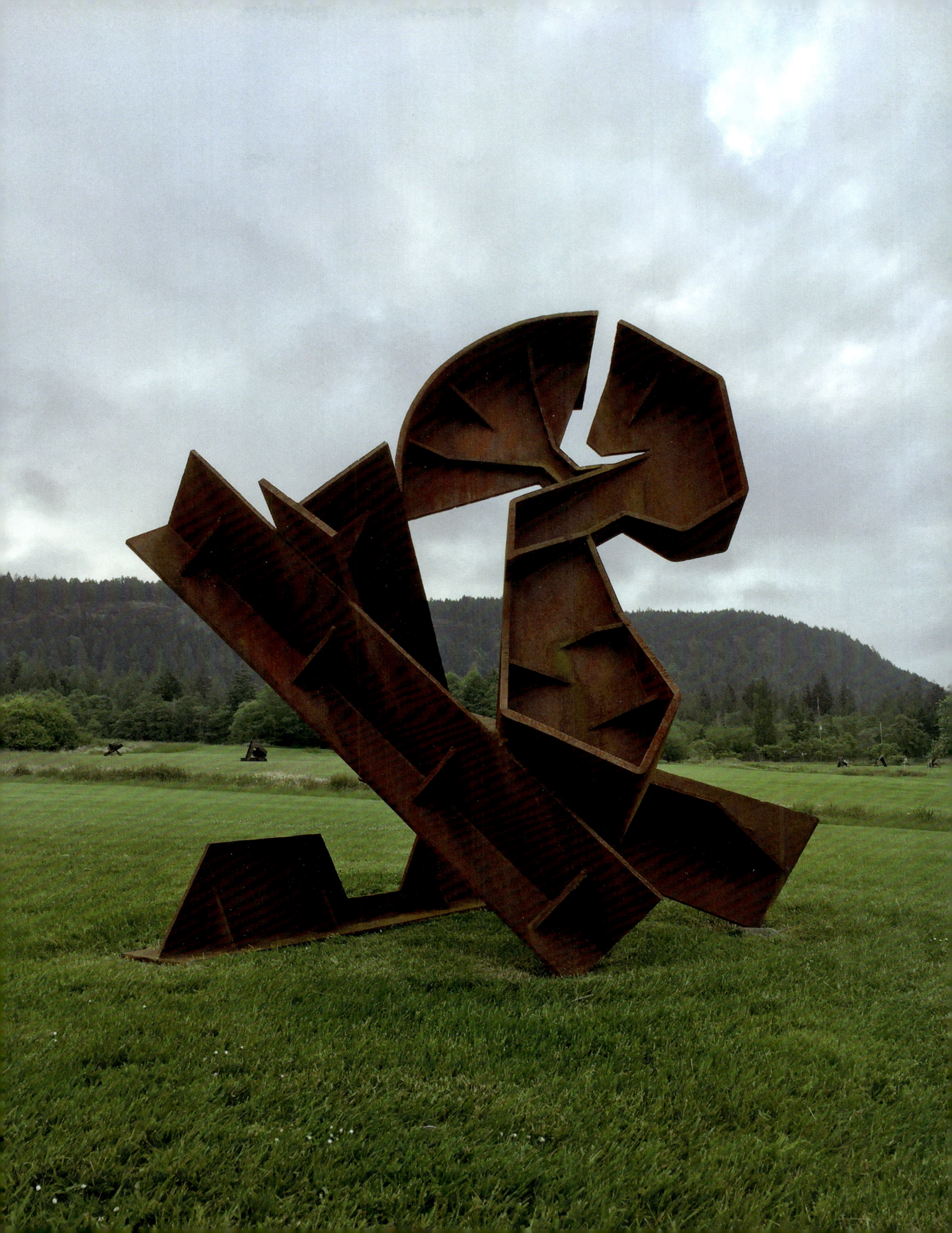

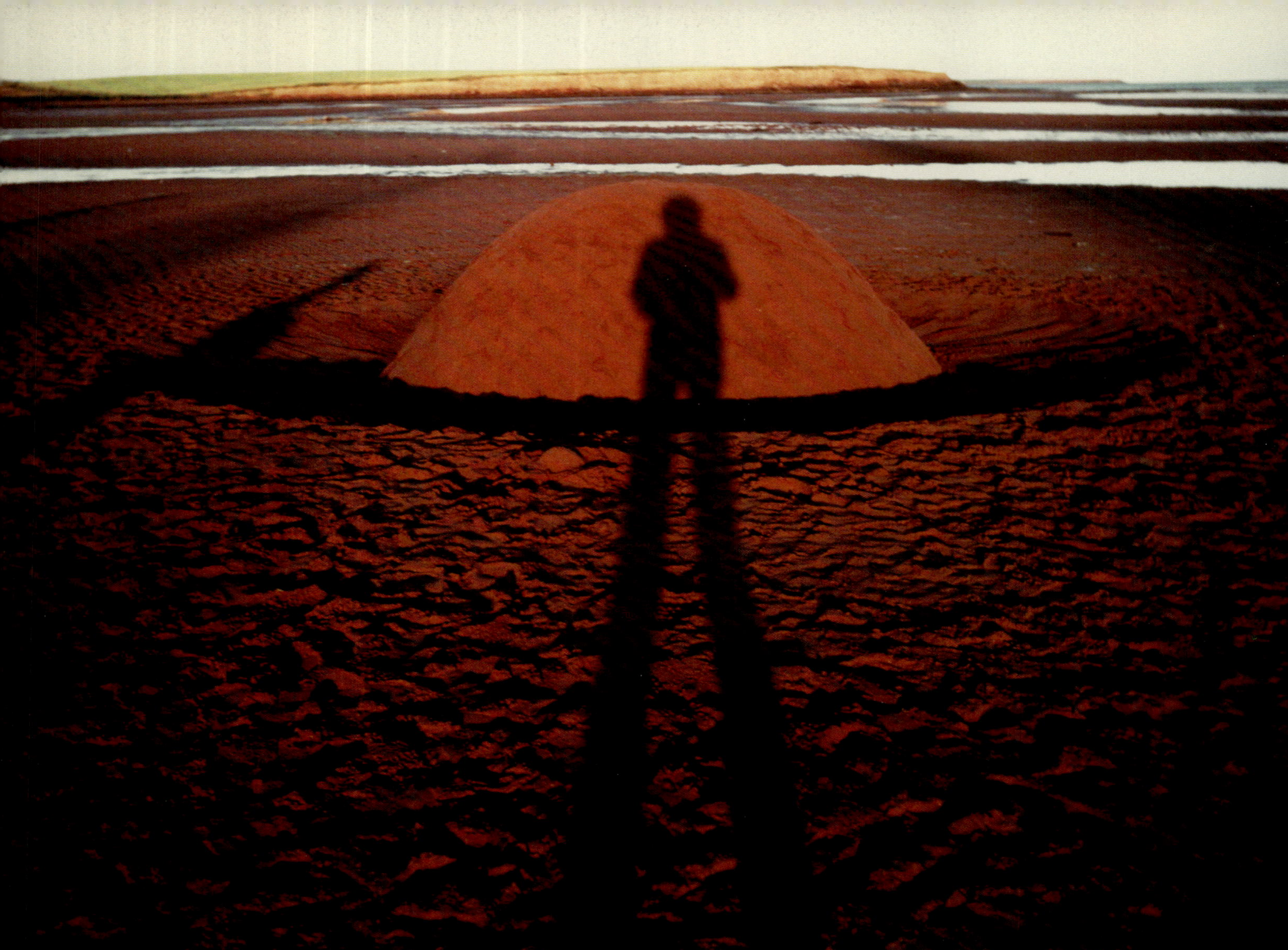

Bill Vazan
*Sand Form Made at Low Tide Sand Flats at Paul's
Bluff Inlet, Victoria Prince Edward Island*, **1969**
In the hope of reconnecting the individual to
nature, Bill Vazan's installations seek to explore the
relationship between humanity and the cosmos.
The Montreal-based sculptor also wanted to give
the viewer of his work a new perception of space
and time and, one might add, of impermanence,
because after several high tides the mound of sand
in this work disappears. The only evidence that *Sand
Form Made at Low Tide Sand Flats* ever existed lies
in the sequence of large format photographs that
document the work's creation—and its destruction.

an artist's engagement with the land to a new level. What the group calls
their "creative wilderness immersions" not only entail exploring and using
the raw materials from a vast unstructured space for their work; they also
have a "deep commitment to social justice and to the environment."[33] At Lac
Preston in the Laurentians the group voiced their concern about acid rain in
the installation *Deadlines/Ça Presse* (1989). In La Minerve forest in Quebec
their installation *À l'Affût* (1994) was a protest against deer hunting. And on
the shores of Henderson Lake, near Clayoquot Sound on Vancouver Island,
Boreal Multimedia gathered seventeen artists from Saskatchewan, British
Columbia and Quebec and joined forces with the Hochuktlisat-h people to
protest against MacMillan Bloedel's logging of an old-growth forest. Working
collectively and individually over a two-week period, Boreal Multimedia
produced *Forêt/Frontière* (1996), comprising site-specific sculptures in stone
and wood. The group also performed; they took photographs and made
videos; and they wrote poetry and sang in an effort to "express the 'spirit'"
of the valley.[34]

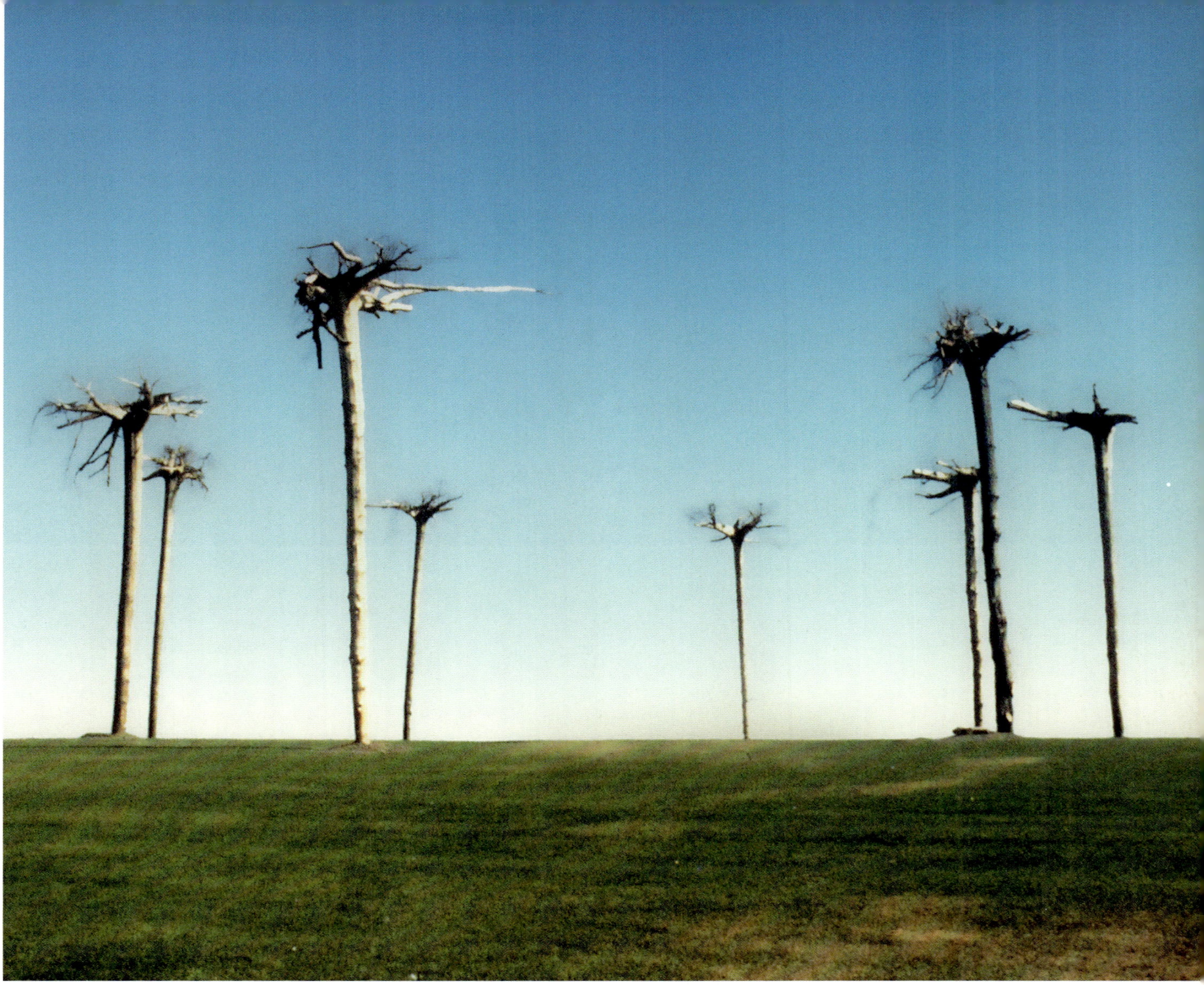

Not every sculptor who produced work during the decades following the 1960s was concerned with making a political, social or theoretical statement. Or with taking their work out of the gallery. Or with creating a work that would vanish with the next tide or the next season. What mattered to Montreal's Gilles Mihalcean (b. 1946) was the seductive ambiguity of the work in progress, bringing out its strengths and physical properties.[35] While Ian Carr-Harris (b. 1941), Royden Rabinowitch (b. 1943), Ian Pratt (b. 1959) and Odette LeBlanc (b. 1961) were determined to eliminate hierarchical relationships by allowing the combination of unrelated found objects to generate their own meaning. And then there is Robert Murray. Long after he moved to the United States in 1960, Murray continued to produce elegant, on-the-ground, open abstract sculptures that exuded an airy lightness that made them independent of any gravitational push or pull. Works like *Swing* (1973) helped to make this unreconstructed

Reinhard Reitzenstein
No Title, 1987
Ever since 1969, when American earthworks sculptor Robert Smithson turned a tree on its head then stuck it into the ground, sculptors have been turning buildings, animals and people upside down. Environmental sculptor Reinhard Reitzenstein is among the couple of hundred contemporary artists to date who are fabricating trees out of metal or transforming living trees into sculptures. After stripping his deciduous trees of their bark and turning them upside down in order to expose their gangly roots, the German-born sculptor and teacher gave this genre a new twist by placing them in a circle. Some call sculptures like *No Title* gimmicky but Reitzenstein prefers to call his work problematic.

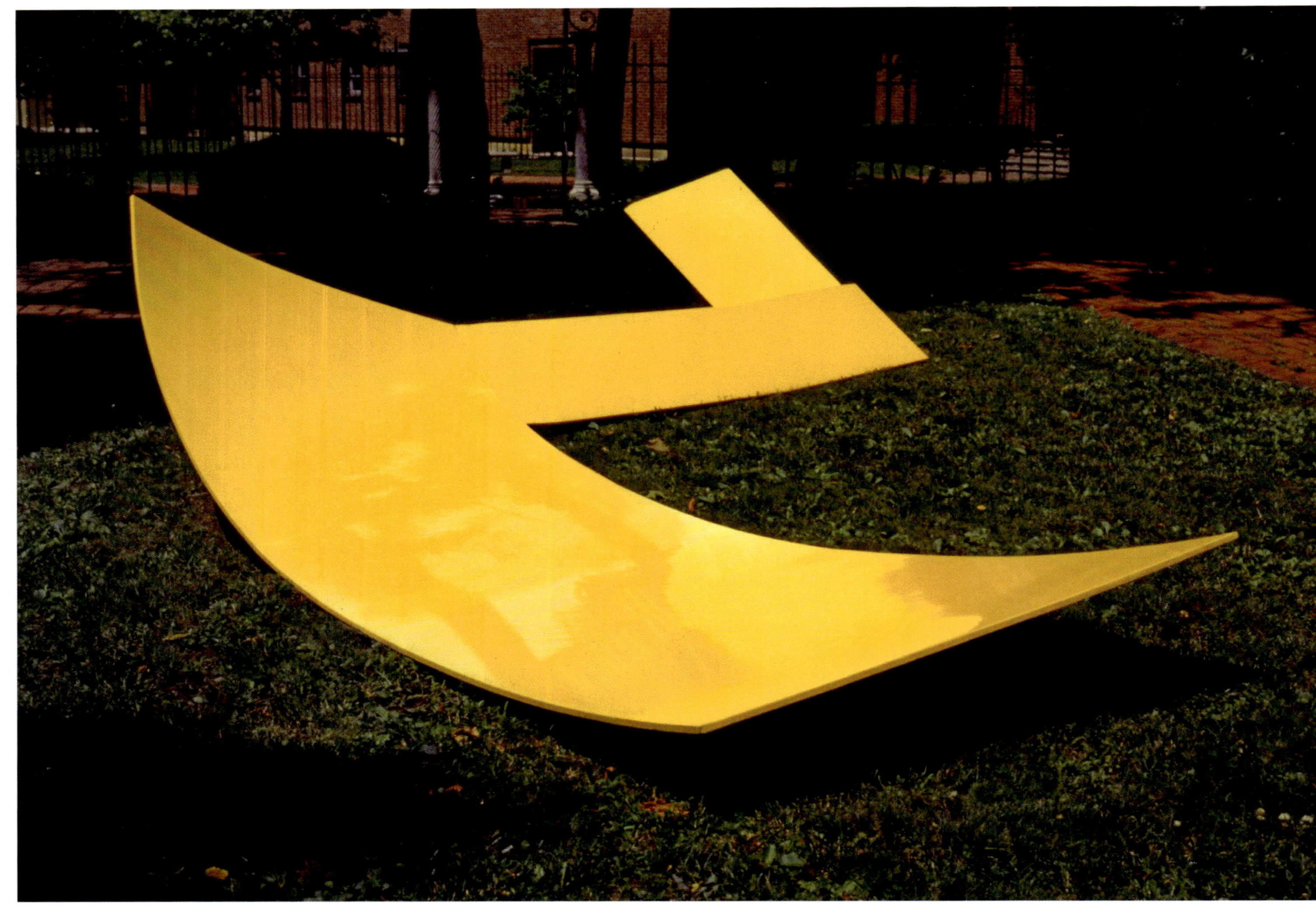

Robert Murray
Swing, 1973

Following Robert Murray's small-scale model, and working on a factory floor, professional welders fabricated this major work, whose components are cut from one sheet of metal. Murray began his artistic career as a landscape painter. When he switched to sculpture in 1959 the one thing that he could not give up was colour. Applied in a painterly way to the aluminum surfaces of his work, Murray's vibrant colours enhance the effects of light and shade and give the work a spontaneity and freshness that is unmatched in the work of any other sculptor in Canada. After settling in New York in 1960, this unreconstructed modernist and master of simplicity and poise rightly earned a reputation for being one of the best-known sculptors in North America.

modernist one of the leading sculptors in the United States and kept his reputation alive in Canada, where he spends his summers at Georgian Bay.

More recently, Douglas Bentham, who was born in Saskatchewan in 1947, turned his back on traditional concepts, such as weight and volume, associated with monolithic sculpture. His imposing pieces, like the stainless-steel sculpture *Unfurled* (2006), possess a lightness and openness that reflects the expansiveness of the Prairie landscape and transcends the physical limitations of the stainless steel from which the work is created.

In their search for new forms and new materials other sculptors drew on the stock components relating to architecture, such as angle-irons, scaffolding or structural beams; they incorporated pipes and ladders and coiled rope; they used spirit levels or fluorescent tubing, along with steel plates and cables and cement. Moving away from the organic, monolithic works of Henry Moore, many Canadians turned to another British sculptor, Anthony Caro, whose large-scale architectural sculptures utilized industrial I-beams, poles, rods and even propeller blades.[36]

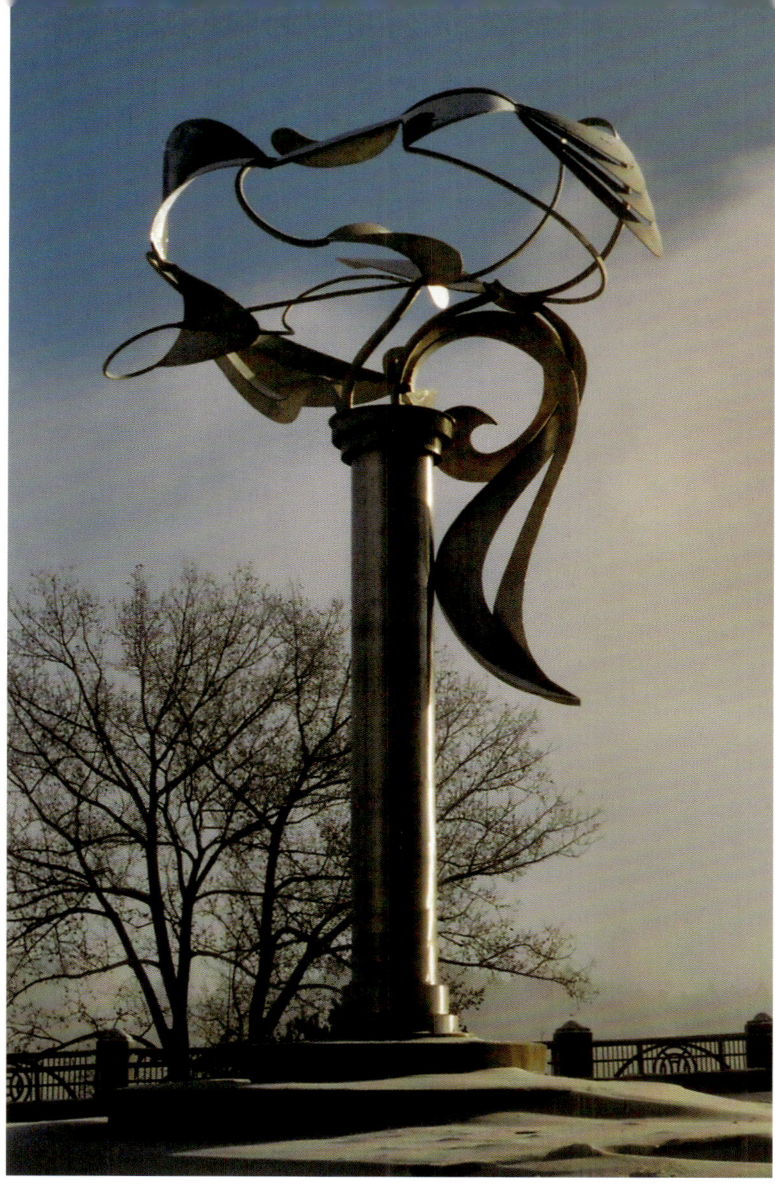

Victoria's Roland Brener (1942–2006), Montreal's Henry Saxe (b. 1937) and Michel Goulet (b. 1944), and Patrick Thibert (b. 1943) from London, Ontario, all followed Caro's—and American sculptor David Smith's—example of drawing the viewer's attention to the mechanization and organization of labour by assembling the components of industrial fabrication. Indeed the haphazard assemblage of architectural elements, including severed columns, broken concrete slabs and fractured beams, in the works by Claude Mongrain (b. 1948) comprising his *Construction* series (1978–1980) evoked, in the mind of one spectator, "a deconstructed construction site."[37] True, Roland Brener's off-the-rack assemblages of bars and braces may resemble industrial scaffolding; yet, stripped of its utilitarian function, his *Wall of Scaffold* (1981), erected in a park in Halifax, is plainly more than a building site—and indeed nothing less than poetic. Likewise, in producing her assemblages of steel, bronze and concrete, Edmonton's Catherine Burgess (b. 1953) thus invited the viewer "to see asymmetries, disjunctions, and elusive visual relationships that resist verbal description."[38]

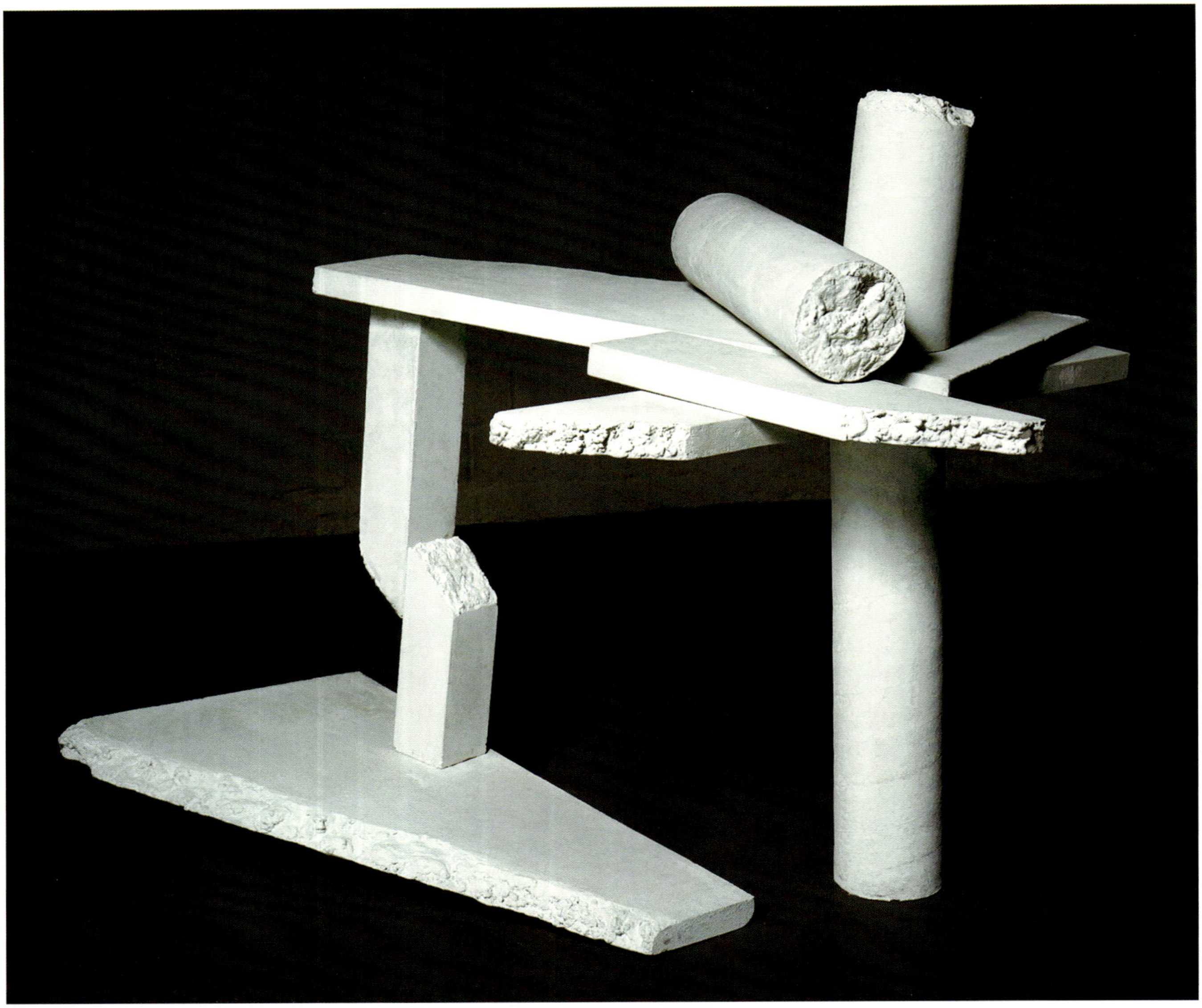

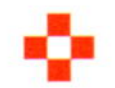

Claude Mongrain
Construction: Vésuve, 1979

Claude Mongrain is fascinated by architectural ruins. Moreover, in common with many postmodernist sculptors, he likes to infuse his work with irony and playfulness, of which his installation *Construction: Vésuve* is the best example. By creating broken slabs of concrete and fractured columns and beams, Mongrain explores the inherent irony associated with a building's stability yet impermanence. It is a moot point whether this assemblage is more like a building site or an archaeological excavation.

The influence of the late Anthony Caro went far beyond the use of particular materials. He had long argued that, because sculpture inhabited the same space as its viewer, the sculptor should make a work "that would involve the whole body of the viewer."[39] He found a warm reception from Canadian art critics like Brian Foss, who agreed that meaning could not be projected from a sculpture: it had to grow "out of the dialogue between the object and the viewer."[40] In short, viewers were "no longer invited to keep a distance, to be absorbed in passive contemplation," but were encouraged to "complete" the work with their own particular imaginative responses. Commenting in the catalogue for the Canadian pavilion at the thirty-fourth Venice Biennale in 1968, Montreal's Ulysse Comtois wrote that his *"transformable colonnes"* should be regarded as "not final," pending the intervention of those who would take an active role in viewing them. "When I leave them, they are still to be made," Comtois suggested. "By manipulating them, the spectator extends the artist's actions."

The example of American kinetic sculptors Alexander Calder (1898–1976) and George Rickey (1907–2002) likewise proved fruitful. In Calgary, Katie Ohe created *Puddle 1* (1976) exemplifying ambitions very much in this tradition. "Through touch, there would be motion," Ohe wrote. "Through motion, there would be infinitely changing perceptions of each work."[41] Mattiussi Iyaituk (b. 1950) similarly invited the viewer of *Singing and Drumming Sounds from the Shaman* (2000) to activate his work.[42] *Fluid Motion* (2001) by Alan Storey (b. 1960), installed at Sapperton metro station in New Westminster, only comes into its own when commuters activate the work's bicycle wheels, which are 5.5 metres in diameter. And in *Spirit Catcher* (1986), Ron Baird (b. 1940) leaves it to the wind to rock the work's sixteen quills back and forth.[43]

Victoria-based sculptor Mowry Baden was another who was dissatisfied with what he called "the stand off and look" tradition associated with most sculptures and installations. He sought to enhance the viewers' perceptual field by challenging them to become "involved in the experience of *their*

Katie Ohe
Puddle I, 1976
There are no "do not touch" signs displayed next to Katie Ohe's *Puddle I*. Instead, this Calgary-born sculptor encourages her viewers to touch the work in order to bring it to life. The sculptor's concern with showing how a work's moveable components can fluctuate in space and create an optical illusion, and how welded steel and cast bronze can have a sense of weightlessness, are central to the success of this highly tactile work. *Puddle I*, like Ohe's other interactive installations, was fabricated in a fine-art foundry in Italy where, over the course of fourteen years, she oversaw every stage of the production of her work.

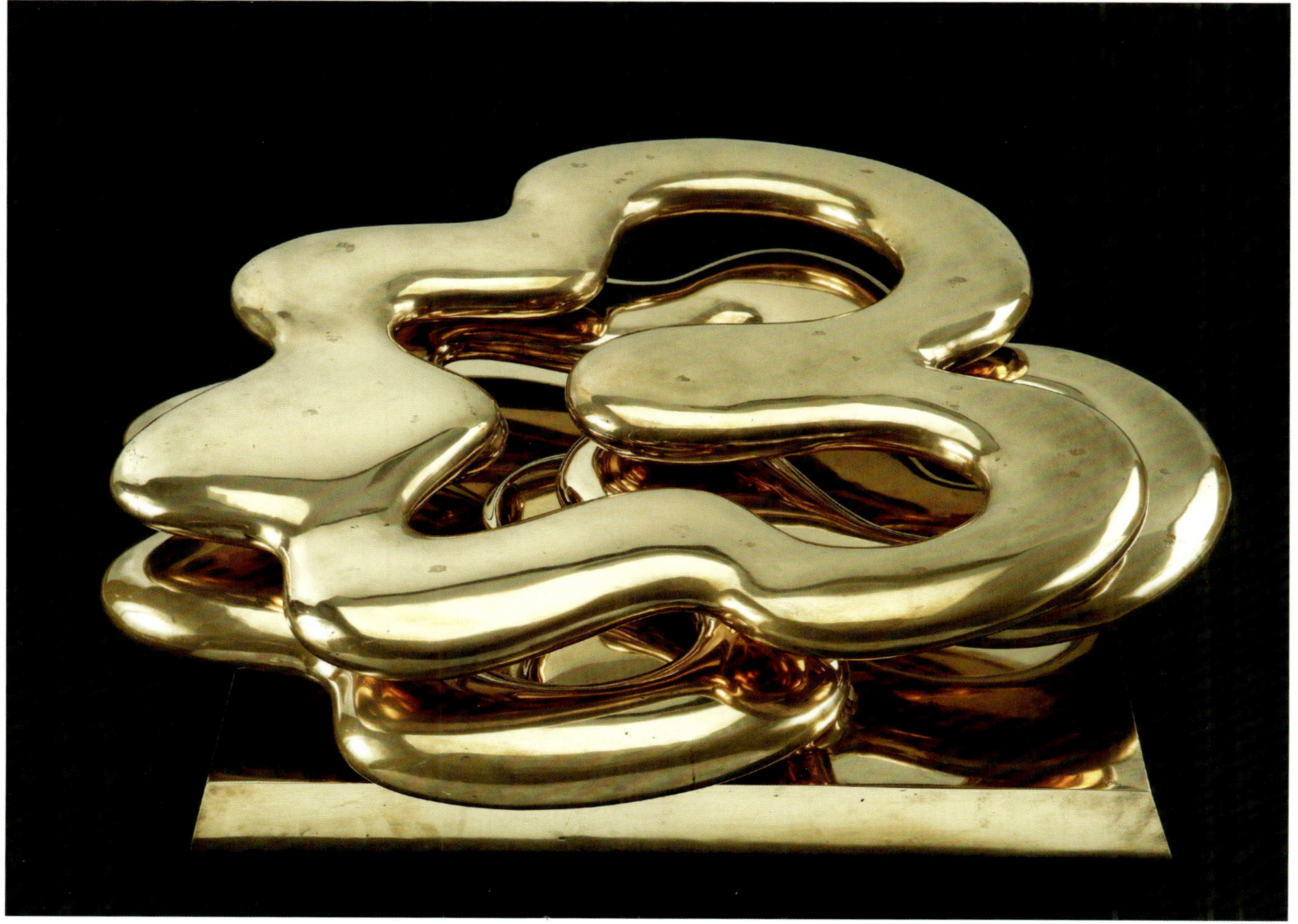

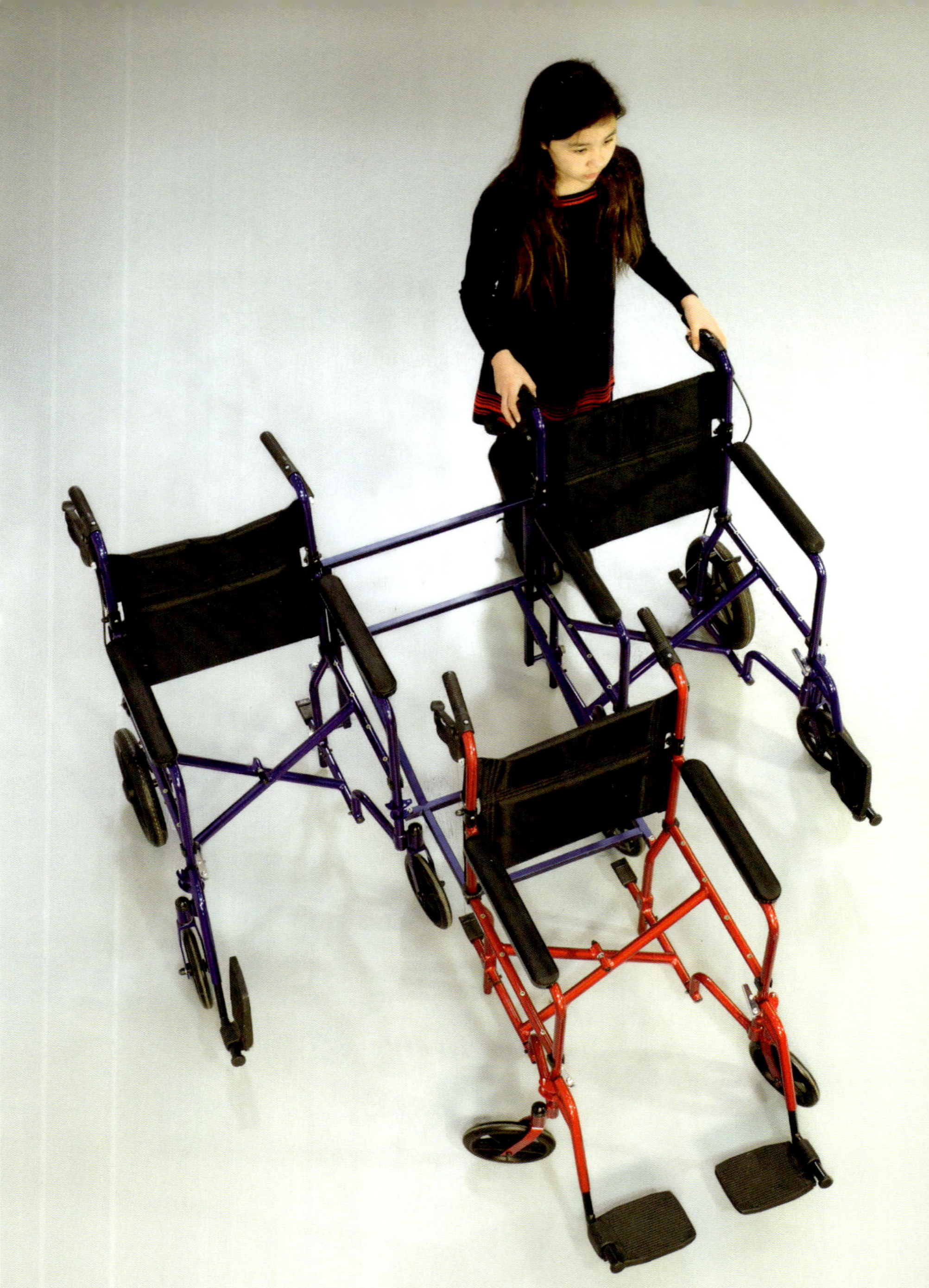

experience."[44] Baden's task-oriented installations incorporate objects that
are at once familiar and unfamiliar to his viewers. In *Beginning, Middle
and End* (2012), for example, viewers are invited to push wheelchairs—that
have no seats. In Baden's mixed-media installation *Ever Pronating* (1996),
the viewer stands in the fold of two upright mattresses, which are as non-
functional as the wheelchairs.[45]

Sculptors working within the traditional realist idiom also sought to
engage the public in their work. But the old conventions—exemplified by
the plinth on which sculpture was traditionally displayed—had a tenacious
hold on viewers, who could not simply be conscripted into a new role as

participants on (literally) level terms with the sculpture with which they were invited to interact.

Self-taught sculptor, restorer and cabinet-maker Fabien Pagé (b. 1959) produced a bronze sculpture of René Lévesque in 1999 that was placed on Parliament Hill in Quebec City. Pagé's on-the-ground, life-sized sculpture enabled the public to share the same social space and thereby "mingle" with the former premier of Quebec. Soon after the sculpture was installed, however, there were problems. Placing the work outdoors and on the ground produced a sculpture some 25 per cent smaller than was conventional on the plinth. Many people professed themselves to be "disheartened by the fact that the monument's size was not in keeping with the symbolic stature of an important person"; it stood in contrast with the other sculptures, invariably larger-than-life, that lined the Promenade des Premiers-Ministres in Quebec City.[46] The on-the-ground location and accurate rendering of Lévesque's 1.6-metre height allowed a viewer to place a cigarette between Lévesque's fingers; it allowed anyone eager for a posthumous photo opportunity with the premier (who had died in November 1987) to lean against the work. This kind of behaviour was unacceptable to the province's government officials. Pagé was commissioned to make a larger, 2.5-metre-high sculpture of Lévesque. This was installed on a platform in 2002, but proved uninspiring and less accessible to the public.

In 2013 Timothy Schmalz (b. 1969), a Toronto sculptor and practising Roman Catholic, produced *Jesus the Homeless* (2013) after seeing a homeless person sleeping on a park bench. He offered the work to Toronto's St. Michael's Cathedral. Church officials rejected the offer of Schmalz's "visual translation" of a verse in the Gospel of Matthew: "as you did it to one of the least of my brothers, you did it to me." However, the University of Toronto's Jesuit School of Theology, Regis College, along with churches and cathedrals in the United States and in Europe, did acquire other castings of Schmalz's realistic rendering of a faceless and homeless Jesus Christ in repose.

Edmonton sculptor Barbara Paterson (b. 1936) found more success in integrating the public into her work. *Women are Persons!* (1999) honoured Irene Parlby, Emily Murphy, Louise McKinney, Henrietta Muir Edwards and Nellie McClung, who succeeded in their campaign to make women eligible for appointment to the Canadian Senate in 1929. Versions of this true-to-life work are installed in both Calgary and Ottawa, and Paterson's addition of a chair invites the public to join and thereby interact with the women. In this case, it seems, the invitation was accepted with thanks.

Dissatisfied with direct engagement with the physical world, a small number of sculptors turned to cyberspace and virtual reality. The computer gave Carol Proulx (b. 1946) a way of exploring "the world of space, the space I live in, the space I move in" by allowing the Montreal artist to fully explore every dimension of a sculpture, from its height, depth and volume to its movement and transparency.[47] Similarly, in *The Salmon Project* (2007–2014) Ontario College of Art and Design professor Claire Brunet

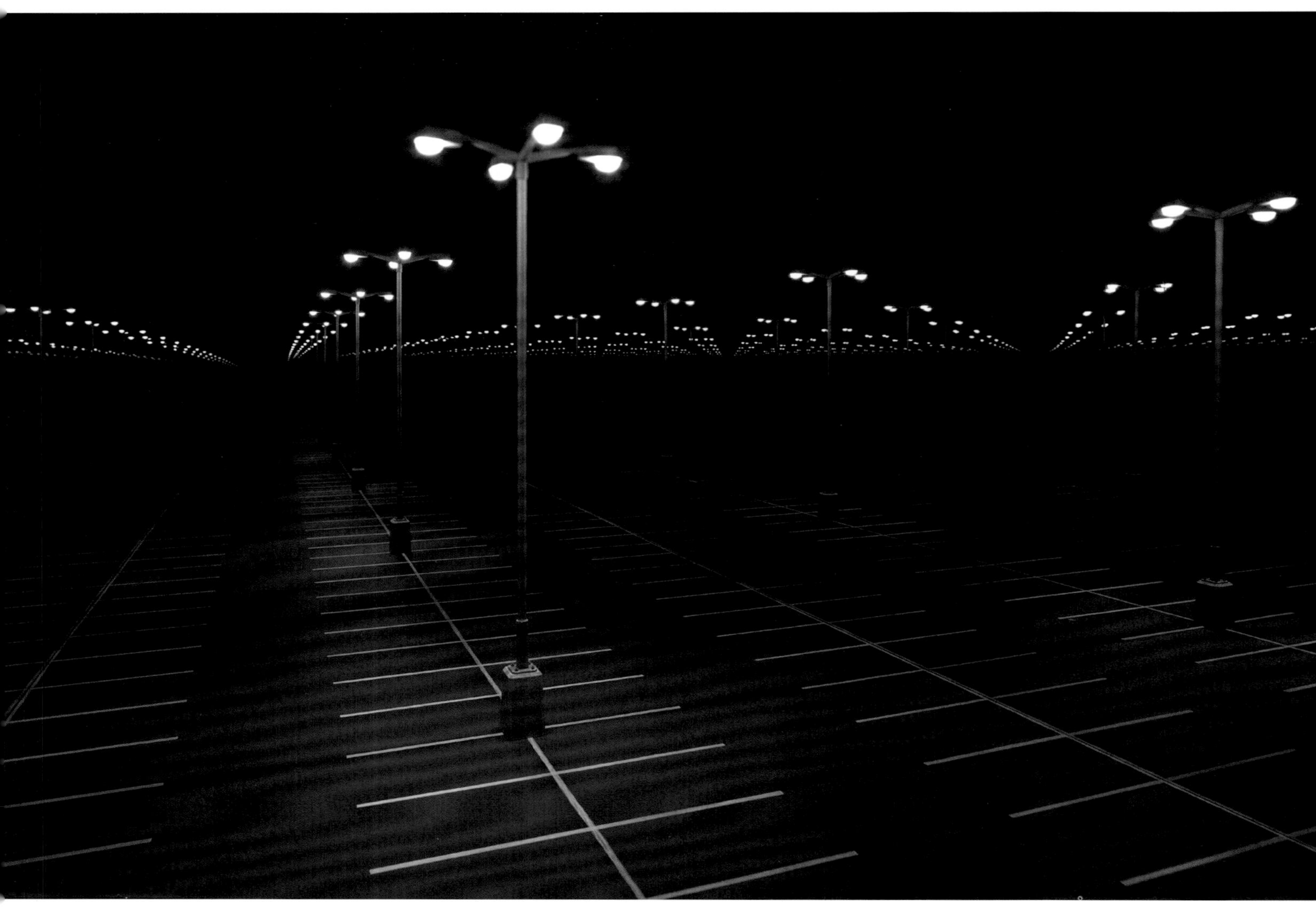

Guillaume Lachapelle
Nuit Étoilée, 2012

The only semblance that Guillaume Lachapelle's works have to traditional sculpture is the plinth on which they sit. Made with the help of 3-D printing technology and composed of mirrors and LED lights, among other materials, the artist's light boxes and dioramas can turn a familiar setting into an eerie film-noir stage set. But these uncanny sculptures elicit more than a sense of fear and of the unknown. Lachapelle's light boxes—just like the receding images of rooms in children's books—evoke a sense of wonder by creating the illusion of infinite space.

(b. 1957) used 3-D technology to explore the difference between variable and established space, while its ulterior purpose was to address the abuses of salmon farming.[48]

In Montreal, Guillaume Lachapelle (b. 1974) built an international reputation using 3-D printing technology. He created models of curved bookshelves, streets and architectural facades and became well known for his mirrored dioramas, or what he calls light or infinity boxes. In all of these works Lachapelle has created an illusion of infinite space that, according to one critic, "opens the conventions of our reality to fresh disposition." When asked if his light boxes were sculptures, Lachapelle replied: "Well, it's an object, so it's a sculpture."[49]

The elasticity of the medium, it seemed, was at least as great as the elasticity of the form. And yet, while many sculptors abandoned conventional materials as much as they now eschewed any literal reference in their work, the received conventions did not simply die or disappear. As French art historian Pierre Francastel argued, "the appearance of a new form does not abolish the validity of the old ones."[50] As already seen in the work of Pagé and Paterson, traditional methods continued to find their adherents; traditional themes, such as human and animal forms, were not neglected, and were certainly not despised—at least, not by those who simply did not care whether their work was considered to be at the cutting edge of their profession. Moreover, a respectful awareness of the art-historical past continued to inspire a number of sculptors whose object was to reconfigure the history of late-twentieth-century sculpture through the depiction of the human figure.

British sculptor Henry Moore kept the human form alive as a subject for the sculptor and won considerable esteem in Canada. This had come first through *Three Way Piece Number Two: The Archer* (1964), installed in Toronto's Nathan Phillips Square in 1966, and was subsequently consolidated by the acceptance of his bequest of more than nine hundred sculptures and works on paper to the Art Gallery of Ontario in 1974. In a similar idiom, Ottawa-based Victor Tolgesy turned his back on what he called "purely design-oriented sculpture in favor of a deliberate involvement with humanity."[51] And there were others of a similar orientation, sometimes difficult to classify.

Joe Fafard (b. 1942), as a young art teacher from the French-Canadian community of Sainte-Marthe in Saskatchewan, trod an interesting path. He found an alternative to the largely abstract kinetic sculptures that he had previously been producing when he arrived to teach pottery and sculpture at the Regina School of Art at Regina College in 1968. It was then that he encountered two West Coast ceramicists, Ric Gomez (b. 1942) and David Gilhooly (1943–2013), whose work introduced him to "funk art" that brought figuration back to painting and sculpture. Under the influence of these American artists, Fafard began producing satirical figures in clay that explored the domestic world. Within a few years Fafard had left his teaching position and was settled in the rural community of Pense near Regina, where he made, painted and glazed realistic portraits of everyone in the community in clay. Workers, merchants, elders—and even farm animals—were all depicted with both irony and dignity. Fafard earned a national reputation when he began making clay sculptural portraits of provincial and national political leaders and of historical figures from the art world.

Though overwhelmingly successful, Fafard paused to wonder if his work was only popular "because it's accessible" and agonize whether "it can't be any good if it's popular."[52] In fact, a number of different issues seem to be at stake here, as can be seen in the statement from the influential— and frequently caustic—Toronto art critic John Bentley Mays, who said that ceramic sculpture did "not constitute art."[53] Was the late art critic claiming that none of the examples he had seen satisfied his own aesthetic criteria? In which case, perhaps newer and better work might cause such a judgment to be revised. Or was there simply a category problem here? True, the editors of the country's leading journal devoted to sculpture, *Espace*, excluded ceramic sculpture from their discourse until 1994.[54] But then they changed their mind.

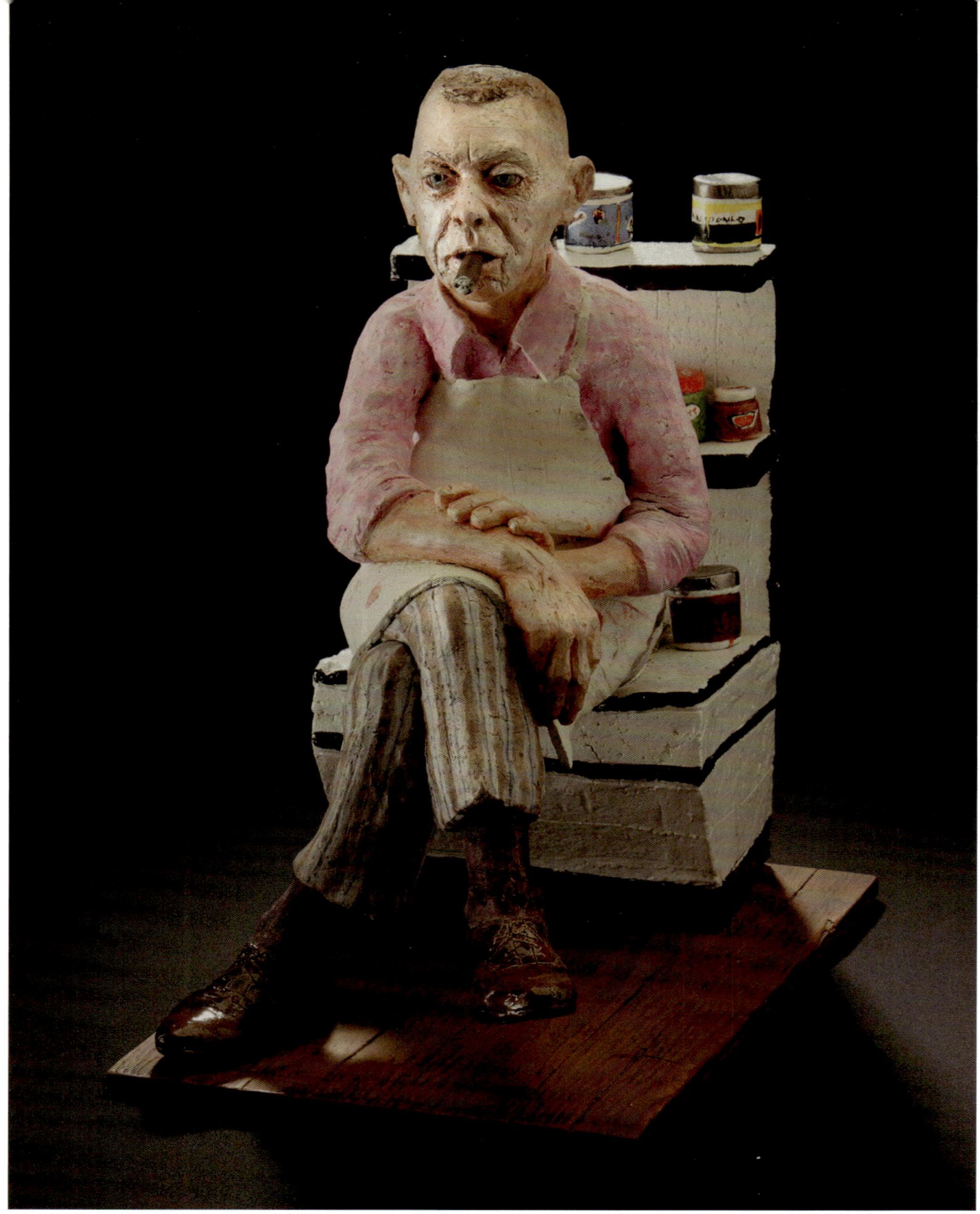

Joe Fafard

The Merchant of Pense, **1973**

It is difficult to believe that Joe Fafard's first sculptural works were abstract and kinetic. It was only after he encountered two anti-Abstract-Expressionist "funk" artists while teaching at Regina College that he began modelling figures in clay. But Fafard did not find the iconic subjects that inhabit his work until he quit his teaching job and moved to the rural community of Pense. There everyone in the community—including animals—became subjects for his figurative sculptures. And beyond the repertoire of characters he found in Pense, he later turned to politicians and famous artists for his subjects.

It was hardly the material itself that constituted the intrinsic difficulty in gaining acceptance. After all, the conceptual ceramic installations of Vancouver artist Gathie Falk (b. 1928), like *Single Right Men's Shoes: Blue Running Shoes* (1973), had been exhibited in public galleries from the early 1970s.[55] And Saskatchewan's Marilyn Levine (1935–2005) enjoyed a successful career after she abandoned the pottery wheel and spent the rest of her career making *trompe l'oeil* sculptures of leather goods. The wrinkles, folds, scrapes, scuffs and stretch marks of Levine's leather bags, jackets and suitcases revealed the personalities of the people who had worn or carried these objects.

These sculptors, one might say, had happened to be working in ceramics as their chosen medium, just as other materials might have been chosen. Montreal painter and sculptor Betty Goodwin (1923–2008) created some effects that could be seen as similar to Levine's work but did so simply by

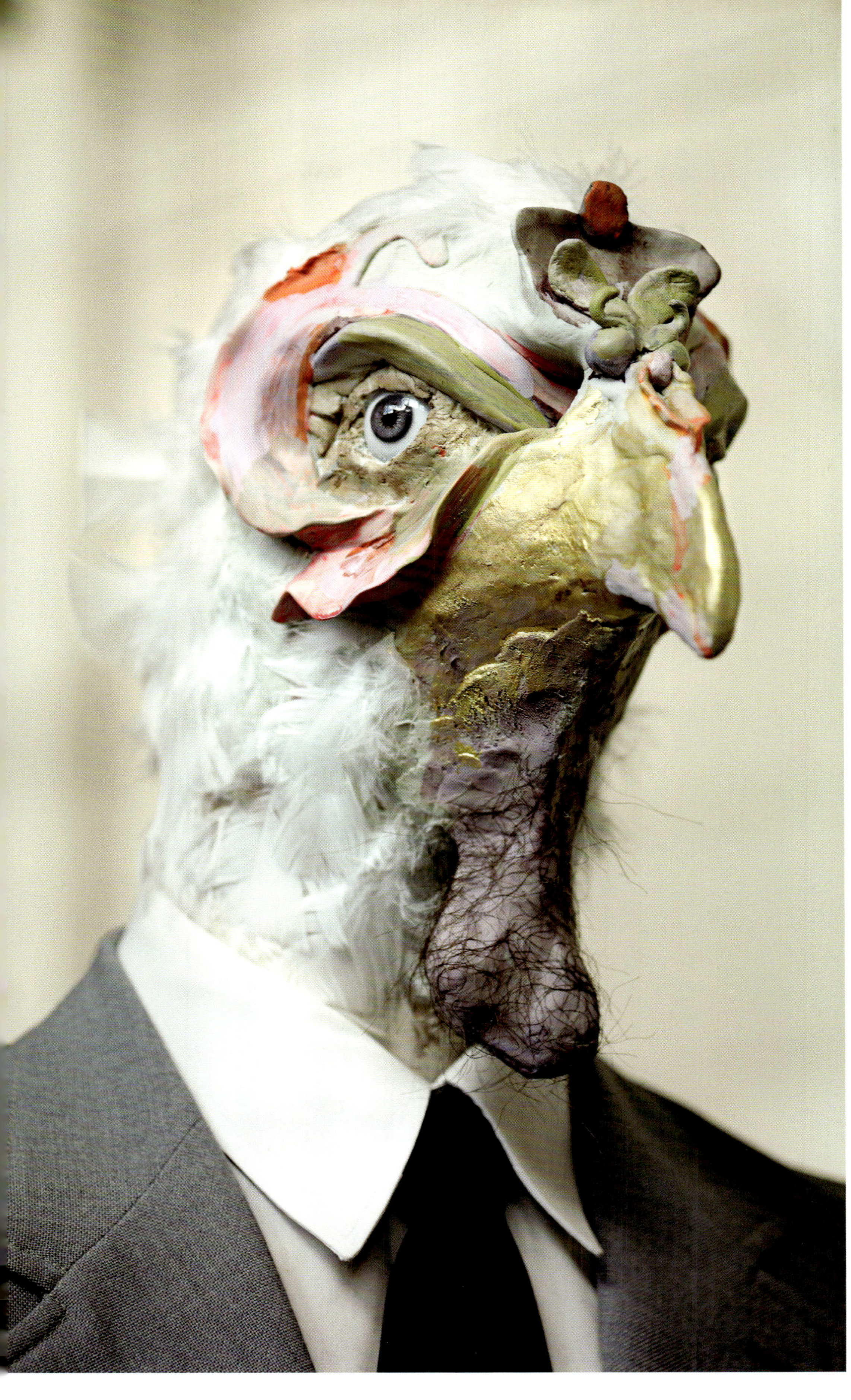

David Altmejd
The Index, 2007
Traditionally student painters and sculptors drew or modelled fragments of the human anatomy fashioned by classical sculptors. Rodin was among the first sculptors in the twentieth century to make body fragments the subject of his work. Montreal-born David Altmejd, who now lives in New York City, not only makes what he calls "monster body parts": the artist's frequently horrific installations also cross the species barrier. He thus presents an elaborate tableau of animalized humans and half-bird human figures.

focusing on men's vests, shirts and gloves—taking the objects themselves as her material. In *John Chinaman* (1991), Sharyn Yuen (b. 1956) combined handmade, photo-emulsion rice paper with internal lighting to create a memorial installation suggesting *tangzhuang* jackets.[56] Using laminated glass, Mary Filer (1920–2016) created murals and free-standing abstract sculptures. Another Vancouver artist, Liz Magor (b. 1948), had earlier presented preserves, glass jars, recipes and other canning equipment in her installation *Time and Mrs. Tiber* (1976). Magor not only told us something about the subject of her work, she explored the brevity of life, thereby setting up "a kind of objective contest: would I outlast the fruit?"[57]

Toronto-based artist Colette Whiten (b. 1945) explored the space that the body occupies and the process of making sculpture by casting both sides of the human body in plaster of Paris.[58] More recently in Montreal, David Altmejd made the body the subject of his work, by taking his installations in directions that some found disturbing. "Haunted by terrible figures and labyrinthine shapes, by desire and revulsion and by the body and its transformation," as one critic put it, Altmejd assembled contrasting elements such as animals and animalized humans, half-bird figures, stuffed squirrels, decapitated werewolf heads and what he refers to as "monster body parts."[59] The unsettling combination of these elements, evident in Altmejd's installation *The Index* (2007), crosses the species barrier, explores the metamorphosis between man and animal, and creates a habitat in which the familiar boundary between human and animal is erased. It is not only aesthetic categories that are being transgressed and questioned here.

A famous article by Francis Fukuyama, published in 1989, controversially declared "the end of history" and the phrase quickly passed into general circulation.[60] It served as a mantra for sculptors who refused to acknowledge that their work was part of the historical tradition. Such bold, sonorous declarations were hardly binding, however, and few evidently felt inhibited in cherry picking from the grand narrative.

Evan Penny, born in South Africa in 1953, was well aware of the difficulty of being a contemporary artist and a figurative sculptor at the same time. "How," he asked, "do I embrace this form, which is often seen to be retrograde and bound up in history, and yet face toward the present and speak to the moment?"[61] Penny found a way around his dilemma. With the help of digital scanning technology and a 3-D computer software program, he made foam prototypes of much-altered photographs that he then modelled and cast into clay. The synthetically generated images seem apparently hyper-realistic, replete with facial blemishes, wrinkles and unwanted hairs; yet they are portraits of people who never existed. In his first and second *No One—In Particular* series (2001–2005; 2004–2007), Penny's larger than life–sized sculptures push the boundaries between the real and the imagined. "I try to situate my sculpture," Penny explains, "somewhere between the way we perceive each other in real time and space and the way we perceive ourselves and each other in an image."[62]

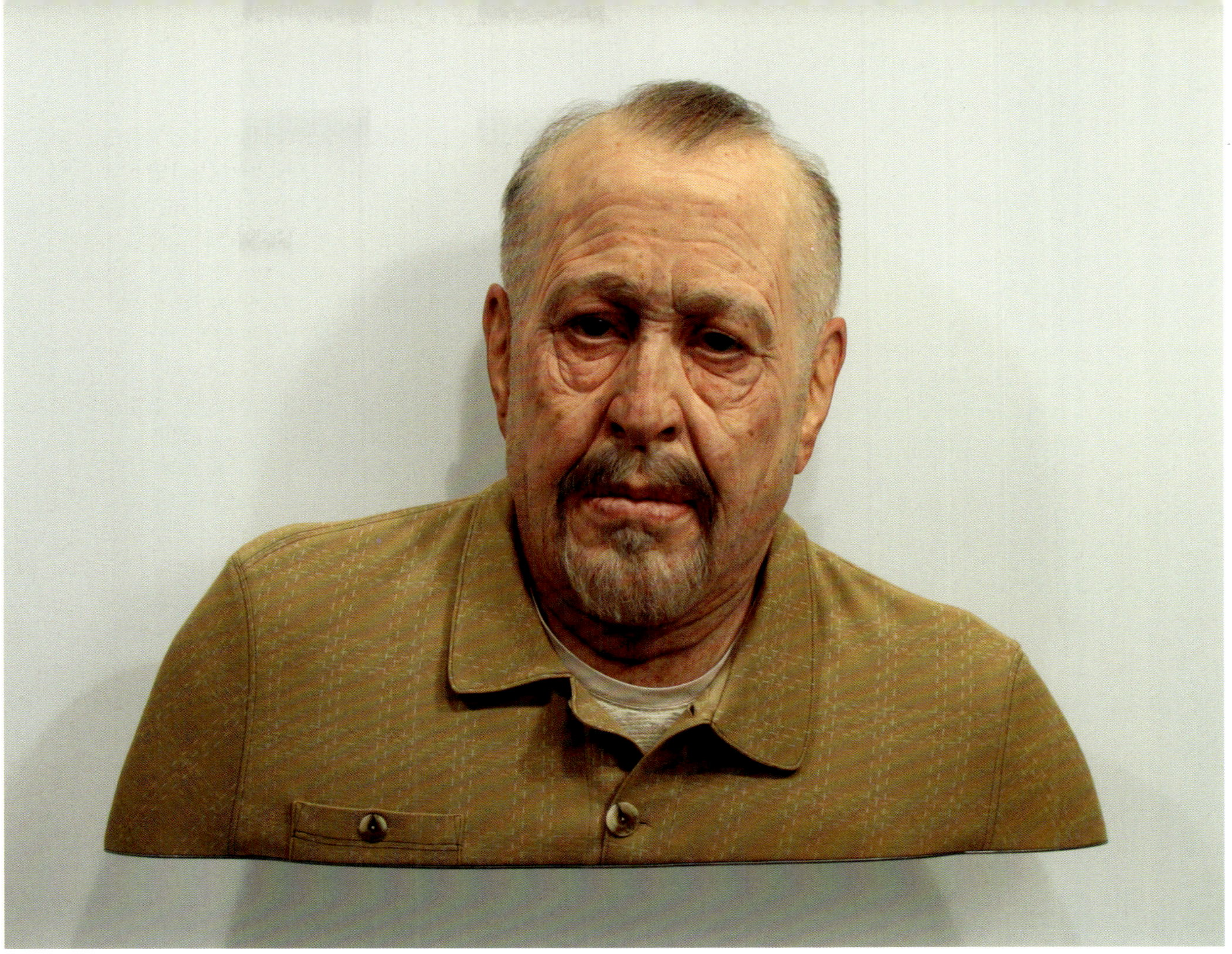

Also of South African origin, Kathy Venter (b. 1951) engages with "a historical continuity that many artists of our times would reject." Her multiple narratives of historical meaning are intended to remind us of "the way civilization adopts, transforms and endlessly reinvents the cultural traces it inherits."[63] Hence the life-sized terracotta figures that float in suspended space from wires might depict people from her present community on Salt Spring Island, British Columbia, but their inspiration comes from Tanagra figurines belonging to the Mycenaean period of ancient Greece. In Vancouver, David Robinson (b. 1964) casts his net even more widely in an attempt to level the playing field between the viewer and his work. Whether standing on a plinth, on the ground, or suspended in the air, each of the sculptor's un-heroic, largely male figures can represent Everyman.

By the new millennium, Halifax's most prominent sculptor, John Greer (b. 1944), made what has been described as post-Conceptualist contemporary sculpture, by looking to ancient Celtic ogham stones, Greek sculpture and ceremonial tomb markers for inspiration. In Toronto, abstract sculptor Ted Bieler produced a series of intricately crafted bronze sculptures inspired by the elaborate Tibetan Buddhist thangka banners and bronze sculptures that he had seen in the Rubin Museum in New

Evan Penny
No One—In Particular #6, Series 2, 2006
This Alberta-born but Toronto-based artist has revived portraiture, even though he believes that the real cannot be represented or symbolized in sculpture. Using digital scanning technology and a 3-D computer program, Penny blends real-life photographic images of people and then transforms them into silicon figurative sculptures that are twice life size. This imaginary hyper-realistic composite of human features belonging to Penny's second *No One—In Particular* series pushes the boundaries between the real and the imagined.

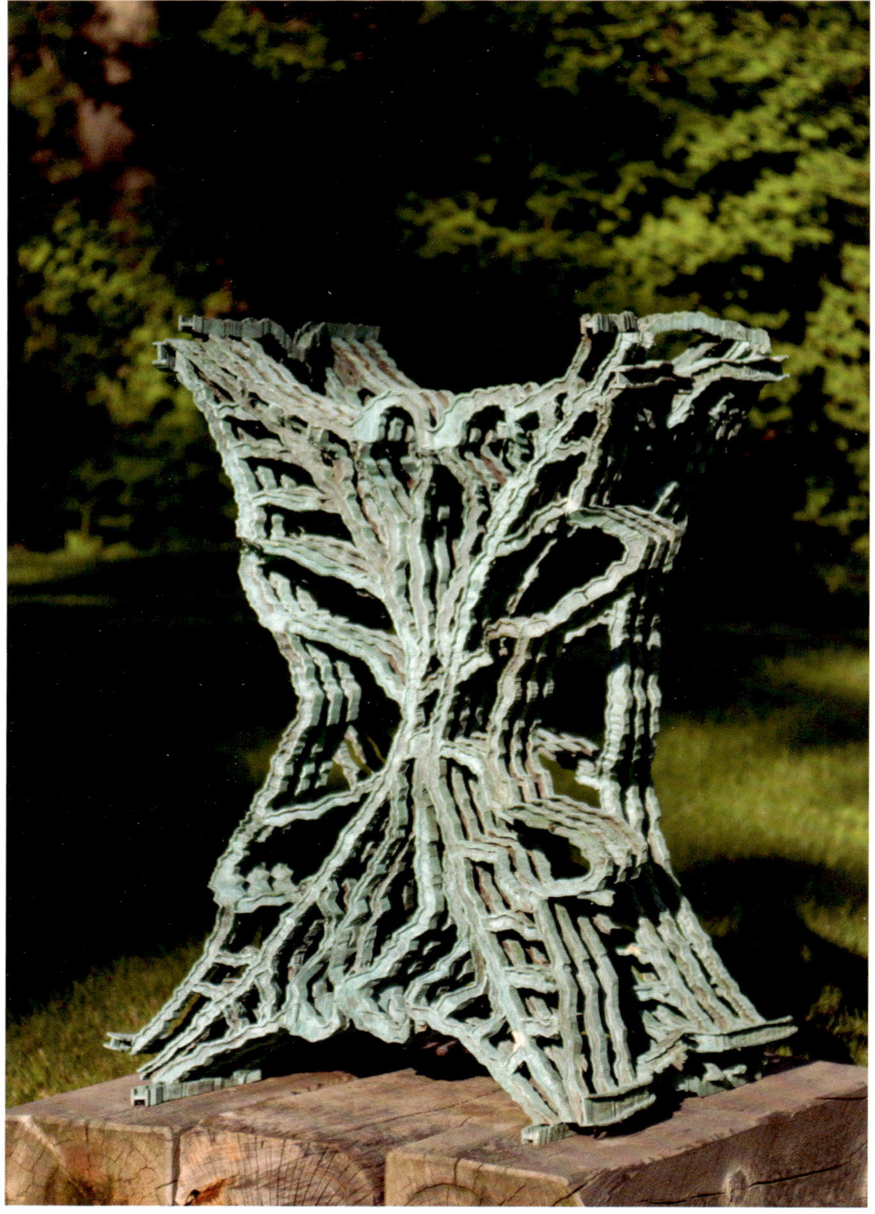

York City. Sources were as diverse as the history that had produced them. Alan Reynolds (b. 1947), based in Edmonton, looked to Oriental art; Yves Louis-Seize (b. 1950), like Greer, to myth and allegory realized through figurative forms; and Richard Prince (b. 1949) to classical sculpture. All of these sculptors were referencing rather than appropriating their historical models, and doing so in order to invigorate their sculpture.

Peter Hide (b. 1944), who had studied and worked with Anthony Caro before immigrating to Edmonton in 1977 to take up a teaching post at the University of Alberta, professed himself aware that "on the large scale of art history, there is no such thing as progress."[64] Seeking to humanize the cold and austere high-abstract language, to get away from the "frontality" and stiffness characteristic of his earlier sculptures, and to get out of the

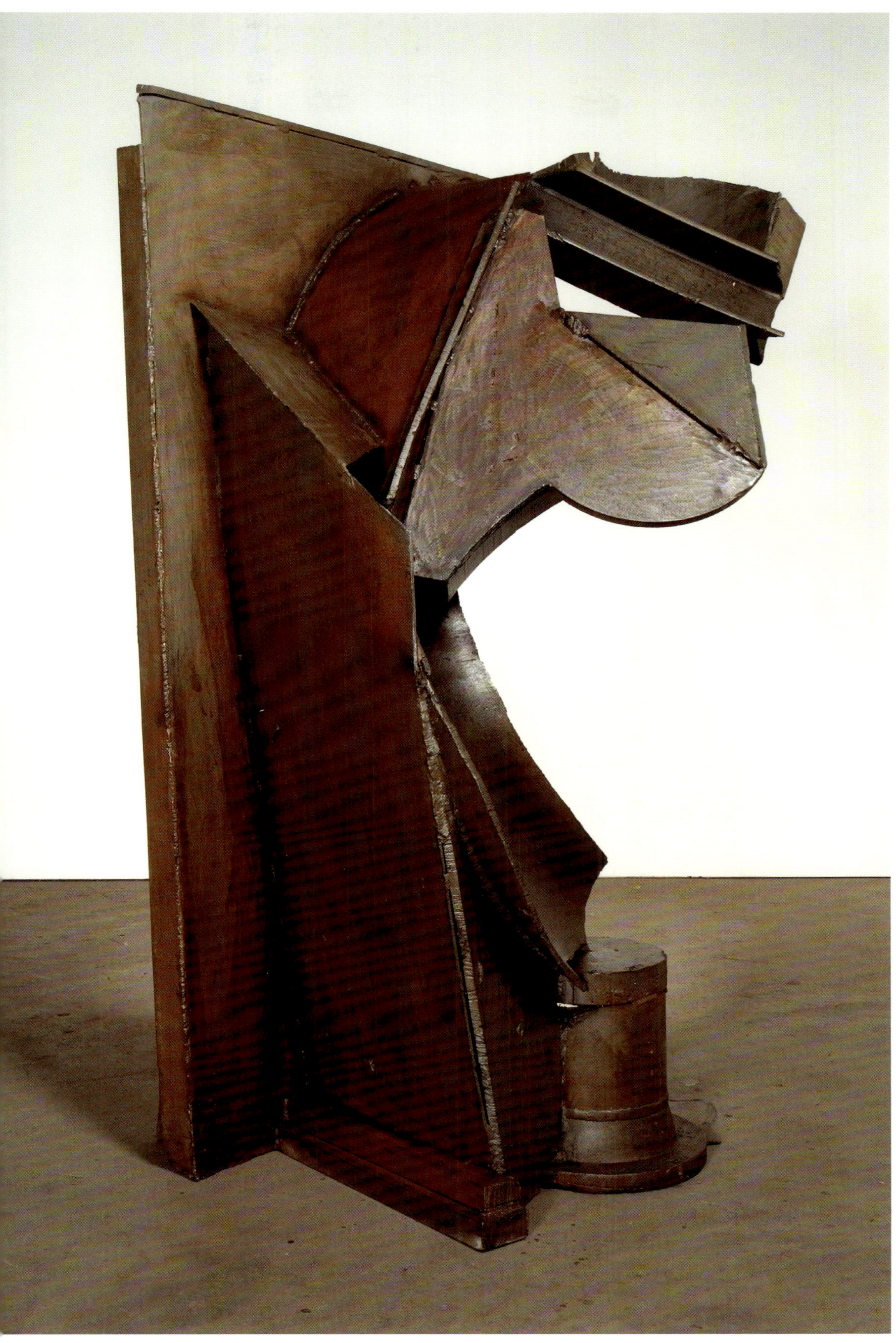

Peter Hide
Madonna, 1988
By the time Peter Hide immigrated to Edmonton in 1977, in order to take up a teaching position at the University of Alberta, he had forsaken the plinth and was using scrap metal for his material. This was much in the manner of his mentor, British sculptor Anthony Caro, but Hide is no mere copyist. His works are monumental and monolithic, dense and compressed. And although they are fabricated in welded steel, and are abstract, they nevertheless have an anthropomorphic feel that brings to mind the work of Henry Moore.

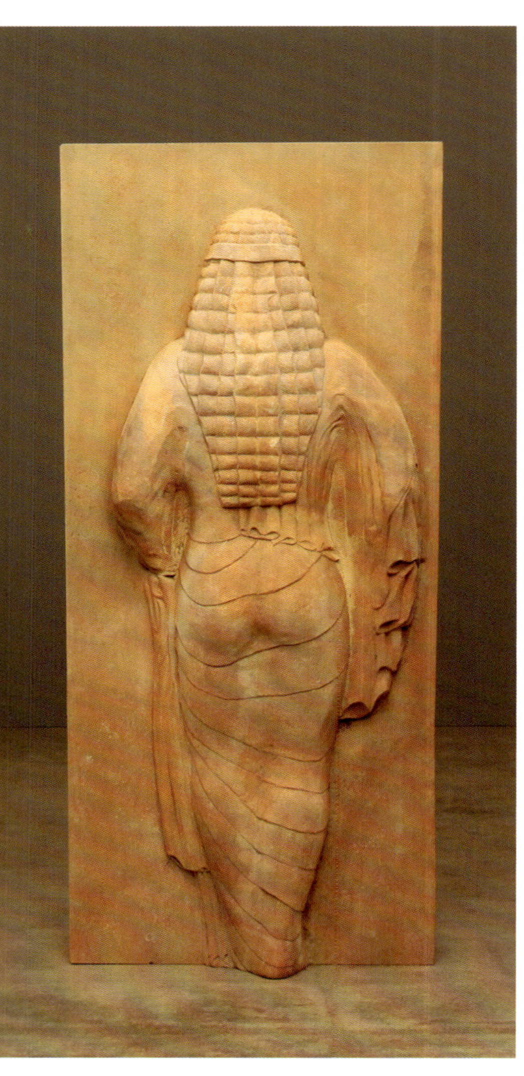

John Greer
Receding, 2007

Nova Scotia artist John Greer rightly believes that creativity comes from reconciling the dynamic between the super-ego and the low self-esteem of a sculptor. As Canada's most philosophically minded artist, he also believes that if humans want to look forward they have to look at the past. Taking its inspiration from the maiden figure of the Greek kore sculpture and its material from limestone quarried on an ancient seabed, this beautifully rendered figurative work brings cultural and natural history together, thereby demonstrating the extent to which the present can embody the entire past in one work.

"stranglehold of Caro-style sculpture," Hide created highly refined works that are both monumental and classical.[65] Adopting the contrapposto pose, with its concept of adjusting the distribution of weight in a standing figure from one leg to another so that one leg bears most of the weight, he injected his figurative abstract sculptures, including *Madonna* (1988), with a liveliness that resembled the animated body.

Sherrard "Sherry" Grauer (b. 1939) was likewise attentive to the historical narrative on which modernist sculptors had turned their backs. Indeed, she arranged the wire-mesh humanoid bodies and canine heads comprising her installation *Dogface Boys' Picnic* (1974–1975) in the same configuration as Édouard Manet (1832–1883) did the picnickers in his painting *Le Déjeuner sur l'Herbe* (*The Luncheon on the Grass*, 1863). In *Van Gogh's Room* (1973–1974), Murray Favro (b. 1940) of London, Ontario, made a less subtle, more mimetic reference to the past. Favro used several versions of Vincent Van Gogh's painting of his room in his "Yellow House" in Arles to make a projected reconstruction of the artist's room that was installed within the National Gallery of Canada.[66]

Other Canadian sculptors reached further back, to the great exemplars of a European tradition to which they self-consciously related even when working in a radically different idiom. Jeffrey Rubinoff was impressed with Italian Renaissance sculptors like Donatello (1386–1466), whose work he encountered on a trip to Florence and Rome in 1980. But while Rubinoff has acknowledged that his own sculptures were in a "dialogue with the ancestors," he did not use them to further a philosophical agenda and his work resisted attempts to invest it with any ulterior meaning in literal, retrospective terms.[67]

First Nations sculptors have always been masters at combining old with contemporary Indigenous designs and concepts, and reflecting the influence of Western art forms and ways of thinking. One of the best-loved sculptures of Haida artist Bill Reid is surely his *Raven and the First Men* (1980), depicting the creation of the Haida nation. It was made for the University of British Columbia's new Museum of Anthropology in Vancouver and was therefore—unlike many of the works in that collection—neither appropriated, nor stolen, nor salvaged, nor purchased for a nominal fee. Reid created the work for Arthur Erickson's building with the assistance of non-Haida First Nations sculptors and Euro-Canadian sculptors, thus breaking down conventional barriers. Traditional Haida design and iconography was combined with Western naturalism, classical renderings of human anatomy with the funky ceramic sculpture of Californians David Gilhooly and Ric Gomez. It was this combination that made the hunched-winged raven look more like the RCA Victor dog, cocking its head while listening to his master's voice, rather than a reconstruction of the mythical raven that dropped the clam shell on Rose Spit in Haida Gwaii, causing the first people of the Haida Nation to emerge from it.[68]

There were other Indigenous artists, including Haida Robert Davidson and Coast Salish Susan Point (b. 1952), who freely appropriated Indigenous and non-Indigenous styles and materials. A sculptor of Haida and Metis descent, Don Yeomans (b. 1958), celebrated the ethnic diversity of British

Columbia by creating a cross-cultural, multi-part totem pole honouring "humankind for transcending our earthbound existence by creating machines that enable us to fly." Commissioned by the Vancouver Airport Authority, *Celebrating Flight* (2007) brought ravens, whales, eagles and bears from Haida mythology together with Celtic knot work, Chinese characters and the latest lighting effects in an effort to reflect both the past and the present.[69]

Inuit sculptor Lucy Tasseor Tutsweetok responded to the country's diversity by including the faces of Inuit, Cree and Euro-Canadians, all of whom reside close to the border between Nunavut and Manitoba, in her limestone sculpture *Inuit, Itqiliit, Unaliit amma Qablunaat* (1991). A conviction that "the creation and appreciation of art is an entirely cross-cultural and international preoccupation" inspired Abraham Apakark Anghik Ruben (b. 1951), an Inuit sculptor from the western Arctic.[70] Some of his sculptures incorporate stylistic elements and motifs from First

Sherry Grauer
Dogface Boys' Picnic, 1974–1975
Sherry Grauer has long thought that dogs are just like people, only nicer. She has always drawn and painted as well as made sculptures. And she has a firm grounding in the history of art. Not surprisingly, then, when she started transforming wire into mesh-like sculptures, as in her *Dogface Boys' Picnic*, she jumbled the traditional art historical categories—giving her human figures dogs' heads within an overall composition that pays homage to Manet's famous painting *Le Dejeuner sur l'Herbe*.

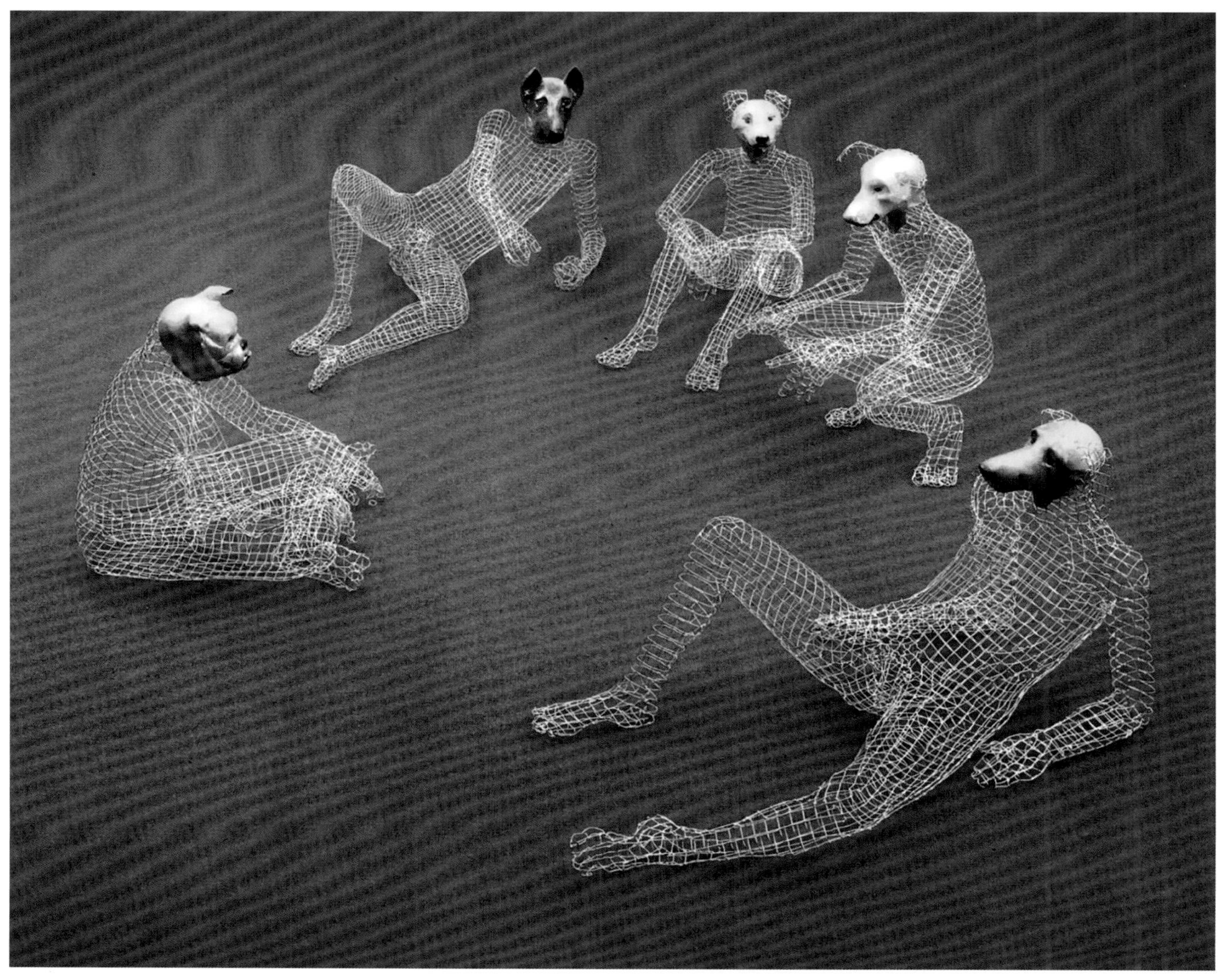

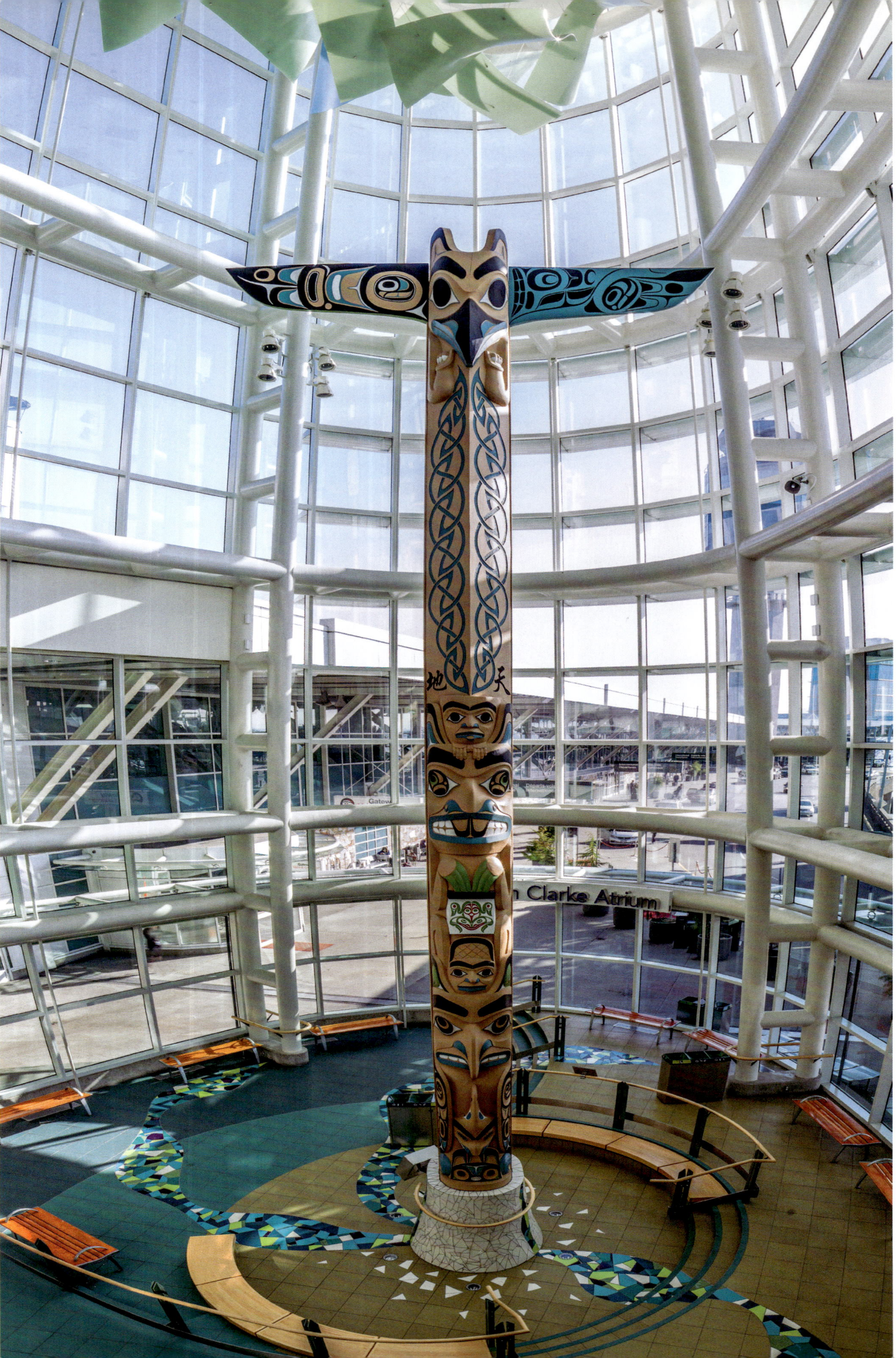

Clarke Atrium

Nations sculpture; others draw on the stories and legends of Viking and Norse mythology.

Few sculptors have ever been able to build—or maintain—their reputations and promote their sculpture without financial assistance, government funding and private patronage. During the formative years of the history of sculpture in Canada, patronage came from the clan or tribe, or from the Church. Then sculptors were paid by itinerant collectors or through public subscriptions and—increasingly—through government funding. The fact is that the great majority of contemporary sculpture, following the Second World War—Indigenous and non-Indigenous—could never have been done without public assistance. As one art critic observed of Installation art in 1986: "[It] exists in Canada because of the funding."[71]

From the late 1950s, then, sculptors had their work commissioned by, supported by and displayed by a number of public institutions across the country and abroad. As mentioned, in 1964 contemporary sculptors were given a boost when Montreal founded the first public gallery in the country devoted exclusively to contemporary art, the Musée d'Art Contemporain de Montréal. (Toronto's Museum of Contemporary Canadian Art was not established until 1999 and Saskatoon's more inclusive Remai Modern Art Gallery of Saskatchewan—featuring contemporary Indigenous and non-Indigenous, Canadian and international artists—followed in 2017.) In 1972, some Canadian sculptors received payment for their work from the Canada Council's Art Bank, an agency that rented their work to government departments, where it was displayed.

Many sculptors, like Peter Hide, Robert Murray, Bill Reid, Marilyn Levine, Mowry Baden and Alberta-born, New York–based Elaine Cameron-Weir (b. 1985), the youngest among this group, have established their careers after being given major solo exhibitions within the walls of public art galleries and museums. For Elza Mayhew in 1964 and for Walter Redinger in 1972, what sealed their reputations was being chosen to represent Canada at the Venice Biennale; as it did later for Tom Dean in 1999, for Jana Sterbak in 2003, for David Altmejd in 2007, for Shary Boyle in 2013, and for Guillaume Lachapelle in 2015. From 1987, sculptors were also aided by having their work illustrated and written about in the Quebec-based *Espace*, a journal devoted entirely to sculpture. In 1992 contemporary First Nations and Inuit sculptors were given an exhibition, *Land, Spirit, Power: First Nations at the National Gallery of Canada*, which was mounted in Ottawa with the assistance of First Nations artists and shown in several venues across the country.

By the end of the twentieth century, then, First Nations sculptors had much more say over how their work was shown. And the wider public could become engaged in the way that Indigenous people were identified, defined and represented in sculpture. During the last decade of the twentieth century, members of the Assembly of First Nations (AFN) led a campaign to remove the Anishinabe scout that had been kneeling at Samuel de Champlain's feet on Hamilton MacCarthy's sculpture since

Opposite:
Don Yeomans
Celebrating Flight, 2007
Don Yeomans knows that Northwest Coast art has never been stagnant: styles, materials, subject matters and methods have always been in flux. So when the Vancouver Airport Authority invited this artist of Haida and Metis heritage to produce a work for the atrium of the newly expanded international terminal, Yeomans created a pole that crossed cultural barriers and included both traditional and non-traditional materials. *Celebrating Flight* gestures towards modern technology yet also speaks to some of the ethnic groups that have made Canada the multicultural society it is today. With this pole, Yeomans has surely broken the barrier between what can and cannot be deemed First Nations art.

1918. In October 1999, the scout was duly removed from the base of the Champlain monument and placed at the north end of Major's Hill Park in Ottawa. First Nations leader Phil Fontaine was pleased that the figure now reflected "the strength of our community and our place in society."[72] Not everyone was happy. Historian Susan Hart argued that, whether on or off the Champlain monument, "the Anishinabe Scout continues to remain a figure in the colonial pageant, a figure without history whose ability to signify cannot exceed the semiotic system set by Western culture."[73]

Who, then, was to determine such issues? Joe Fafard created the laser-cut stainless steel sculpture *Oskana-ka-asateki* (1997), installed in Regina's Market Square, depicting a buffalo rising from a pile of bones. This too came in for criticism from members of the First Nations community, who accused Fafard of appropriating the Cree word *oskana*—meaning "pile o' bones"—for the title of his work. They also questioned his designation of Regina as a buffalo kill site, some claiming that the actual site was northwest of the city at Wascana Creek. And, although Fafard had lived among French-speaking Metis families as a child, it was argued that, as a non-Indigenous sculptor, he was incapable of depicting the true suffering of First Nations people.

Fafard struck back: "Any culture that gets totally self-referential, and will not accept any reference from another culture, eventually speaks only to itself, and cannot participate in the broader dialogue that is the human dialogue."[74] The Regina Public Library's Dunlop Art Gallery proposed holding a forum in order to discuss the role of public art and business in society. Fafard initially agreed to participate, but, sensing a witch hunt, subsequently withdrew. The forum was cancelled. The disputed work remains *in situ* in the centre of Regina, as much a monument to the ongoing, unresolved, conflicting pressures of public funding as to its ostensible subject.

Canadian sculptors, of course, did not have to seek careers that were made within public institutions and programs at home in Canada. Another option, as ever, was to seek fame and fortune abroad, for whatever mixture of reasons. One striking example of this second course is Terence Koh (b. 1977), born in China but trained at the Emily Carr University of Art and Design in Vancouver, who combines porn and punk with queer culture and now lives in New York City. It is doubtful whether his plaster-modelled sculpture *Gone, Yet Still* (2008), depicting Christ with an erect penis, would have been exhibited in a public or private gallery in Canada. It was left to the British and Austrian public, who viewed the tumescent Christ at the Baltic Centre for Contemporary Art in Gateshead in the north of England and at the Wien Secession in Vienna, to provide such a venue—and it did not happen without provoking controversy.[75]

Robert Murray, David Rabinowitch and David Altmejd are all prominent examples of Canadian sculptors who established successful careers in the United States and Europe. But though some of those who took this route have enjoyed financial success and found more sympathetic audiences than might have been the case in Canada, it is not the case that Canadian sculptors have invariably been more successful outside their own country. The story remains much more complex.

From 1983 to 1985 Jeffrey Rubinoff's work was featured in the seminal magazine *Art in America*. And in 1996, now based on Hornby Island, British Columbia, Rubinoff was the first Canadian artist to be given a major one-person exhibition at the Nathan Manilow Sculpture Park in Chicago.[76] During the same decade, Rubinoff was taken on by New York's prestigious Marlborough Gallery. And it was in New York, joining forces with the American-born, Canadian-based sculptor Don Bonham (1940–2014), that he co-founded the Two Sculptors Gallery, which exhibited the work of both Canadian and international sculptors. It proved difficult to establish a gallery devoted entirely to sculpture, not least because Rubinoff was unwilling to succumb to the dictates of the private-gallery system. Instead, Rubinoff returned to Hornby Island where, possessing private means, he was able to focus his energies on producing his work rather than on cultivating what he saw as the rock-star image demanded by the gallery system.

Most sculptors have lacked such freedom to produce whatever they wanted. Walter Redinger, an abstract sculptor from London, Ontario, voiced an inescapable truth when he said in 1973 that the artist was "intimidated by the problem of having to sell his wares."[77] The commemorative sculptor Barbara Paterson likewise spoke from experience: "If you want to be in public art, you have to be willing to bend. After all, someone else is paying for it. It is always a give and take."[78] Sculptors across Canada knew that they had to work with galleries and their curators, with art historians and fine arts journalists, with private and public patrons, if they were going to have their work bought, written about and commissioned. Looking at the art establishment that had grown up around them, working sculptors often felt that they were taking a back seat; or saw it like a spider's web, where few were lucky enough to escape being entangled in the mesh.

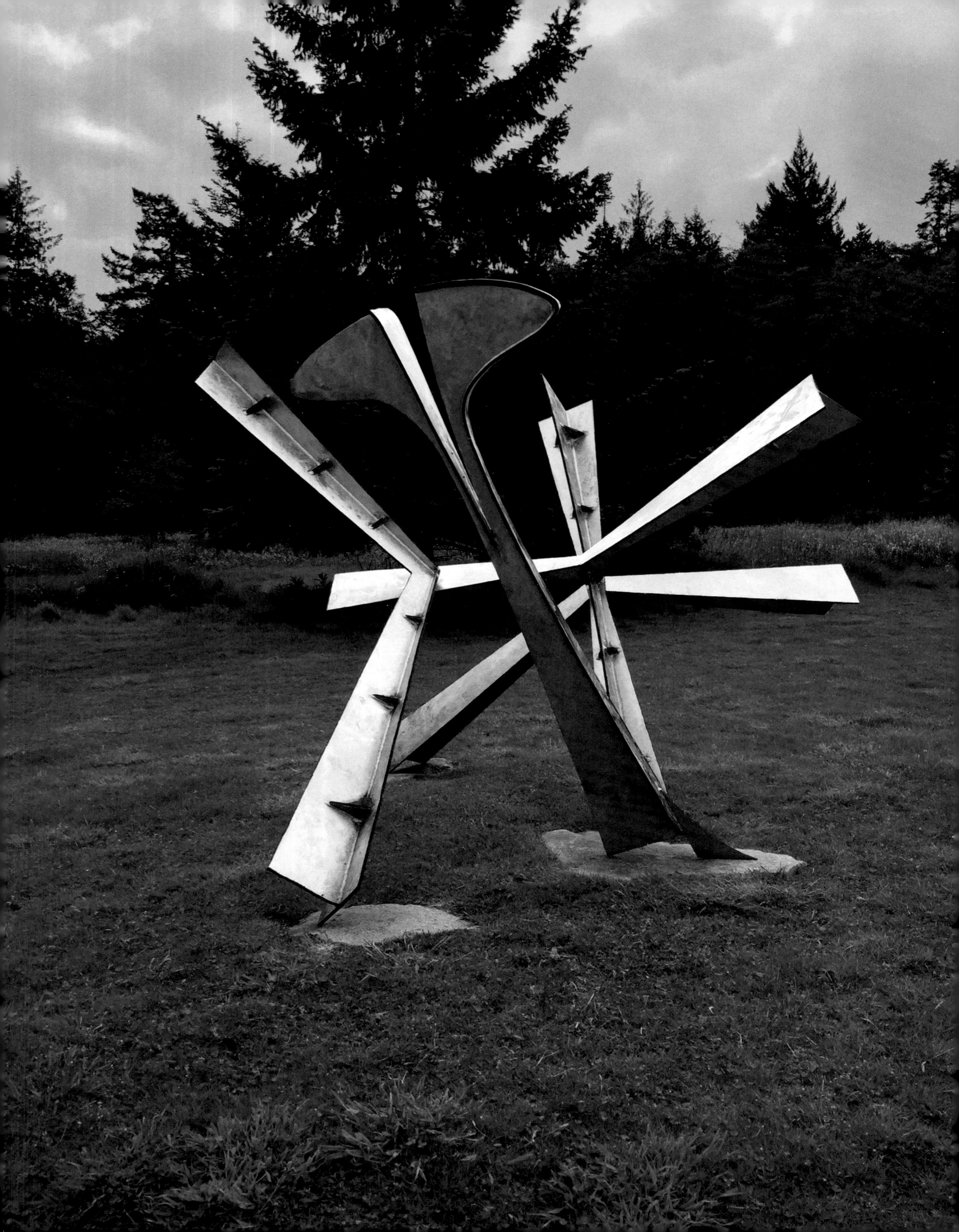

Epilogue

There is more sculpture being produced in Canada today than ever before. You can find it in parks and in sculpture gardens, within and in front of airports, art galleries and university buildings, along riverbanks as well as in city squares and back gardens, and in the most inaccessible areas of the country. And, just as sculpture is appearing everywhere, it is also being produced in an unprecedented range of materials and styles, such as traditional, modernist and postmodernist, and it has become the purview of photographers, video artists and art historians as well as of sculptors themselves. In one sense, such sculptural works have a universal appeal, created with an awareness that transcends national borders, and is informed by travel and now also by images available on the Internet.

Opposite:
Jeffrey Rubinoff
Series 9–3, 2012–2014

Yet many sculptors in Canada have made it their mission to portray or reflect the country in which they live and work. To begin with, there are now numerous commemorative memorials, erected retrospectively, that part with tradition by celebrating the ruled, not the ruler. In Toronto the long overdue *Memorial to Commemorate the Chinese Railroad Workers in Canada* (1989) honours the Chinese labourers who helped build the Canadian Pacific Railway.[1] *The Animals in War Memorial* (2012), a sculpture in Ottawa's Confederation Park, commemorates not only the dogs that detected bombs and the mules and horses that carried troops and hauled field guns and artillery, but also the carrier pigeons that delivered messages during the Boer and First World Wars.[2] Also in Ottawa the *Valiants Memorial* (2006), comprising busts and full-scale figures and created by sculptors Marlene Hilton Moore (b. 1944) and John McEwen (b. 1945), honours fourteen military figures, including Laura Secord. Winnipeg has two sculptures, the *Holocaust Monument* (1990) and *Women Veterans of the Two World Wars* (1976). On the west coast, the Tillicum and Veterans Care Society in Victoria commissioned a six-metre Kwakwaka'wakw totem pole in remembrance of the seven thousand plus First Nations soldiers who fought in the First and Second World Wars.[3] And in 2008 actor and playwright R.H. Thomson (b. 1947) and theatre and lighting consultant Martin Conboy (b. 1942) came up with a novel way to remember the dead of the First World War. Building on the "strategy of absence" used by sculptor Maya Lin (b. 1959), so well achieved in her *Vietnam Memorial* (1982) in Washington, DC, Thomson and Conboy combined their theatrical and lighting skills to create a "light show" that recorded the names of the 68,000 men and women who died on and off the battlefield. This image was projected onto the facades of seven buildings, beginning with Canada House in London's Trafalgar Square. *Vigil 1914–1918* (2008) was then projected onto buildings in Halifax, Fredericton, Ottawa, Toronto, Regina and Edmonton.

Less than six months after four Mounties were shot while investigating a marijuana grow op in northern Alberta on March 3, 2005, artisans Allan and Shane Seib created *Never Forgotten* (2005). The work of this father-and-son team, who were running a steel furniture and functional artwork company in Sylvan Lake, Alberta, at the time of the shooting, exemplified the view that great narratives had come to an end, and it was ordinary men and women who needed appropriate celebration as heroes in the twenty-first century. *Never Forgotten* brought the Canadian flag and the RCMP crest together with the silhouette of a Mountie on horseback in a way that might have struck art critics as aesthetically unimaginative—but one that evidently struck a popular chord. Initially the work was installed at the RCMP headquarters in Edmonton, but it was later moved to Mayerthorpe, near the farm where the officers had been shot.[4] Less than ten years later, the murder of three officers from the Codiac Regional RCMP detachment (Douglas James Larche, David Joseph Ross and Fabrice Georges Gevaudan), who had been shot in Moncton, New Brunswick, evoked a similar response. Morgan MacDonald (b. 1982) a sculptor and owner of a bronze foundry in St. John's, Newfoundland, produced life-sized sculptures of the three men. The *RCMP Memorial* (2015), installed along the river in Moncton, was fitting

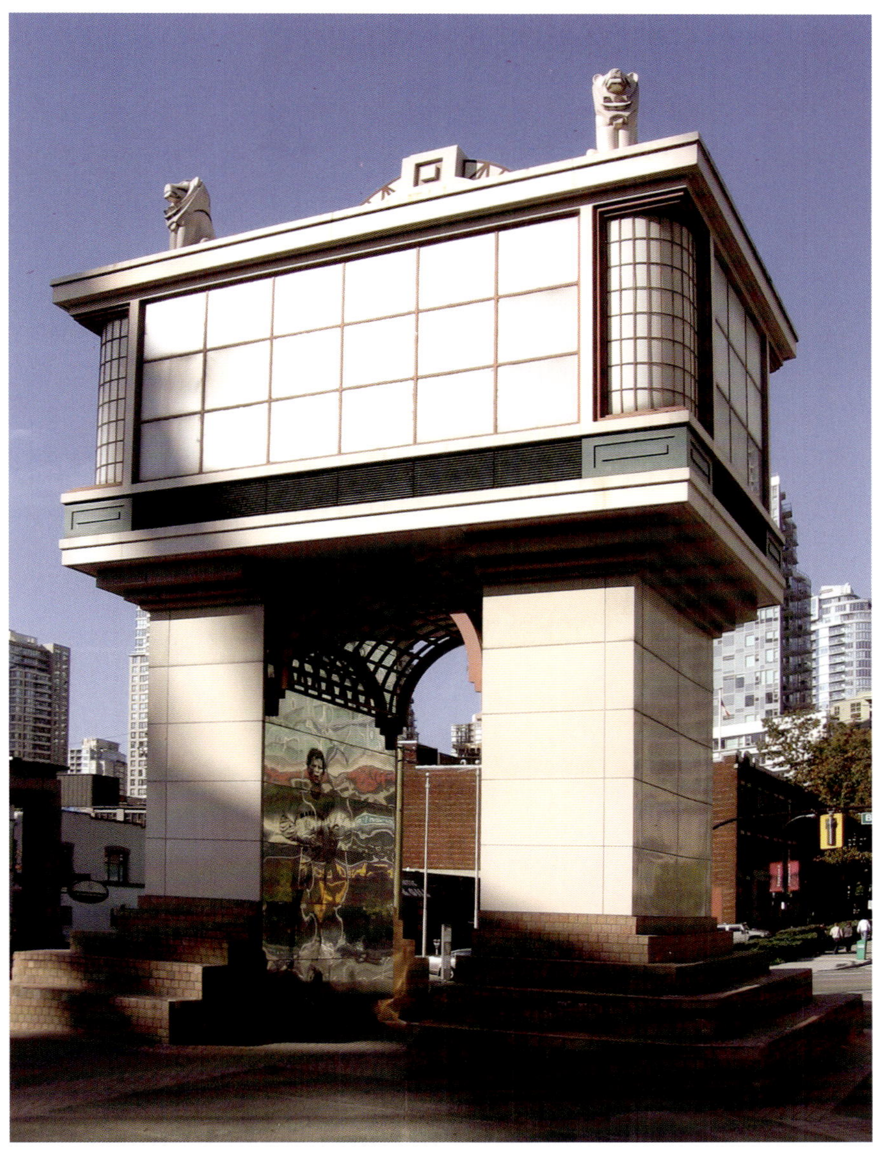

Franklin Allen
Terry Fox Memorial, 1984
The city of Vancouver held a competition for a sculpture to celebrate the marathon-like run across Canada attempted by Terry Fox. The winning submission was for the Roman-style triumphal arch topped by four fibreglass lions, as shown in this 1984 photograph of Franklin Allen's postmodernist "memorial." It did not survive, the public mood remained unhappy and the detractors got what they wanted when it was replaced in 2010 by a series of realistic figurative sculptures that captured Fox's step-hop gait as he ran across the country.

and faithfully rendered in the monumental style popularized by traditional sculptors of an earlier era.

To do otherwise, it seems, would have failed to meet the physical and emotional needs of the general public. This had already become clear in the furor over a monument honouring the return of Terry Fox to Vancouver in 1980 following his aborted run across the country. Designed by American architect Franklin Allen (b. 1932) and installed at present-day BC Place in the heart of Vancouver, the postmodernist *Terry Fox Memorial* (1983) comprised a triumphal arch, rendered in tile, brick and steel and crowned by four fibreglass lions. This was very different from the life-sized figural bronzes of Fox that had already been welcomed in several cities across the country.

Popular bewilderment at the new memorial in Vancouver took many forms. Some were outraged that so much money had been "squandered on so trivial a project." Since local architect Arthur Erickson had chaired the

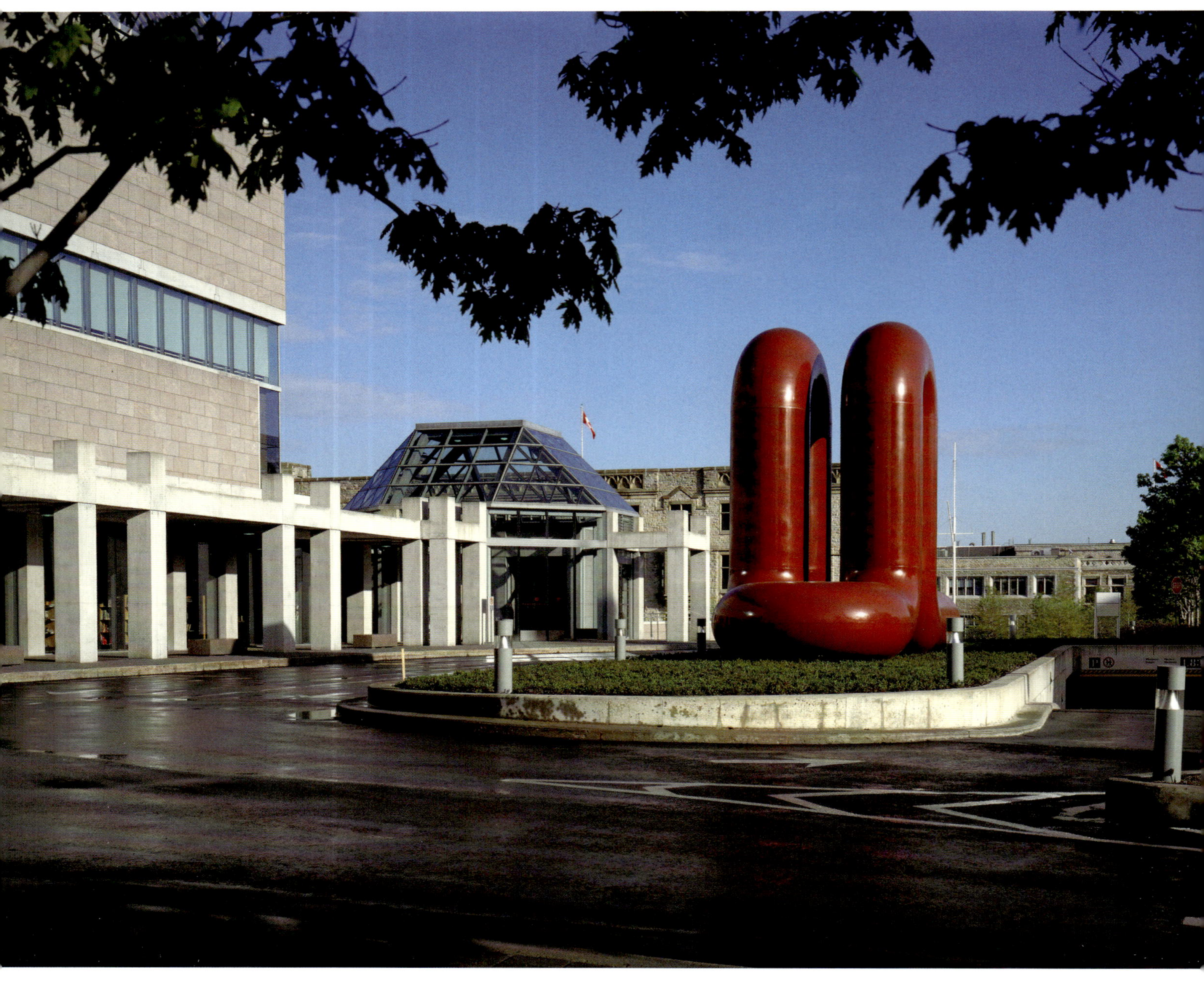

Ed Zelenak
Traffic, 1968–1971

Ed Zelenak's *Traffic* offers a telling example of how a sculpture can move in and out of favour. When this work was installed in Ottawa's Confederation Park in the early 1970s it was vilified. Some called the sculptor's exploration of volume and gestural shapes "the Worm." Yet, after a few years, Zelenak's fibreglass sculpture lost its power to stir controversy, for good or ill. First, when the new National Gallery of Canada was built in 1988, the sculpture was relocated next to the elegant glass-and-granite building, as shown here. But eventually *Traffic* found itself largely forgotten in its less-conspicuous home, the gallery's storage warehouse on the outskirts of the city.

jury, rival architects mounted the sly and sarcastic charge that Allen's design had been chosen "in order to discredit the Post Modern so thoroughly that nothing further would be built in Vancouver in its eclectic image."[5] It was not just the style and the cost of producing the *Terry Fox Memorial* that caused rancour: it was, above all, the absence of figurative representation. Fox was a hero and Vancouverites wanted to "see" him in the form of a bronze statue. In 2010 they got their wish when Allen's triumphal arch was replaced by four bronze figures. Designed by writer and sculptor Douglas Coupland (b. 1961), the first figure was life-sized, with the next three progressively increasing until the final figure was twice as big as the first. These traditionally rendered figurative sculptures faithfully captured Terry Fox's step-hop gait, which became so familiar during his Marathon of Hope, and public approval was finally forthcoming for a lasting and fitting memorial.

Manifestations of public interest in suitable commemoration are not lacking in the second decade of the twenty-first century. For example, in 2013 the minister responsible for Parks Canada approved the construction of a war memorial in Cape Breton's Highlands National Park to mark Canada's 150th birthday in 2017 and to honour the Canadian soldiers who had fought and died abroad. The *Never Forgotten National Memorial* was to comprise a ten-storey statue, inspired by the *Canada "Bereft"* figure on the *Canadian National Vimy Memorial* in France, and to include a car park accommodating three hundred vehicles, an observation deck, a restaurant, an interpretive centre and the inevitable souvenir shop. The brainchild of Toronto-based businessman Tony Trigiani, this project, estimated to cost more than $25 million, was to be paid for by public subscription and federal funding. Stephen Harper's Conservative government pledged $100,000 to get the project off the ground. But many Cape Breton residents and environmentalists were opposed to having the monument constructed at Green Cove, within the boundaries of the national park. They got their way. A few months after coming into office in 2015 the newly elected Liberal government took note of such protests and the project was quashed.

Any new project, of course, is vulnerable to skepticism and even hostility. But it seems that once a sculpture has been installed and has survived a period of immediate impact, it can generate affection as the public begins to identify with the work. When Ed Zelenak's imposing fibreglass sculpture *Traffic* (1968–1971) was placed in Confederation Park in Ottawa there was a public outcry and the modernist work was derided as "the Worm." Eventually, however, Zelenak's sculpture lost its power to sustain controversy. *Traffic* was then moved to the grounds surrounding the new National Gallery of Canada, designed by architect Moshe Safdie, where it became "part of the landscape" and, less flatteringly, "something different to show relatives when they hit town."[6] Similarly, Michael Snow's funky sculpture *The Audience* (1989), depicting oversized baseball fans hanging from the facade of Toronto's SkyDome (now Rogers Centre) was initially disliked. Within five years, however, as one critic commented, Snow's work had caught "the public's attention in a way that most of today's generic 1% public art projects or official monuments seldom do."[7]

In 1999, after a Halloween prankster decapitated Emanuel Hahn's Great

War sculpture *Grieving Soldier*, the citizens of Russell, Manitoba, were outraged, in a way no doubt enhanced by the sculpture's association with the war dead. Restoration was possible when the head was found, and it was repaired and reattached to the figure. A decade earlier, when Vancouver's seventeen-storey Georgia Medical-Dental Building (1929) was slated for demolition, there was a public campaign to save three terracotta Art Deco sculptures of First World War nursing sisters created by British-born Joseph Francis Watson (1885–1967) that were mounted on the three visible corners of the building. Though the campaign was not enough to save the originals, it did induce the developers of the new Shaw Tower to mount replicas on the third-storey level of the building when it was completed in 1991. It was much the same story for Frances Loring's magisterial, stylized *Lion*, installed at the base of a tall column in 1939 to celebrate the completion of Toronto's Queen Elizabeth Way. When the sculpture was designated for demolition due to the construction of the twelve-lane Gardiner Expressway in the early 1960s, public outrage prompted Toronto's city council to save and reinstall the work on the waterfront in Casimir Gzowski Park. However, the relocated sculpture could no longer be seen from the nearby highway.

The Wave (1988) by Donna Hiebert (b. 1961) has been a feature of Halifax's waterfront since 1988. The artist's intention had been "to create

This sculpture may bring to mind the iconic woodcut *Under the Wave off Kanagawa* (ca. 1830–1832) by Katsushika Hokusai (1760–1849). But when Donna Hiebert created *The Wave* she wasn't thinking of Japan's favourite image, but instead of human genitalia. And her object was to create a sensual work that had no pedestal and was psychologically accessible to the public. *The Wave* was originally intended to offer the public shelter from Halifax's exposed waterfront; but instead, with the passage of time, it has become a giant slide entertaining children and adults alike.

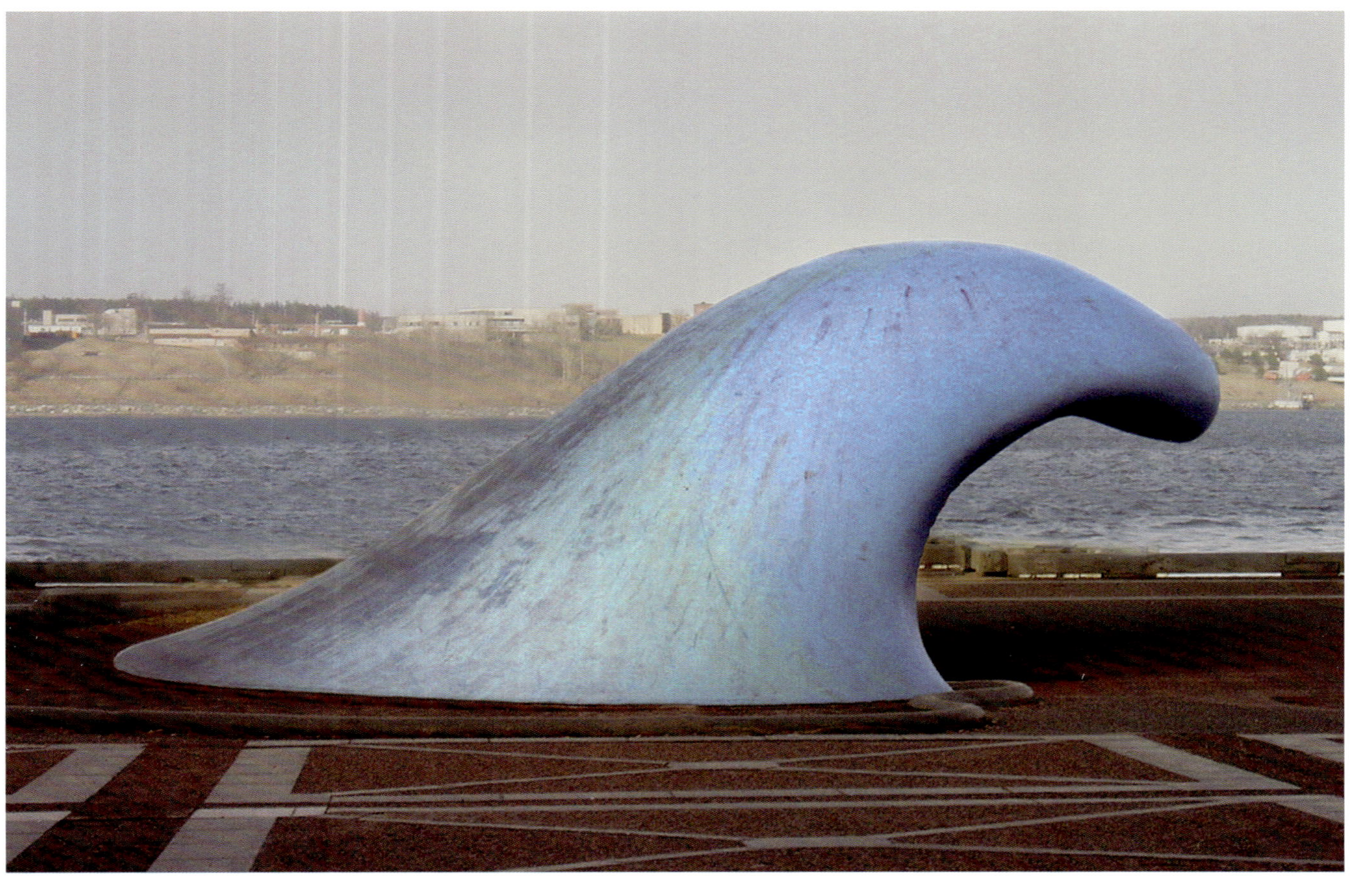

a work that was approachable, to take the sculpture off the base so that psychologically, people—the public—wouldn't be intimidated by it."[8] Here was an innovative work that became vulnerable to its own success when, after a quarter of a century, it faced the threat of relocation to another site because of the possible injury to children—and adults, too—who were using it as a slide. The sculptor threatened legal action if the Halifax Waterfront Development Corporation moved the sculpture to another location.[9] A settlement was finally reached: *The Wave* stayed *in situ* but the concrete surrounding the work was replaced with a rubberized surface to protect anyone who fell on their descent of it. In a fittingly Canadian compromise, everyone had a soft landing.

In 1964 journalist Robert Fulford noted: "Without the grace and humanity of sculpture, our cities and our buildings can be coldly inhuman; with sculpture… they can be infused with life, passion, adventure, and challenge."[10] It may have taken the city of Saskatoon time to meet such expectations, but it did so handsomely in 2015 when it set out its reasons for implementing a plan to support public sculpture. There was the educational element: "to increase awareness, understanding and enjoyment of art as part of everyday life in Saskatoon." There was the politically correct element: to encourage and showcase "a broad range of artists," in particular "encouraging submissions from First Nations, Métis, and new Canadian artists." And there was the recognition that art was "a collaborative creative process between a professional practicing artist(s) and a community."[11] Almost a decade earlier Glenn Gordon, the city of Regina's coordinator of arts, culture and heritage, observed: "When art is part of a community it's not just this homogenous concrete and pavement city." He added a further motivating factor: "Art can act as an identifier, promoter, draw."[12] It was indeed the case that sculpture could provide a source of revenue by drawing tourists to the city—the public installation of almost 350 sculptures in the city's collection had earned Regina the sobriquet of being named a Cultural Capital of Canada in 2004.

City councils, park boards and private agencies have brought more sculpture to their cities in ways that showed the worst and the best aspects of public sculpture. During the 1990s several cities and towns adopted a mascot: Vancouver had its whale, Charlottetown its mice, Toronto its moose and the Trans-Canada Highway its inuksuk. Sculptors, and in many cases volunteers from the general public, were involved in fabricating, painting and installing these emblematic objects throughout their cities and towns, reinforcing the popular assumption that everyone can be an artist. Though some of these sculptures were vandalized, altered or stolen, their general role in promoting civic identity was maintained. In 1999, Truro, Nova Scotia, came up with a novel way to draw tourists and revenue to their city. During the process of "saving" hundred-year-old elm trees that were succumbing to Dutch elm disease, the town council, backed by civic and private funding, paid sculptors to carve historical figures ranging from factory workers to religious and political figures from the trunks of the dying trees. Some of the carvings were done "on site" (at the location of the dying tree), thereby engaging further interest both in sculpture and in the history of Truro's largely blue-collar Hubtown.[13]

In various ways, public agencies have sought to integrate sculpture into the public space, to involve the public in creating the work—and to attract tourists. For example, the organizers of the annual Nunavut Arts Festival in Iqaluit have enabled Inuit sculptors to show, sell and demonstrate their work since 1999. City councils have also supported sculpture symposiums, of which the International Stone Sculpture Symposium held in Vancouver at the VanDusen Botanical Garden in 1975 was among the first in Canada. This was followed in 1980 by a symposium at Chicoutimi, Quebec, that focused on the environment. Since then many other symposiums have come into being.

In Lachine, Quebec, which would later become part of Montreal, a symposium founded in the city's Musée Plein Air in 1985 had installed, by 2004, fifty sculptures along the shore of Lac Saint-Louis. In 1995 the sculpture symposium Terre Gravide—Émergence: Creation d'un Parc des Sculptures, in Parc Marie-Victoria in Longueuil, Quebec, celebrated the work of female sculptors. More recently, the Okanagan-Thompson International Sculpture Symposium, the most geographically extensive in Canada, spread its sculptures over two hundred kilometres.

These symposiums have plainly generated a wider appeal for sculpture. When city officials in Saint John, New Brunswick, invited sculptors from Japan, Germany, Bulgaria and the United States to participate in their symposium in 2012, the event brought "valuable art and experience at so little cost to the community." One of the organizers noted: "I saw people who you would never see at a gallery opening who visited often more than once because they were so interested in what was happening." Since most of the work was created *in situ*, it was literally a hands-on experience. "Many of the men were like kids in a candy shop looking at the tools and how the artists were using them."[14] During the Okanagan-Thompson International Sculpture Symposium in 2002, schoolchildren were bused in to see the sculptures. Local sculptors benefitted from working alongside the officially commissioned international sculptors. And local art galleries increased their sales by featuring the work of local sculptors and inviting them to hold demonstrations and seminars, all of which helped introduce the public to contemporary sculpture.

There was, of course, never any guarantee that the organizers would find every sculpture presented to them during a symposium in keeping with their expectations. During Vancouver's International Sculpture Biennale in 2005, American sculptor Dennis Oppenheim (1938–2011) poised a country church on its steeple in *Device to Root Out Evil* (2005). No one questioned whether or not this qualified as a sculpture. But some people felt that Oppenheim was disrespectful by suggesting that religion was ineffective in rooting out evil. Others simply complained that the upside-down church— sited in a park overlooking Coal Harbour in the centre of the city—blocked the view. Though some people did like the work, the Vancouver Park Board sided with the loudest voices and *Device to Root Out Evil* was removed from its site. In 2008 Oppenheim's orphaned sculpture found a more appreciative home on the grounds of the Glenbow Museum in Calgary, where officials were determined to both inspire and challenge their public.

Towns and cities weren't always willing to create outdoor museums, as Spanish-born sculptor Rafael F. Moreno (b. 1946) discovered. He had asked the Alberta town of Pincher Creek to help him found an International Outdoor Museum of Sculpture that would give Canadian as well as international sculptors an opportunity "to experiment with alternative sources of energy and high technology to develop sculptures."[15] Moreno produced the abstract polychromatic steel sculpture *Cottonwood Tree* (1987) to show the public what could be done if they supported his project; but his attempt to win the public's support polarized opinion. There were negative letters in the press; members of the town council made disparaging remarks. Conversely, twenty protest sculptures were installed on the lawns of the town's most critical adversaries. Moreno promoted the educational and economic benefits of his project, but to no avail.

By the 1980s, not every attempt to establish a sculpture park or garden came to a sticky end. Choosing these venues bypassed the problem of neighbourhood protests because motivated spectators had to travel and sometimes to pay in order to see the work. As one Vancouver Park Board official rightly observed of Dennis Oppenheim's upside-down church: "If it had been placed in a spot that you would have to visit to see it, I don't think anything would have happened, but residents in the area said that they couldn't ignore it and you have to listen to that."[16]

More positively, writer Serge Fisette noted that the sculpture park at the historic Maison Hamel-Bruneau in the Quebec City suburb of Sainte-Foy was successful in offering the local community "daring" exhibitions, thus making the venue "an important focal point for the dissemination of contemporary art in Quebec."[17] It is notable that contemporary sculpture has been sited near the Acacia Gallery on the Saint John River in Gagetown, New Brunswick, as well as at the Parc Jean-Drapeau on the former Expo '67 site in Montreal, and, among other places, in a sculpture park in Windsor, Ontario. This policy has saved many pieces of public sculpture from bumping into controversy while giving city officials an important educational resource and providing the locales with tourists.

Eager to introduce the public to contemporary sculpture, philanthropist Louis Odette, with the assistance of the city of Toronto, transformed a parking lot into the Toronto Sculpture Garden in the centre of the city in 1981. Initially there were group exhibitions; later, individual sculptors were chosen to hold solo exhibitions for four-month periods. In 1983 the Donald Forster Sculpture Park was founded to display the best sculpture being produced in Canada and to attract tourists to the city of Guelph, Ontario. Ottawa's Art Bank provided the first sculptures at Confederation Park, which occupies a former industrial site along both shores of the Gananoque River.

Then in 2004 the Art Bank's sculpture committee, expanding its mission to cultivate an appreciation for arts and culture in their community, started commissioning local sculptors, among them Walter Redinger, the modernist sculptor from London, Ontario, to produce work.

In 1983 the Canadian Centre for Architecture invited sculptor and architect Melvin Charney to combine the history of landscape design with an open-air museum of contemporary sculpture. When the venue was inaugurated in 1988 it was the first public space in Montreal to be created in over fifty years. By 2013 there was even a place for land and environmental sculptors, when Burlington, Ontario, businessman Dan Lawrie instigated the international sculpture collection at Ontario's Royal Botanical Gardens by inviting nine land artists to create ephemeral earth art installations over 2,000 acres of land.[18]

As with public symposiums, sculpture parks and gardens have run into difficulties, some of them inherent. In 2012, during the fourth year of the Canadian Sculpture Competition at Kingsbrae Garden in St. Andrews, New

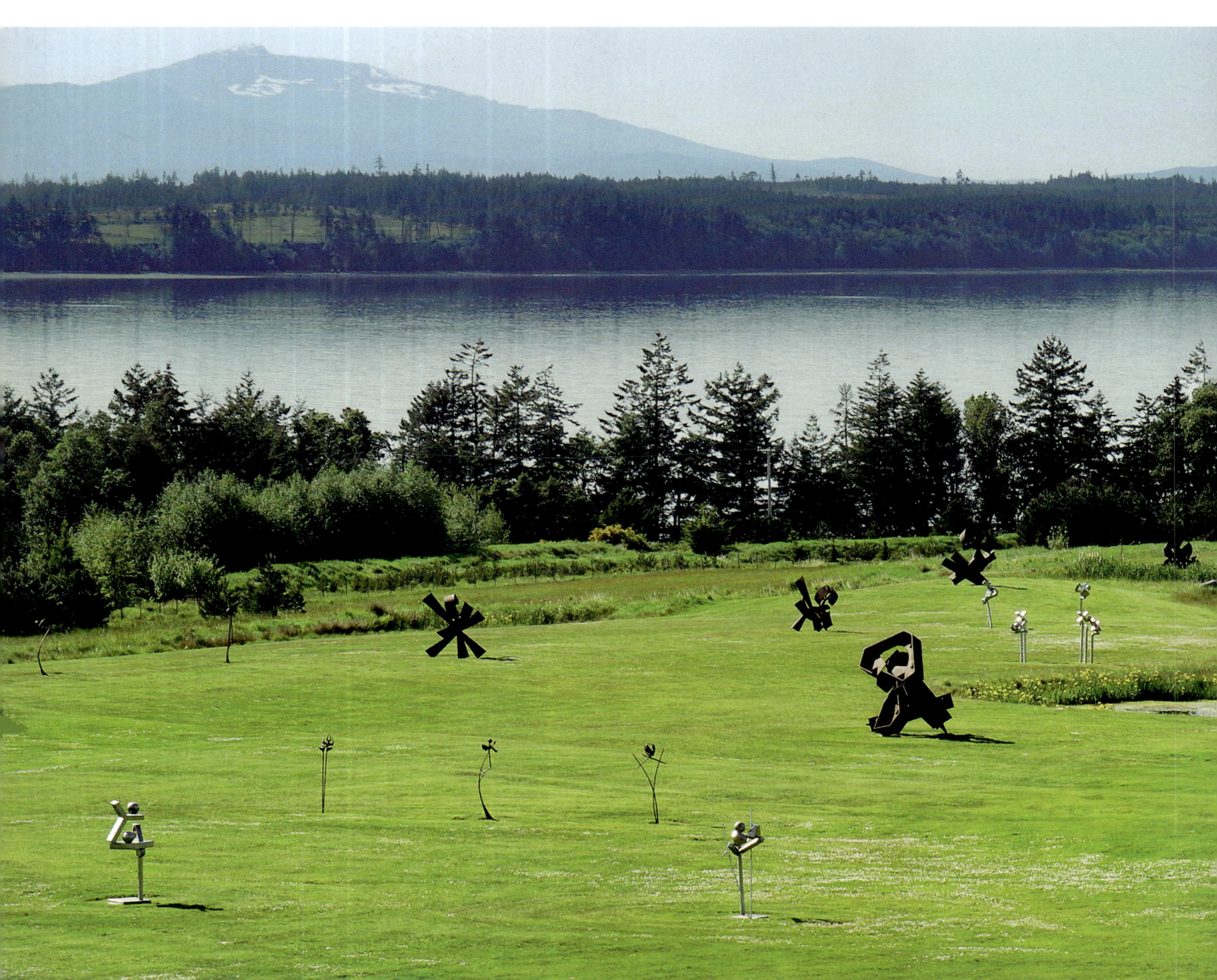

Brunswick, sculptors had competition—from alternative uses of the twenty-seven-acre public garden, with its fifty thousand perennials, children's activities and exotic animals. It was the same in other gardens and parks that sought to expand their activities in order to ensure a good crowd. The achievements, as we have seen, are striking and laudable. But the chores and perils of using publicly controlled spaces are many and various—writing mission statements, outflanking bureaucratic objections, sharing space with other users, winning over a highly critical public and facing caustic reviewers.

Unfortunately, as the history of sculpture in Canada has shown, sculptors have often been bogged down by the agendas of others: those of a commissioning church or government officials, of public and private art galleries, and yes, of art historians. Only a few Canadian sculptors have had the resources to bypass such difficulties by creating specific venues for their work.

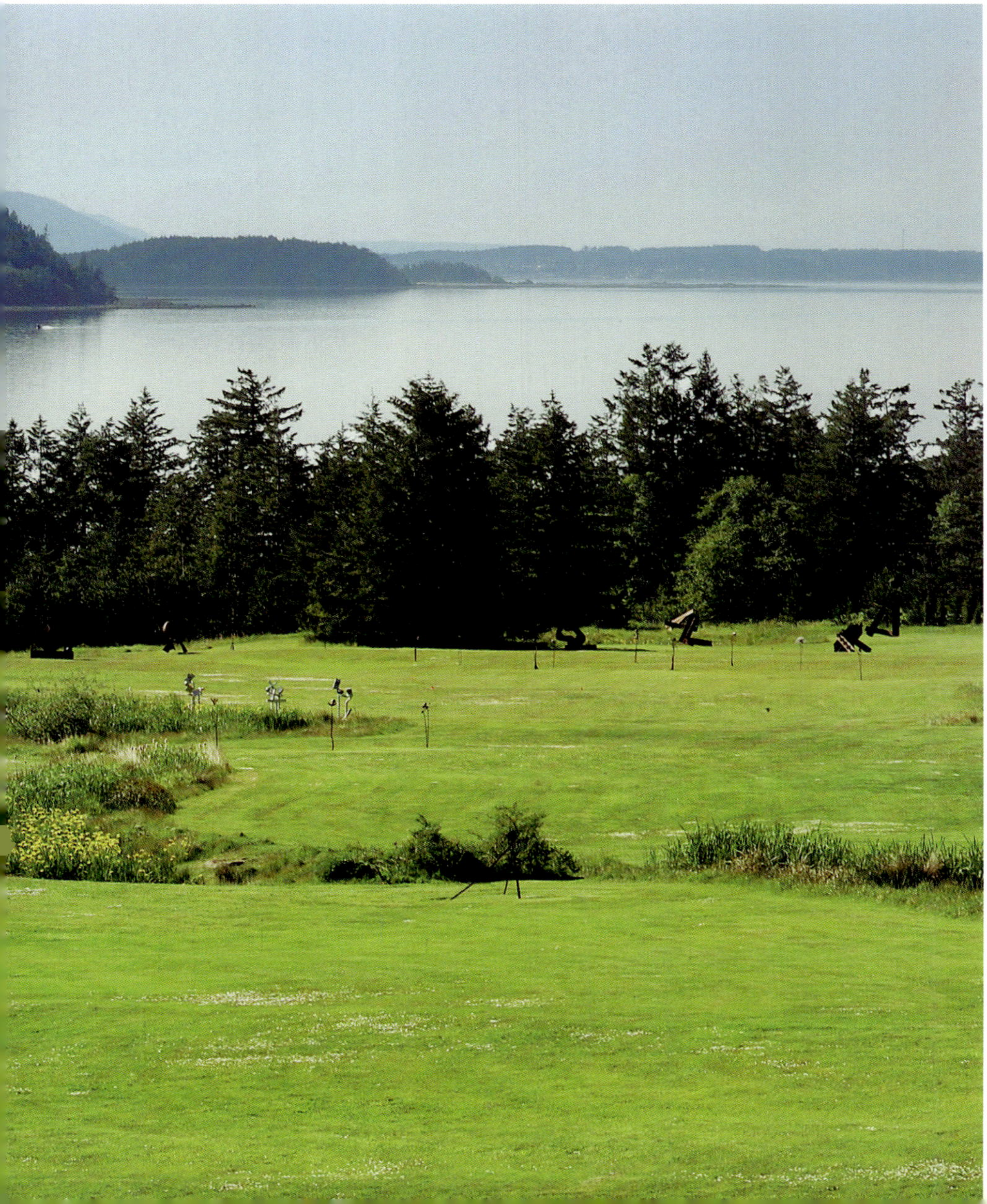

The Jeffrey Rubinoff Sculpture Park, 2004
Storm King Art Center, in upstate New York, can claim to be the first major sculpture park in North America. Likewise, the Jeffrey Rubinoff Sculpture Park is the largest sculpture park devoted to the work of one artist in Canada. Rubinoff spent over forty years on Hornby Island creating berms and ponds, planting irises and levelling fields, in order to transform an old farm into a fitting setting for his work. Today, over one hundred of Rubinoff's modernist sculptures interact with—and are thereby altered by—the vagaries of the weather, the light and the changing seasons.

In 1987 a group of sculptors associated with Vancouver Community College and the Emily Carr College of Art and Design founded the Duenda Sculpture Garden with funding from Employment and Immigration Canada, in a section of Blue Mountain Park near Coquitlam (in the Fraser Valley east of Vancouver). Likewise, in the mid-1990s, self-trained Nova Scotia sculptor Ivan Higgins created an outdoor art gallery for his figurative concrete sculptures at Cosby's Garden Centre on the outskirts of Liverpool on the south shore of Nova Scotia. And Russian-born figurative sculptor Leo Mol (1915–2009), who had made more than two hundred bronze figurative sculptures, donated the collection to the city of Winnipeg. In 1992 the city dedicated over three acres of Assiniboine Park to showing the works, thereby creating the Leo Mol Sculpture Garden.

Other sculptors, notably Katie Ohe, Geert Maas (b. 1944), Luben Boykov (b. 1960) and Jeffrey Rubinoff, have displayed their work in the venues where their sculptures were created. Katie Ohe and her artist-husband Harry Kiyooka (b. 1928) have worked and lived on twenty acres of parkland west of Calgary since 1978. Their aim was not only to provide a permanent home for their work, but also to promote the work of other contemporary artists through a series of exhibitions, lectures and workshops in a specially built pavilion, and to create a botanical sculpture garden and wetlands and woods sanctuary. This project came to fruition when Ohe and Kiyooka donated their land and their work to found a charitable organization, the Kiyooka Ohe Arts Centre society of Calgary.

In a pastoral setting outside of Kelowna, British Columbia, Geert Maas has established a sculpture park where he welcomes visitors to view his sculptures rendered variously in bronze, aluminum, stone and wood. Like Kiyooka and Ohe's arts centre, admission to the Geert Maas Sculpture Gardens and Gallery is by donation. Maas also continues to sell his work to corporations, museums and private collectors.

Needing a permanent location to display his bronze sculptures, Bulgarian-born Luben Boykov joined forces with environmentalist John Evans to found the Boreal Sculpture Garden. Located on six and a half acres of pasture, forest and bog near St. John's, Newfoundland, the garden features Boykov's own abstract work, offers display space to other sculptors and provides workshops for local sculptors wanting to learn how to cast in bronze.

The Jeffrey Rubinoff Sculpture Park (JRSP) is unique in having sufficient funds to run itself without soliciting donations from visitors, governments or fundraising boards. Containing well over one hundred sculptures, the JRSP is the largest privately run sculpture park in Canada. But the JRSP is more than a place where visitors to Hornby Island can spend an afternoon viewing the late artist's modernist sculptures. The JRSP is a centre of learning. Since 2008 scholars from around the world have been invited to discuss the ways in which historians might write and think about the history, exhibition and philosophy of sculpture at the annual Company of Ideas Forum. Building on the educational mandate of the JRSP, Rubinoff also endowed scholarships and fellowships to enable young art historians to find what curator Denis Leclerc described in 1999 as an "appropriate language for speaking about abstract art to the public at large."[19] And, recognizing that music and sculpture share an interest in counterpoint, the JRSP sponsored a series of chamber music concerts. No one viewing Jeffrey Rubinoff's work from the park's glass-walled "concert hall" during a performance can miss the affinity between the notes in Beethoven's late string quartets and the contrapuntal elements in Rubinoff's contemporary sculptures. Following Jeffrey Rubinoff's death in January 2017, an endowment from the Rubinoff estate ensures that the park will continue to bring scholars and musicians together. Moreover, by giving free access, the JRSP offers the general public a unique opportunity to view the work of this remarkable sculptor in the setting in which it was created.

Such achievements are worth saluting, not only in themselves but in indicating what is possible. And it is surely fitting to do so in conclusion of a history that began with the hand-fashioned shards in the Bluefish Caves—work done many thousands of years ago, for motives that we can hardly guess. What has been produced since then has been remarkable: the Nuu-chah-nulth club that Captain James Cook collected on Vancouver Island's west coast in 1778, the gilded liturgical carvings produced in New France, the commemorative First World War memorials, the "landscape" sculptures of the interwar years, and the modernist, postmodernist and contemporary work following the Second World War. Not only does the range of sculptural achievement in Canada deserve due attention: such attention has been long overdue.

Acknowledgements

Books do not write themselves. A work of this scope and complexity owes much to others. From the outset I had two patrons who not only believed that a book of this nature should be written, but were willing to give me tangible support to write it. Thus, Betty Kennedy and Jeffrey Rubinoff were there from the conception; I regret that Jeffrey died before the book was published. Books not only need the foresight of benefactors, they require a publisher who can bring the author's vision to fruition. The Douglas & McIntyre team, including Anna Comfort O'Keeffe, Emma Skagen, Nicola Goshulak, Brianna Cerkiewicz, Patricia Wolfe, and particularly Pam Robertson, among others, did just that.

Others, sculptors and those associated with public and private art institutions, helpfully supplied archival material and illustrations. Among them were Rene Gimpel, Allen MacLeod, Brenda Clairo, Julia Balazs, Larry Camp, Nathalie Galego, Éric Paquette, Marie-Hélène Folsy, Jonathan Lippincott, Jodi Aoki, Mike Patten, Rachel Hand, Vincent Lafond and Erin Gurski, Marie Olinik, Sarah Carr-Locke, Nicole Fletcher, Ninon Gauthier, Craig Willms, Jennifer Longon, Jenifer Medcalf, Richard Siemens, Darlene Wight, Nicole Fletcher, Kit Wallace, Lela Radisevic, Paul Banfield, Sara Carr-Locke, Henry Seaweed, Dwayne Collins, Debbie Miller and Dean Oliver. Artists Robert Murray, Marlene Hilton Moore, John Greer, Donna Hiebert, Mowry Baden, Patrick Thibert, Evan Penny, Ted Bieler, Sherry Grauer, Peter Hide, Robert Davidson, Anne Kahane and Claude Mongrain were among those who gave permission to produce their work and sometimes provided illustrations. Staff and librarians at the University of Victoria, Cambridge University and Pender Island Public Library were particularly helpful. And scholars on both sides of the Atlantic provided essays, exhibition catalogues and books—some of which were brought to my attention by art gallery curator Peter Redpath—that enhanced my knowledge of sculpture. Thank you.

Many people encouraged my efforts on this project. In Canada, friends on Pender Island and in Victoria and Vancouver; in England, friends and colleagues in London and Cambridge, and the Master and Fellows of Churchill College, Cambridge.

At a crucial moment Michel Clairo put his computer skills at my disposal. Sergei Petrov not only came to my rescue when my computer crashed; he provided invaluable photograph assistance throughout the production of this book. H.V. Nelles and John O'Brian read parts of the book. And long-trusted readers Fay Bendall and Peter Clarke read it all—more than once. I thank all of them immensely.

Bibliography

Abell, Walter. "Sculpture," *The Studio* no. 129 (Spring 1945).

Agulhon, Maurice. *Marianne into Battle: Republican Imagery and Symbolism in France, 1789–1880* (Cambridge: Cambridge University Press, 1981, first published 1979).

Anderson, Andrea Karin. "Tom Burrows' 'Sculpture of Concrete, Sculpture of Dreams' or, Looking for the Utopian in the Everyday," master's thesis, University of British Columbia, Vancouver, 1997.

Armstrong, Christopher. *Civic Symbol: Creating Toronto's New City Hall, 1952–1966* (Toronto: University of Toronto Press, 2015).

The Arts and Letters Club of Toronto. *The Year Book of Canadian Art* (Toronto: J.M. Dent, 1913).

Auger, Emily E. *The Way of Inuit Art: Aesthetics and History in and Beyond Inuit Art* (London: McFarland and Company, 2005).

Baker, Marilyn. *Winnipeg School of Art: The Early Years* (Winnipeg: University of Manitoba Press, 1989).

Balkind, Alvin, Robert Bringhurst, Geoffrey James and Russell Keziere. *Visions: Contemporary Art in Canada* (Vancouver: Douglas and McIntyre, 1986).

Bélisle, Josée. *David Rabinowitch* (Montreal: Musée d'Art Contemporain de Montréal; Ottawa: National Gallery of Canada, 2003).

Biéler, André, and Elizabeth Harrison, eds. *The Kingston Conference Proceedings* (Kingston, Ontario, 1941).

Bismanis, Maija, and Timothy Long. *Marilyn Levine: A Retrospective* (Regina: MacKenzie Art Gallery, 1998).

Boas, Franz, "The Decorative Art of the Indians of the North Pacific Coast," *Bulletin of the American Museum of Natural History* vol. 9 (New York: Amerindian Museum of Natural History, 1897).

Boyanoski, Christine. *Loring and Wyle: Sculptors' Legacy* (Toronto: Art Gallery of Ontario, 1987).

Brooke, Janet M. *Henri Hébert 1884–1950: Un Sculpteur Moderne* (Quebec City: Musée de Québec, 2000).

Brooker, Bertram. "Sculpture's New Mood," *Yearbook of the Arts in Canada, 1928–1929* (Toronto: Macmillan, 1929).

Burnett, David, and Marilyn Schiff. *Contemporary Canadian Art* (Edmonton: Hurtig Publishers, 1983).

Cameron, Dorothy. *Sculpture '67* (Ottawa: Queen's Printer, 1968).

Cameron, Elspeth. *And Beauty Answers: The Life of Frances Loring and Florence Wyle* (Toronto: Cormorant Books, 2007).

Capela-Laborde, Cécile. "The Indians of Canada Pavilion at Expo 67: An Expression of Colonialism" essay, Architectural History IV, McGill University, March 29, 2010.

Chevrier, Jean-François, et al. *Melvin Charney: About Reinvention* (Caen, France: Frac Basse-Normandie, 1998).

Cloutier, Nicole. *Laliberté* (Montreal: Montreal Museum of Fine Arts, 1990).

Cole, Douglas. *Captured Heritage: The Scramble for Northwest Coast Artifacts* (Vancouver: Douglas and McIntyre, 1985).

Collins, Judith. *Sculpture Today* (London: Phaidon, 2007).

Corbeil, Danielle. *Claude Tousignant* (Ottawa: National Gallery of Canada, 1973).

Corbett, Gail H. *Katherine E. Wallis (1861–1957): Memoir of a Canadian Sculptor and Artist* (Peterborough: Woodland Publishing, 1997).

Coutu, Joan. "Philanthropy and Propaganda: The Bust of George III in Montreal," *RACAR* vol. 19, nos. 1/2 (1992), 59–67.

Cowan, Susan, ed. *We Don't Live in Snow Houses Now: Reflections of Arctic Bay* (Ottawa: Canadian Arctic Producers, 1976).

Cox, Michael, et al. *Contemporary Art in Manitoba* (Winnipeg: Winnipeg Art Gallery, 1997).

Cronin, J. Keri, and Kirsty Robertson, eds. *Imagining Resistance: Visual Culture and Activism in Canada* (Waterloo: Wilfrid Laurier University Press, 2011).

Currell, Daniel J. "Modernism in Canada: Clement Greenberg and Canadian Art," master's thesis, Concordia University, Montreal, 1995.

Dale, William S.A. "Sculpture," in Malcolm Ross, *The Arts in Canada: Stock-Taking at Mid-Century* (Toronto: MacMillan, 1958).

Dawn, Leslie. *National Visions, National Blindness: Canadian Art and Identities in the 1920s* (Vancouver: UBC Press, 2006).

Demsey, Amy. *Destination Art* (London: Thames and Hudson, 2011).

Douglas, Stan, ed. *Vancouver Anthology: A Project of the Or Gallery* (Vancouver: Talonbooks, Or Gallery, 2011).

Drouin, Daniel, ed. *Louis Philippe Hébert* (Quebec City: Musée du Québec, 2001).

Drouin-Brisebois, Josée. *Otherworld Uprising: Shary Boyle* (Montreal: Conundrum Press, 2008).

Duff, Wilson. *Arts of the Raven: Masterworks by the Northwest Coast Indian* (Vancouver: Vancouver Art Gallery, 1967).

Eber, Dorothy. "Looking for the Artists of Dorset in Eskimo Art," *Canadian Forum* (July/August 1972), 14.

———. *People from Our Side: A Life Story with Photographs by Peter Pitseolak* (Edmonton: Hurtig Publishers, 1975).

Enright, Robert. "Precision, Coercion and Delight: An Interview with Mowry Baden," *Border Crossings* vol. 32, no. 3 (September/October/November 2013), 20–39.

Exhibition of Canadian West Coast Art—Native and Modern, National Gallery of Canada, 1927.

Fabo, Andy. "The Meaning of Flux in the Art of Tom Dean," *Parachute* (April/May/June 1994), 5–13.

Fenton, Terry. *Peter Hide in Canada* (Edmonton: Edmonton Art Gallery, 1986).

Fenton, William N. *The False Faces of the Iroquois* (Norman: University of Oklahoma Press, 1987).

Ferguson, Malcolm Edward Osler. "Canada's Response: The Making and the Remaking of the National War Memorial," master's thesis, Carleton University, 2012.

Fisette, Serge. *La Sculpture et le Vent: Femmes Sculpteures au Québec* (Montreal: Vertiges, 2004)

Fox, James, ed. *The Art of Jeffrey Rubinoff* (Madeira Park: Douglas and McIntyre, 2013).

Fox, James. *British Art and the First World War: 1914–1924* (Cambridge: Cambridge University Press, 2015).

Goodes, Donald, and Kevin Cook. *Olindo Gratton (1855–1941): Religion et Sculpture* (Montreal: Éditions Fides, 1989).

Gordon, Alan. *Making Public Pasts: The Contested Terrain of Montreal's Public Memories, 1891–1930* (Kingston: McGill-Queen's University Press, 2001).

Gordon, Richard. *Katie Ohe* (Calgary: Illingworth Kerr Gallery, 1991).

Graburn, Nelson H.H. "Commentary," *Inuit Art Quarterly* (Spring 1987), 18.

Grande, John K. "Armand Vaillancourt's Social Sculpture," master's thesis, Concordia University, Montreal, 1997.

———. *Kathy Venter: Life* (Toronto: Gardiner Museum, 2013).

———. *Playing with Fire: Armand Vaillancourt, Social Sculptor* (Montreal: Zeit and Geist, 1999).

Greenberg, Clement. "The New Sculpture," *Partisan Review* (June 1949); a revised version of this essay appeared in Greenberg's *Art and Culture* (Boston: Beacon Press, 1961).

Halasz, Piri, et al., *Peter Hide: A Sculptor's Life* (Regina: Hagios Press, 2017).

Hannah, John. "Seated Human Figure Bowls: An Investigation of a Prehistoric Stone Carving Tradition from the Northwest Coast, BC," master's thesis, Department of Archaeology, Simon Fraser University, 1996.

Hart, Susan Elizabeth. "Sculpting a Canadian Hero: Shifting Concepts of National Identity in Ottawa's Core Area Commemorations," master's thesis, Concordia University, Montreal, 2008.

Heinrich, Theodore Allen. *The Painted Constructions 1952–1960 of Sorel Etrog* (Berne: Staempfli and Cie Ltd., 1968).

Holm, Bill. *Smoky-Top: the Art and Times of Willie Seaweed* (Vancouver: Douglas & McIntyre, 1983).

Horrall, Andrew. *Bringing Art to Life: A Biography of Alan Jarvis* (Kingston and Montreal: McGill-Queen's University Press, 2009).

Houston, James A. *Canadian Eskimo Art* (Ottawa: Department of Northern Affairs and National Resources, 1954).

———. "Contemporary Art of the Eskimo," *The Studio* (February 1954).

———. "Eskimo Carvings," *Craft Horizon* (April 1954).

Huneault, Kristina and Janice Anderson *Rethinking Professionalism: Women and Art in Canada, 1850–1970* (Kingston: McGill-Queen's University Press, 2012).

Igloliorte, Heather. "Inuit Art: Makers of Cultural Resilience," *Inuit Art Quarterly* (Spring/Summer 2010), 4.

Inglis, K.S. *Sacred Places: War Memorials in the Australian Landscape* (Melbourne: Melbourne University Press, 1998).

Janson, H.W. *Nineteenth-Century Sculpture* (London: Thames and Hudson, 1985).

Johnson, Carl. "Naissance et Persistance: La Sculpture au Québec de 1946 á 1961," *Espace* 19 (Spring 1992).

Jonaitis, Aldona. *From the Land of the Totem Poles* (New York: American Museum of Natural History, 1988).

Jonaitis, Aldona, and Aaron Glass. *The Totem Pole* (Seattle: University of Washington Press, 2010).

Kerr, Estelle M. "Women Sculptors of Canada," *Women's Saturday Night*, June 20, 1914, 95–96.

Lambert, Richard T. "Eskimo Sculpture," *Canadian Forum* (January 1955), 225–26.

Laurence, Robin. *A Sense of Place: Art at Vancouver International Airport* (Vancouver: Figure 1, 2015).

Lazarus, Eve, Claudia Cornwall and Wendy Newbold Patterson. *The Life and Art of Frank Molnar, Jack Hardman & Leroy Jensen* (Salt Spring Island: Mother Tongue Publishing, 2009).

Leclerc, Denise. *Robert Murray: The Factory as Studio* (Ottawa: National Gallery of Canada, 1999).

Leggo, William. *History of the Administration of the Earl of Dufferin in Canada* (Montreal and Toronto: Lovell, 1878).

Lord, Barry. "Canadian Sculptors at Expo," *Canadian Art* (May 1967).

Lowsborough, John. *The Best Place to Be* (Toronto: Penguin, 2012).

MacCarthy, Hamilton. "The Development of Sculpture in Canada," in J. Castell Hopkins, ed., *Canada: An Encyclopaedia of the Country* (Toronto: Linscott, 1898).

MacLeod, Alan Livingston. *Remembered in Bronze and Stone: Canada's Great War Memorial Statuary* (Victoria: Heritage House, 2016).

MacTavish, Newton. *The Fine Arts in Canada* (Toronto: Macmillan, 1925).

Mantel, Misha P. "A Perspective of Canadian Inuit Art in the Modern Marketplace," bachelor's thesis, University of Leeds, April 2006.

McPherson, Hugo. "The Scope of Sculpture in '64," *Canadian Art* (July/August 1964).

Mitchell, Marybelle. "Making Art in Nunavik: A Brief Historical Overview," *Inuit Art Quarterly* (Fall 1998).

Moroccan, Patrick. "The Making of a Memorial," *War Memorials in Manitoba: An Artistic Legacy* (Regina: Manitoba Historical Society, 2014).

Murray, Joan. *The Best Contemporary Canadian Art* (Edmonton: Hurtig Publishers, 1987).

———. *Canadian Art in the Twentieth Century* (Toronto: Dundurn Press, 1999).

Nasgaard, Roald. *Abstract Painting in Canada* (Vancouver: Douglas and McIntyre, 2007).

Nelles, H.V. *The Art of Nation-Building: Pageantry and Spectacle at Quebec's Tercentenary* (Toronto: University of Toronto Press, 1999).

———. "Camelot in Canada, Or Sir Galahad on Wellington Street," paper presented at the Canadian Historical Association in June 1999, unpublished.

Newton, Eric. *The Diary of English Art Critic Eric Newton: On a North American Lecture Tour in 1937* (New York: Edwin Mellen Press, 1997).

O'Brian, John. *The Flat Side of the Landscape: The Emma Lake Artists' Workshops* (Saskatoon: Mendel Art Gallery, 1989).

O'Brian, John, and Peter White. *Beyond Wilderness: The Group of Seven, Canadian Identity, and Contemporary Art* (Kingston: McGill-Queen's University Press, 2007).

O'Brian, Melanie, ed. *Vancouver Art & Economies* (Vancouver: Arsenal Pulp Press, Artspeak, 2007).

Ord, Douglas. *The National Gallery of Canada: Ideas, Art, Architecture* (Kingston: McGill-Queen's University Press, 2003).

Parker, J. Delisle. "Beatrice Lennie: A Sculptor of the West," *Canadian Review of Music and Art* vol. 5, nos. 6–7 (1946–1947), 22–24.

Pincus-Witten, Robert. *John Nugent: Modernism in Isolation* (Regina: Norman MacKenzie Art Gallery), 1983.

Reinhard Reitzenstein: Escarpment, Valley, Desert (Hamilton: Art Gallery of Hamilton; Oshawa: Robert McLaughlin Gallery, 2002).

Report of Conference on Native Indian Affairs, Acadia Camp, April 1–3, 1948 (Victoria: Provincial Archives, 1948).

Richman, Rhona, et al. *Expo 67: Not Just a Souvenir* (Toronto: University of Toronto Press, 2010).

Roussan, Jacques de. *Signatures: Jordi Bonet* (La Prairie:M. Broquet, 1986).

Rugoff, Ralph, and Matthew Higgs, et al. *Baja to Vancouver: The West Coast and Contemporary Art* (San Francisco: CCA Wattis Institute for Contemporary Arts, 2003).

Salinger, Jehanne Biétry, "Elizabeth Wyn Wood Hahn," *Canadian Forum* vol. 11, no. 128 (May 1931).

Schreiber, Daniel J., ed. *Evan Penny: Re Figured* (Tübingen: Kunsthalle Tübingen, 2010).

Sheehan, Carol. *Breathing Stone: Contemporary Haida Sculpture* (Calgary: Frontenac House, 2008).

Sisler, Rebecca. *The Girls* (Toronto: Clarke, Irwin and Co., 1972).

Skelton, Robin. "Elza Mayhew: A Language for Humanity," *The Malahat Review* 18, University of Victoria, April 1961.

Sloan, Johanne. "Humanists and Modernists at Expo 67," *Revista Mexicana de Estudios Canadienses* no. 13 (Spring/Summer 2007), 71–84.

Stacey, Robert, and Liz Wylie. *Eighty/Twenty: 100 Years of the Nova Scotia College of Art and Design* (Halifax: Art Gallery of Nova Scotia, 1988).

Sturgeon, Graeme. *The Development of Australian Sculpture, 1788–1975* (London: Thames and Hudson, 1978).

Swinton, George. *Sculpture of the Inuit*, 3rd ed. (Toronto: McClelland and Stewart, 1999).

Taft, Lorado. *Modern Tendencies in Sculpture* (Chicago: University of Chicago Press, 1921).

Teitelbaum, Matthew, and Peter White. *Joe Fafard: Cows and Other Luminaries, 1977–1987* (Saskatoon: Mendel Art Gallery; Regina: Dunlop Art Gallery, 1987).

Théirault, Normand. *Claude Tousignant: Sculptures* (Montreal Museum of Fine Arts, 1982).

Tippett, Maria. *Art at the Service of War: Canada, Art and the Great War* (Toronto: University of Toronto Press, 1984, 2013).

———. "'Art Made for Strangers,' Re-thinking Inuit Art," in Roy Calne and William O'Reilly, eds., *Scepticism: Hero and Villain* (New York: Nova Publishers, 2012), 243–52.

———. *Bill Reid: The Making of an Indian* (Toronto: Random House, 2003).

———. *Making Culture: English-Canadian Institutions and the Arts before the Massey Commission* (Toronto: University of Toronto Press, 1990).

Todorov, Todor. *Elemental Sculpture: Theory and Practice* (Newcastle upon Tyne: Cambridge Scholars Publishing, 2014).

Tolles, Thayer, et al. *The American West in Bronze, 1850–1925* (New York: Metropolitan Museum of Art, 2013).

Townsend-Gault, Charlotte, Jennifer Kramer and Ki-Ke-In, eds. *Native Art of the Northwest Coast: A History of Changing Ideas* (Vancouver: UBC Press, 2013).

Urquhart, Jane. *The Stone Carvers* (Toronto: McClelland and Stewart, 2001).

Vance, Jonathan F. *Death So Noble: Memory, Meaning, and the First World War* (Vancouver: UBC Press, 1997).

Varley, Christopher. *Winnipeg West: Painting and Sculpture in Western Canada, 1945–1970* (Edmonton: Edmonton Art Gallery, 1983).

Villeneuve, René. *Baroque to Neo-Classical: Sculpture in Quebec* (Ottawa: National Gallery of Canada, 1997).

Warkentin, John. *Creating Memory: A Guide to Outdoor Public Sculpture in Toronto* (Toronto: Becker Associates, 2010).

Watt, Virginia. "In Retrospect," *Inuit Art Quarterly* (Spring 1987), 17.

Wight, Darlene. *Early Masters: Inuit Sculpture 1949–1955* (Winnipeg: Winnipeg Art Gallery, 2006).

———. *Out of Tradition: Abraham Anghik/David Ruben Piqtoukun* (Winnipeg: Winnipeg Art Gallery, 1989).

Wilkinson, Sarah A. "The Living Monument: A Consideration of the Politics of Indigenous Representation and Public Historical Monuments in Québec," master's thesis, Concordia University, Montreal, 2011.

Withrow, William. *Sculpture Canadienne/Canadian Sculpture, Expo 67* (Montreal: Les Editions d'Orphée, 1967).

Wolfe, Curtis Edward. "Engaging the Public Sphere: The Art and Advocacy of Elizabeth Wyn Wood and Paraskeva Clark Related to their Debate over the Artist's Role in Society," master's thesis, Carleton University, Ottawa, 2010.

Wright, Robin K. *Northern Haida Master Carvers* (Seattle: University of Washington Press, 2001).

Wright, Robin K., and Daina Augaitis, eds. *Charles Edenshaw* (London: Black Dog Publishing, 2013).

Wyn Wood, Elizabeth. "Observations on a Decade, 1938–1948: Ten Years of Canadian Sculpture," *Journal of the Royal Architectural Institute of Canada* 25 (January 1948), 15–19.

Notes

Chapter 1

1 See, for example, Lauriane Bourgeon, "Bluefish Cave II (Yukon Territory, Canada): Taphonomic Study of a Bone Assemblage," *PaleoAmerica* 1, no. 1 (2015): 105–8, and "New Thoughts on the Bones from Bluefish Caves," *Archaeology* (January/February 2015), accessed at www.archaeology.org/news/3011-150213-bluefish-caves-bones.

2 Hamilton MacCarthy, "The Development of Sculpture in Canada," in J. Castell Hopkins, ed., *Canada: An Encyclopaedia of the Country* vol. III (1898), p. 371.

3 Today *La Vierge Druidique de Québec* is in the parish church in Sainte-Marie.

4 Unknown artist, *Angel of the Last Judgment* (c. 1670), is in the Saint-Romuald parish church in Lévis.

5 According to René Villeneuve, over 30 per cent of the settlers in New France lived in Quebec City, Montreal and Trois-Rivières at the end of the seventeenth century, whereas over 90 per cent of the population in France lived in rural areas. René Villeneuve, *Baroque to Neo-Classical: Sculpture in Quebec* (Ottawa: National Gallery of Canada, 1997), 33.

6 The inscription below the bust read: "Temporal and eternal happiness to the sovereign of the British Empire GEORGE III who relieved the distresses of the Inhabitants of his City of Montreal Occasioned by the Fire MD-CCLXV." Joan Coutu, "Philanthropy and Propaganda: The Bust of George III in Montreal," *RACAR* 19, no. l/2 (1992): 59–67.

7 Although some claim that Montreal's Nelson's Column provided a model for the more famous public monument at London's Trafalgar Square, the city of Glasgow erected a forty-two-metre sandstone column honouring Nelson's victory at Trafalgar in 1806, three years before Montreal.

8 Lawrence Durrell, *Selected Poems 1935–1962* (London: Faber, 1964), p. 84.

9 Artist unknown, Haisla *Face Mask* (c. 1830), Seattle Art Museum.

10 Aldona Jonaitis, *From the Land of the Totems* (New York: American Museum of Natural History, 1988), 50.

11 The Six Nations Confederacy, commonly known as the Iroquois, comprised the Mohawk, Cayuga, Onondaga, Oneida, Seneca and Tuscarora peoples.

12 William N. Fenton, *The False Faces of the Iroquois* (Norman: University of Oklahoma Press, 1987), 27.

13 In response to my request to publish an image of a False Face mask, the Royal Ontario Museum wrote, "in respect for First Nations culture we don't grant requests to publish images of false face masks."

14 Alan Gordon, *Making Public Pasts: The Contested Terrain of Montreal's Public Memories, 1891–1930* (Kingston: McGill-Queen's University Press, 2001), xiii.

Chapter 2

1 The *Statue de Notre-Dame-du-Saguenay* was given facelifts in 1913, 1948, 1954 and 1977.

2 I am indebted to Mario Béland's entry on Jobin in the *Dictionary of Canadian Biography* and his catalogue, *Louis Jobin: Maître-Sculpteur*, at the Musée Nationale des Beaux-Arts du Québec (Quebec City: MNBAQ, 1986), and to John K. Grande's "Louis Jobin, 1845–1928," *Espace* 6, no. 2 (Autumn/Winter 1990), 8–11.

3 "Sculpture," *The Canadian Encyclopedia* vol. III (Edmonton: Hurtig Publishers, 1985), 1665.

4 Bernard Mulaire, *Olindo Gratton (1855–1941): Religion et Sculpture* (Montreal: Éditions Fides, 1989), n.p.

5 Gratton's bronze statue *Charles-Joseph Ducharme* (1925) stands in front of the Collège Lionel-Groulx in Sainte-Thérèse, Quebec.

6 W.A. Sherwood, "A National Spirit in Art," *Canadian Magazine* 3, no. 6 (October 1894), 498–50.

7 William Leggo, *History of the Administration of the Earl of Dufferin in Canada* (Montreal and Toronto: Lovell, 1878), 491.

8 Library and Archives Canada, Royal Canadian Academy of Arts Papers, "Minute Books," March 6, 1880, 42.

9 Wilfrid Laurier in "Sir Wilfrid Encourages Art," undated clipping, c. 1903, in RCA Scrapbook, 27, in Library and Archives Canada, Royal Canadian Academy of Arts Papers, vol. 14.

10 John Edgcumbe Staley, "To Foster Canadian Art," *Maclean's* 27, no. 113 (July 1914), 17; Library and Archives Canada, Howick Papers, Grey to Lord Mount Stephen, March 1906.

11 John Warkentin, *Creating Memory: a Guide to Outdoor Public Sculpture in Toronto* (Toronto: Becker Associates, 2010), 15.

12 H.V. Nelles, "Camelot in Canada, Or Sir Galahad on Wellington Street," read at a meeting of the Canadian Historical Association in 1999, unpublished.

13 "Portraits of the Prince and Princess of Wales," *Times* (London), March 1863 and April 1867.

14 The bust of Sir John A. Macdonald, created c. 1867–73, was destroyed in a fire at the Rideau Club in Ottawa.

15 Peter Farrugia, "Convenient Truths: History, Memory, and Identity in Brantford, Ontario," *Journal of Canadian Studies* 46, no. 2 (Spring 2012), 132.

16 *Milwaukee Journal*, April 20, 1929.

17 Ibid.

18 M.H. Spielmann, *British Sculptors and Sculptors of Today* (London: Cassell, 1901), 143.

19 Quoted from a typescript of Hébert's autobiography in Yves Lacasse, "Étapes de ma vie." *Dictionary of Canadian Biography* vol. XIV (1911–20).

20 The Canadian government featured artists in the Dublin Exhibition (1865), the Colonial and Indian Exhibition in London (1886) and the World Columbian Exposition in Chicago (1893), among others.

21 Quoted from a typescript copy of Hébert's autobiography in Yves Lacasse, "Étapes de ma vie," *Dictionary of Canadian Biography* vol. XIV (1911–20).

22 Prior to 1847 there were no professional foundries in North America. Thus, most sculptors had their work cast in Paris, Brussels or Munich. After Jno. Williams Inc. established a foundry in New York City in 1875, many Canadian sculptors, including Hamilton MacCarthy, R. Tait McKenzie and A. Phimister Proctor, sent their models for casting in the United States.

23 Hébert's biographer, Bruno Hébert, cited in Yves Lacasse's entry for the *Dictionary of Canadian Biography* vol. XIV (1911–20).

24 *La Patrie*, September 18, 1912, p. 1, in Nicole Cloutier, *Laliberté* (Montreal: Montreal Museum of Fine Arts, 1990), 53.

25 Hamilton MacCarthy, "The Development of Sculpture in Canada," in J. Castell Hopkins, ed., *Canada: An Encyclopaedia of the Country* (Toronto: Linscott, 1898), 376.

26 Ibid., 374.

27 Ibid., 376.

28 Ibid., 376.

29 "On Sculpture," *St. John Daily Sun*, October 29, 1904.

30 Hamilton MacCarthy, "The Development of Sculpture in Canada," in J. Castell Hopkins, ed., *Canada: An Encyclopaedia of the Country* (Toronto: Linscott, 1898), 381.

31 Ibid., 381.

32 Ibid., 382.

33 Louis-Philippe Hébert, *La Fée Nicotine* (1902), Montreal Museum of Fine Arts.

34 Louis-Philippe Hébert, *Laura Secord* (n.d.), photograph of clay model, Musée du Quebec; *Madeleine de Verchères* (1905), maquette, Musée du Quebec; the finished work is located in Verchères, Quebec; *Évangéline* (1910), Walker Art Gallery, Liverpool, Great Britain.

Chapter 3

1   Katherine Wallis quoted in Gail H. Corbett, *Katherine E. Wallis (1861–1957): Memoir of a Canadian Sculptor and Artist* (Peterborough: Woodland Publishing, 1997), 2.

2   Fidelas [Agnes Machar], "The New Ideal of Womanhood," *Canadian Monthly and National Review* vol. ii (June 1879), 665.

3   Mary Dignam quoted in "Half-Century of Leadership in Canadian Arts," *Christian Science Monitor* (March 18, 1936). In 1890 the Women's Art Club was renamed the Women's Art Association.

4   Katherine Wallis quoted in Gail H. Corbett, *Katherine E. Wallis (1861–1957): Memoir of a Canadian Sculptor and Artist* (Peterborough: Woodland Publishing, 1997), 3.

5   Ibid., 3, 2.

6   Ibid., 3. See also: Katherine Wallis, "Before the West Became the East: Being Reminiscences of the Life of a Canadian Artist," 1938, typescript, Wallis Papers, Trent University Archives.

7   Ibid., 3.

8   Sir Édouard Lantéri, *Modelling: A Guide for Teachers and Students* (London: Chapman and Hall, 1902), 2.

9   Katherine Wallis quoted in Gail H. Corbett, *Katherine E. Wallis (1861–1957): Memoir of a Canadian Sculptor and Artist* (Peterborough: Woodland Publishing, 1997), 42.

10   Ibid., 101.

11   The dates for *Lioness, Mercury* and *Mon Petit Chou* are unknown.

12   Gail H. Corbett, *Katherine E. Wallis (1861–1957): Memoir of a Canadian Sculptor and Artist* (Peterborough: Woodland Publishing, 1997), 5. It should be noted that Wallis used a bronze version of this work as a model for her larger marble carving.

13   Ibid., 102.

14   Quoted from Laliberté's memoir in Nicole Cloutier, *Laliberté* (Montreal: Montreal Museum of Fine Arts, 1990), 17.

15   Gustave Comte, March 16, 1912, cited in Nicole Cloutier, *Laliberté* (Montreal: Montreal Museum of Fine Arts, 1990), 39.

16   F.A. Lamberet, August 4, 1917, cited in Nicole Cloutier, *Laliberté,* (Montreal: Montreal Museum of Fine Arts, 1990), 39.

17   Sarah A. Wilkinson, "The Living Monument: A Consideration of the Politics of Indigenous Representation and Public Historical Monuments in Québec," master's thesis, Concordia University, 2011.

18   Douglas Cole, *Captured Heritage: The Scramble for Northwest Coast Artifacts* (Vancouver: Douglas & McIntyre, 1985), 254.

19   Robert Davidson quoted in Robin K. Wright and Daina Augaitis, eds., *Charles Edenshaw* (London: Black Dog Publishing, 2013), 107.

20   Ibid., 107.

21   Franz Boas, "The Decorative Art of the Indians of the North Pacific Coast," *Bulletin of the American Museum of Natural History* vol. 9 (New York: Amerindian Museum of Natural History, 1897), 123–76.

22   Robin K. Wright, *Northern Haida Master Carvers* (Seattle: University of Washington Press, 2001), 173.

23   Aldona Jonaitis, quoted in *Charles Edenshaw* (London: Black Dog Publishing, 2013), 195–201.

24   Robin K. Wright, *Northern Haida Master Carvers* (Seattle: University of Washington Press, 2001), 21.

Chapter 4

1   Augustus Bridle, "Walter S. Allward, Sculptor," *Toronto Globe*, May 28, 1910, 8.

2   Susan Elizabeth Hart, "Sculpting a Canadian Hero: Shifting Concepts of National Identity in Ottawa's Core Area Commemorations," master's thesis, Concordia University, 2008, 93.

3   McCord Museum, Clarence Gagnon Papers, Box l, Brymner to Gagnon, December 31, 1917.

4   J.E.H. MacDonald, letter to the editor, *Star* (Toronto), March 17, 1916.

5   For Emanuel Hahn's *War the Despoiler* (1915), see the National Gallery of Canada.

6   Patrick Morrocan, "The Making of a Memorial," *War Memorials in Manitoba: An Artistic Legacy* (Regina: Manitoba Historical Society, 2014), 23.

7   For Alfred Laliberté's *Allegory of War* (1917), see the National Gallery of Canada.

8   Frances Loring's *Grief* (1918) was cast in bronze in 1965 and is in the collection of the National Gallery of Canada, no. 40642.

9   Lorado Taft, *Modern Tendencies in Sculpture* (Chicago: University of Chicago Press, 1921), 75.

10   Christine Boyanoski, *Loring and Wyle: Sculptors' Legacy* (Toronto: Art Gallery of Ontario, 1987), 10.

11   Estelle M. Kerr, "Women Sculptors of Canada," *Women's Saturday Night,* June 20, 1914, 95–96.

12   *Manitoba Free Press*, March 10, 1917, in Patrick Moroccan, "The Making of a Memorial," *War Memorials in Manitoba: An Artistic Legacy* (Regina: Manitoba Historical Society, 2014), 3.

13   *Report and Financial Statement for 1917,* the Canadian National Exhibition Association, 36.

14   "Canadian Girl Sculptors Do Unique Work," *Toronto Evening Star*, clipping file of the Art Gallery of Ontario Archives, quoted in Elspeth Cameron, *And Beauty Answers: The Life of Frances Loring and Florence Wyle* (Toronto: Cormorant Books, 2007), p. 107.

15   There were few foundries capable of casting large-scale works in Canada until the early 1920s—the Toronto firm William A. Rogers Limited Company announced in their 1920 catalogue that they were capable of casting large-scale figures. Even so, most Canadian sculptors continued to have models of their work cast or scaled up into marble or bronze by American and European monument firms.

16   See Patrick Moroccan, "The Making of a Memorial," *War Memorials in Manitoba: An Artistic Legacy* (Regina: Manitoba Historical Society, 2014).

17   For a more extensive discussion of the cwmf see Maria Tippett, *Art at the Service of War: Canada, Art and the Great War* (Toronto: University of Toronto Press, 1984, 2013).

18   Records Office, London Guildhall, "Application for Registration in the matter of the War Charities Act, 1916," November 7, 1916.

19   Public Archives of Canada, J.W. Jeffreys Papers, clippings file, *Star* (Toronto), n.d. [November 1917].

20   The three sculptors were Croatia's Ivan Meštrović (1883–1962) and Britain's Clare Sheridan (1885–1970) and Francis Derwent Wood (1871–1926).

21   Eric Brown to Frances Loring, September 10, 1918, National Gallery of Canada Archives.

22   Rebecca Sisler, *The Girls* (Toronto: Clarke, Irwin and Co., 1972), 29.

23   Elspeth Cameron, *And Beauty Answers: The Life of Frances Loring and Florence Wyle* (Toronto: Cormorant Books, 2007), 5.

24   Although most of the guns were melted down, one remains on the memorial in Douglas, Manitoba, and another at the Crowsnest Pass in Alberta.

25   Upon March's death from pneumonia in 1930, his six brothers and only sister completed his work. After being exhibited in London's Hyde Park in 1932, *The Response* was shipped to Ottawa where it was installed in September 1938 and officially commemorated on Parliament Hill by King George vi the following spring.

26   K.S. Inglis, *Sacred Places: War Memorials in the Australian Landscape* (Melbourne: Melbourne University Press, 1998), 173.

27   Curtis Edward Wolfe, "Engaging the Public Sphere: The Art and Advocacy of Elizabeth Wyn Wood and Paraskeva Clark Related to Their Debate over the Artist's Role in Society," master's thesis, Carleton University, 2010, 94; Susan Elizabeth Hart, "Sculpting a Canadian Hero: Shifting Concepts of National Identity in Ottawa's Core Area Commemorations," master's thesis, Concordia University, 2008, 104.

28 Imperial War Museum, London, Canadian War Memorials Papers, n.d. [January 1919].

29 *Daily Express* (London), January 4, 1919.

30 When I curated the exhibition *Lest We Forget* for the London Regional Art Gallery, the Canadian War Museum, still sensitive about showing this work, refused to lend it to me for exhibition.

31 Maria Tippett, *Art at the Service of War: Canada, Art and the Great War* (Toronto: University of Toronto Press, 1984, 2013), 81–87.

32 A.Y. Jackson to Eric Brown, October 30, 1919, National Gallery of Canada Archives.

33 Elspeth Cameron, *And Beauty Answers: The Life of Frances Loring and Florence Wyle* (Toronto: Cormorant Books, 2007), 133. Among Loring's war commissions was the *Galt War Memorial* (1930).

34 Ibid., 128.

35 R.H. Waugh to Elizabeth Wyn Wood, November 11, 1927, Emanuel Hahn–Elizabeth Wyn Wood Fonds, box 4, Queens University Archives. Cited in Curtis Edward Wolfe, "Engaging the Public Sphere: The Art and Advocacy of Elizabeth Wyn Wood and Paraskeva Clark Related to Their Debate over the Artist's Role in Society," master's thesis, Carleton University, 2010, 94.

36 Ibid., 97.

37 The *National Aboriginal Veterans Monument* by First Nations sculptor Noel Lloyd Pinay was erected in Ottawa's Confederation Park in 2001.

38 Estelle M. Kerr, *Canadian Magazine*, 1916, 7; Susan Elizabeth Hart, "Sculpting a Canadian Hero: Shifting Concepts of National Identity in Ottawa's Core Area Commemorations," master's thesis, Concordia University, 2008, 104.

39 Canadian War Museum, Wodehouse File, Eric Brown, "Canada's Own War Memorials' Exhibition in Toronto," October 28, 1919.

40 *Daily Express* (London), January 4, 1919.

41 James Mavor, "Walter Allward, Sculptor," *The Year Book of Canadian Art* (Toronto: J.M. Dent, 1913), 253.

42 Newton MacTavish, *The Fine Arts in Canada* (Toronto: Macmillan, 1925), 83.

43 K.S. Inglis, *Sacred Places: War Memorials in the Australian Landscape* (Melbourne: Melbourne University Press, 1998), 305.

44 Jonathan F. Vance, *Death So Noble: Memory, Meaning, and the First World War* (Vancouver: UBC Press, 1997), 68.

Chapter 5

1 Jane Urquhart, *The Stone Carvers* (Toronto: McClelland and Stewart, 2001), v.

2 Remarkably, Sydney, Australia, mounted the first exhibition devoted entirely to sculpture in 1845.

3 A comment made while in Saskatoon during a lecture tour; *Manchester Guardian*, February 4, 1937, quoted in Eric Newton, *The Diary of English Art Critic Eric Newton: On a North American Lecture Tour in 1937* (New York: Edwin Mellen Press, 1997), 25.

4 Harvey Cowan, "The Ruins of Winter," *City and Country Home* (November 1984), 157.

5 See Chapter 5 in Maria Tippett, *Making Culture: English-Canadian Institutions and the Arts before the Massey Commission* (Toronto: University of Toronto Press, 1990).

6 Brooke, Janet M. *Henri Hébert 1884–1950: Un Sculpteur Moderne* (Quebec City: Musée du Québec, 2000), 224.

7 The ssc was not incorporated until September 1932.

8 Christine Boyanoski, *Loring and Wyle: Sculptors' Legacy* (Toronto: Art Gallery of Ontario, 1987), 43.

9 This would require the academy to lift its quota of five sculptors among its membership of forty. Emanuel Hahn was elected a full academician in 1930 and in 1938 Florence Wyle became the first female sculptor made a full academician of the Royal Canadian Academy.

10 Augustus Bridle, "Big Crowds, Seven Shows as Art Gallery Reopens," *Toronto Daily Star*, October 6, 1928.

11 Arthur Lismer, "Fourth Exhibition of the Sculptors Society of Canada," *Curtain Call* (February 1935), 10.

12 Bertram Brooker, ed., *Yearbook of the Arts in Canada 1928–1929* (Toronto: Macmillan, 1929), 96.

13 Gail H. Corbett, *Katherine E. Wallis (1861–1957): Memoir of a Canadian Sculptor and Artist* (Peterborough: Woodland Publishing, 1997), 100, 102.

14 Fry, Roger, "An Essay in Aesthetics," *New Quarterly*, vol. 2, 1909, 171–90.

15 *Henri Hébert 1884–1950: Un Sculpteur Moderne* (Quebec City: Musée du Québec, 2000), 224.

16 Emanuel Hahn, *Head of Vilhjalmur Stefansson* (1929), National Gallery of Canada.

17 Beatrice Lennie, *Night Flight* (1938), Vancouver Art Gallery.

18 Marilyn Baker, *Winnipeg School of Art: The Early Years* (Winnipeg: University of Manitoba Press, 1989), 104.

19 Wyn Wood intended *Linda* (c. 1932) to be cast either in silver metal or light green bronze. Financial constraints of this work, purchased by Bertram Brooker and donated by him to the Winnipeg Art Gallery, prevented it from being cast in bronze at the time. Following the sculptor's death, however, a bronze cast of *Linda* was made; it is in the Art Gallery of Hamilton. Wyn Wood's *Woman Holding Skein* (1934–1935), Estate of Elizabeth Wyn Wood and Emanuel Hahn.

20 *Young Huron* (1936), bronze, National Gallery of Canada, no. 4915.

21 Frances Loring's *Inuit Mother and Child* (1938), National Gallery of Canada, no. 7790.

22 Florence Wyle's bookends, based on First Nations totem poles viewed in Kispiox, British Columbia, and modelled in 1927, are at the Art Gallery of Ontario.

23 Amateur hockey clubs in the Soviet Union and Canada began playing against one another in the 1920s. At this time Canadian amateur club teams won most of the World Championship and Olympic titles.

24 See Walter Benjamin's essay "The Work of Art in the Age of Mechanical Reproduction," in Howard Eiland and Michael W. Jennings, eds., *Selected Writings: Walter Benjamin, Vol III* (Cambridge, Mass.: Belknap Press, 2002).

25 Elizabeth Wyn Wood, "Reef and Rainbow," *College Times* (Upper Canada College), Christmas 1935, 64, cited in Victoria Baker, *Emanuel Hahn and Elizabeth Wyn Wood: Tradition and Innovation in Canadian Sculpture* (Ottawa: National Gallery of Canada, 1997), 135.

26 Elizabeth Wyn Wood to Robert Ayre, July 1, 1962, in Victoria Baker, *Emanuel Hahn and Elizabeth Wyn Wood: Tradition and Innovation in Canadian Sculpture* (Ottawa: National Gallery of Canada, 1997), 92.

27 Jehanne Biétry Salinger, "Elizabeth Wyn Wood Hahn," *Canadian Forum* vol. 11, no. 128 (May 1931), 302.

28 Elizabeth Wyn Wood's *Northern Island* (1927) and *Dead Tree* (1929) are in the collection of the National Gallery of Canada, and *Reef and Rainbow* (1927) is at the Art Gallery of Ontario.

29 Jehanne Biétry Salinger, "Elizabeth Wyn Wood Hahn," *Canadian Forum* vol. 11, no. 128 (May 1931), 302.

30 Bertram Brooker, "Sculpture's New Mood," *Yearbook of the Arts in Canada 1928–1929* (Toronto: Macmillan, 1929), 104. Seeing her work as bridge between ancient and modern trends in art, Brooker noted that "[Wyn Wood's] work has qualities that relate it at once to the most ancient and the most modern sculpture, so that she becomes a grand-daughter of the Sumerians and a sister of Brancusi."

31 Victoria Baker, *Emanuel Hahn and Elizabeth Wyn Wood: Tradition and Innovation in Canadian Sculpture* (Ottawa: National Gallery of Canada, 1997), 55. *Passing Rain* (1928–1929) is in the collection of the National Gallery of Canada, no. 3715.

32 Blodwen Davies, "Women Artists Helping to Blaze New Trails in Realm of Canadian Creative Work," *Toronto Star*, March 22, 1930.

33 Donald Goodes and Kevin Cook, *Olindo Gratton (1855–1941): Religion et Sculpture*, (Montreal: Éditions Fides, 1989), n.p.

34 See Alfred Laliberté, *Les Artistes de Mon Temps* (1928) and *Légendes, Coutumes, Métiers de la Nouvelle-France* (1934), and the seminal monograph on the eighteenth-century Quebec sculptor Louis Quévillon, *Une Maitrise d'Art en Canada* (1920) by art historian Émile Vaillancourt.

35 Nicole Cloutier, *Laliberté* (Montreal: Montreal Museum of Fine Arts, 1990), 40.

36 Emmanuel Desrosiers in *La Patrie,* cited in Nicole Cloutier, *Laliberté* (Montreal: Montreal Museum of Fine Arts, 1990), 43.

37 Nicole Cloutier, *Laliberté* (Montreal: Montreal Museum of Fine Arts, 1990), 17.

38 Léo-Pol Morin, *La Patrie,* March 28, 1928, cited in Nicole Cloutier, *Laliberté* (Montreal: Montreal Museum of Fine Arts, 1990), 43.

39 Henri Girard, *Le Canada,* December 11, 1931, cited in Nicole Cloutier, *Laliberté* (Montreal: Montreal Museum of Fine Arts), 1990, 43.

40 Quoted from Laliberté's memoir, cited in Nicole Cloutier, *Laliberté* (Montreal: Montreal Museum of Fine Arts, 1990), 17.

41 Newton MacTavish, ed., *The Fine Arts in Canada* (Toronto: Macmillan, 1925). 82.

42 Walter Abell, "Sculpture," *The Studio* 129, no. 625 (April 1945), 132.

43 Bertram Brooker, "Sculpture's New Mood," *Yearbook of the Arts in Canada 1928–1929* (Toronto: Macmillan, 1929), 96.

44 Gail H. Corbett, *Katherine E. Wallis (1861–1957): Memoir of a Canadian Sculptor and Artist* (Peterborough: Woodland Publishing, 1997), 9.

45 Henry Moore quoted in *Architectural Association Journal* (May 1930).

46 Kirk Niergarth, "'What Would He Have Us Do?': Gender and the 'Profession' of Artist in New Brunswick in the 1930s and 1940s," cited in Kristina Huneault and Janice Anderson, *Rethinking Professionalism: Women and Art in Canada, 1850–1970* (Kingston: McGill-Queen's University Press, 2012).

47 J. Delisle Parker, "Beatrice Lennie: A Sculptor of the West," *Canadian Review of Music and Art* 5, nos. 6–7 (1946–1947), 22–24.

48 Ibid., 22–24, 50.

49 Sherry Farrell Racette, "'I Want to Call Their Names in Resistance': Writing Aboriginal Women into Canadian Art History, 1880–1970," in Kristina Huneault and Janice Anderson, *Rethinking Professionalism: Women and Art in Canada, 1850–1970* (Kingston: McGill-Queen's University Press, 2012), 301.

50 Helga Goetz, *The Role of the Department of Indian and Northern Affairs in the Development of Inuit Art*, Inuit Section, Research and Documentation Centre (Ottawa 1985), 7.

51 Harlen Smith, "The Use of Prehistoric Canadian Art for Commercial Design," *Science* no. 46 (1917), 60–66, cited in Leslie Dawn, "Northwest Coast Art and Canadian National Identity, 1900–1950," in Charlotte Townsend-Gault, Jennifer Kramer and Ki-Ke-In, eds., *Native Art of the Northwest Coast: A History of Changing Ideas* (Vancouver: UBC Press, 2013), 313.

52 *Exhibition of Canadian West Coast Art—Native and Modern*, National Gallery of Canada and the Victoria Memorial Museum catalogue, December 1927, 2.

53 Leslie Dawn, "Northwest Coast Art and Canadian National Identity, 1900–1950," in Charlotte Townsend-Gault, Jennifer Kramer and Ki-Ke-In, eds., *Native Art of the Northwest Coast: A History of Changing Ideas* (Vancouver: UBC Press, 2013), 317.

54 See Leslie Dawn, *National Visions, National Blindness: Canadian Art and Identities in the 1920s* (Vancouver: UBC Press, 2006)—especially the chapter "Giving Gitxsan Totem Poles a New Slant," 182–208.

55 *Daily Province* (Vancouver), June 28, 1925, cited in Leslie Dawn, *National Visions, National Blindness: Canadian Art and Identities in the 1920s* (Vancouver: UBC Press, 2006), 199.

56 When the fair ended, Martin's totem poles were donated to New York City's Parks Department, which later donated them to a Boy Scout camp in New Jersey.

57 Maria Tippett, *Making Culture: English-Canadian Institutions and the Arts before the Massey Commission* (Toronto: University of Toronto Press, 1990), 74.

58 Leslie Dawn, "Northwest Coast Art and Canadian National Identity, 1900–1950," in Charlotte Townsend-Gault, Jennifer Kramer and Ki-Ke-In, eds., *Native Art of the Northwest Coast: A History of Changing Ideas* (Vancouver: UBC Press, 2013), 340.

59 Ibid., 332.

60 *Report of Conference on Native Indian Affairs, Acadia Camp, April 1–3, 1948* (Victoria: Provincial Archives, 1948), 12–13.

61 Bill C-4, "An Act to Preserve and Promote Native Indian and Eskimo Arts and Crafts" Third Session, Twenty-Sixth Parliament, April 8, 1965 (Ottawa: Queen's Printer, 1965).

62 Palette, "Girl Carves," *Province* (Vancouver), January 20, 1944, 21.

63 Neel dedicated *Victory Through Honour* to the university's Alma Mater Society, with the hope that they would allow Indigenous people to "take advantage of the opportunity, so that some day our doctors, lawyers, social workers and departmental workers will be fully trained University graduates of our own race." Ellen Neel, *The Native Voice*, November 1948. In 1973 the pole, which had deteriorated and been damaged by vandals, was re-carved by Ellen Neel's nephew Douglas Cranmer; in 2001, subject once again to vandalism, the pole was re-carved by Calvin Hunt, Mervin Child and John Livingston.

64 Elizabeth Wyn Wood, "Observations on a Decade, 1938–1948: Ten Years of Canadian Sculpture," *Journal of the Royal Architectural Institute of Canada* vol. 25 (1948), 15.

65 Page Toles, "Sculptors' Society Exhibition," *Canadian Art* (June/July 1944), 191.

66 Elizabeth Wyn Wood, *Munitions Worker* (1944), National Gallery of Canada, no. 35872.

67 Walter Allward, *Mourning Figure, Female Nude*, National Gallery of Canada, no. 29589.

68 Cited in Kirk Niergarth, "'What Would He Have Us Do?': Gender and the 'Profession' of Artist in New Brunswick in the 1930s and 1940s," in Kristina Huneault and Janice Anderson, *Rethinking Professionalism: Women and Art in Canada, 1850–1970* (Kingston: McGill-Queen's University Press, 2012), 66.

69 André Biéler and Elizabeth Harrison, eds., *The Kingston Conference Proceedings* (Kingston, Ontario, 1941), 111–12.

70 Elizabeth Wyn Wood, "Ten Years of Canadian Sculpture," *Journal of the Royal Architectural Institute of Canada* (September 1948), 15–19.

71 Cited in Kirk Niergarth, "'What Would He Have Us Do?': Gender and the 'Profession' of Artist in New Brunswick in the 1930s and 1940s," in Kristina Huneault and Janice Anderson, *Rethinking Professionalism: Women and Art in Canada, 1850–1970* (Kingston: McGill-Queen's University Press, 2012), 66.

72 Susan Hasbury, "The Sculpture of Elizabeth Wyn Wood," research paper, Carleton University, April 1982, 33.

73 Walter Abell, "Sculpture," *The Studio* vol. 129, no. 625 (April 1945), 132.

Chapter 6

1 Frances Loring, "Hard to Begin Sculpturing Frances Loring Admits," *Toronto Daily Star*, March 22, 1939, 20.

2   Elizabeth Wyn Wood, "Observations on a Decade, 1938–1948: Ten Years of Canadian Sculpture," *Journal of the Royal Architectural Institute of Canada* vol. 25 (January 1948), 16.

3   Lionel Thomas, "An Artist Relates his Skills to Architecture," *Canadian Art* (Autumn 1955), 203.

4   "The Sculptors' Society protests against the Capital Plan which makes no provision for sculptors." *Report of the Royal Commission on National Development in the Arts, Letters and Sciences* (Ottawa, 1951), 214.

5   Up to 1 per cent of the total cost of a public building could be spent on works of art. By 1966, however, only $2 million had been spent on art for government buildings whose total cost was 700 million dollars.

6   Josephine Hambleton, "Canadian Women Sculptors," *Dalhousie Review* vol. xxix, no. 3 (October 1949), 332.

7   Stephen Vickers, "The Architecture in Sculpture," *Journal of the Royal Architectural Institute of Canada* (January 1949), 31–32.

8   Robert Pincus-Witten, *John Nugent: Modernism in Isolation* (Regina: Norman Mackenzie Art Gallery, 1983), 15.

9   Jacques de Roussan, *Signatures: Jordi Bonet* (La Prairie, Quebec: M. Broquet, 1986), 15.

10 Sandra Alfoldy, *Allied Arts: Architecture and Craft in Postwar Canada* (Kingston: McGill-Queen's University Press, 2012), 30.

11 Jacques de Roussan, *Signatures: Jordi Bonet* (La Prairie, Quebec: M. Broquet, 1986), 10.

12 Tolgesy's colleagues were Gerald Trottier, Frank Pen and Dutch-born stained-glass artist Theo Lubbers.

13 Lionel Thomas, "An Artist Relates his Skills to Architecture," *Canadian Art* (Autumn 1955), 204.

14 *Report of the Royal Commission on National Development in the Arts, Letters and Sciences* (Ottawa, 1951), 214.

15 Sara Bowser, "An Interview with Gerald Gladstone," *Canadian Architect* (April 1959), 72, quoted in Denis Leclerc, *The Crisis of Abstraction in Canada* (Ottawa: National Gallery of Canada, 1992), 117.

16 Among the artists chosen in 1966 from a competition to provide works for the Macdonald Building were Louis Archambault, Jack Harman and Paulosie Kanayook.

17 Iris Nowell, "Lives Lived: Walter Yarwood," *Globe and Mail* (Toronto), January 9, 1997.

18 Robert Murray quoted in Ian MacAlpine, "'Will It Be Something Saskatchewan?' Council Divided on City Hall Fountain, Accepts It Anyway," *Saskatoon Star-Phoenix,* August 19, 1959, cited in Denise Leclerc, *Robert Murray: The Factory as Studio* (Ottawa: National Gallery of Canada, 1999), 70.

19 Robert Murray, quoted in Dorothy Cameron, *Sculpture '67* (Ottawa: Queen's Printer, 1968), 10.

20 John K. Grande, *Playing with Fire: Armand Vaillancourt, Social Sculptor* (Montreal: Zeit & Geist, 1999), 26.

21 Unsigned article, "Sculptured Explosions," *Time Magazine,* December 22, 1961, cited in John K. Grande, *Playing with Fire: Armand Vaillancourt, Social Sculptor* (Montreal: Zeit & Geist, 1999), 23.

22 George Swinton, "The Great Winnipeg Controversy," *Canadian Art* (Winter 1956), 244.

23 Charles Daudelin, *Crouching Woman*, limestone, National Gallery of Canada, 1947, no. 28430.

24 Claude Tousignant, quoted in Danielle Corbeil, *Claude Tousignant* (Ottawa: National Gallery of Canada, 1973), 14.

25 See Maria Tippett, *Making Culture: English-Canadian Institutions and the Arts before the Massey Commission* (Toronto: University of Toronto Press, 1990), 35–37.

26 John Ivor Smith, *Florentine*, n.d., Art Gallery of Hamilton.

27 Bill Gladstone, "A Sketch of Artist Gerald Gladstone," at www.billgladstone.ca (Toronto, November 29, 2011), originally published in the *Canadian Jewish News,* 1998.

28 Charles Spencer, "Gerald Gladstone: Spacist Sculptor," *The Studio* no. 830 (June 1962), 214–15.

29 Katie Ohe quoted in Richard Gordon, *Katie Ohe (*Illingworth Kerr Gallery, Calgary, 1991), 9.

30 Ibid., 18.

31 Joan Murray, *Canadian Art in the Twentieth Century* (Toronto: Dundurn Press, 1999), 150.

32 Walter Abell, "Sculpture," *The Studio* vol. 129, no. 625 (April 1945), 132–138.

33 Josephine Hambleton, "Canadian Women Sculptors." *Dalhousie Review* vol. xxix, no. 3 (October 1949), 235.

34 Elizabeth Wyn Wood, "Observations on a Decade, 1938–1948: Ten Years of Canadian Sculpture," *Journal of the Royal Architectural Institute of Canada* vol. 25 (January 1948), 15–19.

35 Joe Plaskett, "Impressions of Art in Europe," speech, Vancouver Art Gallery, 1956, n.p.

36 Andrew Bell, "An Exhibition of Canadian Sculpture," *Canadian Art* (Summer 1949), 155–56.

37 Julien Hébert, "What Themes Are Sculptural?" *Canadian Art* vol. xi, no. 5 (1953), 147.

38 Josephine Hambleton, "Canadian Women Sculptors," *Dalhousie Review* vol. xxix, no. 3 (October 1949), 235.

39 Robin Skelton, "Elza Mayhew: A Language for Humanity," *Malahat Review* no. 18 (April 1961), 63.

40 Jan Zach cited in Dorothy Cameron, *Sculpture '67* (Ottawa: Queen's Printer, 1968), 56.

41 Oliver A.I. Botar, "Biographies," in *An Art at the Mercy of Light: Recent Works by Eli Bornstein* (Saskatoon: Mendel Art Gallery, 2013), 46.

42 An interview with Eli Bornstein, September 21, 2013, in Robert Enright, "Plane Talk: An Interview with Eli Bornstein," *Border Crossings* no. 128 (December 2013), n.p.

43 John Wood, David Hulks and Alex Potts, eds., *Modern Sculpture Reader* (Leeds: Henry Moore Institute, 2007), xxii.

44 Clement Greenberg, "The New Sculpture," *Partisan Review* (June 1949); a revised version of this essay appeared in Greenberg's *Art and Culture* (Boston: Beacon Press, 1961).

45 Christopher Varley, *Winnipeg West: Painting and Sculpture in Western Canada 1945–1970* (Edmonton: Edmonton Art Gallery, 1983), 30.

46 Ibid. It should be noted that by 1968 Judd had turned against Greenbergian modernism. Barnet and Ferren were less enthusiastic too.

47 Roald Nasgaard, *Abstract Painting in Canada* (Vancouver: Douglas and McIntyre, 2007), 143.

48 Judith Collins, *Sculpture Today* (London: Phaidon, 2007), 7.

49 Bruce Barber et al., eds., *Voices of Fire: Art, Rage, Power and the State* (Toronto: University of Toronto Press, 1996), 181.

50 John O'Brian, *The Flat Side of the Landscape: The Emma Lake Artists' Workshops* (Saskatoon: Mendel Art Gallery, 1989), 81.

51 Daniel J. Currell, "Modernism in Canada: Clement Greenberg and Canadian Art," master's thesis, Concordia University, 1995, 56, cited in John D.H. King, "The Emma Lake Workshops, 1955–1970," essay, Brandon University, 51.

52 Florence Rubenfeld, *Clement Greenberg: A Life* (New York: Scribner, 1997), 252.

53 Clement Greenberg, "Clement Greenberg's View of Art on the Prairies," *Canadian Art* (March/April 1963) 90–107.

54 Ibid., 107.

55 John White, *The Birth and Rebirth of Pictorial Space* (New York: Thomas Yoseloff, 1958); Charles Biederman, *The New Cézanne: From Monet to Mondrian* (Red Wing, Minn.: Leicht Press, 1958).

56 John Ivor Smith quoted in Lawrence Sabbath, "Sculpture in Canada; Modellers," *Canadian Art* (July/August 1962), 294.

57 Eve Lazarus et al., *The Life and Art of Frank Molnar, Jack Hardman & LeRoy Jensen* (Salt Spring Island: Mother Tongue Publishing, 2009), 62.

58 Elza Mayhew quoted by Frank Nowosad, "Vertical inspiration," *Monday Magazine*, December 8, 1978.

59 Barry Lord, "What London, Ontario Has that Everywhere Else Needs," *Art in America* vol. 57, no. 5 (September/Octctober 1969), 103–105.

60 Carl Johnson, "Naissance et Persistance: La Sculpture au Québec de 1946 à 1961," *Espace* 19 (Spring 1992), 44.

61 John Grande, "Armand Vaillancourt's Social Sculpture," master's thesis, Concordia University, 1997, 8.

62 Vaillancourt destroyed this work in 1999.

63 Iris Nowell, "Lives Lived: Walter Yarwood," *Globe and Mail* (Toronto), January 9, 1997.

64 See, for example, *Tower* (1965), National Gallery of Canada, and David Burnett and Marilyn Schiff, *Contemporary Canadian Art* (Edmonton: Hurtig Publishers, 1983), 144–45.

65 Joy Carroll, "Walter Yarwood,"' *Canadian Art* vol. 21, no. 4 (1964), p. 236.

66 Theodore Allen Heinrich, *The Painted Constructions 1952–1960 of Sorel Etrog* (Berne: Staempfli & Cie Ltd., 1968), 7–8.

67 Serge Fisette, "Claude Tousignant et la Sculpture," *Espace* no. 86 (Winter 2008/2009), 21.

68 John Ivor Smith quoted in Lawrence Sabbath, "Sculpture in Canada: Modellers" *Canadian Art* (July/August 1962), 290.

69 Robert Fulford, "Now the Sculptors are Starting to Move." *Maclean's* vol. 76, no. 16 (August 24, 1963), 23.

70 Hugo McPherson, "The Scope of Sculpture in '64," *Canadian Art* vol. xxi, no. 4 (July/August 1964), 226.

71 Ibid., 224.

Chapter 7

1 "New Fixture," *Time* (Canadian Edition), August 1, 1955.

2 Elizabeth Wyn Wood, "Observations on a Decade, 1938–1948: Ten Years of Canadian Sculpture," *Journal of the Royal Architectural Institute of Canada* (January 1948), 15.

3 Andrew Horrall, *Bringing Art to Life: A Biography of Alan Jarvis* (Kingston and Montreal: McGill-Queen's University Press, 2009), 244.

4 Ibid.

5 Douglas Ord, *The National Gallery of Canada: Ideas, Art, Architecture* (Kingston: McGill-Queen's University Press, 2003), 151.

6 Charles Comfort quoted in Barrie Hale, "National Gallery Can't See Pop Art," *Telegram* (Toronto) March 6, 1965, cited in Douglas Ord, *The National Gallery of Canada: Ideas, Art, Architecture* (Kingston: McGill-Queen's University Press, 2003), 178.

7 William Townsend, ed., *Canadian Art Today* (Greenwich, Conn.: New York Graphic Society, 1970), 11.

8 John Reeves, *About Face* (Toronto: Exile Editions, 1990).

9 Hugo McPherson, "The Scope of Sculpture in '64," *Canadian Art* vol. xxi, no 4. (July/August1964), 224.

10 Note that in 1956 Frances Loring was commissioned by the federal government to produce a full-scale bronze sculpture of former prime minister Sir Robert Laird Borden for Parliament Hill. Five years later Elizabeth Wyn Wood produced the clay model for a statue of King George vi for Victoria Park at Niagara Falls. (Louis Temporale transformed Wyn Wood's model into a block of Laurentian rose granite.)

11 "Contemporary Canadian Sculpture Show: More Caution than Experiment," *Canadian Art* vol. vii, no. 3 (Spring 1950), 116.

12 Hugo McPherson, "The Scope of Sculpture in '64," *Canadian Art* vol. xxi, no. 4 (July/August 1964), 235.

13 Vincent Price, *Chicago Tribune*, September 24, 1967.

14 Johanne Sloan, "Humanists and Modernists at Expo 67," *Revista Mexicana de Estudios Canadienses* no. 13 (Spring/Summer 2007), 79.

15 William Withrow, *Sculpture Canadienne / Canadian Sculpture, Expo 67* (Montreal: Les Editions d'Orphée, 1967), n.p.

16 Jacques de Roussan, *Signatures: Jordi Bonet* (La Prairie, Quebec: M. Broquet, 1986), 14.

17 Mayhew's *Meditation Piece* is now on the east side of the Rideau Canal in Ottawa.

18 Clement Greenberg, "The New Sculpture," *Partisan Review* (June 1949), reprinted in John O'Brian, *Clement Greenberg: The Collected Essays and Criticism* (Chicago: University of Chicago Press, 1993), 58.

19 Françoise Sullivan quoted in Dorothy Cameron, *Sculpture '67* (Ottawa: Queen's Printer, 1968), 86.

20 Eva H. Turner, "Sculpture in Canada: Welders," *Canadian Art* vol. 19, no. 4 (July/August 1962), 276–83.

21 Kantaroff quoted in Eric J. Stanford, "Preface," *Images of Origins: Sculpture by Maryon Kantaroff* (Toronto: Prince Arthur Galleries, 1979), n.p.

22 Johanne Sloan, "Humanists and Modernists at Expo 67," *Revista Mexicana de Estudios Canadienses* no. 13, (Spring/Summer 2007), 84.

23 These works were acquired by the University of British Columbia following Expo '67.

24 William Withrow, *Sculpture Canadienne / Canadian Sculpture, Expo 67* (Montreal: Les Editions d'Orphée, 1967), n.p.

25 Ibid., Withrow; Alvin Balkind, "The Triumph of the Egg," in Alvin Balkind, et al., *Visions: Contemporary Art in Canada* (Vancouver: Douglas and McIntyre, 1986), 17.

26 Barry Lord, "Canadian Sculptors at Expo," *artscanada* vol. 24, no. 5 (May 1967), 12–16.

27 William Withrow, *Sculpture Canadienne / Canadian Sculpture, Expo 67* (Montreal: Les Editions d'Orphée, 1967), n.p.

28 Willar admitted that the four Atlantic provinces had come to modernism late but the exclusion of all but one artist nevertheless suggested "a real comment on our Maritime insularity." Fred Willar quoted in Dorothy Cameron, *Sculpture '67* (Ottawa: Queen's Printer, 1968), 54.

29 Barry Lord, "Canadian Sculptors at Expo," *Canadian Art* (May 1967), 12.

30 Robert Fulford, "Sculpture '67," *artscanada* no. 89 (August/September 1967), n.p.

31 Ibid.

32 Dorothy Cameron, *Sculpture '67* (Ottawa: Queen's Printer, 1968), 6.

33 Fred Willar quoted in Dorothy Cameron, *Sculpture '67* (Ottawa: Queen's Printer, 1968), 54, 6.

34 Sullivan quoted in Dorothy Cameron, *Sculpture '67* (Ottawa: Queen's Printer, 1968), 86.

35 Joe Bodolai, ed., "Sculpture: Rebirth of Humanism," *artscanada* (Autumn 1974), 43.

36 Walter Abell, "Sculpture," *The Studio* vol. 129, no. 625 (April 1945), 132–37.

37 Jacqueline Hooper, "Arts of the Raven: bc Indian Art Is Something to Shout About," *Post-Intelligencer Weekender Magazine* (Seattle), July 22, 1967.

38 Bill Reid, *Eagle and Bear Box* (1967), ubc Museum of Anthropology.

39 Myra Rutherdale and Jim Miller, "'It's Our Country': First Nations Participation in the Indian Pavilion at Expo 67," *Journal of the Canadian Historical Association* vol. 17, no. 2 (2006), 158.

40 *A Survey of the Contemporary Indians of Canada: Economic, Political, Educational Needs and Policies, Parts 1 and 2* (Ottawa: Indian and Northern Affairs Canada, October 1966 and October 1967).

41 Buffy Sainte-Marie quoted in John Lowsborough, *The Best Place to Be* (Toronto: Penguin, 2012), 205.

42 Ingo Hessel, *Inuit Art: An Introduction* (Toronto: Douglas and McIntyre, 1998), 187.

43 Pearl McCarthy, "Sculptors' Group Honors Eskimo," *Globe and Mail* (Toronto), May 5, 1958.

44 William S.A. Dale, "Sculpture," in Malcolm Ross, *The Arts in Canada: Stock-taking at Mid-century* (Toronto: Macmillan, 1958), 35.

45 George River in Northern Quebec was the first co-operative, although artists in Cape Dorset and Puvirnituq established a sculptors' society with a marketing service in Quebec City in 1962. In 1961 the Canadian Eskimo Art Committee (which became the Canadian Eskimo Arts Council) was founded by the Department of Indian Affairs and Northern Development (DIAND) in order to advise the Dorset co-op and others on technical and design problems and to approve the graphics released.

46 Charles Gimpel, *Coronation Exhibition: Eskimo Carvings* (London: Gimpel Fils, 1953), n.p.

47 Barry Lord, "Canadian Sculptors at Expo," *Canadian Art* (May 1967), 14.

48 In 1911 the Canadian government presented Queen Mary with an ivory kayak during the coronation of George v and in 1951 a carving produced by Cape Dorset artist Mannumi (or Munamee) Shaqu (1917–2000), *Mother and Child,* was presented to Princess Elizabeth during her tour of Canada.

49 James Houston, "Answers to Questions of Arts and Crafts Project, Cape Dorset, 1956," National Archives of Canada, RG 85, vol. 387.

50 Emily E. Auger, *The Way of Inuit Art: Aesthetics and History In and Beyond Inuit Art* (London: McFarland & Co, 2005), 154–66. Also: Dorothy M. Kosinski and Julian Andrews, *Henry Moore: Sculpting the 20th Century,* Dallas Museum of Art, Fine Arts Museums of San Francisco, and National Gallery of Art (New Haven, Conn.: Yale University Press, 2001), 37.

51 See W. Jackson Rushing, *Native American Art in the Twentieth Century: Makers, Meanings, Histories* (New York: Routledge, 1999) and Maria Tippett "'Art Made for Strangers': Re-thinking Inuit Art," in Roy Calne and William O'Reilly, eds., *Scepticism: Hero and Villain* (New York: Nova Publishers, 2012), 243–52.

52 Richard T. Lambert, "Eskimo Sculpture," *Canadian Forum* (January 1955), 225–26. Oshaweetuk Ipeelee, *Stone Mother and Child* (1956), Metropolitan Museum of Art, New York.

53 Sheokjuk Oqutaq quoted in Marybelle Mitchell, "Making Art in Nunavik: A Brief Historical Overview," *Inuit Art Quarterly* (Fall 1998), 6.

54 Manasie Akpaliapik quoted in "On Selling their Work," *Inuit Art Quarterly* (Spring 1990), 9.

55 Marybelle Mitchell, "Making Art in Nunavik: A Brief Historical Overview," *Inuit Art Quarterly* (Fall 1998), 6.

56 Peter Pitseolak quoted in Dorothy Eber, *People from Our Side: A Life Story with Photographs by Peter Pitseolak* (Edmonton: Hurtig Publishers, 1975), 145.

57 Dorothy Eber, "Looking for the Artists of Dorset in Eskimo Art," *Canadian Forum* (July/August 1972), 14.

58 Simon Tookoome quoted in Marybelle Mitchell, "On Selling their Work," *Inuit Art Quarterly* (Spring 1990), 9.

59 Heather Igloliorte, "Inuit Art: Makers of Cultural Resilience," *Inuit Art Quarterly* (Spring/Summer 2010), 4.

60 Manasie Akpaliapik quoted in Marybelle Mitchell, "On Selling their Work," *Inuit Art Quarterly* (Spring 1990), 11.

61 Mannumi Shaqu, *Sea Goddess "Taleolaya"* (1962), stone, Metropolitan Museum of Art, New York, no. 1970.45.25.

62 Susan Cowan, ed., *We Don't Live in Snow Houses Now: Reflections of Arctic Bay* (Canadian Arctic Producers Ltd.: Ottawa, 1976), 134.

63 Nelson H.H. Graburn, "Commentary," *Inuit Art Quarterly* (Spring 1987), 18.

64 Jean Blodgett, *Kenojuak* (Toronto: Mintmark Press, 1985), 23.

65 See, for example, James A. Houston, "Contemporary Art of the Eskimo," *The Studio* (February 1954), "Eskimo Carvings," *Craft Horizon* (April 1954) and *Canadian Eskimo Art* (Ottawa: Department of Northern Affairs and National Resources, 1954, reprinted 1955, 1957, 1959, 1965).

66 James A. Houston, *Canadian Eskimo Art* (Ottawa: Department of Northern Affairs and National Resources, 1959), 38.

67 George Swinton quoted in *Canadian Press,* March 1, 1958, in Virginia Watt, "In Retrospect," *Inuit Art Quarterly* (Spring 1987), 17.

Chapter 8

1 Judith Collins, *Sculpture Today* (London: Phaidon, 2007), 7–8.

2 John Bentley Mays, *Globe and Mail* (Toronto), December 30, 1989.

3 Denise Leclerc, *Robert Murray: The Factory as Studio* (Ottawa: National Gallery of Canada, 1999), 61.

4 Karen Wilkin, "Introduction," *Sculpture '81*, Halifax, August 1981, n.p.

5 Joan Murray, *Canadian Art in the Twentieth Century* (Toronto: Dundurn Press, 1999), 183.

6 David Altmejd quoted in Peter Dubé, "Monstrous Energy," *Espace* no. 79 (Spring 2007), 12.

7 Todor Todorov, *Elemental Sculpture: Theory and Practice* (Newcastle upon Tyne: Cambridge Scholars Publishing, 2014), 95, 96.

8 Rosalind Krauss, "Sculpture in the Expanded Field," *October* vol. 8 (Spring 1979), 30–44.

9 Rosalind Krauss, *Passages in Modern Sculpture* (New York: Viking Press, 1977), 4.

10 Udo Kultermann, *The New Sculpture: Environments and Assemblages* (London: Thames & Hudson, 1968), 6.

11 Arthur Danto, *After the End of Art: Contemporary Art and the Pale of History* (Princeton: Princeton University Press, 1997).

12 David Burnett and Marilyn Schiff, *Contemporary Canadian Art* (Edmonton: Hurtig Publishers, 1983), 181–212.

13 Joan Murray, *Canadian Art in the Twentieth Century* (Toronto: Dundurn Press, 1999) 161–83.

14 André-Louis Paré, "New Espace, New Perspectives," *Espace* no. 107 (2014), 2.

15 See Marshall McLuhan's *The Mechanical Bride* (1951), *The Gutenberg Galaxy* (1962), *Understanding Media* (1964) and *War and Peace in the Global Village* (1968).

16 Robert Stacey and Liz Wylie, *Eighty/Twenty: 100 Years of the Nova Scotia College of Art and Design* (Halifax: Art Gallery of Nova Scotia, 1988), 79.

17 Teresa Marshall cited in Diana Nemiroff, et al., *Land Spirit Power, First Nations at the National Gallery of Canada,* (Ottawa: National Gallery of Canada, 1992), 391.

18 A photograph of Teresa Marshall's *Elitekey* (1990) installation can be found in the National Gallery of Canada.

19 Manasie Akpaliapik quoted in Christine Lalonde, *Inuit Sculpture Now* (Ottawa: National Gallery of Canada, 2005), 15.

20 A photograph of this installation can be found in Douglas Ord, *The National Gallery of Canada: Ideas, Art, Architecture* (Kingston: McGill-Queen's University Press, 2003), 210.

21 Lawrence Sabbath, "Favro Brings Next Wave Excitement to Museum," *Montreal Gazette,* October 15, 1983.

22 Irene Whittome, *The White Museum v* (1975), National Gallery of Canada.

23 A photograph of *Ottawa Room* (1979–1980) appears in Willard Holmes, *Mowry Baden: Maquettes & Other Preparatory Work, 1967–1980* (Victoria: Art Gallery of Greater Victoria, 1985), 42.

24 Lawrence Sabbath, "Favro Brings Next Wave Excitement to Museum," *Montreal Gazette*, October 15, 1983.

25 Josée Drouin-Brisebois, *Otherworld Uprising: Shary Boyle* (Montreal: Conundrum Press, 2008), 28. Shary Boyle, *Untitled* (2004), National Gallery of Canada.

26 Tom Dean, *The Whole Catastrophe* (1999), Art Gallery of Ontario.

27 Robin Metcalfe, "Extremities: Tom Dean prepares for Venice," *Art Matters Magazine* Art Gallery of Ontario, May/August 1999, 38.

28 Louise Dompierre, "Introduction," *Melvin Charney: 1981–1983* (Kingston: Agnes Etherington Art Centre, Queen's University, 1983), 8.

29 Hsio-Yen Shih quoted in Nancy Devitt, "Modern Chinese Art 'Traditional,'" *Windsor Star,* October 13, 1978, cited in Douglas Ord, *The National Gallery of Canada: Ideas, Art, Architecture* (Kingston: McGill-Queen's University Press, 2003), 268.

30 The only record of Tom Burrows's *Mudflat Sculptures* (1971) are gelatin silver photographs of his work, which appear in Scott Watson, "Terminal City: Place, Culture, and the Regional Inflection," *Vancouver: Art and Artists, 1931–1983* (Vancouver: Vancouver Art Gallery, 1983), 228, 229.

31 Jeffrey Rubinoff to Joan Pachner, letter, November 25, 2014, manuscript collection of Joan Pachner.

32 Gary Michael Dault, "Murdering trees and grapevines," *Globe and Mail* (Toronto), August 3, 2002.

33 Greg Beatty, "*Forêt/Frontière*: An Art/Nature Action," *Espace* no. 38 (Winter 1996/1997), 24.

34 Ibid.

35 *Gilles Mihalcean, Recent Sculptures,* Art Gallery of the Cultural Centre of the University of Sherbrooke, March–April, 2016.

36 As Ken Carpenter showed in *The Caro Connection: Sculpture by Sir Anthony Caro from Toronto Collections*, April–June 1995, Koffler Gallery, Toronto, Caro's influence on sculptors in Canada was enormous.

37 John K. Grande, "Claude Mongrain: Sculptures Situations" *Espace* no. 67 (Spring 2004), 42.

38 Stuart Adams, "Art: Nothing Happens by Accident in Catherine Burgess Sculptures," available at www.gigcity.ca/2012/09/04/art-nothing-happens-by-accident-in-catherine-burgess-sculptures.

39 Ken Carpenter, *The Caro Connection: Sculpture by Sir Anthony Caro from Toronto Collections*, April–June 1995, The Koffler Gallery, Toronto, 12.

40 Brian Foss, "Postponed Meanings," *Espace* no. 19 (Spring 1992), 45.

41 Richard Gordon, *Katie Ohe*, Illingworth Kerr Gallery, Alberta College of Art, Calgary, February–March 1991, 24.

42 Mattiussi Iyaituk, *Singing and Drumming Sounds from the Shaman* (2000), National Gallery of Canada, no. 41061.

43 After its exhibition at Expo '86, Ron Baird's *Spirit Catcher* (1986)— a 21.3-metre-high Cor-Ten steel sculpture—was installed at the MacLaren Art Centre in Barrie, Ontario.

44 Mowry Baden cited in *Mowry Baden: Maquettes & Other Preparatory Work, 1967–1980* (Victoria: Art Gallery of Greater Victoria, 1985), 45.

45 Robert Enright, "Precision, Coercion and Delight: An Interview with Mowry Baden," *Border Crossings* vol. 32, no. 3 (September/October/November 2013), 23. This work is in the collection of the artist.

46 Lise Lamarche, "To Small Men," *Espace* 72 (Summer 2005), 7.

47 Serge Fisette and Roch Foitier, "Carol Proulx," *Espace* no. 28 (1994), 14.

48 This work was exhibited at Montreal's Musée d'Art Contemporain in 2014.

49 Jon Sufrin, "The World of Diorama Artist Guillaume Lachapelle Reels Off into Infinity," CBC *Arts*, July 30, 2015.

50 Pierre Francastel, "La Réalité Figurative: Elements Structurels de Sociologie de l'Art," *Médiations* (Paris: Deonël-Gonthier, 1965), 11. Cited in Jocelyne Connolly, "From Analog to Digital: Thinking Sculpture Differently," *Espace* no. 92 (Summer 2010), 9.

51 "Victor Tolgesy," *Canadian Heritage Information Network,* Government of Canada, 3.

52 Matthew Teitelbaum and Peter White, *Joe Fafard: Cows and Other Luminaries* (Saskatoon: Mendel Art Gallery, 1987), 52.

53 John Bentley Mays quoted by Serge Fisette, "Return to Earth," *Espace* no. 27 (Spring 1994), 6.

54 *Espace* no. 27 (Spring 1994).

55 Gathie Falk, *Single Right Men's Shoes: Blue Running Shoes* (1973), Vancouver Art Gallery.

56 This work is in the collection of the artist and was exhibited at the Open Space Gallery in Vancouver in 1993.

57 Liz Magor, *Time and Mrs. Tiber* (1976), National Gallery of Canada.

58 Colette Whiten, *September 1975* (1975), National Gallery of Canada.

59 Peter Dubé, "Monstrous Energy," *Espace* no. 79 (Spring 2007), 6.

60 Francis Fukuyama, "The End of History," *The National Interest* (Summer 1989).

61 Daniel J. Schreiber, *Evan Penny: Re Figured* (Tübingen: Kunsthalle Tübingen, 2011), 19.

62 Ibid., 9.

63 John K. Grande, *Kathy Venter: Life*, Gardiner Museum, May–September 2013, 38.

64 Peter Hide, "Abstraction and the Figure: My Art in Context," *Edmonton Review* vol. 5, issue 1 (1998), 6.

65 Peter Hide quoted in Piri Halasz et al., *Peter Hide: A Sculptor's Life* (Regina: Hagios Press, 2017), 105.

66 Murray Favro, *Van Gogh's Room* (1973–1974), Art Gallery of Ontario.

67 Jeffrey Rubinoff, "Introduction," proceedings of the Company of Ideas Forum 2010, 1; "On the Purposes of the Work and the Sculpture Park," proceedings of the Company of Ideas Forum 2007; and "Introduction," proceedings of the Yale Forum, Hornby Island, 2011, 1.

68 Unfortunately the Bill Reid Foundation denied our request for permission to publish a photo of *Raven and the First Men.*

69 Don Yeomans, "Artist's statement, 2007," in Robin Laurence, *A Sense of Place: Art at Vancouver International Airport* (Vancouver: Figure 1, 2015), 98.

70 Darlene Coward Wight, *Abraham Anghik Ruben* (Winnipeg: Winnipeg Art Gallery, 2002), 12.

71 Ross Skoggard, "Canadian Artists in the Big Apple," *Canadian Art* (Summer 1986).

72 Susan Hart, "Lurking in the Bushes: Ottawa's *Anishinabe Scout*," *Espace* no. 72 (Summer 2005), 16.

73 Ibid., 17.

74 Greg Beatty, "Joe Fafard: Anatomy of a Controversy," *Espace* no. 48 (Summer 1999), 15.

75 "Sculpture offends," *Windsor Star,* January 12, 2008; "Christian Sues Gallery over 'Blasphemous' Erection," *Guardian* (London), September 3, 2008.

76 Nathan Manilow Sculpture Park, "Nathan Manilow Sculpture Park: An Introduction," (1996), *Nathan Manilow Sculpture Park Guides and Videos*, paper 1, available at opus.govst.edu/nmsp_documents/1.

77 Walter Redinger quoted in Joe Bodolai, ed., "Sculpture: Rebirth of Humanism," *artscanada* (Autumn 1974), 45.

78 Angelique Rodrigues, "Commissioned Art: Risk vs. Reward," *Curious Arts* (Calgary), September 16, 2015.

Epilogue

1 Ontario College of Art and Design sculptor and teacher Eldon Garnet (b. 1946) produced this work.

2 David Clendining, *The Animals in War Memorial* (2012), Confederation Park, Ottawa.

3 Calvin Hunt (b. 1956), Mervyn Child (b. 1955) and John Livingstone (b. 1951), *Veterans Pole* (2003), Victoria.

4   Another sculpture duo, Don Begg and Shirley Stephens-Begg, who run Studio West Foundry and Art Gallery in Cochrane, Alberta, produced four life-sized bronzes to be installed in Mayerthorpe.

5   Paul Delany, ed., *Vancouver: Representing the Postmodern City* (Vancouver: Arsenal Pulp Press, 1994), 29.

6   "Sculpture in Conjunction with Art," *Ottawa Citizen*, September 28, 1999, D4.

7   John K. Grande, "What is Public? Whose Art?," *Espace* no. 29 (Fall, 1994), 17.

8   Hilary Beaumont, "The Wave Has Left its Mark," *Chronicle Herald* (Halifax), December 13, 2013.

9   "Rumour about Relocation of Well-Known Sculpture Makes Waves in Halifax," CTV Atlantic, September 17, 2013.

10 Robert Fulford cited in Joe Bodolai, ed., "Sculpture: Rebirth of Humanism," *artscanada* (Autumn 1974), 41.

11 City of Saskatoon, Council Policy no. C10-025, January 1, 2015, 1–2.

12 Glenn Gordon quoted in "Interaction Benefits Reichert," *Leader-Post* (Regina), February 2, 2006.

13 *Truro Tree Sculpture Guide (1999–2000)*, published by the city of Truro.

14 Meghan Barton quoted in "Intern Inspired by Sculpture Symposium," *Telegraph-Journal* (Saint John), October 17, 2012.

15 Lee Montgomery, "International Outdoor Museum of Sculpture," *Espace* vol. 5, no. 4 (Summer 1989), 18.

16 Gerry Bellett, "Controversial sculpture to be removed," *Vancouver Sun,* April 2, 2008, 2.

17 Serge Fisette, "Photos… in the Garden," *Espace* no. 38 (Winter 1996/1997), 12.

18 Among the artists included were Lance Betanger, Kitty Mykka, Alfino Bonanno, Chris Booth, Firman Djamil, Pilar Ovalle, Charles Pachter, Laura Santini and Richard Watts.

19 Denise Leclerc, *Robert Murray: The Factory as Studio* (Ottawa: National Gallery of Canada, 1999), 61.

List of Works

Listed in order of appearance. Materials and dimensions given when available.

Figure of Man and Child (n.d.), Unknown Artist, ivory, Collection of the Cambridge University Museum of Archaeology and Anthropology, 1950.405. Photo courtesy of the Cambridge University Museum of Archaeology and Anthropology. **p. 2, 15**

Construction: Vésuve (1979), Claude Mongrain, white concrete and metal wire, 155 × 122 × 130 cm, Collection of the Musée d'Art de Joliette. © Claude Mongrain. Photo by Paul Litherland. **p. 6**

Scraper (c. 13,000 BCE), Unknown Artist, Collection of the Canadian Museum of History, MgVo-2:H5-1-1, s91-922. Photo courtesy of the Canadian Museum of History. **p. 10**

Miniature Mask (c. 1500 BCE), Unknown Artist, bone, 6.3 × 3.2 cm, Collection of the Cambridge University Museum of Archaeology and Anthropology, 1950.366. Photo courtesy of the Cambridge University Museum of Archaeology and Anthropology. **p. 13**

Seated Human Figure Bowl, "Qelemteleq" (1200–200 BCE), Unknown Artist, stone, 23.4 × 8.9 × 13.9 cm, Collection of the Museum of Vancouver, QAA 1077. Reproduced with permission of the Katzie First Nation. Illustration by Joelly Cright. **p. 14**

Floating or Flying Bear (c. 500 BCE–1200 CE), Unknown Artist, ivory, 15.6 × 3.6 × 3.4 cm, Collection of the Canadian Museum of History, NhHd-1:2655. Photo courtesy of the Canadian Museum of History. **p. 15**

Inuksuit at Inuksugasalik Point, Nunavut (n.d.), Unknown Artist. Photo by Charles Gimpel, courtesy of the estate of E.R. Gimpel. **p. 16**

Stone Club (n.d.), Unknown Artist, stone, Collection of the Royal BC Museum and Archives, GhSvw-y:2. Photo courtesy of the Royal BC Museum and Archives. **p. 17**

La Vierge Druidique de Québec (c. 1671–1695), Marie Lemaire des Anges. Église Sainte-Marie de Beauce. **p. 18**

Sacred Heart Altar (1790), Philippe Liébert, Collection of the Montreal Museum of Fine Arts, Gift of Concordia University in honour of the legacy of the Sisters of Charity of Montreal, "Grey Nuns," 2009.14. Photo courtesy of the Montreal Museum of Fine Arts. **p. 19**

Saint Joseph (c. 1750), Pierre-Noël Levasseur, wood with gilt, 92 × 49 × 27.4 cm with base, Collection of the National Gallery of Canada, 9995. Photo courtesy of the National Gallery of Canada. **p. 20**

Saint Joachim (1793), François Baillairgé, wood with gilt, 31 × 12 × 7.6 cm, Collection of the National Gallery of Canada, 18528. Photo courtesy of the National Gallery of Canada. **p. 20**

Bust of King George III (c. 1765–1766), Joseph Wilton, painted bronze, 33 × 26 × 28 cm, Collection of the McCord Museum, Gift of the Natural History Society of Montreal, M15885. Photo courtesy of the McCord Museum. **p. 23**

Nelson's Column (1809), Coade and Sealy of London. Illustration: *Nelson's Pillar, Montreal* (1839–1842), print, Collection of the McCord Museum, Gift of Miss Moodie, M928.94.1.42. **p. 24**

Monument to Wolfe and Montcalm (1827), John Phillips, stonemason. Illustration: *Monument to Wolfe and Montcalm, Quebec* (1840), print by Robert Wallis: steel engraving on wove paper, 22 × 28 cm, John Clarence Webster Canadiana Collection of the New Brunswick Museum, W1930. **p. 25**

Crimean War Monument (1860), George Laing. St. Paul's Church Cemetery, Halifax, NS. Photo by Meunierd / Shutterstock. **p. 26**

Whalebone Club (c. 1778), Unknown Artist, bone and bark, 58 × 10 cm, Collection of the Cambridge Museum of Archaeology and Anthropology, 1921.567.1. Photo courtesy of the Cambridge Museum of Archaeology and Anthropology. **p. 29**

Carved Panel Pipe (early 1800s), Unknown Artist, argillite, 30 × 2 × 9.4 cm, Collection of the Cambridge Museum of Archaeology and Anthropology, 1949.208. Photo courtesy of the Cambridge Museum of Archaeology and Anthropology. **p. 30**

Thirteen Saints (1892–1900), Olindo Gratton. Marie-Reine-du-Monde Cathedral, Montreal, QC. **p. 34** photo by Norman Pogson / Alamy Stock Photo, BMRRG5. **p. 39** photo by NiKreative / Alamy Stock Photo, C5B989.

Statue de Notre-Dame-du-Saguenay (c. 1881), Louis Jobin. Photo: Collection Initiale of the Bibliothèque et Archives Nationales du Québec. **p. 37**

Le Chanteur (c. 1865), Jean-Baptiste Côté, polychromed wood, 81 × 20 × 21.5 cm, Paul Gouin Collection of the Montreal Museum of Fine Arts, 2010.856. Photo courtesy of the Montreal Museum of Fine Arts. **p. 38**

Queen Victoria (1871), Marshall Wood. Photo © Library of Parliament. **p. 42**

Joseph Brant Memorial (1886), Percy Wood. Brantford, Ontario. Photo by Michael Jenner, Alamy, AJ845R. **p. 43**

Maisonneuve Monument (1895), Louis-Philippe Hébert. Photo: *Maisonneuve Monument, Place d'Armes, Montreal* (1869), Wm. Notman & Son, Collection of the McCord Museum, view-2787. **p. 47**

Samuel de Champlain (1915), Hamilton MacCarthy. Ottawa, Ontario. Photo courtesy of Library and Archives Canada, PA-034433. **p. 51**

L'Arbre de la Rue Durocher (1953–1954), Armand Vaillancourt, elm, 518.7 × 188 × 158 cm, Collection of the Musée National des Beaux-Arts du Québec, 1976.268. © Armand Vaillancourt / SODRAC (2017). **p. 164**

Woman with Labret (1975), Robert Davidson, alder, acrylic paint, abalone. Photo courtesy of the artist. **p. 166**

Une Grande Couple (1967), Louis Archambault, University of Toronto. Photo © Bill Dutfield. **p. 172**

Flight (1963–1964), Sorel Etrog. © Estate of Sorel Etrog. **p. 173**

Walking Woman (1967), Michael Snow. Photo courtesy of Library and Archives Canada, e000990948. **p. 174**

Robot (1967), Germain Bergeron. Photo by George Lenko, the University of British Columbia Photograph Collection, UBC 1.1/15948. **p. 175**

Le Phare du Cosmos (1967), Yves Trudeau. Photo courtesy of Library and Archives Canada, MIKAN no. 3198313. **p. 176**

UKI (1967), Gerald Gladstone. Photo © Bill Dutfield. **p. 177**

Poles and Houses at the Haida Village (1959–1962). Bill Reid and Douglas Cranmer. Photo by Michael Wheatley / Alamy Stock Photo, DXMK75. **p. 181**

Mother and Children (c. 1960), Lucy Tasseor Tutsweetok, stone, 45.8 × 25.9 × 33.3 cm, Collection of the Winnipeg Art Gallery, Twomey Collection, with appreciation to the Province of Manitoba and Government of Canada, 1118.71. © Public Trustee for Nunavut, E/L Lucy Tasseor Tutsweetok (aka Tutsuituk). All rights reserved. Photo by Ernest Mayer. **p. 185**

Hawk (1968), Osuitok Ipeelee, stone, 47 × 15.8 × 27.8 cm, Collection of the Winnipeg Art Gallery, Twomey Collection, with appreciation to the Province of Manitoba and Government of Canada, 1118.71. Photo by Ernest Mayer. **p. 187**

Migration (c. 1965), Joe Talirunili, stone, bone, gut and sinew, 22 × 30.2 × 14.8 cm, Collection of the Winnipeg Art Gallery, Twomey Collection, with the appreciation to the Province of Manitoba and Government of Canada, 1951.71. Photo by Ernest Mayer. **p. 188–89**

Bear (1962), Pauta Saila, stone, 41× 26.7 × 7.8 cm, Collection of the Winnipeg Art Gallery, Twomey Collection, with appreciation of the Province of Manitoba and Government of Canada, 1042.71. Reproduced with the permission of Dorset Fine Arts. Photo by Ernest Mayer. **p. 190**

Sand Form Made at Low Tide Sand Flats at Paul's Bluff Inlet, Victoria, Prince Edward Island, Knob was Completely Erased after Seven Hightides. Self-portrait (1969), Bill Vazan. AZO dye print (Cibachrome), 40.6 × 51.1 cm, Reproduced with the permission of Bill Vazan. Photo courtesy of the National Gallery of Canada, 17238. **p. 192, 210**

1,000,000 Pennies (1979), Gerald Ferguson, one million Canadian pennies, dimensions variable, Collection of the Art Gallery of Nova Scotia, 2002.126. Photo courtesy of the Art Gallery of Nova Scotia. **p. 198–99**

Untitled (1991), Manasie Akpaliapik, whalebone, Brazilian soapstone, antler, ivory, musk-ox horn and shell, 41.5 × 24.2 × 25.8 cm, Collection of the National Gallery of Canada, 37354.1-2. Reproduced with permission of the Inuit Art Foundation. Photo courtesy of the National Gallery of Canada. **p. 200**

Prototype for New Understanding #2 (1998), Brian Jungen. Nike Air Jordans and hair, 23 × 21 × 25.5 cm, Collection of the Vancouver Art Gallery, VAG 99.20.1. Photo by Trevor Mills, Vancouver Art Gallery. **p. 202**

One Day of AZT/One Year of AZT (1991), General Idea. Installation in two parts: Five elements, fibreglas and enamel; and 1,825 elements, vacuum-formed styrene with vinyl, Collection of the National Gallery of Canada. Reproduced with permission of A.A. Bronson. Photo by Cheryl O'Brien **p. 203**

Vanitas: Flesh Dress for an Albino Anorectic (1987), Jana Sterbak, mannequin, flank steak, salt, thread, 158.1 × 41.9 × 30.2 cm, Collection of the Walker Art Center, 1993.54.1.3. Reproduced with permission of the artist. Photo courtesy of the Walker Art Center. **p. 204**

Series 3-5 (1983), Jeffrey Rubinoff, Cor-Ten steel, 2.1 × 2.4 × 2.4 m, © Estate of Jeffrey Rubinoff. Photo by Sergei Petrov. **p. 207**

Series 4-9 (1986), Jeffrey Rubinoff, Cor-Ten welded plate, 2.1 × 1.5 × 1.4 m, © Estate of Jeffrey Rubinoff. Photo by Sergei Petrov. **p. 209**

No Title (1987), Reinhard Reitzenstein. Artist wishes to acknowledge the role of Dane Pine, who was the principle advisor and involved in the site selection for the project. Photo courtesy of the artist. **p. 211**

Swing (1973), Robert Murray. Sculpture and photo reproduced with permission of the artist. **p. 212**

Unfurled (2006), Doug Bentham. Saskatoon, Saskatchewan. Sculpture and photo reproduced with permission of the artist. **p. 213**

Construction: Vésuve (1979), Claude Mongrain, white concrete and metal wire, 155 × 122 × 130 cm, Collection of the Musée d'Art de Joliette. © Claude Mongrain. Photo by Paul Litherland. **p. 214**

Puddle I (1976), Katie Ohe, bronze, Collection of the Glenbow Museum. Reproduced with permission of the artist. **p. 215**

Beginning, Middle and End (2012), Mowry Baden, collection of the artist. Photo by Mark Alldritt. **p. 216**

Nuit Étoilée (2012), Guillaume Lachapelle, Nulon, paint, MDF, Plexiglas, electrical components and LEDS, 50 × 70 × 70 cm, Collection of Galerie Art Mûr. **p. 218**

Merchant of Pense (1973), Joe Fafard, glazed ceramic, wood and acrylic, Collection of the Glenbow Museum, 73.9. Photo courtesy of the Glenbow Museum. **p. 220**

The Index (2007), David Altmejd, mixed media, 332.7 × 129.7 × 923 cm, Collection of the Art Gallery of Toronto, gift of George Hartman and Arlene Goldman, 2014, 2014/378. © David Altmejd. Photo courtesy of the Art Gallery of Ontario. **p. 221**

No One—In Particular #6, Series 2 (2006), Evan Penny, silicone, pigment, hair aluminum, 100 × 80 × 19 cm, collection of the artist. **p. 223**

Butterfly Torso (1989), Ted Bieler, cast bronze, 94 × 61 × 64 cm, collection of the artist. **p. 224**

Madonna (1988), Peter Hide, mild steel welded, 170 × 90 × 40.6 cm, collection of the artist. Photo courtesy of Richard Siemens. **p. 225**

Receding (2007), John Greer, limestone, 213.4 × 96.5 × 40.6 cm, collection of the artist. **p. 226**

Dogface Boys' Picnic (1974–1975), Sherry Grauer, wire mesh, fibreglas putty, styrofoam, urethane foam, white glue, gauze, adhesive bandage, acrylic and aluminum paint, 91.4 × 254 × 304.8 cm, Collection of the National Gallery of Canada, 18460.1-5. Photo courtesy of the artist. **p. 227**

Celebrating Flight (2007), Don Yeomans. Collection of the Vancouver Airport Authority. Photo by Dave Nunuk. **p. 228**

Series 9–3 (2012–2014), Jeffrey Rubinoff, stainless 304, 2.1 × 3 × 3 m. © Estate of Jeffrey Rubinoff. Photo by Sergei Petrov. **p. 232**

Terry Fox Memorial (1984), Franklin Allen (architect), Ian Bateson (inside illustration). Formerly in Vancouver, British Columbia. Photo by Ian Bateson. **p. 235**

Traffic (1968–1971), Ed Zelenak, fibreglas-reinforced plastic, 6.71 × 9.75 × 3.66 m, Collection of the National Gallery of Canada, 16908. Reproduced with permission of the artist. Photo courtesy of the National Gallery of Canada. **p. 236**

The Wave (1988), Donna Hiebert, ferro-cement, 3.7 × 9.1 m. Reproduced with permission of the artist. Photo by RicLaf on Flickr. **p. 238**

Index